FUNDAMENTALS OF
HUMAN RESOURCE
MANAGEMENT

To my wife, Marie, and our six children,
Jesse, Justin, Danielle, Nicole, Brian, and Renee

R.N.L.

For my father, Charles "Chuck" Hendon, who taught me perseverance

J.R.H.

FUNDAMENTALS OF HUMAN RESOURCE MANAGEMENT

FUNCTIONS, APPLICATIONS, SKILL DEVELOPMENT

ROBERT N. LUSSIER
Springfield College

JOHN R. HENDON
University of Arkansas at Little Rock

SAGE

Los Angeles | London | New Delhi
Singapore | Washington DC

Los Angeles | London | New Delhi
Singapore | Washington DC

FOR INFORMATION:

SAGE Publications, Inc.
2455 Teller Road
Thousand Oaks, California 91320
E-mail: order@sagepub.com

SAGE Publications Ltd.
1 Oliver's Yard
55 City Road
London EC1Y 1SP
United Kingdom

SAGE Publications India Pvt. Ltd.
B 1/I 1 Mohan Cooperative Industrial Area
Mathura Road, New Delhi 110 044
India

SAGE Publications Asia-Pacific Pte. Ltd.
3 Church Street
#10-04 Samsung Hub
Singapore 049483

Acquisitions Editor: Maggie Stanley
Associate Editor: Abbie Rickard
Editorial Assistant: Nicole Mangona
eLearning Editor: Katie Bierach
Production Editor: Laura Barrett
Copy Editor: Melinda Masson
Typesetter: C&M Digitals (P) Ltd.
Proofreader: Dennis W. Webb
Indexer: Wendy Allex
Cover Designer: Gail Buschman
Marketing Manager: Ashlee Blunk

Printed in Canada

All trademarks depicted within this book, including trademarks appearing as part of a screenshot, figure, or other image are included solely for the purpose of illustration and are the property of their respective holders. The use of the trademarks in no way indicates any relationship with, or endorsement by, the holders of said trademarks.

Library of Congress Cataloging-in-Publication Data

Names: Lussier, Robert N., author. | Hendon, John R., author.

Title: Fundamentals of human resource management: functions, applications, skill development / Robert N. Lussier, John R. Hendon.

Description: Los Angeles : Sage, [2017] | Includes bibliographical references and index.

Identifiers: LCCN 2015035721 | ISBN 978-1-4833-5850-5 (pbk. : alk. paper)

Subjects: LCSH: Personnel management.

Classification: LCC HF5549 .L8247 2017 | DDC 658.3--dc23
LC record available at http://lccn.loc.gov/2015035721

This book is printed on acid-free paper.

15 16 17 18 19 10 9 8 7 6 5 4 3 2 1

··· Brief Contents

SAGE was founded in 1965 by Sara Miller McCune to support the dissemination of usable knowledge by publishing innovative and high-quality research and teaching content. Today, we publish over 900 journals, including those of more than 400 learned societies, more than 800 new books per year, and a growing range of library products including archives, data, case studies, reports, and video. SAGE remains majority-owned by our founder, and after Sara's lifetime will become owned by a charitable trust that secures our continued independence.

Los Angeles | London | New Delhi | Singapore | Washington DC

··· Detailed Contents

Chapter 3. The Legal Environment and Diversity Management 54

PART II • STAFFING 83

Chapter 4. Matching Employees and Jobs: Job Analysis and Design 84

©iStockphoto.com/
asiseeit

Chapter 5. Recruiting Job Candidates 112

©iStockphoto.com/ shironosov

PART III • DEVELOPING AND MANAGING　161

©iStockphoto.com/track5

PART IV • COMPENSATING 245

©iStockphoto.com/minemero

Chapter 10. Compensation Management 246

©iStockphoto.com/Georgijevic

Chapter 11. Employee Incentives and Benefits 274

PART V • PROTECTING AND EXPANDING ORGANIZATIONAL OUTREACH   301

Chapter 12. Workplace Safety, Health, and Security   302

Chapter 13. Organizational Ethics, Sustainability, and Social Responsibility   326

Chapter 14.   Global Issues for Human Resource Managers   350

··· Preface

In his book *Power Tools,* John Nirenberg asks, "Why are so many well-intended students learning so much and yet able to apply so little in their personal and professional lives?" The world of business and human resource management (HRM) has changed, and so should how it is taught. Increasing numbers of students want more than lectures to gain an understanding of the concepts of HRM. They want their courses to be relevant and to apply what they learn, and they want to develop skills they can use in their everyday life and at work. It's not enough to learn about HRM; they want to learn how to be HR managers. This is why we wrote the book. After reviewing and using a variety of HRM books for more than a decade, we didn't find any that (1) could be easily read and understood by students and (2) effectively taught students how to be HR managers. We wrote this text out of our desire to prepare students to be successful HR managers and/or to use HRM skills as line managers or employees. As the subtitle states, this book not only presents the important HRM concepts and functions, but also takes students to the next level by actually engaging them by teaching them to apply the concepts through critical thinking and to develop HRM skills they can use in their personal and professional lives.

MARKET AND COURSE

This book is for undergraduate and graduate-level courses in human resource management (HRM) including personnel management. It is appropriate for a first course in an HRM major, as well as required and elective courses found in business schools. This textbook is also appropriate for HRM courses taught in other disciplines such as education and psychology, particularly Industrial Psychology and Organizational Psychology, and can be utilized for training courses in Supervision. The level of the text assumes no prior background in business or HRM. This book is an excellent choice for online and hybrid courses in HRM.

LEARNING BY DOING: A PRACTICAL APPROACH

I (Lussier) started writing management textbooks in 1988—prior to the calls by the Association to Advance Collegiate Schools of Business (AACSB) for skill development—to help professors teach their students how to apply concepts and develop management skills. Pfeffer and Sutton (*The Knowing-Doing Gap,* 2000) concluded that the most important insight from their research is that knowledge that is actually implemented is much more likely to be acquired from learning by doing than from learning by reading, listening, or thinking. We designed this book to give students the opportunity to "learn by doing" with the following approaches:

- A practical **"how-to-manage"** approach which is strategy driven.

- The only HR text where primary content areas identified in the Society of Human Resource Management **2013 Curriculum Guidebook** as *required* for undergraduate students is specifically identified in the text where the material is covered (over 150 items). In addition, many of the *secondary* and *graduate students only* items are also identified as they occur in the text.

- Six types of high-quality **application materials** use the concepts to develop critical-thinking skills.

- Four types of high-quality **skill-builder exercises** help to actually develop HR management skills that can be utilized in students' professional and personal lives.

- A selection of **videos** that reinforce HRM-related abilities and skills.

- A flexible approach which meets the preferred teaching style of professors and learning styles of today's students who want to be engaged with active learning.

A NEW GENERATION OF LEARNERS

Today's students, including "Millennials" and "Generation Z" or the Postmillennials, succeed when they are fully engaged in learning on multiple levels; traditional methods of teaching do not always meet their needs. Our text is flexible enough to accompany lecture-based teaching, and also offers a wide range of engaging activities which accommodate a variety of contemporary learning styles. Many of the specific learning preferences of today's students have been addressed in the book's overall approach, organization, and distinctive features:

- **Active Learning**

    A desire for **active learning** is addressed with a large variety of activities and skill-building tools.

- **Practical Approaches**

    A desire for **application and skills** in personal and professional realms is addressed by a variety of features throughout the text. **Immediate application and ongoing self-assessment** are found in the Work Application prompts and self-assessment tools. Organization tools such as **checklists, summaries, and "how to"** instructions are integrated throughout: for example, the marginal references to SHRM curriculum guidelines.

- **Accessible Content**

    Chunking of content into easily digested segments helps students to organize study time. **Visual learning** preferences are accommodated in colorful exhibits, models, and figures throughout the text, along with an ancillary package which includes visual learning options. **Internet learning** preferences are recognized in a robust web-based package which includes video and interactive features for students.

A THREE-PRONGED APPROACH

We have created a concise textbook intended to develop the full range of HRM competencies. As the title of this book implies, we provide a balanced, three-pronged approach to the curriculum:

Concepts/Functions

The following features are provided to support the first step in the three-pronged approach.

HRM functions. Chapter 1 presents eight major HRM functions identified by SHRM with questions that need to be answered. The book is structured around the eight functions in five parts; see the table of contents for details. These functions are emphasized in order to show students the depth of knowledge that is required of a 21st century HR manager.

Pedagogical aids. Each chapter includes Learning Outcomes, Chapter Summary and Key Terms, and Review Questions. Marginal icons also indicate points at which (1) International Human Resources and (2) Ethics, Sustainability, and Social Responsibility are discussed in the text.

SHRM's Required Content, as well as many Secondary and Graduate-only HR Content Areas from the *SHRM Human Resource Curriculum: Guidebook and Templates for Undergraduate and Graduate Programs* (SHRM, 2013), are annotated for easy reference where they appear in each chapter of the text. A margin note seen here identifies the Curriculum Guide topic being covered, and a reference number links to an appendix covering the entire SHRM Curriculum Guide. *Nearly all of the Primary Content Areas and Subtopics* identified in the SHRM Curriculum Guidebook are introduced within the text.

`SHRM`

Applications

The following features are provided to support the second step in the three-pronged approach.

Opening Vignettes illustrate how a real-life Human Resources manager currently employed by the state of Arkansas works within the various HRM functions in her daily activities.

Organizational examples of HRM concepts and functions appear throughout the book.

Work Applications incorporate open-ended questions which require students to explain how the HRM concepts apply to their own work experience. Student experience can be present, past, summer, full-time, part-time employment, or volunteer work.

Applying the Concept features ask the student to determine the most appropriate HRM concept to be used in a specific short example.

Ethical Dilemma features give students examples of real-world situations in which they need to make a choice using the concepts and skills from the chapter.

Cases at the end of each chapter illustrate how specific organizations use the HRM functions. Critical thinking questions challenge the students to identify and apply the chapter concepts which are illustrated in each case. Several longer and more comprehensive cases are also available to the instructor on the website, either for testing material or to allow students to apply what they have learned over a significant part of the course.

Skill Development

The following features are provided to support the third step in the three-pronged approach.

Self-Assessments help students to gain personal knowledge of how they will complete the HRM functions in the real world. All information for completing and scoring is contained within the text.

Communication Skills at the end of each chapter include questions for class discussion, presentations, and/or written assignments to develop critical thinking communication skills; they are based on HR Content Areas.

Behavior Modeling showing step-by-step actions to follow when implementing HRM functions, such as how to conduct a job interview, performance appraisals, and coaching and disciplining, are presented throughout the text.

Skill Development Exercises develop skills that can be used in students' personal and professional lives. Many of the competitor exercises tend to be discussion-oriented exercises that don't actually develop a skill that can be used immediately on the job.

ANCILLARIES

http://edge.sagepub.com/fundamentalsofhrm

$SAGE edge™

SAGE edge offers a robust online environment featuring an impressive array of tools and resources for review, study, and further exploration, keeping both instructors and students on the cutting edge of teaching and learning.

SAGE edge for Instructors supports teaching by making it easy to integrate quality content, creating a rich learning environment for students.

- **Test banks** built on Bloom's taxonomy and tied to the book's learning objectives provide a diverse range of pre-written options as well as the opportunity to edit any question and/or insert personalized questions to effectively assess students' progress and understanding.

- **Sample course syllabi** for semester and quarter courses provide suggested models for structuring one's course.

- Editable, chapter-specific **PowerPoint® slides** offer complete flexibility for creating a multimedia presentation for the course.

- EXCLUSIVE! Access to full-text **SAGE journal articles** that have been carefully selected to support and expand on the concepts presented in each chapter to encourage students to think critically. Each article has open-ended discussion questions to prompt deeper engagement with the material.

- **Multimedia content** includes videos that appeal to students with different learning styles.

- The **Instructor's Manual** provides answers to in-text questions and case notes.

SAGE edge for Students provides a personalized approach to help students accomplish their coursework goals in an easy-to-use learning environment.

- Mobile-friendly **eFlashcards** strengthen understanding of key terms and concepts.

- Mobile-friendly practice **quizzes** allow for independent assessment by students of their mastery of course material.

- A customized online **action plan** helps track progress through the course and materials to enhance the learning experience.

- **Chapter learning objectives** help students reinforce the most important material.

- **Multimedia content** includes video and web resources that appeal to students with different learning styles.

- EXCLUSIVE! Access to full-text **SAGE journal articles** that have been carefully selected to support and expand on the concepts presented in each chapter.

··· Acknowledgments

We would like to thank our team at SAGE Publications, which helped bring this book to fruition. Our first executive editor, Patricia Quinlin, who brought us to SAGE, and editor Lisa Cuevas Shaw have shepherded the development of the first edition of *Human Resource Management* from its inception. Our current editor, Maggie Stanley, as well as Abbie Rickard, Nicole Mangona, and Katie Bierach, provided additional assistance and support. We are grateful to Janet Kiesel for a cover and interior design that sets this book apart. During the production process, Laura Barrett provided professionalism and valuable support. Liz Thornton lent her marketing experience and skills to promoting the book.

We would like to acknowledge our colleagues at SHRM who provided organizational resources—in particular the 2013 *SHRM Human Resource Curriculum*—to ensure that *Fundamentals of Human Resource Management* is *the* textbook of choice for future HR practitioners. We would also like to recognize Cindy Wright of the Department of Human Services for Arkansas for her vital contribution of chapter opening vignettes, which feature her personal insight and experience as an HR professional. Excellent case material has been provided by Can Guler, Komal Thakker, and Herbert Sherman of the Department of Management Sciences, School of Business Brooklyn Campus, Long Island University, and by Robert Wayland, University of Arkansas at Little Rock.

Thanks to the following reviewers who participated throughout all stages of the book's development:

Wai Kwan (Elaine) Lau, *Marshall University*

Tony Daniel, *Shorter University*

Samuel L. Rohr, *Purdue University North Central*

Marie A. Valentin, *Texas A&M University*

Brian Martinson, *Tarleton State University*

Cindy Lanphear, *University of the Ozarks*

Tony Bledsoe, *Meredith College*

Joni Koegel, *Cazenovia College*

Andrea Smith-Hunter, *Siena College*

Reggie Hall, *Tarleton State University*

Richard Bahner, *Kean University*

Katina Sawyer, *Villanova University*

Hudson Nwakanma, *Florida A&M University*

Kelly Hall, *Stetson University*

Julie Palmer, *Webster University*

Kelly Mollica, *University of Memphis*

··· About the Authors

Robert N. Lussier is a professor of management at Springfield College. Through teaching management courses for more than 25 years, he has developed innovative methods for applying concepts and developing skills that can be used both personally and professionally. A prolific writer, Dr. Lussier has more than 425 publications to his credit, including *Management* 7e (SAGE), *Human Relations* 10e (McGraw-Hill), and *Leadership* 6e (South Western/Cengage) and has published in top tier academic journals. He holds a bachelor of science in business administration from Salem State College, master's degrees in business and education from Suffolk University, and a doctorate in management from the University of New Haven. He served as founding director of Israel Programs and has taught courses in Israel.

John R. Hendon is a seven-time entrepreneur and former director of operations for a $60 million company. He brought his experience and interests to the classroom full time in 1994 and has been a Management faculty member at the University of Arkansas at Little Rock for over 17 years. An active member of the Society for Human Resource Management, he teaches in the areas of Human Resources Management, Strategy, and Organizational Management, and researches in a number of areas in the Management field, specializing in Entrepreneurial research. John is also currently the President of "The VMP Group," an Arkansas-based business consulting firm. John's company consults with a variety of businesses on human resources, family business, strategic planning, organizational design, and leadership. He has provided professional assistance in the start-up and operation of dozens of Arkansas and California-based businesses and non-profits, government agencies, and utilities. John holds an MBA degree from San Diego State University and a BS in Education from the University of Central Arkansas.

Part I

21st Century Human Resource Management Strategic Planning and Legal Issues

1. The New Human Resource Management Process

2. Strategy-Driven Human Resource Management

3. The Legal Environment and Diversity Management

PRACTITIONER'S MODEL

- ↑ Productivity
- ↑ Satisfaction
- ↓ Absenteeism
- ↓ Turnover

PART V: Protecting and Expanding Organizational Outreach
How do you PROTECT and EXPAND your Human Resources?

Chapter 12	Chapter 13	Chapter 14
Workplace Safety, Health, and Security	Organizational Ethics, Sustainability, and Social Responsibility	Global Issues for Human Resource Managers

PART IV: Compensating
How do you REWARD and MAINTAIN your Human Resources?

Chapter 10	Chapter 11
Compensation Management	Employee Incentives and Benefits

PART III: Developing and Managing
How do you MANAGE your Human Resources?

Chapter 7	Chapter 8	Chapter 9
Training, Learning, Talent Management & Development	Performance Management and Appraisal	Employee Rights and Labor Relations

PART II: Staffing
What HRM Functions do you NEED for sustainability?

Chapter 4	Chapter 5	Chapter 6
Matching Employees and Jobs	Recruiting Job Candidates	Selecting New Employees

PART I: 21st Century Human Resource Management Strategic Planning and Legal Issues
What HRM issues are CRITICAL to your organization's long-term sustainability?

Chapter 1	Chapter 2	Chapter 3
The New Human Resource Management Process	Strategy-Driven Human Resource Management	The Legal Environment and Diversity Management

©iStockphoto.com/pixdeluxe

1 THE NEW HUMAN RESOURCE MANAGEMENT PROCESS

• • • LEARNING OUTCOMES

After studying this chapter, you should be able to do the following:

1-1 Explain why all managers need to understand the basics of HRM. PAGE 4

1-2 Discuss how HRM helps improve organizational revenues in a 21st century organization. PAGE 6

1-3 Describe the major HRM discipline areas. PAGE 10

1-4 Recall the primary difference between line and staff managers and their major HR responsibilities. PAGE 13

1-5 Summarize the major HRM skill sets. PAGE 16

1-6 Identify the most common HRM certification programs and their parent organizations. PAGE 17

1-7 Explain the practitioner's model for HRM and how it applies to this book. PAGE 19

Practitioner's Perspective

Cindy reflected on the current state of the HR field: Choice and change—two things you can rely on today! No longer merely concerned with hiring, firing, and record keeping, the average human resources department (HR) increasingly partners with the strategic planners in the executive suite, thanks to HR-based education and certifications. HR certification is available through HRCI with PHR, SPHR, and GPHR designations, and SHRM also offers its own program of certification with SHRM-CP and SHRM-SCP.

My professional progress began with membership in HR organizations. First, I became a SHRM student member, which provided access to SHRM's website—which was in turn valuable for research while I was a student. I still use it frequently. Next, my involvement spread to the local HR association. The chapter meetings provided excellent opportunities for education through the monthly programs, as well as for networking and swapping "best practices" with my colleagues. My involvement inspired me to become certified as a professional. But beyond that, I have found that those who invest in certification tend to become more involved in their profession and, by extension, more successful.

I invite you to join me as we explore the field of human resource management (HRM). Chapter 1 gives an overview of HRM as a profession.

● ● ●

Cindy Wright, PHR, came late to the Human Resources profession, and perhaps that explains some of her passion for the field. Wright graduated summa cum laude with a Business Administration degree, HR emphasis. She was recognized as "Outstanding Graduate" by the Human Resources Management department. After employment as a benefits administrator for seven thousand telecommunication's retirees, then as an HR Generalist

©Cindy Wright

● ● ● CHAPTER OUTLINE

Why Study Human Resource Management (HRM)?
21st Century HRM
  HRM Then and Now
  HRM Challenges
  Critical Dependent Variables
  Technology and Knowledge
  Labor Demographics
Disciplines Within HRM
  The Legal Environment: EEO and Diversity Management
  Staffing
  Training and Development
  Employee Relations
  Labor and Industrial Relations
  Compensation and Benefits
  Safety and Security
  Ethics and Sustainability

HRM Responsibilities
  Line Versus Staff Management
  Major HR Responsibilities of HR Staff and Line Management
HRM Skills
  Technical Skills
  Human Relations Skills
  Conceptual and Design Skills
  Business Skills
HRM Careers
  Society for Human Resource Management (SHRM)
  Other HR Organizations
  Professional Liability
Practitioner's Model for HRM
  The Model
Trends and Issues in HRM
  Creating an Engaged Workforce
  Reverse Discrimination Rulings Continue to Evolve

for a gas well drilling company of 500 employees, Wright is now working in personnel management for the Department of Human Services in the Division of Behavior Health Services. Besides membership in the profession's national organization—the Society for Human Resource Management (SHRM), Wright has been active in the local affiliated chapter—the Central Arkansas Human Resources Association (CAHRA). Wright served as Vice President of Administration for the chapter's Board as well as Chair of the College Relation Committee. She was recognized by her peers with the "Rising Star" award for her work in creating a student chapter membership and was involved in the initial efforts to create satellite CAHRA chapters. Wright's mission is to provide assistance to others interested in entering into and advancing within the Human Resources profession.

LO 1-1

Explain why all managers need to understand the basics of HRM.

Human resources (HR) The people within an organization

WHY STUDY HUMAN RESOURCE MANAGEMENT (HRM)?

It's natural to think, "What can I get from this book?" or "What's in it for me?" Success in our professional and personal lives is about creating relationships,[1] and students generally understand the importance of relationships.[2] The better you can work with people, the more successful you will be in your personal and professional lives—whether as an employee, a line manager, or a human resource manager. And that's what this book is all about.

In the 21st century organization, **human resources (HR)**—*the people within an organization*—are one of the primary means of creating a competitive advantage for the organization, because the ways we manage people directly affect their performance.[3] This is because most organizations of comparable size and scope within an industry generally have access to the same material and facilities-based resources that any other organization within the industry may have, making it

SHRM HR CONTENT

See Appendix: *SHRM 2013 Curriculum Guidebook* for the complete list

A. Employee and Labor Relations (required)

4. Employee engagement
5. Employee involvement
6. Employee retention
20. Attendance

B. Employment Law (required)

21. Professional liability

C. Ethics (required)

8. Codes of ethics

D. HR's Role in Organizations (required)

1. Generally . . . discuss HR's role with regard to each of the individual HR disciplines

F. Managing a Diverse Workforce (required)

8. Reverse discrimination

J. Strategic HR (required)

5. Sustainability/corporate social responsibility
6. Internal consulting (required—graduate students only)
9. Ethics (integrated)
11. Organizational effectiveness

O. Globalization (required—graduate students only)

8. Global labor markets

Q. Organizational Development (required—graduate students only)

5. Improving organizational effectiveness
6. Knowledge management
9. Ongoing performance and productivity initiatives
10. Organizational effectiveness

very difficult to create a competitive advantage based on material, facility, or other tangible resources. What this frequently leaves is people as the organization's most valuable asset.[4] If the organization can manage its people more successfully than its competitors do, if it can get its employees *engaged* in the day-to-day success of the organization, and if it can get them to stay with the organization, then it has a much greater chance of being successful—with the term *successful* defined in this case as being more productive and more profitable than the competition.[5] Managers are responsible for getting the job done through employees,[6] so the organization's human resources are nearly always its most valuable resource. (As you can see, there are SHRM Guide boxes next to this section. We will explain them in the sixth section of this chapter, "HRM Careers.")

While job satisfaction (which we will talk about at length later) can be an important aspect of employee engagement, the overall concept of **employee engagement** is much larger. It is *a combination of job satisfaction, ability, and a willingness to perform for the organization at a high level and over an extended period of time.* **Google** is an example of an organization that takes the concept of employee engagement very seriously. Google's "Project Oxygen" is one attempt to analyze what makes a better boss and use that information to train managers to be more consistent and interactive.[7] This training is designed to create greater employee satisfaction and engagement, for very practical reasons. According to *HR Magazine*, companies that fall into "the top 10% on employee engagement beat their competition by 72% in earnings per share during 2007–08."[8] Companies with high levels of satisfaction and engagement outperformed those with less engaged employees in return on investment (ROI), operating income, growth rate, and long-term company valuation.[9]

Today's students want courses to be directly applicable to their lives outside of school.[10] Organizations also want managers to have the ability to apply concepts at work.[11] The role of modern managers also continues to change, requiring today's organizational leaders to deal with increasingly dynamic and complex environments.[12] Because of these issues, this book uses a three-pronged approach, with these objectives:

- To teach you the important functions and concepts of HRM
- To develop your ability to apply HRM functions and concepts through critical thinking
- To develop your HRM skills in your personal and professional lives
- To offer some unique features to further each of the three objectives, as summarized in Exhibit 1-1

SHRM Guide boxes (tied to Appendix) throughout the text will show you what SHRM says a college curriculum should teach in an HRM major.

A: 5
Employee Involvement

Employee engagement A combination of job satisfaction, ability, and a willingness to perform for the organization at a high level and over an extended period of time

EXHIBIT 1-1   FEATURES OF THIS BOOK'S THREE-PRONGED APPROACH

Features That Present HRM Functions and Important Concepts	Features to Apply the HRM Functions and Concepts That You Learn	Features That Foster Skill Development
• Learning Outcomes	• Practitioner's Perspective	• Self-Assessments
• Key terms	• Organizational examples	• Communication Skills Questions
• Step-by-step behavior models	• Work Applications	• Ethical Dilemmas
• Chapter summaries with glossaries	• Applying the Concepts	• Skill Builder Exercises
• Review questions	• Cases	
	• Videos	

WORK
APPLICATION 1-1

How can this course help you in your personal and professional lives? What are your goals, or what do you want to get out of this course?

LO 1-2

Discuss how HRM helps improve organizational revenues in a 21st century organization.

SHRM

A: 4
Employee Engagement

SHRM

Q: 9
Ongoing Performance and Productivity

Cost center A division or department that brings in no revenue or profit for the organization—running this function only costs the organization money

Revenue centers Divisions or departments that generate monetary returns for the organization

Productivity center A revenue center that enhances the profitability of the organization through enhancing the productivity of the people within the organization

Productivity The amount of output that an organization gets per unit of input, with human input usually expressed in terms of units of time

Effectiveness A function of getting the job done whenever and however it must be done

Efficiency A function of how many organizational resources we used in getting the job done

This book will teach you how to get people engaged and get the results necessary to succeed against tough competitors in the new century.[13] We will focus on HR management, but the principles within this text apply to any form of management. The bottom line is that if you learn these skills and apply them successfully in any manager role, you will get your employees engaged and improve productivity. That is what will get you noticed by senior management and allow you to move up the organizational ladder. So let's get started!

21ST CENTURY HRM

HRM Then and Now

Back in the mid-1970s—when there weren't even any computers available to most managers!—the human resource manager (we usually called them personnel managers then) was sometimes selected for the job because that person had limited skills as an operational manager. Many times they were not considered capable of managing line functions in *real* operations, so we put them in HR. This was because HRM was considered to be a bit easier than other management jobs. HR managers were only expected to be paper pushers who could keep all of the personnel files straight. They had very little to do with the management of the organization's business processes.

Cost Centers. In these types of organizations, the HR department was considered a cost center. A cost center *is a division or department that brings in no revenue or profit for the organization—running this function only costs the organization money.* As you can easily see, we don't want many (or any) cost centers if we can help it. We need revenue centers instead.

Revenue Centers. Revenue centers, however, *are divisions or departments that generate monetary returns for the organization.* Where cost centers eat up available funds, revenue centers provide funds for the organization to operate. So, what's a good HR manager to do? HR departments are not able to generate revenue *directly* because of their tasking within the organization, but they can generate significant revenue and profit in an indirect fashion as *productivity centers.*

Productivity Centers. A **productivity center** is *a revenue center that enhances the profitability of the organization through enhancing the productivity of the people within the organization.* Today's HR managers are no longer running an organizational cost center. HRM enhances the revenues of the organization—by being a productivity center. Productivity is *the amount of output that an organization gets per unit of input, with human input usually expressed in terms of units of time.*

But how can we become more productive? Productivity is the end result of two components that managers work to create and improve within the organization:

- Effectiveness—*a function of getting the job done whenever and however it must be done.* It answers the question, "Did we do the right things?"

- Efficiency—*a function of how many organizational resources we used in getting the job done.* It answers the question, "Did we do things right?"

Both of these are important, but most of the time, we are focused on efficiency. Our people allow us to be more efficient as an organization *if* they are used in the correct manner. This course is about how to make our people more efficient.

Companies around the world are taking this need for efficiency very seriously, and a few examples will quickly show how seriously. Teresa Taylor of **CenturyLink**, Lisa Brummel of **Microsoft**, and Leslie Locke of **Athenahealth** were all line managers with significant experience, but *none of them had senior HRM experience* when their organizations asked them to become HR leaders. Each of the companies was concerned about employee engagement and productivity, and especially about improving efficiency,[14] so the companies put some of their best managers in the HRM job. In addition to improving efficiency, some fairly new research has shown that among Fortune 500 firms, having a senior HR manager in the "C-suite"—meaning having a chief of human resources operations (CHRO) in addition to having a chief operations officer (COO), a chief finance officer (CFO), etc.—increased profitability by 105% over peer companies that did not have a CHRO![15]

HR management deals primarily with improving the efficiency of the people within our organization—getting more per unit of time. If our people are inefficient, it can literally kill the organization.

HRM Challenges

A recent SHRM survey of HR professionals asked what challenges they think will be most significant over the next 10 years. Here is what they said.[16]

The three biggest challenges:

1. Retaining and rewarding the best employees
2. Developing the next generation of corporate leaders
3. Creating a corporate culture that attracts the best employees

The HR competencies and subcompetencies that will be the most critical:

1. Business acumen
    a. HR metrics/analytics/business indicators
    b. Knowledge of business operations and logistics
    c. Strategic agility
2. Organizational leadership and navigation
3. Relationship management
4. Communication

Can you see how these challenges and the competencies could have an effect on productivity? We have pursued better selection and retention strategies for a number of years, and we have recently become much better at identifying future leaders and managing organizational relationships, culture, and structure.

Where we have not done as well—at least in most organizations to this point—is in business acumen, especially in quantitative areas dealing with metrics and data analytics. This is an area that will explode in the next few years in HR departments all over the world. The ability to analyze large data sets will allow HRMs to work toward overcoming another of their challenges—creating strategic agility *and* greater productivity. We will introduce you to some of the basic HR metrics as we go through this text so that you have a working understanding of how they might be used in each functional area of HRM.

SHRM

Q: 5, 10, J:11
Improving Organizational Effectiveness; Organizational Effectiveness

WORK
APPLICATION 1-2

Recall your most recent job. Did you work in a traditional cost center, a revenue center, or a productivity center? Briefly describe the firm and department and what made it a cost, revenue, or productivity center.

©iStockphoto.com/Yuri_Arcurs

Today's technology improves the effectiveness and efficiency of HR managers, leading to higher levels of productivity throughout the organization.

WORK
APPLICATION 1-3

How would you rate your level of productivity, job satisfaction, turnover, and absenteeism on your current job or a past job?

SHRM

A:6
Employee Retention

SHRM

A:20
Attendance

Job satisfaction The feeling of well-being that we experience in our jobs—basically whether or not we like what we do and the immediate environment surrounding us and our jobs

Turnover The permanent loss of workers from the organization

Absenteeism The failure of an employee to report to the workplace as scheduled

Information Age An era that began around 1980, in which information became one of the main products used in organizations; it is characterized by exponential increases in available information in all industries

Critical Dependent Variables

Before we go further, let's look at some of the things that managers tell us they *must* control to compete in today's business environment but that they can't *directly* manipulate. Every time that we survey managers in any industry or any department about managing others, they bring up the following issues as being among the most important and most difficult things that they deal with:[17]

1. *Productivity*—defined above
2. *Job satisfaction*—a feeling of well-being and acceptance of our place in the organization
3. *Turnover*—permanent loss of workers from the organization. When people quit, it is considered voluntary turnover, while when people are fired, it is involuntary turnover.
4. *Absenteeism*—temporary absence of employees from the workplace

Note that all of these issues deal with people: not computers, not buildings, not finances—people! We have already introduced you to productivity, but what about the other three items? Why do we care about job satisfaction, turnover, and absenteeism? Let's take a moment for a more detailed look at each of them.

Job satisfaction, as noted above, is *the feeling of well-being that we experience in our jobs—it's basically whether or not we like what we do and the immediate environment surrounding us and our jobs*, or "the extent to which people like (satisfaction) or dislike (dissatisfaction) their jobs."[18] There is a wealth of research that shows that if our employees are highly dissatisfied with their jobs, they will be far more likely to voluntarily leave and create turnover.[19] They will typically also have lower than average productivity, so we want to maintain reasonably high job satisfaction.

Turnover *is the permanent loss of workers from the organization.* There is strong and "growing recognition that collective turnover can have important consequences for organizational productivity, performance, and—potentially—competitive advantage."[20] As we will discuss throughout the book, turnover is very costly, so we want to minimize turnover.

How about absenteeism? **Absenteeism** *is the failure of an employee to report to the workplace as scheduled.* On an annual basis, absenteeism costs in the United States went from an estimated $30 billion in 1984[21] to anywhere from $100 to $150 billion per year in 2011.[22,23] We likely lose productivity, and if some of our workers are frequently absent, it causes lower job satisfaction in others who have to continually "take up the slack" for their absent coworker.

Note that these four issues are interrelated. Absenteeism is costly, is often due to a lack of job satisfaction, and leads to lower productivity.[24] People tend to leave their jobs (turnover) when they don't have job satisfaction, and while they are being replaced and sometimes after, organizational productivity goes down.[25] Seeing that job satisfaction can affect absenteeism, turnover, and productivity, we will discuss job satisfaction in some more detail in Chapter 9.

So the bottom line is this: As managers, we always need to be doing things that will improve productivity and job satisfaction and that will reduce absenteeism and turnover. These items are critical. Everything in HRM revolves around these four things.

Technology and Knowledge

The 20th century saw the growth and decline of the Industrial Age in the United States and most other developed countries around the world. However, as we neared the end of the 20th century, we started to enter the Information Age—*an era that began around 1980, in which information became one of the main products used in organizations; it is characterized by exponential increases in available information in all industries.* This was when assembly line work began to be taken over more and more by computers, robots, and other machines, and it was when the humans in our organizations were beginning to provide more than just labor; they started to provide intelligence—or knowledge. In the Information Age, we began to see a new kind of worker—knowledge workers.

Knowledge Workers and the Knowledge-Based Firm. **Knowledge** workers are *workers who "use their head more than their hands" and who gather and interpret information to improve a product or process for their organizations.* There has been a lot written in the past 20 years on knowledge workers, but we can boil it down to the fact that most workers in 21st century organizations are not working primarily with their hands; they work with their minds. In essence, knowledge workers manage knowledge for the firm.

The Pace of Technological Change. Technology is currently outstripping our ability to use it. Computers get faster and faster, but the human beings that have to use them don't. What does this mean to a business? It means that if we can figure out ways to take advantage of the technology better and quicker than our competitors can, then we can create a sustainable competitive advantage. We must continually figure out ways to use the technology more successfully through hiring and training better and more capable employees—our *human* resources. If we do this, then our people will continually figure out ways to take advantage of it before our competitors.

Knowledge Workers Are in Short Supply. However, there is a continuous shortage of knowledge workers available. In fact, "The majority of jobs being created in the United States require skills possessed by only 20% of the current workforce."[26] And the news is the same globally. This means that for the foreseeable future, we will have a shortage of knowledge workers. So each HR manager is going to be competing with every other HR manager in the world for that 20% of the workforce that comprises the pool of knowledge workers. Only if the organization manages its people successfully and maintains a reasonable working environment will it have any chance of filling most of the jobs that it has available.

Knowledge workers Workers who "use their head more than their hands" and who gather and interpret information to improve a product or process for their organizations

Labor Demographics

In addition to the issues of knowledge workers and knowledge-based organizations, we face significant demographic changes in the labor force that will be available to our companies over the next 20 years.

Companies are already seeing a reduction in the number and quality of potential employees, as well as greater gender, ethnic, and age diversity than at any time in the past. The lack of skilled workers for increasingly complex jobs is considered to be a major, ongoing problem.[27,28] Partly as a result of this shortage of skilled labor, we are seeing more older employees with high-level skill sets remain in the workforce. Some agencies estimate that over 90% of the growth in the US labor force between 2006 and 2016 will be from workers ages 55 and older.[29] So as a manager in a 21st century organization, your workforce will look much older than it has historically.

©Colorblind/Cardinal/Corbis

Part of the diversity in today's workforce is people retiring later in life and working part-time.

SHRM

0:8
Global Labor Markets

Your organization will also look more culturally diverse—even compared to today. The growth in immigrant workers will be substantial. Hispanic workers (of all nationalities) alone are predicted to be approximately 24% of the workforce in 2050, but today, they only make up about 14% of the workforce. Asian workers are expected to move up from about 4% now to about 8% of the workforce in 2050. But the gender mix will stay fairly close to what it is today. The percentage of women in the workforce has stabilized at about 47% or 48%.[30]

All of this means that managers of a 21st century organization will need to be more culturally aware and able to deal with individuals with significantly different work ethics, cultural norms, and even languages.

LO 1-3

Describe the major HRM discipline areas.

DISCIPLINES WITHIN HRM

HRM is an exciting field with many different paths that you can take over the course of your career. The field is so broad that you could do something different each year for a 40-year career and never exactly duplicate an earlier job. Although there are many different jobs in the field, most of them fall into a few categories. Let's briefly take a look at each of these disciplines or specialties. But first, complete the self-assessment below to help you better understand your overall interest in HR and which specialties interest you more. This section presents the disciplines discussed in detail throughout the book, so we will keep it short here.

The Legal Environment: EEO and Diversity Management

Equal employment opportunity (EEO) and diversity management specialists ensure compliance with equal opportunity laws and regulations as well as organizational affirmative action plans (when such plans are required or desired). They also have responsibilities related to the management of diverse employee groups within the company.

The HR legal and regulatory environment is critical to every organization today. This is also quite likely the area that changes more than any other in HRM. Every court case that deals with the HR environment inside any organization has the potential to affect every organization. Even if the court ruling doesn't change the way a company has to do business, if a federal or state legislature sees that ruling as unfair, then it may change the law and thus affect each organization under its jurisdiction.

Staffing

Staffing includes all of the things that we need to do to get people interested in working for our company—going through the recruiting process, selecting the best candidates who apply, and getting them settled into their new jobs. However, this area can literally make or break the organization in its ability to be productive.[31] If we attract and hire the right types of people with the right attitudes and skills, then the organization will have a good start at being successful.

Training and Development

Next, we have the training and development discipline. We train people for a variety of reasons, from teaching them their basic job to teaching them the things that they will need in order to move up in the organization as people above them resign or retire.

As a training and development specialist, you would have responsibility for the training processes within the organization as well as for the development of curricula and lesson plans and the delivery of training courses. You would also be involved with the development of talent within the company so that employees are trained and ready to move into more senior positions as those positions become vacant.

Employee Relations

This specialty covers a wide array of items such as coaching, counseling, and disciplining the workforce as needed. It also involves leadership and team-building efforts within the organization. We also measure and evaluate job satisfaction and employee engagement as part of employee relations. HR managers in this function have to keep up with the many and varied laws relating to employee relations, and this specialty also involves the management of employee communication.

Recycling contributes to our present and future sustainability.

Labor and Industrial Relations

The labor and industrial relations specialist works with the laws and regulations that control the organization's labor-related relationships with their workforce. HR managers who work in this area might be involved in union votes, negotiations for union agreements, collective bargaining, grievances, and other items that affect the union/management relationship within the organization. This area also includes all labor relations activities, even in nonunion businesses.

Compensation and Benefits

The compensation and benefits specialist helps decide the total compensation package that the organization will use to attract and retain the best mix of people with skills that are specifically suited to the organization. A manager will have to understand the federal and state laws that deal with compensation. You would also deal directly with all of the federal and state compensation laws to ensure compliance in organizational pay and benefits procedures.

Safety and Security

In the safety and security discipline, you might work in the area of occupational safety and/or health to make sure we don't injure our people or cause them to become sick because of exposure to some substance they work with. This discipline also includes fields such as stress management and employee assistance programs, which help employees cope with the demands of their jobs on a daily basis. And finally, this function works to ensure that employees are secure from physical harm inflicted by other workers, outsiders, or even acts of nature.

Ethics and Sustainability

In this specialty, you would bear responsibility for seeing to it that the organization acts in an ethical and socially responsible manner. You might work on codes of ethics and also make sure employees live by those codes, such as by maintaining ways in which employees can report violations of ethics (also known as *whistle-blowing*).

Sustainability is meeting the needs of today without sacrificing future generations' ability to meet their needs.[32] Some companies have historically done a relatively poor job of maintaining the environment in some countries in which they operated.

J:5
Sustainability/Corporate Social Responsibility

J:9
Ethics (integrated)

C:8
Codes of Ethics

1-1 SELF ASSESSMENT

HR Disciplines

Following are 24 HR activities that you could be involved in. Rate your interest in each specialty with a number (1–7) that represents your interest in the activity.

I'm not really interested in doing this					I'm really interested in doing this	
1	**2**	**3**	**4**	**5**	**6**	**7**

1. _____ Working to make sure everyone in the firm is treated fairly
2. _____ Working against discrimination and helping minorities to get hired and promoted
3. _____ Knowing the laws, helping the firm implement laws, and reporting how the firm complies with the HR laws
4. _____ Working to get people to apply for jobs, such as writing advertisements and attending job fairs
5. _____ Interviewing job candidates
6. _____ Orienting new employees to the firm and their jobs
7. _____ Teaching employees how to do their current jobs
8. _____ Developing employees' general skills so they can progress in the firm
9. _____ Designing curricula and lesson plans for others to teach employees
10. _____ Coaching, counseling, and disciplining employees whose work quality is not up to standards
11. _____ Working with teams and helping resolve conflicts
12. _____ Working to understand and improve the level of job satisfaction throughout the firm
13. _____ Working with union employees
14. _____ Collective bargaining with unions
15. _____ Solving employee complaints
16. _____ Working to determine fair pay for different jobs, including investigating competitors' pay scales
17. _____ Creating incentives to motivate and reward productive employees
18. _____ Finding good benefits providers, such as lower-cost and higher-quality health insurance providers
19. _____ Making sure that employees don't get hurt on the job
20. _____ Working to keep employees healthy, such as developing diet and exercise programs
21. _____ Ensuring the security of the facilities and employees, issuing IDs, and keeping employee records confidential
22. _____ Ensuring that employees are ethical, such as developing and enforcing codes of ethics
23. _____ Enforcing ethical standards, such as maintaining methods for employees to confidentially report ethics violations
24. _____ Working to help the organization develop methods to improve efficiency while protecting our environment

Scoring and Interpreting Individual Discipline Results

Place your rating numbers (1–7) below and total the three scores for each discipline. Then rank your totals from 1 to 8 to determine which disciplines interest you most:

Legal Environment:
EEO and Diversity Management

1 _____

2 _____

3 _____

_____ Total (Rank this total: _____ [1–8])

Staffing

4 _____

5 _____

6 _____

_____ Total (Rank this total: _____ [1–8])

If you take a look at the table of contents as well as the practitioner's model below, you will realize that this book is organized to discuss the eight areas of HRM listed above. Next, let's take a look at some of the professional organizations that are out there to help you get where you want to go in an HRM career.

Training and Development

7 _____
8 _____
9 _____
_____ Total (Rank this total: _____ [1–8])

Compensation and Benefits

16 _____
17 _____
18 _____
_____ Total (Rank this total: _____ [1–8])

Employee Relations

10 _____
11 _____
12 _____
_____ Total (Rank this total: _____ [1–8])

Safety and Security

19 _____
20 _____
21 _____
_____ Total (Rank this total: _____ [1–8])

Labor and Industrial Relations

13 _____
14 _____
15 _____
_____ Total (Rank this total: _____ [1–8])

Ethics and Sustainability

22 _____
23 _____
24 _____
_____ Total (Rank this total: _____ [1–8])

The higher your total in each discipline, the greater your interest in that area of HR at this point in time. Of course, your interest levels can change as you learn more about each discipline. You will also be doing self-assessments in all the other chapters that relate to these eight disciplines.

Scoring and Interpreting Total Discipline Results

Now add up your grand total interest score from all 24 activities and write it here: _____. Then compare it to the continuum below to gauge your overall level of interest in working in human resources:

Low interest in HR						High interest in HR
24	50	75	100	125	150	168

The higher your score, the greater is your overall interest in HR, again at this time only.

You should realize that this self-assessment is only designed to show your current level of interest. It may not predict how much you will enjoy working in any HR discipline in the future. For example, if you get a real job in an area where you gave yourself a low score today, you could end up finding it very interesting. The self-assessments throughout this book are designed to give you a better understanding of your interest and aptitudes at the present time, and they are open to your interpretations. For example, some people tend to rate themselves much lower or higher than others even though they have the same level of interest—so don't be too concerned about your score. There are *no* correct answers or scores. Some people with lower scores may actually enjoy the course more than those with higher scores. The purpose of these self-assessments is to help you gain self-knowledge and get you thinking about how the topic of HRM relates to you.

So at this point, you should have a better idea of what the eight HR disciplines are and which areas are of more and less interest to you. But as you read the rest of this chapter and the others and learn more about each discipline, you may change your mind.

HRM RESPONSIBILITIES

Now that we know the HR disciplines, it's time to learn the difference between line and staff managers and how their HR responsibilities within the disciplines are different while being related.

LO 1-4

Recall the primary difference between line and staff managers and their major HR responsibilities

1-1 APPLYING THE CONCEPT

HRM Disciplines

Identify each HRM discipline and write the letter corresponding to it before the activity involving it:

a. Legal Environment: EEO and Diversity Management

b. Staffing

c. Training and Development

d. Employee Relations

e. Labor and Industrial Relations

f. Compensation and Benefits

g. Safety and Security

h. Ethics and Sustainability

_____ 1. The HR manager is writing an ad to recruit a job candidate.

_____ 2. The HR manager is investigating an employee complaint of racial discrimination.

_____ 3. The HR manager is taking a class in preparation for the exam to become certified as a Professional in Human Resources (PHR).

_____ 4. The HR manager is working with an insurance company to try to keep the high cost of health insurance down.

_____ 5. The HR manager is replacing the office copier with a more energy-efficient model.

_____ 6. The HR manager is having a new software program installed to protect employee records from theft.

_____ 7. The HR manager is working on the new collective bargaining contract with the Teamsters Union.

_____ 8. The HR manager is looking for potential new employees at the LinkedIn website.

_____ 9. The HR manager is filling out an accident report with a production worker who got hurt on the job.

_____ 10. The HR manager is reviewing a report that compares its wages and salaries to other businesses in the area.

_____ 11. The HR manager is giving priority to promoting a member of a minority group to a management position.

_____ 12. The HR manager is teaching the new employee how to use the HR software program.

_____ 13. The HR manager is referring an employee to a marriage counselor.

1-1 ETHICAL DILEMMA: WHAT WOULD YOU DO?

Our first HR discipline is to know and obey the laws, and the last discipline is ethics and sustainability. A long debated issue is: (a) should a company focus on making a profit and doing so within the law, or (b) should a company go beyond the law to be ethical and socially responsible? Some experts state that (c) by being ethical and socially responsible the firm will be more profitable, whereas (d) others say that one shouldn't consider profits—a company should be ethical and socially responsible simply because it is the right thing to do. **Apple**'s cofounder Steve Jobs primarily believed in focusing on profits, whereas current CEO Tim Cook has changed policies to be more socially responsible by giving more resources to nonprofit organizations.

1. Do you agree with (a) focusing on profits, or (b) going beyond to be ethical and socially responsible?
2. Do you agree with (c) being ethical and socially responsible if it is profitable, or (d) that a company should be ethical simply because it is the right thing to do?
3. Review the HR disciplines and describe how a company can be ethical and socially responsible in performing these functions.

WORK
APPLICATION 1-4

Give brief examples of the HR disciplines performed by the HR department (or individuals responsible for HR) where you work or have worked.

Line Versus Staff Management

Line managers are *the individuals who create, manage, and maintain the people and organizational processes that create whatever it is that the business sells.* Put simply, they are the people who control the actual operations of the organization. A line manager may have direct control over staff employees, but a staff manager would not generally have any direct control of line employees. HR managers, on the other hand, would generally be **staff managers**, *individuals who advise line managers in some field of expertise.* These managers, including accountants, lawyers, and HR staff, act basically as internal consultants for the company. So HR managers have staff authority to *advise* the operational managers concerning the HR disciplines, as we discuss next.

Major HR Responsibilities of HR Staff and Line Management

All managers are responsible for meeting the organization's goals through effective management of its human resources. However, their major HR responsibilities are different. The HR staff has the primary responsibility of developing the HR policies and programs for everyone in the organization to implement on a daily basis. The line managers, therefore, are responsible for implementing the HR policies within their departments. Let's review the HR disciplines and discuss some differences.

- **The Legal Environment: EEO and Diversity Management.** The HR staff needs to know the laws and train the line managers how to operate within the law, such as what line managers can and can't ask during the interview process to follow EEO laws. HR staff may develop diversity programs and teach line managers how to work with a diversity of employees.

- **Staffing.** The HR staff generally recruits employees, but line managers select who is hired.

- **Training and Development.** HR staff develop training programs, including training line managers how to be effective managers. HR may teach many employees how to do their jobs, but line managers tend to provide ongoing on-the-job training.

- **Employee Relations.** HR staff develop policies, but line managers are constantly dealing with employee relations. HR may train line managers on how to coach and discipline employees.

- **Labor and Industrial Relations.** HR is responsible for policies and training to making sure the labor laws are followed, and line managers implement them. If the organization has a union, HR often helps in the contract negotiations.

- **Compensation and Benefits.** HR is responsible for developing the pay system including salary and benefits, but line managers can often have some input into how much an individual is paid, including raises.

- **Safety and Security.** HR is responsible for knowing the safety laws (OSHA) and ensuring that line managers train and manage their employees to follow the safety rules.

- **Ethics and Sustainability.** HR may develop Ethics Codes for everyone in the organization to follow, and line managers are responsible for making ethical decisions and helping their employees do likewise.

Line and staff employees can work more effectively together with today's technology.

WORK
APPLICATION 1-5

Give examples of line and staff positions at an organization where you work or have worked.

J:6
Internal Consulting

D:1
HR's Role in Organizations

Line managers The individuals who create, manage, and maintain the people and organizational processes that create whatever it is that the business sells

Staff managers Individuals who advise line managers in some field of expertise

LO 1-5

Summarize the major HRM skill sets.

WORK
APPLICATION 1-6

Give examples of HR responsibilities performed by your present boss or a past boss.

Technical skills The ability to use methods and techniques to perform a task

---

Human relations skills The ability to understand, communicate, and work well with individuals and groups through developing effective relationships

Empathy Being able to put yourself in another person's place—to understand not only what that person is saying but why the individual is communicating that information to you

Conceptual and design skills The ability to evaluate a situation, identify alternatives, select a reasonable alternative, and make a decision to implement a solution to a problem

Business skills The analytical and quantitative skills—including in-depth knowledge of how the business works and its budgeting and strategic planning processes—that are necessary for a manager to understand and contribute to the profitability of the organization.

HRM SKILLS

All managers require a mix of technical, human relations, conceptual and design, and business skills in order to successfully carry out their jobs (see Exhibit 1-2).[33] The set of necessary HR skills is similar to the skills needed by other managers, but of course it emphasizes people skills more than some other management positions do.

Technical Skills

The first skill set that an HR manager must develop to be successful, and the easiest one to develop, is technical skills.[34] Technical skills are *the ability to use methods and techniques to perform a task*. HR managers require many skills, including comprehensive knowledge of laws, rules, and regulations relating to HR; computer skills; interviewing and training skills; understanding of performance appraisal processes; and many others. We will cover many of these skills in the remaining chapters of this book.

Human Relations Skills

The second major skill set is human relations skills, which comprise *the ability to understand, communicate, and work well with individuals and groups through developing effective relationships*. The resources you need to get the job done are made available through relationships with people both inside the organization (i.e., coworkers and supervisors) and outside the organization (i.e., customers, suppliers, and others).[35] We will focus on interpersonal skills throughout this book, and you will have the opportunity to develop your human relations skills through this course.

HR managers must have strong people skills, including being *empathetic*. Empathy *is simply being able to put yourself in another person's place—to understand not only what that person is saying but why the individual is communicating that information to you*. Empathy involves the ability to consider what the individual is feeling while remaining emotionally detached from the situation.

Conceptual and Design Skills

Conceptual and design skills help in decision making. Leaders' decisions determine the success or failure of the organization.[36] So organizations train their people to improve their decision-making skills.[37] Conceptual and design skills *include the ability to evaluate a situation, identify alternatives, select a reasonable alternative, and make a decision to implement a solution to a problem*.

Business Skills

Lastly, HR managers must have strong general business skills. Business skills *are the analytical and quantitative skills—including in-depth knowledge of how the*

EXHIBIT 1-2   HRM SKILLS

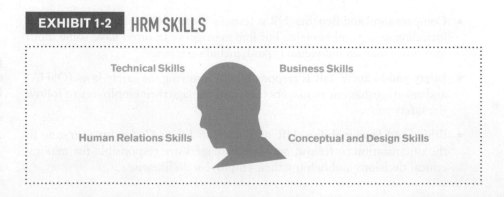

business works and its budgeting and strategic planning processes—that are necessary for a manager to understand and contribute to the profitability of the organization. HR professionals must have knowledge of the organization and its strategies if they are to contribute strategically. This also means that they must have understanding of the financial, technological, and other facets of the industry and the organization. Today, HR managers must gain the capability to manipulate large amounts of data using data analytics programs and HR metrics.

HRM CAREERS

If you are interested in HRM as a career, there are several professional associations and certification programs associated with HR management that will help you get into these jobs and help you advance more quickly in the future. We've listed some of them below, and there are several others within specific HR disciplines that are not discussed here.

Society for Human Resource Management (SHRM)

The **Society for Human Resource Management (SHRM)** *is the largest and most recognized of the HRM advocacy organizations in the United States.* According to its website, SHRM is "the world's largest association devoted to human resource management . . . representing more than 250,000 members in over 140 countries."[38]

What does SHRM do? Probably the biggest part of its work is dedicated to (1) advocacy for national HR laws and policies for organizations and (2) training and certification of HR professionals in a number of specialty areas. SHRM's new "competency-based" certification programs include the SHRM Certified Professional and Senior Certified Professional (SHRM-CP and SHRM-SCP).

SHRM is an outstanding organization that anyone thinking about a career in human resources should consider joining. Student memberships have always been and continue to be very inexpensive, especially considering all that is available to members of the organization.

SHRM also provides a curriculum guide for colleges and universities that offer HRM degree programs. The guide identifies specific areas in which SHRM believes students should gain competence as HRM majors. Because SHRM is such

WORK
APPLICATION 1-7

Give examples of how a present or past boss of yours used each of the four HRM skills.

LO 1-6

Identify the HRM certification programs and their parent organizations.

Society for Human Resource Management (SHRM) The largest and most recognized of the HRM advocacy organizations in the United States

1-2 APPLYING THE CONCEPT

HRM Skills

Identify each activity as being one of the following types of HRM skills and write the letter corresponding to each skill before the activity or activities describing it:

a. technical
b. human relations
c. conceptual and design
d. business

____ 14. The HR manager is working on the strategic planning process.

____ 15. The HR manager is working on determining why more employees have been coming to work late recently.

____ 16. The HR manager is filling out a complex government form.

____ 17. The HR manager is talking socially with a few of her staff members.

____ 18. The HR manager is praising a staff member for finishing a job analysis ahead of schedule.

____ 19. The HR manager is assigning projects to various staff members.

____ 20. The HR manager is communicating with employees throughout the company via email.

Taking and passing the SHRM Assurance of Learning Exam is an important step on the path to becoming an HR Manager.

a significant force in each of the HRM fields, we have decided to show you where each of the required curriculum areas is covered within this text. In each chapter, you will see notes on the side of the page when a *SHRM required* topic is discussed. These notes are alphanumerically keyed to the information in the Appendix *SHRM Curriculum Guide 2013*. You might want to pay special attention to these side notes if you have plans to become an HR manager.

If you do decide to work toward a goal of becoming an HR manager, you will need to think about taking the SHRM Assurance of Learning Exam. According to the SHRM website, "First and foremost, passing the assessment will help students show potential employers they have acquired the minimum knowledge required to enter the HR profession at the entry level."[39] To get more information about the Assurance of Learning Exam, go to the SHRM website at http://www.shrm.org/assessment.

Other HR Organizations

In addition to SHRM, there are three organizations that have certification programs that are recognized in many countries around the world. The first one is the **Association for Talent Development (ATD)**. As its name implies, ATD primarily focuses on the training and development functions of HR managers.[40] Its major certifications include the Certified Professional in Learning and Performance (CPLP) and the Human Performance Improvement (HPI) certification.

Second, the **Human Resource Certification Institute** (HRCI) provides some of the most respected certifications for HR personnel anywhere in the world. The three biggest certification programs are the PHR, SPHR, and GPHR certifications. PHR stands for Professional in Human Resources, SPHR stands for Senior Professional in Human Resources, and GPHR stands for Global Professional in Human Resources. These certifications are recognized by organizations worldwide as verification of a high level of training.

The third organization is **WorldatWork,** whose certifications mainly cover compensation and performance management programs.[41] Certifications from this organization include Certified Compensation Professional (CCP), Certified Benefits Professional (CBP), Global Remuneration Professional (GRP), Work-Life Certified Professional (WLCP), Certified Sales Compensation Professional (CSCP), and Certified Executive Compensation Professional (CECP).

WORK
APPLICATION 1–8

Are you joining or will you join a professional association, and will you seek certification? Explain why or why not.

Professional Liability

Do you realize that you can be held personally liable for your actions on the job? If you break the law, you can be sued and possibly face criminal charges. This is one of the many reasons why you really want to understand all of the HRM concepts. You need to be aware of the potential for personal liability, and in some cases, you may even need to consider professional liability insurance—for instance, if you are an HRM consultant to outside organizations.

PRACTITIONER'S MODEL FOR HRM

We have given you a (very) brief history of the HRM world and what HR management does for the organization. Now we need to start talking about some of the detailed information that you will need to know in order to be a successful HR (or other) manager for your organization. How will we do that? We are going to work through what you need to know using a practitioner's model for HRM, shown in Exhibit 1-3, which is the foundation for this book.

The Model

The practitioner's model is designed to show you how each of the areas within HRM interact and which items you must deal with before you can go on to successfully work on the next section—kind of like building a foundation before you build a house. Let's discuss the details of each section of the model separately. As we discuss each section, refer back to Exhibit 1-3 for a visual of the section.

LO 1-7

Explain the practitioner's model for HRM and how it applies to this book.

B:21

Professional Liability

EXHIBIT 1-3   THE PRACTITIONER'S MODEL FOR HRM

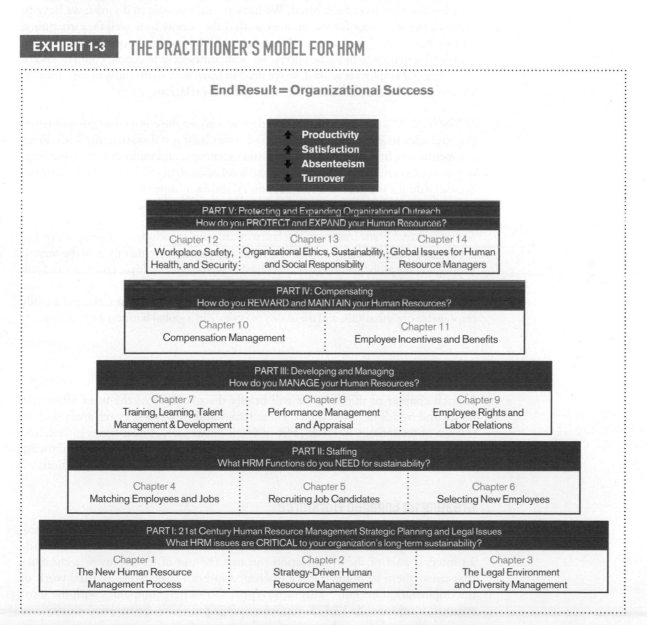

Section I: 21st Century HRM, Strategic Planning, and HR Laws. You have already begun Section I, where we talk about HRM in the 21st century, including the necessity of having strategy-driven HRM and a strong understanding of the basic HR legal environment. This is the basis for everything else that a 21st century HR manager will do, so it is the foundation of our diagram. These are the things that are *most critical* to the organization's basic stability and success, because if we don't get them right, we will probably not be around long enough as an organization to be successful in the sections resting on this one.

Section II: Staffing. Now that we have a stable organization with some form of direction, we start to look at getting the right people into the right jobs We first look at identifying the jobs that will need to be filled and then work through how to recruit the right numbers and types of people to fill those jobs. Finally, we find out what our options are concerning methods to select the best of those job candidates whom we have recruited.

Section III: Developing and Managing. In the third section, we learn how to manage our people once they have been hired. We have to train people to do jobs; we have to evaluate them in some formal manner so that they know how well they are doing; and we have to develop them so that they can fill higher-level positions as we need people to step up into those positions. We sometimes have to coach, counsel, and/or discipline our employees as well, so we need to learn how to do those things. Finally, Section III addresses the role of employee and labor relations.

Section IV: Compensating. The fourth section will cover the compensation and benefits packages to keep our people satisfied (or at least not dissatisfied). Both direct compensation, in the form of base pay and incentives, and indirect pay, in the form of worker benefits, provide us with some level of control over what our employees decide to do for the organization. Section IV shows us how to *reward and maintain* our workforce, since they are so critical to our ongoing success.

Section V: Protecting and Expanding. The last section's topics include managing safety and health, providing ethical and social responsibility guidelines to members of the organization, and the globalization issues involved in working in multiple countries and cultures. In addition to safety and health, two areas have become far more important since the beginning of the information age in the early 1980s: ethical, sustainable, and socially responsible organizations; and the ability to operate in a global business environment.

TRENDS AND ISSUES IN HRM

In each chapter of this text, we will briefly discuss some of the most important issues and trends in HRM today. These issues and trends will cover areas such as the use of technology in HRM, HR in small businesses, ethical issues in HR, and diversity and equal opportunity. For this chapter, we have chosen the following issues: creating an engaged workforce and the issue of reverse discrimination.

Creating an Engaged Workforce

Many of our employees are highly talented and extremely difficult to replace, but according to a recent Gallup report, 70% of them just aren't being made an integral part of the organization through the use of management techniques that cause them to become more interested in both their work and the work of the organization overall.[42] This same report shows that companies with the most engaged workforce had 147% higher earnings per share, better productivity and profitability, and lower absenteeism and turnover than their competitors, so there is certainly strong reason to work toward a more engaged workforce.

Higher rates of pay are not the answer, or at least not the *complete* answer. Evidence shows that increases in pay do not provide the motivational potential that most employees and managers believe they do.[43]

The first and most important thing that companies must do to improve engagement is to find, hire, and *train* managers on how to create employee engagement. Train them to communicate and be empathetic, and to provide feedback so that employees know that their managers recognize good work.[44] The evidence says that poorly trained managers are likely the biggest reason for employees being actively disengaged.

The second thing is to create and adhere to company values and goals that make employees feel they are part of something that is important and much bigger than they could do on their own.[45] They will be required to engage with others in order to have access to coworkers who will be available to help in reaching those goals.

Third, you have to make the hard decision to get the actively disengaged employees out of the company. This *is* a case of "one bad apple spoiling the whole barrel." Actively dissatisfied employees create tension in the workplace, which converts to disengagement among other employees who were just recently excellent workers.[46]

Reverse Discrimination Rulings Continue to Evolve

In 2009, a case claiming "reverse discrimination" (*Ricci v. DeStefano*.[47]) came to the Supreme Court. *What is reverse discrimination?* It is discrimination against a majority group rather than a minority group. In general in the United States, this would be discrimination against white male employees or applicants. We protect many different racial, ethnic, gender and other groups within the United States, but how do we, and should we, protect the majority group? At what point does the protection of minority groups cross over to discrimination against the majority?

Ricci v. DeStefano renewed the discussion of race-based decision making in employment. And while there were many nuances to the case, the end result was that reverse discrimination was deemed to have occurred. A written promotion exam for firefighters was considered discriminatory when no black and only one Hispanic test-taker passed the exam. As a result, the city of New Haven threw the entire exam out and didn't promote anyone. The firefighters who scored highest on the exam sued based on reverse discrimination.

Was the decision right or wrong? We can't make that determination here, but employment discrimination of all types continues to be something that HR managers have to be very aware of and guard against to the best of their ability. Nobody in your workforce likes feeling that they have been treated unfairly. Fairness is one of the critical themes you will see dealt with throughout this book. The HR department is, and will continue to be, the organization's watchdog on the topic of workforce discrimination and fairness to all employees.

SHRM

F:8

Reverse Discrimination

• • • CHAPTER SUMMARY

1-1   Explain why all managers need to understand the basics of HRM.

In a modern organization, human resources are one of the primary means of creating a competitive advantage for the organization, because the ways we manage people directly affects their performance. Engaged employees have also been shown to directly contribute to the bottom line (the top 10% on employee engagement beat their competition by 72% in earnings per share during 2007–2008). HRM provides all managers with tools to engage their employees and as a result increase employee productivity and company profitability.

1-2   Discuss how HRM helps improve organizational revenues in a 21st century organization.

Today's HR department acts as a productivity center rather than a cost center, enhancing the profitability of the company by improving employee productivity. HRM practices primarily help to improve organizational efficiency. Employees become more efficient if they are used correctly, which means that managers don't use up their time (the valuable resource that we get from employees) in an inefficient manner.

1-3   Describe the major HRM discipline areas.

- *The legal environment: EEO and diversity management.* This discipline deals with equal opportunity laws and regulations as well as management of a diverse workforce.
- *Staffing.* This discipline manages the processes involved in job analysis, recruiting, and selection into the organization.
- *Training and development.* This discipline has responsibility for the training processes within the organization, for developing curricula and lesson plans, and for delivery of training courses. It is also involved with development of talent within the company to provide a group of employees who will be able to move into more senior positions that become vacant.
- *Employee relations.* This area involves the coaching, counseling, and discipline processes, along with employee communication and stress management. It is also typically responsible for the management of job satisfaction and employee engagement.
- *Labor and industrial relations.* This discipline works with the laws and regulations that control the organization's relationships with its workforce. It also works with any union-management contracts, including but not limited to union

votes, grievances, contract negotiations, and bargaining with union representatives.

- *Compensation and benefits.* This discipline works with pay of various types and with benefits packages, all of which are designed to attract and keep the right mix of employees in the organization. It also deals directly with all of the federal and state compensation laws to ensure compliance.
- *Safety and security.* This discipline works to ensure that the environment on the job is safe for all workers so that on-the-job injuries and illnesses are minimized to the greatest extent possible. It also involves managing the organization's planning for securing the workforce, both from being harmed by other people and from natural disasters such as earthquakes or tornados.
- *Ethics and sustainability.* This discipline bears responsibility for seeing to it that the organization acts in an ethical and socially responsible manner, to minimize harm to the environment and its various stakeholders. It involves managing the sustainability efforts in the organization to minimize the depletion of worldwide resources caused by the organization carrying out its processes.

1-4   Recall the primary difference between line and staff managers and their major HR responsibilities.

The HR staff has the primary responsibility of developing the policies and programs with its HR disciplines for everyone in the organization to implement on a daily basis. The line managers are responsible for implementing the HR policies within their departments.

1-5   Summarize the major HRM skill sets.

The HRM skill sets include technical skills, human relations skills, conceptual and design skills, and business skills. *Technical skills* include the ability to use specialized knowledge, methods, and techniques to perform a task. *Human relations skills* provide the ability to understand, communicate, and work well with individuals and groups through developing effective relationships. *Conceptual and design skills* provide the ability to evaluate a situation, identify alternatives, select an alternative, and implement a solution to the problem. Finally, *business skills* provide analytical and quantitative skills, including the in-depth knowledge of how the business works and of its budgeting and strategic planning processes.

1-6   Identify the most common HRM certification programs and their parent organizations.

The primary certifications are carried out by SHRM, ATD, HRCI, and WorldatWork. SHRM's "competency-based" certification programs include the SHRM Certified Professional and Senior Certified Professional (SHRM-CP and SHRM-SCP). ATD training and development certifications include the Certified Professional in Learning and Performance (CPLP) and the Human Performance Improvement (HPI) certification. HRCI maintains certification programs for Professional in Human Resources (PHR), a senior version (SPHR), and a global version (GPHR). Finally, certifications from WorldatWork include Certified Compensation Professional (CCP), Certified Benefits Professional (CBP), Global Remuneration Professional (GRP), Work-Life Certified Professional (WLCP), Certified Sales Compensation Professional (CSCP), and Certified Executive Compensation Professional (CECP).

1-7 Explain the practitioner's model for HRM and how it applies to this book.

The practitioner's model shows the relationships between each of the functions and disciplines within HRM. On the first level are the items that are absolutely critical to the organization if it is going to continue to operate (and stay within federal and state laws while doing so) and be stable and successful for a significant period of time. The second level encompasses those things that are required to identify the kinds of jobs that must be filled and then recruit and select the right types of people into those jobs so the company can maximize productivity over the long term. These items will allow the organization to get its work done successfully over long periods of time. In the third tier, we concern ourselves with management of the human resources that we selected in the second level. We have to get them training to do their jobs and allow them to perform those jobs for a period of time. We then have to appraise their performance and, if necessary, correct behaviors that are not allowing them to reach their maximum potential. As this is occurring, we need to ensure that we maintain positive relationships with our employees so that they remain engaged and productive. In the fourth tier, we want to make sure that we reward our workforce reasonably through fair and reasonable compensation planning to minimize unnecessary turnover and dissatisfaction. In the last tier we provide for employee safety and health, and also turn our attention to organizational ethics and the issues surrounding global business operations because these issues will allow us to sustain our workforce and thrive in the 21st century.

KEY TERMS

absenteeism, 8
business skills, 16
conceptual and design skills, 16
cost center, 6
effectiveness, 6
efficiency, 6
empathy, 16
employee engagement, 5

human relations skills, 16
human resources, 4
Information Age, 8
job satisfaction, 8
knowledge worker, 9
line manager, 14
productivity, 6
productivity center, 6

revenue center, 6
Society for Human Resource Management (SHRM), 17
staff manager, 15
technical skills, 16
turnover, 8

KEY TERMS REVIEW

Complete each of the following statements using one of this chapter's key terms.

1. _____ the people within an organization.

2. _____ is a combination of job satisfaction, ability, and a "willingness to perform" for the organization at a high level, and over an extended period of time.

3. _____ a division or department within an organization that brings in no revenue or profit – in other words it costs money for the organization to run this function.

4. _____ a division or department that generates monetary returns for the organization.

5. _____ a revenue center that enhances profitability of the organization through enhancing the productivity of the people within the organization.

6. _____ the amount of output that an organization gets per unit of input, with human input usually expressed in terms of units of time.

7. _____ answers the question "Did we do the right things?"; it is a function of getting the job done whenever and however it must be done.

8. _____ is a function of how many organizational resources we used in getting the job done; it answers the question "Did we do things right?"

9. _____ is the feeling of well-being that we experience in our work—basically whether or not we like what we do and the immediate environment surrounding us and our work.

10. _____ is the permanent loss of workers from the organization.

11. _____ is the failure of an employee to report to the workplace as scheduled.

12. _____ is an era that began around 1980 in which information became one of the main products used in organizations; it is characterized by exponential increases in available information in all industries.

13. _____ are workers who "use their head more than their hands" to gather and interpret information in order to improve a product or process for their organizations.

14. _____ include the ability to use methods and techniques to perform a task.

15. _____ are the ability to understand, communicate, and work well with individuals and groups through developing effective relationships.

16. _____ is being able to put yourself in another person's place—to understand not only what they are saying but why they are communicating that information to you.

17. _____ are made up of the ability to evaluate a situation, identify alternatives, select an alternative and make a decision to implement a solution to a problem.

18. _____ are the analytical and quantitative skills, including in-depth knowledge of how the business works and its budgeting and strategic planning processes that are necessary for a manager to understand and contribute to the profitability of their organization.

19. _____ create and manage the organizational processes and the people that create whatever it is that a business sells.

20. _____ are the individuals that *advise* line management of the firm in their area of expertise.

21. _____ is the largest and most recognized of the HRM advocacy organizations in the United States.

● ● ● COMMUNICATION SKILLS

The following critical-thinking questions can be used for class discussion and/or for written assignments to develop communication skills. Be sure to give complete explanations for all answers.

1. Why is it important for all business majors to take this course in HRM?

2. Are you interested in becoming an HR manager? Why or why not?

3. Do you agree with the statement "Effectively utilizing the human resources within the organization is one of the few ways to create a competitive advantage in a modern business"? Why or why not?

4. Is employee engagement possible in an age when people tend to have very little loyalty to their employers and vice versa? How would you work to increase employee engagement as a manager?

5. Can HRM really create revenue for the organization? If so, how?

6. Identify some things that could be done by a manager to increase productivity and job satisfaction and decrease absenteeism and turnover. Make a list for each item.

7. If you were the HR manager for your organization, what would you do to increase the number of applicants who apply for "knowledge worker" positions in your organization? Assume you can't pay them more.

8. Is there anything that an individual within an organization can do to help improve relations among diverse workers? If so, what?

9. Some say that for managers, hard skills (technical and business skills) are more important than soft skills (human relations and conceptual and design skills). What do you think, and why?

10 Are external certification programs (in all jobs) becoming more important? Why?

● ● ● CASE 1–1 BA–ZYNGA! ZYNGA FACES TROUBLE IN FARMVILLE

In late 2011, Zynga's employees were showing serious frustration with long hours, high-stress deadlines, and especially the leadership of the company. Responses to a quarterly staff satisfaction survey provided lots of criticism of both the company culture and Mr. Mark Pincus—the CEO. One individual was so disenchanted that he openly expressed his intent to "cash out" and leave after the company's initial public offering (IPO) in December 2011.

Zynga was one of the fastest growing web-based companies at that point in time. It operated with an almost military command-and-control structure, with autonomous units in charge of each game (most of you will recognize the games FarmVille and CityVille). At times, it was "a messy and ruthless war."[48] Employees worked long hours while "managers relentlessly track[ed] progress, and the weak links [were] demoted or let go."[49] The entire environment could be described as intense.

There were serious concerns about the long-term viability of this culture, though. "While some staff members thrive in this environment, others find it crushing. Several former employees describe emotionally charged encounters, including loud outbursts from Mr. Pincus, threats from senior leaders, and moments when colleagues broke down [in] tears."[50] A number of former employees spoke about how the high-pressure culture might become a major liability as the company continued to grow. The consensus of these former workers appeared to be that the company might not continue to be able to attract and retain the top engineering and programming talent that they would need going forward.

"While from the outside Zynga may have the fun and whimsy of the Willy Wonka chocolate factory, the organization thrives on numbers, relentlessly aggregating performance data, from the upper ranks to the cafeteria staff."[51] Everything was measured and mapped, and results were used to identify the top performers along with the "not-so-top" performers and their groups. (Top teams had been known to be rewarded with vacations for the entire team, with spending money provided by the company!) Mr. Pincus personally tracked large amounts of data showing performance levels for the 3,000 employees and their work teams.

It wasn't that Zynga was failing, or even that there was an open fear of failure. Zynga was one of the rare Internet start-ups that were actually making money. Zynga had garnered $828.9 million in revenue in the first nine months of 2011 and had earned $121 million since the start of 2010. However, the company culture was purely performance driven. The best employees were rewarded very well, while people who couldn't "hit the numbers" were likely to disappear.

Other local companies and their human resources managers were looking on in anticipation. They also had talent acquisition problems, but many had a much more collaborative culture than Zynga did, and they thought they would be able to use these cultural attributes to steal talent from Zynga after the IPO concluded. They knew that most of Zynga's early employees who had some type of stock or options in the company would not be likely to leave until the IPO was finalized, but that many would be looking around soon after.

Questions

1. Imagine you are the new HR director at Zynga. What do you think you might do in this situation to limit the potential loss of a large number of very talented employees?

2. Are there any benefits or incentives that you can think of that might make more people want to stay on at Zynga after the IPO is complete and they can "get their money"?

3. HR managers frequently have to teach other senior managers how to deal with their employees better. What do you think you would do about Mr. Pincus? Is there anything you *could* do? Could you coach him concerning his management style? Do you think this would be effective?

4. Do you think that big cash and stock rewards for top performers and "the boot" for poor performers is the appropriate way to manage talent in this type of high-tech business? Why or why not?

••• SKILL BUILDER 1–1 GETTING TO KNOW YOU

Objectives

1. To get acquainted with some of your classmates
2. To gain a better understanding of what the course covers
3. To get to know more about your instructor

Skills

The primary skills developed through this exercise are as follows:

1. *HR management skill*—Human relations
2. *SHRM 2013 Curriculum Guidebook*—A: Employee Relations

Procedure 1 (5–8 minutes)

Break into groups of five or six, preferably with people you do not know. Have each member tell the group their name and two or three significant things about themselves. Then have all group members ask each other questions to get to know each other better.

Procedure 2 (4–8 minutes)

Can everyone in the group address every other person by name? If not, have each member repeat their name. Then each person in the group should repeat the names of all the group members until each person knows everyone's first name.

Application

What can you do to improve your ability to remember people's names?

_____

_____

_____

_____

Procedure 3 (5–10 minutes)

Elect a spokesperson for your group. Look over the following categories and decide on some specific questions you would like your spokesperson to ask the instructor from one or more of the categories. The spokesperson will not identify who asked the questions. You do not have to have questions for each area.

- *Course expectations*. What do you expect to cover or hope to learn from this course?

- *Doubts or concerns*. Is there anything about the course that you don't understand?
- *Questions about the instructor*. List questions you'd like to ask the instructor to get to know them better.

Procedure 4 (10–20 minutes)

Each spokesperson asks the instructor one question at a time until all questions have been answered. Spokespeople should skip questions already asked by other groups.

Apply It

What did I learn from this experience? How will I use this knowledge in the future?

_____

_____

_____

• • • SKILL BUILDER 1–2 COMPARING HR MANAGEMENT SKILLS AND HR RESPONSIBILITIES

Objective

To better understand the importance of good HR management skills and implementing HR responsibilities effectively

Skills

The primary skills developed through this exercise are as follows:

1. *HR management skills*—Conceptual and design
2. *SHRM 2013 Curriculum Guidebook*—A: Employee Relations

Compare Your Supervisors' HR Management Skills and HR Responsibilities Effectiveness

Recall the best supervisor or boss you ever worked for and the worst one you ever worked for (preferably line managers, not HR managers). Compare these two people by writing brief notes in the following chart about each person's HR management skills and HR responsibilities.

HR Management Skills and HR Responsibilities

Best Supervisor or Boss		Worst Supervisor or Boss
	Technical	
	Human Relations	
	Conceptual and Design	
	Business Skills	
	Legal Considerations	
	Staffing	
	Training and Development	
	Employee and Labor Relations	
	Safety and Security	
	Ethics	

Based on your own experiences with a good boss and a poor one, what do you believe are the key differences between good and poor managers?

Apply It

What did I learn from this exercise? How will I use this knowledge in the future?

_____

_____

_____

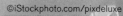
©iStockphoto.com/pixdeluxe

©iStockphoto.com/Photo_Concepts

2 STRATEGY-DRIVEN HUMAN RESOURCE MANAGEMENT

• • • LEARNING OUTCOMES

After studying this chapter, you should be able to do the following:

2-1 Classify the major components of the external environment. PAGE 31

2-2 Discuss the three major organizational factors that affect our strategic options. PAGE 33

2-3 Summarize the major components of organizational structure and why it is important to understand them. PAGE 39

2-4 Describe organizational culture and how it affects the members of the organization. PAGE 40

2-5 Define data analytics and explain how it helps organizations make important decisions. PAGE 42

2-6 Identify how human resource information systems (HRIS) can help HR make decisions. PAGE 44

2-7 Recall the common measurement tools for strategic human resource management (HRM). PAGE 45

2-8 Define the key terms found in the chapter margins and listed following the Chapter Summary. PAGE 49

Practitioner's Perspective

Cindy notes that one thing many family get-togethers have in common is storytelling—reminiscing about common experiences and outstanding members. These stories are part of the ties that bind and define the group, and the same is true for your work "family."

For example, take this story about Bill, an executive who started work as an emergency medical technician (EMT). One time while Bill was moving a nursing home resident, the resident's bedridden roommate feebly attempted to say good-bye. Young and impatient, Bill didn't stop to let the two talk but hurried off to the hospital with his passenger. The next time he was at that location, Bill was pulled aside by a nurse who said, "What I am about to say will break your heart, but it will make you a better man. The woman you transported died in the hospital that night. The roommate was her husband of 70 years, and you didn't give him time to say good-bye." Ever afterward in his career, Bill's motto was "Patients First," and that goal permeates his institution even today in everything it does.

What else defines company culture? Chapter 2 examines strategies, mission statements, vision, and values—all important pieces of a company's identity.

● ● ●

STRATEGY AND STRATEGIC PLANNING IN THE 21ST CENTURY: THE ORGANIZATION AND THE ENVIRONMENT

Strategy and strategic planning provide us with a process of looking at our organization and its environment—both today and in the expected future—and determining what we as an organization want to do to meet the requirements of that expected future (see Exhibit 2-1). This process of strategic analysis and building a coherent strategy is more critical today than it has ever been before.[1,2,3,4] This is

● ● ● CHAPTER OUTLINE

EXHIBIT 2-1   STRATEGIC CHOICE

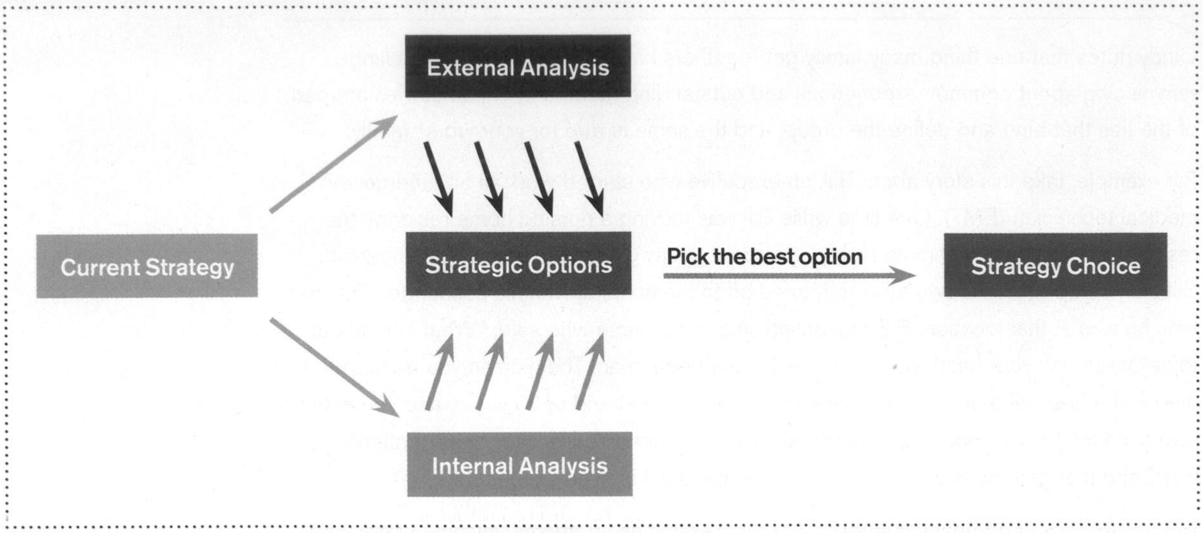

because in most worldwide industries today, we have far more competition and capacity than ever before, making it more difficult to create the sustainable competitive advantage that we need in order to survive over the long term.

There is an old saying: "When you fail to plan, you plan to fail." Research supports this saying and confirms the importance of planning.[5] Some managers complain that they don't have time to plan, yet research shows that managers who plan are more effective and efficient than nonplanners. Before we get into the details of strategic planning, complete Self-Assessment 2-1 to determine your level of planning.

HRM is a critical component of strategic planning, because without the right people with the right types of education, skills, and mind-set, we cannot expect to accomplish the objectives that we set for ourselves.[6] In this chapter, we focus on the

SHRM HR CONTENT

See Appendix: *SHRM 2013 Curriculum Guidebook* for the complete list

A. Employee and Labor Relations (required)

   3. Managing/creating a positive organizational culture

C. Ethics (required)

   3. Individual versus group behavior

E. Job Analysis/Job Design (required)

   9. Organization design (missions, functions, and other aspects of work units for horizontal and vertical differentiation)

G. Outcomes: Metrics and Measurement of HR (required)

   1. Economic value added

   7. Return on investment (ROI)

J. Strategic HR (required)

   1. Strategic management

   2. Enhancing firm competitiveness

   3. Strategy formulation

   7. Competitive advantage

   8. Competitive strategy

   10. Linking HR strategy to organizational strategy

   13. Mission and vision

Q. Organizational Development (required–graduate students only)

   12. Organizational structure and job design

| EXHIBIT 2-2 | THE EXTERNAL ENVIRONMENT |

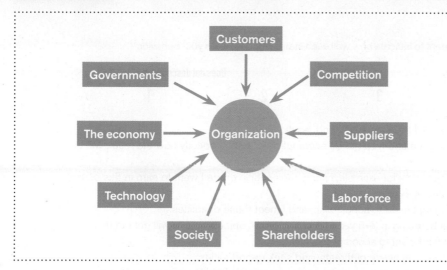

organization's environment. The environment has two parts: internal and external. First, we briefly discuss the external environment. Then we describe in detail three key aspects of the internal environment: strategy, structure, and culture.

THE EXTERNAL ENVIRONMENT

The external environment consists of a series of influences that originate outside the organization and that the company cannot control. Each of these forces acts on the firm and causes the firm to have to change and adapt, usually in the form of strategic responses to environmental changes.[7] The nine major forces originating in the external environment are shown in Exhibit 2-2, along with an explanation of each (below).

LO 2-1

Classify the major components of the external environment.

- *Customers*. Without customers, there's no need for an organization. Therefore, companies must continually improve products and services to create value for their customers.[8] This process of product improvement requires skilled employees who are willing to use their creativity to add to the organization's knowledge and thereby help create new products and services for customers.

- *Competition*. Businesses must compete for customers, and their performance is not simply a function of their own actions. Each firm's performance must be understood relative to the actions of its *competitors*.[9] Organizations also frequently compete for the same employees and sometimes for suppliers.[10] Also, changes in competitors' strategies often affect the performance of the organization.

- *Suppliers*. Organizations buy resources from suppliers. Therefore, partnerships with *suppliers* also affect firm performance.[11] The Japanese earthquake and tsunami in Fukushima affected virtually every company in the auto industry because electronic components made in northern Japan were unavailable for an extended period of time.[12] It is important to develop close working relationships with your suppliers.

- *Labor force*. The talent pool available to an organization from which to hire new employees has a direct effect on the organization's performance. Living Social is an example of a fast-growing company that is recruiting thousands of new workers.[13]

2-1 SELF ASSESSMENT

Level of Planning

Write a number from 1 to 5 before each statement to indicate how well each statement describes your behavior.

Describes me				Does not describe me
5	4	3	2	1

_____ 1. Whenever I start a project of any kind, I have a specific end result in mind.

_____ 2. When setting objectives, I state only the end result to be accomplished; I don't specify how the result will be accomplished.

_____ 3. I have specific and measurable objectives; for example, I know the specific grade I want to earn in this course.

_____ 4. I set objectives that are difficult but achievable.

_____ 5. I set deadlines when I have something I need to accomplish, and I meet those deadlines.

_____ 6. I have a long-term goal (what I will be doing in 3–5 years) and short-term objectives that will get me there.

_____ 7. I have written objectives stating what I want to accomplish.

_____ 8. I know my strengths and weaknesses, am aware of threats, and seek opportunities.

_____ 9. I analyze a problem and consider alternative actions, rather than immediately jumping in with a solution.

_____ 10. I spend most of my day doing what I plan to do, rather than dealing with emergencies and trying to get organized.

_____ 11. I use a calendar, appointment book, or some form of to-do list.

_____ 12. I ask others for advice.

_____ 13. I follow appropriate policies, procedures, and rules.

_____ 14. I develop contingency plans in case my plans do not work out as I expect them to.

_____ 15. I implement my plans and determine if I have met my objectives.

Add up the numbers you assigned to the statements to see where you fall on the continuum below.

Planner						Nonplanner
75	65	55	45	35	25	15

Don't be too disappointed if your score isn't as high as you would like. All of these items are characteristics of effective planning. Review the items that did not describe you and consider making an effort to implement those characteristics of planning.

WORK
APPLICATION 2-1

Give examples of how the external environment have affected an organization where you work or have worked.

- *Shareholders.* The owners of a corporation, known as shareholders, influence management. Most shareholders of large corporations are not involved in the day-to-day operation of the firm, but they do vote for the directors of the corporation. The board of directors is also generally not involved in the day-to-day management of the firm, but may hire or fire top management. The top manager reports to the board of directors, and if the organization does not perform well, the board can fire that manager and others.[14]

- *Society.* Our society, to a great extent, determines what acceptable business practices are.[15] Individuals and various groups of stakeholders work to pressure businesses to make changes. For example, Pepsi has been pressured by **Oxfam International** to identify its sugar suppliers and investigate suspected land theft by those suppliers from poor farmers.[16]

- *Technology.* Few organizations operate today as they did even a decade ago. Products not envisioned a few years ago are now being mass-produced, which creates new business opportunities. Businesses that don't keep up with technology, like **BlackBerry** (a one-time cell phone leader), lose business to those creating the latest business innovations, like **Apple** and **Samsung**.

- *Economic.* No organization has control over economic growth, inflation, interest rates, foreign exchange rates, and so on; thus, the economy has a direct impact on the firm's performance and profits. We always have to take the economy into account when performing strategic planning activities.

- *Government.* As a business owner or manager, you can't just run your business any way you want to because the federal, state, and local governments develop the laws and regulations that determine what your business can and can't do.[17] So although you can try to influence the government, it clearly affects your business. To learn more about the US federal government, visit its official web portal at http://www.usa.gov/.

Technology is one of the nine major forces originating in the external environment. Companies that continue to innovate their technology, like Apple, will have an advantage over the competition.

In addition to our analysis of the major external environmental factors above, we need to review some internal organizational factors to decide what we want to do as an organization as we move into the future. The major factors in our analysis of our internal environment are shown in Exhibit 2-3 and are discussed in this and the next two sections.

STRATEGY

Strategy and the strategic planning process have a long history, and businesses have adapted these principles to their own use. "Many military historians and contemporary business students view the Chinese military strategist Sun Tzu (ca. 500 BCE) as the developer of "the Bible" of strategy . . . Sun Tzu's principles are divided into two components: 1) knowing oneself and 2) knowing the enemy."[18]

LO 2-2

Discuss the three major organizational factors that affect our strategic options.

SHRM

J:8
Competitive Strategy

EXHIBIT 2-3   THE INTERNAL ENVIRONMENT

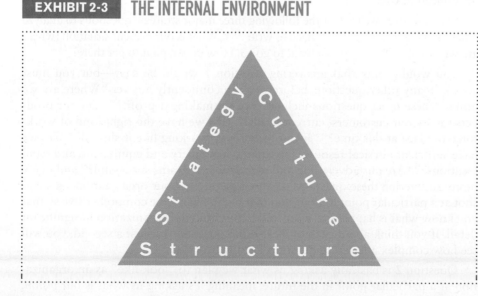

2-1 APPLYING THE CONCEPT

The External Environment

Read each statement and write in the letter corresponding to the external environmental factor it refers to.

a. customers

b. competition

c. suppliers

d. labor force

e. shareholders

f. society

g. technology

h. the economy

i. governments

_____ 1. The CEO was fired by the owners because our company is not profitable.

_____ 2. GE wanted to acquire our company, but the SEC said that would be in violation of antitrust laws, thereby preventing the deal.

_____ 3. Karen bought a new oven that will cook our pizza in half the time and make it taste even better.

_____ 4. **eHarmony,** an online dating service, is losing some customers to other services focusing on Christian, African-American, and older people seeking matches.

_____ 5. Our purchasing agent just closed a deal that will let us buy sugar for a few cents less per pound, saving us thousands of dollars per year.

To put Sun Tzu's words in a contemporary business context, we need to know our internal and external environments. But how does a modern business go about creating and implementing a strategic plan? Well, strategic planning follows a process,[19] so let's discuss that process now.

SHRM

J:1

Strategic Management

What Is Strategy?

Research has shown that HRM is an important strategic business function that influences the performance of both large and small firms.[20] But what is strategy? At its most basic level, a **strategy** is *a plan of action designed to achieve a particular set of objectives.* It looks at the external (industry and macro-) environment and the internal (organizational) environment in order to create strategic advantage. Strategic advantage occurs when you analyze the environment better and react to it quicker than your competitors do while using all of your internal resources efficiently, thus creating the sustainable competitive advantage that we introduced in Chapter 1.

In this section, we look at the following three major strategic questions to analyze what kind of strategic plan we need to write:[21] 1. What is our present situation (where are we now)? 2. Where do we want to go? 3. How do we plan to get there?

You would think that answering question 1 would be easy—but you must answer many other questions before you can confidently answer "Where are we now?" These other questions include "Are we making a profit?" "Do our products satisfy our customers' current needs?" "Do we have the right kind of workforce in place at this time?" "Is our technology working like it should?" "Do we have sufficient physical resources like plant, machinery and equipment, and retail locations?" "Are our advertising and marketing programs successful?" and many more. Answering these questions creates a picture of your organization—a snapshot at a particular point in time, and that picture has to be comprehensive so that you know what is happening, good and bad, within the organization in significant detail. If you think about each of these other questions for just a second, you will see how complex answering question 1 really becomes.

Question 2 is basically asking us what we plan to "look like" as an organization at a particular point in the future, meaning it's asking us what is our *vision,*

Strategy A plan of action designed to achieve a particular set of objectives

mission, and objectives for the organization. Answering question 3 gives us the necessary information to create the plan that will allow us to reach the goals that we identify in our answer to question 2 so that we can become the organization that we envision and at the same time create a sustainable competitive advantage.

SHRM

J:7

Competitive Advantage

Visions, Missions, and Objectives

A vision and a mission are two of the most critical components of any successful corporate strategy. Together, they provide the information necessary to focus every employee on the company's goals and objectives.

SHRM

J:13

Mission and Vision

The Vision. A **vision** is *what we expect to become as an organization at a particular point in time in the future.* The vision by necessity is a fuzzy thing; it is not specific in that it doesn't say *how* we're going to achieve it. It is who we are, what we stand for, what we believe in, and what we want to become. Despite their fuzziness, visions are very powerful when used correctly. A vision provides a focus point for the future; it tells the company where it is headed.[22] If everyone is focused on the same future end state, they will work toward that same end state.

So the vision answers the question "What do we want to become as an organization?" But the firm is only successful when the followers share the leader's vision,[23] and HR is where many organizations perform the culture training that promotes a shared vision within the organization.

The Mission. In contrast, the mission is where we start to become specific. The **mission statement** *lays out our expectations of what we're going to do in order to become the organization that we have envisioned.*
The mission is more specific than the vision, which means that it generally must be a bit longer-winded. The mission statement takes into account things like whom we serve (in terms of customer groups, types of products and services, technologies we use, etc.) and how we serve them. Fundamentally, it answers the question "What do we need to do in order to become what we have envisioned?"

@iStockphoto.com/sljbo

Putting the Vision and Mission Together. Let's use as an example the vision and mission statements of the **College of Business of the University of Arkansas at Little Rock.** Its vision statement is as follows: "The College of Business serves as a catalyst to advance education and economic development in the State of Arkansas."[24] Notice that this vision statement does not tell you how the college will be a catalyst, or what it is going to do. But what is a catalyst? It's "a substance that modifies and increases the rate of a reaction without being consumed in the process."[25] So, that means the college is going to be an organization that increases the rate of change in education and economic development in its home state.

Trader Joe's is known for its strong company vision and mission.

We then look at the mission of the organization, which tells us how the organization expects to do what the vision puts forth. The mission statement of this college of business says, "The mission of the College of Business is to prepare students to succeed as business professionals in a global economy and to contribute to the growth and viability of the region we serve."[26] So the college of business will achieve its vision by providing education that gives its students the tools they

Vision What we expect to become as an organization at a particular point in time in the future

Mission statement A statement laying out our expectation of what we're going to do in order to become the organization that we have envisioned

WORK
APPLICATION 2-2

Identify the vision and mission of an organization where you work or have worked.

need to succeed in business and create change in the state. This, in turn, will act to improve the state's economic fortunes.

When you put the vision and mission together, all the people in the organization get a more complete picture of the direction in which they are expected to go. This allows them all to focus on going in that direction, and that in turn makes it much easier for them to help the organization achieve its goals. *The fact that they create a focus is the thing that makes a vision and mission so powerful.* If everyone in the organization is focused on the same end result, it is much more likely that the organization will achieve that end result.

A strong vision and a good mission statement are critical parts of the strategic planning process. *Everything* else in strategic planning comes from the vision and mission.

$$\text{Vision} + \text{Mission} = \text{FOCUS!}$$

The next task is to go through a series of analyses of both external and internal factors to come up with the plan of action that answers question 3. Strategic planners look at each of the environmental factors that we noted above, and they analyze the company's capabilities and limitations to come up with objectives and a workable plan. We will discuss some of this process in the following sections.

WORK
APPLICATION 2-3

Write an objective for an organization where you work or have worked that is specific, that is measurable, and that has a target date.

Setting Objectives. After developing our vision and mission, the next step is to set objectives that flow from the mission to address strategic issues. Successful managers have a goal orientation,[27] which means they set and achieve objectives. Goal orientation can also be learned.[28] You must begin with the end in mind, and objectives do not state how they will be accomplished—just the end result you want to accomplish.[29] Objectives *state what is to be accomplished in singular, specific, and measurable terms, with a target date.*

Here is a model adapted from Max Weber to help you write effective objectives, followed by a few company examples.

Objectives Statements of what is to be accomplished in singular, specific, and measurable terms, with a target date

To + action verb + singular, specific, measureable result + target date

Honda:[30] To + introduce + 12 new Honda models for Chinese markets + over 3 years, beginning in 2013

Nike:[31] To + increase + annual revenues to $36 billion + by 2017

Dell:[32] To + cut + costs by $4 billion + by 2018

2-2 APPLYING THE CONCEPT

Writing Objectives

For each objective, write in the letter corresponding to which "must" criteria is not met.

a. single result

b. specific

c. measurable

d. target date

_____ 6. To start working out aerobically within a few weeks

_____ 7. To double ticket sales

_____ 8. To sell 7% more sandwiches and 15% more chips in 2016

_____ 9. To decrease the number of sales returns by year end of 2016

_____ 10. To be perceived as the best restaurant in the Boston area by 2017

2-1   ETHICAL DILEMMA: WHAT WOULD YOU DO?

A major objective of all business corporations is to make a profit and to develop strategies to increase profits. Some US corporations have used the strategy of inversion, to acquire a foreign company and move headquarters overseas to reduce paying corporate taxes. Several members of Congress stated that although inversions are legal, it is unethical to avoid paying US taxes. The **US Department of the Treasury** drafted new rules to make it harder for companies to avoid federal taxes by buying foreign enterprises. The feds stopped short of blocking companies from shifting profits overseas.[33] The announcement didn't stop **Burger King Worldwide's** acquisition of Canada's **Tim Hortons**,[34] as many corporations don't believe inversions are unethical. Some members of Congress also say that individuals also use legal tax loopholes to lower their personal income taxes and that this is unethical, but most people take all the deductions they can to pay less taxes.

1. Are inversions ethical or unethical?
2. If you became the new CEO of Burger King, would you have the company pay the corporate tax even though it is not required to do so by law?
3. As an individual taxpayer, will (or do you) take deductions to lower the amount you pay in taxes or not?
4. Are your answers to questions 2 and 3 consistent, or do you believe businesses should pay the extra taxes but individuals shouldn't?
5. Review the HR disciplines and describe how a company can be ethical and socially responsible in performing these functions.

Types of Strategies

There are several generic strategy types that we are able to categorize. However, we will keep this simple and break the types of strategies down into three common categories: cost leadership, differentiation, and focus or niche strategies.[35]

Cost Leadership. Cost leaders do everything that they can to lower the internal organizational costs required to produce their products or services. **Walmart** has had great success with this strategy, and during the recent recession and even afterward, Walmart reduced its prices even more aggressively to combat loss of business to "dollar" stores.[36] However, low-cost strategies can have a downside as well. **Tata Motors'** cheap Nano automobile at first failed because potential customers saw it as "too cheap" and therefore thought, "It must be unreliable." So, Tata is now building more expensive Nanos, hoping that they will catch on with young buyers.[37]

Differentiation. This strategy attempts to create an impression of difference for the company's product or service in the mind of the customer. The differentiator company stresses its advantage over its competitors.[38] If the company like **Apple** is successful in creating this impression, it can charge a higher price for its product or service than can its competitors. **Nike, Harley Davidson, Margaritaville,** and others place their corporate name prominently on their products to differentiate those products from those of the competition.

Focus or Niche. With this strategy, the company focuses on a specific portion of a larger market. For instance, the company may focus on a regional market, a particular product line, or a buyer group. Within a particular target segment or market niche, the firm may use either a differentiation or a cost leadership strategy. It is hard to compete head-on with the big companies like **Coca-Cola** and **Pepsi,** but the much smaller **Dr Pepper Snapple Group's** two non-colas have a differentiated taste for a much smaller target market, but it is still very profitable.[39]

WORK
APPLICATION 2-4

Identify the strategy of an organization where you work or have worked and explain how the organization uses the strategy against its competitors to gain customers.

2-3 APPLYING THE CONCEPT

Identify which strategy is used by each brand or company listed and write the letter corresponding to the company's strategy by the company's name.

a. cost leadership

b. differentiation

c. focus or niche

_____ 11. **Gucci** handbags

_____ 12. **Bodybuilder** magazine

_____ 13. **Rolex** watches

_____ 14. **TOMS** shoes

_____ 15. **Target** stores

©iStockphoto.com/ProArtWork

Companies that have a specific focus or niche can garner a target audience looking for something specific, allowing the company to profit alongside larger, more dominant competitors.

How Strategy Affects HRM

There are several areas where the generic corporate strategy affects how we do our jobs within HR. Let's take a look at a few of the significant differences between generic strategies. We will continue to discuss these areas in greater detail as we progress through the book.

HRM and Cost Leadership. If our organization is following a generic cost leadership strategy, we are going to be most interested in minimizing all internal costs, including employee costs, to maximize efficiency and effectiveness.[40] We will probably create specific job descriptions that are highly specialized within the organization so that we have people doing the same thing repeatedly, like **McDonald's.** We will also have a specific job description for each position and job-specific training with very little, if any, cross-training. We may provide incentives that emphasize cost controls and efficiency.

HRM and Differentiation. On the other hand, if our organization is following a differentiator strategy, we're going to be more concerned with employees who have the ability to innovate and create new processes, and who can work in uncertain environments within cross-functional teams.[41] In a differentiator organization, we will most likely have much broader job classifications, as well as broader work-planning processes. Individuals will be hired and paid based on individual knowledge and capabilities, not specifically based on skills related to the job they fill upon entering the organization. Here, incentive programs will more often reward innovation and creativity. So you can see very quickly that HRM will need to do its job in a significantly different way based on the type of generic strategy that the company decides to follow.

How HRM Promotes Strategy

So, HR managers need to recruit, select, train, evaluate, and interact with employees differently based on different organizational strategies. The same holds true when looking at different sets of company objectives, different competitors, and many other industry and company characteristics.

HR managers have to evaluate all of the organizational characteristics to determine what kinds of people to bring into the organization and then how to maintain those people once they have become a part of the company. This is the reason that it's so critical for HR managers to understand organizational strategy.[42] In fact, as you go through the remainder of this book, you will see continuing references to how HRM will affect the company's ability to do its work over the long term. Everything that HR does must mesh with the chosen strategy to provide the right kinds of employees, who will learn and do the right types of jobs so that the company can achieve its goals.

STRUCTURE

The selection of a proper organizational structure is critical to successfully implement strategy.[43] **Organizational structure** *refers to the way in which an organization groups its resources to accomplish its mission.*

In HRM, managers need to have an understanding of organizational structure to do their jobs correctly. An organization is a system that is typically, but not always, structured into departments such as finance, marketing, production, human resources, and so on. Each of these departments affects the organization as a whole, and each department is affected by the other departments. All of an organization's resources must be structured effectively if it is to achieve its mission.[44]

Basics of Organizational Structure

One way to look at organizational structure is to identify a series of fundamental components. Each of these components identifies part of how we divide the organization up and group its resources to make them more efficient and effective. Let's discuss complexity, formalization, and centralization as structural components.

Complexity. **Complexity** is *the degree to which different parts of the organization are segregated from one another.* Organizations can be broken up vertically using management layers, horizontally with departments or divisions, and separated physically from each other—for instance with marketing functions in New York and manufacturing in Guadalajara. Each of these demonstrates a way in which we break the organization up into smaller and more differentiated pieces.

We want to minimize complexity as much as possible in order to minimize organizational costs. For example, **Microsoft** is currently working through changes to its organizational complexity under new CEO Satya Nadella because its historical structure has become too expensive.[45]

Formalization. **Formalization** is *the degree to which jobs are standardized within an organization, meaning the degree to which we have created policies, procedures, and rules that "program" the jobs of the employees.* If we make things routine by creating standard operating procedures and other standard processes, we can usually increase the efficiency and effectiveness of the people within the organization.[46]

How much we're able to formalize jobs within the organization, though, depends on what the organization is designed to do. If the organization is designed to do the same thing over and over, such as producing a low-cost commodity, then we can usually formalize many of its procedures. On the other hand, if the organization is designed to do unique and nonroutine things, then we will probably not be able to formalize very much of what the organization does.[47]

Centralization. Centralization, the third major component of organizational structure, is *the degree to which decision making is concentrated within the organization.* The degree of centralization in an organization has to do with dispersion of authority for decision making and delegation of authority. If we can concentrate authority in decision making with one or a few individuals, we can concentrate on hiring people who are very good at making business decisions in those few positions and not worry about the decision-making skills of the rest of our employees.[48]

LO 2-3

Summarize the major components of organizational structure and why it is important to understand them.

SHRM

J:10
Linking HR Strategy to Organizational Strategy

J:2
Enhancing Firm Competitiveness

J:3
Strategy Formulation

E:9
Organizational Design

WORK
APPLICATION 2-5

Briefly describe some of the organizational culture artifacts where you work or have worked.

Organizational structure The way in which an organization groups its resources to accomplish its mission

Complexity Degree to which different parts of the organization are segregated from one another

Formalization Degree to which jobs are standardized within an organization, meaning the degree to which we have created policies, procedures, and rules that "program" the jobs of the employees

Centralization Degree to which decision making is concentrated within the organization

However, there's a trade-off to centralized decision making. As the organization gets larger, we may have to go through many layers of the organization in order to get a decision made. This can slow down the processes within the firm. For example, **TEPCO** was criticized for having a complex bureaucratic decision-making process that led to the meltdown of three reactors at one of its nuclear plants in Japan.[49]

Is There One "Best" Structure? No. The best structure is one that fits the firm's current competitive situation as well as its internal capabilities and that enables it to implement its strategies successfully. Warren Buffett advises businesses to keep things simple,[50] and Peter Drucker may have said it as well as anyone when he noted, "The simplest organization structure that will do the job is the best one."[51]

How Does Structure Affect Employee Behavior?

SHRM

C:3
Individual vs. Group Behavior

SHRM

Q:2
Organizational Structure and Job Design

Here is a general answer to how structure affects our employees' behavior. With high complexity, formalization, and centralization, employees focus on following the policies and rules within the limited scope of their highly specialize jobs without making decisions—like **McDonald's**. With low complexity, formalization, and centralization, employees can be more creative to get the job done the way they want to—like **Zappos**, where there are no departments or standard procedures and employees are expected to "think on your feet" and make decisions.

How Does Structure Affect HRM?

As the HR manager, would your job change if your organization adopted the structure of one of the two companies above? Would you need to recruit and hire different types of people in a bureaucratic organization like **McDonald's** than you would in an entrepreneurial organization like **Zappos**? Indeed, you would. In the more bureaucratic organization, you would most likely hire people who had significant depth of expertise in a narrow area within their field of knowledge so that they could apply that expertise in a highly efficient manner. Your training programs would also probably be more specific and geared toward particular jobs. In fact, the organizational structure will affect virtually every function of the HR manager. So in order to be a successful HR manager, you have to understand and adapt to the particular organizational structure of your firm.

LO 2-4

Describe organizational culture and how it affects the members of the organization.

SHRM

A:3
Managing/Creating a Positive Organizational Culture

ORGANIZATIONAL CULTURE

Organizational culture is another characteristic that affects how the HR manager operates within the firm. Fostering the right organizational culture is one of the most important responsibilities of the CEO and other corporate executives.[52] Management needs to be involved in establishing shared values, beliefs, and assumptions so that employees know how to behave.[53] Every group of humans that gather together anywhere at any point in time create a unique group culture. They have their own group standards, called norms, which create pressure for the group's members to conform. Social groups have societal cultures, nations have national cultures, and organizations have their own distinct organizational cultures.

What Is Organizational Culture?

Organizational culture The values, beliefs, and assumptions about appropriate behavior that members of an organization share

Organizational culture consists of *the values, beliefs, and assumptions about appropriate behavior that members of an organization share.* Culture describes how employees do what they do (behavior) and why they do what they do (values, profits, customers, employees, society). Every organization has a culture, and success depends on the health and strength of its culture.[54] Therefore, leaders should spend a lot of time building the organization's culture.[55] Organizational culture is primarily learned through observing people and events in the organization.

Artifacts of Organizational Culture. There are five artifacts of organizational culture that help employees learn the culture:

1. *Heroes*, such as founders Steve Jobs of Apple, Sam Walton of Walmart, Herb Kelleher of Southwest Airlines, Frederick Smith of FedEx, and others who have made outstanding contributions to their organizations.

2. *Stories*, often about founders and others who have made extraordinary efforts. These include stories about Sam Walton visiting every Walmart store yearly, or someone driving through a blizzard to deliver a product or service. Public statements and speeches can also be considered stories.

3. *Slogans*, such as at McDonald's. Q, S, C, V (or quality, service, cleanliness, and value).

4. *Symbols*, such as logos, and plaques, pens, jackets, or a pink Cadillac at the cosmetics firm Mary Kay.

5. *Ceremonies*, such as awards dinners for top achievers at Mary Kay.

How Culture Controls Employee Behavior in Organizations

Organizational culture is a very powerful force in controlling how people act within its boundaries. For instance, if the culture says that we value hard work and productivity but an individual on one of the teams fails to do his or her part, then the other members of the team are quite likely to pressure that individual to conform to the culture. Since assumptions, values, and beliefs are so strong, all individuals will most likely conform to those behaviors that the culture values.

Do you believe that culture has the ability to cause you to change the way you act? Have you ever done something to fit in, or have you ever done something you really didn't want to do because of peer pressure? Doesn't peer pressure control most people—at least sometimes? Think about the way you act as part of your family, and then compare that to the way you act as a student at school, with a group of your friends, or as an employee at work. Chances are quite high that you act differently within these different "cultures." We all act to conform, for the most part, to the culture that we happen to be in at that point in time, because the culture's values push us to act that way.

Social Media and Culture Management

Recall that each organization has an internal and an external environment. Exhibit 2-4 puts together the internal and external components making up that environment.

Social media is one of the mechanisms that we now use to both monitor and—at least partially—control organizational environments.[56] Companies can monitor

In a strong organizational culture, employees tend to dress and behave in similar ways.

the internal environment using social media venues, which gives management a feel for the culture within the organization. They can also actively seek out information internally using various forms of social media[57] and can even ask company members to interact on social media platforms such as LinkedIn and Facebook. Have you ever known a friend whose organization asked employees to "like" them on Facebook? This mechanism is becoming more important every day and will continue to do so for the immediate future.

The same is true for the external environment, from following competitors on social media sites to utilizing government Web pages and media links. Governments and other entities are even using social media to extend their reach into communities that are generally hard to reach because they don't pay much attention to standard methods of communication like State of the Union addresses and regulatory bulletins. In the United States, President Obama's administration turned to social media to attract younger individuals (who don't tend to get as involved with government issues) to the federal health care exchanges. The administration did this because the new health care law required younger members to sign up to offset the higher cost of insuring older individuals.[58]

Social media continues to become more important to even traditional businesses and governments. You can bet that governments will pay more attention to social media in the future, since many of the "Arab Spring" uprisings were coordinated via social media.[59] This is just one example of the power of social media sites.

WORK
APPLICATION 2-8

Give examples of how you, or an organization, have used social media at work.

2-4 APPLYING THE CONCEPT

The Internal Environment

Identify which internal environmental factor is referred to in each statement and then write the letter corresponding to that factor before the statement.

a. strategy

b. structure

c. culture

_____ 16. "At **Victoria's Secret**, we focus on selling clothes and other products to women."

_____ 17. "At the **SEC**, we have several layers of management."

_____ 18. "At **Ford**, quality is job one."

_____ 19. "Walking around the office at **Bank of America**, I realized that I would have to wear a jacket and tie every day."

_____ 20. "I work in the production department at **Ford**, and she works in the marketing department."

LO 2-5

Define data analytics and explain how it helps organizations make important decisions.

Data analytics Process of accessing large amounts of data in order to analyze those data and gain insight into significant trends or patterns within organizations or industries

AN INTRODUCTION TO DATA ANALYTICS FOR HRM

Data analytics is *the process of accessing large amounts of data in order to analyze those data and gain insight into significant trends or patterns within organizations or industries.* Computing power has obviously been increasing at a remarkable rate for the past 20 years, as has the ability to both create and store large amounts of data and information. This ability to create huge amounts of data has led to the concept of "big data."

Big data involves the collection of extremely large data sets—so large, in fact, that data analytics on these data sets would have been impossible until very recently, since we just did not have the computing power or the programs available. With the advent of faster computers and new analytics programs, we can now find patterns in these massive data sets that allow us to make important organizational decisions—especially strategic decisions.

EXHIBIT 2-4   THE INTERNAL AND EXTERNAL ENVIRONMENT

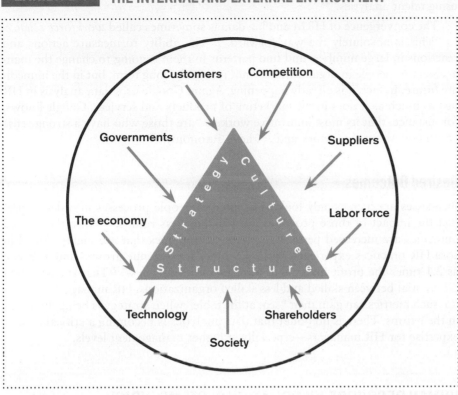

A Brief on Data Analytics

Companies like **Google** grew up on data analytics. Director of Research Peter Norvig said recently, "We don't have better algorithms than anyone else; we just have more data."[60] And Google analyzes *all* of that data looking for patterns that it can use. Many other companies have also jumped on this bandwagon, including some powerful outsourcers like **IBM** and **Oracle**, who are selling big data services.[61] Other companies are doing their own big data analysis, using big data as a competitive weapon, according to a **McKinsey & Company** report.[62]

Analysis of big data is providing information that HR managers can immediately act on as well. A recent analysis showed that "the communication skills and personal warmth of an employee's supervisor are often crucial in determining the employee's tenure and performance."[63] A lot of HR managers have anecdotally passed this information on to their line managers for many years.

Because of big data, we can now analyze thousands or even millions of instances of interaction between people in and between organizations and look for patterns to those interactions. So "We can measure, and therefore manage, more precisely than ever."[64] If we find a pattern, it may tell us what we should do based on data rather than instinct. We can "directly translate that [pattern] knowledge into improved decision making and performance."[65]

HR Analytics

HR managers must become comfortable with collecting and analyzing big data to drive results.[66] Analytics tools and processes can be used for many HR functions, such as talent acquisition and management, training and development, work and job analysis, productivity analysis, motivation, retention, and engagement.[67] However, organizational silos, skills shortages, and suspicion about reducing human beings to data points are "preventing HR departments from effectively using talent analytics."[68]

The convergence of HRM and big data is sometimes called *workforce science,* as "This is absolutely the way forward."[69] The ability to measure actions and reactions in large numbers and find patterns in them is going to change the management of people in organizations—not just in the long term, but in the immediate future. In fact, it is already happening. Again, **Google** uses data analysis in HR just as much as it does in the marketing of products and services. Google knows, for instance, that its most innovative workers "are those who have a strong sense of mission about their work and . . . have autonomy."[70]

Desired Outcomes

Businesses are increasingly looking at internal people processes in order to predict the impact of those processes on their business results.[71] Thus, the desired outcomes are increased performance, and "companies that are highly skilled in core HR practices experience up to 3.5 times the revenue growth and as much as 2.1 times the profit margins of less capable companies."[72] That is a shocking differential between skilled and less skilled organizations. HR managers who can use such metrics can gain their "seat at the table" when strategy is being discussed in their firms. There is no doubt that data analytics is becoming a critical area of expertise for HR managers—especially at higher management levels.

LO 2-6

Identify how human resource information systems (HRIS) can help HR make decisions.

HUMAN RESOURCE INFORMATION SYSTEMS (HRIS)

Human resource information systems (HRIS) are one type of system used to manage and analyze data in organizations, as HR uses data to influence business performance.[73] Most organizations today use complex computer systems to manage and manipulate those data.

What Are HRIS?

Human resource information systems (HRIS) are *interacting database systems that "aim at generating and delivering HR information and allow us to automate some human resource management functions."*[74] Some of the most common features in HRIS include modules for tracking attendance and leave, job, and pay history and logging appraisal scores and review dates. Others include modules for benefits enrollment and tracking, succession management, training management, and time logging. There are additional modules available depending on the size and type of the organization.[75]

How Do HRIS Assist in Making Decisions?

HRIS allow us to maintain control of our HR information, and they make it available for our use during the strategic planning process. Organizations can access things such as training records, job descriptions, work histories, and much more. Having this aggregate information immediately available makes the strategic planning process both quicker and smoother. We can use the information stored in the database to make daily decisions within the HR department. For example, since training records are available in the HRIS, if we need to determine who has completed conflict management coursework for a new team being created in the company, we can quickly identify those individuals with that skill set. We can also use the same databases when considering promotions, transfers, and many other daily activities that are required inside the organization.

Human resource information systems (HRIS) Interacting database systems that aim at generating and delivering HR information and allow us to automate some human resource management functions

MEASUREMENT TOOLS FOR STRATEGIC HRM

Housed within many HRIS are statistical packages for HRM. Just as we have to quantify and measure other parts of the organization, we also have measurement tools specific to HRM. Two of the most common tools are economic value added (EVA) and return on investment (ROI). Let's take a brief look at each of these tools.

Economic Value Added (EVA)

Economic value added (EVA) is designed as a method for calculating the creation of value for the organization's shareholders. **Economic value added (EVA)** *is a measure of profits that remain after the cost of capital has been deducted from operating profits.* It provides shareholders and managers with a better understanding of how the business is performing overall. As an equation, EVA would look like this:[76]

$$\text{EVA} = \text{Net operating profit after tax} - (\text{Capital used} \times \text{Cost of capital})$$

So EVA is a measure of how much money we made through our operations minus the amount of money that we had to spend or borrow (at a particular interest rate) in order to perform those operations. For a company to grow, it must generate average returns higher than its capital costs.

Return on Investment (ROI)

Return on investment (ROI) *is a measure of the financial return we receive because of something that we do to invest in our organization or its people.* ROI is most commonly used in financial analyses, but many areas of HR lend themselves to ROI calculations. These areas include training, outsourcing, benefits, diversity, and many others. In each of these areas, we can calculate the cost of the process—whether that process is training, diversity management, or anything else—and compare that to the returns we get from the process.

To calculate ROI, you need two figures: the cost of the investment and the gain that you receive from making the investment. From there, the calculation is pretty simple:

$$\text{ROI} = \frac{\text{Gain from investment} - \text{Cost of investment}}{\text{Cost of investment}}$$

So, as an example, if we create a training course to improve the skills of our assembly workers and send all of the workers through the training, that training will cost us $1,000,000. We know that historically, during a normal year of production, the assembly workers have been able to assemble $5,000,000 worth of our product. However, after the training is complete, we measure our assembly process over the ensuing year and find that our amount of product created that year has increased to $8,000,000. This gives us a $3,000,000 gain from the investment. We can plug these numbers into our calculation and find out the following:

$$\text{ROI} = \frac{\$3,000,000 - \$1,000,000}{\$1,000,000} = \frac{\$2,000,000}{\$1,000,000} = 2 \text{ or } 200\%$$

So in this case, our return on investment over the course of 1 year is 2 times the cost of the investment.

It is always important to calculate at least a rough ROI for any investment in organizational resources. There's a definite need to understand how much we get in return for an investment. Don't just assume that the return on investment is always positive—because it's not.

LO 2-7

Recall the common measurement tools for strategic human resource management (HRM).

G:1

Economic Value Added

G:7

Return on Investment (ROI)

Economic value added (EVA) Measure of profits that remain after the cost of capital has been deducted from operating profits

Return on investment (ROI) Measure of the financial return we receive because of something that we do to invest in our organization or its people

Taking a company global requires effective strategic and HRM planning.

TRENDS AND ISSUES IN HRM

Here we continue our discussion of some of the most important issues and trends in HRM today. In this chapter, we chose the following issues: managing data to improve structure, culture, and staffing, and the continuing globalization of business, which increases the need for strategic planning. Let's discuss each of these topics next.

Everything Old Is New Again: Managing Data for HRM Decision Making

As we noted in the section on big data, there have been new advances in both computing power and storage in the past few years, and we now have the ability to do data analysis that we could not attempt before. These improvements in data capability have in turn led to improvements in virtually every area of strategic and HRM planning as a component of strategy. In all areas, data are leading us to new conclusions concerning our people and their work. For instance, when **Xerox** had problems staffing a call center, it analyzed a large data set that identified successful employees, and consequently found that the company was hiring based on the wrong characteristics.[77] Xerox had assumed that people with call center experience would do better, but unexpectedly that was not true. People who were more creative did better in Xerox's call center environment.

Data analysis is being used around the world to find the right type of workers for specific jobs, and when done correctly, it allows companies to lower turnover and manage engagement better than ever. The data are there to help you make better business decisions; the challenge is to use the data to improve workplace attractiveness to employees, who can then increase the company's chances of success through increased engagement with their employer.

Continuing Globalization Increases the Need for Strategic and HRM Planning

As business in most industries continues to globalize, competition will continue to increase. This is primarily due to the fact that as industries globalize, competitors who used to be limited to one region, country, or group of countries gain access to many more markets. As more and more competitors gain access to more and more markets, competition is likely to increase. This increasing competition puts pressure on businesses to create a plan to overcome their competitors' advantages.

As we noted earlier in this chapter, the process of strategic planning is designed to analyze the competitive landscape that our organization faces and create a workable plan that will allow us to compete within that landscape. So as competition increases, developing a good, solid "global" strategy and implementing continuous reviews of our strategic plans become more and more significant.

Companies must become more competent global competitors. For HRM, this means that HR managers will need to become better at managing expatriate employees, paying wages across national borders, managing disparate country laws and regulations, and much more. We will discuss the globalization issues for HRM in more detail in Chapter 14.

• • • CHAPTER SUMMARY

2-1   Classify the major components of the external environment.

There are nine major external forces: customers, competition, suppliers, the labor force and unions, shareholders, society, technology, the economy, and governments. Each factor is briefly discussed below.

- *Customers.* Companies must continually improve products to create value for their customers.

- *Competition.* Organizations must compete against each other for customers, for the same employees, and sometimes for suppliers. Competitors' changing strategic moves affect the performance of the organization.

- *Suppliers.* The firm's performance is affected by its suppliers. Therefore, it is important to develop close working relationships with your suppliers, and close relationships require employees who have the ability to communicate, empathize, negotiate, and come to mutually advantageous agreements.

- *Labor force.* The recruits available to and the employees of an organization have a direct effect on its performance. Management recruits human resources from the available labor force outside the company's boundaries.

- *Shareholders.* The owners of a corporation, known as shareholders, influence management. Most shareholders of large corporations are not involved in the day-to-day operation of the firm, but they do vote for the board of directors, and the top manager reports to the board of directors.

- *Society.* Individuals and groups within society have formed to pressure business for changes. People who live in the same area with the business do not want it to pollute the air or water or otherwise abuse natural resources.

- *Technology.* Computers and the Internet have changed the speed and the manner in which organizations conduct and transact business, and they're often a major part of the firm's systems processes. Changing technologies require technologically savvy employees who have the ability to adapt to new processes.

- *Economic.* No organization has control over economic growth, inflation, interest rates, foreign exchange rates, and so on. In general, as measured by gross domestic product (GDP), businesses do better when the economy is growing than they do during recessions.

- *Governments.* National, state, and local governments all set laws and regulations that businesses must obey. Governments create both opportunities and obstacles for businesses. To a large extent, business may not do whatever it wants to do; the government tells business what it can and cannot do.

2-2   Discuss the three major organizational factors that affect our strategic options.

Our strategic options are governed to a great extent by our current strategy, our organizational structure, and our culture. Strategy deals with how the organization competes within its industry. *Strategy* is just a plan of action to achieve a particular set of objectives. It looks at the external environment and the organizational environment to create strategic advantage. Strategic advantage occurs when you analyze the environment better and react quicker than your competitors do, thus creating a sustainable competitive advantage.

Organizational structure refers to the way in which an organization groups its resources to accomplish its mission. Organizations structure their resources to transform inputs and outputs. All of an organization's resources must be structured effectively to achieve its mission. As a manager in any department, you will be responsible for part of the organization's structure.

Organizational culture consists of the shared values, beliefs, and assumptions about appropriate behavior among members of an organization. Organizational culture is primarily learned through observing people and events in the organization.

2-3   Summarize the major components of organizational structure and why it is important to understand them.

All of an organization's resources must be structured effectively if it is to achieve its mission. Structure is made up of three major components:

- *Complexity*, which is the degree to which three types of differentiation exist within the organization. These three types are vertical differentiation, horizontal differentiation, and spatial differentiation. The more the organization is divided—whether vertically, horizontally, or spatially—the more difficult it is to manage.

- *Formalization*, which is the degree to which jobs are standardized within an organization. The more we can standardize the organization and its processes, the easier it is to control those processes.

- *Centralization*, which is the degree to which decision making is concentrated within the organization at a single point—usually at the top. A highly centralized organization would have all authority concentrated at the top, while a decentralized organization would have authority spread throughout. If authority can be centralized, we can take advantage of learning curve effects that help to improve our decision making over time.

2-4   Describe organizational culture and how it affects the members of the organization.

Organizational culture consists of the values, beliefs, and assumptions about appropriate behavior that members of an organization share. Organizational culture is primarily learned through observing people and events in the organization.

Because organizational culture is based at least partly on assumptions, values, and beliefs, the culture can control how people act within its boundaries. Since assumptions, values, and beliefs are such strong influences, individuals will generally act to conform to the culture. For the most part, we all act

to conform to the culture that we happen to be in at any given point in time, and that's because cultural values push us to act that way.

2-5   Define data analytics and explain how it helps organizations make important decisions.

Data analytics is the process of accessing large amounts of data in order to analyze those data and gain insight into significant trends or patterns within organizations or industries. Analytics tools and processes can be used to guide decision making for many HR functions, such as talent acquisition and management, training and development, work and job analysis, productivity analysis, motivation, retention, and engagement. Data analytics on a large scale, or *big data*, will change how people are managed within organizations, and ideally lead to increased performance of the organization.

2-6   Identify how HRIS can help HR make decisions.

Human resource information systems (HRIS) are interacting database systems that aim to generate and deliver HR information and allow us to automate some HRM functions. They are primarily database management systems, designed especially for use in HR functions.

HRIS allow us to maintain control of our HR information and make it available for use during the strategic planning process. Having this information immediately available makes the strategic planning process both quicker and smoother. We can also use the information stored in the database to make daily decisions within the HR department, such as a decision on whom to send to a particular training class. We can also use these databases when considering promotions, transfers, team assignments, and many other daily activities that are required inside the organization.

2-7   Recall the common measurement tools for strategic HRM.

We discussed two common tools in this chapter: economic value added (EVA) and return on investment (ROI).

EVA is a measure of profits that remain after the cost of capital has been deducted from operating profits. ROI is a measure of the financial return we receive because of something that we do to invest in our organization or its people.

2-8   Define the key terms found in the chapter margins and listed following the Chapter Summary.

Complete the Key Terms Review to test your understanding of this chapter's key terms.

● ● ● KEY TERMS

centralization, 39
complexity, 39
data analytics, 42
economic value added (EVA), 45
formalization, 39

human resource
    information systems (HRIS), 44
mission statement, 35
objectives, 36
organizational culture, 40

organizational structure, 39
return on investment (ROI), 45
strategy, 34
vision, 35

● ● ● KEY TERMS REVIEW

Complete each of the following statements using one of this chapter's key terms.

1. _____ is a plan of action to achieve a particular set of objectives.

2. _____ is what we expect to become as an organization at a particular future point in time.

3. _____ is our expectations of what we're going to do in order to become the organization that we envisioned.

4. _____ state what is to be accomplished in singular, specific, and measurable terms with a target date.

5. _____ refers to the way in which an organization groups its resources to accomplish its mission.

6. _____ is the degree of three types of differentiation within the organization.

7. _____ is the degree to which jobs are standardized within an organization.

8. _____ is the degree to which decision-making is concentrated within the organization at a single point - usually at the top of the organization.

9. _____ consists of the values, beliefs, and assumptions about appropriate behavior that members of an organization share.

10. _____ is the process of accessing large amounts of data in order to analyze those data and gain insights into significant trends or patterns within organizations or industries.

11. _____ are interacting database systems that aim at generating and delivering HR information and allow us to automate some human resource management functions.

12. _____ is a measure of profits that remain after the cost of capital has been deducted from operating profits.

13. _____ is a measure of the financial return we receive because of something that we do to invest in our organization or its people.

● ● ● COMMUNICATION SKILLS

The following critical-thinking questions can be used for class discussion and/or for written assignments to develop communication skills. Be sure to give complete explanations for all answers.

1. Can you name a business that you know of in which competition has increased significantly in the past few years? Why do you think competition has increased in this case?

2. What are some of the ways in which the environmental factors that we discussed in this chapter directly affect the organization?

3. Do you agree that every organization needs a strategic plan? Why or why not?

4. Think about the technological changes that have occurred since you were born. Do you think those changes have affected the strategic planning process? How?

5. What should a mission statement focus on—customers, competitors, products/services, the employee environment, or something else? Identify why you chose a particular answer.

6. We discussed the three major generic strategies in this chapter. Can you think of examples of each of the three strategies in specific businesses you know of? In your opinion, how successful have these companies been with their strategy?

7. If you were going to design the structure for a new, innovative start-up company, what kind of structure would you try to create in regard to level of complexity, formalization, and centralization? Why would you set up this type of structure?

8. Which of the five artifacts, or important ways in which employees learn about culture, do you think is most important? Why?

9. Name some situations in HRM when you would want to use either economic value added (EVA) or return on investment (ROI) as an analytical tool.

• • • CASE 2-1 STRATEGY-DRIVEN HR MANAGEMENT: NETFLIX, A BEHIND-THE-SCENES LOOK AT DELIVERING ENTERTAINMENT

Netflix is a highly successful retailer of movie rental services, with a market value of over $25 billion. It offers a subscription service that allows its members to stream shows and movies instantly over the Internet on game consoles, Blu-ray players, HDTVs, set-top boxes, home theater systems, phones, and tablets. Netflix also includes a subscription service for those who prefer to receive discs via the US mail (rather than streaming), without the hassle of due dates or late fees.

The idea of a home delivery movie service came to CEO Read Hastings when he was forced to pay $40 in overdue fines after returning a video of the movie *Apollo 13* to Blockbuster. He realized that he could capitalize on an existing distribution system (the US Post Office) that did not require renters to leave their homes. The Netflix website was launched on August 29, 1997, with only 30 employees and 925 movies available for rent. It used a traditional pay-per-rental model, charging $0.50 per rental plus US postage, and late fees applied. Netflix introduced the monthly subscription concept in September 1999, and then it dropped the single-rental model in early 2000. Since that time, the company has built its reputation on the business model of flat-fee unlimited rentals without due dates, late fees, or shipping and handling fees. In addition, its online streaming service doesn't have per title rental fees.[78] Throughout 2014, Netflix's total sales grew by 21%, generating a net income of $112 million.[79] Subscribers increased by almost 40% that year, reaching 46 million, and the stock value tripled from 2012 to 2014. But how did they reach that point?[80]

There are many reasons why Netflix's strategy is successful, yet the numbers tell only the results and not the behind-the-scenes story. According to Read Hastings and former chief talent officer (CTO) Patty McCord, this success is not a surprise at all given Netflix's business model. But more important, they say, is Netflix's HR strategy, which is to create an environment of fully motivated employees who understand the culture of the company and perform exceptionally well within it. Hastings and McCord had the foresight to document their HR strategy via PowerPoint, and soon these slides went viral, with more than 5 million views on the Web. McCord described Netflix's HR strategy as consisting of the following steps:

1. *Selecting new employees/recruiting.* Hire employees who care about, understand, and then prioritize the company's interests. This will eliminate the need for formal regulations and policies because these employees will strive to grow the company for their own self-satisfaction. This sets Netflix apart from the many companies that do not hire employees who would be a great fit with the company's culture and that therefore still spend great amounts of time and money on enforcing their HR policies—policies that target only 3% of their workforce.[81]

2. *Talent management/matching employees with jobs.* To avoid high employee turnover, a company must recruit talented people with the right skills, although mismatches may occur. Layoffs and firings are also inevitable given changing business cycles. In such cases, it is HR's duty to place employees in departments that match the employees' skill sets, as well as to train employees to meet changing business needs.[82]

3. *Send the right messages.* To boost overall employee morale, most HR departments throw parties or give away free items. But when stock prices are decreasing or sales numbers are not as high as predicted, what use would a company have for an office party? Netflix executives stated that they have not seen an HR initiative that truly improved morale. Instead of cheerleading, employees need to be educated about how the company earns its revenue and what behaviors will drive its success. By receiving clear messages about how employees should execute and commit to their duties, employees will be more informed about the criteria they will need to meet to receive their bonuses, and they will therefore be more apt to receive those bonuses. Knowing what to do and how to do it, employees' motivation will increase, and with increased motivation, morale and performance will improve.[83]

4. *Performance evaluation.* Netflix implemented informal 360-degree reviews after realizing that formal review sessions were not effective. These informal 360-degree sessions allowed workers to give honest opinions about themselves and colleagues—focusing on whether certain policies should stop, start, continue, or change. Instead of relying on bureaucratic measures, employees valued these conversations as an organic part of their work, and those conversations have been demonstrated to increase employee performance.[84] For example, Netflix found that when its employees perceived their bosses as less than expert in their field, employee performance dropped. Employees indicated that managers who relied on charm or IQ were not trusted and received low subordinate appraisals.

Questions

1. Netflix was a pioneer in the online video rental market, making "old-fashioned" DVD rentals a thing of the past and putting Blockbuster out of business. Describe how Netflix changed the entertainment rental industry.

2. What is Netflix's competitive strategy? What does it believe is the driving force that makes this strategy so successful? Do you agree?

3. In terms of sustaining the company's competitive advantage, what is the most important step that Netflix has taken, as noted by Hastings and McCord?

4. "Where we want to be, how to get there, and where are we now" are key points of a successful company's strategy. How do the company's HR policies support the firm's strategy?

5. How does Netflix monitor its employees' performance?

6. How would you create a link between customers and the way employees perform to assure that incentives are distributed evenly and equally at Netflix?

Case created by Herbert Sherman, PhD, and Theodore Vallas, Department of Management Sciences, Long Island University School of Business, Brooklyn Campus

• • • SKILL BUILDER 2–1 WRITING OBJECTIVES

For this exercise, you will first work at improving ineffective objectives. Then you will write nine objectives for yourself.

Objective

To develop your skill at writing objectives

Skills

The primary skills developed through this exercise are as follows:

1. *HR Management skills* — conceptual and design
2. *SHRM 2013 Curriculum Guidebook*—J: Strategic HR

Part 1

Indicate which of the criteria each of the following objectives fails to meet in the model and rewrite the objective so that it meets all those criteria. When writing objectives, use the following model:

To + action verb + single, specific, and measurable result + target date

1. To improve our company image by the end of 2017

   Criteria not met: _____

   Improved objective: _____

2. To increase the number of customers by 10%

   Criteria not met: _____

   Improved objective: _____

   To increase profits during 2017

   Criteria not met: _____

Improved objective: _____

To sell 5% more hot dogs and 13% more soda at the baseball game on Sunday, June 14, 2016

Criteria not met: _____

Improved objective: _____

Part 2

Write three educational, three personal, and three career objectives you want to accomplish. These may be short-term (something you want to accomplish today), long-term (something you want to have accomplished 20 years from now), or medium-term objectives. Be sure to structure your objectives using the model and meeting the criteria for effective objectives.

- Educational Objectives
- Personal Objectives
- Career Objectives

Apply It

What did I learn from this experience? How will I use this knowledge in the future?

_____

_____

Your instructor may ask you to do this Skill Builder in class in a group. If so, the instructor will provide you with any necessary information or additional instructions.

Case created by Herbert Sherman, PhD, and Theodore Vallas, Department of Management Sciences, Long Island University School of Business, Brooklyn Campus

• • • SKILL BUILDER 2–2 STRATEGIC PLANNING AT YOUR COLLEGE

This exercise enables you to apply the strategic planning process to your college or university as an individual and/or a group. Complete each step by typing or writing out your answers. You can also conduct this exercise for another organization.

Objective

To develop your strategic planning skills by analyzing the internal environment of strategy, structure, and culture

Skills

The primary skills developed through this exercise are as follows:

1. *HR Management skills*—conceptual and design
2. *SHRM 2013 Curriculum Guidebook*—J: Strategic HR

PART A: STRATEGY

Step 1: Develop a Mission

1. What is the vision and mission statement of your university/college or school/department?

2. Is the mission statement easy to understand and remember?

3. How would you improve the mission statement?

Step 2: Identify a Strategy

Which of the three generic strategies does your school or department use?

Step 3: Conduct Strategic Analysis

1. Complete a SWOT analysis by identifying the strengths, weaknesses, opportunities, and threats facing your school.

2. Determine the competitive advantage (if any) of your university/college or school/department.

Step 4: Set Objectives

What are some objectives of your university/college or school/department?

Step 5: Implement, Monitor, and Evaluate Strategies

How would you rate your university/college's or school/department's strategic planning? How could it be improved?

PART B: STRUCTURE

Describe your school or department's organizational structure in terms of its complexity, formalization, and centralization.

PART C: CULTURE

Identify artifacts in each of the categories of heroes, stories, slogans, symbols, and ceremonies.

Identify the cultural levels of the organization's behaviors, values and beliefs, and assumptions.

Apply It

What did I learn from this experience? How will I use this knowledge in the future?

_____

_____

_____

Your instructor may ask you to do this Skill Builder in class in a group. If so, the instructor will provide you with any necessary information or additional instructions.

©iStockphoto.com/bbourdages

3

THE LEGAL ENVIRONMENT AND DIVERSITY MANAGEMENT

• • • LEARNING OUTCOMES

After studying this chapter, you should be able to do the following:

3-1 Describe the OUCH test and its four components and identify when it is useful in an organizational setting. PAGE 56

3-2 Identify the major equal employment opportunity (EEO) laws and the groups of people that each law protects. PAGE 59

3-3 Briefly discuss the major functions of the Equal Employment Opportunity Commission (EEOC). PAGE 66

3-4 Contrast the concepts of equal employment opportunity, affirmative action, and diversity. PAGE 68

3-5 Compare the two primary types of sexual harassment. PAGE 70

3-6 Briefly discuss the employer's requirements concerning avoidance of religious discrimination in the workplace. PAGE 73

3-7 Define the key terms found in the chapter margins and listed following the Chapter Summary. PAGE 76

Practitioner's Perspective

Cindy says: One of the reasons some agree with the Dilbert comic strip depiction of the HR manager as devoid of feeling is due to the necessity of fair and uniform enforcement of government rules and regulations, as well as the company's own policies and procedures. Aaron—a favorite with the patients and a willing overtime worker—misread the schedule and missed a day of work at the hospital. A no-call/no-show merits a written warning, but Aaron's supervisor didn't want to administer the discipline.

"Well," I asked, "what if we were talking about another less exemplary employee? What about, oh, let's say—Sandy? What would you do if she was NC/NS?"

"Hey, no problem there—I'd write up Sandy in an instant!" replied the supervisor.

"Wait—wouldn't that be discrimination?" Different treatment of individuals who are in similar circumstances opens the door to legal liability. In Chapter 3, we'll explore why HR is required to advise and assist with compliance issues—no matter how "heartless" it may appear.

● ● ●

THE LEGAL ENVIRONMENT FOR HRM: PROTECTING YOUR ORGANIZATION

We all have to obey the law. In this chapter, we will explore some of the laws that HR managers have to work with on a daily basis, and we will also look in some more depth at diversity and why it is valuable in an organization.

WORK
APPLICATION 3-1

Give examples of how you and other employees legally discriminate at work.

● ● ● CHAPTER OUTLINE

The Legal Environment for HRM: Protecting Your Organization

A User's Guide to Managing People: The OUCH Test

   Objective

   Uniform in Application

   Consistent in Effect

   Has Job Relatedness

Major Employment Laws

   Equal Pay Act of 1963

   Title VII of the Civil Rights Act of 1964 (CRA)

   Age Discrimination in Employment Act of 1967 (ADEA)

   Vietnam Era Veterans Readjustment Assistance Act of 1974 (VEVRAA)

   Pregnancy Discrimination Act of 1978 (PDA)

   Americans with Disabilities Act of 1990 (ADA), as Amended in 2008

   Civil Rights Act of 1991

   Uniformed Services Employment and Reemployment Rights Act of 1994 (USERRA)

   Veterans Benefits Improvement Act of 2004 (VBIA)

   Title II of the Genetic Information Nondiscrimination Act of 2008 (GINA)

   Lilly Ledbetter Fair Pay Act of 2009 (LLFPA)

Equal Employment Opportunity Commission (EEOC)

   What Does the EEOC Do?

   Employee Rights Under the EEOC

   Employer Rights and Prohibitions

EEO, Affirmative Action, and Diversity: What's the Difference?

   Affirmative Action (AA)

   Diversity in the Workforce

Sexual Harassment: A Special Type of Discrimination

   Types of Sexual Harassment

   What Constitutes Sexual Harassment?

   Reducing Organizational Risk From Sexual Harassment Lawsuits

Trends and Issues in HRM

   Federal Agencies Are Becoming More Activist in Pursuing Discrimination Claims

   The ADA and the ADA Amendments Act (ADAAA)

We have grown to believe in the value of a diverse workforce,[1] and one of the primary jobs of an HR manager is to assist in avoiding any discriminatory employment situations that can create legal, ethical, or social problems with organizational stakeholders. As a result, one of the first things we need to do in this chapter is define discrimination, which is *the act of making distinctions or choosing one thing over another; in HR, it is making distinctions among people*. So you can see that if managers don't discriminate, then they're not doing their job. However, we want to avoid *illegal* discrimination based on a person's membership in a protected class, and we want to avoid unfair treatment of any of our employees at all times. Illegal discrimination *is making distinctions that harm people and that are based on those people's membership in a protected class*. This chapter will teach you some of the tools that we can use to avoid illegal discrimination.

LO 3-1

Describe the OUCH test and its four components and identify when it is useful in an organizational setting.

Discrimination The act of making distinctions or choosing one thing over another; in HR, it is making distinctions among people

Illegal discrimination The act of making distinctions that harm people and that are based on those people's membership in a protected class

OUCH test A rule of thumb rule used whenever you are contemplating any employment action, to maintain fairness and equity for all of your employees or applicants

A USER'S GUIDE TO MANAGING PEOPLE: THE OUCH TEST

Before we start talking about equal employment opportunity and all of the forms of illegal discrimination in the workplace, let's take the opportunity to introduce you to the OUCH test.[2] The OUCH test *is a rule of thumb rule used whenever you are contemplating any employment action, to maintain fairness and equity for all of your employees or applicants*. You should use this test whenever you are contemplating any action that involves your employees.

SHRM HR CONTENT

See Appendix: *SHRM 2013 Curriculum Guidebook* for the complete list

B. Employment Law (required)
1. Age Discrimination in Employment Act of 1967
2. Americans with Disabilities Act of 1990 and as amended in 2008
3. Equal Pay Act of 1963
4. Pregnancy Discrimination Act of 1978
5. Title VII of the Civil Rights Act of 1964 and 1991
6. Executive Order 11246 (1965)
15. Uniformed Services Employment and Reemployment Rights Act of 1994 (USERRA)
17. Enforcement agencies (EEOC, OFCCP)
24. Disparate impact
25. Disparate treatment
27. Unlawful harassment
    Sexual
    Religious
    Disability
    Race
    Color
    Nation of origin
28. Whistle-blowing/retaliation

29. Reasonable accommodation
    ADA
    Religious
31. Lilly Ledbetter Fair Pay Act
32. Genetic Information Nondiscrimination Act (GINA)

E. Job Analysis/Job Design (required)
6. Compliance with legal requirements
    Equal employment (job-relatedness, bona fide occupational qualifications and the reasonable accommodation process)

F. Managing a Diverse Workforce (required)
1. Equal opportunity employment
2. Affirmative action
4. Individuals with disabilities
6. Racial/ethnic diversity
7. Religion
9. Sex/gender issues
12. Business case for diversity

I. Staffing: Recruitment and Selection (required)
15. Bona fide occupational qualifications (BFOQs)

EXHIBIT 3-1   THE OUCH TEST

Objective	Fact-based and quantifiable, not subjective or emotional
Uniform in Application	Apply the same "tests" in the same ways
Consistent in Effect	Ensure the result is not significantly different for different groups
Has Job Relatedness	Action must relate to the essential job functions

OUCH is an acronym that stands for (see Exhibit 3-1):

- Objective
- Uniform in application
- Consistent in effect
- Has job relatedness

Objective

Is the action objective, or is it subjective? Something that is objective is based on fact, or quantifiable evidence. Something that is subjective is based on your emotional state/feelings or opinion. You should make your employment actions as objective as possible, in all cases.

Uniform in Application

Is the action being uniformly applied? If you apply an action in an employment situation, are you applying that same action in all cases of the same type? If you ask someone to perform a test, you need to create the exact same testing circumstances, as much as you can control them. For instance, if one person took an exam in a quiet room and the other in a noisy hallway, you would not be uniform in application.

Consistent in Effect

Does the action have a significantly different effect on one or more protected groups than it has on the majority group? We have to try to make sure that we don't affect one of the many protected groups disproportionately with an employment action. But how can we know?

The Department of Labor and the EEOC have given us the **Four-Fifths Rule**,[3] *a test used by various federal courts, the Department of Labor, and the EEOC to determine whether disparate impact exists in an employment test.* If the selection ratio for any group (e.g., Asian males) is less than four-fifths of the selection rate for the majority group (e.g., white males) in any employment action, then it constitutes evidence of potential disparate impact.

For an example, take a look at Exhibit 3-2. Let's suppose that we live in an area that is basically evenly split between African-American and White, non-Hispanic populations. You are planning on hiring about 40 new employees for a general position in your company. You decide to give each of the potential employees a written test. If the results of the test disproportionately rule out the African-American applicants, then your written test is not consistent in effect. So let's look at the numbers in Exhibit 3-2.

Four-Fifths Rule A test used by various federal courts, the Department of Labor, and the EEOC to determine whether disparate impact exists in an employment test

EXHIBIT 3-2   THE FOUR-FIFTHS RULE

Example 1: You are planning to hire about 40 new employees. The statistical information on applicants is below:

	White Males	African American Males
Applicants	100	100
Selected	20	17
Selection rate	20% (20/100)	17% (17/100)

4/5ths = 80%, so 80% of 20% (0.80 × 0.20) = 16%.

The selection rate of 17% is greater than 16%, so the Four-Fifths Rule is met.

Example 2: What if you didn't have equal numbers of applicants in each group?

	White Males	African American Males
Applicants	100	40
Selected	29	9
Selection rate	29%	22.5% of 40

4/5ths = 80%, so 0.80 × 0.29 = 0.232 or 23.2%

The selection rate of 22.5% is *less* than the 23.2% required, so the Four-Fifths Rule is *not* met.

You would have to hire 9.28 or more people (23.2% of 40 = 9.28) in this case to be in compliance with the Four-Fifths Rule. You can't have 28% of a person, so you need to round up to 10 to be within the requirement. Therefore, you need one more African American male (10 − 9 selected) to meet the 4/5 ratio requirement.

In the first example, the selection rate of African American males (the protected group in this case) was 17%, which is above the Four-Fifths Rule threshold of 16%. Therefore, we are "consistent in effect," based on the Four-Fifths Rule.

However, in the second example, the selection rate of African American males was 22.5%, and the minimum value by the Four-Fifths Rule was 23.2%. As a result, we would be outside the boundaries of being consistent in effect in this case.

If we are out of compliance with the Four-Fifths Rule, have we automatically broken the law? No.[4] We do have to investigate why we are outside the four-fifths parameter, though. If there is a legitimate reason for the discrepancy that we can prove in a court case, then we are probably OK with a selection rate that is outside the parameters. We *can* also look at six fifths to determine the possibility of reverse discrimination, so we would want to have between 16 and 24 African-American males selected in the first example, since 6/5 of 20 is 24.

Consistency in effect is by far the most complex of the four OUCH test factors. However, it is also very important for us to show consistency in our actions as managers in an organization.

WORK
APPLICATION 3-2

Select an employment policy at the company where you work or at a company where you have worked. Give it the OUCH test, stating whether it does or does not meet each of the four criteria.

Has Job Relatedness

Is the action directly related to the primary aspects, or essential functions of the job in question?[5] In other words, if your job has nothing to do with making coffee for the office in the morning, I cannot base any employment action such as a hiring or firing on whether or not you can make coffee.

Remember that the OUCH test is a rule of thumb and does not work perfectly. It is not a legal test by itself. It is a good guide to nondiscriminatory practices, but it is only a guide.

MAJOR EMPLOYMENT LAWS

Managers need a basic understanding of the major employment laws that are currently in effect. If you don't understand what is legal and what isn't, you can inadvertently make mistakes that may cost your employer significant amounts of money and time. Let's take a chronological look at some of the laws listed in Exhibit 3-3.

LO 3-2

Identify the major equal employment opportunity (EEO) laws and the groups of people that each law protects.

Equal Pay Act of 1963

The Equal Pay Act requires that women who do the same job as men, in the same organization, must receive the same pay. It defines *equal* in terms of "equal skill, effort, and responsibility, and . . . performed under similar working conditions."[6] However, if pay differences are the result of differences in *seniority, merit, quantity or quality of production,* or *any factor other than sex* (e.g., shift differentials and training programs), then pay differences are legally allowable.[7] While designed to equalize pay between men and women, the act was never fully successful, but our next law added serious consequences to such unequal treatment.

SHRM

B:3

Equal Pay Act of 1963

EXHIBIT 3-3   MAJOR EEO LAWS IN CHRONOLOGICAL ORDER

Law	Description
Equal Pay Act of 1963	Requires that women be paid equal to men if they are doing the same work
Title VII of the Civil Rights Act of 1964	Prohibits discrimination on the basis of race, color, religion, sex, or national origin in all areas of the employment relationship
Age Discrimination in Employment Act of 1967	Prohibits age discrimination against people 40 years of age or older and restricts mandatory retirement
Vietnam Era Veterans Readjustment Assistance Act of 1974	Prohibits discrimination against Vietnam veterans by all employers with federal contracts or subcontracts of $100,000 or more. Also requires that affirmative action be taken
Pregnancy Discrimination Act of 1978	Prohibits discrimination against women affected by pregnancy, childbirth, or related medical conditions
Americans with Disabilities Act of 1990	Strengthened the Rehabilitation Act of 1973 to require employers to provide "reasonable accommodations" to allow disabled employees to work
Civil Rights Act of 1991	Strengthened civil rights by providing for possible compensatory and punitive damages for discrimination
Uniformed Services Employment and Reemployment Rights Act (USERRA) of 1994	Ensures the civilian reemployment rights of military members who were called away from their regular (nonmilitary) jobs by US government orders
Veterans Benefits Improvement Act of 2004	Amends USERRA to extend health care coverage while away on duty, and requires employers to post a notice of benefits, duties, and rights of reemployment
Genetic Information Nondiscrimination Act of 2008	Prohibits the use of genetic information in employment, prohibits intentional acquisition of same, and imposes confidentiality requirements
Lilly Ledbetter Fair Pay Act of 2009	Amends the 1964 CRA to extend the period of time in which an employee is allowed to file a lawsuit over pay discrimination

President Barack Obama signed the Lilly Ledbetter Fair Pay Act into law in 2009.

Joyce N. Boghosian/BrokenSphere/CreativeCommons

SHRM

B:5

Title VII of the Civil Rights Act of 1964 and 1991

SHRM

B:25

Disparate Treatment

SHRM

B:24

Disparate Impact

Disparate treatment When individuals in similar situations are intentionally treated differently and the different treatment is based on an individual's membership in a protected class

Disparate impact When an officially neutral employment practice disproportionately excludes the members of a protected group; it is generally considered to be unintentional, but intent is irrelevant

Pattern or practice discrimination When a person or group engages in a sequence of actions over a significant period of time that is intended to deny the rights provided by Title VII of the 1964 CRA to a member of a protected class

Title VII of the Civil Rights Act of 1964 (CRA)

This act changed the way that virtually every organization in the country did business, and it also helped change employers' attitudes about discrimination. The 1964 CRA states that it is illegal for an employer "(1) to fail or refuse to hire or to discharge any individual, or otherwise to discriminate against any individual with respect to his compensation, terms, conditions, or privileges of employment, because of such individual's race, color, religion, sex, or national origin; or (2) to limit, segregate, or classify his employees or applicants for employment in any way which would deprive or tend to deprive any individual of employment opportunities or otherwise adversely affect his status as an employee, because of such individual's race, color, religion, sex, or national origin."[8]

The act applies to organizations with 15 or more employees who are working 20 or more weeks a year and who are involved in interstate commerce. The law also generally applies to state and local governments; educational institutions, public or private; all employment agencies; and all labor associations of any type.

Let's discuss some of the important concepts introduced by the CRA of 1964.

Types of Discrimination. The 1964 CRA identified three types of discrimination. Subsequent court rulings helped to further define the three types: disparate treatment; disparate impact; and pattern or practice.

Disparate (Adverse) Treatment. **Disparate treatment** *exists when individuals in similar situations are intentionally treated differently and the different treatment is based on an individual's membership in a protected class.* In a court case, the plaintiff must prove that the employer intended to discriminate in order to prove disparate treatment.[9] Disparate treatment is generally illegal unless the employer can show that there was a "bona fide occupational qualification" (or BFOQ) that caused the need to intentionally disallow members of a protected group from applying for or getting the job.

Disparate (Adverse) Impact. **Disparate impact** *occurs when an officially neutral employment practice disproportionately excludes the members of a protected group; it is generally considered to be unintentional, but intent is irrelevant.*[10]

Disparate impact is generally judged by use of the Four-Fifths Rule. If our investigation shows that an employment test or measure was biased toward or against a certain group, then we have to correct the test or measure unless there was a legitimate reason to measure that particular characteristic. However, if our investigation shows that the test was valid and reliable and that there was some other legitimate reason why we did not meet the four-fifths standard, then illegal discrimination *may* not exist.

Pattern or Practice. **Pattern or practice discrimination** *occurs when a person or group engages in a sequence of actions over a significant period of time that is intended to deny the rights provided by Title VII of the 1964 CRA to a member of a protected class.* If there is reasonable cause to believe that any organization is engaging in a pattern or practice that denies the rights provided by Title VII, the US Attorney General may bring a federal lawsuit against it.[11] In general, no individual can directly bring a pattern-or-practice lawsuit against an organization. As with the disparate treatment concept, it must be proven that the employer intended to discriminate against a particular class of individuals and did so over a protracted period of time.

See Exhibit 3-4 for types of discrimination and types of organizational defenses against illegal discrimination charges.

Organizational Defenses Against Discrimination Charges. The organization can defend itself against discrimination charges by showing either that there was a need for a particular characteristic or qualification for a specific job or that there was a *requirement* that the business do certain things in order to remain viable and profitable so that we didn't harm *all* of our employees by failing and shutting down. Let's review these defenses.

Bona Fide Occupational Qualification (BFOQs). The first defense is a **bona fide occupational qualification (BFOQ)**, *a qualification that is absolutely required in order for an individual to be able to successfully do a particular job.* The qualification cannot just be a desirable quality within the job applicant—it must be mandatory.[12] A BFOQ defense can be used against both disparate impact and disparate treatment allegations.

Business Necessity. **Business necessity** exists *when a particular practice is necessary for the safe and efficient operation of the business and when there is a specific business purpose for applying a particular standard that may, in fact, be discriminatory.* A business necessity defense is applied by an employer in order to show that a particular practice was necessary for the safe and efficient operation of the business and that there is a specific business purpose for applying a particular standard that may, in fact, be discriminatory. Business necessity defenses must be combined with a test for job relatedness. However, business necessity is specifically prohibited as a defense against disparate treatment.[13]

Job Relatedness. **Job relatedness** exists *when a test for employment is a legitimate measure of an individual's ability to do the essential functions of a job.* For job relatedness to act as a defense against a charge of discrimination, it first has to be a business necessity, and then the employer must be able to show that the test for the employment action was a legitimate (valid) measure of an individual's ability to do the job.[14]

WORK APPLICATION 3-3

Give examples of BFOQ for jobs at an organization where you work or have worked.

SHRM

I:15
Bona Fide Occupational Qualifications (BFOQs)

Bona fide occupational qualification (BFOQ) A qualification that is absolutely required in order for an individual to be able to successfully do a particular job

Business necessity When a particular practice is necessary for the safe and efficient operation of the business and when there is a specific business purpose for applying a particular standard that may, in fact, be discriminatory

Job relatedness When a test for employment is a legitimate measure of an individual's ability to do the essential functions of a job

EXHIBIT 3-4   ORGANIZATIONAL DEFENSES TO DISCRIMINATION CHARGES

Discrimination Type	Intent	Organizational Defense
Disparate Treatment	Intentional	BFOQ
Disparate Impact	Unintentional	BFOQ or business necessity and job relatedness
Pattern or Practice	Intentional	BFOQ (unlikely defense)

3-1   APPLYING THE CONCEPT

BFOQ

State if each of the following would or wouldn't meet the test of a BFOQ:

a. It is a legal BFOQ
b. It is NOT a legal BFOQ

_____ 1. For the job of modeling women's clothing, applicants must be female.

_____ 2. For a job of loading packages onto trucks to be delivered, applicants must be able to lift 35 pounds.

_____ 3. For the job of teaching business at a Catholic college, applicants must be practicing Catholics.

_____ 4. For the job of attendant in a men's locker facility at a gym, applicants must be male.

_____ 5. For the job of a guard in a prison with male inmates, applicants must be men.

SHRM

B:1

Age Discrimination in Employment
Act of 1967 (1967)

Age Discrimination in Employment Act of 1967 (ADEA)

The ADEA prohibits discrimination against employees age 40 or older, so it added the "protected class" of *age*. In this case, it applies if the organization has 20 or more workers instead of 15. The wording of this act almost exactly mirrors Title VII with the exception of the 20-worker minimum. This mirroring of the 1964 CRA is true of nearly all of the protected class discrimination laws that came about after 1964.

Vietnam Era Veterans Readjustment Assistance Act of 1974 (VEVRAA)

This act again provides basically the same protection as the CRA does, but for Vietnam veterans. However, it only applies to federal contractors. It requires that "employers with federal contracts or subcontracts of $100,000 or more provide equal opportunity *and* affirmative action for Vietnam era veterans, special disabled veterans, and veterans who served on active duty during a war or in a campaign or expedition for which a campaign badge has been authorized."[15]

SHRM

B:4

Pregnancy Discrimination Act of
1978

Pregnancy Discrimination Act of 1978 (PDA)

The Pregnancy Discrimination Act prohibits discrimination against women affected by pregnancy, childbirth, or related medical conditions as unlawful sex discrimination under Title VII and requires that they be treated as all other employees for employment-related purposes, including benefits.[16] Again, this law is mandatory for companies with 15 or more employees, including employment agencies, labor organizations, and state and local governments.

SHRM

B:2

Americans with Disabilities Act
(ADA)

F:4

Individuals With Disabilities

B:29

Reasonable Accommodation–ADA

Americans with Disabilities Act of 1990 (ADA), as Amended in 2008

The ADA is one of the most significant employment laws ever passed in the United States. It prohibits discrimination based on disability in all employment practices, such as job application procedures, hiring, firing, promotions, compensation, and training. It applies to virtually *all* employers with 15 or more employees in the same basic ways as the CRA of 1964 does.

There are, however, many things about the ADA that make it difficult for employers to implement. The first of these is the definition of the word "disability." The ADA defines a **disability** as *a physical or mental impairment that substantially limits one or more major life activities, a record of having such an impairment, or being regarded as having such an impairment.*[17]

What Does the ADA Require of Employers? An organization must make "reasonable accommodations" to the physical or mental limitations of an individual with a disability who was otherwise qualified to perform the "essential functions" of the job, unless it would impose an "undue hardship" on the organization's operation.[18]

Disability A physical or mental impairment that substantially limits one or more major life activities, a record of having such an impairment, or being regarded as having such an impairment

Reasonable accommodation An accommodation made by an employer to allow someone who is disabled but otherwise qualified to do the essential functions of a job to be able to perform that job

A **reasonable accommodation** is *an accommodation made by an employer to allow someone who is disabled but otherwise qualified to do the essential functions of a job to be able to perform that job.* Reasonable accommodations are usually inexpensive and easy to implement. For example, if a job requires that the employee use a computer keyboard and a blind individual applies for that job, the organization can make a reasonable accommodation by purchasing a Braille keyboard. In this case, Braille keyboards are inexpensive and provide the blind individual with the ability to do the job based on the reasonable accommodation provided.

In defining reasonable accommodations, it is also necessary to distinguish between "essential" and "marginal" job functions. **Essential functions** *are the fundamental duties of the position.* Based on many court decisions, a function can generally be considered essential if it meets one of the following criteria:

1. The function is something that is done routinely and frequently in the job.

2. The function is done only on occasion, but it is an important part of the job.

3. The function may never be performed by the employee, but if it were necessary, it would be critical that it be done right.

Marginal job functions, on the other hand, *are those functions that may be performed on the job but need not be performed by all holders of the job.* Individuals with disabilities *cannot* be denied employment if they cannot perform marginal job functions.[19]

Under the ADA, employers are:[20]

- Not required to make reasonable accommodations if the applicant or employee does not request it;

- Not required to make reasonable accommodations if applicants don't meet required qualifications for a job;

- Not required to lower quality standards or provide personal use items such as glasses or hearing aids to make reasonable accommodations; and

- Not required to make reasonable accommodations if to do so would be an undue hardship.

An **undue hardship** exists *when the level of difficulty for an organization to provide accommodations, determined by looking at the nature and cost of the accommodation and the overall financial resources of the facility, becomes a significant burden on the organization.* However, an undue hardship may be different for different companies. For instance, a small company may have an undue burden based on a relatively low-cost accommodation to a disabled individual, while a larger company could not claim undue hardship for the same accommodation.

The biggest problem that employers have with the ADA is the fact that it contains a number of words and phrases that can be interpreted in a variety of ways. Because of these poorly defined terms, companies have had a difficult time in applying the ADA in a consistent manner, and as a result, they have quite likely been involved in more lawsuits per disabled employee than with any other protected group.[21]

Civil Rights Act of 1991

The CRA of 1991 was enacted as an amendment designed to correct a few major omissions of the 1964 CRA as well as to overturn several US Court decisions.[22] One of the major changes in the amendment was the addition of compensatory and punitive damages in cases of intentional discrimination under Title VII and the ADA, when intentional or reckless discrimination is proven. **Compensatory damages** are *monetary damages awarded by the court that compensate the injured person for losses.* Such losses can include future pecuniary loss (potential future monetary losses like loss of earnings capacity), emotional pain, suffering, and loss of enjoyment of life. **Punitive damages** are *monetary damages awarded by the*

SHRM

B:5
Title VII of the Civil Rights Act of 1991

Essential functions The fundamental duties of the position

Marginal job functions Those functions that may be performed on the job but need not be performed by all holders of the job

Undue hardship When the level of difficulty for an organization to provide accommodations, determined by looking at the nature and cost of the accommodation and the overall financial resources of the facility, becomes a significant burden on the organization

Compensatory damages Monetary damages awarded by the court that compensate the injured person for losses

Punitive damages Monetary damages awarded by the court that are designed to punish an injuring party that has intentionally inflicted harm on others

©iStockphoto.com/MivPiv

The Uniformed Services Employment and Reemployment Rights Act (or USERRA) was passed in 1994. This measure protects military members from losing their civilian jobs should they be called away by US government orders.

court that are designed to punish an injuring party that has intentionally inflicted harm on others. They are meant to discourage employers from intentionally discriminating, and they do this by providing for payments to the plaintiff beyond the actual damages suffered.

However, the act also provides for a sliding scale of upper limits or "caps" on the combined amount of compensatory and punitive damages based on the number of employees employed by the employer. The limitations are shown in Exhibit 3-5.[23]

Another major area in which the 1991 Act changed the original CRA is in the application of quotas for protected group members. Quotas were made explicitly illegal by the 1991 act. The act also prohibits "discriminatory use" of test scores, which is also called race norming. **Race norming** *exists when different groups of people have different scores designated as "passing" grades on a test for employment.* The 1991 act basically equated this with quotas and, as such, made it illegal.[24] So you can't have different passing grades for any group.

SHRM

B:15

Uniformed Services Employment and Reemployment Rights Act of 1994 (USERRA)

Race norming When different groups of people have different scores designated as "passing" grades on a test for employment

Uniformed Services Employment and Reemployment Rights Act of 1994 (USERRA)

USERRA was passed to ensure the civilian reemployment rights of military members who were called away from their regular (nonmilitary) jobs by US government orders. Unlike other EEO laws, there is no minimum number of employees required for coverage by USERRA.[25] Per the US Department of Labor website, "USERRA is intended to minimize the disadvantages to an individual that occur when that person needs to be absent from his or her civilian employment to serve in this country's uniformed services. USERRA makes major improvements in protecting service member rights and benefits by clarifying the law and improving enforcement mechanisms."[26]

USERRA covers virtually every individual in the country who serves or has served in the uniformed services, and it applies to all employers in the public and private sectors, including federal employers. It also provides protection for disabled veterans, requiring employers to make reasonable efforts to accommodate their disabilities.[27]

| EXHIBIT 3-5 | CAPS ON COMPENSATORY AND PUNITIVE DAMAGES BY EMPLOYER SIZE | |

Employer Size	Caps on Damages
15 to 100 employees	$50,000
101 to 200 employees	$100,000
201 to 500 employees	$200,000
501 employees or more	$300,000

Veterans Benefits Improvement Act of 2004 (VBIA)

The VBIA was enacted as an amendment to USERRA. It extended the requirement for employers to maintain health care coverage for employees who were serving on active duty in the military (originally, this period was 18 months, but the VBIA changed it to 2 years), and it also required employers to post a notice of benefits, duties, and rights under USERRA/VBIA in a place where it would be visible to all employees who might be affected.[28]

Title II of the Genetic Information Nondiscrimination Act of 2008 (GINA)

Title II of the Genetic Information Nondiscrimination Act of 2008 (GINA) "prohibits the use of genetic information in employment, prohibits the intentional acquisition of genetic information about applicants and employees, and imposes strict confidentiality requirements."[29]

Because companies were starting to use genetic tests to make employment and health care decisions, Congress decided to address their use so that the general public would not fear adverse employment-related or health coverage–related consequences for having a genetic test or participating in research studies that examine genetic information.[30] The result was GINA.

Lilly Ledbetter Fair Pay Act of 2009 (LLFPA)

This law amended Title VII of the 1964 CRA. In practical terms, the LLFPA extends the period of time in which an employee is allowed to file a lawsuit for compensation (pay) discrimination. The 1964 CRA only allowed 180 days from

WORK
APPLICATION 3-4

Give examples of how major employment laws have affected an organization where you work or have worked, preferably as the law relates directly to you. Be sure to specify the law and what the firm does or doesn't do because of the law.

B:32

Genetic Information
Nondiscrimination Act (GINA)

B:31

Lilly Ledbetter Fair Pay Act

3-2 APPLYING THE CONCEPT

Employment Laws

Review the laws listed below and then write the letter corresponding to each law before the statement(s) describing a situation where that law would apply.

a. Equal Pay

b. Title VII CRA 1964

c. ADEA

d. VEVRAA

e. PDA

f. ADA

g. CRA 1991

h. USERRA

i. VBIA

j. GINA

k. LLFPA

_____ 6. I had to take a medical test, and the company found out that I am at high risk to get cancer. So it decided not to hire me so it could save money on medical insurance.

_____ 7. Although I was the best qualified, I was intentionally not promoted because I am a woman.

_____ 8. I can't understand why this firm doesn't want to hire me just because I served my country. I didn't want to go and fight overseas, but I was drafted into the Army in 1969 and had no choice; I didn't want to go to jail for draft evasion.

_____ 9. My boss is laying me off because I serve in the National Guard and will be deployed overseas for six months. As a result, I will have to find a new job when I get back.

_____ 10. The firm is laying me off to hire some younger person to save money. Is this what I deserve for my 20 years of dedication?

_____ 11. I'm being paid less than the men who do the same jobs, just because I'm a woman.

_____ 12. The firm hired this new guy and bought a special low desk because he is so short.

_____ 13. I'm suing the firm for lost wages because they intentionally discriminated against me and fired me when I complained about it.

the time of the discriminatory action for an individual employee to file a lawsuit. The LLFPA allows an individual to file a lawsuit within 180 days after "any application" of that discriminatory compensation decision, including every time the individual gets paid, as long as the discrimination is continuing, which would usually be for the entire period of their employment.

LO 3-3

Briefly discuss the major functions of the Equal Employment Opportunity Commission (EEOC).

EQUAL EMPLOYMENT OPPORTUNITY COMMISSION (EEOC)

The various federal equal employment opportunity (EEO) laws are enforced by the Equal Employment Opportunity Commission (EEOC). The EEOC is a federal agency that has significant power over employers in the process of investigating complaints of illegal discrimination.[31]

What Does the EEOC Do?

B:17

Enforcement Agencies—EEOC

E:6

Compliance With Legal Requirements

The EEOC basically has three significant responsibilities: (1) investigating and resolving discrimination complaints through either conciliation or litigation, (2) gathering and compiling statistical information on such complaints, and (3) running education and outreach programs on what constitutes illegal discrimination.[32] Additionally, every company with more than 100 employees or with more than 50 employees *and* with federal contracts totaling $50,000 or more must file an EEO-1 Report with the EEOC each year.[33] The EEO-1 identifies the company's EEO compliance data based on protected classifications within federal law.

Generally, a discrimination complaint must be filed with the EEOC within 180 days of the date of discrimination. If the EEOC determines that discrimination has taken place, it will attempt to provide reconciliation between the parties. If the EEOC cannot come to an agreement with the organization, there are two options:

1. The agency may aid the alleged victim in bringing suit in federal court.

2. It can issue a "right-to-sue" letter to the alleged victim. A right-to-sue is *a notice from the EEOC, issued if it elects not to prosecute an individual discrimination complaint within the agency, that gives the recipient the right to go directly to the courts with the complaint.*

F:1

Equal Opportunity Employment

B:27

Unlawful Harassment

B:28

Whistle-blowing/Retaliation

Employee Rights Under the EEOC

Employees have the right to bring discrimination complaints against their employer by filing a complaint with the EEOC. They also have the right to participate in an EEOC investigation, hearing, or other proceeding without threat of retaliation; rights related to the arbitration and settlement of the complaint; and the right to sue the employer directly in court over claims of illegal discrimination, even if the EEOC does not support their claim. For information on how to submit a written complaint, see the EEOC website link (http://www.eeoc.gov/employees/howtofile.cfm).

Right-to-sue A notice from the EEOC, issued if it elects not to prosecute an individual discrimination complaint within the agency, that gives the recipient the right to go directly to the courts with the complaint

Employer Rights and Prohibitions

The employer has a right to defend the organization using the defenses noted earlier: BFOQ, business necessity, and job relatedness. However, the employer does not have a right to *retaliate* against individuals who participate in an EEOC action. The employer also is prohibited from creating a work environment that would lead to charges of *constructive discharge.*

Retaliation. In addition to providing defenses against discrimination claims, the 1964 civil rights act identifies a situation in which organizations can be held liable for harming the employee because of retaliation.[34] Retaliation *is a situation where the organization takes an "adverse employment action" against an employee because the employee brought discrimination charges against the organization or supported someone who brought discrimination charges against the company.* An adverse employment action *is any action such as firings, demotions, schedule reductions, or changes that would harm the individual employee.*

Retaliation is a form of harassment based on an individual filing a discrimination claim. Each of the EEO laws identifies retaliation as illegal harassment based on the protected class identified within that law.

Managers need to be aware that there are severe penalties for engaging in retaliation against an employee or applicant for participating in protected activity. In 2013, over 40% of all EEOC complaints had a retaliation claim as at least a component of the complaint.[35]

Constructive Discharge. The organization can also be accused of "constructive discharge" due to discriminatory actions on the job. Constructive discharge exists *when an employee is put under such extreme pressure by management that continued employment becomes intolerable and, as a result, the employee quits, or resigns from the organization.* In a Supreme Court decision in 2004,[36] the court noted that the US Court of Appeals had identified constructive discharge as the following: "(1) he or she suffered harassment or discrimination so intolerable that a reasonable person in the same position would have felt compelled to resign . . . ; and (2) the employee's reaction to the workplace situation—that is, his or her decision to resign—was reasonable given the totality of circumstances."

So if an individual can show that constructive discharge caused them to resign from the organization, then the individual would be eligible for all employee rights associated with being involuntarily terminated from the company.

EEO, AFFIRMATIVE ACTION, AND DIVERSITY: WHAT'S THE DIFFERENCE?

Managers need to understand the terms *equal employment opportunity* (EEO), *affirmative action*, and *diversity*. These are significantly different concepts and they should not be used interchangeably. *EEO* is the term that deals with a series of laws

WORK
APPLICATION 3-5

Has an organization where you work or have worked had any potential or actual cases brought to the EEOC against it? If so, explain the complaint(s). The HR staff at your employer may not be too eager to talk about this, but you can do some research on larger corporations.

Retaliation A situation where the organization takes an "adverse employment action" against an employee because the employee brought discrimination charges against the organization or supported someone who brought discrimination charges against the company

Adverse employment action Any action such as firings, demotions, schedule reductions, or changes that would harm the individual employee

Constructive discharge When an employee is put under such extreme pressure by management that continued employment becomes intolerable and, as a result, the employee quits, or resigns from the organization

---

3-1   ETHICAL DILEMMA: WHAT WOULD YOU DO?

The United States was once known as the "melting pot," as people from all over the world came to the country and adjusted to its culture. In the past, generally, immigrants had to learn English to get a job. Today, however, many organizations hire people who can't speak English, and they use translators and have policies written in multiple languages for these employees. Government agencies at the federal, state, and local levels are also providing translators and written materials in other languages.

1. Why are some organizations no longer requiring workers to speak English?
2. Should a worker be required to be able to speak English to get a job in the United States?
3. Is it ethical to (or not to) hire people who can't speak English and to provide translators and policies written in multiple languages?

Affirmitive Action programs and policies are intended to prefer the hiring of individuals from protected groups in an attempt to mitigate past discrimination.

LO 3-4

Contrast the concepts of equal employment opportunity, affirmative action, and diversity.

SHRM

F:2

Affirmative Action

SHRM

B:6

Executive Order 11246 (1965)

Affirmative action A series of policies, programs, and initiatives that have been instituted by various entities within both government and the private sector that are designed to prefer hiring of individuals from protected groups in certain circumstances, in an attempt to mitigate past discrimination

and regulations put in place at the federal and state government level over the last 45 years. As such, EEO is very specific and narrowly defined within federal and state laws.

On the other hand, affirmative action was created in the 1960s through a series of policies at the presidential and legislative levels in the United States. Affirmative action, except in a few circumstances, does not have the effect of law.[37] Therefore, affirmative action is a much broader concept based on policies and executive orders (orders from the president) to help legally protected groups.

Finally, diversity is not law, nor *necessarily* even policy within organizations. Diversity is a very broad set of concepts that deal with the differences among people within organizations. Today's organizations view diversity as a valuable part of their human resources makeup. However, there are no specific federal laws that deal with requirements for diversity within organizations, beyond the EEO laws that specifically identify protected class members and require that organizations deal with those protected class members in an equal way when compared to all other members of the organization.

Let's take a closer look at EEO, affirmative action, and diversity. Exhibit 3-6 provides a summary of these three concepts.

Affirmative Action (AA)

Affirmative action is *a series of policies, programs, and initiatives that have been instituted by various entities within both government and the private sector that are designed to prefer hiring of individuals from protected groups in certain circumstances, in an attempt to mitigate past discrimination.* There are only two specific cases in which AA can be mandated or required within an organization.[38] In all other cases AA is strictly voluntary. The two situations where affirmative action is mandatory are:

Executive Order 11246. If the company is a contractor to the federal government and receives more than $10,000 per year, they are required by presidential order (Executive Order 11246) to maintain an affirmative action program. Exemptions from this order include the following:

- "(A) Government contractor or subcontractor that is a religious corporation, association, educational institution, or society, with respect to the employment

| EXHIBIT 3-6 | EQUAL EMPLOYMENT OPPORTUNITY, AFFIRMATIVE ACTION, AND DIVERSITY |

Topic	Governance	Concept
EEO	Federal (and state) law	Narrow, specific requirements and prohibitions
Affirmative Action	Executive orders, federal court orders, or voluntary	Policies that broadly define situations in which actions should be taken to balance a workforce with its surroundings
Diversity	Organizational voluntary policies	No legal requirement; designed to better serve a more diverse customer base

of individuals of a particular religion to perform work connected with the carrying on by such corporation, association, educational institution, or society of its activities . . . "[39]

- " . . . facilities of a contractor that are in all respects separate and distinct from activities of the contractor related to the performance of the (federal government) contract . . . "[40]

Federal Court Orders for AA Programs. If an organization is presented with a federal court order to create an affirmative action program to correct past discriminatory practices, it must comply. This is usually only done when there is a history of past discriminatory practices in the organization.

The *Bakke v. California* decision of 1978 is the basis for the concept of **reverse discrimination**, which is *discrimination against members of the majority group by an organization, generally resulting from affirmative action policies within an organization.* And there have been a number of other recent AA rulings in federal courts For example, the Supreme Court ordered a lower court to reconsider a "race-conscious" admissions plan at Texas state universities,[41] and it also upheld a voter-backed AA ban in Michigan's universities.[42]

Diversity in the Workforce

Diversity *is simply the existence of differences—in HRM, it deals with different types of people in an organization.* Let's discuss why organizations are embracing diversity as it provides both opportunities and challenges.[43]

Demographic Diversity. Is diversity really all that important? The answer is yes.[44] There is currently a shortage of skilled workers—and there will be for the foreseeable future, so to exclude a qualified person because that individual is different in some way is counterproductive to business success. Increasing cultural diversity in the workforce poses one of the most challenging human resource and organizational issues of our time.[45]

Why Do We Need Diversity? Diversity helps increase sales, revenues, and profits—in other words, embracing diversity creates business opportunities.[46] Diverse employees allow us to see the diversity around us, in our customers and other stakeholders, much better than we would if our work groups were more homogenous.[47] As a result, we are better able to provide products and services that will appeal to the larger and more diverse groups that we come into contact with during the course of doing business.[48]

What Are the Advantages of a Diverse Workforce? The primary advantages of a diverse workforce come from the ability to stimulate and provide more creative and innovative solutions to organizational problems.[49] **Creativity** *is a basic ability to think in unique and different ways and apply those thought processes to existing problems,* and **innovation** *is the act of creating useful processes or products based on creative thought processes.*

A diverse group looking at a problem will analyze the problem from different directions and in different ways, and will discover more of the aspects of the problem than would a single person or a more homogeneous work group.[50]

Why is it so hard to be innovative and creative? Most of us have learned not to be creative—we have been told over and over as we grow up that we should do things the way everyone else does them. In other words, we have been *trained* not to be innovative! Over time, this has the effect of causing most of us to lose the ability to think differently. This ability, called divergent thinking, is necessary in

---

SHRM

F:6
Racial/Ethnic Diversity

SHRM

F:12
Business Case for Diversity

Reverse discrimination
Discrimination against members of the majority group by an organization, generally resulting from affirmative action policies within an organization

Diversity The existence of differences—in HRM, it deals with different types of people in an organization

Creativity A basic ability to think in unique and different ways and apply those thought processes to existing problems

Innovation The act of creating useful processes or products based on creative thought processes

WORK
APPLICATION 3-7

Discuss how demographic diversity and the need for diversity is affecting an organization you work for or have worked for. What are some of the advantages and challenges faced by the firm? Also, describe how diversity is managed at the organization.

order to come up with creative solutions to a problem.[51] **Divergent thinking** *is the ability to find many possible solutions to a particular problem, including unique, untested solutions.*

By introducing diversity into our workforce, we assist the process of divergent thinking. Different people think differently because they have different backgrounds and have solved problems differently in the past, so this has the effect of increasing the creativity and innovation in the organization without the individual having to relearn the ability to be highly creative.

Are There Any Challenges to Diversity? There are several things that can cause diversity to break down the organization instead of allowing it to become better and more creative.[52] The first issue is conflict. **Conflict** *is simply the act of being opposed to another.* Conflict occurs in interactions between individuals. There are many reasons for conflict, but it is typically greater when people are significantly different from each other, which means that if we create a more diverse workforce, there's a greater likelihood for more conflict.

The second big issue is group cohesiveness. **Cohesiveness** *is an intent and desire for group members to stick together in their actions.* In organizations, we have learned that in order for a work group to become as good as it possibly can be, the group has to become cohesive. The members have to learn to *want* to be part of the group and want to interact with other members of the group in order for the group to perform at a high level. However, the more diversity there is within the group, the more difficult it is to create the cohesiveness necessary for high performance. So, more diverse groups tend to be less cohesive—not always, but as a general rule.[53]

Managing Diversity. Diversity affects bottom-line profits, but so do some of the challenges associated with diversity, like conflict and reduced cohesiveness. In other words, if all of our diverse employees don't work well together, the organization does not work well.[54] Managing diversity so that we gain the benefits available is one of the most critical jobs of a 21st century manager. Diversity can be managed successfully only in an organizational culture that values diversity.[55]

Through managing diversity, affirmative action and diversity programs have been used to help women and minorities advance in organizations. Complete Self-Assessment 3-1 to determine your attitude toward women and minorities advancing at work.

SHRM

F:9
Sex/Gender Issues

LO 3-5

Compare the two primary types of sexual harassment.

Divergent thinking The ability to find many possible solutions to a particular problem, including unique, untested solutions

Conflict The act of being opposed to another

Cohesiveness An intent and desire for group members to stick together in their actions

Sexual harassment "unwelcome sexual advances, requests for sexual favors, and other verbal or physical conduct of a sexual nature constitutes sexual harassment when submission to or rejection of this conduct explicitly or implicitly affects an individual's employment, unreasonably interferes with an individual's work performance or creates an intimidating, hostile or offensive work environment"

SEXUAL HARASSMENT: A SPECIAL TYPE OF DISCRIMINATION

Sexual harassment is part of the 1964 CRA (the prohibition of discrimination based on sex), but it is one of the two items we mentioned earlier in the chapter that was not specifically recognized as a separate type of discrimination until federal courts started hearing cases on the act. Sexual harassment is a pervasive issue in organizations, and we all need to understand what it is and how to avoid creating a situation where it can occur at work.

Types of Sexual Harassment

Sexual harassment is defined by the EEOC as "*unwelcome sexual advances, requests for sexual favors, and other verbal or physical conduct of a sexual nature constitutes sexual harassment when submission to or rejection of this conduct explicitly or implicitly affects an individual's employment, unreasonably interferes with an individual's work performance or creates an intimidating, hostile or offensive work environment.*"[56] There are two types of sexual harassment specifically delineated in law: quid pro quo harassment and hostile work environment.[57] Both are discussed below.

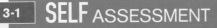

Attitudes About Women and Minorities Advancing

Be honest in this self-assessment, as your assessment will not be accurate if you aren't. Also, you should not be asked to share your score with others.

Each question below is actually two questions. It asks you about your attitude toward women, and it also asks you about your attitude toward minorities. Therefore, you should give two answers to each question: one regarding women and the other regarding minorities. Write the number corresponding to your answer (5 = agree, 3 = don't know, 1 = disagree) about women in the Women column, and write the number corresponding to your answer about minorities in the Minorities column.

Agree				Disagree
5	4	3	2	1

Women   Minorities

_____ 1. Women/Minorities lack motivation to get ahead.   1. ____

_____ 2. Women/Minorities lack the education necessary to get ahead.   2. ____

_____ 3. Women/Minorities working has caused rising unemployment among white men.   3. ____

_____ 4. Women/Minorities are not strong enough or emotionally stable enough to succeed in
high-pressure jobs.   4. ____

_____ 5. Women/Minorities have a lower commitment to work than do white men.   5. ____

_____ 6. Women/Minorities are too emotional to be effective managers.   6. ____

_____ 7. Women/Minority managers have difficulty in situations calling for quick and precise decisions.   7. ____

_____ 8. Women/Minorities have a higher turnover rate than do white men.   8. ____

_____ 9. Women/Minorities are out of work more often than are white men.   9. ____

____ 10. Women/Minorities have less interest in advancing than do white men.   10. ____

____ Total   Total ____

Women: To determine your attitude score toward women, add up the total of your 10 answers in the Women column and place the total on the Total line and on the following continuum. The higher your total score, the more negative your attitude.

10 _____ 20 _____ 30 _____ 40 _____ 50
Positive attitude   Negative attitude

Minorities: To determine your attitude score toward minorities, add up the total of your 10 answers from the Minorities column and place the total on the Total line and on the following continuum. The higher your total score, the more negative your attitude.

10 _____ 20 _____ 30 _____ 40 _____ 50
Positive attitude   Negative attitude

Each statement is a negative attitude about women and minorities at work. However, research has shown all of these statements to be false; they are considered myths. Such statements stereotype women and minorities unfairly and prevent them from advancing in organizations through gaining salary increases and promotions. Thus, part of managing diversity and diversity training is to help overcome these negative attitudes to provide equal opportunities for ALL.

Quid Pro Quo Harassment. Literally, quid pro quo means "This for that." Quid pro quo harassment is *harassment that occurs when some type of benefit or punishment is made contingent upon the employee submitting to sexual advances.* "If you do something sexual for me, I will do something for you." Quid pro quo is a direct form of harassment aimed at an individual and is most commonly seen in supervisor-subordinate relationships, although this is not always the case. It is, however, based on the power of one individual over another.

Quid pro quo harassment Harassment that occurs when some type of benefit or punishment is made contingent upon the employee submitting to sexual advances

WORK
APPLICATION 3-8

A high percentage of people, especially women, have been sexually harassed. Have you or anyone you know been sexually harassed at work? Briefly describe the situation, stating if it was quid pro quo or a hostile work environment.

Hostile Work Environment. **Hostile work environment** is *harassment that occurs when someone's behavior at work creates an environment that is sexual in nature and that makes it difficult for someone of a particular sex to work in that environment.* Hostile work environment sexual harassment happens when a "reasonable person" determines that the behavior in question goes beyond normal human interaction and the jokes and kidding that accompany such interaction, instead rising to a level that such a reasonable person would consider the act or acts to be both harassing and sexual in nature.[58] For the purposes of the law, a **reasonable person** is *the "average" person who would look at the situation and its intensity to determine whether the accused person was wrong in their actions.*

What Constitutes Sexual Harassment?

Sexual harassment does not have to occur between a male and female or between a supervisor and subordinates. Same-sex harassment also occurs at work.[59]

As in other forms of illegal discrimination, the plaintiff only has to show a prima facie (literally "on the face of it," meaning it looks like harassment to our reasonable person) case that harassment has occurred. To qualify as a prima facie case of sexual harassment, the work situation must include the following characteristics:[60]

1. The plaintiff is a member of a protected class;
2. The harassment was based on sex;
3. The person was subject to unwelcome sexual advances; *or*
4. The harassment was sufficiently severe enough to alter the terms, conditions, or privileges of employment.

In order for the organization to be considered for liability, two critical conditions must exist:[61]

1. The plaintiff did not solicit or incite the advances.
2. The harassment was undesirable, and was severe enough to alter the terms, conditions, and privileges of employment.

Hostile work environment Harassment that occurs when someone's behavior at work creates an environment that is sexual in nature and that makes it difficult for someone of a particular sex to work in that environment

Reasonable person The "average" person who would look at the situation and its intensity to determine whether the accused person was wrong in their actions

---

3-3 APPLYING THE CONCEPT

Sexual Harassment

Write the letter and number codes listed below before each statement to indicate the kind of behavior it describes.

a. sexual harassment: After the harassment letter, write in if it is (1) quid pro quo or (2) hostile work environment harassment (i.e., write a/1 or a/2).

b. not sexual harassment

_____ 14. Karen tells her coworker Jim an explicitly sexual joke, even though twice before, Jim told her not to tell him any dirty jokes.

_____ 15. Ricky-Joe typically puts his hand on his secretary's shoulder as he talks to her, and she is comfortable with this behavior.

_____ 16. José, the supervisor, tells his secretary, Latoya, that he'd like to take her out for the first time today.

_____ 17. Cindy tells her assistant, Juan, that he will have to go to a motel with her if he wants to be recommended for a promotion.

_____ 18. Jack and Jill have each hung up pictures of nude men and women on the walls near their desks, in view of other employees who walk by.

_____ 19. As coworker Rachel talks to Carlos, he is surprised and uncomfortable because she gently rubbed his buttock.

EXHIBIT 3-7 **LIMITING ORGANIZATIONAL LIABILITY FOR SEXUAL HARASSMENT**

1. Develop a policy statement making it clear that sexual harassment will not be tolerated. You have to delineate what is acceptable and what is not. The policy should also state that anyone participating in a sexual harassment complaint or investigation should not be retaliated against.

2. Communicate the policy by training all employees to identify inappropriate workplace behavior. Make sure that everyone is aware of the policy.

3. Develop a mechanism for reporting sexual harassment that encourages people to speak out. It is critical in this case to create a mechanism outside of the normal chain of command. The typical case of harassment is between an individual and the immediate supervisor. Because of this, if the organization does not have a way to report the behavior outside the normal supervisory chain of command, the courts will consider that the company does not have a mechanism for reporting.

4. Ensure that just cause procedures (we will talk about these in Chapter 9) are followed when investigating the complaint.

5. Prepare to carry out prompt disciplinary action against those who commit sexual harassment.

Reducing Organizational Risk From Sexual Harassment Lawsuits

Once the plaintiff has shown a prima facie case for the accusation, the courts will determine whether the organization is liable for the actions of its employee based on the answers to two primary questions:

1. Did the employer know about, or should the employer have known about, the harassment?

2. Did the employer act to stop the behavior?

In general, if the employer knew or should have known about the harassment and did nothing to stop the behavior, then the employer can be held liable. Sexual harassment should be treated very seriously, because the consequences can be grave for the organization if it doesn't do what it should to prevent the harassment.

So how do you protect your organization from liability in case of a charge of sexual harassment? Exhibit 3-7 shows five important steps to follow.[62]

RELIGIOUS DISCRIMINATION

Religion-based discrimination and the ability of employers to create work rules that may affect religious freedom continue to be an issue in the workplace.[63] The issue of standards of dress in a number of religions, most notably Islam's standards for women's attire in public (including the hijab or niqab), has become a point of contention in some workplaces. If an employer sees the niqab as a symbol of repression, can the employer deny the right to wear such head coverings and use the antidiscrimination statutes concerning gender as justification? Can an employer require drivers that work for them to deliver alcohol to customer warehouses when the drivers may have a religious opposition to drinking alcohol?[64] There are many religious freedom questions that we are dealing with in companies today, and there are certainly no easy answers.

Remember that religious discrimination is a violation of the 1964 CRA because it identifies religion as a protected class. Because religion was specifically identified in the CRA, we can't use it as a factor in making "any employment decision" with our employees. Religion is a less obvious characteristic than gender or race, so it is usually not a characteristic on which we base decisions. However, if a person's religion requires a certain type of dress or observation of religious holidays or days of worship that is not in keeping with the normal workday practices of the

WORK
APPLICATION 3-9

Describe the sexual harassment policy where you work or have worked. If you are not sure, check the company HR handbook or talk to an HR department staff member to get the answer.

LO 3-6

Briefly discuss the employer's requirements concerning avoidance of religious discrimination in the workplace.

©iStockphoto.com/JohnnyGreig

organization, and if the individual requests accommodation for these religious beliefs, then we generally would need to make every reasonable effort to accommodate such requests.

TRENDS AND ISSUES IN HRM

We again end this chapter with two significant issues that are affecting HRM. These issues include increasing federal agency activism in reinterpreting laws that have been in effect for as many as 80 years, and the 2008 amendment to the ADA.

Religion is identified as a protected class in the 1964 Civil Rights Act, meaning that an employer cannot consider an individual's religion when making employment decisions.

SHRM

B:29

Reasonable Accommodation–
Religious

SHRM

F:7

Religion

Federal Agencies Are Becoming More Activist in Pursuing Discrimination Claims

A number of federal agencies have become much more active over the past few years in pursuing large-scale claims against US businesses. The EEOC, the Occupational Safety and Health Administration (OSHA), the National Labor Relations Board (NLRB), and other agencies have begun to act directly against companies in many cases without a complaint being filed. Systemic discrimination investigations constitute one type of investigation that has increased dramatically.[65]

Systemic discrimination (23% of EEOC's active cases in 2013)[66] is defined by the EEOC as "a pattern or practice, policy, or class case where the alleged discrimination has a broad impact on an industry, profession, company, or geographic area."[67] In one year alone, more than 300 systemic investigations resulted in 63 settlements or conciliation agreements worth more than $40 million.[68]

As the HR manager, you need to know that there is no longer a minimal chance of being investigated for potential wrongdoing if there isn't an employee complaint. Federal agencies are actively seeking out evidence of "pattern or practice" forms of discrimination and then prosecuting those cases. So you will need to be more diligent than ever in maintaining a fair and nondiscriminatory workplace.

The ADA and the ADA Amendments Act (ADAAA)

Claims under the ADA increased from 17,734 in 2007 to more than 25,000 in 2011, mostly due to the changes in the ADAAA.[69] This increase is at least in part due to the increase in *association discrimination* claims—claims that one has been discriminated against because one is, for example, associated with a partner who has HIV or has a family member who is disabled and needs care.[70]

Recent EEOC guidance also notes several conditions that may be episodic or in remission where the changes in the ADAAA have made it clear that those conditions are covered by the law. Among these conditions are cancer, diabetes, and epilepsy.[71] The Midwest Regional Medical Center in Oklahoma was charged by the EEOC with firing an employee because of her ongoing cancer treatments.[72] The EEOC filed suit on behalf of the individual when she was terminated, noting that she could have returned to work after a short period of sick leave if she had been allowed to do so.

Enforcement actions based on the ADAAA revisions will almost certainly continue to evolve. As an HR manager, you will need to keep apprised of the developments in this amendment to the ADA to provide good counsel to the executives and managers in your company or other organization.

• • • CHAPTER SUMMARY

3-1   Describe the OUCH test and its four components and identify when it is useful in an organizational setting.

The OUCH Test is a rule of thumb you should use whenever you are contemplating any employment action. You use it to maintain equity for all of your employees or applicants. OUCH is an acronym that stands for Objective, Uniform in application, Consistent in effect, and Has job relatedness. An employment action should generally be objective instead of subjective; we should apply all employment tests the same way, every time, with everyone, to the best of our ability; the employment action should not have an inconsistent effect on any protected groups; and the test must be directly related to the job to which we are applying it.

3-2   Identify the major equal employment opportunity (EEO) laws and the groups of people that each law protects.

The Equal Pay Act of 1963 requires that women be paid equal to men if they are doing the same work.

The Civil Rights Act of 1964 prohibits discrimination on the basis of race, color, religion, sex, or national origin, in all areas of the employment relationship.

The Age Discrimination in Employment Act of 1967 prohibits age discrimination against people 40 years of age or older, and it restricts mandatory retirement.

The Vietnam Era Veterans Readjustment Assistance Act of 1974 prohibits discrimination against Vietnam veterans by all employers with federal contracts or subcontracts of $100,000 or more. It also requires that affirmative action be taken.

The Pregnancy Discrimination Act of 1978 prohibits discrimination against women affected by pregnancy, childbirth, or related medical conditions, and it treats such discrimination as unlawful sex discrimination.

The Americans with Disabilities Act of 1990 requires employers to provide "reasonable accommodations" to allow disabled employees to work.

The Civil Rights Act of 1991 strengthened civil rights by providing for possible compensatory and punitive damages for discrimination.

The Uniformed Services Employment and Reemployment Rights Act (USERRA) ensures the civilian reemployment rights of military members who were called away from their regular (nonmilitary) jobs by US government orders.

The Veterans Benefits Improvement Act of 2004 amends USERRA to extend health care coverage while away on duty, and it requires employers to post a notice of benefits, duties, and rights of reemployment.

The Genetic Information Nondiscrimination Act of 2008 prohibits the use of genetic information in employment, prohibits intentional acquisition of the same, and imposes confidentiality requirements.

The Lilly Ledbetter Fair Pay Act of 2009 amends the 1964 CRA to extend the period of time in which an employee is allowed to file a lawsuit over pay discrimination.

3-3   Briefly discuss the major functions of the Equal Employment Opportunity Commission (EEOC).

The EEOC is a federal agency that investigates complaints of illegal discrimination based on race, color, religion, sex (including pregnancy), national origin, age (40 or older), disability, or genetic information.

The EEOC has three significant functions: investigating and resolving discrimination complaints through either conciliation or litigation, gathering and compiling statistical information on such complaints, and running education and outreach programs on what constitutes illegal discrimination.

3-4   Discuss the differences among equal employment opportunity, affirmative action, and diversity.

Equal employment opportunity deals with a series of laws and regulations put in place at the federal and state government levels in the last 45 years. As such, equal employment opportunity is very specific and narrowly defined within US law and various state laws.

Affirmative action, except in a few circumstances, does not have the effect of law. Therefore, affirmative action is a much broader concept based on policy than is EEO, which is more narrowly based on law.

Finally, diversity is not law, nor *necessarily* even policy within organizations. Diversity is a very broad set of concepts that deal with the differences among people within organizations. Today's organizations view diversity as a valuable part of their human resources makeup, but there are no specific laws that deal with requirements for diversity within organizations beyond the EEO laws.

3-5   Compare the two primary types of sexual harassment.

Quid pro quo harassment occurs when some type of benefit or punishment is made contingent upon the employee submitting to sexual advances. In other words, if you do something for me, I will do something for you, or conversely, if you refuse to do something for me, I will harm you.

Hostile work environment harassment occurs when someone's behavior at work creates an environment that is sexual in nature and makes it difficult for someone of a particular sex to work in that environment. Hostile environment sexual harassment happens when a "reasonable person" would determine that the environment went beyond normal human interactions and the jokes and kidding that go with those interactions and rose to the level that such a reasonable person would consider the act or acts to be both harassing and sexual in nature.

3-6   Briefly discuss the employer's requirements concerning avoidance of religious discrimination in the workplace.

Religious discrimination is one of the identified protected classes in the 1964 Civil Rights Act. As such, we can't use it as a factor in making "any employment decision" with our employees. Issues such as standards of dress, time off for religious holidays, adherence to strongly held religious beliefs, and other questions of religious freedom should be accommodated to the best of our ability to avoid inadvertent violation of the law.

3-7   Define the key terms found in the chapter margins and listed following the Chapter Summary.

Complete the Key Terms Review to test your understanding of this chapter's key terms.

• • • KEY TERMS

adverse employment action, 67	disparate impact, 60	pattern or practice
affirmative action, 68	disparate treatment, 60	discrimination, 60
bona fide occupational qualification	divergent thinking, 70	punitive damages, 63
(BFOQ), 61	diversity, 69	quid pro quo harassment, 71
business necessity, 61	essential functions, 63	race norming, 64
cohesiveness, 70	Four-Fifths Rule, 57	reasonable accommodation, 62
compensatory damages, 63	hostile work environment, 72	reasonable person, 72
conflict, 70	illegal discrimination, 56	retaliation, 67
constructive discharge, 67	innovation, 69	reverse discrimination, 69
creativity, 69	job relatedness, 61	right-to-sue, 66
disability, 62	marginal job functions, 63	sexual harassment, 70
discrimination, 56	OUCH test, 56	undue hardship, 63

• • • KEY TERMS REVIEW

Complete each of the following statements using one of this chapter's key terms.

1. _____ is the act of making distinctions or choosing one thing over another—in HR, it is distinctions among people.

2. _____ is making distinctions that harm people by using a person's membership in a protected class.

3. _____ is a rule of thumb used whenever you are contemplating any employment action, to maintain fairness and equity for all of your employees or applicants.

4. _____ is a test used by various federal courts, the Department of Labor, and the EEOC to determine whether disparate impact exists in an employment test.

5. _____ exists when individuals in similar situations are intentionally treated differently and the different treatment is based on an individual's membership in a protected class.

6. _____ occurs when an officially neutral employment practice disproportionately excludes the members of a protected group; it is generally considered to be unintentional, but intent is irrelevant.

7. _____ occurs when, over a significant period of time, a person or group engages in a sequence of actions that is intended to deny the rights provided by Title VII (the 1964 CRA) to a member of a protected class.

8. _____ is a qualification that is absolutely required for an individual to successfully do a particular job.

9. _____ exists when a particular practice is necessary for the safe and efficient operation of the business, and when there is a specific business purpose for applying a particular standard that may, in fact, be discriminatory.

10. _____ exists when a test for employment is a legitimate measure of an individual's ability to do the essential functions of a job.

11. _____ is a physical or mental impairment that substantially limits one or more major life activities, a record of having such an impairment, or a condition of being regarded as having such an impairment.

12. _____ is an accommodation made by an employer to allow someone who is disabled but otherwise qualified to do the essential functions of a job to be able to perform that job.

13. _____ consist of the fundamental duties of the position.

14. _____ are those functions that may be performed on the job but need not be performed by all holders of the job.

15. _____ occurs when the level of difficulty for an organization to provide accommodations, determined by looking at the nature and cost of the accommodation and the overall financial resources of the facility, becomes a significant burden on the organization.

16. _____ consists of monetary damages awarded by the court that compensate the person who was injured for their losses.

17. _____ consist of monetary damages awarded by the court that are designed to punish an injuring party that intentionally inflicted harm on others.

18. _____ occurs when different groups of people have different scores designated as "passing" grades on a test for employment.

19. _____ is a notice from the EEOC, if they elect not to prosecute an individual discrimination complaint within the agency, that gives the recipient the right to go directly to the courts with a complaint.

20. _____ is a situation in which the organization takes an "adverse employment action" against an employee because the employee brought discrimination charges against the organization or supported someone who brought discrimination charges against the company.

21. _____ consist of any actions such as firings, demotions, schedule reductions, or changes that would harm the individual employee.

22. _____ exists when an employee is put under such extreme pressure by management that continued employment becomes intolerable for the employee and, as a result of the intolerable conditions, the employee resigns from the organization.

23. _____ is a series of policies, programs, and initiatives that have been instituted by various entities within both government and the private sector to create preferential hiring of individuals from protected groups in certain circumstances, in an attempt to mitigate past discrimination.

24. _____ is discrimination against members of the majority group by an organization, generally resulting from affirmative action policies within an organization.

25. _____ is the existence of differences—in HRM, it deals with different types of people in an organization.

26. _____ is a basic ability to think in unique and different ways and apply those thought processes to existing problems.

27. _____ is the act of creating useful processes or products based on creative thought processes.

28. _____ is the ability to find many possible solutions to a particular problem, including unique, untested solutions.

29. _____ is the act of being opposed to another.

30. _____ is an intent and desire for group members to stick together in their actions.

31. _____ consists of unwelcome sexual advances, requests for sexual favors, and other verbal or physical conduct of a sexual nature; when submission to or rejection of this conduct explicitly or implicitly affects an individual's employment; unreasonably interferes with an individual's work performance; or creates an intimidating, hostile, or offensive work environment.

32. _____ is harassment that occurs when some type of benefit or punishment is made contingent upon the employee submitting to sexual advances.

33. _____ is harassment that occurs when someone's behavior at work creates an environment that is sexual in nature and makes it difficult for someone of a particular sex to work in that environment.

34. _____ is the "average" person who would look at the situation and its intensity to determine whether the accused person was wrong in their actions.

• • • COMMUNICATION SKILLS

The following critical-thinking questions can be used for class discussion and/or for written assignments to develop communication skills. Be sure to give complete explanations for all answers.

1. Do you agree that applying the OUCH test to an employment situation will minimize illegal discrimination? Why or why not?

2. Are there any groups of people in the United States that you think should be covered by federal laws as a protected group but are not currently covered? Why or why not?

3. In your opinion, is most discrimination in the United States unintentional (disparate impact), or is most discrimination intentional (disparate treatment)? Why do you think so?

4. What is your opinion of organizations using bona fide occupational qualifications (BFOQs) to limit who they will consider for a job?

5. Do you agree that most employers probably *want* to obey the Americans with Disabilities Act but don't know exactly what they are required to do under the law? Do you think that most employers would rather not hire disabled people? Justify your answer.

6. How would *you* define the terms "reasonable accommodation" and "undue hardship" if you were asked by one of your company managers?

7. Has affirmative action gone too far in creating a *preference* for historically underrepresented groups over other employees and applicants instead of treating everyone equally?

8. Do you think that sexual harassment in the workplace is overreported or underreported? Justify your answer.

• • • CASE 3-1 ENGLISH-ONLY: ONE HOTEL'S DILEMMA

Erica, the Human Resource Manager, was frustrated by many of her hotel staff speaking Spanish in the hallways and rooms as they were cleaning them.

The Sawmill Hotel where Erica works is situated in downtown Minneapolis, Minnesota. Its target market includes sports enthusiasts attending nearby professional (Twins, Vikings, Timberwolves, Wild) games but also business professionals and families. This four-star hotel features an indoor and outdoor swimming pool, a message center, three stores, two restaurants, and a beauty shop. Total staff includes about 10 managers, 30 cleaning assistants to take care of rooms, 10 front desk specialists, and 25 who are involved with the stores, restaurants, and beauty shop. All are required to focus on customer service as their number-one value.

Erica hires everyone in the hotel except for the Chief Executive Officer, Vice President of Finance, and Vice President of Marketing. For the rest of the managers, the 30 cleaning assistants, and the store, restaurant, and beauty shop workers, she advertises for openings with the local job service and the Minneapolis *Star Tribune* (with the associated website). A typical *Tribune* ad for a cleaning assistant reads as follows: Cleaning Assistants Wanted, Sawmill Hotel, $9–$11/hour. Prepare rooms for customers and prepare laundry. Contact: Erica Hollie, Human Resource Manager, 555-805-1234.

As a result of the advertising, Erica has been able to obtain good help through the local target market. Twenty-seven of the 30 cleaning assistants are women. Twenty of the 30 have a Hispanic background. Of the Hispanics, all can speak English at varying levels.

Rachel, the lead cleaning assistant, believes that maximizing communication among employees helps the assistants become more productive and stable within the hotel system. She uses both English and Spanish to talk to assistants under her. Spanish is useful with many assistants because they know Spanish much better than English. Spanish also is the "good friends" language that allows the Spanish speakers to freely catch up on each other's affairs and that motivates them to stay working at the hotel. The use of the Spanish language among cleaning assistants has been common practice among them for the two years since the hotel opened.

In the last few months, top management decided to have an even greater focus on customer service by ensuring customer comment cards are available in each room and at the front desk. Customers also can comment online about their stay at the hotel.

There have been several customer complaints that cleaning assistants have been laughing about them behind their back in Spanish. One customer, Kathy, thought that staffers negatively commented about her tight pink stretch pants covering her overweight legs. Other customers have complained they didn't think asking staff for help was easy given the amount of Spanish spoken. In all, about 15 out of 42 complaints in a typical month were associated with the use of the Spanish language.

Though bellhops and front desk clerks are typically the workers who handle complaints first, Erica, the Human Resource Manager, has the main responsibility to notify workers about customer complaint patterns and to set policy in dealing with the complaints. The prevalence of complaints concerning workers speaking Spanish each month led Erica to make a significant change in policy concerning the use of Spanish. In consultation with top management, Erica instituted the following employee handbook policy effective immediately:

"English is the main language spoken at the hotel. Any communication among employees shall be in English. Use of Spanish or other languages is prohibited unless specifically requested by management or the customer."

In an e-mail explanation for the new policy, Erica stated the number of complaints that had come from the use of Spanish and the need for customer courtesy and communication.

Rachel immediately responded to Erica's e-mail by stating that the new policy was too harsh on the native Spanish-speaking assistants at the hotel. She thought that a better policy is to allow her assistants to communicate with each other through Spanish but by quietly doing so away from customer earshot. If there is a general discussion in front of a customer, it is recommended to speak English. There should never be discussions in any language about customer appearances.

Though Rachel grumbled, the policy stuck because Erica and top management wanted to stop customer complaints. As a result of the policy, 10 of the 20 Spanish-speaking assistants quit within two months. These were high-quality assistants who had been with the hotel since the start. Their replacements came from a job service and have not worked out as well in their performance.

Questions

1. What law(s) do you think might apply in this case?

2. Should a complete ban of Spanish be instituted among staff of the hotel unless customers use Spanish themselves, or should the use of Spanish be completely allowed by staff among themselves as long as it is quiet (why or why not)?

3. What rules, if any, would you put into effect in this situation, knowing about the customer complaints? Explain your answer.

Case created by Gundars Kaupins of Boise State University

• • • SKILL BUILDER 3-1 THE FOUR-FIFTHS RULE

For this exercise, you will do some math.

Objective

To develop your skill at understanding and calculating the Four-Fifths Rule

Skills

The primary skills developed through this exercise are as follows:

1. *HR management skill*—Analytical and quantitative business skills

2. *SHRM 2013 Curriculum Guidebook*—G: Outcomes: Metrics and Measurement in HR

Complete the following Four-Fifths Problems

1:

	Males	Females
Applicants	100	100
Selected	50	40
Selection rate	50% (50/100)	40% (40/100)

4/5 = _____ %.

The selection rate of _____% is equal to, less than, or greater than _____% or 4/5.

Therefore, the Four-Fifths Rule is or is not met. How many total females and how many more females should be hired? _____ _____

2:

	White	Nonwhite
Applicants	120	75
Selected	80	25
Selection rate	_____	_____

4/5 = _____ %.

The selection rate of _____% is equal to, less than, or greater than _____% or 4/5.

Therefore, the Four-Fifths Rule is or is not met. How many total and how many more nonwhites should be hired? _____ _____

3:

	White Females	Nonwhite Females
Applicants	63	109
Selected	17	22
Selection rate	_____	_____

4/5 = _____ %.

The selection rate of _____% is equal to, less than, or greater than _____% or 4/5.

Therefore, the Four-Fifths Rule is or is not met. How many total and how many more nonwhite females should be hired? _____ _____

• • • SKILL BUILDER 3–2 DIVERSITY TRAINING

Objective

To become more aware of and sensitive to diversity

Skills

The primary skills developed through this exercise are as follows:

1. *HR management skill*—Human relations skills
2. *SHRM 2013 Curriculum Guidebook*—L: Training and Development

Answer the following questions:

Race and Ethnicity

1. My race (ethnicity) is ____.
2. My name, ____, is significant because it means ____. [or]
   My name, ____, is significant because I was named after ____.
3. One positive thing about my racial/ethnic background is ____.
4. One difficult thing about my racial/ethnic background is ____.

Religion

5. My religion is ____.
6. One positive thing about my religious background is ____.
7. One difficult thing about my religious background is ____.

Gender

8. I am ____ (male/female).

9. One positive thing about being (male/female) is ____.
10. One difficult thing about being (male/female) is ____.

Age

11. I am ____ years old.
12. One positive thing about being this age is ____.
13. One difficult thing about being this age is ____.

Other

14. One way in which I am different from other people is ____.
15. One positive thing about being different in this way is ____.
16. One negative thing about being different in this way is ____.

Prejudice, Stereotypes, and Discrimination

17. Describe an incident in which you were prejudged, stereotyped, or discriminated against. It could be something minor, such as having a comment made to you about your wearing the wrong type of clothes/sneakers or being the last one picked when selecting teams.

Apply It

What did I learn from this experience? How will I use this knowledge in the future?

Your instructor may ask you to do this Skill Builder in class in a group. If so, the instructor will provide you with any necessary information or additional instructions.

_____

_____

_____

Part II

Staffing

4 Matching Employees and Jobs: Job Analysis and Design

5 Recruiting Job Candidates

6 Selecting New Employees

PRACTITIONER'S MODEL

↑ Productivity
↑ Satisfaction
↓ Absenteeism
↓ Turnover

PART V: Protecting and Expanding Organizational Outreach
How do you PROTECT and EXPAND your Human Resources?

Chapter 12	Chapter 13	Chapter 14
Workplace Safety, Health, and Security	Organizational Ethics, Sustainability, and Social Responsibility	Global Issues for Human Resource Managers

PART IV: Compensating
How do you REWARD and MAINTAIN your Human Resources?

Chapter 10	Chapter 11
Compensation Management	Employee Incentives and Benefits

PART III: Developing and Managing
How do you MANAGE your Human Resources?

Chapter 7	Chapter 8	Chapter 9
Training, Learning, Talent Management & Development	Performance Management and Appraisal	Employee Rights and Labor Relations

PART II: Staffing
What HRM Functions do you NEED for sustainability?

Chapter 4	Chapter 5	Chapter 6
Matching Employees and Jobs	Recruiting Job Candidates	Selecting New Employees

PART I: 21st Century Human Resource Management Strategic Planning and Legal Issues
What HRM issues are CRITICAL to your organization's long-term sustainability?

Chapter 1	Chapter 2	Chapter 3
The New Human Resource Management Process	Strategy-Driven Human Resource Management	The Legal Environment and Diversity Management

©BuckStudio/Crave/Corbis

4

MATCHING EMPLOYEES AND JOBS

Job Analysis and Design

• • • LEARNING OUTCOMES

After studying this chapter, you should be able to do the following:

4-1 Describe the process of workflow analysis and identify why it is important to HRM. PAGE 86

4-2 Summarize the four major options available for the job analysis process. PAGE 87

4-3 Discuss the four major approaches to job design. PAGE 91

4-4 Identify and briefly describe the components of the job characteristics model (JCM). PAGE 94

4-5 Explain the three major tools for motivational job design. PAGE 96

4-6 Discuss the three most common quantitative HR forecasting methods. PAGE 98

4-7 Name the seven major options for managing a labor surplus and the seven options for overcoming a labor shortage. PAGE 100

4-8 Define the key terms found in the chapter margins and listed following the Chapter Summary. PAGE 108

Master the content.

Use the online study tools at
edge.sagepub.com/fundamentalsofhrm
to review, practice, and improve your skills.

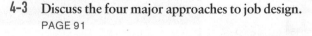

Practitioner's Perspective

Cindy's day started when an executive burst into the HR office. "Hold everything!" he shouted. "Doug just announced he's retiring unexpectedly, and we've got to start advertising for someone to replace him immediately. I don't know how we can manage without him!"

"Calm down—we can do this," she replied. "Just send us your succession planning matrix and his functional job description, and we'll start the process to replace him."

"I hate to admit it, but I never completed that matrix, and I don't have an updated job description for Doug," the manager replied sheepishly. "There have been so many changes with the department reorganizations this year that we need to reconfigure everything."

While hiring someone new is the perfect time to update the job description for a position, it is not the best time to create one. Why is it important to have a current job description, and how does one go about writing one? Chapter 4 shows how to successfully identify and document motivational positions.

• • •

EMPLOYEE AND JOB MATCHING

Now that we have learned some of the basics concerning how to treat our human resources fairly and equitably, we need to start putting people to work in the organization. Let's start with the realization that in order for the organization to maximize productivity, we must match the right people with the right jobs.[1] Why? Because mismatched workers tend to have low job satisfaction, leading to absenteeism, higher turnover, and lower levels of productivity than those who are matched effectively.[2] The first step to matching people to the right jobs is to determine what jobs we need to have performed and the qualifications needed to do the jobs. Then we can match employees to those jobs. Let's start by taking a brief look at workflow analysis.

• • • **CHAPTER OUTLINE**

Employee and Job Matching

Workflow Analysis
  Organizational Output
  Tasks and Inputs

Job Analysis
  Why Do We Need to Analyze Jobs?
  Databases
  Job Analysis Methods
  Outcomes: Job Description and Job Specification

Job Design/Redesign
  Organizational Structure and Job Design
  Approaches to Job Design and Redesign

The Job Characteristics Model (JCM)

Designing Motivational Jobs
  Job Simplification
  Job Expansion
  Job Design for Flexibility

HR Forecasting
  Forecasting Methods

Reconciling Internal Labor Supply and Demand
  Options for a Labor Surplus
  Options for a Labor Shortage

Trends and Issues in HRM
  O*Net as a Tool for Job Analysis
  Workflows and Job Design for Sustainability

LO 4-1

Describe the process of workflow analysis and identify why it is important to HRM.

WORKFLOW ANALYSIS

Imagine that we are starting up a brand new company. The first thing we have to know is what we expect the organization to do. Do we plan to make products (e.g., **Samsung**), or do we plan to provide services (e.g., **Netflix**)? Per our discussion of organizational structure in Chapter 2, the way in which we put the organization together will depend on what we expect it to do, and that in turn will help determine the workflow. **Workflow analysis** is *the tool that we use to identify what has to be done within the organization to produce a product or service.* For each product or service that we provide in the organization, we have to identify the work processes that create that product or service.

Organizational Output

The first thing we analyze is the end result of our processes: our expected organizational outputs, or what the customer wants from us.[3] So we are actually working backward. If we decide that we are going to make desks but we don't identify what kind of desks we're going to make, then do we need skilled craftsman, metalworkers, or just unskilled assemblers? The answer is, of course, that it depends on what kind of desk we plan to make. So identifying the end result is a critical first step in identifying the workflows needed to create that result.

Tasks and Inputs

Once we identify the result we expect, we can then determine the steps or activities required to create the end result we've identified. Finally, based on the steps that we identify and the tasks that will have to be performed, we can identify the inputs that are going to be necessary to carry out the steps and perform the same tasks.[4]

SHRM

E:8

Work Management (Work Processes and Outsourcing)

Workflow analysis The tool that we use to identify what has to be done within the organization to produce a product or service

SHRM HR CONTENT

See Appendix: *SHRM 2013 Curriculum Guidebook* for the complete list

E.   Job Analysis/Job Design (required)

  1. Job/role design (roles, duties, and responsibilities)
  7. HR planning (skill inventories and supply/demand forecasting)
  8. Work management (work processes and outsourcing)

G.   Outcomes: Metrics and Measurement of HR (required)

  5. Trend and ratio analysis projections
  10. Quantitative analysis
  12. Analyzing and interpreting metrics
  13. Forecasting

I.   Staffing: Recruitment and Selection (required)

  1. The employment relationship: Employees, contractors, temporary workers

J.   Strategic HR (required)

  12. Trends and forecasting in HR

M.   Workforce Planning and Talent Management (required)

  1. Downsizing/rightsizing (secondary)
  2. Planning: Forecasting requirements and availabilities, gap analysis, action planning, core/flexible workforce
  6. Labor supply and demand

S.   Downsizing/Rightsizing (secondary)

  1. Employment downsizing
  2. Alternatives to employment downsizing
  4. Why downsizing happens
  5. When downsizing is the answer
  7. Alternatives to downsizing
  8. Consequences of employment downsizing
  9. Approaches to reducing staff size
  13. Importance of focusing on individual jobs versus individual staff members
  14. Layoffs

There is a simple mnemonic (a memory tool) available to remember what resource inputs we have available. It is called the 4 Ms:[5]

1. *Machines*—resources such as tools, equipment, manufacturing machinery, and other machines that are used in completing work

2. *Material*—any physical resource (e.g., wood, metal, buildings, real estate, etc.) that we use in production

3. *Manpower*—the people that are needed in a particular production process—both quantity and types

4. *Money*—the capital that must be spent to perform our processes

These four large categories of resources are what we use up in doing what we intend to do.[6] Whenever we look at workflow analysis, we have to identify which of the 4 Ms and how much of each we are using up in a particular process. The final result of our workflow analysis is shown in Exhibit 4-1.

JOB ANALYSIS

Once we understand the workflows in the organization, the next thing that we need to do is figure out which parts of the workflows are done by each person. This is the concept of job analysis. **Job analysis** *is the process used to identify the work performed and the working conditions for each of the jobs within our organizations.* Job analysis results will include duties, responsibilities, skills, knowledge

WORK
APPLICATION 4-1

Using Exhibit 4-1 as an example, identify the output and 4 Ms inputs for an organization that you work for or have worked for.

LO 4-2

Summarize the four major options available for the job analysis process.

Job analysis The process used to identify the work performed and the working conditions for each of the jobs within our organizations

EXHIBIT 4-1   WORKFLOW ANALYSIS

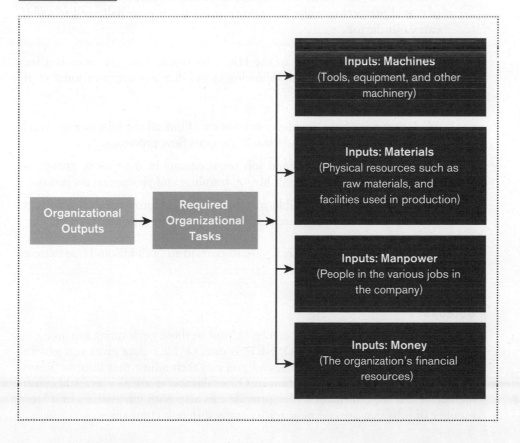

required, outcomes, conditions under which the worker must operate, and possibly other factors.[7]

The two primary outcomes for most job analysis projects are the job description and the job specification. The **job description** *identifies the major tasks, duties, and responsibilities that are components of a job*, while the **job specification** *identifies the qualifications of a person who should be capable of doing the job tasks noted in the job description.*

Why Do We Need to Analyze Jobs?

Job analysis is the basis of just about everything that HR does.[8] If you think about it, you will realize that we need to identify and correctly analyze the jobs in the organization in order to perform *any* of the following functions:

1. *Human resource planning.* Job analysis helps us design jobs better to get the results that we need. (We will talk about job design shortly.)

2. *Job evaluation for compensation.* If we don't know what the job consists of, how can we determine how much the job is worth to the organization so we know how much to pay the person?

3. *Staffing (recruiting and selection).* If we don't know what an employee is going to do and how much we will pay that employee, then how do we know whom to recruit and hire?

4. *Training.* If we don't know what the job consists of, how can we teach people to do the job?

5. *Performance management.* How can we evaluate performance if we don't know what the worker's job consists of?

6. *Maintain a safe work environment.* Job analysis will help us identify hazards that the job incumbent will need to understand, as well as any required personal protective equipment and training the person will need to safely carry out the job.

So job analysis is important to the HR department, but how does it affect other managers? Think about the following issues that *any* organizational manager may face on a routine basis:

1. Managers must have detailed information about all the jobs in their work groups so that they can understand the workflow processes.

2. Managers need to understand job requirements in their work groups so that they can make intelligent hiring, training, and promotion decisions.

3. Every manager is responsible for conducting performance evaluations to ensure that all employees are performing their jobs satisfactorily.

So we can see that job analysis is very important to both HR and line managers. But how do you analyze a job?

Databases

There are various databases that can be helpful to those performing job analysis. The **US Department of Labor's O*NET**[9] is one. O*NET data gives you general information on over 900 job titles, and you can then adjust that information to your company's specific circumstances. Other databases are also available commercially, and the information they provide can help with job analysis of a large number of jobs that are common across many different companies.

Job description Identification of the major tasks, duties, and responsibilities that are components of a job

Job specification Identification of the qualifications of a person who should be capable of doing the job tasks noted in the job description

Using a database can be a good starting point for job analysis. However, each job analysis will most likely need to be customized, and if you can't find one on a database, you need to conduct your own job analysis. How to do so is our next topic.

Job Analysis Methods

Four commonly used methods of job analysis include the use of questionnaires, interviews, diaries, and observation.[10,11] The necessary result that we are looking for with all four methods is a job description and specification for a person to be successful in the position. Let's discuss the four methods.

Questionnaires. A number of highly valid and reliable questionnaires can be given to different people in order to analyze the job in question. A questionnaire may be given to the current jobholder (the incumbent), the supervisor, or others who are affected by the way the job is done in the organization. Most of the questionnaires follow similar processes. Each asks questions that help to identify the functions that are a part of a particular job, and then, in most cases, assigns a point value to that function.[12] The *Position Analysis Questionnaire* and the *Management Position Description Questionnaire* are two examples of this type of job analysis.[13]

Questionnaire Advantages

- Quick way to get information from large number of sources
- Usually easy to quantify
- Relatively low cost
- Generally valid and reliable instruments
- No need for a trained interviewer or observer

Questionnaire Disadvantages

- Incomplete responses (nobody is interviewing or observing actions, so there is no follow-up)
- Responses may be hard to interpret
- Low response rates are possible if there is no supervisory follow-up

Interviews. In job analysis interviews, questions are usually asked by trained interviewers of the incumbent and the answers are compiled into a profile of the job. The interviewer asks job-related questions, and the incumbent describes the job based on the questions asked.

Interview Advantages

- The incumbent is most familiar with the job
- Can include qualitative data
- Allows the interviewer to follow up confusing or incomplete answers
- Simple, quick, and more comprehensive than some other forms
- Provides an opportunity to explain the need for the analysis and answer questions

An employee's diary or log outlining their daily tasks and activities can be used as the basis for a job description.

Interview Disadvantages

- Dependent on trained interviewer and well-designed questions
- Workers may exaggerate their job duties
- Time-consuming and may not be cost efficient

Diaries. Here the worker maintains a work log, or *diary*, in which the employee writes down the tasks accomplished while going about the job.[14] This log becomes the document from which we build the description of the job.

Diary Advantages

- Participatory form of analysis
- May collect data as they happen
- The worker knows the job and what is important
- Useful for jobs that are difficult to observe

Diary Disadvantages

- Relies on worker writing all work down
- Worker may rely on memory of things done earlier in the day
- Information distortion
- Data are not in a standard format—makes quantifying difficult

Observation. We can also use observation of the person at work, in which an observer shadows the worker and logs tasks that the worker performs over a period of time. A trained observer will usually identify tasks that workers don't even think about doing and therefore wouldn't have noted in a log or diary.

Observation Advantages

- Firsthand knowledge
- Allows the analyst to see the work environment, view the tools and equipment the worker uses, observe the worker's interrelationships with other workers, and gauge the complexity of the job
- Reduces information distortion common in some other methods
- Relatively simple to use

Observation Disadvantages

- Observer may affect the job incumbent's performance
- Inappropriate for jobs that involve significant mental effort
- May lack validity and reliability
- Time-consuming
- Requires a trained observer

The four methods listed above are certainly not the only methods of job analysis, and they may not even be the best options for any particular situation. There are many other options, including the use of subject matter experts, work sampling, videotaping of jobs, and others. However, these four types of analysis demonstrate the basic process of job analysis. We can also use multiple methods if one method alone will not provide a good analysis.

Outcomes: Job Description and Job Specification

The primary outcomes that we are looking for in any job analysis are the creation of a job description and a job specification.[15] These two outcomes are routinely written into one document. The job description part describes the job itself, not the person who will do the job. The job specification part identifies the qualifications needed by the person who is to fill a position. We will use the job specification to go out and recruit when we have an opening for the job. Exhibit 4-2 shows a sample job description and specification.

WORK APPLICATION 4-2

Which of the four job analysis processes would be the most appropriate to use to write the job description and job specifications for a job you hold or have held? Explain why it has advantages over the other methods.

WORK APPLICATION 4-3

Complete a job analysis for a job you hold or have held; write a brief job description and job specifications

---

4-1 APPLYING THE CONCEPT

Job Analysis Methods

Review the following job analysis methods and then write the letter corresponding to each method before the situation in which it would be the most appropriate.

a. questionnaire

b. interview

c. diary

d. observation

____ 1. On your staff, you have an industrial engineer who is an efficiency expert. You want her to improve the productivity of your machinists.

____ 2. You have professionals who work independently using different methods of developing computer games.

____ 3. In your call center, where hundreds of employees make cold calls to sell your products, there is a high turnover rate that you want to improve.

____ 4. You have several service call employees who repair a variety of computers. You would like to have a better idea of what types of computers they are fixing.

JOB DESIGN/REDESIGN

Tasks are grouped by the organization, usually into functional departments, and the tasks are further grouped into jobs for each employee, providing structures and processes. **Job design** *is the process of identifying tasks that each employee is responsible for completing, as well as identifying how those tasks will be accomplished.* Job design is crucial because it affects job satisfaction and productivity, along with a large number of other functions in HRM.[16]

Job redesign refers to changing the tasks or the way work is performed in an existing job. Job design, which includes redesign, is about working smarter, not harder, to find new ways of doing things that boost productivity.[17]

Organizational Structure and Job Design

The way we combine the components of an organizational structure causes employees to act in different ways (Chapter 2). Jobs in the organization have to be designed to fit within the confines of the structure that we have designed.[18]

If we have a more relaxed, flatter structure with lots of autonomy for our workers, we will need to design our jobs to take advantage of that autonomy or

LO 4-3

Discuss the four major approaches to job design.

Job design The process of identifying tasks that each employee is responsible for completing, as well as identifying how those tasks will be accomplished

EXHIBIT 4-2   JOB DESCRIPTION—APPLE "CHANNEL COMPLIANCE REPORTING MANAGER"

Jobs at Apple

Requisition Number 4391934

Job title: Channel Compliance Reporting Manager

Location: Santa Clara Valley

Country: United States

City: Cupertino

State/Province: California

Job type: Full Time

Job description: Team up with Apple, one of the most influential technology leaders in the industry. Join the Apple Finance organization and make a positive impact on a company that is known for its impressive lineup of products, including Mac, iPod, iPhone, iTunes, and iLife. At Apple, you'll share in a commitment to excellence by partnering with world-class managers, all with one unified vision—creating innovative products that delight customers. Finance is about "fueling innovation." We do this by hiring quality individuals with integrity, personal accountability, teamwork, excellence, and proactive thinking. If you exemplify our values and want to be part of something big, contact us today.

Summary of the position: Reporting to Channel Compliance Management, this role has the responsibility for the global development, deployment and maintenance of channel member regulatory compliance training program. This individual will be a key resource to introduce and implement best practices, reusability and streamlining online and classroom compliance training for channel member employees.

Key Duties and Responsibilities:

- Responsible to develop, implement and maintain a comprehensive global compliance training program to deliver training to applicable channel member employees
- Identify the training needs based on local regulatory guidelines (Laws & Regulations), global and US regulations and Apple Policy
- Collaborate with subject matter experts to ensure the compliance training material is current and reflects changes in Regulations/Policies
- Manage the training content localization and deployment of the material
- Schedule and implement a risk based and effective training calendar
- Develop a process and system to track classroom training accomplishments
- Ensure effective document and record keeping for all Channel Compliance related training programs
- Develop and implement an effective and efficient management reporting for compliance training program
- Efficiently manage the training resources within allocated budget

Key Skills and Competencies:

- Successful implementation and management of channel member training programs in large and global distribution model
- Must have excellent project management and time management skills
- Exercise good business judgment and excellence in problem solving
- Possess strong writing, editing, communication, and negotiation skills
- Demonstrated ability to maintain and develop relationships across a large virtual team
- Experienced in managing external parties—vendors, resellers, distributors, etc.
- Strong data analysis skills and obsessive about details and accuracy
- Advanced Excel user
- BA/BS degree or higher
- 5 to 8 years in areas of Analysis & Reporting, Working cross-functionally, and Project Management.

self-direction on the part of our employees. If, on the other hand, we have a rigid, bureaucratic organizational structure with strong centralized decision making and control, then our jobs have to be designed so that they can be readily controlled by a central authority.

SHRM

E:1

Job/Role Design (Roles, Duties, and Responsibilities)

Approaches to Job Design and Redesign

Job design/redesign can take several forms, depending on what we are trying to accomplish in the organization. There are four primary approaches to job design: mechanistic, biological, perceptual-motor, and motivational.[19]

SELF ASSESSMENT

Organizational Structure and Job Design Preference

Individuals differ in the type of organizations and job designs in which they prefer to work. To determine your preference, evaluate each of the following 12 statements, using the scale below. Assign each statement a number from 1 to 5, representing your level of agreement with the statement (5 = strong agreement, 3 = not sure, 1 = strong disagreement).

I agree				I disagree
5	4	3	2	1

_____ 1. I prefer having just one boss telling me what to do, rather than multiple people.

_____ 2. I prefer to just perform my job, rather than being concerned about organizational objectives and being involved in setting them.

_____ 3. I prefer knowing the reporting relationship, knowing who is whose boss, and working through proper channels—rather than just working directly with a variety of people based on the situation.

_____ 4. I prefer having a clear job description so I know just what I need to do at work, rather than having the ambiguity of not being sure and doing whatever needs to be done.

_____ 5. I prefer being a specialist doing one job really well, rather than being a generalist doing several things not as well.

_____ 6. I prefer doing my own thing that contributes to the organization, rather than coordinating the work I do with that of others in teams.

_____ 7. I prefer slow change, rather than regular fast changes.

_____ 8. I prefer routine at work, rather than being delegated new tasks to perform.

_____ 9. I prefer doing more simple tasks, rather than more complex tasks that take more time and effort.

_____ 10. I prefer that people get promoted based primarily on seniority, rather than based on performance.

_____ Total

Scoring: To determine your preference, add up the numbers you assigned to the statements (the total will be between 10 and 50) and place your total score on the continuum below:

10	15	20	25	30	35	40	45	50
Organic								Mechanistic

An organization that is minimally or moderately complex, highly formalized, and centralized is a mechanistic organization. Organic organizations are even more complex but lower on formalization and centralization. This exercise tests the type of structure with which you feel most comfortable. You will learn more about mechanistic and organic structures throughout this chapter. The higher your score, the more you prefer to work in a more traditional, mechanistic, stable structure and job design. The lower your score, the more you prefer to work in a more contemporary, organic, changing structure and job design.

Review your answers, knowing that the opening statement applies to mechanistic and the opposite statement (after "rather than") applies to organic organizational structure and job design. Most firms and people prefer organizations somewhere between the two extremes.

1. Mechanistic job design *focuses on designing jobs around the concepts of task specialization, skill simplification, and repetition.* When we design a mechanistic job, we will try to make the job simple and repetitive so that the worker can get very good and very fast at doing it. An example of mechanistic job design in manufacturing would be attaching the desktop to its base using six fasteners and then going to the next desk to do the same thing again. The biggest problem in mechanistic job design is that we might overspecialize the work to the point that it becomes too repetitive and thus very boring.[20]

2. Biological job design *focuses on minimizing the physical strain on the worker by structuring the physical work environment around the way the body works.* Here

Mechanistic job design Designing jobs around the concepts of task specialization, skill simplification, and repetition

Biological job design Designing jobs by focusing on minimizing the physical strain on the worker by structuring the physical work environment around the way the body works

WORK
APPLICATION 4-4

Which of the four approaches to job design/redesign best describes a job you hold or have held? Explain how the job incorporates the features of the approach.

we make the job physically easier so that workers can be more efficient and so that it is less likely that they will be injured and have to miss work. An example of biological job design would involve installing a conveyor belt that lifts and adjusts to the correct level so each person can assemble their parts of the final product within a comfortable range of motion. This allows the workers to do their jobs with minimal physical strain. Again, though, this approach does little to make workers more motivated or satisfied with their work.

3. Perceptual-motor job design *focuses on designing jobs with tasks that remain within the worker's normal mental capabilities and limitations.* Instead of trying to minimize the physical strain on the workforce, the goal is to design jobs in a way that ensures they moderate the mental strain on a worker.[21] For example, we might use it to break down an executive assistant's job into a report writer and a scheduler job, because the sets of skills needed in these two areas are significantly different. One more time, we may create jobs that are not very motivating.

4. Motivational job design *focuses on the job characteristics that affect the psychological meaning and motivational potential of the job, and it views attitudinal variables as the most important outcomes of job design.* The theory is that if workers are more motivated, they will produce more work. It is to this last approach to job design that we can apply the job characteristics model, which we will discuss next.

LO 4-4

Identify and briefly describe the components of the job characteristics model (JCM).

THE JOB CHARACTERISTICS MODEL (JCM)

The job characteristics model (JCM) *provides a conceptual framework for designing or enriching jobs based on core job characteristics.*[22] Use of the JCM improves employee motivation and job satisfaction,[23] and it can increase performance.[24] As Exhibit 4-3 illustrates, users of the JCM focus on core job dimensions, the psychological states of employees, and the strength of employees' need for growth to improve employee motivation, performance, and job satisfaction and reduces absenteeism and job turnover. Research supports the idea that use of the JCM increases performance by meeting employee needs to grow and develop on the job.[25]

In the JCM, the five core job characteristics can be fine-tuned to improve the outcomes of a job in terms of employees' productivity and their quality of working life:

1. *Skill variety* is the number of diverse tasks that make up a job and the number of skills used to perform the job.

2. *Task identity* is the degree to which an employee performs a whole identifiable task. For example, does the employee put together an entire television or just place the screen in the set?

3. *Task significance* is an employee's perception of the importance of the task to others—the organization, the department, coworkers, and/or customers.

4. *Autonomy* is the degree to which the employee has discretion to make decisions in planning, organizing, and controlling the task performed.

5. *Feedback* is the extent to which employees find out how well they perform their tasks.

Note that if employees are not interested in enriching their jobs, the job characteristics model will fail.

The first three of the core job characteristics lead collectively to the psychological state (in the second column of Exhibit 4-3) of *experienced meaningfulness of work* to provide workers with a variety of things to do. If they can identify what it is that they are accomplishing, and if they think that their job is a significant endeavor, then they will think that their work has meaning and thus be more likely to stay in the job and do it well.

Perceptual-motor job design Designing jobs with tasks that remain within the worker's normal mental capabilities and limitations

Motivational job design Designing jobs by focusing on the job characteristics that affect the psychological meaning and motivational potential of the job; this approach views attitudinal variables as the most important outcomes of job design

Job characteristics model A conceptual framework for designing or enriching jobs based on core job characteristics

4-2 APPLYING THE CONCEPT

Job Design

Review the list of job design techniques below and write the letter corresponding to each technique before the statement exemplifying that technique.

a. mechanistic

b. organic

c. biological

d. perceptual-motor

e. motivational

_____ 5. We are required to wear these special belts when we unload the trucks at **Target.**

_____ 6. We have added enough employees so that we are breaking the human resources function into its own department. Jack will now focus on compensation and benefits, and Jill will conduct the training. Latoya will be responsible for safety and security.

_____ 7. Here at **Intel,** we are going to change your job so that you can develop new skills and complete entire jobs by yourself. We're doing this to make the job more meaningful to you and so that you can do the job the way you want to and know how you are doing.

_____ 8. I just finished the Casey project. What should I do now?

_____ 9. This is the 30th customer I've checked out at **Stop & Shop** supermarket today.

The core characteristic of *autonomy* leads to the psychological state of *experienced responsibility for outcomes.* If we give people the ability to make some decisions on their own, it is likely that they will feel more responsible for the outcome of the decisions that they make.

Finally, *feedback* leads to the psychological state of *knowledge of results.* However, it is not the knowledge of the result itself that matters. Remember that the second column is *psychological* states! It is the psychological feeling that we get from knowing the results that create the state of, for lack of a better term, satisfaction with the results of our work.

EXHIBIT 4-3   THE JOB CHARACTERISTICS MODEL (JCM)

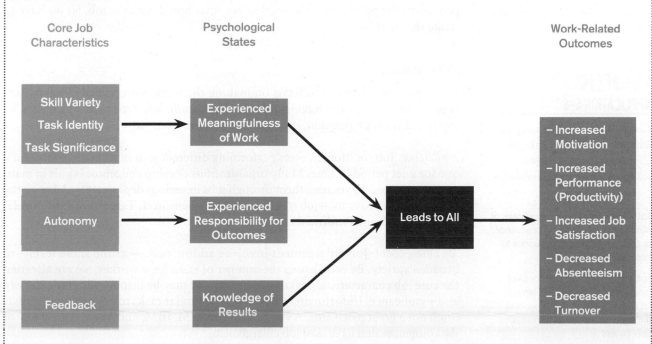

All of the psychological states *collectively* lead to all of the outcomes noted on the right side of the diagram. It is an interesting list. If the job is designed correctly, the model says that the worker will quite possibly be more motivated and more productive and have higher job satisfaction while also being less likely to be absent or leave the organization. The use of the JCM is even more critical for motivating young millennials (than older workers) that are looking for meaning in their work; they don't want, and will leave, boring jobs.[26]

DESIGNING MOTIVATIONAL JOBS

A variety of different job tools can be used in different circumstances to design or redesign motivational jobs. Our tools include job simplification, job expansion, and flexible work. These are discussed next.

Job Simplification

The best advice golfer **Tiger Woods** ever got was to simplify.[27] **Job simplification** *is the process of eliminating or combining tasks and/or changing the work sequence to improve performance.* Job simplification makes jobs more specialized. Job simplification breaks a job down into steps using a flowchart, and then employees analyze the steps to see if they can do the following:

- *Eliminate.* Does the task, or do parts of it, have to be done at all? If not, don't waste time on them.

- *Combine.* Doing similar things together often saves time. Make one trip to the mailroom at the end of the day instead of several throughout the day.

- *Change sequence.* Often, a change in the order of doing things, or designing new systems, results in a lower total time spent on tasks.

Work simplification may be motivational when an individual is overwhelmed by a job because it can allow that employee to understand the job better, and the job therefore becomes more motivational. However, we don't want to simplify the process to the point where the worker becomes bored with the job. So we have to strike the right balance.[28]

Job Expansion

Job expansion allows us to focus on making the work more varied.[29] **Job expansion** is *the process of making jobs broader, with less repetition.* Jobs can be *expanded through rotation, enlargement, and enrichment.*

Job Rotation. Job rotation involves performing different jobs in some sequence, each one for a set period of time. Many organizations develop conceptual skills in management trainees by rotating them through jobs in various departments. A few of the companies that have used job rotation are **Bethlehem Steel**, **Target**, **Ford**, **Motorola**, **National Steel**, and **Prudential Insurance**.

Job Enlargement. Job enlargement involves adding tasks—at the same level—to broaden variety. By broadening the number of tasks for a worker, we are affecting the core job characteristic of skill variety, and we may be helping with task identity and significance. Unfortunately, adding more similar tasks to an employee's job is often not a great motivator. **AT&T, Chrysler, GM, IBM,** and **Maytag** are a few of the companies that have used job enlargement.

Job Enrichment. Job enrichment is the process of building motivators into the job itself to make it more interesting and challenging, frequently through increasing autonomy.[30] A simple way to enrich jobs is for the manager to delegate more authority to employees[31] by making them more autonomous (another core job characteristic) to make some decisions that were reserved for management.[32] An enriched job may also help the employee with the JCM characteristics of task identity and significance in some cases. **Maytag, Monsanto, Motorola, and Travelers Insurance** have successfully used job enrichment.

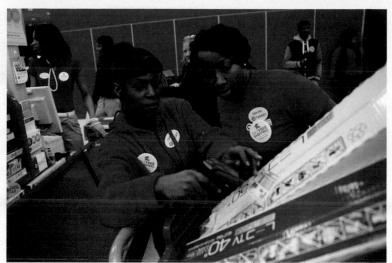

Job Design for Flexibility

In addition to the primary tools for designing and redesigning specific jobs above, we have another set of tools that can be used in the workplace to improve motivation in entire groups of jobs or maybe even the entire workforce.[33] These tools include flextime, job sharing, telecommuting, and compressed workweeks.[34]

Flextime allows us to provide workers with a flexible set of work hours. We usually create a set of *core hours* where everyone is at work, *bandwidth* or *work hours* available, and then a set of *flex hours* when people can be at work or can take time off. Individuals have the opportunity to modify their schedule within the work hours as long as they complete a set number of hours per day or week at work. Flextime has the potential to motivate workers because it allows them much greater autonomy with regard to their schedule. Take a look at Exhibit 4-5 for a sample flextime schedule.

In *job sharing* (also called work sharing) we allow two (or more) people to share one whole job, including the workload and any benefits that are associated with that job. Job sharing again allows greater autonomy in the individual's job.

Telecommuting allows workers to work from a location other than the corporate office, usually from home. Telecommuting is another form of autonomy,

Target employees will rotate through a number of positions on the job, giving them a range of skills and experiences.

WORK
APPLICATION 4-7

Give one example of how an organization, preferably one you work for or have worked for, uses any of the flexible job design tools. State which one is used, explain how it is implemented, and discuss how it affects employee motivation.

4-3   APPLYING THE CONCEPT

Designing Motivational Jobs

Review the following job design techniques and write the letter corresponding to each technique before the statement exemplifying it.

   a. job simplification

   b. job rotation

   c. job enlargement

   d. job enrichment

   e. work teams

_____ 10. Would you like more job variety? If so, I can add three new tasks to your job to make it less repetitive.

_____ 11. I'm going to teach you to balance the accounts so that you can do it for Carlos while he is on vacation.

_____ 12. Would you like me to delegate a new task to you to make your job more challenging?

_____ 13. **Domino's Pizza** stopped requiring customers to sign a credit card slip for under $25.

_____ 14. I'm creating a new crew with the seven of you. There will not be a formal manager; you will share that responsibility. From now on, you don't have a manager. So share the job together.

EXHIBIT 4-4 JOB DESIGN OPTIONS, PROCESSES, AND THE JCM

Option	Process	Core Characteristics Affected (JCM)
Job simplification	Eliminate tasks	Task identity and significance
	Combine tasks	
	Change task sequence	
Job expansion	Rotate jobs	Skill variety, task identity, and significance
	Enlarge jobs	Possibly feedback
	Enrich jobs	
Work teams	Integrated	Skill variety, task identity, and significance
	Self-managed	Feedback

EXHIBIT 4-5   SAMPLE FLEXTIME WORK SCHEDULE[35]

Acmemegadyne Corporation Flextime Work Schedule
Normal operating hours: 8:30 a.m.–5:30 p.m. Monday through Friday (1 hour for lunch)
Full-time workers (40 hours per week):
Core hours: 9:00–11:00 a.m.; 1:00–3:00 p.m.
Flexible hours: 7:30–9:00 a.m.; 11:00 a.m.–1:00 p.m.; 3:00–6:30 p.m.
Work hours (bandwidth): 7:30 a.m.–6:30 p.m.
"A flextime arrangement may be suspended or cancelled at any time. Exempt employees must depart from any flextime schedule to perform their jobs. Nonexempt employees may be asked to work overtime regardless of a flextime schedule" (from SHRM flextime policy sample).

but we need to make sure that telecommuters get opportunities to engage with coworkers and receive feedback concerning their work, since an absence of these opportunities are two of the major drawbacks to telecommuting.[36]

Finally, a *compressed workweek* means that we take the normal 5-day, 40-hour workweek and compress it down to less than 5 days. One common example would be a 4-day, 10-hour per day workweek.

Each of these additional tools allows us to design greater flexibility into our organization in one way or another. As a result, in many cases, we can improve both productivity and job satisfaction and in turn lower rates of absenteeism and turnover—a win-win for the organization and the employee within it.

HR FORECASTING

LO 4-6

Discuss the three most common quantitative HR forecasting methods.

HR forecasting and labor requirements planning are at the core of determining our future employment needs.[37] Through forecasting, we will make determinations—based on both quantitative and qualitative information—of what types of jobs and how many of each type we will need to fill over a particular period of time. If we fail to get it right, we won't get the right people in place at the time when they are needed and will always be chasing turnover, which causes lower organizational productivity. **HR forecasting** *identifies the estimated supply and demand for the different types of human resources in the organization over some future period, based on analysis of past and present demand.*

Before we get into forecasting, we need to understand a couple of terms. You always need to make sure that any analytical process you use includes *valid* and *reliable* measures. If you don't, then your results will always be suspect and will generally be of very little value. So what do these terms mean?

Reliability. Reliability identifies how consistent a particular measure is. In other words, does the measure give a similar result every time it is used? If it does, then it is probably reliable. For instance, if you give a test of comprehension on a set of company terms after teaching those terms in the same manner to several groups of employees, and if the results in each group are similar, then the test is most likely reliable.

Validity. Validity refers to whether or not we measured what we thought we measured. It is not as easy as it sounds for subjective measures. For example, does a motivational test actually, and accurately, measure the level of motivation? If we don't measure what we meant to measure, our test was not valid.

Also, a measure can be reliable but not valid, but it can't be valid if it is not reliable. For example, if you step on a low-quality home scale and weigh 175, get off and on again several times, and weigh 175 every time, then the scale is reliable. However, if you go to a high-quality scale and weigh 180 repeatedly, then the measurements you got from the home scale are reliable but not valid. So remember validity and reliability as you decide on the tools that you are going to use in the forecasting process.

Forecasting Methods

Forecasting should be completed in two distinct steps. First, we complete a quantitative analysis of our workforce using one or more of several methods, and then we adjust the results of the quantitative (math) analysis using qualitative methods. Experience is needed when analyzing situations that are unique or different from what has happened in our business environment in the past, and qualitative analysis looks at the differences between the "historical" and the "now." Let's define each type.

Quantitative Forecasting. A **quantitative forecast** *utilizes mathematics to forecast future events based on historical data.* Three common quantitative methods of forecasting are trend analysis, ratio analysis, and regression analysis.[38] Let's take a quick look at each method in Exhibit 4-6.

Trend analysis is *a process of reviewing historical items such as revenues and relating changes in those items to some business factor to form a predictive chart.* For example, we could look at historical revenues and relate those revenue volumes to the number of people in the organization for each year, or alternatively, we could analyze historical production levels and relate those levels to the number of people used to accomplish those levels of production. Either of these would give us a historical trend that we could then extend into the future to predict the number of people that would be required for a particular sales or production level.[39]

Ratio analysis is *the process of reviewing historical data and calculating specific proportions between a business factor (such as production) and the number of employees needed.* It generally gives us very similar results to trend analysis, but it should be a bit more precise because we are computing an exact value for the ratio.

Regression analysis is *a statistical technique that identifies the relationship between a series of variable data points for use in forecasting future variables.* We can use statistical software to create the regression diagram (most HRIS include

M:2

Forecasting Requirements and Availabilities, Gap Analysis, etc.

SHRM

E:7

HR Planning (Skill Inventories and Supply/Demand Forecasting)

SHRM

G:13

Forecasting

HR forecasting Identifying the estimated supply and demand for the different types of human resources in the organization over some future period, based on analysis of past and present demand

Quantitative forecast Utilizing mathematics to forecast future events based on historical data

Trend analysis A process of reviewing historical items such as revenues and relating changes in those items to some business factor to form a predictive chart

Ratio analysis The process of reviewing historical data and calculating specific proportions between a business factor (such as production) and the number of employees needed

Regression analysis A statistical technique that identifies the relationship between a series of variable data points for use in forecasting future variables

this capability). Then it is just a process of looking at the values along the line and applying them to your company's situation in a given year.

Qualitative Forecasting. **Qualitative forecasting** *is the use of nonquantitative methods to forecast the future, usually based on the knowledge of a pool of experts in a subject or an industry.* We provide our group of experts with the quantitative predictions that we have created and ask for their assessment of the data, taking into account circumstances within our industry and the general economic climate while comparing the present situation with the historical environment on which the quantitative evaluations are based. The experts will then come to a consensus about how to adjust the quantitative data for today's environment.

We need to use both quantitative and qualitative analysis to get good forecasts for the future needs of the organization and its human resources. We will look at both forecasting methods and identify whether we expect to have a surplus or a shortage of people in the organization over the next few years. More likely, we will find that we will have a surplus of some types of people and a shortage of others. Regardless of the situation, once we know what to expect, we can set up procedures to correct the expected problem.

4-4 APPLYING THE CONCEPT

Quantitative Methods

Complete each problem below:

_____ 15. Turn to the Regression Analysis section of Exhibit 4-6. Assume that in 2012, you expect a recession and revenues to drop to $24MM. Around how many employees will you need?

 a. 160   b. 180   c. 210   d. 230

_____ 16. You have 253 employees. Over the past year, there were 26 absences. What is the approximate percentage and ratio of absenteeism?

 a. 9.7%, 1–10   b. 10%, 1–10   c. 10%, 1–100
 d. 12%, 1–12

_____ 17. You have 1,215 employees. Over the past year, 298 left the firm. What is the approximate percentage and ratio of turnover?

 a. 4%, 1–20   b. 40%, 4–10   c. 22%, 22–100
 d. 25%, 1–4

_____ 18. Turn to the Trend Analysis section of Exhibit 4-6. Assume that in 2012, you expect revenues to be $35MM. Around how many employees will you need?

 a. 210   b. 230   c. 250   d. 270

_____ 19. Turn to the Ratio Analysis section of Exhibit 4-6. Assume that in 2015, you expect the production level to increase to $22,000,000. Around how many employees will you need, and how many new workers do you need to add?

 a. 2 and 11   b. 73 and 12   c. 74 and 13
 d. 75 and 14

Qualitative forecasting The use of nonquantitative methods to forecast the future, usually based on the knowledge of a pool of experts in a subject or an industry

RECONCILING INTERNAL LABOR SUPPLY AND DEMAND

After completion of the labor requirements planning process, we end up with either an expected shortage or a surplus of people in each type of job in the organization. External job supply and demand affect the frequency with which people leave their jobs, and high turnover negatively affects organizational performance.[40] Therefore, balancing our supply and demand for labor affects our firm's productivity. We have to figure out how to make supply match up with our expected demand.

Regardless of whether we have a shortage or a surplus, we have to attempt to get the right numbers of people with the right skill sets into our organization at the right time. What are our options to accomplish this, and how does each option affect the company and its workforce?

EXHIBIT 4-6   QUANTITATIVE FORECASTING ANALYSIS

Trend Analysis

Historical Data	2010	2011	2012	2013	2014
Revenues ($MM)	27.84	29.92	25.48	26.3	30.12
Total # of Employees	225	244	215	214	240

We then estimate the number of employees needed based on the historical trend. In this case, how many total employees would you say we need if we expect 2014 revenues to be $31.8 million? You likely said something around 250 people, because you looked at the historical trend.

Ratio Analysis

Historical Data	2010	2011	2012	2013	2014
Production Levels ($MM)	18.62	20.58	17.44	17.23	19.16
Avg. # Production Workers/Year	62	71	61	55	61
$ Production/Worker (000's)	300	290	286	313	314

The average production per worker for the 5 years listed would be just under $301,000, so $301,000:worker is our ratio. If we expect production requirements to be $20.2MM in 2015, we could divide $20,200,000 by $301,000 and get approximately 67 production workers as an expected complement for 2015. If we had 61 workers at the end of 2014, we would need to recruit 6 more for 2015—assuming no voluntary turnover during the year.

Regression Analysis

A regression diagram of all of the companies in our industry by year for the past 10 years, plotted with the number of employees on the x-axis and revenues on the y-axis, might look like this:

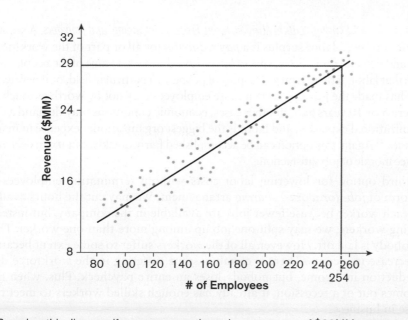

Based on this diagram, if we were expecting to have revenues of $29MM next year, we would need approximately 254 employees.

A company may choose to downsize, or lay off employees, if they face a labor surplus. This means they can terminate a group of employees with little warning or justification.

SHRM

M:6

Labor Supply and Demand

S:1

Employment Downsizing

S:5

When Downsizing Is the Answer

S:9

Approaches to Reducing Staff Size

M:1

Downsizing/Rightsizing

S:13

Importance of Focusing on Individual Jobs vs. Individual Staff Members

S:14

Layoffs

S:4

Why Downsizing Happens

Layoff A process of terminating a group of employees, usually due to some business downturn or perhaps a technological change, with intent to improve organizational efficiency and effectiveness

Options for a Labor Surplus

If we are predicting a surplus of people going into the future, what can we do about it? We can't usually just hang on to employees that aren't needed, because it is too expensive. However, we don't necessarily have to get rid of a large number of employees, either. How we handle the situation will depend on how soon we are able to predict that there will be a surplus, and it will also depend on our strategy, values, and philosophy. We have to understand the consequences of each option and choose wisely.

Downsizing and Layoffs. Our first option *may* be a layoff, especially if we have large numbers of surplus people. A layoff is *a process of terminating a group of employees, usually due to some business downturn or perhaps a technological change, with intent to improve organizational efficiency and effectiveness.* In a layoff, we are generally allowed to terminate the employment of a group of individuals with very little advance warning, and we usually don't have to provide any disciplinary or other justification for what we are doing. We may have to comply with the Worker Adjustment and Retraining Notification Act (WARN Act), which we will discuss in some detail in Chapter 9, but other than that, we have few documentation needs other than ensuring that there is no illegal discrimination in a layoff event.[41] We do have to document the method by which we determined who should be in the layoff, and it would be wise not to be arbitrary in our selection of individuals.

The most valuable result of a layoff is that the resulting savings are immediately added to bottom-line corporate performance.[42] However, layoffs create many potential problems, including lower employee morale and job satisfaction.[43] So we end up with a lot of stress issues in layoffs, and these create problems for the organization.

Pay Reduction, Work Sharing, Natural Attrition, Hiring Freezes, Retraining, and Transfers. A second option for cutting a labor surplus is a *pay reduction* for all or part of the workforce. Supply and demand for various types of labor drive the market value of the people who provide that labor. If there is an oversupply of people in a particular field, or if new technology has made the job easier, then those employees may not be worth as much as they were 5 or 10 years ago. In other cases, economic conditions may demand a cut in organizational expenses, and labor is the biggest organizational expense in many companies.[44] Again, this option can be accomplished fairly quickly, but it can decrease employee morale or job satisfaction.

A third option for lowering labor costs without terminating employees is some form of *job- (or work-) sharing* arrangement. We may cut the hours available to each worker because fewer jobs are available in the company, but instead of cutting workers, we may split one job up among more than one worker. This way, nobody is laid off. However, all of the workers suffer to some extent because of a decrease in income. There is certainly some suffering in the workforce due to a reduction in income, but nobody loses an entire paycheck. Plus, when the firm comes out of a recession, it already has enough skilled workers to meet the increase in business.

Next, we have the option to allow *natural attrition* to lower organizational numbers without the need for a layoff or pay reduction. We can just allow positions to stay unfilled as turnover occurs. This option, along with the slightly more stringent option of a *hiring freeze*, causes our number of employees to drop slowly. Therefore, it can't be used in a situation where speed in reducing expenses is critical, but if we have done our job forecasting, we may have enough time for this option to work for us without putting massive stress on our workforce.

Retraining workers and *transferring* them from one job to another may be options in some circumstances. However, this option will only work if we have too many employees in one type of job and too few in another. If there are no positions where we have a shortage, retraining workers will not work. Again, the process is a little slow due to the fact that the person has to be retrained in a new field. But if we have a good worker who is willing to try a new job, and if a position is available, then using this option can allow us to retain that good employee.

Early Retirement. The last option that we will discuss here is *early retirement*. Early retirement can be a valuable option in some cases. However, there can be many pitfalls to using early retirement to reduce our workforce.[45] In an early retirement offer, employees are given the choice of leaving the company before they would ordinarily do so (reaching the "normal" retirement age of 65, for instance), and in exchange for leaving, the employee will receive benefits of some type from the organization.

There are some good reasons to use early retirement as an option to reduce an employee surplus, but it is a slow method of getting rid of people, and we have to be careful in planning for and offering early retirements. Problems with early retirement may include too many or too few people taking the offer, or the perception of being forced out of work due to age, among other issues.[46]

In a surplus situation, we want to use the options that we discussed in this section from the bottom up—starting with things like early retirements and attrition, because they are the least disruptive to the workforce and allow us to maintain motivation and job satisfaction levels much better than things like layoffs and pay reductions. This will provide us with the best long term results.

SHRM

S:8
Consequences of Employment Downsizing

S:2
Alternatives to Employment Downsizing

S:7
Alternatives to Downsizing

4-1 ETHICAL DILEMMA: WHAT WOULD YOU DO?

As firms struggle to compete in the global economy, many have downsized, especially since the last recession. In some firms, the positions formerly held by full-time employees are filled by part-time workers. Using part-time employees saves companies money because such employees do not receive many benefits (e.g. health insurance) in contrast to full-time employees. **Walmart** is known for maintaining a very high ratio of part-time to full-time employees as a way of keeping costs down. Walmart's policy of using mostly part-time workers at minimum or near minimum wage is one of the reasons the chain can offer lower prices.

1. Is downsizing ethical and socially responsible?
2. Is using part-time employees rather than full-time ones ethically and socially responsible?
3. Would you be willing to pay higher prices at stores, such as Walmart, so that more full-time workers could replace part-time workers?

Options for a Labor Shortage

What if our forecasts show an expected shortage? What we need to analyze here is how fast we can solve the problem, but also how quickly we can lower our number of employees again if we need to. The best options here are methods that are really fast in solving the shortage but that also can be reversed quickly if a surplus of employees starts to take form. As opposed to the surplus situation in the last section, we want to work here from the first options down to the bottom. We would start with asking for or requiring overtime and work down the list as we have to, because again, we want the smallest possible disruption to our workforce.

Overtime. Our first option—the quickest and easiest way to fix a personnel shortage—is *overtime.* Can we force you to work overtime? The answer is yes. No federal law limits the option to require you to work a "reasonable amount" of overtime if you are an employee of the organization.[47] It works until we get to the point where we start to stress our people too much because the overtime becomes excessive. When stress levels get too high, employees' work will suffer.[48] So, if we start to see too much stress among our workforce, we need to do something else to relieve our personnel shortage. What other options do we have?

Temporary or Contract Workers. We can frequently use *temporary or contract workers* to overcome a short-term shortage, but we probably don't want to use temporary workers for more than a year at most, for reasons we will discuss shortly. Since the recession of 2008, many employers are reluctant to hire full-time employees, so many firms are using temps and independent contractors who are not legally employed by the firm. At more than 7% of the workforce, contractors are an important and growing segment of the US population and are increasingly prevalent throughout the developed world.[49]

Hiring temporary and contract workers is a quick fix for shortages. And the upside is that hiring temporary help is easy to take back. When we no longer need the temporary worker, we just release that individual back to the temp agency. For contract workers, we allow the contract to lapse in order to release them.

However, there are some common problems. First, temporary and contract workers have little or no loyalty to you and your organization and may not be motivated to work hard because they aren't staying.[50] They may not know the specific jobs in your company, and they generally don't know the company as well as do your permanent workers.[51] There can also sometimes be a clash between temp workers and permanent employees.

Temps and contractors can also create legal problems for the organization. If an organization classifies a worker as an "independent contractor," and exerts significant control over the actions of that worker, then the organization can be judged guilty of misclassification of the worker.[52] That means the government can penalize the organization for not withholding employment taxes on the "employee" and not paying for required benefits, such as workers' compensation insurance and Social Security withholding.

Along the same lines, if the company keeps "temporary" employees longer than a year, then those workers are probably not really temporary, and they may be eligible for full-time employment benefits. **Microsoft** had to pay almost $100 million to about 10,000 workers that it had classified as temporary,[53] and **FedEx** was charged $319 million in unpaid employment taxes and penalties in 2007 because it misclassified drivers as contract workers.[54] These are just some of the problems with temporary and contract workers. However, both are highly revocable if we no longer need them.

Retraining Workers, Outsourcing, and Turnover Reduction. These options take a bit longer to put into effect. We can *retrain workers*, but doing so isn't a quick response to a shortage.[55] This option is especially useful if we have a surplus of employees somewhere

---

SHRM

I:1

Employment Relationship: Employees, Contractors, Temporary Workers

---

SHRM

E:8

Work Management (Work Processes and Outsourcing)

else. It is moderately fast and generally easy to revoke, because the workers are still trained to do their old jobs.

Outsourcing may be another option. We can outsource an entire function that we currently do in-house.[56] For instance, we might outsource all of our computer-programming jobs to an outsourcing company that specializes in computer programming. This option is moderately fast, but it is not extremely fast because we have to find a company that can do the job, research the company, negotiate with it, come up with a contract, and then finally get it to do the work when we want it done.

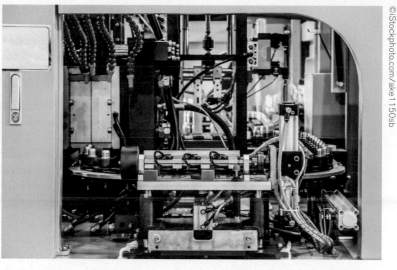

Technological innovations can help a company deal with a labor shortage by automating processes normally performed by people.

Next is *turnover reduction*. If fewer people voluntarily leave than we have predicted, we can reduce a projected shortage.[57] But how can we reduce turnover? We can improve working conditions or do other things that may cause our workforce to become more satisfied. We can adjust work hours (minimally), make benefits packages better, and maybe make work schedules a little better. As discussed, we can also use job design flexibility. Any of these might cause turnover to go down. But this won't happen overnight because it takes some time to change people's opinions of the organization. In addition, this option is very difficult to take back later.

New Hires and Technological Innovation. Our next option is to *hire new employees*. But this option takes a while, doesn't it? We have to go through a long process of analyzing the job, recruiting people, selecting employees, training, and working through a learning curve to get them capable of doing the work. We can see that this is a slow method of resolving a worker shortage. It is also not easy to take back.

Finally, we may be able to overcome a shortage of personnel through *technological innovation*. In other words, we may be able to use machinery that can do the job of people. But again, this is a slow process, and it also cannot be revoked. We can't create or find new equipment, install it, and make it operational overnight. Also, if we create a group of robots that are capable of assembling our product, we are not going to stop using them and hire a bunch of new assembly workers again.

TRENDS AND ISSUES IN HRM

In this chapter's trends and issues section, we will review O*Net as a job analysis tool in some more detail. Secondly, we will brief you on how organizations can "think sustainability" in their workflow analysis and job design processes.

O*Net as a Tool for Job Analysis

HR managers need large amounts of information to analyze the jobs in their organization. O*Net and its partner site, O*Net OnLine, provide information on nearly 1,000 jobs that are common to many different businesses and industries. Using the O*Net Toolkit (http://www.onetcenter.org/toolkit.html), managers can learn how the O*Net website works.[58] Once you have reviewed the toolkit, you might want to take a look at O*Net OnLine at http://www.onetonline.org/. This site provides a search interface with the O*Net database, using a variety of search options.[59] HR managers can then use this information to complete a job analysis and create job descriptions and specifications. In addition, the O*Net characteristics help in pricing each job to provide a competitive compensation system and lower voluntary turnover in the company. So O*Net is a handy free resource for job analysis, job descriptions, and job specifications.

Workflows and Job Design for Sustainability

As in many other areas of business today, we can frequently incorporate sustainability initiatives into our work design processes to help us limit our effect on the environment as well as save the organization time and money. If we design work processes with sustainability in mind, we can identify process changes that will lower our impact on critical natural resources.[60] For example, we may be able to use less water in a cooling operation by using a more open design that allows for radiational cooling instead of using water to cool those same parts.

We can also utilize some of our job design options, such as telecommuting, compressed workweeks, and flextime opportunities, to lower the need for our workers to commute to and from work.[61] We may also be able to lower our effect on the environment by using a technique called hoteling.[62] Hoteling *occurs when the organization has less office space than it would have in a traditional office arrangement (where everyone has an assigned space), so it uses a software program that allows employees to "reserve" office space for particular parts of the workweek when they will need it.* Hoteling can lower the total amount of office space that we need, and lower the usage of all of the common services that are needed for that office space. All it takes is a little thought to change the effect of a company on its environment.

Hoteling When an organization uses a software program that allows employees to "reserve" office space for particular parts of the workweek when they will need it

---

Get the edge on your studies at edge.sagepub.com/fundamentalsofhrm

Read the chapter and then take advantage of the open-access site to

- take a quiz to find out what you've mastered;
- test your knowledge with key term flashcards;
- watch videos to capture key chapter content.

REVIEW, **PRACTICE**, and **IMPROVE** your critical thinking with the tools and resources at **SAGE edge**.

⑤SAGE edge™

••• CHAPTER SUMMARY

4-1   Describe the process of workflow analysis and identify why it is important to HRM.

We start our workflow analysis by determining the end result. Once we identify the result we expect, we can determine the steps or activities required to create the end result that we've identified. This is basically an analysis of the tasks that are going to have to be performed in order to create the output that we expect. Finally, we can identify the inputs that are going to be necessary to carry out the steps and perform the tasks. The inputs are known as the 4 Ms: machines (tools, equipment, and machines), material (physical resources used in production), manpower (the people needed in a particular production process), and money (the capital that must be spent to perform our processes).

4-2   Summarize the four major options available for the job analysis process.

Questionnaires ask questions that help to identify the functions that are a part of a particular job, and then, in most cases, they assign a point value to each of those functions. In the job analysis *interview*, questions are asked verbally, usually of the incumbent, and the answers are compiled into a profile of the job. *Diaries* have the workers maintain a work log, or diary, in which they write down the tasks that they accomplish as they go about their job. This log becomes the document from which we build the description of the job. We can also use *observation* of the worker at work, where an observer shadows the worker and logs tasks that are performed over a period of time.

4-3   Discuss the four major approaches to job design.

Mechanistic job design focuses on designing jobs around the concepts of task specialization, skill simplification, and repetition. *Biological job design* focuses on minimizing the physical strain on the worker by structuring the physical work environment around the way the body works. *Perceptual-motor job design* attempts to make sure that workers remain within their normal mental capabilities and limitations. *Motivational job design* focuses on the job characteristics that affect psychological meaning and motivational potential, and it views attitudinal variables as the most important outcomes of job design.

4-4   Identify and briefly describe the components of the job characteristics model (JCM).

The five core job characteristics include skill variety, task identity, task significance, autonomy, and feedback. The first three lead collectively to the psychological state of *experienced meaningfulness of work*, in which workers think that their work has meaning. The fourth core characteristic of autonomy leads to the psychological state of *experienced responsibility for outcomes*. Finally, feedback leads to the psychological state of *knowledge of results*—the psychological feeling that we get from knowing the results and that in turn creates *satisfaction* with the results of our work.

All of the psychological states *collectively* lead to the outcomes: motivation, performance, job satisfaction, absenteeism, and turnover. These can go up or down depending on the design of the job.

4-5   Explain the three major tools for motivational job design.

Job simplification is the process of eliminating or combining tasks and/or changing the work sequence to improve performance. It makes jobs more specialized. However, we might make the job less motivational if we simplify the work to the point where the worker gets bored. *Job expansion*, on the other hand, makes jobs less specialized. Jobs can be expanded through rotation, enlargement, and enrichment. *Flexibility in job design* includes flextime, job sharing, telecommuting, and compressed workweeks, and allows the manager to use these tools to increase worker motivation.

4-6   Discuss the three most common quantitative HR forecasting methods.

Trend analysis allows the company to look at historical trends—for instance, whether employment went up or down in a given year and how the number of employees related to revenue or productivity—and make judgments from those trends. *Ratio analysis* calculates specific values by comparing a business factor with the number of employees needed. *Regression analysis* is a statistical technique in which we use a regression diagram made from historical data points to predict future needs presented with a *y*- and *x*-axis.

4-7   Name the seven major options for managing a labor surplus and the seven options for overcoming a labor shortage.

The major options for managing surplus include: a *layoff*, terminating a group of employees; *pay reduction*, which lowers the rate of pay for groups of employees; *work sharing*, where we cut hours available to each worker; *natural attrition*, where we lower employee numbers by not refilling jobs when turnover occurs; a *hiring freeze*, where we allow natural attrition, but in addition, we don't create any new jobs, even if they are needed; *retraining and transferring workers* from one job to another; and *early retirement*, where employees are given the choice of leaving the company before they would normally retire.

Options for a shortage include: *overtime*, our best option until we get to the point where we are starting to stress our people too much; or *temporary workers* who can be used for short periods. Other options include: *retrained workers, outsourcing, turnover reduction, new hire employees,* or *technological innovation.*

4-8   Define the key terms found in the chapter margins and listed following the Chapter Summary.

Complete the Key Terms Review to test your understanding of this chapter's key terms.

••• KEY TERMS

••• KEY TERMS REVIEW

Complete each of the following statements using one of this chapter's key terms.

1. _____ is the tool that we use to identify what has to be done within the organization to produce a product or service.

2. _____ is the process used to identify the work performed and the working conditions for each of the jobs within our organizations.

3. _____ identifies the major tasks, duties, and responsibilities that are components of a job.

4. _____ identifies the qualifications of a person who should be capable of doing the job tasks noted in the job description.

5. _____ is the process of identifying tasks that each employee is responsible for completing as well as how those tasks will be accomplished.

6. _____ focuses on designing jobs around the concepts of task specialization, skill simplification, and repetition.

7. _____ focuses on minimizing the physical strain on the worker by structuring the physical work environment around the way the body works.

8. _____ focuses on designing jobs in which the tasks remain within the worker's normal mental capabilities and limitations.

9. _____ focuses on the job characteristics that affect the psychological meaning and motivational potential, and it views attitudinal variables as the most important outcomes of job design.

10. _____ provides a conceptual framework for designing or enriching jobs based on core job characteristics.

11. _____ is the process of eliminating or combining tasks and/or changing the work sequence to improve performance.

12. _____ is the process of making jobs broader, with less repetition.

13. _____ identifies the estimated supply and demand for the different types of human resources in the organization over some future period, based on analysis of past and present demand.

14. _____ utilizes mathematics to forecast future events based on historical data.

15. _____ is a process of reviewing historical items such as revenues, and relating those changes to some business factor to form a predictive chart.

16. _____ is the process of reviewing historical data and calculating specific proportions between a business factor (such as production) and the number of employees needed.

17. _____ is a statistical technique that identifies the relationship between a series of variable data points for use in forecasting future variables.

18. _____ uses nonquantitative methods to forecast the future, usually based on the knowledge of a pool of experts in a subject or an industry.

19. _____ is a process of terminating a group of employees, usually due to some business downturn or perhaps a technological change, with intent to improve organizational efficiency and effectiveness.

20. _____ occurs when the organization has less office space than it would in a traditional office arrangement (where everyone has an assigned space) and uses a software program that allows employees to reserve office space for particular parts of the workweek when they will need it.

••• COMMUNICATION SKILLS

The following critical-thinking questions can be used for class discussion and/or for written assignments to develop communication skills. Be sure to give complete explanations for all answers.

1. Think of something you could make or build. Now analyze the workflows to make that item, using the information in the book. Don't forget to identify what you would need in each category of the 4 Ms.

2. Think of a job that you have held or that was held by someone you know. If you were going to analyze that job using one of the methods in the book, which method would you use and why?

3. Can more than one of the four main approaches to job design be used at the same time to design a job? Can you provide an example of how this could work?

4. Are there any situations in which you might design a job using the JCM and yet the job would still not be motivational? What circumstances might cause this to happen?

5. Do you think that using flextime, telecommuting, job sharing, or compressed workweeks is really going to motivate employees? Why or why not?

6. Have you seen job simplification, job rotation, or job expansion being used in your workplace? (If you aren't currently working, use a workplace that you are familiar with.) Did it work to motivate the employees? Why?

7. Which of the three quantitative forecasting methods do you think would give you the most accurate forecast? Explain your choice.

8. Is a layoff, or downsizing, ever the best option to resolve a projected surplus in an organization? Justify your answer.

9. How much overtime is reasonable in a week? How long can the company expect workers to continue to work overtime before they see employee stress levels getting significantly higher than normal?

• • • CASE 4-1 GAUGING EMPLOYMENT AT HONEYWELL

Honeywell is a diverse, differentiated industrial conglomerate with segments such as transportation systems, performance materials and technologies, aerospace, and automation and control solutions, yet the company is best known for its thermostats. According to the 2013 Fortune 500 list, Honeywell ranked 78th out of all US companies, with a revenue of $39 billion.

In 1999, Honeywell merged with AlliedSignal and Pittway but encountered problems when they realized that each company possessed its own unique corporate culture. During the next several years, Honeywell found itself addressing new challenges while trying to absorb its acquisitions. For example, environmental-related business liabilities had never been addressed and now required real attention, while managers were disinvesting in research and development because their divisions showed higher profits. New product development ceased. Honeywell also experienced high turnover in upper management, having three different CEOs in 4 years.[63]

Honeywell's main focus in the past decade has been on resolving these issues by first implementing their "One Honeywell" culture. This strategy increased overseas sales by 10% while also helping the company become more aware of and responsive to its environmental responsibilities. Investments in new products and services increased while turnover started to decrease, with employees filling more than 85% of the vacancies in top-level positions. Just as Honeywell turned the corner in 2008, the United States entered a recession and Honeywell's orders were being cancelled or postponed. No new orders were being placed, and sales were decreasing. As a result, direct costs of production were decreasing because the company simply did not need to purchase raw materials to make new products.[64]

In the manufacturing industry, the cost of people covers more than 30% of total expenses, and most firms responded to the recession by restructuring their workforce by firing thousands of employees. Cutting costs for production was not an option because a loss of customers is a major risk for the company; therefore, the only option left was cutting costs through employees. Honeywell knew that even the worst recessions usually last about 12 to 18 months, but the company wanted to be prepared when the economy started to heal.

With its new culture in place, Honeywell took a different approach than its competitors did. Honeywell projected the possible impact of economic recovery on its business, noting that it would have to rehire many of the employees it would lay off during the recession. Given this projection, Honeywell then followed a different method of restructuring and let its workers take furloughs, that is, temporary unpaid leaves of absence. Honeywell also knew that furloughs would harm the morale and loyalty of its employees. Even the employees who stayed would be distracted, thinking that their own jobs might be at stake. To benefit from furloughs, Honeywell limited their use by implementing more diligent performance reviews and avoiding hiring for new positions.

Honeywell CEO David Cote believed that most of his managers still overestimated the savings from layoffs and underestimated how disruptive layoffs would be given that the average employee received 6 months' worth of severance pay, meaning that Honeywell would only start saving money 6 months after the firm laid off an employee. However, the value of the employees' contributions was intangible since the firm might be losing its most skilled employees. The results of keeping the valuable employees were that Honeywell bounced back quicker than its competitors did after the recession and its business increased at a quicker pace.[65]

1. How does the use of HR forecasting reflect Honeywell's strategy and culture?

2. Which quantitative or qualitative manpower forecasting method do you believe Honeywell used to decide to move forward with furloughs rather than layoffs? Explain.

3. What options did Honeywell use to overcome the projected labor surplus during the recession? Were there other available options?

4. Compared to layoffs, do you expect the impact of furloughs to be higher on the turnover rate or lower? Explain your reasoning.

5. How might job analysis and job design minimize the impact of furloughs on organizational performance and productivity? How does hoteling fit into this scenario?

6. How could CEO Cote use trend/ratio/regression analysis to support his contention that most Honeywell managers overestimated their savings and underestimated how disruptive layoffs would be to the firm's operations?

Case created by Herbert Sherman, PhD, and Theodore Vallas, Department of Management Sciences, Long Island University School of Business, Brooklyn Campus

••• SKILL BUILDER 4–1 JOB ANALYSIS

Objective

To develop your skill at completing a job analysis; to improve your ability to get ready

Skills

The primary skills developed through this exercise are as follows:

1. *HR management skills*—technical, business, and conceptual and design skills

2. *SHRM 2013 Curriculum Guidebook*—E: Job Analysis/Job Design

Overview

Your output is to arrive at school or work. Your inputs (4 Ms) are each and every task you perform until you arrive at your destination. Through your job analysis flowchart, improve the efficiency of your inputs so you can get more done in less time, with better results.

Step 1. Make a Flowchart

List step-by-step exactly what you do from the time you get up (or start your routine) until the time you start school or work. Get up or start earlier, say 15 minutes, to give you time to complete your flowchart without making you late. Be sure to number each step and list each activity separately with its M (don't just say go to the bathroom—list each activity in sequence while in there). For example:

1. Get up at 7:00—manpower

2. Go to bathroom—manpower

3. Take shower—material

4. Dry hair—material

. . .

18. Drive car—material

19. Buy coffee—money

20. Walk in to school at 8:00—manpower

Step 2. Analyze the Flowchart

Later in the day, when you have time, do a job simplification analysis of your flowchart of activities to determine if you can do the following:

— Eliminate: Are you doing anything that you don't need to do?

— Combine: Can you multitask any simple tasks, make fewer trips to the bathroom, etc.?

— Change Sequence: Will you be more efficient if you rearrange your flowchart of tasks?

3. Develop a New Flowchart

Based on your analysis, make a new flowchart that eliminates, combines, and changes the sequence of tasks you will perform to get ready more efficiently.

4. Change Your Routine

Consciously follow the steps of your new flowchart until it becomes your new habit.

Apply It

What did I learn from this experience? How will I use this knowledge in the future?

_____

_____

Your instructor may ask you to do this Skill Builder in class in a group. If so, the instructor will provide you with any necessary information or additional instructions.

• • • SKILL BUILDER 4–2 JOB CHARACTERISTICS MODEL (JCM)

Objective

To develop your skill at implementing the JCM

Skills

The primary skills developed through this exercise are as follows:

1. *HR management skills*—technical, business, and conceptual and design skills

2. *SHRM 2013 Curriculum Guidebook*—E: Job Analysis/Job Design

Preparation

Select a job you have now or have held in the past. Using Exhibit 4-3: The Job Characteristics Model and Exhibit 4-4: Job Design Options, Processes, and the JCM, apply these concepts to do a job analysis for your job. Be sure to use the exact terms from the text. The two exhibits provide a good summary of the process and terminology.

Apply It

What did I learn from this experience? How will I use this knowledge in the future?

_____

_____

Would you change your job to make it more motivational? If so, how and why?

Your instructor may ask you to do this Skill Builder in class in a group. If so, the instructor will provide you with any necessary information or additional instructions.

• • • SKILL BUILDER 4–3 O*NET

Objective

To visit O*Net and learn how to use Career Exploration Tools and/or to learn more about a job.

Skills

The primary skills developed through this exercise are as follows:

1. *HR Management skills*—technical, business, and conceptual and design skills

2. *SHRM 2013 Curriculum Guidebook*—E: Job Analysis/Job Design

Preparation

The instructor or student selects one or both options:

a. Select a job you would like to learn more about, visit http://www.onetonline.org, and search for the job. Write a brief report identifying your job search and state what you learned about the job.

b. Go to http://www.onetcenter.org. Click the "Products—Career Exploration Tools" link. From the drop-down menu, select "Computerized Interest Profile." In the overview, click either the full O*NET Interest Profiler or the Interest Profiler Short Form. Click "on the Web." Then take the Interest Profile and complete the self-assessment as instructed and get your results and print them. Write a brief report including your results and identifying what you learned about yourself.

Apply It

What did I learn from this experience? How will I use this knowledge in the future?

_____

_____

Your instructor may ask you to discuss your results in a group or as a class. If so, the instructor will provide you with any necessary information or additional instructions.

©iStockphoto.com/asiseeit

5 RECRUITING JOB CANDIDATES

••• LEARNING OUTCOMES

After studying this chapter, you should be able to do the following:

5-1 Describe the main external forces acting on recruiting efforts. PAGE 113

5-2 Name the five main organizational recruiting considerations. PAGE 115

5-3 Identify the major advantages and disadvantages of both internal and external recruiting. PAGE 116

5-4 Summarize the major challenges and constraints involved in the recruiting process. PAGE 121

5-5 Discuss the basic methods available for evaluating the recruiting process. PAGE 124

5-6 Define the key terms found in the chapter margins and listed following the Chapter Summary. PAGE 128

Practitioner's Perspective

Cindy describes the day that Angie timidly knocked at her door before she came into her office. Angie said, "I know I just started here last month, but I'm giving you my two weeks' notice. I just can't do this anymore."

"What seems to be the problem?" she asked.

"Well, when I accepted the job of quality administrative assistant, I never expected to actually have to go to the units to gather information as part of my work. Being around the patients makes me uncomfortable."

Uh-oh. Angie and Cindy just experienced the fallout from a process breakdown that apparently prevented her from getting a realistic preview of her job duties. Why does an honest exchange of information matter when you are recruiting? How does a high turnover rate impact your company? The factors you need to consider as you endeavor to attract and retain the best qualified candidates are highlighted in Chapter 5.

● ● ●

THE RECRUITING PROCESS

Recruiting *is the process of creating a reasonable pool of qualified candidates for a job opening.* Notice that this definition identifies the fact that we need *qualified* applicants.[1] The process doesn't work if the candidates we attract are not qualified to do the work. Thus, a good job analysis (Chapter 4) is necessary to help everyone involved to know whether a given candidate is a qualified match for a given job opening.

The costs associated with recruiting, selecting, and training new employees often add up to more than 100% of their annual salary,[2] so it is important to get it right the first time. It's not about how many candidates we can attract, it's about finding "qualified" recruits. If you think about it, you will realize that if you find too many applicants, it costs the organization too much to go through the selection process. On the other hand, finding too few candidates allows no real *selection* process.

LO 5-1

Describe the main external forces acting on recruiting efforts.

Recruiting The process of creating a reasonable pool of qualified candidates for a job opening

---

Typically, a good rule of thumb might be to recruit about 15 to 25 qualified candidates *for each job opening*. That's just a rule of thumb, but it is probably going to allow a reasonable applicant pool. However, you may get more or less if you don't target your recruiting correctly.

To fill an opening, potential job candidates must generally be made aware that the organization is seeking employees. They must then be persuaded to apply for the jobs. In HR recruiting, we want to use a series of tools to show the candidates why they might want to become a part of the organization. We will discuss these tools as we go through the remainder of this chapter.

SHRM

I:2

External Influences on Staffing: Labor Markets, Unions, Economic Conditions, Technology

External Forces Acting on Recruiting Efforts

Think about what is happening around you right now. Is the unemployment rate high or low? Are there government incentives to increase hiring of the unemployed, or is government doing very little to increase employment? Is the available supply of people with advanced skills very large, or are there not enough people with high-level skill sets available to companies? Generally, the external forces acting on recruiting fall into two large categories: the available labor market and the social and legal environment.

The Labor Market. The availability of talent to fill our needs depends on several items in the labor market.[3] The **labor market** *is the external pool of candidates from which we draw our recruits.*

Supply and demand and the unemployment rate. First, we must consider the *supply and demand* factors in a particular category of jobs. This issue usually ties in directly with the *unemployment rate* in an area. Every business recruits primarily from an identifiable geographic area. So we need to identify our recruiting area, whether that is local, regional, national, or international, and then determine what the unemployment rate is in that area. If unemployment is high, the job of recruiting is generally easier than if unemployment is very low.

WORK
APPLICATION 5-1

Select one of your jobs and discuss the supply and demand issues (the unemployment rate and competition between employers) that had an effect on your job search.

Competitors. If recruiting competition is very strong for available talent such as mechanical engineers—for instance, if there are a significant number of competitors and each competitor needs a large number of engineers—then it will be a more difficult recruiting environment.[4]

Labor market The external pool of candidates from which we draw our recruits

Social and Legal Environment. The social environment also affects our ability to recruit new people.[5] Today, people put more weight on "me time" and job satisfaction than they did in past years, and as a result, candidates look at the firm's social environment

SHRM HR CONTENT

See Appendix: *SHRM 2013 Curriculum Guidebook* for the complete list

G. Outcomes Metrics and Measurements of HR
6. Calculating and Interpreting Yield Ratios

I. Staffing: Recruitment and Selection (required)
2. External influences on staffing: labor markets, unions, economic conditions, technology

3. External recruitment: recruiters, open vs. targeted recruitment, recruitment sources, applicant reactions, medium (electronic, advertisement), fraud/misrepresentation

when deciding whether or not to apply for a job there. In many cases, new employees also expect a high level of benefits and good opportunities for training and development.[6]

We also have to take into account the legal environment and abide by all of the EEO laws that we discussed in Chapter 3. Recall that we must avoid illegal discrimination in our recruiting efforts. There are also laws in some situations that limit our ability to lure employees away from competitor firms. In other cases, labor agreements may limit our ability to recruit, or a union may be able to place limits on our ability to recruit from outside of the union's ranks. Many other factors, such as state laws, noncompete agreements, and other requirements may also limit our ability to recruit in a particular environment.

When planning to recruit new employees, an organization needs to decide how it will utilize social media in recruitment efforts.

ORGANIZATIONAL RECRUITING CONSIDERATIONS

Based on our knowledge of the labor market and the legal environment, we can start to consider the internal issues that control our recruiting processes. We have to set recruiting policies in order to be consistent, in order to be fair and equitable, and so that we can defend our processes legally if it becomes necessary. So, what do we have to think about, and in what level of detail?

LO 5-2

Name the five main organizational recruiting considerations.

What Policies to Set

We always have to determine *how* we are going to go through the recruiting process before we start trying to recruit new members into our workforce. The policies that we set will determine our actions on the other four major recruiting considerations. Among other things, we have to answer questions concerning when we will recruit new members into the organization, alternatives to new recruits, where we recruit (local, national, global), and how to incorporate social media into our efforts. Let's discuss these four primary items we will need to consider before the recruiting process starts.

When to Recruit

Yes! We recruit when we need someone to fill a job. But it's not that simple. There are alternatives to recruitment to mitigate a worker shortage, and which one we choose depends on a bunch of different factors. We need to identify the points at which we would generally go through the process of starting and carrying out a recruitment campaign. We don't want to go through a long recruiting process and then figure out that we didn't need to—we would just be wasting time and money.

Alternatives to Recruitment

Do we have a viable and financially feasible way to solve our shortage other than through recruitment? Is the alternative less expensive or better for our circumstances in some other way? Alternatives may include using overtime, outsourcing some work, or using temporary or contract workers or other options to mitigate a shortage—at least temporarily, which are common with seasonal businesses. We

WORK
APPLICATION 5-2

Select a future job (preferably after graduation) and describe your social expectations when job searching. What type of organization do you want to work for? Also, will there be any legal restrictions on your job search?

need to analyze each of these options before deciding on new hires, and we need to create a policy concerning when each of these options is useful.

Reach of the Recruiting Effort

Next, we need to identify our effective labor market. Do we plan to recruit only from local sources? Should we consider people all over a particular region (e.g., the mid-South or New England)? Do we need to recruit nationally or even globally?[7] The answer, again, is "It depends." Can we find the right number and types of employees if we only recruit locally? If not, we may be forced to recruit from a broader pool of talent. Is the job that we are recruiting for so specialized that we need to recruit from all over the world? We must remember that it is time-consuming and expensive to bring people to the organization from far away though. So we only expand our geographic recruiting area when we need to.

Social Media Recruiting

Many firms are now heavily using social media sites, which can provide recruiters with much more reach than they had in the past.[8] However, this reach also brings with it some significant issues for the business—such as having to pore over thousands of résumés in response to a single job opening. So to avoid this problem, you have to understand social media's reach and use it selectively, whether you're a job seeker or a recruiter. Social media provides a number of valuable recruiting services. First, it provides a reach that the company may not get with other means such as advertising in local newspapers or on radio or television. Second, social media sites like Facebook can also provide the candidate with information on our company values and culture.[9] Corporate profile information can help individuals make a better decision concerning whether or not they would be comfortable in our organization, which in turn lowers the possibility that they will take the job and then end up leaving within a few weeks or months. Additionally, in many cases, the recruiter or the individual candidate has connections on LinkedIn or Facebook that allow the recruiter to get information on the other party and, sometimes, get an introduction.[10]

There *are* problems with social media recruiting, and some of them are significant dangers to the company. For instance, there is the potential for discrimination through disparate treatment of individuals because of information posted on their Facebook or LinkedIn sites or on their Twitter feed.[11] Pictures can also potentially identify individuals as members of a protected class, and those pictures may cause subconscious bias on the part of some recruiters. Any bias, whether intentional or unintentional, is a danger to the organization during the recruiting and hiring process.

INTERNAL OR EXTERNAL RECRUITING?

A general internal recruiting policy like "we promote from within" sounds good, but we also have to recruit externally to fill at least some jobs. So the question is, which jobs do we fill with current employees, and which jobs do we recruit from outside the firm? If we say our policy is to promote from within and we hire an outsider to fill a management position, many of our employees will begin to think that we don't follow our policy. They might show less loyalty to the organization because they feel that the organization failed to show them loyalty. However, if our policies say that we will go outside for recruits when it is unlikely that anyone in the organization would have the skill set necessary to do the job identified in our job specification, then we can provide a legitimate answer to someone who questions our recruiting process.

WORK
APPLICATION 5-3

Select a future job (preferably after graduation) and state the geographic area in which you will apply for jobs.

LO 5-3

Identify the major advantages and disadvantages of both internal and external recruiting.

When we are instituting new processes or we have identified significant resistance to change as an issue in a section of the organization, we may bring in new people with new ideas and different skills. We may also identify specific occupations in our organization that will typically be recruited from outside, usually due to the need for a specialized skill set (e.g., nuclear plant operator, corporate attorney, or emergency medical technician). It is unlikely that we would promote from within to these types of positions.

In this section, we discuss internal versus external recruiting efforts and the advantages and disadvantages of each approach.

Internal Recruiting

Internal recruiting *involves filling job openings with current employees or people the employees know.*

Internal Recruiting Sources. There are two common types of internal recruiting:

- *Promotions from within.* Many organizations post job openings on physical or electronic bulletin boards, in company newsletters, and so on. Current employees may apply or bid for the open positions.

- *Employee referrals.* Employees may be encouraged to refer friends and relatives for positions. About 40% of new hires at **Groupon** historically come from employee referrals.[12] For hard-to-recruit-for jobs, some firms pay a bonus to employees when their referred applicant is hired.

Advantages and Disadvantages of Internal Recruiting. Is it generally a good idea to recruit from inside the organization? What are the major advantages and disadvantages of internal recruiting?

Advantages include the following:

- Possible increases in organizational commitment and job satisfaction based on the opportunity to advance with commensurate increases in pay.

- The internal recruit will be able to learn more about the "big picture" in the company and become more valuable.

- The individual also has shown at least some interest in the organization, has knowledge of our operations and processes, and feels comfortable continuing employment within the company.

- The company has existing knowledge of the applicant and a record of that person's previous work.

- The organization can save money by recruiting internally because of both lower advertisement costs and lower training costs.

- Internal recruiting is usually faster than external recruiting.

And here are some of the disadvantages:

- The pool of applicants is significantly smaller in internal recruiting.

- There will still be a job to fill—the employee will move from somewhere else in the organization into the new job, so that employee's old job will need to be filled as well.

- Success in one job doesn't necessarily mean success in a significantly different job, especially if the employee is promoted to supervise former coworkers.

Internal recruiting Filling job openings with current employees or people the employees know

- An external candidate may have better qualifications for the job opening.

- Current employees may feel that they are entitled to the job whether they are capable and qualified or not, especially if we have a strong policy of preferring internal candidates.

- And the biggest threat to the company: We may create or perpetuate a strong resistance to change or stifle creativity and innovation because everyone in the organization, even the "new hires," are part of the old organizational culture.

External Recruiting

Companies commonly recruit people from other firms to satisfy their HR needs.[13] *External recruiting is the process of engaging individuals from the labor market outside the firm to apply for a job.*

SHRM

I:3

External Recruitment: Recruiters, Open vs. Targeted, Sources, etc.

External Recruiting Sources. To recruit qualified external candidates, we have to look at the type of person that we are trying to find and then go to the source or sources that will most likely provide that type of person. Our external recruiting options are listed with a summary of strengths in Exhibit 5-1.

Walk-ins. Qualified candidates may come to an organization "cold" and ask for a job. Walk-ins may be good recruits for a couple of reasons. First, they have already selected your organization as an employment target, and second, there are no advertising costs associated with walk-ins. So the process can occur much more quickly than it would with other external recruiting methods. However, candidates seeking professional and management-level positions generally send a résumé and cover letter asking for an interview.

Educational institutions. They are good places to recruit people who have little or no prior experience but have a good general skill set, such as a degree. Do recruiters come to your college to interview and hire graduates?

Employment agencies. There are three major types of employment agencies:

Temporary agencies, like **Kelly Services,** provide part- or full-time help for limited periods. They are useful for replacing employees who will be out for a short period of time or for supplementing the regular workforce during busy periods. Some HR experts expect the number of short- and long-term temps to continue to increase.[14] However, make sure your temps are not really full-time employees, like in our **Microsoft** discussion in Chapter 4, or you too can face a lawsuit.

Public agencies are state employment services. They generally provide job candidates to employers at no cost or very low cost. Too often, the public agencies get reputations as havens for the hard-core unemployed—those who do not want to work. However, they can be a strong source of good-quality employees, especially in bad economic conditions when many good workers lose their jobs.

Private employment agencies. They are privately owned and charge a fee for their services of recruiting candidates for you. Private agencies are generally used for recruiting people with prior experience, and here are some different types you can use:

- *General employment agencies.* Some of them charge job seekers for their services, and others charge the employer. They are generally used for lower level jobs that require experience.

External recruiting The process of engaging individuals from the labor market outside the firm to apply for a job

- *Contingency agencies.* They offer candidates to the employer and are paid when the job candidate is hired by the employer. Contingency agencies frequently work with a more skilled set of clients, such as high-level manufacturing skills or mid-level management experience.

- *Retained search firms or executive recruiters.* They are paid to search for a specific type of recruit for the organization and will be paid regardless of success in their recruiting efforts. Often referred to as "headhunters," they specialize in recruiting senior managers and/or those with specific high-level technical skills, like highly specialized engineers and IT/computer experts. They tend to charge the employer a large fee and will be at least partially paid whether or not there is a successful hire.

Job fairs can be an effective way to reach a large number of potential external recruits.

Advertising. A simple "Help Wanted" sign in the window is an advertisement. Newspapers are places to advertise positions, but advertising in professional and trade magazines may be more suitable for specific professional recruiting. There are also several online job search websites, such as Indeed.com, Monster.com, and CareerBuilder.com. Here are some ad options:

Local mass media. Is the *Daily Planet* (Thanks, Superman!), Channel 5, or the oldies FM radio station a good option for your recruiting dollars? As usual, it depends on what kind of candidate you are looking for. Local advertising generally works to recruit semiskilled or skilled line employees but may not work as well for highly skilled managers. Ads are especially useful if you need a large number of recruits for a specific type of job.

Specialized publications. These target specific groups—the *Wall Street Journal* or *APICS Magazine* are two examples. There are many types of industry trade and professional publications you can use to recruit the niche candidates you are looking for.

The Internet. Should your company put every job opening up on the Internet? In many cases, companies are discovering that they may not want to advertise every job opening on the Internet because of its reach.[15] They just don't have the time to wade through possibly thousands of applications for a single opening. Jobs requiring computer or other high-level technical skills would probably have good potential for Internet recruitment. But you may not find a five-star chef on the Internet because they may use other job search methods.

See Exhibit 5-1 for a review of internal and external recruiting sources.

Advantages and Disadvantages of External Recruiting. So, what are the advantages and disadvantages of external recruiting?

Advantages include the following:

- The first and biggest advantage is the mirror image of the biggest disadvantage in internal recruiting—we *avoid* creating or perpetuating resistance to change, allowing a foothold for innovative new ways of operating.

- We may be able to find individuals with complex skill sets who are not available internally.

- We can lower training costs for skilled positions by externally hiring someone with the requisite skills.

- External hires will frequently increase organizational diversity.

EXHIBIT 5-1   MAJOR RECRUITING SOURCES

Internal Sources	Strengths
A. Promotion from within	Provides current employees new job opportunities within the firm
B. Employee referral	Inexpensive recruiting based on employee knowledge of the candidate

External Sources	Strengths
C. Walk-ins	Inexpensive and self-selected
D. Educational institutions	Good basic skill sets; typically less expensive than others with more experience
E. Temporary agencies	Prescreened workers; useful in short-term shortage situations
F. Public agencies	At least some prescreening; public employment agencies are very inexpensive
G. Private agencies	Heavy prescreening of recruits, lowering organizational prescreening costs; typically very well targeted; good for experienced recruits
H. Local mass media	Fairly broad reach if searching for many recruits; cost per person is low; good for semiskilled or skilled line employees
I. Specialized publications	Good for targeting specific types of recruits; fairly good reach; fairly low cost per person
J. Internet	Very broad reach; beginning to be able to target to specific audiences as many professional organizations have sites

5-1 APPLYING THE CONCEPT

Recruiting Sources

Using Exhibit 5-1: Major Recruiting Sources, write the letter (A–J) of which recruiting source is most appropriate in each of the following recruiting situations:

_____ 1. You need a CEO from outside the company.

_____ 2. "We need more employees, Jean. Do you know anyone interested in working for us?"

_____ 3. We need to hire a new history professor.

_____ 4. We need another computer programmer.

_____ 5. A worker got hurt on the job and will be out for a week.

_____ 6. We need an experienced clerical worker, but we don't have any money for ads.

_____ 7. We need a person to perform routine cleaning services, and experience is not necessary.

_____ 8. The VP of finance needs a new administrative assistant.

_____ 9. We have a supervisor retiring in a month.

_____ 10. We like to hire young people without experience in order to train them to sell using a unique approach.

What about disadvantages? There are certainly potential problems in bringing outsiders into the company:

- Disruption of the work team due to introducing significantly different ways of operating.

- External recruiting takes much longer, which means it costs more.

- Might adversely affect current employees' motivation and satisfaction due to the perceived inability to move up in the organization.

- Likely will incur higher orientation and training costs than internal recruiting.

- The candidate may look great on paper, but we have no organizational history on the individual.

WORK
APPLICATION 5-4

Identify the recruiting source that was used to hire you for your current job or a past job and explain how it was used.

CHALLENGES AND CONSTRAINTS IN RECRUITING

The process of recruiting is time-consuming and expensive. As a result, we want to pay attention to the effectiveness of our recruiting methods. We have budgetary and other constraints, so we face the challenge of balance in finding qualified candidates without spending too much and without recruiting too many or too few candidates. So let's discuss these issues in this section.

LO 5-4

Summarize the major challenges and constraints involved in the recruiting process.

Budgetary Constraints

We obviously have to live within our budgets in all cases, and recruiting is no exception. There are times when we would like to fly half a dozen top-notch recruits in from around the world to interview for a position, but such costs add up very quickly. Generally, the more value the recruit brings to the firm, the more we can afford to spend.

Policy Constraints and Organizational Image

There are many *organizational policies* that can affect our recruiting efforts. Whether we have a *promote-from-within* policy or not affects how we recruit. Our policies on *temporary-to-permanent* employees would also affect how we recruit in most cases. Do we have policies concerning *recruiting and hiring relatives* of current employees? If so, this would affect our recruiting efforts. Do we have an *affirmative action policy* in the organization? If so, it will dictate many of our recruiting procedures. And we can have other policies that affect recruiting.

We are also affected in our recruiting efforts by our *organizational image* in the markets from which we source our recruits.[16] You may know of a company in your local community that you would not apply to because of its bad reputation, and others you want to work for. This is just one of many reasons why we want to maintain a strong reputation in the communities that we serve.

WORK
APPLICATION 5-5

Explain how a firm's image played a role in your applying for and accepting a job you currently hold or have held.

Job Characteristics and the Realistic Job Preview (RJP)

Let's face it. Not every job we need to fill is glamorous, and every job has some aspects we'd rather not deal with. We need to realize that not everyone wants, or can get, great jobs. Some people are very happy in low level jobs you may find boring, and they do a great job. The key is to recruit "qualified" candidates—people that actually want the job and will stay with the company. One mistake companies have made is to make the job sound better than what it really is. They

Job candidates need a realistic job preview to understand what the job is all about.

©iStockphoto.com/PeopleImages

WORK
APPLICATION 5-6

Briefly describe the RJP you received for your present job or a past job. How could the RJP be improved?

Realistic job preview (RJP) A review of all of the tasks and requirements of the job, both good and bad

may successfully recruit and hire, but when the employee realizes what the job really is, they leave. This turnover wastes recruiting time and expenses, as well as training costs, which becomes a vicious cycle.

Most companies have come to the conclusion that realistic job previews are a necessary part of the recruiting process to recruit a qualified candidate that will stay with the firm. A **realistic job preview (RJP)** *is a review of all of the tasks and requirements of the job, both good and bad.* A good job analysis (Chapter 4) with a clear job description should provide a good RJP. We have found that "giving applicants a warts-and-all preview of what a job entails on a day-to-day basis can reduce turnover effectively by making sure the applicant is really a good fit for the job."[17] There is strong research evidence that early turnover in a job is directly related to failure to provide an RJP for that job.[18]

The Recruiter–Candidate Interaction

Does the recruiter (or recruiters) affect the job candidates and their willingness to apply for a job in our organization? The obvious answer is yes. The recruiter is one of the primary factors responsible for an applicant showing interest in our organization and our jobs.[19] According to one report, "Recruiters with higher degrees of engagement and job fit dramatically outperform their peers who score lower in those areas. That's measured both in the quality of hires and in productivity."[20] So we have to be sure to hire qualified candidates to be our recruiters; experienced internal people usually work out better than external candidates because knowing the organization helps them give an RJP.

It takes good communications skills for recruiters to accurately assess if job candidates are actually qualified for the job—including whether or not they fit the organizational culture and are likely to stay with the firm. So when hiring recruiters, make sure they have a strong set of communication skills. The recruiter must be able to talk with the recruits "on their level" in order to make them feel comfortable with the process. Recruiters need to learn when to ask probing

5-1 SELF ASSESSMENT

Career Development

Indicate how accurately each statement describes you by placing a number from 1 to 7 on the line before the statement. 7 = strong agreement; 1 = strong disagreement.

Describes me						Does not describe me
7	6	5	4	3	2	1

_____ 1. I know my strengths, and I can list several of them.

_____ 2. I can list several skills that I have to offer an employer.

_____ 3. I have career objectives.

_____ 4. I know the type of full-time job that I want next.

_____ 5. I have analyzed help-wanted ads or job descriptions, and I have determined the most important skills I will need to get the type of full-time job I want.

_____ 6. I have or plan to get a part-time job, summer job, internship, or full-time job related to my career objectives.

_____ 7. I know the proper terms to use on my résumé to help me get the next job I want.

_____ 8. I understand how my strengths and skills are transferable, or how they can be used on jobs I apply for, and I can give examples on a résumé and in an interview.

_____ 9. I can give examples (on a résumé and in an interview) of suggestions or direct contributions I made that increased performance for my employer.

_____ 10. My résumé focuses on the skills I have developed and on how they relate to the job I am applying for, rather than on job titles.

_____ 11. My résumé gives details of how my college education and the skills developed in college relate to the job I am applying for.

_____ 12. I have a résumé that is customized to each part-time job, summer job, or internship I apply for, rather than one generic résumé.

Add up the numbers you assigned to the statements and place the total on the continuum below:

84	74	64	54	44	34	24	12
Career ready						In need of career development	

---

questions and when to lie back and let a recruit talk. Role-playing training for the recruiter is particularly effective in teaching this skill.[21] Another important communication skill to assess is **active listening,** _which is the intention and ability to listen to others, use the content and context of the communication, and respond appropriately._ This means that recruiters have to want to listen and must have developed their active listening skills so that they not only hear the words that recruits are saying but also understand the context of the conversations (what the circumstances are and why the other person is communicating this information) so that they can empathize with recruits and visualize why they are providing this information.[22] Empathy in this situation (putting yourself in another's position) allows the recruiter to visualize why something is being communicated and is critical if the recruiter is to respond correctly.

The recruiter's job also includes successfully communicating with the hiring managers in the organization. The same active listening skills that serve recruiters in interactions with an applicant can allow them to more clearly define what the hiring manager wants and needs in the new organizational recruit. So we need to create strong training programs in communication with recruiters in the organization.[23]

WORK
APPLICATION 5-7

Briefly describe the interaction you had with the recruiter for your current job or a past job. How could the interaction have been improved?

Active listening The intention and ability to listen to others, use the content and context of the communication, and respond appropriately

We also have to train recruiters in the process of the RJP. They need to understand the job in detail so that they can give honest answers and an RJP of the job to the potential candidate. In many cases today, we may have a recruiting team with one person on the team having the "technical" knowledge of the job (maybe the supervisor of the job) and the other person having the HR-related knowledge that keeps us from inadvertently violating any laws, regulations, or internal policies. This helps us with the RJP because the technical person can explain details that the HR recruiter would generally not know or understand.

So recruiting, selecting, and then training our recruiters is a major factor in our overall recruiting success with both the hiring manager and the candidates.

EVALUATION OF RECRUITING PROGRAMS

LO 5-5

Discuss the basic methods available for evaluating the recruiting process.

We need to measure our recruiting processes the same as we measure every other process in the organization. This is another point at which HR analytics skills are becoming significantly more important. As we noted above, the recruitment process is expensive, and unless we identify and control those costs, the beneficial results may end up being outweighed by the costs. But recruitment and salary cost are an investment. If you hire the best people, like **Google**, their productivity will more than pay for itself.

See Exhibit 5-2 for an overview of five evaluation methods that we discuss in this section.

Yield Ratio

SHRM
G:6
Calculating and Interpreting Yield Ratios

Our first measurement option is the recruiting **yield ratio**—*a calculation of how many people make it through the recruiting step to the next step in the hiring process.* For example, we advertise for a job opening and receive 100 résumés and applications. Of these applicants, 50 are judged to have the basic qualifications for the job. As a result, our yield ratio on the advertisement would be 50% (50 of our 100 applicants made it through the first recruiting step). As with most metrics, we then compare to historical data or to other company benchmarks to see how we are doing in the process. If our historic yield ratio for advertisements is 40%, then our ad was much more effective than average.

Cost per Hire

Another measure that you probably want to use is how much it costs to get each person hired, or *cost per hire*—which is calculated based on this formula:[24]

Advertising + Agency fees + Employee referrals + Travel cost of applicants and staff + Relocation costs + Recruiter pay and benefits = Total cost

Total cost ÷ Number of hires = Cost per hire

For example, when needing several new customer service representatives, we were successful in recruiting and hiring 15 fully qualified applicants for the open positions. During the recruiting campaign, the company spent $140,000 on all of the recruiting costs combined. The cost per hire was therefore $140,000/15 = $9,333.33.

Time Required to Hire

Time required to hire is pretty self-explanatory. How many days/weeks/months did it take to get someone hired into an open position? If our company has a new

Yield ratio A calculation of how many people make it through the recruiting step to the next step in the hiring process

| EXHIBIT 5-2 | RECRUITING EVALUATION METHODS |

Generally, all recruiting evaluation methods are comparisons to historical averages to see whether the organization is improving in its recruiting efforts or is less successful than in the past.

Yield ratio:

Divide the number of qualified applicants by the number of applicants.

An advertisement yielded 40 applications, and 28 have the basic qualifications. The yield ratio is 28:40, or 70%.

Cost per hire:

Divide the total cost by the number of applicants hired.

$60,000/10 = $6,000

Time to hire:

The total time required from a position coming open until a new hire is in place.

A new opening on October 15 was filled on December 5, so our time to hire was 51 days.

New hire turnover:

Divide the number of recruits that left within a specified time frame by the number of new hires.

Last year 84 people were hired, and 13 of those left again within 3 months. Our new hire turnover would be 13/84, or 15.5%.

New hire performance:

Divide the difference in performance by new recruits into the average for all employees in the same category to determine the percentage above or below average.

The average of all new hire appraisals last year was 3.1 on a 4 point grading scale. The average of all appraisals in the organization last year was 3.2. Therefore, new recruits are 3.3% below average (3.2 − 3.1 = 0.1; 0.1/3.2 = 3.3%).

opening on June 10 and we are able to fill the position on August 28, our time to hire was 79 days ([June] 30 − 10 = 20 + [July] 31 + [August] 28 = 79).

New Hire Turnover

Employee retention remains a critical issue for organizations and HR managers.[25] In measuring new-hire turnover, we need to identify a time frame. We would usually look at turnover within the first 3 to 6 months. So we identify our time frame and then measure how many new recruits compared to all hires during that period chose to leave the organization.

If we had 30 new hires in the past year and two of them left again within 6 months of being hired (we are identifying our turnover window as 6 months), we can calculate the turnover percentage and then compare it to historical averages: 2/30 = 6.7% new-hire turnover rate. If our historical new-hire turnover is 10%, then we have improved, at least during this annual cycle.

New Hire Performance

We can also analyze the performance ratings of new hires versus all employees. There are many ways to evaluate employees, but suppose you evaluate employees on an overall 4.0 scale (as in college). Further, let's assume the average employee in the organization is judged to be a 3.0 on our 4-point scale. If our new hires are performing significantly below the average (say, at 2.4), we may want to analyze where

WORK
APPLICATION 5-8

Discuss how your present employer or a past employer evaluates its recruiting programs. If you don't know, contact the HR department to find out.

It is important to evaluate the performance of new hires against all employees to understand how they fit in the organization, and make adjustments as necessary.

they are not being successful and provide training opportunities to them and all new hires going forward to increase their chances for long-term success.

To make the measure more objective, we can calculate the percentage of new recruits who perform above or below average. You divide the difference in performance by new recruits compared to the average. Let's use the new recruit average of 2.4 compared to the 3.0 average: $3.0 - 2.4 = 0.6$; $0.6/3.0 = 0.2$ or 20% below average. Don't bother working with negative numbers. You can easily see if the new recruits are above or below average, so just subtract the smaller from the larger number.

TRENDS AND ISSUES IN HRM

The first issue that we will cover here is the looming worldwide talent war. Closely connected to this is our second trend, creating "massively flexible" on-demand workforces.

Talent Wars

In a recent study, **Accenture** noted that "34 percent of employers worldwide are having difficulty filling open positions, and 73 percent cite lack of experience, skills, or knowledge as the primary obstacle to recruiting."[26] HR executives are also projecting significant worker shortages in many professions in 10 major industries by 2020 and 2030.[27]

As a result of this lack of skills and experience, a global war for talent has become a reality. With the shortage of skilled 21st century workers, the only way to have any real chance of recruiting for open knowledge-worker positions is to recruit in every corner of the globe. How do we find these highly skilled individuals and get them to apply for jobs in our organization? We have to understand labor regulations in all markets where we recruit, immigration laws concerning employment, and how people search for work in each area where we recruit so that we can advertise "where they look."

5-2   APPLYING THE CONCEPT

Recruiting Evaluation Methods

Do the math.

11. Your company had a new opening on May 5 and you filled the position on June 25. Your time to hire was _____ days.

12. Your company hired 24 people last year, and 14 of those left again within 3 months. Your new hire turnover is _____.

13. The average of all new hire appraisals last year was 4.3 on a 5-point grading scale. The average of all appraisals in the organization last year was 4.1. Therefore, new recruits are _____ % above or ___ % below average.

14. An advertisement for a job opening receives 62 applications. Of these, 48 have the basic qualifications required for the job. The yield ratio would be _____.

15. You hired 7 workers and it cost you $72,000. The cost per hire is _____.

HR analytics again comes to the forefront in this effort. Employment forecasting uses more robust data modeling and analytics tools than we have in the past, and we are also able to use analytical searches to find and source the types of people who have been identified through these forecasts.

So global recruiting is a potential method for winning the talent war. More and more, we are going to find that global searches are the only methods of finding those skilled workers that we need for our 21st century company.

WORK
APPLICATION 5-9

Discuss how your present employer or a past employer uses technology in recruiting. If you don't know, contact the HR department to find out.

Global Knowledge Workers as an On-Demand Workforce

Closely related to the global talent war, we will increasingly see a much larger number of contingent workers as a segment of our overall workforce. The core group of employees will do the work that requires continuity, but they will be surrounded by large groups of contractors, temporary workers, consultants, vendors on premises, outsourcing organizations, and other individuals.[28,29] HR will also need to become more adept at managing these contingent workforces.[30]

Right now, there is evidence that the contingent workforce in the United States is somewhere between 20% and 25% of all individuals doing economic work.[31] These workers can be available to the company on demand, through websites such as **Elance** and **Guru**, through temporary agencies and other services, or through a company database of available individuals.

According to **Accenture**, this "new extended workforce is increasingly mobile, global, and borderless,"[32] and assists the organization with two critical items: agility in numbers and types of workers and access to skilled talent. Access to this talent will become a much more important part of HR recruiting in the near future. We will need to create partnerships with organizations such as temporary agencies, schools, outsourcers, and even suppliers who can assist us with this sourcing. We will also need to become much better at matching workers with discrete tasks and following the assignments to make sure that results are satisfactory. This process of analysis, job matching, and follow-up is going to be a long-term requirement for 21st century HR departments.

• • • CHAPTER SUMMARY

5-1 Describe the main external forces acting on recruiting efforts.

The main external forces are the effective labor market and the social and legal forces that act on us as well as our potential recruits. These forces include (1) supply and demand, meaning whether there are plenty of candidates for the available jobs or whether there are more jobs than candidates, (2) the unemployment rate in the recruiting area, (3) competitors and whether competition for available workers is strong or weak, and (4) the social and legal environments, meaning the social factors that recruits emphasize when weighing whether or not to accept employment in a particular company and what limits are placed on recruiting efforts by laws and regulations.

5-2   Name the five main organizational recruiting considerations.

The five considerations are organizational policies, when we should recruit new employees, alternatives to recruiting, the reach of the recruiting effort, and how to use social media. *Policies* set the other four items. *When to recruit* tells us whether or not we should first mitigate a shortage with other organizational tactics, such as overtime. *Alternatives* include using overtime, outsourcing some work, or using temporary or contract workers or other options to mitigate a shortage. *Reach* determines the geographic locations that we will search for new employees. Finally, we need to determine how we are willing to use *social media* to assist in our recruiting efforts.

5-3   Identify the major advantages and disadvantages of internal and external recruiting.

The major advantages of internal recruiting include increases in organizational commitment and job satisfaction, the ability to learn more about the "big picture" in the company, the fact that the individual feels comfortable working for the company, the fact that the company knows the individual and that person's work history, lower recruiting costs, and a relatively speedy process compared to external recruiting. Disadvantages include the facts that the pool of applicants is smaller, you will have to fill the old job of the person you hire, success in one job doesn't necessarily mean success in a different job, external candidates may be more qualified, internal candidates may feel that they are entitled to the job, and we may perpetuate resistance to change and stifle innovation and creativity.

Advantages of external recruiting are that we avoid perpetuating resistance to change and encourage innovation and creativity, we may be able to find individuals with complex skill sets who are not available internally, there will be lower training costs for complex positions, and we have the potential to increase diversity. Disadvantages include potential disruption of the work team, the fact that it takes longer than internal recruiting and costs more, the fact that it may adversely affect current employees' motivation and satisfaction, higher orientation and training costs, and the fact that the candidate may look great on paper but may not perform after being hired.

5-4   Summarize the major challenges and constraints involved in the recruiting process.

The most obvious constraint is money. We have to avoid spending too much on the recruiting process. Additionally, organizational policies also affect how we recruit. Our organization's image also plays a significant role in our ability to source the people we need from the communities around us. Next is the type of job. Not all jobs are clean or fun. Finally, our selection and training of the recruiter and their delivery of an RJP is a major factor in recruiting success. We have to find an individual who has the ability to actively listen and empathize with the candidate.

5-5   Discuss the basic methods available for evaluating the recruiting process.

The recruiting *yield ratio* calculates how many people make it through the recruiting step to the next step in the hiring process. Another measure is *cost per hire*. You also may want to analyze *time required to hire*. *New-hire turnover* is another measure of success. If we have high rates of turnover immediately after recruitment and selection, we probably need to reevaluate our recruiting and selection process. Finally, we can also analyze *new-hire performance ratings* and compare them to the organizational norms. If our new hires perform at a significantly lower level than the norm, we may want to analyze where they are not being successful and provide training opportunities to increase their chances for long-term success.

5-6   Define the key terms found in the chapter margins and listed following the Chapter Summary.

Complete the Key Terms Review to test your understanding of this chapter's key terms.

• • • KEY TERMS

active listening, 123
external recruiting, 118
internal recruiting, 117

labor market, 114
realistic job preview (RJP), 122
recruiting, 113

yield ratio, 124

• • • KEY TERMS REVIEW

Complete each of the following statements using one of this chapter's key terms.

1. _____ is the process of creating a reasonable pool of qualified candidates for a job opening.

2. _____ is the term for the external pool of candidates from which we draw our recruits.

3. _____ involves filling job openings with current employees or people they know.

4. _____ is the process of engaging individuals from the labor market outside the firm to apply for a job.

5. _____ is a review of all of the tasks and requirements of the job, both good and bad.

6. _____ is the intention and ability to listen to others, use the content and context of the communication, and respond appropriately.

7. _____ is a calculation of how many people make it through the recruiting step to the next step in the hiring process.

● ● ● COMMUNICATION SKILLS

The following critical-thinking questions can be used for class discussion and/or for written assignments to develop communication skills. Be sure to give complete explanations for all answers.

1. Should you "shop" for good employees who are out of work in a bad economy, and then should you terminate existing employees who aren't doing their jobs very well after finding a good replacement? What consequences of this course of action can you see?

2. If you were in charge of your company, would you rather recruit new employees, or would you rather use some of the other tools for addressing a shortage of employees that were discussed in this and the last chapter? Why?

3. In your personal experience, do you think that internal recruiting really improves organizational morale, job satisfaction, and productivity? Why or why not?

4. Do you think that targeted or closed recruiting leads to the potential for discrimination in recruiting efforts? Why or why not?

5. When would you *definitely* use the Internet as a recruiting tool, and when would you definitely *not* use the Internet to recruit? Why?

6. What could an organization do to improve its image if it has a bad reputation with recruits? Categorize your efforts into immediate-term and longer-term items.

7. If you were in charge of your company, what would you tell recruiters to do or not do to enhance their recruiting efforts? Why?

8. Do you think that you are a good "active listener"? Why or why not, and what could you do to become better?

9. What options do you see as alternatives to recruiting globally for knowledge-based jobs in the coming years?

● ● ● CASE 5-1 LINKEDIN: HOW DOES THE WORLD'S LARGEST PROFESSIONAL NETWORK NETWORK?

In 2003, LinkedIn was launched to help those who felt a bit disconnected in the business world by creating a professional network where members could find jobs from the labor market, locate business opportunities, and connect with other professionals. Given its differentiation approach, LinkedIn became the dominant player, with over 300 million members in more than 200 countries. It has continued its growth strategy through acquisitions, such as the 2012 purchase of SlideShare—an application that allows users to share slideshow presentations—for some $119 million. In addition, the company has launched its Talent Pipeline offering, a new recruiter product. Mobile applications are another area of focus for the company; in 2011, about 15% of member visits came from mobile devices, and mobile page views were up more than 300% year over year. LinkedIn is also ramping up its international expansion activities, having experienced growth in India, Brazil, and China. About 60% of its member base comes from outside the United States, and its service is available in French, German, Italian, Portuguese, and Spanish. As a reflection of its global focus, LinkedIn recently opened offices in London, Mumbai, and Sydney in addition to its presence in Canada, Ireland, and the Netherlands.[33]

Through this giant network, members are able to find jobs from the labor market, locate business opportunities, and connect with other professionals. LinkedIn has become a powerful tool for large companies to find new talent as well. Unlike the other job-hunting search engines like **Monster** or **Indeed**, LinkedIn provides the opportunity for users and employers to network with each other. Companies like **Google** or **HP** use their own resources and their own search tools for headhunting; however, for the majority of the hiring process, LinkedIn is used to gather more information about candidates. LinkedIn can count executives from all Fortune 500 companies among its members, and it is believed that 90% of Fortune 100 companies use LinkedIn's corporate talent solutions to recruit employees.[34]

Successful growth requires hiring new employees. Ironically, to meet the increasing demand for their services, LinkedIn itself needed to hire new software engineers, salespeople, and corporate managers. LinkedIn may have a lot to teach its corporate users about how to benefit from its services, yet how does LinkedIn hire its own employees?

When LinkedIn needs an immediate hire for a vacant position, it requires its HR team to design, implement, and maintain the network configurations, but it also requires them to collaborate with business leaders to recruit applicants who meet the company's objectives. LinkedIn uses its own website along with a plan to recruit only the best for the company in the least amount of time possible. Whenever a user checks the profile of a LinkedIn employee, it is likely that the user will see an advertisement for a possible opening in the company. The goal is to reach the whole labor market about this vacancy and announce it to users familiar with the firm's services. The job seekers then realize it would be easier to "follow" LinkedIn's page to catch further openings, so it is not a surprise that LinkedIn's number of followers has multiplied by a factor of 10 during the past 3 years. LinkedIn also uses its database to generate links between local job listings and job seekers for specific industries—not only to search for talent in nearby locations or where the job turnover is high, as in New York City or Silicon Valley, but in places where labor supply/demand is more in balance, as in Washington, D.C., or Dallas.[35]

Key positions in the company, in one case a data center manager, required far more targeted recruiting given the technical nature of the jobs. Job specifications included 15+ years of managerial experience, at least 3 years in a similar job, a PhD in computer science, and proven leadership in the IT world. Knowing it could take more than a year and a half to persuade people to leave their current job and join LinkedIn, LinkedIn narrowed down its search by focusing on only current job seekers. In the end, the search result provided only seven résumés that matched the job's criteria—only seven identifiable people on the planet![36]

Questions

1. How does LinkedIn's growth strategy impact the recruitment function of its HR department?

2. One way that LinkedIn has grown is through acquisition. From a recruitment viewpoint, why use this method of growth rather than internal development?

3. Why would a firm use LinkedIn's services rather than those of a traditional headhunter or their in-house recruitment specialists?

4. What are alternative methods that firms can employ to recruit new employees besides using LinkedIn's services?

5. What is a realistic job preview, and how might LinkedIn be used by firms to provide such a preview to potential employees?

6. Evaluate LinkedIn's search for a data center manager. How might the company have handled this search differently in order to increase the number of potential applicants?

Case created by Herbert Sherman, PhD, and Theodore Vallas, Department of Management Sciences, Long Island University School of Business, Brooklyn Campus

• • • SKILL BUILDER 5-1 ONLINE JOB SEARCH

Objectives

To develop your job search skills and to learn more about job descriptions and specifications

To get you thinking about your career

Skills

The primary skills developed through this exercise are as follows:

1. *HR management skills*—technical, business, and conceptual and design skills
2. *SHRM 2013 Curriculum Guidebook*—I: Staffing: Recruitment and Selection

Preparation

Study the steps in the job search, which is preparation for the written assignment.

Let's do an exercise related to your professional development. Employers recruit job candidates, so we focus on you.

1. Think about a job or internship you would like to have. You may also get ideas when you go to a job search website.

2. Go to a job search website of your choice. You may use http://www.collegejournal.com (jobs and tips for new college grads), http://www.collegerecruiter.com (career tests to identify possible jobs, internships, and entry-level jobs), http://www.shrm.org (HR jobs and advice), http://www.monster.com (simply a listing of all types of jobs), and http://www.careerbuilder.com (jobs and advice). You may want to search using other websites and use more than one job search engine. If you are interested in working for a specific business or nonprofit organization, you may also visit its website.

3. Read about the job, job description, and specifications.

4. Your professor may want the URLs you used in your job search.

Written Assignment Instructions

Type the answers to these three questions.

1. What job(s) were you searching for, and which web-site(s) did you use to search?

2. List three or four things that you learned about job searching.

3. How will you use this information to get a job?

Apply It

What did I learn from this experience? How will I use this knowledge in the future?

_____

_____

_____

Your instructor may ask you to do this Skill Builder in class in a group by sharing your answers. If so, the instructor will provide you with any necessary information or additional instructions.

• • • SKILL BUILDER 5–2 RÉSUMÉ

Objective

To develop a résumé you can use for internships and part-time, summer, and full-time employment

Skills

The primary skills developed through this exercise are as follows:

1. *HR management skills*—technical, business, and conceptual and design skills

2. *SHRM 2013 Curriculum Guidebook*—I: Staffing: Recruitment and Selection

Preparation

Writing the résumé:

You may go to your college's Career Center and/or visit Proven Résumés at http://www.provenresumes.com for help. You should read the tips below before writing your résumé:

Type out your résumé, and keep it to one page, unless you have extensive "relevant" experience. Before finalizing your résumé, improve it by using the résumé assessment below, which may be used to grade your résumé.

Answer these résumé questions with Yes, Somewhat, or No:

- Within 10 seconds, can a recruiter understand what job you are applying for and that you have the qualifications (skills/experience and education) to get the position? You should not use the word *I* or *me* on a résumé.

Objective

- Does your résumé have an objective that clearly states the position being applied for (such as sales

rep)? The job applied for affects all sections of your résumé because your résumé needs to state how you are qualified for the job. If you don't list the job you are applying for, your résumé will most likely be tossed out and you will not get a job with the firm.

Education (describe relevant courses)

- If education is your major qualification for the job, is there detail that states the skills developed and courses taken in school that qualify you for the position you're applying for?

- Be sure to state your degree, major, and minor and concentration, if you have them. Don't write Bachelor of Science or Master of Business Administration—use BS and name of degree or MBA. Be sure to list your month and year of graduation.

- Your résumé should do a good job of filling one page. If you don't have extensive experience, list relevant courses that prepared you for the job you are applying for. For relevant courses, don't just include a shopping list. Pick a few "relevant" courses and describe how each course qualifies you for the job listed in your objective. So if you want to be a sales rep, you should state that you are a marketing major (or that you pursued a marketing concentration) and that you have taken the Sales and Selling course. Describe the skills you developed in the sales and other relevant courses.

- If you list computer courses/skills, be sure to list programs such as Microsoft Word, Excel, Access, PowerPoint (it is *one* word, not two), Windows, SPSS, HTML, etc. If you've used them on the job, say so with the program you used.

Experience

- Does your résumé list experience or skills that support the fact that you can do the job stated in your objective?

- Be sure to list names and addresses of employers, with months and years on the job. If you want the company to which you are applying to contact your boss for a reference, list your boss's name and telephone number on your résumé.

- Don't just list activities, such as cutting grass. Focus on general skills that can be applied to the job you want. Try to show skills. Did you do any planning, organizing, leading (influencing others, communicating, and motivating), and controlling? Give examples of your skills.

- For the sales job example, if any of your past jobs don't include sales experience, list sales skills developed on the job. List communication skills that you used while interacting with customers stating how you used them. Also state that you enjoy meeting new people and that you have the ability to easily converse with people you don't know.

Accomplishments (NOT *necessarily a separate section and heading*)

- Does your résumé clearly list your accomplishments and valuable contributions you made while attaining your education and/or experience?

- If you have a high GPA, you should list it with your education.

- If you are on a college sports team, be sure to list it with any accomplishments (such as Maroon of the Week, captain, MVP, or selection to conference teams). A good place to list sports is in the education section.

- List job accomplishments like "Increased sales by 10% from May to August 2010," "Employee of the Month," and "Earned highest tips based on superior sales skills and excellent communication skills used with customers."

- Is your résumé neat, attractive, and free of errors? Have neat columns and use tables without gridlines. Use high-quality bond paper and ink colors for hard copies.

Apply It

What did I learn from this experience? How will I use this knowledge in the future?

_____

_____

_____

Your instructor may ask you to do this Skill Builder in class in a group by showing others your résumé. If so, the instructor will provide you with any necessary information or additional instructions.

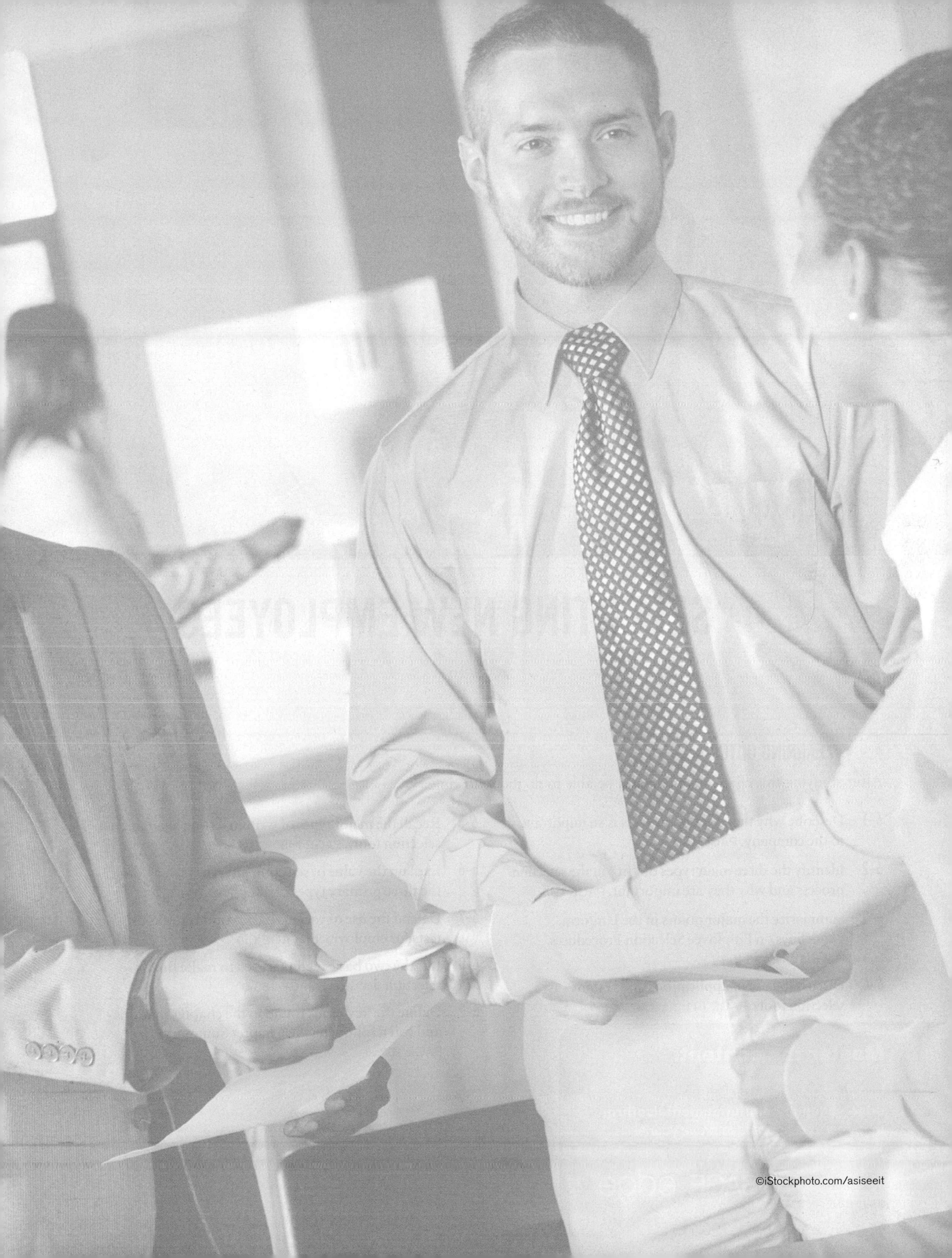

©iStockphoto.com/shironosov

6 SELECTING NEW EMPLOYEES

Practitioner's Perspective

In a discussion of hiring, Cindy notes that the process of moving a person from job candidate to employee is a matching game for both the candidate and the company. Job candidates want to emphasize their attractive qualities while minimizing any drawbacks. Sometimes, it is hard for an employer to determine if "what you see is really what you get." Is there a line that shouldn't be crossed in the attempt to gather information about a job candidate?

She says, "When Sacha, our finance manager, started talking about vetting the candidates for her open position by checking their Facebook accounts, I knew we needed to talk. 'But you find out so much about people by looking at their page—mostly whether or not they have done something that would disqualify them,' Sacha said."

Is there real potential to access via the Internet candidate information that an employer should not have prior to offering a position? What are the pitfalls to avoid and legal restrictions that must be respected during hiring? Chapter 6 covers the process one should follow to properly select employees.

● ● ●

THE SELECTION PROCESS

After completing the recruiting process, we need to select one person from the pool to fill our job opening. Selection is important because bad hires can be costly.[1] Firms should always seek to hire the most highly skilled employees to maximize their output,[2] but there is often a mismatch when the job and person don't fit together, and productivity suffers as a result.[3] Remember that in most organizations today, at least one of our competitive advantages will be our employees, so if we put the wrong people into the wrong jobs, we can have great difficulty in carrying out our strategic plans. So we need to focus on fit.[4]

LO 6-1

Describe why the selection process is so important to the company.

● ● ● **CHAPTER OUTLINE**

Selection is the process of choosing the best-qualified applicant who was recruited for a given job. As with all other employee organizational decisions, we can apply the OUCH test to determine whether or not we should use a particular tool or measure in the selection process. The OUCH test will give us an initial analysis of the measure being used, and whether we need to do some more investigation before we decide to use that specific measure in the selection process.

The Importance of the Selection Process

Why is the selection process so critical to the organization? Because of the negative consequences of bad hiring decisions, which are essentially the results of mismatches between jobs and employees. Here are three of those reasons.

Bad Hires Cost Time and Money. First and probably most notably, if we hire someone who is not willing or able to do the job successfully, we will most likely have to go through the whole process again in a very short time. Because recruiting and selection is so expensive, we must work to avoid this.

Bad Hires Result in Lower Productivity. Have you ever seen or worked with a bad employee who did a poor job doing the minimum amount of work possible, resulting in poor customer service, and creating extra work for you and/or coworkers? Just a few new hires who show this lack of concern for the organization and its customers can be highly contagious. Pretty soon, others may decide, "If they can do the absolute minimum and still get paid what I get paid, then why should I work so hard?" Once this occurs, morale, job satisfaction, and organizational commitment can drop very quickly. You don't want to put yourself and your organization in such a position, so you must give your full attention to making sure you hire only candidates who fit the jobs.

Selection The process of choosing the best-qualified applicant who was recruited for a given job

SHRM HR CONTENT

See Appendix: *SHRM 2013 Curriculum Guidebook* for the complete list

B. Employment Law (required)

32. The Genetic Information Nondiscrimination Act (GINA)
36. Fair Credit Reporting Act (FCRA)
39. Negligent hiring

E. Job Analysis/Job Design (required)

3. Employment practices (recruitment, selection, and placement)

I. Staffing: Recruitment and Selection (required)

6. Initial assessment methods: Résumés, cover letters, application blanks, biographical information, reference/background checks, genetic screening, initial interviews, minimum qualifications
7. Discretionary assessment methods
8. Ability/job knowledge tests, assessment centers

9. Noncognitive assessments (e.g., personality assessments, integrity tests, situational judgment tests, interest inventories)
10. Structured interviews
11. Contingent assessment methods: Drug testing, medical exams
12. Measurement concepts: Predictors/criteria, reliability, validity
13. Selection decisions: Ranking, grouping/banding, random selection

Q. Organizational Development (required–graduate students only)

14. Social networking

X. Workplace Health, Safety, and Security (secondary)

10. Testing for substance abuse

Bad Hires Can Be Negligent Hires. Almost every state in America recognizes this legal concept, so HR managers must understand it as well.[5] A **negligent hire** *is a legal concept that says if the organization hires someone who may pose a danger to coworkers, customers, suppliers, or other third parties, and if that person then harms someone else in the course of working for the company, then the company can be held liable for the individual's actions.*

For example, if you hired a salesperson who had a criminal record for assault and they then assaulted a customer, the company could be held liable for the harm done to the customer who was assaulted. So we have to make every legitimate attempt to find out if candidates have the potential to be a danger to others and weed them out during our selection process.

Steps in the Selection Process

The selection process follows a series of steps that are illustrated in Exhibit 6-1. Note that this is a general guide and that one may skip some steps in the process or perhaps not follow them in the exact sequence shown. For example, there may not be any preliminary testing or initial interviewing, and there may not be any drug screening or physical exam.

If you think about it for a minute, the process steps make logical sense. People apply for jobs, and then the firm screens the job candidates to narrow down the selection. This screening may include a test of some type and an initial interview for the top candidates.

Before we get into those selection steps though, let's discuss the importance of selecting the applicant who best matches the job, or what we call "looking for fit." We also need to briefly discuss the federal Uniform Guidelines on Employment Selection Procedures (UGESP) that affect how we conduct each of the steps in the selection process. Once we have covered these two items, we can go into the actual steps of the selection process.

LOOKING FOR "FIT"

"We hold these truths to be self-evident, that all men are created equal."[6] Is this a true statement? It is what the US Declaration of Independence says! However, we all know that people are not equal. We also know that as managers, if we treat people equally (the same), then we really aren't doing our job. Managers are supposed to get the best productivity out of their workforce, but not everyone can do everything equally well. So we have to treat people differently *but fairly* in order to be successful in our jobs. We need to attempt to assess three things in this process: personality-job fit, ability-job fit, and person-organization fit. Let's take a look at these items.

Personality-Job Fit

Our personality defines to a great extent who we are and how we act and react in certain situations. We all have unique personalities. Some of us are strongly extroverted and enjoy "working the crowd" in a social setting, while others may be fairly introverted and feel extremely uncomfortable in such an environment. Some of us desire to try new things constantly, while others don't like change. Personality affects the things people enjoy doing and even affects the way that they work. So you have to do your best to identify candidates' personality types and put them in positions that will be enhanced by their particular personality traits, such as an outgoing extrovert in sales. This is called *personality-job fit.*[7]

B:39
Negligent Hiring

I:7
Discretionary Assessment Methods

E:3
Employment Practices (Recruitment, Selection, Placement)

WORK
APPLICATION 6-1
Select an organization you work for now or worked for in the past and give an example of how a mismatch of a job and an employee resulted in a negative outcome.

WORK
APPLICATION 6-2
Select a job you hold at present or held in the past, list each step in the selection process, and state if it was or was not used to hire you.

LO 6-2
Identify the three main types of "fit" in the selection process and why they are important.

Negligent hire A legal concept that says if the organization hires someone who may pose a danger to coworkers, customers, suppliers, or other third parties, and if that person then harms someone else in the course of working for the company, then the company can be held liable for the individual's actions

EXHIBIT 6-1   STEPS IN THE SELECTION PROCESS

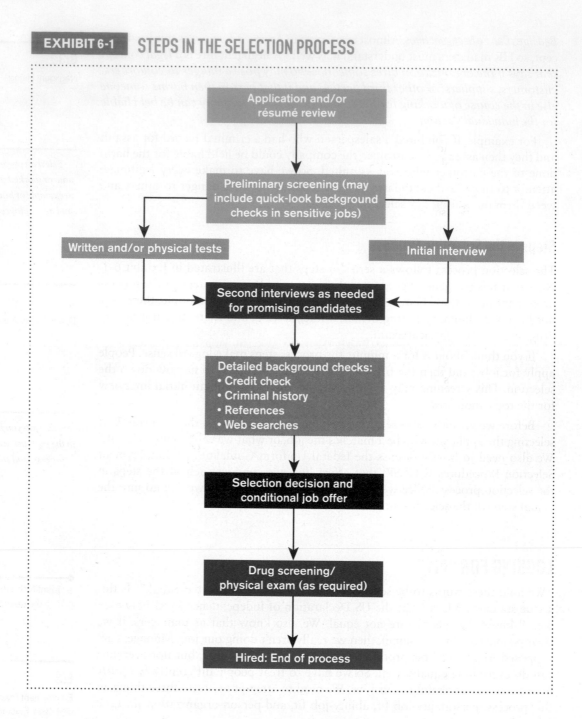

WORK
APPLICATION 6-3

Select a present or past job of yours and explain in detail how well your personality and ability fit or did not fit the job and how well you fit the organization.

Ability-Job Fit

All of us have a certain set of physical and intellectual skills, and no two people are exactly alike. Some of us are very capable at working with computers, while others are more capable at sales or physical work. Each of us is more skilled at some things than others.

Managers have to analyze a candidate's abilities and limitations. Using this information, the manager must hire the right people and then assign them to the types of jobs for which they are best suited. Here again, if we assign the wrong person to a job, we can easily frustrate that employee and as a result cause motivation and job satisfaction to drop, which in turn will likely cause losses in productivity. So we have to get the ability-job fit right.[8]

Person-Organization Fit

Finally, we have to assess the person-organization fit when deciding on which candidate to select.[9] Person-organization fit deals with the cultural and structural characteristics of the organization and how well the candidate will fit within that structure and culture.[10] If a candidate works best in a decentralized organization with strong individual reward systems, and if we are hiring people to work in a tightly controlled and centralized team-based division, then it is unlikely that the candidate will be able or willing to conform to the requirements of the company structure and culture. As a result, such candidates will likely be unhappy in this situation and will be more likely to leave as soon as they can find another opportunity that more closely matches their personality.

UNIFORM GUIDELINES ON EMPLOYEE SELECTION PROCEDURES

The Uniform Guidelines on Employee Selection Procedures (UGESP) *provide information that can be used to avoid discriminatory hiring practices as well as discrimination in other employment decisions.* Most often called simply the "Uniform Guidelines," they were created to guide employers in their efforts to comply with the federal laws concerning all employment decisions, and especially the selection process.[11]

LO 6-3

Summarize the major points in the Uniform Guidelines on Employee Selection Procedures (UGESP).

What Qualifies as an Employment Test?

The UGESP formalize and standardize the way in which the federal government identifies and deals with discriminatory employment practices. They define the concept of "tests for employment" that are used in either the selection process or other employment actions. But what is a *test for employment*? It is a pretty broad term. The guidelines define it as applying to

> . . . tests and other selection procedures which are used as a basis for any employment decision. Employment decisions include but are not limited to hiring, promotion, demotion, membership (for example, in a labor organization), referral, retention, and licensing and certification . . . Training or transfer may also be considered employment decisions if they lead to any of the decisions listed above.[12]

Although the guidelines specifically say that they "apply only to selection procedures which are used as a basis for making employment decisions,"[13] if we look closely at the definition of *employment decision* above, pretty much any employment procedure that we would use becomes a test for employment, which means that we need to follow the UGESP guidelines during every step of the selection process and all other actions with employees.

Valid and Reliable Measures

The UGESP also discusses the need for any employment test to be valid and reliable. In simple language, **validity** *is the extent to which a test measures what it claims to measure.* The UGESP notes that "users may rely upon criterion-related validity studies, content validity studies, or construct validity studies"[14] to validate a particular selection procedure. But what are these validity measures?

Criterion-Related Validity. **Criterion-related validity** *is an assessment of the ability of a test to measure some other factor related to the test.* For example, SAT scores are

Uniform Guidelines on Employee Selection Procedures (UGESP) Guidelines that provide information that can be used to avoid discriminatory hiring practices as well as discrimination in other employment decisions

Validity The extent to which a test measures what it claims to measure

Criterion-related validity An assessment of the ability of a test to measure some other factor related to the test

Employment tests must be designed to have valid and reliable measures, meaning the test should actually measure what it claims to, and that it tests these measures consistently for all participants. Otherwise, the test may not provide accurate results.

WORK
APPLICATION 6-4

Select a present or past job of yours and explain which one of the three types of validity would be the most relevant to that job.

SHRM

I:12

Measurement Concepts: Predictors/ Criteria, Reliability, Validity

Content validity An assessment of whether a test measures knowledge or understanding of the items it is supposed to measure

Construct validity An assessment that measures a theoretical concept or trait that is not directly observable

Reliability The consistency of a test measurement

designed to be one of the predictors of college success. In employment, criterion-related validity occurs when we can show a strong relationship between job candidates' scores on a test and on-the-job performance of those candidates after they are hired.[15]

Content Validity. **Content validity** *is an assessment of whether a test measures knowledge or understanding of the items it is supposed to measure.* So we have to show that "the content of a selection procedure is representative of [measures] important aspects of performance on the job."[16] In other words, our test has to be a valid measure of knowledge, skills, or abilities that are directly applicable to the job, such as an essay test that contains intentional English errors to determine how many errors the editor candidate can correct in a set period of time.

Construct Validity. **Construct validity** *measures a theoretical concept or trait that is not directly observable.* For construct validity to be applicable, we must demonstrate that "(a) a selection procedure measures a construct (something believed to be an underlying human trait or characteristic, such as personality and honesty) and (b) the construct is important for successful job performance."[17] For example, intelligence is a construct that is measured by an IQ test, and research has supported the IQ test's validity. Intelligence is a major predictor of job performance. However, the UGESP says that this method of validation is far more difficult to demonstrate than are the other two options, so it would be best if you can show that a measure has criterion-related or content validity. Large corporations often use personality, honesty, and IQ types of tests, but the tests are usually developed and tested with supporting validity by consulting firms, and there is a fee for every test given, so it can be expensive.

Reliability. **Reliability** *is the consistency of a test measure.* In addition to being valid, for a measure to be useful in any type of employment testing, it needs to be *reliable.*

Reliability means that the measure is consistent in some way—perhaps consistent when used by two different people (called inter-rater reliability) or consistent over time (called test-retest reliability). We want our measures when we are working with people to be reliable measures, meaning they should be consistent over time and between people.[18]

The Relationship Between Reliability and Validity. Let's put validity and reliability together. If a test is not reliable, it can't be valid. For example, if a job candidate steps on our company scale and weighs 150 pounds, then steps off and on again and weighs 155, the scale is not reliable. How much does the candidate actually weigh? A test can be reliable but not valid, but it can't be valid without being reliable. If a job candidate steps on the company scale and weighs 150 pounds and then weighs 150 pounds three more times, our scale is reliable. However, what if we place the person on a more expensive, better scale and the person weighs 155? Then our scale is reliable but not valid because it doesn't accurately measure a person's weight.

Now that we understand that we need to select for fit and follow the UGESP, we are ready to discuss the selection steps illustrated in Exhibit 6-1.

6-1 APPLYING THE CONCEPT

Validity and Reliability

Write the letter corresponding to each of the following before the situation in which it is discussed.

  a. criterion-related validity

  b. content validity

  c. construct validity

  d. reliability

_____ 1. A job candidate failed a job application test, but she claims that the test is not fair and that she can do the job. What type of evidence do you need to ensure that the test is in fact a good predictor of job performance?

_____ 2. You are running a law firm and require all your lawyers to pass the bar exam. What does the bar exam need to do to indicate it is a good test?

_____ 3. You have developed a new system for predicting future company sales. Your boss wants some proof that it works.

_____ 4. An NFL team makes a recruit take an intelligence test. The recruit's score is below the acceptable level, so the team refuses to hire the player. The player complains, stating that his intelligence score has nothing to do with playing football. What evidence do you need to support not hiring the player?

_____ 5. You decided to let the job candidate in situation 1 above take the application test again. The next day she took the test again, and the score was within a couple of points of her score on the first test. So you again decide not to hire her. What evidence do you need to support this decision?

APPLICATIONS AND PRELIMINARY SCREENING

The first step in the selection process is to get job applicants to fill out an application or send in their résumé. Then we do preliminary screening that may include a quick background check, testing, and initial interviewing to narrow down the applicants to the best matches, or fit, for the job. Let's discuss the application and résumé and what you generally can and can't ask during the pre-employment inquiries.

Applications and Résumés

Candidates are typically asked to complete an application form to provide biographical data.[19] We need data to aid in selecting the best person for the job.[20] Even in cases where résumés are appropriate, many companies today require a completed application in order to be able to compare candidates easier because the information is in a standard format; this is needed for computer scanning of applications, which is commonly used in large organizations. The application and/or résumé allows us to identify your basic skill set, background, work history, education, and other general information.

Whether it is an application or a résumé, we need to verify the information. There is anecdotal evidence from professional recruiters and background screeners that between one third and one half of all applications and résumés include significant fictitious information.[21] And companies have started to check these documents much more thoroughly because they know that many of their applicants will embellish and outright lie—and the problem has gotten worse over the years.[22]

Pre-employment Inquiries

On a job application or during an interview, no member of an organization should ask any questions that can be used to illegally discriminate against an applicant, unless the questions are bona fide occupational qualifications (BFOQs). Exhibit 6-2 lists some information on what generally can and cannot be asked during the selection process.

LO 6-4

Discuss the use of applications and résumés as selection tools.

SHRM

I:6

Initial Assessment Methods: Résumés, etc.

EXHIBIT 6-2   PRE-EMPLOYMENT INQUIRIES

Topic	Generally Acceptable	Generally Unacceptable or Risky
Name	Current legal name and whether the candidate has ever worked under a different name	Maiden name or whether the person has ever changed their name
Address	Current residence	Whether the candidate owns or rents their home
Age	Only whether the candidate's age is within a certain range (if required for a particular job); for example, an employee may need to be 21 to serve alcoholic beverages	How old are you? What is your date of birth? Can you provide a birth certificate? How much longer do you plan to work before retiring?
Sex	Candidate to indicate sex on an application only if sex is a BFOQ	Candidate's sexual preference, orientation or gender identity
Marital and Family Status	None	Specific questions about marital status or any question regarding children or other family issues
National Origin, Citizenship, or Race	Whether the candidate is legally eligible to work in the United States, and whether the candidate can provide proof of status if hired	Specific questions about national origin, citizenship, or race
Language	What languages the candidate speaks and/or writes; can ask candidate to identify specific language(s) if these are BFOQs	What language the candidate speaks when not on the job or how the candidate learned the language
Criminal Record	Whether the candidate has been convicted of a felony; if the answer is yes, can ask other information about the conviction if the conviction is job-related	Whether the candidate has ever been arrested (an arrest does not prove guilt), or charged with a crime
Height and Weight	Generally none unless a BFOQ	Candidate's height or weight if these are not BFOQs
Religion	None unless a BFOQ	Candidate's religious preference, affiliation, or denomination if not a BFOQ
Education and Work Experience	Academic degrees or other professional credentials if information is job related	For information that is not job related
References	Names of people who can verify applicant's training and experience	A reference from a religious leader
Military Record	Information about candidate's military service	Dates and conditions of discharge from the military; draft classification; National Guard or reserve unit of candidate
Organizations	About membership in job-related organizations, such as unions or professional or trade associations	About membership in any non-job-related organization
Disabilities	Are you capable of performing the essential tasks of the job with or without any accommodation?	General questions about disabilities or medical condition

6-2 APPLYING THE CONCEPT

Pre-employment Questions

Using Exhibit 6-2 and the general guideline not to ask any questions that are not job related unless they are BFOQs, identify whether each question can or cannot be asked on an application form or during a job interview.

  a. Legal (can ask)

  b. Illegal (cannot ask during pre-employment)

_____ 6. What languages do you speak?

_____ 7. Are you married or single?

_____ 8. How many children do you have?

_____ 9. So you want to be a truck driver. Are you a member of the Teamsters Union representing truck drivers?

_____ 10. Are you straight or a homosexual?

_____ 11. Have you ever belonged to a union?

_____ 12. What is your date of birth?

_____ 13. Have you been arrested for stealing on the job?

_____ 14. Do you own your own car?

_____ 15. Do you have any form of disability?

_____ 16. Are you a member of the Knights of Columbus?

_____ 17. Can you prove you are legally eligible to work?

_____ 18. Are you currently a member of the military reserve?

_____ 19. What is your religion?

_____ 20. How much do you weigh?

It may be hard to memorize the list, but to keep it simple, everyone in the firm that is involved in recruiting and selecting, not just HR, should follow two major rules of thumb to avoid discrimination and a possible lawsuit:

1. Every question asked should be job related. If the question is not job related, there is no reason to ask it, so don't.

2. Any general question that you ask is one you should ask of all candidates.

WORK
APPLICATION 6-5

Have you or anyone you know ever been asked an illegal question on an application form or during a job interview? What was the question?

TESTING AND LEGAL ISSUES

As we noted in Chapter 3, all of the federal EEO laws apply to "any employment action," so clearly, they apply in all selection tests. Managers must also know that there are some other significant laws dealing with allowable hiring practices. Let's complete a quick review of EEOC rules and various testing options.

LO 6-5

Recall the major types of written testing available as selection tools.

The EEOC and Employment Testing

The UGESP (covered above) were created to provide a "uniform federal position in the area of prohibiting discrimination in employment practices on grounds of race, color, religion, sex, or national origin."[23] The guidelines have been formally adopted by the federal Equal Employment Opportunity Commission (EEOC), the Department of Labor, the Department of Justice, and the Civil Service Commission. As such, the EEOC will use these guidelines any time it is faced with a discrimination-in-hiring complaint. If the EEOC investigates a complaint about employment testing being discriminatory, the company will have to provide evidence to support the validity of the test for the job being filled. If the company can't support that the measure is valid, it is likely that the EEOC will consider the test a discriminatory hiring practice.

Polygraphs and Genetic Testing

Polygraph testing can only be used in a few circumstances. The 1988 Employee Polygraph Protection Act (EPPA) made it illegal to use a polygraph to test employee honesty in most circumstances. However, there are two exceptions for corporations and other businesses (there are other exceptions for government and national security).[24] See Exhibit 6-3 for a summary of some of the exceptions.

 SHRM

B:32

The Genetic Information Nondiscrimination Act (GINA)

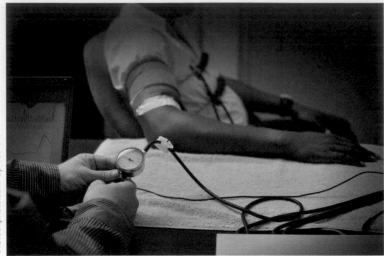

Polygraph testing can only be used in a few circumstances.

Genetic testing. As discussed in Chapter 3, GINA is the Genetic Information Non-discrimination Act (GINA),[25] which protects people from discrimination by health insurers and employers on the basis of their DNA information. We have to remember that this information is protected and not use it in selection processes.

Written Testing

Written tests can be used to predict job success, as long as the tests meet EEOC guidelines for validity and reliability. Today, written tests are a common part of the selection process.[26] In fact, 80% of midsize and large companies use personality and ability assessments for entry and midlevel management positions to help ensure the right fit between the job candidate and the job.[27]

Skills Tests. **Skills tests** can be either written or done in physical form. A written **skills test** is simply an assessment instrument designed to determine if you have the ability to apply a particular knowledge set to do the job you are applying for. Have you ever taken a written test on Microsoft Word or PowerPoint? If so, you have taken a written skills test.

Let's use the OUCH test to find out if we should use a test. Is a skills test *objective*? Can we give you a test on Microsoft Word, for example, and then answer yes or no as to whether you know how to indent and italicize? If so, the test is objective. Is a skills test *uniform in application*? If we give the same test to everyone in the same situation, it is. Is it *consistent in effect*? In general, the answer is yes. However, we can certainly design skills tests that are not consistent in effect, whether we do so intentionally or unintentionally, so we have to validate the test. Does it *have job relatedness*—a direct relationship to the primary aspects of job performance? If the answer is yes, it meets the OUCH test.

Personality and Interest Tests. **Personality** tests measure the psychological traits or characteristics of applicants to determine suitability for performance in a specific type of job. The Myers-Briggs Type Indicator and the Birkman Method are two common personality tests. Interest tests are similar, but they measure a person's intellectual curiosity and

 SHRM

I:9

Noncognitive Assessments (e.g., Personality Assessments, etc.)

Skills test An assessment instrument designed to determine if you have the ability to apply a particular knowledge set

Personality test A test measuring the psychological traits or characteristics of applicants to determine suitability for performance in a specific type of job

Interest test A test measuring a person's intellectual curiosity and motivation in a particular field

EXHIBIT 6-3	EXCEPTIONS TO THE EPPA FOR POLYGRAPH TESTING

General Exception	Specific Exception—can request the employee to submit when:
1. For armored car personnel; personnel engaged in the design, installation, and maintenance of security alarm systems; or other uniformed or plainclothes security personnel	1. There is an active investigation involving economic loss or injury to the employer's business.
2. Use by any employer authorized to manufacture, distribute, or dispense a controlled substance listed in Schedule I, II, III, or IV of Section 202 of the Controlled Substances Act	2. The employee had access to the property.
	3. The employer has reasonable suspicion that the employee was involved in the incident or activity under investigation.
	4. The employer executes and maintains a statement of the facts for a period of 3 years and provides a copy of the statement to the employee.

motivation in a particular field. If there is a legitimate reason for having a person with a particular type of personality or certain set of interests in a job, then we need to support the validity and reliability of the test for those personality traits or interests. If we can't support a relationship between these items and the job, then an applicant could potentially take the company to court for discriminatory hiring practices.[28]

Cognitive Ability Tests. **Cognitive ability tests** *are assessments of general intelligence or of some type of aptitude for a particular job.* Here again, we need to ensure that the tests that may be used are professionally developed, reliable, and valid indicators of a particular ability or knowledge set. Courts have upheld the use of cognitive ability testing, even when such testing had a potential disparate impact, as long as the ability being tested was directly related to a business necessity and was job related.[29] If you can't validate the test, don't use it.

Honesty or Integrity Tests. There are actually two types of honesty tests: pen-and-paper tests and polygraph tests, also known as lie detector tests—which as stated have very limited legal use. Dishonest employees can be negligent hires and often steal from the company or hurt its image, which can be very costly, so you want to do your best not to hire them. Honesty and integrity tests are certainly not infallible, and they can be faked in some cases. But the evidence supports that they have value in identifying people who may be less honest and allowing the employer to weed some of these individuals out of the selection process.[30]

Physical Testing

Physical testing can also help us select the best candidate for certain jobs. **Physical tests are designed to ensure that applicants are capable of performing in ways defined by the job specification and description.** Physical testing will generally be valuable where there are significant physical skills required to perform the job or where there is a significant safety risk, creating danger for the employee or others by working in a job for which they are physically unqualified. There are many types of physical testing, but we will limit our discussion to some of the most common forms.

Physical Skills Tests. They are designed to determine whether you have the skills and abilities to perform a particular set of physical tasks. Physical skills tests may include tests of strength and/or endurance, tests of eye-hand coordination, or other physical abilities. These tests can also be conducted in several different forms, including work sample tests, assessment centers, and simulations.

Let's take a closer look at some of the common forms of physical testing. **Work samples** *provide a sample of the work that the candidate would perform on the job and ask the candidate to perform the tasks under some type of controlled conditions.* A simple example of a work sample test might be asking the candidate to type a particular letter and then judging the speed and accuracy of the results.

An assessment center provides a more rigorous physical testing environment. **Assessment centers** *are places where job applicants undergo a series of tests, interviews, and simulated experiences to determine their potential for a particular job.* For example, at **T-Mobile**, you might have to assist a fictitious customer who is mad about his bill, or you might have to provide customers with information about new company services. So an assessment center used by T-Mobile might give tests designed to make candidates demonstrate how well they can use several different computer systems designed to obtain and communicate the information that customers need.

We can also use **simulations**, which allow us to put the person into a high-pressure situation but still control the environment so that we limit the danger and cost. Simulations are very valuable in cases where a real event could be dangerous, or emotionally taxing or cost a lot of money. Simulators and even virtual reality

WORK
APPLICATION 6-6

Have you or anyone you know taken a written test when applying for a job or on the job? If so, state the type of test and describe its content.

I:8

Ability/Job Knowledge Tests, Assessment Centers

Cognitive ability test An assessment of general intelligence or of some type of aptitude for a particular job

Physical test A test designed to ensure that applicants are capable of performing on the job in ways defined by the job specification and description

Work sample A test conducted by providing a sample of the work that the candidate would perform on the job and asking the candidate to perform the tasks under some type of controlled conditions

Assessment center A place where job applicants undergo a series of tests, interviews, and simulated experiences to determine their potential for a particular job

Simulation A test where a candidate is put into a high-pressure situation in a controlled environment so that the danger and cost are limited

environments are beginning to be used in many situations such as military training and teaching new doctors how to perform different types of surgery.[31]

Physical Exams. If the job will require heavy physical exertion, there may be a legitimate need to have individuals submit to a physical exam to ensure that they are healthy enough for the stress. (Think NFL lineman!) In other cases, we may be required by the state or federal government to have individuals who work in specific fields take a physical exam before they are allowed to work in certain jobs such as driving a heavy truck (DOT physical) or flying a plane (FAA physical).

However, we have to be very aware of the potential for discrimination based on disability if we require a physical exam as a prerequisite to work in our organization, so make sure any physical test is valid or don't use it.

Drug Testing. Although not required, most employers have the right to test for a wide variety of substances in the workplace.[32] The primary reasons for drug testing will generally be workplace safety and productivity—substance abusers commonly have more workplace accidents, make more errors, and miss more days of work, which also places a burden on coworkers.

But employers need to follow some guidelines to stay within the law in implementation and maintenance of any drug-testing program they choose to implement. In general, testing must be done systematically in one of two forms: either "random" or "universal." Testing can't be selective in most states. In other words, we can't decide we want to test "Amy Jones" because we just want to. Testing can be universal in some situations (e.g., after a workplace accident or on initial offer of employment) and random in others (e.g., quarterly drug testing of a sample of the workforce), but it has to be one or the other and we have to specify which option we use in each situation.

Most states now require prior authorization for drug testing. In the case of applicants, this authorization is usually part of the legal notices on the job application. For existing employees, it will usually be part of the employee handbook. The drug-testing policy must include full-disclosure of substance abuse training, when testing will occur, substances to be detected, and disciplinary action if testing positive. The policy may also require the employer to "reasonably accommodate" employees who voluntarily submit to an alcohol or drug rehabilitation program. In most states, the policy is not allowed to exempt managerial employees from testing.

There continues to be discussion of recent state laws legalizing medicinal or even recreational marijuana and how this affects company drug-testing policies. The simplest answer is that these laws do not currently affect company drug policies. In each case where an individual has challenged a detrimental employment action (including termination for a positive drug test) in court, all the way up to the US Supreme Court (*Ashcroft v. Raich*), the decision has been that employers can "safely refuse to accept medical marijuana as a reasonable medical explanation for a positive drug test result."[33] Employers are also not required to accommodate employee use of medical marijuana under the ADA.

Fitness-for-Duty Testing. A significant number of companies today are turning to fitness-for-duty tests in place of more invasive drug testing. A **fitness-for-duty test** simply *identifies whether or not an employee is physically capable at a particular point in time of performing a specific type of work.*[34] Federal law notes that we can use a medical examination "if it is job related and consistent with business necessity."[35] For instance, some trucking firms use fitness-for-duty testing before drivers are allowed to take an 18-wheel truck out of their terminals. Another plus for this type of testing is that it is much more acceptable to employees than drug testing.

Testing, in all forms, can be time-consuming and expensive. Therefore, testing has to pay for itself through its ability to help you hire applicants who are in fact

Fitness-for-duty test A test identifying whether or not an employee is physically capable at a particular point in time of performing a specific type of work

6-3 APPLYING THE CONCEPT

Type of Test

Write before each job situation below the letter corresponding to the type of test described.

a. genetic

b. skills

c. personality and interest

d. cognitive ability

e. honesty or integrity–polygraph

f. physical skills

g. physical exam

h. drug

_____ 21. As part of the selection process, you will have to answer questions while being monitored by this machine.

_____ 22. A paper-and-pencil test is administered so that we can determine whether you have the right characteristics to succeed on the job.

_____ 23. You have to undergo an exam by our doctor to determine whether you can handle the job.

_____ 24. To get the drywalling job, you will have to hang, tape, and paste 10 sheets while doing a quality job, all in 3 hours.

_____ 25. Part of the selection process is to take our intelligence test.

_____ 26. Part of the firefighter test is to carry this 50-pound dummy up this ladder in 2 minutes or less.

_____ 27. You have to go in the bathroom now and put a sample of your urine in this cup so we can test it.

_____ 28. You need to take a test so that we can determine if you might get any known illnesses or diseases in the future.

a good fit for the job and the organization. It may save you time and money by preventing you from hiring and then immediately losing employees who are a bad fit, preventing negligent hires, and improving worker productivity by maximizing the chance of hiring good-fit employees. This justifies the investment in the test. So as an HR manager, you will have to make decisions about whether or not testing is a good investment in your particular industry and for helping you select the best candidate for the specific jobs you need to fill.

SELECTION INTERVIEWS

Remember that during the selection process, some of the usual steps may be skipped or completed out of sequence. While the initial interview may be skipped, rarely will a candidate get a job without being interviewed by at least one person. Many organizations today, such as **Nike, PricewaterhouseCoopers,** and **Google,** are using technology to enhance their ability to quickly complete screening interviews.[36]

LO 6-6

Explain the value of selection interviews, including the three primary types of interviews.

Interviewing

The interview is usually the most heavily weighted and one of the last steps in the selection process.[37] To get a job, you need to be able to ace the interview,[38] but as a manager, you will need to know how to conduct a job interview. So this part of the section can help you do both well. You can practice this skill in Skill Builder 6-2.

An important focus of the interview is to assess the applicant's fit (personality-, ability-, and person-organization fit). More than half of HR professionals rank culture (person-organization) fit as the most important criterion at the interview stage.[39] You can also practice your interviewer skills in Skill Builder 6-1.

I:10

Structured Interviews

Types of Interviews and Questions

Exhibit 6-4 shows the various types of interviews and questions, which we discuss in this section.

Many companies now use computers to conduct the first round of interviews.

Types of Interviews. Three basic types of interviews are based on structure. In a structured interview, all candidates are asked the same list of prepared questions. In an unstructured interview, there are no preplanned questions or sequence of topics. In a semistructured interview, the interviewer has a list of questions but also asks unplanned questions. The semistructured interview is generally preferred by most interviewers. It helps avoid discrimination (because the interviewer has a list of prepared questions to ask all candidates), but it also allows the interviewer to ask each candidate questions relating to that person's own situation. The interviewer departs from the structure when appropriate. At the same time, using a standard set of questions makes it easier to compare candidates. The amount of structure you should use depends on your experience as an interviewer. The less experience you have, the more structure you need.

Types of Questions. Developing a set of consistent questions to ask all candidates can help you objectively compare the candidates and select the most qualified.[40] The questions you ask give you control over the interview; they allow you to get the information you need to make your decision. Remember, though, that all questions should have a purpose and should be job related.

You may use four types of questions during an interview:

1. *Closed-ended questions* require a limited response, often a yes or no answer, and are appropriate for dealing with fixed aspects of the job. Examples include "Do you have a class-one license?" and "Can you produce it if hired?"

2. *Open-ended questions* require detailed responses and are appropriate for determining candidate abilities and motivation. Examples include "Why do you want to be a computer programmer for our company?" and "What do you see as a major strength you can bring to our company?"

3. *Hypothetical questions* require candidates to describe what they would do and say in a given situation. These questions are appropriate for assessing capabilities. An example would be "What would the problem be if the machine made a ringing sound?"

4. *Probing questions* require a clarification response and are appropriate for improving the interviewer's understanding. Probing questions are not planned. They are used to clarify the candidate's response to an open-ended or hypothetical question. Examples include "What do you mean by 'it was tough'?" and "What was the dollar increase in sales you achieved?"

Today, HR interviewers prefer behavior-based questions that ask candidates to describe how they handled specific situations. Laszlo Bock, **Google**'s vice president of people operations, noted in a recent interview that "what works well are structured behavioral interviews, where you have a consistent rubric for how you assess people, rather than having each interviewer just make stuff up." One of his sample questions is "Give me an example of a time when you solved an analytically difficult problem."[41]

There are two basic types of behavior-based questions: situational questions and behavioral-descriptive questions. A *situational question* puts you in a hypothetical

**WORK
APPLICATION 6-8**

Select one of your jobs and identify the type of interview you had to get it. Describe how the interview went in terms of its structure.

**WORK
APPLICATION 6-9**

Select one of your jobs and identify the type of interview questions you were asked. For each type of question, state some of the questions you were actually asked during the interview.

EXHIBIT 6-4   TYPES OF INTERVIEWS AND QUESTIONS

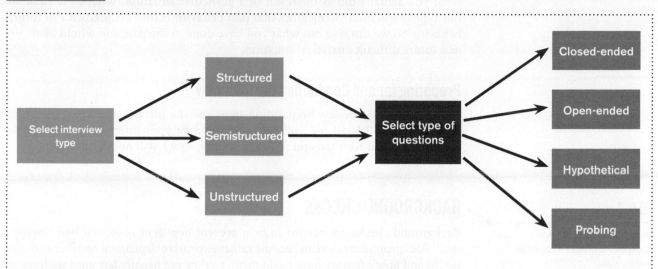

Common Interview Questions

Answering these questions prior to going to a job interview is good preparation that will help you get the job. Written answers are better preparation than verbal ones.

- How would you describe yourself?
- What two or three things are most important to you in your job and career?
- Why did you choose this job and career?
- What do you consider to be your greatest strengths and weaknesses?
- What have you learned from your mistakes?
- What would your last boss say about your work performance?
- What motivates you to go the extra mile on a project or job?
- What have you accomplished that shows your initiative and willingness to work?
- What two or three accomplishments have given you the most satisfaction? Why?
- Why should I hire you?
- What skills do you have?
- What makes you qualified for this position?
- In what ways do you think you can make a contribution to our company?
- Do you consider yourself a leader?
- How do you work under pressure?
- Why did you decide to seek a position in this company?
- What can you tell us about our company?
- What are your expectations regarding promotions and salary increases?
- Are you willing to travel and relocate?
- What are your long-range and short-range goals and objectives?
- What do you see yourself doing 5 years from now? Ten years from now?
- What do you expect to be earning in 5 years?

situation that you would likely face in the job you are applying for, and it asks, "What is your solution to this problem?" An example would be "You lead a team of marketing, operations, and engineering people working on an engineering design problem. Two of the engineers have significantly different views concerning the method of solving a problem in the design of the item. How would you interact with the two engineers to resolve the problem?" Using this question, the interviewer is trying to figure out what you would most likely do in real life to resolve a complex conflict within a team.[42]

On the other hand, a *behavioral descriptive question* asks about something specific that you have done in the past. Mr. Bock's question above—"Give me an example of a time when you solved an analytically difficult problem"—is an example of a behavioral descriptive question. It asks you to tell the interviewer what you actually did as the result of a particular situation. What's the value of this type of question? Remember that past behavior is the best predictor of future behavior. So we can find out what you have done in the past and would likely do in a future difficult analytical situation.

Preparing for and Conducting the Interview

Completing the interview preparation steps and the interviewing steps shown in Model 6-1 and Model 6-2 will help you improve your interviewing skills. The steps are straight forward and self-explanatory, so we will not discuss them.

LO 6-7

Defend the use of various background checks as tests for employment.

BACKGROUND CHECKS

Background checks are needed to help prevent negligent hires and bad employees.[43] Background checks can become rather expensive depending on which checks we do and how often we have to do them, so they are usually left until we have at least narrowed down the list of candidates to a final few, or in some cases even to the final candidate. We may then offer employment to the candidate conditioned on passing various background checks. Remember, though, that you cannot use a background check to discriminate in violation of federal or state laws.[44]

Common background checks include credit checks, criminal background checks, reference checks, and Web searches. In this section, we describe them, and provide guidelines on when to use them.

Credit Checks

B:36

Fair Credit Reporting Act (FCRA)

Although several states have recently put limits on its use,[45] one of the most commonly used background checks is the credit check. Credit checks are subject to the Fair Credit Reporting Act (FCRA),[46] which requires that employers disclose to the applicant that they will use credit reports for employment decisions. The act also says that if the information on the credit report results in an adverse employment action, the employer has to give a copy of the report to the person and inform the applicant of rights under FCRA, including the right to dispute the report. FCRA lawsuits have been on the rise over the past few years, with companies such as **Disney**, **Domino's Pizza**, **Kmart**, and **Dillard's** being accused of FCRA violations in hiring.[47]

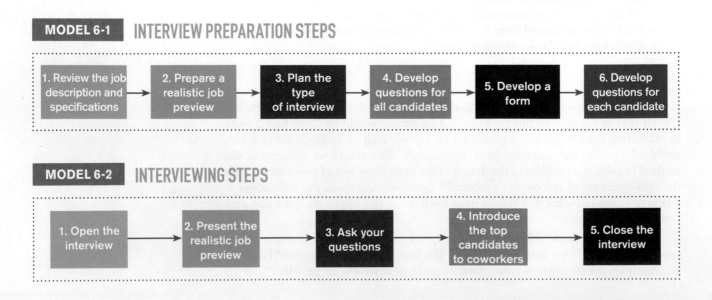

MODEL 6-1   INTERVIEW PREPARATION STEPS

1. Review the job description and specifications → 2. Prepare a realistic job preview → 3. Plan the type of interview → 4. Develop questions for all candidates → 5. Develop a form → 6. Develop questions for each candidate

MODEL 6-2   INTERVIEWING STEPS

1. Open the interview → 2. Present the realistic job preview → 3. Ask your questions → 4. Introduce the top candidates to coworkers → 5. Close the interview

SELF ASSESSMENT

Interview Readiness

Select a professional job you would like to apply for. On a scale of 1 to 7 (1 = not confident, 7 = totally confident), indicate for each question how confident you are that you can give an answer that would make a positive impression on an interviewer.

I am confident that I have an answer   **I am not confident that I have an answer**

7_____6_____5_____4_____3_____2_____1

_____ 1. Why did you choose the job for which you are applying?

_____ 2. What are your long-range career goals over the next 5 to 10 years?

_____ 3. What are your short-range goals and objectives for the next 1 to 2 years?

_____ 4. How do you plan to achieve your career goals?

_____ 5. What are your strengths and weaknesses?

_____ 6. What motivates you to put forth your greatest effort? Describe a situation in which you did so.

_____ 7. What two or three accomplishments have given you the most satisfaction? Why?

_____ 8. Why do you want this job?

_____ 9. In what kind of an organizational culture do you want to work?

_____ 10. Why did you decide to apply for a position with our organization?

_____ 11. What do you know about our organization?

_____ 12. In what ways do you think you can make a contribution to our organization?

_____ 13. What two or three things would be most important to you in your job?

_____ 14. Are you willing to relocate for the job? Do you have any constraints on relocation?

_____ 15. Describe a situation in which you had to work with a difficult person (another student, a coworker, a customer, a supervisor, etc.). How did you handle the situation?

_____ Total. Add up the numbers you assigned to each question and place the total on this line and on the continuum below.

105   95   85   75   65   55   45   35   25   15

Ready for the job interview   **Not ready for the job interview**

These are common interview questions, so you should be prepared to give a good, confident answer to each of them. Your career services office may offer mock interviews to help you with your interview skills to help you get the job you are looking for.

Credit checks will most likely be done if applicants will have access to any money or if they will work with the company's financial information. Credit checks may also be done with other employees to evaluate their personal responsibility—to see if they have a habit of being dishonest in credit transactions.

A history of not paying bills tells the organization that the person is likely to be dishonest in other ways as well. Does something like a bankruptcy on your credit report automatically knock you out of contention for a job? No. In fact, by law, the company can't refuse to hire you solely because of a bankruptcy.[48] However, again, if your credit report shows a pattern of failure to live up to your credit obligations, the company can and probably will use that information to remove you from the applicant pool, as long as state laws allow it.

Criminal Background Checks

All states allow criminal background checks in at least some cases. However, laws vary so significantly across jurisdictions that it is difficult to enumerate the circumstances in which criminal background checks are allowed. However, due to the issue of negligent hiring, most companies today will generally complete a criminal background check when it is allowed. Can or should a criminal record keep an individual from being hired? Again, it depends on what type of conviction it was, how long ago it occurred, and what type of job the individual is being considered for now.

We would have a much easier time defending the use of a criminal background check for an individual who would have access to products or funds that are easily stolen than we would in the case of someone with no access to anything of significant value in the company. Similarly, we would be more likely to be able to use a violent criminal history to rule out an applicant if the applicant would have access to children or other innocent persons who could easily be harmed by the employee. As always, we have to look at all the circumstances and make a decision based on the OUCH test and the defensibility of the selection tool that we are considering.

Reference Checks

Reference checks include not only calls to references that are provided by the applicant but also reference letters from employers, personal letters of recommendation, and possibly cold calls to previous employers and coworkers. But is a reference check going to be of any value, or are the references that the applicant provides going to say only good things about the applicant?

The basic answer is that a reference letter that is requested by the applicant is almost always going to say good things. The applicant will almost never ask anybody to provide a reference unless the applicant knows that the reference will be good. In addition, though, we want to check references that might not have been given to us by the applicant but instead by people such as former employers and coworkers.

What is a previous employer most likely going to tell you if you call for a reference check? The most common HR answer will be in the form of "Yes, he/she worked at this company, from (date) to (date) in (job type) job." This is to protect the company from being sued for providing defamatory information about the former employee—in other words, for hurting the individual's reputation unfairly. Over time, company lawyers have found that if companies provide more information than noted above, we can become the target of lawsuits. So most companies won't provide more information than they have to. A phone conversation may get you some useful info, but don't expect it in writing.

Web Searches

SHRM

Q:14
Social Networking

Finally, with the ability to access very large amounts of information, more and more organizations are using the Internet to do research on job candidates. "Googling" a candidate's name is becoming a standard practice in many organizations.[49] And it is truly amazing what the company finds in many cases.

Should social media be used as a selection device? HR departments are going to use the tools that they have available to get the best possible people, so social media will most likely continue to be one tool that is used in the recruiting and selection process. However, we need to be very careful to avoid using information that would be illegal in consideration for employment. It would be very easy to find out information on someone's religion, race, gender, or other facets of that individual's personal life—factors that would be illegal to consider in the hiring process—that might allow a company representative to make a biased and even discriminatory choice.[50] Most legal opinions seem to favor the employer in cases where there might be a question of violation of privacy if the employer is doing a check of social media to avoid negligent hires, but companies need to make sure that they are doing so in an ethical and legal equitable manner, or they can be considered liable for invasions of off-duty privacy.[51]

WORK
APPLICATION 6-10

Do an Internet search on yourself. Did you find any material that you or others posted that you would not want a prospective employer to find? Are your email address and telephone message professional?

Two ways that companies have found to avoid illegal bias are to have either an outside agency do the social media search or have a company insider who has no decision authority in hiring do that same search and bring only relevant information to the person or persons doing the selection.[52] This separates the search (and any items found that would be illegal to consider) from the selection process.

On a personal note, as a potential job applicant, make sure that everything on the Web about you is information that you are comfortable with a company discovering in a Web search. You may not be putting negative things about yourself online, but you also need to make sure your friends aren't, either. Employers *will* most likely do a Web search on you as a candidate in today's world. Also, make sure your email address and telephone message are professional for job searching.

Web searches should be used carefully in the recruiting process, as the results of a web search may reveal factors that employers cannot legally consider when making a hiring decision (such as religion, race, gender, marital status, etc.).

SELECTING THE CANDIDATE AND OFFERING THE JOB

Even when you follow all the steps in the selection process, you can't find out everything about a potential job candidate. You may want to just discover some basics that tell you whether or not the individual is a *really* good fit for the job. These might include the following three things:

1. Does the candidate have the basic qualifications for the job—right personality, ability, and person-organization fit?

2. Does the candidate actually *want* to do the job, or does this person want just *any* job? In other words, will the candidate be satisfied with the job and stay for some time and be a productive hire?

3. Is the candidate basically honest, and is this person telling the truth? If not, you could be looking at a problem employee.

LO 6-8
List the two basic methods used to make final selection decisions

I:13

Selection Decisions: Ranking, Grouping/Banding, Random Selection

6-1 ETHICAL DILEMMA: WHAT WOULD YOU DO?

Several recent state laws and executive orders at the federal level have brought the topic of LGBT individuals to the forefront of attention in many businesses, but as of the writing of this text, there is no federal law that currently prohibits workplace discrimination on the basis of sexual orientation.[53] A presidential amendment to Executive Orders 11246 and 11478 did, however, recently make it illegal for *federal agencies* and *federal contractors* to discriminate based on sexual orientation or gender identity, but not in other cases.[54]

Assume that you are the hiring authority at a company which is not affected by a state law or presidential order protecting LGBT individuals. You decide to complete a Web search of the two primary candidates for a job opening and find that one of the two is obviously and very publicly transgender. Information on LGBT issues are all over their personal Facebook and other social media pages. They appear to be very much an activist for the cause.

1. Would it be unethical to use this information in your hiring decision? Why or why not?
2. How would you use the information to sway your hiring decision?
3. Would you decide to hire this person if they were the best qualified candidate? Justify your answer.

The recruiter may know that by finding out these three basic things, the candidate will be a valuable addition to the organization and can be trained to do any specific job that is necessary.

There are two basic methods that we use to make final selection decisions for the organization. The **multiple-hurdle selection model** *requires that each applicant must pass a particular selection test in order to go on to the next test.* If an applicant fails to pass any test in the process, that person is immediately removed from the running. On the other hand, the **compensatory selection model** *allows an individual to do poorly on one test but make up for that poor grade by doing exceptionally well on other tests.* Again, each step in the selection process (interviews and background checks) is a test. Using the compensatory model allows the employer to rank each of the candidates based on their overall score from all of the testing. The employer can also group candidates based on this same information.

Hiring

So after all selection activities are completed, compare each candidate's qualifications to the job specifications, identify whether or not this person really wants to do the job, and analyze whether or not the individual has been basically honest during the selection process. Do all this to determine who would be the best fit for the job. Be sure to get coworkers' impressions of each candidate when appropriate because they will have to work and get along with whomever you hire (person-organization fit), and they can tell you if they think the person fits and if they want the person on their team or not. Diversity should also be considered when selecting a candidate.

To bring the selection process to an end, contact the best candidate and offer that person the job. If the candidate does not accept the job or accepts but leaves after a short period of time, you can frequently offer the next-best candidate the job.

TRENDS AND ISSUES IN HRM

Let's take a brief look at the issue of selection with a global workforce and the use of HRIS in the selection process. Each of these issues has affected the process of selection in a significant way during the past decade, which in turn has caused HR managers to change the way they work.

Selection With a Global Workforce

HR has to be very careful not to violate any laws when recruiting and selecting anyone locally and especially internationally. There are several issues of significance when selecting individuals from all over the world. The first major issue is the process of immigration and work visas. Each country has its own requirements for immigration and for foreign workers who want to gain employment in that country. The HR manager is typically the responsible individual for identifying the requirements and making sure that the individual fulfills them.

The organization, through the HR department, is typically responsible for assisting the individual with filling out the forms and in many cases for sponsoring the individual's work visa. The most common type of professional work visa in the United States is the H-1B visa for professional employees. The HR department also has to maintain records of the company's employees showing a legal right to work in the United States in accordance with the Immigration Reform and Control Act of 1986.

In addition to the immigration and visa requirements, organizations that hire workers in other countries face issues with the selection process itself. How difficult is it to go through the process of identification of recruits, selection testing,

Multiple-hurdle selection model Model requiring that each applicant must pass a particular selection test in order to go on to the next test

Compensatory selection model Model allowing an individual to do poorly on one test but make up for that poor grade by doing exceptionally well on other tests

interviewing, and the other pieces of the selection process? In many cases, the HR representative may never even see the individual who's being hired. There may also be a language barrier, and there are almost certainly cultural differences between the candidate's home country and the organization in the hiring country. Each of these barriers must be overcome, and every company handles these issues a little bit differently. However, the HR managers must understand and be able to work within the global hiring environment.

HRIS and the Selection Process

Human resource information systems (HRIS) continue to become increasingly valuable to the organization in all HRM functions, including the selection process. HRIS allow the organization to automate many of the selection processes such as applications, initial screening, testing, interviewing, and corresponding with the candidate. The application process can even be varied for different types of jobs within the organization. Once the applications are in, many of the systems can automatically alert each applicant to the need to log in to the company's site for any initial testing that may be required for the position. The system can be set up to score the testing and provide the HR representative with a list of the highest-scoring candidates.

As you can quickly see, the HRIS can save significant amounts of money and time in the selection process. In addition, the fact that the initial application and testing are done in an automated form allows the organization to limit any human bias that might occur from face-to-face interaction between the HR representative and the candidate, which is obviously something that the HR department needs to be concerned with.

Get the edge on your studies at **edge.sagepub.com/fundamentalsofhrm**

Read the chapter and then take advantage of the open-access site to

- take a quiz to find out what you've mastered;
- test your knowledge with key term flashcards;
- watch videos to capture key chapter content.

REVIEW, **PRACTICE**, and **IMPROVE** your critical thinking with the tools and resources at **SAGE edge**.

$SAGE edge™

• • • CHAPTER SUMMARY

6-1 **Describe why the selection process is so important to the company.**

Selection is important primarily because we need the best possible person in each job in order to maximize productivity. Unproductive members of the organization can cause lower motivation and job satisfaction in all of a company's employees. Second, organizations have a responsibility to avoid negligent hires—people who may pose a danger to others within the organization. The company can incur legal liability if we don't screen potential applicants carefully.

6-2 **Identify the three main types of "fit" in the selection process and why they are important.**

The three types of fit are personality-job fit, ability-job fit, and person-job fit. They are important because managers are supposed to get the best productivity out of their workforce. But not everyone can do everything equally well, so managers have to treat people differently, but fairly, in order to put the right person in the right job. They do this by assessing the three types of fit between the person and the company.

6-3   Summarize the major points in the Uniform Guidelines on Employee Selection Procedures (UGESP).

The UGESP provides guidelines on how to avoid discriminatory hiring practices. It identifies what the federal government considers to be an employment test and how those tests can be used in making employment decisions. The UGESP also identifies the acceptable types of validity that can be used to validate employment tests, and it notes that these tests must be reliable.

6-4   Discuss the use of applications and résumés as selection tools.

Applications and résumés are used in a fairly interchangeable manner, except that the application gives the company information on the applicant that is in a standard format. This makes it easier to quickly scan and evaluate the different applicants. Applications also typically have some legal language or disclosures that must be agreed to by the applicant. Both documents should be used to review and verify both the work experience and the education of the applicant. This experience and education should always be verified, though, because evidence shows that a high percentage of people exaggerate or lie on applications and résumés.

6-5   Recall the major types of written testing available as selection tools.

The major types of written tests are *skills tests*, which evaluate the candidates' ability to apply their knowledge to a specific type of problem; *personality tests*, which evaluate the applicants' personal traits or characteristics so that they can be matched up with appropriate types of jobs; *interest tests,* which identify what an applicant is interested in and therefore most likely motivated to learn; *cognitive ability tests,* which are assessments of intelligence or aptitude for a specific type of work; and *honesty or integrity tests,* which evaluate the individual's philosophy concerning theft and other forms of dishonesty.

6-6   Explain the value of selection interviews, including the three primary types of interviews.

The interview gives the manager a chance to make a face-to-face assessment of the candidate, including the person's ability to communicate, and personality, appearance, and motivation. It also gives the candidate a chance to learn about the job and the organization. The three primary types of interviews are the *unstructured interview*, in which the interviewer has no preplanned questions or topics; the *semistructured interview*, where the interviewer may ask both planned and unplanned questions; and the *structured interview*, where all candidates are asked the same set of questions. Most interviewers prefer the semistructured interview.

6-7   Defend the use of various background checks as tests for employment.

Credit checks are one of the most commonly used background checks. They should not automatically disqualify a person for a job, but if a credit report shows a pattern of dishonesty, then it can be valuable as a tool for selection. Criminal background checks may or may not be allowed by state law. Any criminal conviction should have something to do with the essential job functions, or we should not use it to disqualify an individual. Reference checks will usually not provide a lot of information, but we should complete them anyway in case they do provide valuable information. And, finally, Web searches frequently turn up information on the morals, values, or honesty of potential employees; companies use these when they are allowed under state and local laws.

6-8   List the two basic methods used to make final selection decisions.

There are two basic methods that can be used to make final selection decisions for the organization. The *multiple-hurdle selection model* requires that each applicant must pass a particular selection test in order to go on to the next test. If an applicant fails to pass any test in the process, that person is immediately removed from the running. The *compensatory selection model* allows an individual to do poorly on one test but make up for that poor grade by doing exceptionally well on other tests. Using the compensatory model allows the employer to rank each of the candidates based on their overall score from all of the testing.

6-9   Define the key terms found in the chapter margins and listed following the Chapter Summary.

Complete the Key Terms Review to test your understanding of this chapter's key terms.

• • • KEY TERMS

assessment center, 145
cognitive ability test, 145
compensatory selection model, 154
construct validity, 140

content validity, 140
criterion-related validity, 139
fitness-for-duty test, 146
interest test, 144

multiple-hurdle selection model, 154
negligent hire, 137
personality test, 144
physical test, 145

reliability, 140
selection, 136
simulation, 145

skills test, 144
Uniform Guidelines on Employee
Selection Procedures (UGESP), 139

validity, 139
work sample, 145

• • • KEY TERMS REVIEW

Complete each of the following statements using one of this chapter's key terms.

1. _____ is the process of choosing the best-qualified applicant recruited for a job.

2. _____ is a legal concept that says if the organization selects someone who may pose a danger to coworkers, customers, suppliers, or other third parties, and if that person then harms someone else in the course of working for the company, then the company can be held liable for the individual's actions.

3. _____ provides information that can be used to avoid discriminatory hiring practices as well as discrimination in other employment decisions.

4. _____ is the extent to which a test measures what it claims to measure.

5. _____ is an assessment of the ability of a test to measure some other factor related to the test.

6. _____ is an assessment of whether a test measures knowledge or understanding of the items it is supposed to measure.

7. _____ measures a theoretical concept or trait that is not directly observable.

8. _____ is the consistency of a test measurement.

9. _____ is an assessment instrument designed to determine whether you have the ability to apply a particular knowledge set.

10. _____ measures the psychological traits or characteristics of applicants to determine suitability for performance in a specific type of job.

11. _____ measures a person's intellectual curiosity and motivation in a particular field.

12. _____ is an assessment of general intelligence or of some type of aptitude for a particular job.

13. _____ ensures that applicants are capable of performing on the job in ways defined by the job specification and description.

14. _____ means that we provide a sample of the work that the candidate would perform on the job and ask the candidate to perform the tasks under controlled conditions.

15. _____ are places where job applicants undergo a series of tests, interviews, and simulated experiences to determine their potential for a particular job.

16. _____ allows us to put a candidate in a high-pressure situation but still control the environment so as to limit the danger and cost.

17. _____ identifies whether or not an employee is physically capable at a particular point in time of performing a specific type of work.

18. _____ requires that each applicant must pass a particular selection test in order to go on to the next test.

19. _____ allows an individual to do poorly on one test but make up for that poor grade by doing exceptionally well on other tests.

• • • COMMUNICATION SKILLS

The following critical thinking questions can be used for class discussion and/or for written assignments to develop communication skills. Be sure to give complete explanations for all answers.

1. Do you agree that selection of a top-quality candidate is a critical process in organizations, or do you think intensive training after the person is selected is more valuable? Explain your answer.

2. Should organizations be held liable by the justice system for negligent hires? Why or why not?

3. In your mind, how critical is the concept of person-organization fit? Why do you think so?

4. Are there cases other than the two instances noted in the chapter when companies should be

allowed to use polygraph tests on employees? When and why?

5. Do you feel that it's OK to tell "little white lies" on résumés and applications? Why or why not?

6. Are companies overtesting applicants by using the processes that were discussed in this chapter? Explain your answer.

7. Are background checks—including credit checks, criminal history checks, and looking at a candidate's Facebook page—too invasive? Explain your answer.

8. Is the use of HRIS for narrowing down the list of candidates and sending form letters, including rejection letters, too impersonal? Why or why not?

• • • CASE 6-1 NOT GETTING FACE TIME AT FACEBOOK—AND GETTING THE LAST LAUGH!

In August 2009, Facebook turned down job applicant Brian Acton, an experienced engineer who had previously worked at **Yahoo** and **Apple**. More than 4 years later, Facebook paid him $3 billion to acquire his 20% stake of **WhatsApp**, a start-up he had cofounded immediately after Facebook rejected his job application.[55] WhatsApp Messenger is a proprietary, cross-platform instant-messaging subscription service for smartphones and selected feature phones that use the Internet for communication. In addition to text messaging, users can send each other images, video, and audio media messages as well as their location using integrated mapping features.[56] How could Facebook, a highly successful firm, have made such a drastic mistake?

Back in 2009, Brian Acton was a software engineer who was out of work for what seemed like a very long time. He believed he had what it took to make a difference in the industry, but his career did not work out as planned. Even though he spent years at Apple and Yahoo, he got rejected many times by **Twitter** and Facebook.[57] Acton described the details of the interview process that he failed to do well in as follows:

First of all, interviewing a person for a job that requires technical skills is difficult for both the interviewer and the interviewee. Facebook is a highly desirable firm to work for and requires the best skills and talents from all of their potential employees. It is therefore not surprising that the selection process rivals, if not tops, any company in the industry. The process starts with an email or a phone call from a recruiter in response to an online application or [to] a recommendation from a friend who may work for Facebook. Sometimes, in the initial chat online, timed software coding challenges are set to find the best performers. If this chat goes well, an applicant will go on to the next level—an initial in-person interview or phone screening.[58]

In this next hurdle, the applicant will have a 45-minute chat with a fellow engineer/potential coworker, [with] whom he or she shares the same area of expertise. They will tell you about their job and what their role is in Facebook; then they ask about the applicant's résumé, motivation, and interests. Additionally, the applicant will be tested about his or her technical skills, coding exercises, and programming abilities.[59]

If successful, the applicant will be invited for back-to-back interviews. This part of the process is very grueling and stressful since all the interviews take place throughout a single day. The candidate will also be asked to manually write a program on a whiteboard to make sure that the applicant is knowledgeable about program writing. The goal in this final step is to see how one approaches a problem and comes up with a solution [that] is simple enough to solve in 10–30 minutes and can be easily explained.[60]

As a potential coworker, the applicant will be tested in terms of understanding and explaining complex ideas, with most tasks project related and constantly changing. This requires employees to possess a diversified set of skills. That is the reason why the applicant is not only tested in coding skills . . . but also to gauge enthusiasm and motivation. The applicant's leadership and decision-making skills are also evaluated as the company seeks to find someone who can make a large impact on the industry and make quick decisions.[61]

After going through this arduous process, Brian Acton was one of the engineers who received an email that "regretted to inform" him that he didn't get the position. Yet he stayed positive and took a different path, which led him to start his own company, WhatsApp. Teaming up with Yahoo alumni, he developed the most popular text-messaging application, and the company was sold to Facebook for a total of $19 billion in 2014.[62] This epic comeback proves how persistence and ambition play a huge role in job hunting, but it also proves how difficult it is to hire the right employee even when that person has the best skill set.[63]

Questions

1. The selection process at Facebook consists of three steps. What are those three steps, and which type of written tests are applicable for each?

2. If you were the recruiter responsible for the preliminary screening of applicants to Facebook, how would you prepare for the interview?

3. Facebook gives a battery of tests to the applicant along several steps of the selection process. What are those tests, what are they testing for, and how might Facebook ensure the validity and reliability of those tests?

4. Psychological testing did not seem to be part of Facebook's selection process. How might it use this testing, which tests might it use, and where in the process might it use them?

5. From what you have read, what are the criteria of selection employed by Facebook? Are they valid and reliable? How might this explain why Acton was not hired?

6. Agree or disagree with this statement based upon this case: "Not hiring the right person is still better than hiring the wrong person."

Case created by Herbert Sherman, PhD, and Theodore Vallas, Department of Management Sciences, Long Island University School of Business, Brooklyn Campus

• • • SKILL BUILDER 6-1 INTERVIEW QUESTIONS FOR USE WHEN HIRING A PROFESSOR TO TEACH THIS COURSE

Objective

To develop your ability to develop interview questions

Skills

The primary skills developed through this exercise are as follows:

1. *HR management skills*—technical, business, and conceptual and design skills
2. *SHRM 2013 Curriculum Guidebook*—I: Staffing: Recruitment and Selection

Preparation

Assume you are the dean of your college and you need to hire a professor to teach this course next semester. Develop a list of at least 10 questions you would ask the candidates during a job interview for the position.

Apply It

What did I learn from this experience? How will I use this knowledge in the future?

_____

_____

_____

Your instructor may ask you to do this Skill Builder in class in a group by sharing your interview questions and coming up with a group list of questions. If so, the instructor will provide you with any necessary information or additional instructions. This may be followed by the professor actually being interviewed by answering group questions. One of the coauthors prefers taking one question from each group at a time until all questions (without repeat) are answered or the time is up. Of course, I get the job every time.

• • • SKILL BUILDER 6-2 INTERVIEWING

Objective

To develop your ability to develop interview questions

To develop your ability to interview and to be interviewed

Skills

The primary skills developed through this exercise are as follows:

1. *HR management skills*—technical, human relations, business, and conceptual and design skills
2. *SHRM 2013 Curriculum Guidebook*—I: Staffing: Recruitment and Selection

Preparation

Assume you are the HR director and you need to hire a new college grad for an entry-level HR position. Because you are not a large company, you have a small staff and

the new hire will help out in a wide variety of HR functions. Develop a list of at least 10 questions you would ask the candidates during a job interview for the position.

Apply It

What did I learn from this experience? How will I use this knowledge in the future?

_____

_____

_____

Your instructor may ask you to do this Skill Builder in class by breaking into groups of two or three and actually conducting interviews using your questions. If so, the instructor will provide you with any necessary information or additional instructions.

Part III

Developing and Managing

7   Training, Learning, Talent Management, and Development

8   Performance Management and Appraisal

9   Employee Rights and Labor Relations

PRACTITIONER'S MODEL

⬆ Productivity
⬆ Satisfaction
⬇ Absenteeism
⬇ Turnover

PART V: Protecting and Expanding Organizational Outreach
How do you PROTECT and EXPAND your Human Resources?

Chapter 12	Chapter 13	Chapter 14
Workplace Safety, Health, and Security	Organizational Ethics, Sustainability, and Social Responsibility	Global Issues for Human Resource Managers

PART IV: Compensating
How do you REWARD and MAINTAIN your Human Resources?

Chapter 10	Chapter 11
Compensation Management	Employee Incentives and Benefits

PART III: Developing and Managing
How do you MANAGE your Human Resources?

Chapter 7	Chapter 8	Chapter 9
Training, Learning, Talent Management & Development	Performance Management and Appraisal	Employee Rights and Labor Relations

PART II: Staffing
What HRM Functions do you NEED for sustainability?

Chapter 4	Chapter 5	Chapter 6
Matching Employees and Jobs	Recruiting Job Candidates	Selecting New Employees

PART I: 21st Century Human Resource Management Strategic Planning and Legal Issues
What HRM issues are CRITICAL to your organization's long-term sustainability?

Chapter 1	Chapter 2	Chapter 3
The New Human Resource Management Process	Strategy-Driven Human Resource Management	The Legal Environment and Diversity Management

©PeterM.Fisher/Crave/Corbis

7 TRAINING, LEARNING, TALENT MANAGEMENT, AND DEVELOPMENT

• • • **LEARNING OUTCOMES**

After studying this chapter, you should be able to do the following:

7-1 Identify each of the common points in the tenure of employees within the organization where training may be needed. PAGE 163

7-2 Describe the steps in the training process and their interrelationship. PAGE 166

7-3 Summarize the four methods for shaping behavior. PAGE 168

7-4 Compare each of the major training delivery types. PAGE 171

7-5 Discuss the Four-Level Evaluation Method for assessing training programs. PAGE 175

7-6 List some of the individual and organizational consequences that can occur as a result of organizational career planning processes. PAGE 177

7-7 Define the key terms found in the chapter margins and listed following the Chapter Summary. PAGE 183

Practitioner's Perspective

Cindy told the story of Jennifer, who had worked in the same position for 10 years. Jennifer had always been a valuable employee, but lately, her productivity and performance had started to decline. Her supervisor, Mandy, finally called her in to find out what was wrong.

After some hesitation, Jennifer said, "To tell the truth, I feel like I am in a rut. I just don't get the same satisfaction from doing my job that I used to get."

"I wish we'd had this talk sooner," Mandy replied, "but now that I know how you feel, there is something we can do. Let's take a look at some of the training opportunities coming up this quarter. Tell me what training classes you might be interested in taking."

What if Jennifer and Mandy never had that talk? Do you think Jennifer would have remained at her job? Chapter 7 looks at the ins and outs of managing and retaining talent through training and development.

● ● ●

THE NEED FOR TRAINING AND DEVELOPMENT

After we hire new employees, we need to teach them about the organization and its routine processes and to do their new jobs. There is a relationship between training and job satisfaction;[1] it decreases expensive turnover[2] and makes it less likely that employees will engage in neglectful behavior.[3]

Effective training and development are investments, not expenses, as they pay for themselves through competitive advantage and increased performance.[4] This is why companies worldwide are investing heavily in training and long-term employee development.[5] As managers' skills should also be developed,[6] leadership programs and courses are currently popular.[7] This is why best-practice companies (e.g., GE, IBM, and **Johnson & Johnson**) provide leadership programs.[8]

Let's begin by discussing training and development and the difference between them, followed by when training is needed.

LO 7-1

Identify each of the common points in the tenure of employees within the organization where training may be needed.

● ● ● **CHAPTER OUTLINE**

SHRM

E:5

Training and Development

Q:16

Training Employees to Meet Current
and Future Job Needs

Q:2

Developing Human Resources

Training and Development

In this chapter, we will discuss both organizational training and the concept of employee development. The two are related but separate pieces of the organization's processes involving the management of its employees. **Training** *is the process of teaching employees the skills necessary to perform a job*. We train employees to provide them with the knowledge, skills, and abilities (KSAs) that they can put to immediate use.

Somewhat in contrast to training is the process of employee development. Both colleges and corporations have been criticized for not doing a good job of developing our business leaders.[9] This is one of the reasons why this book focuses on developing HR *skills*, not just knowledge. **Employee development** *is ongoing education to improve knowledge and skills for present and future jobs*. So, employee development teaches our workers skills at those tasks that they will need to know to move into higher level jobs. To remain competitive in today's dynamic environment, organizations must have employees who maintain up-to-date knowledge and skills, and development plays an important role in this effort.[10]

When Is Training Needed?

Training The process of teaching employees the skills necessary to perform a job

Employee development Ongoing education to improve knowledge and skills for present and future jobs

Orientation The process of introducing new employees to the organization and their jobs

HR managers should begin by completing a *needs assessment*. We will discuss needs assessments shortly, but let's review some common points at which we should probably complete a needs assessment and at least consider providing training.

New Employee Orientation. **Orientation**, usually called *onboarding* today, *is the process of introducing new employees to the organization and their jobs*. Our orientation introduces the new employee to all of the things that exist within the organizational society in order to be able to go about their daily lives. Onboarding socialization done effectively increases job satisfaction and performance and reduces turnover

SHRM HR CONTENT

See Appendix: *SHRM 2013 Curriculum Guidebook* for the complete list

rates.[11,12] Many orientations emphasize corporate values, culture, and strengths.[13] This socialization process is important to both newcomers and organizations, as the new employees learn the ropes and understand what is expected from them as they assimilate into the organization and attempt to become productive members.[14] Thus, job and career orientation have long-lasting effects on new employee job attitudes and satisfaction, behavior, work mastery, and performance.[15]

Orientation is an introduction of the person to the company. What do we need to think about when we introduce somebody to the company? We need to think about introducing the new employee to all of the things that exist within the organizational society that they are entering. The process is very similar to someone moving to a different country and having to assimilate into a new culture. What do people need to know in order to be able to go about their daily lives, do the routine things that they need to do, and provide for their own personal needs? Orientation should be designed to answer all of the questions necessary to allow new employees to integrate into the "society" that they are entering.

First, the new employee needs to learn the organization's policies, procedures, rules, and regulations—much like learning the laws in society. The second thing that people would probably want to know is how to act and interact with others in the new society, so in addition to introducing the employee to the job and how to perform it within the organization, we would want to talk to the individual about the underlying organizational structure and culture, plus where to go and whom to talk to in order to get certain things done. So when they have questions, who do they go to for answers? Safety and security issues will vary with the type of environment, but need to be covered.

They would also likely need to fill out paperwork with HR, such as home address and payroll information, and to get an employee ID. We also need to tell them about their pay and benefits, including whom to contact with HR questions.

Part of the problem of high turnover rates today is poor orientation. Effective orientation results in lower turnover rates,[16] so orientation should be provided over a significant period of time, anywhere from 1 to 4 weeks or even more, depending on the complexity of the organization and the jobs. Southwest Airlines has a 90-day orientation, Toyota has a 5-week orientation, and Honda has a 6-week orientation.

However, in most organizations, the orientation process is significantly shorter than this and one reason that our 21st century organizations suffer significant early turnover of new hires. If our new employee is frustrated due to not knowing how to do the job or how to fix an issue with pay, the likelihood of that person leaving the organization goes up drastically. Many organizations could significantly reduce new-hire turnover by modestly increasing the orientation period for new hires.

New Job Requirements or Processes. The second common point where training may be necessary occurs when jobs change in some form, either the same job or transferring to a new one. The change may be based on discovery of new techniques or technologies to perform particular work to make the work more efficient. The organization may require new processes or procedures or entirely new jobs. With any major job changes, we should conduct a training needs assessment, and when needed, an appropriate training program can be designed and implemented.

Remediation. The third common point at which managers need to investigate the requirement for additional training occurs when there has been some failure of an employee or some employees to perform successfully and meet organizational standards. Remediation *is the correction of a deficiency or failure in a process or procedure.* In remediation, we work to correct the actions of the individual or individuals responsible for the process or procedure so that they can successfully carry out the action in the future.

WORK
APPLICATION 7-1

Select a job you hold in the present or held in the past. Did you receive both training and development or just training? Explain in some detail why it was one or both.

WORK
APPLICATION 7-2

Briefly describe the orientation you received for a job. How could it be improved?

Remediation The correction of a deficiency or failure in a process or procedure

Employee Development for Advancement. Finally, we need to develop current employee skills and abilities so that employees can move into higher level jobs within the organization. Offering development opportunities generally decreases turnover.[17] Providing development opportunities and succession planning is the only way the organization can be sustainable over long periods of time. It requires identifying high-potential individuals for development and ultimately advancement into managerial and executive slots. So succession is an important function of the HR department. Organizations that neglect succession processes and employee development can find themselves at a competitive disadvantage when senior personnel leave the firm through either retirement or resignation. Although both training and development are critically important to company success, in this chapter we will focus more on training than development.

THE TRAINING PROCESS AND NEEDS ASSESSMENT

LO 7-2

Describe the steps in the training process and their interrelationship.

How do we know who needs what training, in what forms, and at what point; if employees are ready for training; and if our training has been effective? We answer these questions in this section, as we plan our training processes very carefully. We need to look at what's currently going on in the organization and how that differs from what needs to happen in the future to accomplish our strategic business goals. Once we do this, we can analyze the types of training that will be necessary to build new knowledge, skills, and abilities for our workforce.

Steps in the Training Process

This chapter is primarily organized to follow the steps in the training process. Let's take a look at how we go through the training process in Exhibit 7-1. Here is a brief description of the steps, and we provide more detail of each step throughout the chapter with titles similar to the steps.

Step 1: Assessing needs. We conduct a needs assessment to determine what training is necessary to improve performance.

Step 2: Selecting how to shape behavior. We select a method based on learning theories so that we can change employee behavior to improve performance.

Step 3: Designing training. We design the training and development based on the needs assessment. We must determine which training methods we will use to shape employee behavior, and we must select the delivery method.

Step 4: Delivering training. Before we actually conduct the training and development, we must select the delivery method.

Step 5: Assessing training. After we complete the training, our last step is to assess how effective the training was at developing the needed skills to determine our success at shaping behavior.

Interrelationship of the Training Process Steps. Note in Exhibit 7-1 that each of steps 2-3-4-5 has a double-headed arrow; this is because

The training process begins with assessing the needs of the new hire.

all the steps are so closely related and based on each other that they are commonly planned together before actually delivering the training. In other words, you are constantly thinking ahead and behind your current step in the training process. If the assessment of the training reveals that the behavior has not been shaped (changed) as needed, we may have to go back to step 1 and start the training process again.

Needs Assessment

The first major step in the training process is the needs assessment. A **needs assessment** *is the process of analyzing the difference between what is currently occurring within a job or jobs and what is required—either now or in the future—based on the organization's operations and strategic goals.* If management does not make the correct diagnosis—like a mechanic working on your car—they may create training solutions that don't solve the existing problem. So if a needs assessment is not done correctly, none of the other steps will be successful. We may not shape the behavior needed, the design and delivery can be wrong, training may not even be needed, and the assessment of training may not measure the desired outcome we wanted to begin with. Only by diligently going through the process of looking at that chain of events in the status quo can a manager identify where the process can be changed to improve organizational productivity and reach the organization's goals.

Employee Readiness

As part of our needs assessment, the manager needs to evaluate the employees who would be taking part in the training. Employees may feel insecure about their ability to learn, and they may therefore be unwilling to participate in training for new processes. We must also evaluate whether the employees are physically and mentally ready to go through the training process successfully. In other words, are they *able and willing* to learn?[18] Do they have the skills and competencies necessary to succeed in this training process?

Ability. We have to determine whether or not our employees feel that they are *able* to participate in the training process—do they believe they can do it. **Self-efficacy** *is whether or not a person believes that they have the capability to do something or attain a particular goal.* As Henry Ford said, if you believe you can or cannot do something—you are correct.

SHRM

Q:4
Equipping the Organization for Present and Future Talent Needs

SHRM

E:5, L:1
Needs Assessment

Needs assessment The process of analyzing the difference between what is currently occurring within a job or jobs and what is required—either now or in the future—based on the organization's operations and strategic goals

Self-efficacy Whether or not a person believes that they have the capability to do something or attain a particular goal

---

EXHIBIT 7-1   **THE TRAINING PROCESS**

1. Assessing the Needs for Training and Development
2. Selecting How to Shape Behavior Through Training and Development
3. Designing the Training and Development
4. Delivering the Training and Development
5. Assessing the Training and Development

WORK
APPLICATION 7-3

Describe your self-efficacy for a job you have or have had. How does or did your self-efficacy affect your job performance?

If employees feel that they are unable to learn, then the job of the manager becomes one of upgrading the employees' abilities if necessary and then convincing them of their capabilities. In addition, the manager has to analyze the true abilities and limitations of each of the employees who may participate in the training process. Each of us has physical and intellectual abilities, but at different levels. Managers must match abilities to jobs, so don't put employees in jobs they can't do at the desired level of performance—never set up a person to fail and be demoted or fired.

Willingness. The second major piece in the employee readiness equation is whether or not employees are *willing* to learn what's being taught in a training program. In other words, we have to determine their motivation to learn. There are many reasons why employees resist change, including if they believe the training is necessary or not. A significant part of willingness to learn is based on the support the individual gets from the people around them, including coworkers, supervisors, and even family members. So managers need to clearly explain why the training is needed and how the employee and organization will benefit.

LO 7-3

Summarize the four methods for shaping behavior.

LEARNING AND SHAPING BEHAVIOR

Step 2 of the training process consists of selecting how to shape or change employee behavior. To do this, trainers have to understand how people learn. So in this section, we begin by explaining learning. Then we discuss a common learning theory used to shape employee behavior. Next, we put the theory into practice in Exhibit 7-2 and discuss how to shape or change employee behavior.

Q:11 `SHRM`

Organizational Learning

L:3 `SHRM`

Learning Theories: Behaviorism, etc.

Learning

Learning can be many different things, but in a business, we usually need to *know* that our employees have mastered something that we are trying to train them to do. How do we know that they have learned a particular thing, then? We know because of changes in their behavior at work. So in our case, learning *is any relatively permanent change in behavior that occurs as a result of experience or practice.*[19] There is visible evidence that individuals have learned something because they *changed behavior*—the way they act, or what they do and say. There are three types of learning theories: *classical conditioning, operant conditioning, and social learning.*

WORK
APPLICATION 7-4

Do you like to learn new things? Describe your willingness to learn in college and to train on the job. Will you voluntarily sign up for company training and development programs that are not required for your job?

Operant Conditioning and Reinforcement

Let's take some time now to discuss one of the most common learning theories: operant conditioning and reinforcement. Using this tool, we will then show you how to cause employees to do more of the things that you need them to do, and do less of others behaviors that lower productivity in the organization.

Classical conditioning says we will react *involuntarily* to a stimulus in the environment if we associate that stimulus with something else. For example, if you heard a sound it can cause you to be afraid because you realize that the sound indicates danger to you. You have been involuntarily conditioned to the feeling of danger associated with that sound. *Operant conditioning* is B. F. Skinner's theory that behavior is based on the consequences received from behaving in a similar way at an earlier point in time. Skinner figured out how to get people to behave based on the reinforcement they receive. In other words, if we acted in a certain way previously and received a reward, we will likely repeat that behavior. If, however, we acted in a particular way and received a negative consequence (punishment), then we will probably not repeat the behavior. *Social learning* is experienced through watching the actions of another person and witnessing the consequences of those actions. If you see a person work hard and get a raise, you may also work hard to get a pay increase.

Learning Any relatively permanent change in behavior that occurs as a result of experience or practice

7-1 APPLYING THE CONCEPT

Learning Theories

Review the three learning theories below and write the letter corresponding to each theory before the statement(s) illustrating it:

a. classical conditioning

b. operant conditioning

c. social learning

___ 1. My parents continuously told me how to behave properly as I was growing up. Could that be why customers comment on my good manners and social skills?

___ 2. I got caught smoking in a no-smoking area and was given a verbal warning. I'm not doing it again because I don't want to get into more trouble and possibly end up losing my job.

___ 3. Shelly is a very hard worker, but I've never even seen her get as much as a thank-you for her performance. So why should I work?

___ 4. After seeing what happened to Sean, you better believe that I'm keeping my goggles on when I'm on the job.

___ 5. I completed the project ahead of schedule and did an excellent job. As a result, my boss gave me a sincere thanks and a $100 gift certificate to Amazon.com. I learned that it is worth putting in extra effort for the boss.

Shaping Behavior

We can use Skinner's concept of operant conditioning to shape the behaviors of the employees by providing reinforcement (rewards) or punishment or, as a third alternative, provide neither. Take a look at Exhibit 7-2 and the four methods of shaping behavior. We can break these methods down into a process of applying a reward, removing a reward, applying punishment, removing punishment, or providing no response to the actions of the individual. If we understand each of the four methods, we can use them to cause workers to act in ways that are conducive to the improvement and ultimate success of the organization. Let's discuss each part of the exhibit.

Positive Reinforcement. It is shown in the upper left quadrant A in Exhibit 7-2. Positive reinforcement *is providing a reward in return for a constructive action on the part of the subject.* For example, if our employees do something that improves productivity,

WORK
APPLICATION 7-5

Give examples of what you learned in an organization through classical conditioning, operant conditioning, and social learning.

Positive reinforcement Providing a reward in return for a constructive action on the part of the subject

EXHIBIT 7-2   SHAPING BEHAVIOR

	Reward	Noxious stimulus
Apply	**(A)** Positive Reinforcement — Apply a reward	**(B)** Punishment — Apply a noxious stimulus— Give bad consequence
Withdraw	**(C)** Punishment — Remove a reward	**(D)** Negative Reinforcement — Avoid or remove a noxious stimulus

Extinction (E) = The absence of a response, designed to avoid reinforcing negative behaviors
Shaping (changing) behavior:

A, D = Increasing target behaviors
B, C, E = Decreasing target behaviors

WORK
APPLICATION 7-6

Give examples of how an organization uses positive reinforcement, punishment, negative reinforcement, and extinction to shape employee behavior.

we give them a positive reinforcement bonus as a reward to encourage repeat performance of more suggested improvements. We should realize that positive reinforcement is the most commonly used method of shaping employee behavior when we train new employees to do their jobs and when existing employees need to learn new job requirements and processes. It is generally considered the best form of reinforcement but is not always the best option based on the situation.

Negative Reinforcement. Our second option would be to *avoid or remove* a *noxious stimulus* (the lower right quadrant D in the exhibit), a process called negative reinforcement. **Negative reinforcement** *is the withdrawal of a harmful thing from the environment in response to a positive action on the part of the subject.* Negative reinforcement is commonly based on rules, with punishment being given for breaking the rules. A rule itself is not a punishment; it is a means of getting people to do or avoid a specific behavior, such as coming to work on time. But if the rule is broken, punishment is usually the consequence, such as after coming to work late four times (rule) you get fired (punishment). We certainly don't want to punish employees for breaking a rule that they don't know exists, so during new employee orientation make sure employees know the expected behaviors and the consequences for breaking rules.

Punishment. In contrast to reinforcement, we may punish bad behaviors. **Punishment** is the application of an adverse consequence, or the removal of a reward, in order to decrease an unwanted behavior. One method of punishment would be to remove a reward (the lower left quadrant C in the exhibit) as a result of people doing something that they shouldn't have done. Think of the New England Patriot's Tom Brady being initially told he couldn't play in the first four games of the 2015 football season.

Alternatively, we can *apply a noxious stimulus* (the upper right quadrant B in the exhibit), which is also considered to be punishment. An example here would be suspending a worker without pay because of excessive absenteeism. By suspending the worker, we're applying a negative response. The negative response received by the worker is designed to cause a decline in the behavior that created such a response. So in other words, punishment can be the application of something bad (a noxious stimulus) or the removal of something good (a reward).

We should realize that punishment is not commonly used during training of employees; rather, it is commonly used when employees know how to do the job but just will not meet the job standards, or when employees break a rule and get disciplined for doing so. We will learn more about when and how to discipline employees in Chapter 9.

Extinction. The last option doesn't fit in the diagram itself, because it's the absence of reinforcement or punishment of any kind. **Extinction** *is the lack of response, either positive or negative, in order to avoid reinforcing an undesirable behavior.* You may have heard the phrase "Ignore it and it will go away." How does a lack of response cause behavior to be shaped in a way that we desire?

Employees will sometimes exhibit problem behavior to cause a reaction from the manager or fellow employees. The employee who exhibits the behavior may delight in causing others concern or consternation. For example, the male employee who continually asks his female manager about organizational sexual harassment policies in front of other workers to cause her discomfort as she explains the policy is most likely *intentionally* acting to cause her embarrassment. In such a case, the female manager may be able to ignore the stimulus behavior and provide no reinforcement. The employee's behavior will most likely decline or go away completely because it is not having the desired negative effect on the manager.

Negative reinforcement
Withdrawal of a harmful thing from the environment in response to a positive action on the part of the subject

Punishment The application of an adverse consequence, or the removal of a reward, in order to decrease an unwanted behavior

Extinction The lack of response, either positive or negative, in order to avoid reinforcing an undesirable behavior

Shaping (Changing) Behavior. If you understand these methods of shaping behavior, they become powerful tools in your managerial toolbox for changing behavior to increase performance. These tools allow you to *cause* your employees to act in ways you want them to and avoid acting in ways that are detrimental to themselves, their division or department, or the organization as a whole. Now let's discuss how to increase and decrease behaviors to increase performance.

Increasing Targeted Behavior. If we want to cause the behavior to increase, then we want to use positive or negative reinforcement (quadrant A or D in Exhibit 7-2). Reinforcement, whether positive or negative, is designed to cause an increase in the targeted behavior.

Managers can shape the behavior of their employees to improve performance.

Decreasing Targeted Behavior. If, on the other hand, we want to cause a particular behavior to decrease, we would use punishment (in either of its forms) or extinction (quadrant B, C, or E in Exhibit 7-2). Punishment and extinction are designed to cause a targeted behavior to decrease over time.

DESIGN AND DELIVERY OF TRAINING

Recall that back in Chapter 1 we identified four important HRM skills: technical, human relations, conceptual and design (decision making), and business skills. Essentially, all of the training methods are used to develop specific skills that can be classified into one of these four skills categories. Once we have completed our needs assessment and selected how we plan to shape behavior, we are ready to complete step 3 of the training process: designing the training by selecting training methods and then delivering the training. So in this section, we will present which

LO 7-4

Compare each of the major training delivery types.

7-2 APPLYING THE CONCEPT

Shaping Behavior

Review the following methods of shaping employee behavior and write the letter corresponding to each before the situation(s) illustrating it.

a. positive reinforcement

b. punishment—give bad consequence

c. punishment—remove reward

d. negative reinforcement

e. extinction

_____ 6. Betty used to give me that intimidating look when I assigned her a task she didn't want to do, and that behavior made me uncomfortable. So I just ignored it and didn't let her make me feel uncomfortable, and she stopped giving me the look.

_____ 7. You know the rules. That behavior is going to cost you $25.

_____ 8. You got that angry lady to calm down and leave the store as a happy customer. This behavior leads to keeping our customers. Thanks, keep up the good work.

_____ 9. If you don't stop breaking the pricing gun, you will have to buy a new one.

_____ 10. I know you like to get out of work for a while and get our lunches, but because you mixed up the order today, Santana will go tomorrow.

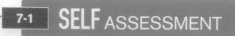

7-1   SELF ASSESSMENT

Your Learning Style

Below are 10 statements. For each statement, distribute 5 points between the A and B alternatives. If the A statement is very characteristic of you and the B statement is not, place a 5 on the A line and a 0 on the B line. If the A statement is characteristic of you and the B statement is occasionally or somewhat characteristic of you, place a 4 on the A line and a 1 on the B line. If both statements are characteristic of you, place a 3 on the line that is more characteristic of you and a 2 on the line that is less characteristic of you. Be sure to distribute 5 points between each A and B alternative for each of the 10 statements. When distributing the 5 points, try to recall recent situations on the job or in school.

1. When learning:
   _____ A. I watch and listen.
   _____ B. I get involved and participate.

2. When learning:
   _____ A. I rely on my hunches and feelings.
   _____ B. I rely on logical and rational thinking.

3. When making decisions:
   _____ A. I take my time.
   _____ B. I make them quickly.

4. When making decisions:
   _____ A. I rely on my gut feelings about the best alternative course of action.
   _____ B. I rely on a logical analysis of the situation.

5. When doing things:
   _____ A. I am careful.
   _____ B. I am practical.

6. When doing things:
   _____ A. I have strong feelings and reactions.
   _____ B. I reason things out.

7. I would describe myself in the following way:
   _____ A. I am a reflective person.
   _____ B. I am an active person.

8. I would describe myself in the following way:
   _____ A. I am influenced by my emotions.
   _____ B. I am influenced by my thoughts.

9. When interacting in small groups:
   _____ A. I listen, watch, and get involved slowly.
   _____ B. I am quick to get involved.

10. When interacting in small groups:
    _____ A. I express what I am feeling.
    _____ B. I say what I am thinking.

Scoring: Place your answer numbers (0–5) on the lines below. Then add the numbers in each column vertically. Each of the four columns should have a total number between 0 and 25. The total of the two A and B columns should equal 25.

1. _____ A. _____ B. (5)	2. _____ A. _____ B. (5)
3. _____ A. _____ B. (5)	4. _____ A. _____ B. (5)
5. _____ A. _____ B. (5)	6. _____ A. _____ B. (5)
7. _____ A. _____ B. (5)	8. _____ A. _____ B. (5)
9. _____ A. _____ B. (5)	10. _____ A. _____ B. (5)

Totals: _____ A. _____ B. (25)   _____ A. _____ B. (25)

Style: Observing   Doing   Feeling   Thinking

There is no best or right learning style; each of the four learning styles has its pros and cons. The more evenly distributed your scores are between the A's and B's, the more flexible you are at changing styles. Understanding your preferred learning style can help you get the most from your learning experiences.

Determining Your Preferred Learning Style

The five odd-numbered A statements refer to your self-description as being "observing," and the five odd-numbered B statements refer to your self-description as "doing." The column with the highest number is your preferred style of learning. Write that style here: _____

The five even-numbered A statements refer to your self-description as being a "feeling" person, and the five even-numbered B statements refer to your self-description as being a "thinking" person. The column with the highest number is your preferred style. Write that style here: _____

Putting the two preferences together gives you your preferred learning style. Check it off below:

_____ Accommodator (combines doing and feeling)

_____ Diverger (combines observing and feeling)

_____ Converger (combines doing and thinking)

_____ Assimilator (combines observing and thinking)

training methods to use based on which types of skills we are developing. Exhibit 7-3 presents the type of skills, the training methods appropriate for developing each skill, and descriptions of the training methods.

Before we actually conduct the training, in step 4, the HR department or other trainers also have to select the methods for training delivery. The choice will depend to some extent on what information is being transferred, as well as on the options that are available to the particular organization. We also need to look at the best type of training to use in order to maximize transfer of knowledge while minimizing the cost of the training process. In the next sections, we discuss our four options: on-the-job, classroom, distance, and simulation training.

WORK
APPLICATION 7–7

Identify and describe the training method(s) used to train and develop you for a job you have or have had.

On-the-Job Training (OJT)

On-the-job training (OJT) is done at the work site with the resources the employee uses to perform the job. The manager, or an employee selected by the manager, usually conducts the training one-on-one with the trainee. Because of its proven record of success, job instructional training (JIT)—a specific type of on-the-job training—is a popular training type used worldwide. See Model 7-1 for the self-explanatory steps of JIT.

SHRM

L:6
On-the-Job Training (OJT)

EXHIBIT 7-3	SKILLS AND TRAINING METHODS

Skills Developed	Methods	Description
Technical Skills	a. Written material, lectures, videotapes, question-and-answer sessions, discussions, demonstrations	Questions or problems related to previously presented material are presented to the trainee in a booklet or on a computer screen. The trainee is asked to select a response to each question or problem and is given feedback on the response.
	b. Programmed Learning	Depending on the material presented, programmed learning may also develop interpersonal and communication skills.
	c. Job Rotation	Employees are trained to perform different jobs. Job rotation also develops trainees' conceptual skills.
	d. Projects	Trainees are given special assignments, such as developing a new product or preparing a report. Certain projects may also develop trainees' interpersonal skills and conceptual skills.
Human Relations Skills	e. Role-Playing	Trainees act out situations that might occur on the job, such as handling a customer complaint, to develop skill at handling such situations on the job.
	f. Behavior Modeling	Trainees observe how to perform a task correctly, by watching either a live demonstration or a videotape. Trainees role-play the observed skills and receive feedback on their performance. Trainees develop plans for using the observed skills on the job.
Conceptual and Design/ Business Skills	g. Cases	The trainee is presented with a simulated situation and asked to diagnose and solve the problems involved. Trainees usually must also answer questions about their diagnosis and solution.
	h. In-Basket Exercises	The trainee is given actual or simulated letters, memos, reports, and so forth that would typically come to the person holding the job. The trainee must determine what action each item would require and must assign priorities to the actions.
	i. Management Games	Trainees work as part of a team to "manage" a simulated company over a period of several game "quarters" or "years."
	j. Interactive Videos	Trainees can view videotapes that present situations requiring conceptual skills or decision making.

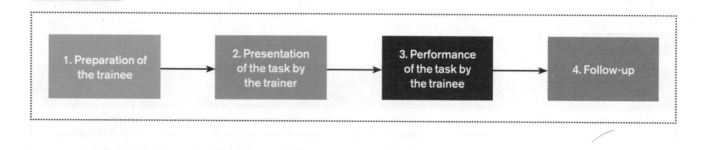

7-3 APPLYING THE CONCEPT

Training Methods

For each of the training situations below, identify the most appropriate training method. Use the letters a through j from Exhibit 7-3 as your answers.

___ 11. You want your customer service staff to do a better job of handling customer complaints.

___ 12. Your large department has a high turnover rate, and new employees need to learn several rules and regulations to perform their jobs.

___ 13. You need your new employees to learn how to handle the typical daily problems they will face on the job.

___ 14. You need an employee to conduct an Internet search to find out more about a new product you want to buy for the department; you want a special report.

___ 15. You want employees to be able to do each other's job when they take vacations.

___ 16. You want to improve your employees' ability to sell products to customers in the store so that customers don't end up leaving and buying the products online.

___ 17. You need to prepare middle managers to advance to upper-level managers. You are considering having them run a simulated company getting quarterly results.

MODEL 7-1 JOB INSTRUCTIONAL TRAINING STEPS

1. Preparation of the trainee → 2. Presentation of the task by the trainer → 3. Performance of the task by the trainee → 4. Follow-up

Classroom Training

Our second common training option is classroom training. A training course includes content, instruction methods, lesson plans, and instructor materials—and provides all these materials to a qualified instructor who will teach the class.

©iStockphoto.com/track5

Organizations can use classroom training to share knowledge, skills, or ideas consistently with a range of employees at once.

Classroom training is generally very good for consistently transferring general knowledge or theories about a topic to a large number of people. It is generally not very good for teaching specific hands-on skills because of the passive nature of learning in a classroom. However, it is effective when using the same equipment that is used on the job.

Distance or E-Learning

Our third option is some form of distance learning—also called e-learning—in either a synchronous or an asynchronous format. *Synchronous distance learning* occurs when all of the trainees sign in to a particular website where their instructor then interacts with them and teaches the topics for the day. In contrast, *asynchronous distance learning* is a process in which the student can sign in to the training site at any point in time and materials are available for their studies. The instructor may or may not be online at the same time as the

EXHIBIT 7-4   CAREER STAGES AND THE HIERARCHY OF NEEDS

Exploration	Establishment	Maintenance	Disengagement
Meet personal needs	Career entry	Personal satisfaction	Lower output
Identify interests	Building skills	Continue advancement	Coach/mentor as desired
Evaluate skills	Security/stabilization	Coach/mentor	Balance between work and nonwork
Tentative work choice	Work relationships	Improve policies and procedures	
	Work contributions		
	Advancement		

MASLOW'S HIERARCHY OF NEEDS

Physiological	Safety/Security	Social	Esteem	Self-Actualization
Air, food, water, sleep, etc.	Physical shelter, physical security, financial security, stability, etc.	Friendship, love, relationships, family, belonging to social groups, etc.	Social status, recognition, self-respect, reputation, achievement, etc.	Wisdom and justice—pass knowledge to others because *you* think it is valuable.

Disengagement. The fourth stage is the *disengagement* stage. This stage typically shows lower levels of output and productivity as the individual prepares for life after work. During this stage, because of the desire to balance nonwork with work activities, the individual may begin to choose to work only on efforts they feel are necessary or worthy of their attention. They may continue to mentor or sponsor other individuals' progression through their own careers. This stage goes from the early 60s to whenever the individual finally completely disengages from the organization.

Let's take a look now at the second part of Exhibit 7-4 to illustrate why career stages matter so much to managers in the organization, and especially to HR management. We have added Abraham Maslow's Hierarchy of Needs below each of the career stages. It's rather surprising how closely Maslow's needs hierarchy matches up with our career stages.

What are people most concerned with at the earliest career stage? They are typically most concerned with physical and safety issues, right? Are they physically able to get the *basic things* that they need in order to live and work—like money for shelter, food to eat, fuel for their car? Are they getting paid enough to *survive and be safe*? Then, as they get into the establishment and maintenance stages, they become more concerned with *social interactions* and then gaining *status and recognition*. Finally, as they move to the disengagement stage, they are more concerned with higher-level esteem needs such as *self-respect, achievement* of personal goals, and being able to do the *things that they think are important*. So, we see people go through these different motivational points in their life as they go through their career.

Now that we understand career stages and how those stages identify what might motivate workers in a particular stage, let's match those up with organizational HR strategies that are available to reinforce employee behavior. This will give us a general working model of how organizational HR strategies can create either positive or negative consequences for both the individual and the organization, depending on how the HR strategies are applied in a particular situation. Take a look at Exhibit 7-5. We have individual career stages identified on the left side of the diagram. On the right side are some of the major organizational

WORK
APPLICATION 7-9

Identify the level of career development you are on. Using Exhibit 7-4, but in your own words, describe your career stage and the Maslow motivational issues you are dealing with now.

EXHIBIT 7-5   CONSEQUENCES OF CAREER PLANNING

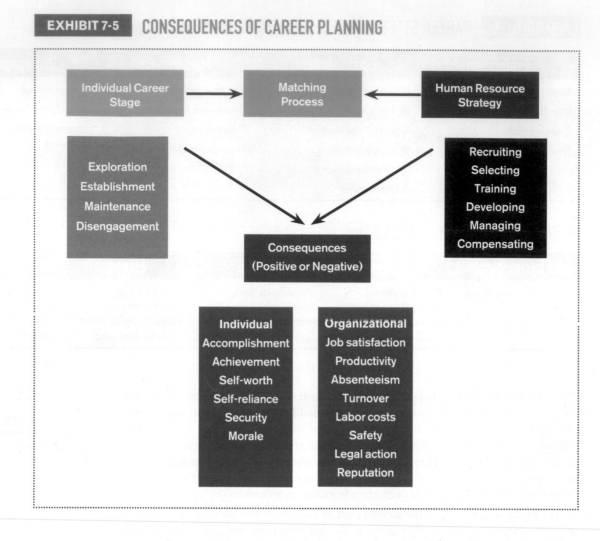

HR strategies that are available. Depending on how the HR strategies are applied, and based on the individual's career stage and motivating factors, we end up with either positive or negative consequences to both the individual and the organization.

If we apply the correct HR strategy or strategies to an individual employee based on the factors that motivate the employee, we can improve each of the major organizational dependent variables that we identified in Chapter 1—job satisfaction, productivity, absenteeism, and turnover. In addition, there are several other organizational factors that can either improve or decline based on the application (or lack thereof) of the correct HR strategy. These factors include labor costs, organizational safety, employee lawsuits, and organizational reputation, among others. So as you can see, if the organization fails to apply the correct strategy to motivate the employee (based on the employee's current career stage), the consequences can be severe.

On the other side of the diagram, the consequences to the employee are equally significant. If the organization applies the correct types of HR strategies to develop the employee successfully over time, individual feelings of accomplishment and achievement increase, self-worth and self-reliance increase, the employee's sense of security increases, and their morale is likely to increase due to higher individual satisfaction levels. Again, if the strategies applied are unsuccessful, each of these individual consequences can become negative. After looking at the model, it should become obvious that successfully applying HR strategies to individual employees based on their personal motivating factors and career stage is critical to overall organizational success over time.

So now you know why it's so important to create career paths for our employees within the organization and provide employee development opportunities. If we do these things successfully, we end up with a series of positive consequences for both the organization and the individuals involved. We have better productivity, better job satisfaction and employee engagement, and lower absenteeism and turnover. However, if we fail to do these things successfully, a series of negative consequences can occur that ultimately cost both the organization and the individual time and money. Employee development is a critical piece in the organizational puzzle in order to provide long-term success.

TRENDS AND ISSUES IN HRM

The first issue that we will discuss involves the "gamification" of training and development. Then we will briefly look at the ever-more-common trend of outsourcing training and development and other functions in organizations.

The Gamification of Training and Development

One of the trends in training and development in today's organizations is "gamification." In fact, the *Financial Post* of Toronto said it is a "revolution" in educating workers.[27] In the training world, gamification is the process of designing and utilizing video and other game technology to teach the player a business concept.

What is the value gained from gamification? The major advantage that is gained through gamification of training is trainee engagement in the training process, especially with the millennial-generation employees. However, we are finding that gamification also works with other generations of employees to more actively engage them in the training process. One of the key challenges with training always has been to get people engaged in the process. Using gamification is proving to be one of the most important measures to get people to learn.

Outsourcing Employee Training and Development

As we've noted earlier in the book, outsourcing has become the major topic of interest to organizations of all sizes. In fact, based on a recent survey by **ADP**, "91 percent of large companies and 80 percent of midsized companies" say that outsourcing one or more HR functions provides "real value."[28] Outsourcing of the training and development function significantly lags other functions in the HR department, though.[29] Even so, modern organizations must evaluate whether or not outsourcing of the training and development functions makes sense. If the company can reduce costs for training and development as well as improve the quality of the training function, it may make sense for the organization to consider outsourcing of these functions.

However, the organization must carefully evaluate all of the information in an analysis for potential outsourcing of the training and development function. Without this careful evaluation, significant mistakes can be made and large amounts of money may be spent without the organization receiving the requisite benefits from the process.

SHRM

L:7; Q:13
Outsourcing Employee
Development

WORK
APPLICATION 7-10

Select an organization you work for or have worked for. What, if any, training and development functions do or did it outsource—including bringing in consults to develop and conduct training and development? If you are not sure, ask the HR training specialist.

• • • CHAPTER SUMMARY

7-1   Identify each of the common points in the tenure of employees within the organization where training may be needed.

The most common points at which managers should consider workforce training include new-employee *orientation,* which is used to acculturate new employees to the organization and its culture and to prepare them to do their own job within the organization; when *processes or procedures have changed;* whenever there has been some *failure to perform* successfully (remedial training); or when *employee development* opportunities come up, allowing the company to develop current employees' skills and abilities so that they are able to move into higher-level jobs within the organization.

7-2   Describe the steps in the training process and their interrelationship.

The first step involves conducting a needs assessment to identify the type of training needed. The second step involves selecting how to shape employee behavior. The third step involves designing the training by selecting training methods. The fourth step involves selecting the delivery method and delivering the training. The last step involves assessing the training to determine if employee behavior has changed to improve performance—if not, return to step one. The steps are so closely related and based on each other that they are commonly planned together before actually delivering the training.

7-3   Summarize the four methods for shaping behavior.

The four options for shaping behavior include positive reinforcement, negative reinforcement, punishment, and extinction. Positive reinforcement involves the application of a reward in response to a person's behavior in order to increase the chances

that that behavior will be repeated. Negative reinforcement involves the withdrawal or avoidance of a noxious stimulus, or a negative thing, in response to a person's positive behavior to increase the chances that the behavior will be repeated. Punishment occurs either when a noxious stimulus is applied or when a reward is taken away in response to a negative behavior. Extinction provides no reinforcement, either positive or negative, to the actions of the subject.

7-4   Compare each of the major training delivery types.

On-the-job training (OJT) is done at the work site with the resources the employee uses to perform the job, and it is conducted one-on-one with the trainee. In *classroom training,* the organization creates a training course and provides a qualified instructor to teach the class in a single location at a specific time. *Distance learning,* also called e-learning, allows the students to sign in to the training site and provides materials to them for their studies. There's typically less interaction between an instructor and trainee than in OJT or classroom training.

7-5   Discuss the Four-Level Evaluation Method for assessing training programs.

The four-level evaluation method measures *reaction, learning, behaviors,* and *results.* In *reaction evaluations,* we ask the participants how they feel about the training process, including the content provided, the instructor(s), and the knowledge that they gained. *Learning evaluations* are designed to determine what knowledge was gained by the individual, whether any new skills have been learned, and whether attitudes have changed as a result of the training. *Behavior evaluations* are designed to determine whether or not the trainee's on-the-job behaviors changed as a result of the training. In a *results evaluation*, we try to determine whether or not individual behavioral changes have improved organizational results. This is the level at which ROI will be measured and evaluated.

7-6   List some of the individual and organizational consequences that can occur as a result of organizational career planning processes.

Organizational consequences include all of the major organizational dependent variables that we identified in Chapter 1: job satisfaction, productivity, absenteeism, and turnover. In addition, labor costs, organizational safety, employee lawsuits, and organizational reputation can either improve

or decline based on the application (or lack thereof) of the correct HR strategy. On the employee side of the diagram, if the organization applies the correct HR strategies, individual feelings of accomplishment and achievement increase, self-worth and self-reliance increase, the employee's sense of security increases, and employee morale is likely to increase due to higher individual satisfaction levels. If the strategies are unsuccessful, each of these individual consequences can become negative.

7-7   Define the key terms found in the chapter margins and listed following the Chapter Summary.

Complete the Key Terms Review to test your understanding of this chapter's key terms.

• • • KEY TERMS

career, 177
employee development, 164
extinction, 170
learning, 168

needs assessment, 167
negative reinforcement, 170
orientation, 164
positive reinforcement, 169

punishment, 170
remediation, 165
self-efficacy, 167
training, 164

• • • KEY TERMS REVIEW

Complete each of the following statements using one of this chapter's key terms.

1. _____ is the process of teaching employees the skills necessary to perform a job.

2. _____ is ongoing education to improve knowledge and skills for present and future jobs.

3. _____ is the process of introducing new employees to the organization and their jobs.

4. _____ is the correction of a deficiency or failure in a process or procedure.

5. _____ is the process of analyzing the difference between what is currently occurring within a job or jobs in comparison with what is required—either now or in the future—based on the organization's operations and strategic goals.

6. _____ is whether people believe that they have the capability to do something or attain a particular goal.

7. _____ is any relatively permanent change in behavior that occurs as a result of experience or practice.

8. _____ is providing a reward in return for a constructive action on the part of the subject.

9. _____ is the withdrawal of a harmful thing from the environment in response to a positive action on the part of the subject.

10. _____ is the application of an adverse consequence or removal of a reward in order to decrease an unwanted behavior.

11. _____ is the total lack of response, either positive or negative, to avoid reinforcing an undesirable behavior.

12. _____ is the individually perceived sequence of attitudes and behaviors associated with work-related experiences and activities over the span of a person's life.

• • • COMMUNICATION SKILLS

The following critical-thinking questions can be used for class discussion and/or for written assignments to develop communication skills. Be sure to give complete explanations for all answers.

1. Is the currently available workforce really not sufficiently trained to participate in knowledge-intensive jobs? Why or why not?

2. Think of and then list all of the items that you think should be included in a new employee orientation. Briefly justify why each item should be included.

3. Briefly describe a job you have or had. If you were promoted, which training method(s) would you use to train the person to do your current job?

4. Which one of the primary delivery of training types would you use to teach basic accounting to a group of employees? Justify your answer.

5. Have you ever filled out an evaluation form for an employee training class? Which type of evaluation was it? What evidence led you to think it was this type?

6. What management tools or processes would you use in order to evaluate your employees for remediation training?

7. Do you agree with the definition of a *career* presented in the text? Why or why not? How would you change it?

8. Which method of development, formal education, experience, or assessment do you think is most valuable? Justify your choice.

9. Identify and discuss two or three ways in which poor application of HR strategies (Exhibit 7-5) would create negative *employee* consequences.

• • • CASE 7-1 GOOGLE SEARCH: BUILDING THE PROGRAM THAT WRITES THE CODE TO FIND FEMALE TALENT

Google Inc. took Web searching to a much more sophisticated level when it offered targeted search results from billions of Web pages, based on a proprietary algorithm that allowed for greater customization than did prior engines like **Web Crawler** and **Dogpile**. Employing more than 50,000 people, Google generates most of its revenue from advertising sales. In 2013, its net income was close to $13 billion, and the company showed 60% revenue growth between 2012 and 2014. Added to that, Google has been on the top of the Fortune "Best Places to Work" list since 2012.[30] Google is one of the best firms at making employees feel welcomed and supported, but being in the technology field, the company had become a "boys' club," with women constituting only 30% of its entire workforce.

Alongside Google, other Silicon Valley technology giants like **Facebook, Yahoo,** and **LinkedIn** recently disclosed their gender and racial diversity ratios in their workplaces. On average, Google's workforce consists of more than 65% males, 55% whites, and 35% Asians. The gaps between these numbers are even wider in technology-related positions. As shown in its May 2014 report, it employs only 2% blacks and 3% Hispanics. Google admitted that this problem required immediate action. Google's sharing of demographic information is a promising sign that it is willing to change, but action speaks louder than words.

Google took quick action and performed its own search. It found that women were losing interest in computer sciences as a career at an alarming rate. Only 14% of the computer science graduates were women in 2013, and surveys indicated that less than 1% of women expressed any interest in majoring in computer sciences in college.[31] Google then recognized that it could not use traditional recruitment techniques to hire women since they were just not present in the labor pool.

Google also examined its own unique hiring processes and concluded that they were both difficult and tedious—women were not emerging through these processes, and Google could not just sit back and hope to gain new female employees from a labor pool that could not supply them.[32]

Google decided to be far more proactive in the area of women employee development and committed $50 million for both research and solution strategies. Its research indicated that if women were exposed to coding at an early age, they would more likely look favorably at a career path in computer science.[33] Google's research also noted that compared to the companies led by men, tech companies led by women achieved a 35% higher return on investment and 12% higher revenue.[34]

Google understood that its answer to this labor shortage, as well as to greater profitability, was to show young girls how interesting aspects of computer science could be, as well as how lucrative, and to inspire them to pursue a career in this field. Secondly, only 10% of the schools in the United States offered computer science courses, so access to this field was a major problem. To achieve its goal of more women in the workforce, Google initiated a project called "Made With Code" (MWC) that was designed to attract women to the sciences and in the long run diminish possible gender biases in its own organization, as well as in the field.[35]

MWC was launched as an event in New York City, with the participation of teenage girls from local public schools; famous female entrepreneurs; and many professional women who utilized coding in the film, music, and fashion industries. To increase exposure and inspiration, Google is working closely with producers and writers in the **Science & Entertainment Exchange** to have more female coders in movies and television series.[36]

With the MWC program targeting the people who normally did not have the access or the opportunity to pursue a career in computer science, Google provided accelerated tech-training programs to help them succeed in high-level tech jobs. Google did this by offering free coding classes online to pull extraordinary talent from the cities surrounding Silicon Valley.[37] It also provided workshops that fostered student collaboration on simple coding projects like 3-D printed bracelets. Research has noted that women thrive in team environments, and Google wanted them to understand that teamwork is the cornerstone of software development. To this end, Google gave an additional 3 months of free access to its Code School to women.[38] Google hopes that the outcome of its programs will increase younger girls' involvement in computer science and in the long run increase women's visibility in the profession and at Google.

Questions

1. What is a needs assessment, and how might Google use this tool to increase the presence of women in its workforce?

2. Some might argue that Google's "Made With Code" program has redefined the concept of employee development. Agree or disagree and provide an explanation supporting your position.

3. Explain how Google's particular situation demonstrates the relationship between employee recruitment and employee development, given the above discussion.

4. Explain how Google's "Made With Code" has become an integral part of its career planning.

5. How might the concepts of self-efficacy and reinforcement theory help us better understand schoolgirls' relative lack of interest in computer science?

6. Assume that Google is ultimately successful and receives more female applicants, whom it then hires. What suggestions do you have for managing this new talent pool?

Case created by Herbert Sherman, PhD, and Theodore Vallas, Department of Management Sciences, Long Island University School of Business, Brooklyn Campus

• • • SKILL BUILDER 7-1 THE TRAINING PROCESS

Objective

To develop your ability to conduct a needs assessment, to select how to shape employee behavior, to design a training program by selecting training methods, to select a method to deliver training, and to choose an assessment method

Skills

The primary skills developed through this exercise are as follows:

1. *HR management skill*—conceptual and design skills
2. *SHRM 2013 Curriculum Guidebook*—L: Training and development

Assignment

As an individual or group, select a job and write out your answers. Follow the steps in the training process below to train a person to do the job.

Step 1: Needs assessment. Conduct a needs assessment for the job by developing a competency model identifying the knowledge, skills, and abilities needed to do the job successfully.

Step 2: Select how you will shape behavior. Be sure to specify if you will use positive reinforcement, punishment,

negative reinforcement, or extinction. State the rewards and/or punishment.

Step 3: Design the training. Select and describe in detail the training method(s) you will use to shape the behavior.

Step 4: Deliver the training. Just select one of the four methods of delivery that you will use to conduct the actual training and describe how you will deliver the training.

Step 5: Assessment of training. Just select one of the four assessment methods and describe in detail how you will determine if the training did in fact shape the behavior.

Apply It

What did I learn from this experience? How will I use this knowledge in the future?

_____

_____

_____

Your instructor may ask you to do this Skill Builder in class by breaking into groups of four to six and doing the preparation. If so, the instructor will provide you with any necessary information or additional instructions.

• • • SKILL BUILDER 7-2 CAREER DEVELOPMENT

Objective

To begin to think about and develop your career plan

Skills

The primary skills developed through this exercise are as follows:

1. *HR management skill*—conceptual and design skills
2. *SHRM 2013 Curriculum Guidebook*—L: Training and development

Assignment

Write out your answers to the following questions.

1. Do you now, or do you want to work in HRM? Why? If not, what career do you want to pursue, and why?
2. If you want to work in HR, based on your self-assessment back in Chapter 1 or other knowledge, list your highest levels of interest in HR disciplines. If not, what are your highest levels of interests, functions, or disciplines within your chosen career?
3. What methods of employee development (formal education, experience-internships and jobs, and assessment) are you using to prepare for your career?

Apply It

What did I learn from this exercise? How will I use this knowledge in the future?

_____

_____

_____

Your instructor may ask you to do this Skill Builder in class by breaking into groups of two to three and discussing your career plans. If so, the instructor will provide you with any necessary information or additional instructions.

©iStockphoto.com/monkeybusinessimages

©iStockphoto.com/laflor

8 PERFORMANCE MANAGEMENT AND APPRAISAL

Master the content.

Use the online study tools at
edge.sagepub.com/fundamentalsofhrm
to review, practice, and improve your skills.

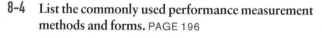
⑤SAGE edge™

Practitioner's Perspective

Cindy remarks that although performance evaluation can be uncomfortable for both managers and employees, failure to accurately and honestly evaluate performance is never a good choice. She recalls the time that a supervisor, Annette, came to see her.

"I want to fire Christine," Annette said angrily. "She entered the wrong invoice numbers again, and now I have to stay and correct her mistakes—again!"

"Is this common?" Cindy asked. "Have you expressed your concerns or initiated a performance improvement plan?"

"She does it all the time, but I usually don't catch it until after she is off for the day," Annette replied. "By morning, it doesn't seem worth my time go over it with her."

"How about her performance evaluation?" she asked next. "Have you brought Christine's poor performance to her attention at her annual evaluation?"

"Well, no, I always give all my employees a satisfactory rating—it's easier that way," answered Annette.

Without ever bringing Christine's unacceptable performance to her attention and thus giving her a chance to change, firing or otherwise severely disciplining Christine at this point would be questionable. How can this problem be avoided? In Chapter 8, you will learn how to create and utilize a performance evaluation process that works.

• • •

• • • CHAPTER OUTLINE

Performance Management Systems
Performance Management Versus Performance Appraisal
The Performance Appraisal Process
Accurate Performance Measures

Why Do We Conduct Performance Appraisals?
Communication (Informing)
Decision Making (Evaluating)
Motivation (Engaging)

What Do We Assess?
Trait Appraisals
Behavioral Appraisals
Results Appraisals

How Do We Use Appraisal Methods and Forms?
Critical Incidents Method
Management by Objectives (MBO) Method
Narrative Method or Form
Graphic Rating Scale Form
Behaviorally Anchored Rating Scale (BARS) Form
Ranking Method
Which Option Is Best?

Who Should Assess Performance?
Supervisor
Peers
Subordinates
Self
Customers
360-Degree Evaluations

Performance Appraisal Problems
Common Problems Within the Performance Appraisal Process
Avoiding Performance Appraisal Process Problems

Debriefing the Appraisal
The Evaluative Performance Appraisal Interview
The Developmental Performance Appraisal Interview

Trends and Issues in HRM
Is It Time to Do Continuous Appraisals?
Competency-Based Performance Management

LO 8-1

Summarize the necessary characteristics of accurate performance management tools.

SHRM

Q:5

Improving Organizational Effectiveness

Performance management The process of identifying, measuring, managing, and developing the performance of the human resources in an organization

PERFORMANCE MANAGEMENT SYSTEMS

It is critical to evaluate how well our newly trained employees perform their job. Therefore, performance evaluation is an important part of the jobs of managers and HRM staff.[1,2] In this section we discuss the difference between performance management and performance appraisal, and we present the performance appraisal process.

Performance Management Versus Performance Appraisal

The most common part of the performance management process, and the one with which we are most familiar, is the performance appraisal, or evaluation. (In this chapter, we will use the terms *performance evaluation*, *performance appraisal*, and just *appraisal* interchangeably.) However, the performance appraisal process is not the only part of performance management. **Performance management** *is the process of identifying, measuring, managing, and developing the performance of the human resources in an organization.* Performance management is a systematic analysis and measurement of worker performance (*and* communication of that assessment to the individual) that we use to improve performance over time.

Netflix is one company that has stopped doing formal performance appraisals.

©iStockphoto.com/JasonDoiy

SHRM HR CONTENT

See Appendix: *SHRM 2013 Curriculum Guidebook* for the complete list

E.   Job Analysis/Job Design (required)

    4. Performance management (performance criteria and appraisal)

H.   Performance Management (required)

    1. Identifying and measuring employee performance

    2. Sources of information (e.g., managers, peers, clients)

    3. Rater errors in performance measurement

    5. Performance appraisals

    6. Appraisal feedback

    7. Managing performance

Q.   Organization Development (required—graduate students only)

    5. Improving organizational effectiveness

    9. Ongoing performance and productivity initiatives

Performance appraisal (PA), on the other hand, *is the ongoing process of evaluating employee performance.* Performance appraisal should not be simply a once- or twice-a-year formal interview. It should be an ongoing process. Employees need regular feedback on their performance,[3] so give routine and candid assessments.[4] Although we will spend most of the chapter discussing performance appraisals, there are several other significant pieces to performance management that we already covered in past chapters and will cover in future chapters.

We discussed "strategic planning," which provides inputs into what we want to evaluate in our performance management system, in Chapter 2, and the major method of identifying performance requirements in a particular job when we went through "job analysis and design" in Chapter 4. In Chapter 7, we discussed "training and development." Additionally, we will discuss motivating employees, coaching and counseling, employee relations, compensation, and other pieces in Chapters 9 through 14. Now that we understand the difference between performance management and performance appraisal, let's look at the performance appraisal process.

The Performance Appraisal Process

Exhibit 8-1 illustrates the performance appraisal process. Note the connection between the organization's mission and objectives and the performance appraisal (PA) process. Here we briefly discuss each step of the process.

Step 1: Job analysis. If we don't know what a job consists of, how can we possibly evaluate an employee's performance in that job? We learned how to do a job analysis in Chapter 4.

Step 2: Develop standards and measurement methods. We can't assess performance without standards and measuring to see if standards are met.[5] We will discuss PA methods in the next part of this section, and in the section "How Do We Use Appraisal Methods and Forms?" we will discuss these topics in more detail.

Step 3: Informal performance appraisal—Coaching and disciplining. As its definition states, PA is an ongoing process. While a formal evaluation may only take place once or

SHRM

E:4
Performance Management
(Performance Criteria and Appraisal)

SHRM

Q:9
Ongoing Performance and
Productivity Initiatives

WORK
APPLICATION 8-1

Select a job you have or have had. Do you or did you know the organization's mission and objectives? Briefly state the mission. If you don't know it, find out. Do you understand how your job fits or helps to meet the organization's mission and objectives? Explain in some detail.

Performance appraisal The ongoing process of evaluating employee performance

---

8-1 ETHICAL DILEMMA: WHAT WOULD YOU DO?

Academic Standards

The academic credit-hour system was set up many years ago to ensure that there would be some standardization across colleges throughout the country and that academics and employers had the same understanding of the workload that a college student had carried to earn a degree. The credit-hour system was based on the assumption that a student would spend 2 hours of preparation for each hour of in-class time. So a student taking five classes should spend 15 hours per week in classes and about 30 hours preparing for classes, or a total of about 45 hours a week—which is a full-time schedule.

1. How many hours outside of class, on average, do you and other students you know spend preparing for class each week?
2. Are college professors today assigning students 2 hours of preparation for every hour in class? If not, why do you think they have dropped this standard?
3. Are students who are essentially doing part-time work (that is, attending classes but doing little academic work outside of class) during college being prepared for a career after graduation (with a 40- to 60-hour workweek)?
4. Is it ethical and socially responsible for professors to drop standards and for colleges to award degrees for doing less work than students did 5, 10, or 20 years ago?
5. Are professors that inflate grades being ethical and socially responsible?

EXHIBIT 8-1   THE PERFORMANCE APPRAISAL PROCESS

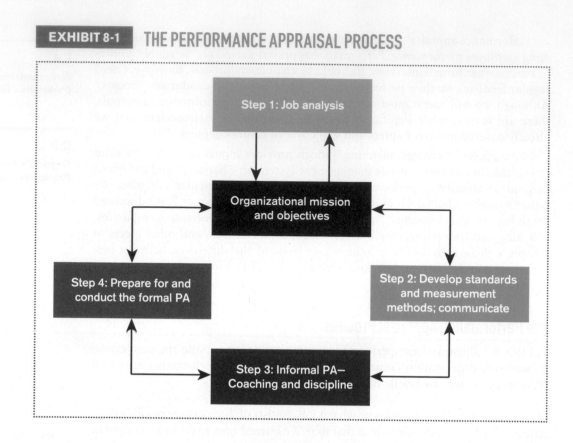

twice a year, people need regular feedback on their performance to know how they are doing.[6]

Step 4: Prepare for and conduct the formal performance appraisal. The formal PA review with the boss usually occurs once or sometimes twice a year, using measurement forms. We will discuss them later in this chapter along with the steps of preparing for and conducting the PA.

Accurate Performance Measures

We need accurate standards and measures of employee performance both to effectively assess performance and to let employees know where they can improve.[7] This in turn should lead to training employees to develop the skills they need to improve their performance.[8]

Also, to be an accurate measure of performance, our measure must be valid, reliable, acceptable and feasible, specific, and based on the mission and objectives. Let's discuss each of those requirements here.

Valid and Reliable. We have to create valid and reliable measurement to be accurate. Recall that we discussed reliability and validity in Chapter 4 and Chapter 6. *Valid* means that a measure accurately measures what you wanted to measure. *Reliable* means the measure is consistent each time we use it.[9]

Acceptable and Feasible. Acceptability means that the use of the measure is satisfactory or appropriate to the people who must use it. To be acceptable, an evaluation tool must also be feasible.[10] Is it possible to reasonably apply the evaluation tool in a particular case, or is it too complex or lengthy to work well? As an example, if the manager must fill out a 25-page form that has very little to do with the job being evaluated, the manager may not feel that the form is acceptable or feasible, at least partially due to its length, even if the employees do. Conversely, if the manager fills out a two-page evaluation and feels it is a true measure of performance in an employee's job, but the employee feels that the evaluation leaves out large segments of what is done in the work routine, the employee may not feel that the form is acceptable and feasible. If either management or employees feel that the form is unacceptable, it most likely will not be used successfully.

Specific. The evaluation measure must be specific enough so that everyone involved completely understands what is going well and what needs to be improved.

Based on the Mission and Objectives. Finally, as with everything else we do in HR, we need to ensure that the performance management process guides our employees toward achievement of the company's mission and objectives. Thus, stating specific objectives saying exactly what each person in each job should achieve, or their performance outcomes, leads to accurate assessment that can increase performance. For some examples of inaccurate measures of performance, complete Applying the Concept 8-1.

WORK
APPLICATION 8-2

Assess the accuracy of the measurements of your performance on your last performance appraisal. Be sure to describe the measures' validity, reliability, acceptability, and feasibility plus whether the measures were specific and based on the organization's mission and objectives.

WHY DO WE CONDUCT PERFORMANCE APPRAISALS?

Let's discuss three major reasons (communicating, decision making, and motivating) why performance evaluations are completed, and why they are so critical to continually improving organizations' performance.[11]

LO 8-2

Identify and briefly discuss the purposes of performance appraisals.

Communication (Informing)

The first major reason for PA is to provide an opportunity for formal communication between management and the employees concerning how the supervisor believes each employee is performing. "Organizations can prevent or remedy the majority of performance problems by ensuring that two way conversation occurs between the manager and the employee, resulting in a complete understanding of what is required, when it is required, and how the employee's contribution measures up."[12] Within this two-way interaction, the process requires that we provide the opportunity for the employee to speak to us concerning factors that inhibit their ability to successfully perform to expectations.

8-1 APPLYING THE CONCEPT

Measurement Accuracy

Before each of the situation descriptions below, write the letter corresponding to the accuracy criterion for a measure that is NOT met in the situation.

a. valid   d. feasible

b. reliable   e. specific

c. accepted   f. based on the mission and objectives

_____ 1. My boss is on my case because I'm not producing as much as I used to. But it's not my fault that the machine jams more often and then I have to stop working to fix it.

_____ 2. My boss said I have to evaluate all 25 of my employees four times a year instead of only once. I told her I don't

have the time to do it that many times. It's just not possible to do a good review that often without cutting back on other things that are more important.

_____ 3. My boss said I have a bad attitude and gave me a lower overall performance rating. I questioned what my attitude had to do with my performance because I get all my work done well, and by the deadline.

_____ 4. My boss asked me to complete a self-evaluation form rating my performance. But I didn't do it because it is her job—I let her do it.

_____ 5. My boss told me that I was not doing a very good job. But when I asked him why, he never gave me any details to support his assessment. Good answer.

Factors in a job that management may not know about can include lack of training, poorly maintained equipment, lack of necessary tools, conflict within work groups, and many other things that management may not see on a daily basis. We can only resolve problems when we know about them. So you need two-way communication with your employees to find out when issues within the work environment are causing a loss of productivity so they can be fixed.

Decision Making (Evaluating)

Accurate information is necessary for management decision making and is absolutely critical to allow the manager to improve organizational productivity.[13] We use information from annual PAs to make evaluative decisions concerning our workforce, including such things as pay raises, promotions, training, and termination. When we have valid and reliable information concerning each individual we supervise, we have the ability to make administrative and performance decisions that can enhance productivity for the firm.

SHRM

H:7

Managing Performance

Motivation (Engaging)

We need to motivate our employees to improve the way they work, which in turn will improve organizational productivity overall.[14] But what is motivation, and are PAs normally motivational? We define motivation here as *the willingness to achieve organizational objectives*. We need to increase this willingness to achieve the organization's objectives, which will in turn increase organizational productivity.

LO 8-3

Discuss the options for what to evaluate in a performance appraisal.

WHAT DO WE ASSESS?

Our next step is to figure out what needs to be evaluated in our PA. In HR terms, the PA should be based on our job analysis.[15] However, we can't evaluate everything, so we have to choose what we will focus on because what gets measured and evaluated gets done.[16] Our three primary options for what to evaluate are traits, behaviors, and results, so let's discuss them in this section.

Trait Appraisals

Traits *identify the physical or psychological characteristics of a person*. Traits of an individual can be part of the PA process. There is evidence that traits, including inquisitiveness, conscientiousness, and general cognitive ability, are valuable in jobs that require management and leadership skills.[17,18] However, we must ensure that we focus on traits that have a direct relationship to the essential functions of the job, that they are within the control of the individual, and that they are accurate measures.

Give Traits the OUCH Test. When measuring traits, it's difficult to meet the *objective* requirement of the OUCH test because it is difficult to create a quantifiable and factual link between characteristics like height or job enthusiasm and job performance. If we utilized these measures in all cases in employee evaluations, we would be able to meet the *uniform in application* requirement of the OUCH test. The third test—*consistent in effect*—would be extremely difficult to meet due to the fact that different racial, ethnic, social, and gender groups tend to have different physical and personality characteristics. Remember, reliability is a measure of consistency. Physical and personality characteristics have less to do with success in the job than certain behaviors do. So it's difficult to meet the *has job relatedness* test in most

Motivation The willingness to achieve organizational objectives

Traits The physical or psychological characteristics of a person

cases. Finally, it would be very difficult to get different supervisors to evaluate subjective traits the same because of their own personality traits.

Should We Measure Traits? Author Ken Blanchard said that there are too many evaluation items that can't be objectively measured—such as attitude, initiative, and promotability. Therefore, it's important to ask whether both managers and employees will agree with the measured rating as being accurate. The bottom-line test (we will call it the Blanchard test) is this: Does everyone understand why they are assessed at a specific level (evaluation) and what it takes to get a higher rating (development)?[19] We should only assess traits that meet the bottom-line test of having a direct and obvious objective measureable relationship between the trait and success in the job.

Behavioral Appraisals

Our second option in the assessment process is to evaluate employees based on behaviors. You will recall that behaviors *are simply the actions taken by an individual*—the things that they do. Behavioral appraisals measure what individuals *do* at work, not their personal traits and characteristics. Behaviors can be directly observed, and as a result, are more likely to be a valid assessment of the individual's performance than traits.

Give Behavior the OUCH Test. **Let's take a look at a behavioral evaluation using the OUCH test.** In general, directly observing and evaluating an action is significantly more *objective* than making an attempt to judge a trait like individual effort. If we applied the same evaluation of behaviors to all of the individuals in the same type of job, we would have a reasonable certainty that we were being *uniform in application*. The same thing would be true here in evaluating the concept of *consistent in effect*. To meet the test of *has job relatedness*, we would need to make sure that we chose behaviors that were necessarily a part of successfully accomplishing a task; the behaviors need to be directly related to the essential functions of the job. So the behavioral evaluation process is generally more *valid and reliable*.

Should We Measure Behavior? The most useful and therefore most acceptable feedback to employees is feedback on specific job-related behaviors.[20] As managers, though, we still need to be cognizant of the fact that a behavioral evaluation can be a poor measure of work performance if the behaviors chosen are not directly applicable to being successful in the job; and Blanchard says it happens more often than you may think. So as with traits, the Blanchard test asks whether employees understand why they are assessed at a specific level (evaluation) and what it takes to get a higher rating (development).[21]

Results Appraisals

Our final option is to evaluate the results, or outcomes, of the work process. Results are simply *a measure of the goals achieved through a work process*. Using results as an evaluation measure provides management with an assessment of the goals that were achieved in a particular job over time.

Can We Accurately Measure Results That Affect Job Performance? Results are certainly concrete measures of performance. However, the results of a job could have been skewed based on factors that were outside the control of the individual. For example, standards could be set too low or high, and equipment and machines don't always work correctly, and as a result, employees can't do as much, or any work. But done correctly, results provide the company with its return on investment—its investment in the people in the organization. So, organizations measure results.

Behaviors The actions taken by an individual

Results A measure of the goals achieved through a work process

Give Results the OUCH Test. Results are a very *objective* measure of performance. If we apply the same results-based measure to each similar job, then our measure is *uniform in application.* The measure of results would almost certainly be consistent across different groups of employees, so we would also meet the *consistency in effect* requirement of the OUCH test. And of course, if we are measuring the results of what happens in a job, we are certainly providing a measure that *has job relatedness.* So with a quick scan, we can see that a results-based performance appraisal meets the requirements of the OUCH test better than traits and behavior options.

Should We Measure Results? Results-based evaluations, like behavior-based evaluations, are typically very acceptable to both the employee and the manager. We can better defend results appraisals than we can defend the other two options, even in court. It tends to be very easy for the organization to go into a courtroom and show that an individual's results were objectively lower than those achieved by others in the same or similar jobs, if necessary. The results-based evaluation would most likely be valid and would usually be reliable, assuming that we were able to take into account factors outside the individual's control that nonetheless affect job performance. So again, the Blanchard test asks: Does everyone understand why they are assessed at a specific level (evaluation) and what it takes to get a higher rating (development)?[22]

LO 8-4

List the commonly used performance measurement methods and forms.

H:5
Performance Appraisals

HOW DO WE USE APPRAISAL METHODS AND FORMS?

The formal performance appraisal usually involves the use of a standard form, selected or developed by the HR department, to measure employee performance. Employees need to know the standards and understand what good performance looks like, and they need to be able to measure their own performance. If you are stuck with a form that has subjective sections, work with your employees to develop clear, accurate standards.

Exhibit 8-2 lists the commonly used performance appraisal measurement methods and forms and displays them on a continuum based on their use in evaluative and developmental decisions. In this section, we discuss each of the measurement methods and forms, starting with the developmental methods and working toward the evaluative ones.

8-2 APPLYING THE CONCEPT

Assessment Options

Write the letter corresponding to each of the following assessment options for measuring performance before the situation describing it.

a. traits

b. behavior

c. results

_____ 6. On the assessment form question number 7, "willingness to take responsibility," I'm giving you an average rating.

_____ 7. You have to stay calm and stop yelling at your coworkers.

_____ 8. You only sold 25 units 3 weeks in a row. You know the standard is 35, so I'm giving you a formal warning that if you don't get up to standard in 2 weeks, you will be fired.

_____ 9. When you promote one of the women, make sure she is attractive.

_____ 10. I'm pleased with your performance. It is only your second week on the job, and you are already producing the standard 10 units per day. I don't think it will be long before you exceed the standard and get bonus pay.

EXHIBIT 8-2   PERFORMANCE APPRAISAL MEASUREMENT METHODS AND FORMS

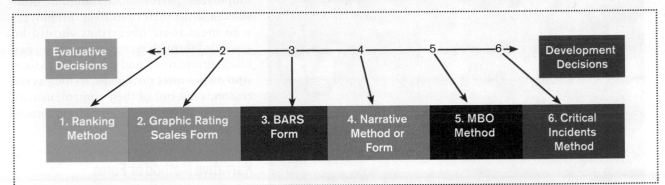

Critical Incidents Method

The critical incidents method is a performance appraisal method in which a manager keeps a written record of the positive and negative performance of employees throughout the performance period. There is no standard form used, so it is a method. Every time an employee does something very well, like beating a tough deadline or keeping an angry customer from terminating a business relationship with the firm, a note goes in the employee's file. Notes also go into the file every time the employee's behavior hurts performance. Most of us can't remember events that happened more than a few weeks ago, so we record significant critical incidents over the entire period in order to do a good assessment.

Although critical incidents are commonly used for developmental decisions, they are also used for evaluative decisions. For legal purposes, a list of documented critical incidents is especially important to have leading up the evaluative decision of firing employees. We will discuss discipline and documentation in Chapter 9.

One error managers tend to make in critical incidents evaluation is focusing on the negative actions of employees. Remember that a good, balanced evaluation includes both positive and negative feedback, so look for good performance, not just poor performance, and praise it when you see it.[23] **Robert Graham** CEO Michael Buckly does it the old fashioned way with a file folder for each of his direct reports,[24] but there are software programs to track performance that should be used during the formal review.

Management by Objectives (MBO) Method

The management by objectives (MBO) method is a process in which managers and employees jointly set objectives for the employees, periodically evaluate performance, and reward employees according to the results. MBO is a three-step process, discussed below.

Step 1: Set individual objectives and plans. The manager sets objectives jointly with each individual employee.[25] The objectives are the heart of the MBO process and should be accurate measures of performance results. To be accurate, objectives should be SMART: Specific, Measurable, Attainable, Relevant, and Time based.[26] We developed a model based on the work of Max E. Douglas, and we have provided two examples in Model 8-1 that we can use when setting objectives for ourselves or others.

Step 2: Give feedback and continually evaluate performance. Communication is the key factor in determining MBO's success or failure, and employees should continually critique their own performance.[27] Thus, the manager and employee must communicate often to review progress.[28]

Managers and employees can set objectives together.

Step 3: Reward according to performance. Employees' performance should be measured against their objectives. Employees who meet their objectives should be rewarded through recognition, praise, pay raises, promotions, and so on.[29] Employees who do not meet their goals, so long as the reason is not out of their control, usually have rewards withheld and even punishment given when necessary.

Narrative Method or Form

The narrative method or form *requires a manager to write a statement about the employee's performance.* There may not be an actual standard form used, especially for high-level professional and executive positions, but there can be a form, so it can be a method or a form. A narrative gives the manager the opportunity to give the evaluative assessment in a written form that can go beyond simply checking a box to describe an assessment item. Narratives can be used alone, but they often follow an objective part of the form. Although the narrative is ongoing, it is commonly used during the formal review. A letter of recommendation is often a narrative method.

Graphic Rating Scale Form

The graphic rating scale form is a performance appraisal checklist form on which a manager simply rates performance on a continuum such as excellent, good, average, fair, and poor. The continuum often includes a numerical scale, for example from level 1 (lowest performance level) to 5 (highest). The self-assessment and Skill Builder exercise 8-1 use a graphic rating scale form.

The graphic rating scale form is probably the most commonly used form during the formal performance appraisal because it can be used for many different types of jobs, making this a kind of one-size-fits-all (or none) form that requires minimal time, effort, cost, and training. But on the negative side, graphic rating scales are not very accurate measures of performance because the selection of one rating over another, such as an excellent versus good rating, is very subjective.

Behaviorally Anchored Rating Scale (BARS) Form

A behaviorally anchored rating scale (BARS) form *is a performance appraisal that provides a description of each assessment along a continuum.* As with graphic rating scales, the continuum often includes a numerical scale that runs from low to high. However, BARS forms overcome the problem of subjectivity by providing

Narrative method or form Method in which the manager is required to write a statement about the employee's performance

Graphic rating scale form A performance appraisal checklist form on which a manager simply rates performance on a continuum such as excellent, good, average, fair, and poor

Behaviorally anchored rating scale (BARS) form A performance appraisal that provides a description of each assessment along a continuum

MODEL 8-1   SETTING OBJECTIVES MODEL

(1) To +   (2) Action Verb +   (3) Specific and Measurable Result +   (4) Target Date

To +   produce +   20 units + per day

To increase widget productivity 5% by December 31, 2017

an actual description of the performance (behavior) for each rating along the continuum, rather than that one simple word (*excellent, good*, etc.) that graphic rating scales provide. A description of each level of performance makes the assessment a more objective, accurate measure.

Why are BARS forms probably less commonly used than graphic rating scales? It's partly economics and partly expertise. The graphic rating scale can be used for many different jobs, but BARS forms have to be customized to every different type of job. And developing potentially hundreds of different BARS forms takes a lot of time, money, and expertise. Even when a firm has an HR staff, the question becomes "Is developing BARS forms the most effective use of our time?" Obviously, the answer depends on the types of jobs being evaluated and the resources available to complete the evaluation process.

Here is a very simple example of making a graphic rating scale item into the more objective BARS.

Attendance—excellent, good, average, fair, poor

becomes

Attendance—number of days missed 1, 2, 3–4, 5, 6 or more

In education, the trend is to require teachers to develop BARS, called grading rubrics, so that subjective grading of essays and case studies are more objective. Students use the rubric to do the work by meeting the written descriptive of how each part will be graded. When getting it back with a grade, students better understand why they got the grade they did and how to improve in the future. Have you seen and used one?

Ranking Method

Ranking *is a performance appraisal method that is used to evaluate employee performance from best to worst.* There often is no actual standard form used, and we don't always have to rank all employees. This method can be contentious, as evidenced by recent announcements by Microsoft and Yahoo. In late 2013, Yahoo announced that it was adopting a ranking system,[30] but later the same day, Microsoft announced that it was dropping its forced-ranking system.[31] Dell tried forced-ranking and it turned good employees into politicians, bad employees into backstabbers, colleagues into enemies, and destroyed collaboration—so Dell dropped it.[32]

Under the ranking method, the manager compares an employee to other similar employees, rather than to a standard measurement. An offshoot of ranking is the forced distribution method, which is similar to grading on a curve. Predetermined percentages of employees are placed in various performance categories—for example, excellent, 5%; above average, 15%; average, 60%; below average, 15%; and poor, 5%. The employees ranked in the top group usually get the rewards (a raise, a bonus, or a promotion), those not in the top tend to have rewards withheld, and the ones in the bottom group sometimes get punished. In Skill Builder 8-1, you are asked to rank the performance of your peers.

Which Option Is Best?

Using a combination of the methods and forms is usually superior to using just one. For developmental objectives, the critical incidents, MBO, and narrative methods work well. Alternately, you can't decide who gets the promotion or merit raise without an evaluative method. So for administrative decisions, a ranking method based on the evaluative methods, and especially graphic rating scales or BARS forms, works well.

8-3 APPLYING THE CONCEPT

Appraisal Methods and Forms

State which of the following assessments is being described in each of the given situations, writing each assessment's corresponding letter before the situation(s) in which it is described.

a. critical incidents method

b. MBO method

c. narrative method and forms

d. BARS forms

e. graphic rating scale forms

f. ranking method

_____ 11. Hank is not doing a good job, so you decided to talk to him about it and keep track of his performance regularly.

_____ 12. Your employees perform different tasks. You want to create a system for developing each of them.

_____ 13. Sara is moving, has applied for a job at another company, and asked you for a letter of recommendation.

_____ 14. You started a new business a year ago, and you are extremely busy focusing on sales, but you want to develop a performance appraisal form you can use with all 14 of your employees, who do a variety of jobs.

_____ 15. You have been promoted, and you have been asked to select your replacement.

Remember that the success of the performance appraisal process does not just lie in the formal method or form used once or twice a year. It depends on the manager's human relations skills in ongoing critical incidents coaching, and it also depends on effective measures of performance that are accurate enough to let everyone know why they are rated at a given level (evaluative) and how they should improve (developmental) for the next assessment.[33]

LO 8-5

Describe the available options for the rater/evaluator.

WHO SHOULD ASSESS PERFORMANCE?

Now that we've learned the why, what, and how of the performance appraisal process, we need to discuss the options for choosing a rater or evaluator. There are a number of different options concerning who should evaluate the individual employee, and the decision needs to be based on a series of factors. Let's take a look at six options for deciding who should evaluate an employee.

SHRM

H:2

Sources of Information (e.g., Managers, Peers, Clients)

Supervisor

The most commonly used evaluator is the immediate supervisor because supervisors are supposed to know the level of performance of their employees. However, this is not always the case due to problems with supervisor performance assessments.

Problems With Supervisor Evaluations. Many times today, supervisors have little or no direct contact with their employees because they may be in a different building, city, state, or even country. Virtual teams, Internet-linked offices, telecommuting, and other factors cause supervisors to not be in constant touch with their employees. What if the supervisor doesn't even know what you're supposed to be doing in your job? What if there's a personality conflict?

Avoiding Supervisor Review Problems. A simple way to overcome these problems is to have others in addition to (or in place of) the supervisor assess performance. Also, multiple measures can make a performance assessment more accurate—valid and reliable. Using other evaluators and multiple measures can help overcome personal bias and provide information that supervisors don't always know about.

Peers

In addition to, or in place of, supervisors, the trend is to using more teams, and teams commonly evaluate each member's performance.[34] Why? Peers often know the job of the individual employee better than the supervisor does, and they are more directly affected by the employee's actions, either positive or negative. In addition, peers can evaluate the ability of the individual to interact with others successfully in a group or team setting—something that may be very difficult for the supervisor to see unless they are intimately involved with the group.

Problems With Peer Reviews. Peer evaluations can cause problems because the process can become less objective. Also, the validity of peer evaluations is really unclear.[35] Personality conflicts and personal biases can affect how individual employees rate their peers. A major problem is with perception, because most of us see ourselves as being better at our job than our boss and peers.

Avoiding Peer Review Problems. Because we know that problems can occur within a peer evaluation, the manager can take the issues into account and adjust rating values as necessary. For example, if a personality conflict has occurred between two group members that caused them to lower each other's grades, those grades can be adjusted based on feedback from other group members. Some research shows that as peers evaluate each other more, their ability to provide relevant and valuable feedback increases, as does their personal confidence. So giving employees practice in peer evaluations can improve the validity and reliability of such evaluations.[36] Even with the potential for personality conflicts and bias, peer evaluations can give us good insight into the inner workings of a group or team when the supervisor has infrequent contact with the team.

Subordinates

We can also have the employees evaluate their boss. Subordinate evaluations can give us good insight into the managerial practices and potential missteps of people who oversee others. As a result, subordinate evaluations may give us valuable information that we would be unable to find out using any other means. Have you filled out a form that assesses professors?

Problems With Subordinate Reviews. There is potential for bias here, especially from subordinates who have been disciplined by their supervisor. Obviously, the subordinates may try to get back at their supervisor for giving them tasks that they did not want to perform or for disciplining them for failure in their jobs. There may also be a personality conflict, or some subordinates may be biased against their supervisor or manager for other reasons—recall perception problems.

On the other end of the scale, the subordinates may inflate the capabilities of their manager, at least partly because of a lack of understanding of all the tasks and duties required of the manager. In fact, in a recent survey, about two thirds of employees rated their managers higher than the managers rated themselves.[37]

Avoiding Subordinate Review Problems. In many cases, as we go through a group of subordinate evaluations, we will see one or two outliers providing either very high or very low marks for the supervisor. In such a case, we should probably throw those outliers out of the calculation when determining overall marks for the supervisor. It's surprising how often these outliers are extremely easy to spot in a subordinate evaluation process. Another significant issue in the case of subordinate evaluations is confidentiality. Subordinate evaluations *must* be anonymous or it is unlikely that the subordinates will provide an honest evaluation of their supervisor. Despite potential problems, subordinate evaluations can provide us with valuable information about the supervisor's capabilities.

Self

Ever done a self-assessment at work? Virtually all of us have informally evaluated how we perceive we are doing on the job, and it can be part of the formal PA process. As you know, every chapter of this book has one or more self-assessments, and in one for this chapter—Skill Builder 8-1 at the end of the chapter—you will assess your performance on a group project. If you want to, you can do the skill-builder now.

Problems With Self-Assessments. Let's face it, we tend to be biased in our self-perception because we all want to view our self positively. A significant portion of the research evidence seems to show that individuals with lower overall levels of knowledge and skills tend to inflate the self-assessment of their abilities.[38] Conversely, as individuals become more knowledgeable and more skilled, the evidence tends to show that they will either accurately estimate or even underestimate their capabilities in their jobs.[39,40,41]

Avoiding Self-Assessment Problems. Here again, if we know that self-evaluations tend to be skewed, we can most likely adjust for that. In addition, receiving information from the individual concerning their perception of their skill set is extremely valuable in a number of management processes—including plans for training and development opportunities, providing work assignments, and counseling and disciplinary measures. As stated in the Blanchard test, both the manager and employee need to agree on the level of performance and what it takes to get to the next level—it's called *perception congruence.*

Customers

We may want to use customers as evaluators when the individual being evaluated has frequent contact with internal or external customers. It does not matter what else we do successfully if our customers are uncomfortable with their interactions with our employees because they can usually take their business elsewhere. And even *internal* customers can create significant problems within the firm due to conflict between departments or divisions. So we may want to ask internal and external customers to evaluate the individuals with whom they come into contact.

Problems With Customer Assessments. One problem with customer evaluations is that they commonly use simple graphic rating scales, which we discussed as being very subjective. Also, customers are usually not trained to do an accurate assessment, so bias is a problem. For these and other reasons, the popular opinion is that customer evaluations are negatively skewed. However, research shows that in some situations, customer evaluations actually exceed internal evaluations.[42]

Avoiding Customer Assessment Problems. Regardless of problems, customer evaluations provide us with valuable information concerning our employees who have direct customer contact. And we can always adjust the evaluation process knowing that customer evaluations may be biased. Haven't we all been on the phone and heard something like "this conversation will be recorded and used for training purposes"? This is true, but it's also usually an evaluation and employees are rewarded or punished based on how they deal with customers.

360-Degree Evaluations

In some cases, the evaluation is expanded to everyone that an employee comes into contact with through 360-degree feedback.[43] The 360-degree evaluation *analyzes individuals' performance from all sides—from their supervisor's viewpoint, from their subordinates' viewpoint, from their customers (if applicable), from their peers, and from their own self-evaluation.* The 360-degree evaluation would generally give us the most accurate analysis of performance.

Problems With 360-Degree Evaluations. Although considered the best, 360-degree evaluations are not the most popular method because of the time, effort and money needed to use them. Also, some employees have little contact with others, making them unnecessary anyway.

Avoiding 360-Degree Problems. Unfortunately, there really is no simple way to avoid these problems besides what is commonly done—simply not using 360-degree evaluations. The 360-degree evaluation format tends to be most valuable if it is used for purposes of individual development, rather than to make administrative evaluative decisions.[44] A good 360-degree feedback system can provide specific suggestions about how to improve individual competencies."[45] It can also go a long way toward minimizing some of the most common problems with the performance appraisal process, which we will review in the next section.

Employees who frequently interact with customers may be evaluated based on customer evaluations, but this method may present issues of subjectivity.

PERFORMANCE APPRAISAL PROBLEMS

During the PA process, we face some common problems. However, we can take measures to avoid them if we know about them. So in this section, we discuss the problems first with simple ways to avoid each of them as an individual. Then we discuss what the organization can do to overcome these problems on an organization-wide basis. We can actually overcome multiple problems with the same method.

Common Problems Within the Performance Appraisal Process

Let's briefly discuss each of the common problems during the performance appraisal process listed in Exhibit 8-3.

Bias. **Bias** *is simply a personality-based tendency, either toward or against something.* PA bias is toward or against an individual employee. We all have biases, but supervisors especially cannot afford to allow their biases to enter into their evaluation of subordinates. This is easier said than done. Biases make the PA process subjective rather than objective, and they certainly provide the opportunity for a lack of consistency in effect on different groups of employees. So we need to be objective and not let our feelings of liking or disliking an individual influence our assessment of that person.

Stereotyping. **Stereotyping** *is mentally classifying a person into an affinity group and then identifying the person as having the same assumed characteristics as the group.* Making any assumptions about individual employee characteristics based on their supposed membership in a group, rather than explicitly identifying the performance of the individual, creates the potential for significant error in evaluations. So we need to get to know each employee as an individual and objectively evaluate actual performance.

LO 8-6

Name some of the common problems with the performance appraisal process.

SHRM

H:3

Rater Errors in Performance Measurement

Bias A personality-based tendency, either toward or against something

Stereotyping Mentally classifying a person into an affinity group and then identifying the person as having the same assumed characteristics as the group

EXHIBIT 8-3 — PERFORMANCE APPRAISAL PROBLEMS AND AVOIDING THEM

Common Problems	How to Avoid Problems
Bias	Develop accurate performance measures
Stereotyping	Use multiple criteria
Halo error	Minimize the use of trait-based evaluations
Distributional errors	Use the OUCH and Blanchard tests
Similarity	Train your evaluators
Proximity	Use multiple raters
Recency	
Contrast	

Halo Error. This occurs when the evaluator forms a *generally* positive impression of an individual and then artificially extends that general impression to an overall evaluation of the individual.[46] (Alternatively, the evaluator can form a negative initial impression and extend it to form an overall negative evaluation—this is sometimes called the "horns error.") So we need to remember that employees are often strong in some areas and weaker in others, and we need to objectively evaluate their actual performance for each and every item of assessment.

Distributional Errors. These errors occur in three forms: severity or strictness, central tendency, and leniency. They are based on a standard normal distribution, or the bell curve that we are all so familiar with. In *severity* or *strictness* error, the rater evaluates just about everyone as below average. *Central tendency* error occurs when just about everyone is rated average. Finally, *leniency* error occurs when just about everyone is rated as above average—like grade inflation. So we need to give a range of evaluations because we really aren't all equal in our level of performance, and everyone can't be the worst or the best.

Similarity Error. This error, also called "like me," occurs when the rater gives better evaluations to subordinates whom they consider more similar to themselves and poorer evaluations to subordinates whom they consider to be different from themselves. We all have a tendency to feel more comfortable with people who we feel are more similar to ourselves,[47] and if we are not careful, we can allow this feeling of comfort with similar individuals to be reflected in the performance appraisal process. So we need to evaluate all employees based on their actual performance, even if they are different from us and don't do things the same way that we do.

Proximity Error. This error states that similar marks may be given to items that are near (in other words, proximate to) each other on the performance appraisal form, regardless of differences in performance on those measures. For instance, if we mark the first three items as "meets expectations," we tend to continue marking the same way on down the form. So we need to be objective in evaluating employees' actual performance on each and every item on the assessment form, and having *reverse item scales* really helps.

Recency Error. This occurs when the rater uses only the last few weeks of a rating period as evidence when putting together performance ratings. For instance, if a warehouse worker has been a strong performer for most of the appraisal period, but right before his annual evaluation he accidentally set a fire, he may be rated poorly due to recency error. So we need to evaluate the employee based on their performance during the entire assessment period. Using the critical incident evaluation method really helps avoid recency error.

Contrast Error. Here the rater compares and contrasts performance between two employees, rather than using absolute measures of performance to assess each employee. For example, the rater may contrast a good performer with an outstanding performer; then, as a result of the significant contrast, the good performer seems to be "below average." So we need to evaluate the individual based on their actual performance against an objective standard.

Avoiding Performance Appraisal Process Problems

As discussed, PA can fail to provide an accurate assessment of the capabilities and behaviors of individual employees. Thus far, we have only provided simple solutions to help us overcome these problems as individuals. But how can a firm avoid these problems on an organization-wide basis? Let's discuss how the firm can limit the potential for the appraisal process to go astray by developing accurate performance measures, training evaluators, and using multiple raters.

Develop Accurate Performance Measures. As discussed, if the PA methods and forms are not accurate measures, then the entire process will have problems. Therefore, the organization should have its own HR specialist or hired consultants develop an objective assessment process and measures. Let's discuss three things HR specialists commonly do to help ensure accurate measures.

Use Multiple Criteria. HR must ensure that we focus on more than one or two criteria to evaluate an individual's performance. We should generally have at least one evaluation criterion for each major function within an individual job so that we have the ability to lower the incidence of halo, recency, and contrast errors, and we may even be able to affect bias and stereotyping because of the fact that many criteria, not just one or two, are being analyzed.

Minimize the Use of Trait-Based Evaluations. As noted, trait-based evaluations tend to be more subjective than behavior and results-based evaluations, and as a result, they should generally not be used unless there is a *specific reason* why employees must

WORK
APPLICATION 8-6

Select your current job or a past job. Identify common mistakes your supervisor made when assessing your performance, during either an informal coaching or a formal appraisal review.

8-4 **APPLYING** THE CONCEPT

Avoiding Appraisal Problems

Review the list of common problems or errors and then write the letter corresponding to each one before the statement describing or involving it.

a. bias   e. similarity error

b. stereotyping   f. proximity error

c. halo error   g. recency error

d. distributional error   h. contrast error

_____ 16. I got a lower rating than I deserve because I'm not afraid to speak my mind to the boss, and she doesn't like it.

_____ 17. I'm sick and tired of hearing how many units Sally produces and that I should be more like her.

_____ 18. I told my boss that I thought I deserve an excellent rating, but she said that she gives everyone a good rating.

_____ 19. I tend to take it easy during the year, but I make sure to really push and do a good job for the month of December, and that's why I got a good performance review.

_____ 20. I attended all the classes and participated in the class discussions, so the professor gave me an A even though my final average on my test scores was a B.

WORK
APPLICATION 8-7

Select your current job or a past job. Identify and explain how the organization's performance appraisal process does or doesn't use each of the three methods of overcoming common performance appraisal problems. How can the organization improve the process?

exhibit a particular trait to be successful in a job. By eliminating traits, we lower the incidence of bias, stereotyping, and similarity errors.

Give the Measures the OUCH and Blanchard Tests. We already stated this, but these two tests are so important that they bear repeating here. With the OUCH test, the measure has to be objective, uniform in application, consistent in effect, and have job relatedness. With the Blanchard test, everyone must understand why they are assessed at a specific level (evaluation) and what it takes to get a higher rating (development).[48]

Train Evaluators. Next, we should train our evaluators to avoid the common errors and problems that occur in performance assessment and in how to use the various methods and forms.

Train Evaluators to Overcome the Common Problems of Assessment. Through training, the evaluator becomes aware that the common errors occur with some regularity, so they can guard against them. Most employees want to do a good job, and once they know that these errors are routinely made, they will make attempts to correct them.

Train Evaluators to Use the Measurement Methods and Forms. Evaluators should also be trained to use the various PA methods and forms. Because the critical incident method is not commonly used as a formal assessment method, evaluators should be taught to use it to help overcome recency error. Evaluators also need training to effectively use MBO and to write a good narrative. When using a graphic rating scale, the organization should provide some training for the raters so they better understand the differences between the word descriptors along the continuum (excellent, good, etc.). BARS forms and ranking are fairly straightforward, but supervisors need to realize that they too are subject to common problems when selecting each rating.

Use Multiple Raters. At least in some cases, we can have multiple raters evaluate an individual. As we noted earlier, this becomes expensive very quickly, so we must decide whether or not the value inherent in using multiple evaluators overcomes the cost of the process. However, if it does, using multiple evaluators can conquer some significant problems in the appraisal process, including bias and stereotyping. In addition, halo, similarity, and contrast errors become less likely, and distributional errors tend to even out among multiple raters. It is for these reasons that 360-degree evaluations have gained favor in many organizations.

LO 8-7

Contrast evaluative performance reviews and developmental performance reviews.

H:6

Appraisal Feedback

DEBRIEFING THE APPRAISAL

The debriefing process is where we communicate to individuals our analysis of their performance. **Facebook** managers are being told that performance reviews should be 80% focused on strengths.[49] Recall that there are two major reasons for assessing performance: for evaluative decisions and for development. We also suggested breaking the formal performance appraisal debriefing into two separate interviews. In this section, we will briefly describe how to conduct both reviews.

The Evaluative Performance Appraisal Interview

When preparing for an evaluative interview, follow the steps outlined in Model 8-2. Our evaluation should be fair (meaning ethically and legally not based on any of the problems discussed).[50] If we have had regular coaching conversations with our employees, they know where they stand,[51] and our preparation is mostly done except for filling out the form. So our relationship with the employee will directly affect the outcome.[52] Employees should also critique their own performance through a self-assessment using the same form as the evaluator prior to the meeting.[53]

MODEL 8-2   THE EVALUATIVE PERFORMANCE APPRAISAL INTERVIEW

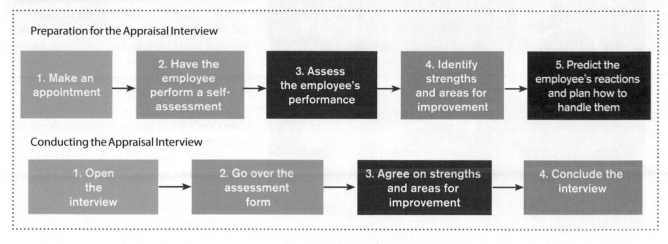

Preparation for the Appraisal Interview

1. Make an appointment → 2. Have the employee perform a self-assessment → 3. Assess the employee's performance → 4. Identify strengths and areas for improvement → 5. Predict the employee's reactions and plan how to handle them

Conducting the Appraisal Interview

1. Open the interview → 2. Go over the assessment form → 3. Agree on strengths and areas for improvement → 4. Conclude the interview

Conducting an Evaluative Interview. During the interview, encourage the employee to talk and also listen to the critique of their performance.[54] Model 8-2 lists the steps for conducting an evaluative performance appraisal interview. In step 1, we open the meeting with some small talk to put the person at ease. Then in step 2, we go over our evaluation of the items on the assessment form. In step 3, we identify the employee's strengths and weaknesses, discuss them, and agree on them. Finally, in step 4, we conclude the interview, which may involve making the appointment for the developmental interview.

MODEL 8-3   THE DEVELOPMENTAL PERFORMANCE APPRAISAL INTERVIEW

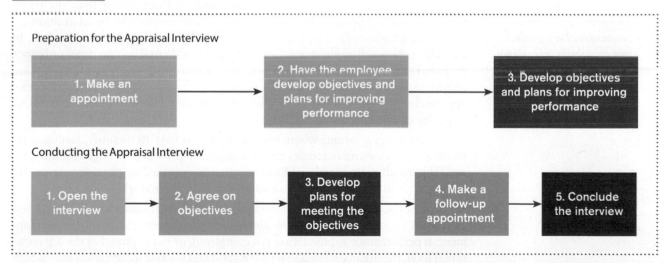

Preparation for the Appraisal Interview

1. Make an appointment → 2. Have the employee develop objectives and plans for improving performance → 3. Develop objectives and plans for improving performance

Conducting the Appraisal Interview

1. Open the interview → 2. Agree on objectives → 3. Develop plans for meeting the objectives → 4. Make a follow-up appointment → 5. Conclude the interview

The Developmental Performance Appraisal Interview

After the employee's performance evaluation is completed, you should prepare for the developmental interview based on targeting areas for improvement you already discussed in the evaluative interview. Yes, as a manager you are busy, and you may question the need for coaching and the cost of separate formal developmental interviews, but the benefit of spending time developing employees will lead to increased performance and lower turnover in your organization.[55]

Conducting a Developmental Interview. The steps are listed in Model 8-3. Again, step 1 starts with small talk to open the interview. In step 2, it is important to agree on

Developmental performance appraisals can be time consuming, but will ultimately lead to increased performance and lower turnover.

developmental objectives. As part of step 3, the employee needs to be made aware of exactly what he or she must do to improve and increase the rating on the next review, and you must also let the employee know that follow-up progress feedback is essential for changing behavior.[56] So step 4 is to set up a follow-up meeting to review the employee's progress. When conducting steps 3 and 4, we don't want the employee working on too many things at once, so we should keep the number of objectives down to three or fewer related issues. We can always add new objectives later. We end in step 5 by concluding the interview with some positive encouragement to reach the objectives.

TRENDS AND ISSUES IN HRM

The first item in this trends and issues section asks whether we can and should provide employees with continuous evaluations of their performance. Then we discuss the relative merits of competency-based performance management and the more traditional task-based evaluation of performance.

WORK
APPLICATION 8-9

Select an organization you work for or have worked for. Does it use formal evaluations? Do you believe the organization should or should not conduct formal evaluations?

Is It Time to Do Continuous Appraisals?

One of the more recent performance measurement ideas gaining traction is to use continuous technology-based appraisal and feedback rather than the traditional evaluation process. In organizations where results can be quantitatively measured, *results-only-work-environments* (ROWE) are beginning to be seen. In a results-only-work-environment, employees are evaluated on outcomes only (not on behaviors or traits as in most traditional evaluation processes). Outcomes are continuously evaluated, and there is no waiting for an end-of-year performance appraisal. For a ROWE system to work, though, goals have to be quantifiable so that they can be specifically measured.

In other organizations where results are not as easy to quantify, feedback on member behavior and outcomes can be constantly provided through technologies available to all team members. Each member is expected to provide meaningful feedback to all other members as a routine part of their work.

One problem with the above methods is that organizations legitimately use appraisals to make good decisions about their employees and employee development. If performance appraisals are not completed, or not captured at the organizational level, the organization doesn't have valid and reliable information with which to make good decisions about things such as training, promotions, and pay raises.

WORK
APPLICATION 8-10

Select an organization you work for or have worked for. Does it use competency-based performance management? Do you believe the organization should or should not use it?

Competency-Based Performance Management

Historically, the performance appraisal process evaluates specific employee skills and the employee's success in using those skills. Competency-based performance, on the other hand, evaluates large sets of capabilities and knowledge that, if put to good use, can improve organizational productivity to a much greater extent than just doing a job using an existing skill set.

Because of the nature of work in today's companies, and the fact that competencies are becoming a significant issue, performance management systems need to be redesigned so that we can evaluate the skills and capabilities that are most important to the business. However, to successfully use competency-based performance management, the organization has to move from an analysis and measurement of the *individual tasks* within a process to a more holistic evaluation of the *ability to combine and improve activities* to create the most successful organizational outcomes.

SHRM notes that doing competency-based evaluations is necessary to align performance with rewards if the organization is going to use a competency-based pay and incentives program.[57] Competency-based pay programs have been shown to align individual goals more closely with the organization's overall strategic goals. Because of these factors, competency-based performance appraisals will likely continue to increase as a percentage of overall performance appraisal processes.

WORK
APPLICATION 8-11

For a change, let's look at your college professors' grading habits. Are some professors hard graders (meaning they give few As), are others easy graders (meaning they give lots of As), or are they all consistent? Assuming there is inconsistency, should the college administration dictate a forced grade distribution?

Get the edge on your studies at edge.sagepub.com/fundamentalsofhrm

Read the chapter and then take advantage of the open-access site to

- take a quiz to find out what you've mastered;
- test your knowledge with key term flashcards;
- watch videos to capture key chapter content.

REVIEW, **PRACTICE**, and **IMPROVE** your critical thinking with the tools and resources at **SAGE edge**.

$SAGE edge™

• • • CHAPTER SUMMARY

8-1   Summarize the necessary characteristics of accurate performance management tools.

The performance management tools and measures that we use need to be valid, reliable, acceptable/feasible, and specific. A *valid* tool measures the process that you want it to measure. A *reliable* tool works in a generally consistent way each time you use it. *Acceptability* and *feasibility* deal with the tool being satisfactory and reasonable to the people who use it and also capable of being successfully applied in a particular situation. Finally, a *specific* measure defines the performance well enough that we understand the current level of performance achieved and what, if anything, the employees need to do to improve their performance to comply with standards.

8-2   Identify and briefly discuss the purposes of performance appraisals.

Communication is the first purpose. Appraisals need to provide an opportunity for formal two-way communication between management and the employee concerning how the organization feels the employee is performing. The second purpose is to

gain information for evaluative decisions. We need good information on how employees are performing so that we can take fair and equitable actions with our workforce to improve organizational productivity. Providing motivation for development is the last major purpose. Used correctly, appraisals can motivate by providing opportunities for the employees to improve their performance over time.

8-3   Discuss the options for what to evaluate in a performance appraisal.

Our three primary options for what to evaluate are traits, behaviors, and results. There is *some* evidence that particular types of traits are valuable in jobs that require management and leadership skills, but many traits have been shown to have very little bearing on job performance, meaning they are not valid measures of performance. We can also use behaviors to evaluate our workers. Measuring behaviors is usually a much better appraisal option because physical actions or behaviors can be directly observed, and as a result, they are more likely to be a valid assessment of the individual's performance. Finally, we can evaluate performance based on results. Results are a concrete measure of what has happened in the organization. However, results may be skewed based on factors that are outside the control of the individual who is being evaluated.

8-4   List the commonly used performance measurement methods and forms.

The *critical incidents* method utilizes records of major employee actions over the course of the appraisal period to complete the employee evaluation. *MBO* uses objectives jointly set by the manager and employee to gauge employee performance during the evaluation period. In the *narrative method*, the manager writes either a structured or unstructured paragraph about the employee's performance. *Graphic rating scales* provide a numerical scale so that the manager can check off where an employee falls on the continuum. *BARS* forms provide a description of the behaviors that make up acceptable performance at each level on the scale. Finally, *ranking* creates a hierarchy of employees, from best to worst.

8-5   Describe the available options for the rater/ evaluator.

It is logical to choose *supervisors* as evaluators when they have ongoing contact with the subordinate and know the subordinate's job. When the supervisor may not spend lots of time with the individual employee, *peers* may make better evaluators because they may know the job of the individual employee better than the supervisor does and may be more directly affected by the employee's actions. *Subordinate* evaluations can give us good insight into the managers who control employees in our

organization. We may want to use *customers* as evaluators when the individual being evaluated has frequent contact with those customers, because we need to know how customers feel about their interactions with our employees. *Self-evaluation* is valuable in a number of management processes, from training and development to counseling and disciplinary measures, among others.

8-6   Name some of the common problems with the performance appraisal process.

Personal biases and stereotyping are two of the most significant appraisal problems. Other problems include halo error, distributional errors (either the grading is too harsh or too lenient, or everyone is judged to be average), similarity error, proximity error, recency error, and contrast error.

8-7   Contrast evaluative performance reviews and developmental performance reviews.

The *evaluative interview* is a review of the individual employee's performance over a certain period. The evaluation needs to be fair and equitable, not based on bias. The employee must be given the opportunity to talk as well as listen to the critique of their performance. The *developmental interview*, on the other hand, focuses on areas for improvement over time. You should have employees come up with their own objectives and strategies for improvement, and you should develop your own objectives for them.

8-8   Define the key terms found in the chapter margins and listed following the Chapter Summary.

Complete the Key Terms Review to test your understanding of this chapter's key terms.

● ● ● KEY TERMS

behaviorally anchored rating scale (BARS) form, 198
behaviors, 195
bias, 203
critical incidents method, 197
graphic rating scale form, 198

management by objectives (MBO) method, 197
motivation, 194
narrative method or form, 198
performance appraisal, 191
performance management, 190

ranking, 199
results, 195
stereotyping, 203
360-degree evaluation, 202
traits, 194

● ● ● KEY TERMS REVIEW

Complete each of the following statements using one of this chapter's key terms.

1. _____ is the process of identifying, measuring, managing, and developing the performance of the human resources in an organization.

2. _____ is the ongoing process of evaluating employee performance.

3. _____ is the willingness to achieve organizational objectives.

4. _____ identify the physical or psychological characteristics of a person.

5. _____ are the actions taken by an individual.

6. _____ is a measure of the goals achieved through a work process.

7. _____ is a performance appraisal method in which a manager keeps a written record of positive and negative performance of employees throughout the performance period.

8. _____ is a process in which managers and employees jointly set objectives for the employees, periodically evaluate performance, and give rewards according to the results.

9. _____ requires a manager to write a statement about the employee's performance.

10. _____ is a performance appraisal checklist on which a manager simply rates performance on a continuum such as excellent, good, average, fair, and poor.

11. _____ is a performance appraisal that provides a description of each assessment along a continuum.

12. _____ is a performance appraisal method that is used to evaluate employee performance from best to worst.

13. _____ analyzes individual performance from all sides—from the supervisor's viewpoint, from the subordinates' viewpoint, from customers' viewpoints (if applicable), from peers, and using the employee's own self-evaluation.

14. _____ is a personality-based tendency, either toward or against something.

15. _____ consists of mentally classifying a person into an affinity group and then identifying the person as having the same assumed characteristics as that group.

• • • COMMUNICATION SKILLS

The following critical-thinking questions can be used for class discussion and/or for written assignments to develop communication skills. Be sure to give complete explanations for all answers.

1. Other than giving an annual evaluation, what would you do to manage the performance of your employees? Explain why.

2. What would you do as the manager in order to make sure that your employees knew the standards that they would be evaluated against? Explain your answer.

3. Do you really think that it is possible for a performance appraisal to be motivational? Why or why not?

4. Can you think of a situation in which a trait-based evaluation would be necessary? Explain your answer.

5. You are in charge and you want to evaluate a group of assembly workers. Who would you choose as the evaluator(s)? What about evaluating the Director of Operations—who would you choose to do that? Explain your answer.

6. How would you minimize the chances that stereotyping could affect the evaluation process in your company?

7. Which of the solutions to performance appraisal problems would you implement first if you were in charge? Second? Why?

8. What would you do to make the performance appraisal debriefing more comfortable and less confrontational for your employees? How do you think this would help?

9. Do you agree that annual performance appraisals should be discontinued in companies? Defend your answer.

• • • CASE 8-1 AMAZON.COM: SELLING EMPLOYEE PERFORMANCE WITH ORGANIZATION AND LEADERSHIP REVIEW

Amazon.com, which started as the biggest online bookstore, has become a household name by expanding rapidly in the retail market. It offers millions of movies, games, music, electronics, and other general merchandise products in several categories, including apparel and accessories, auto parts, home furnishings, health and beauty aids, toys, and groceries. Shoppers can also download e-books, games, MP3s, and films to their computers or handheld devices, including Amazon's own portable e-reader, the Kindle. Amazon also offers products and services, such as self-publishing, online advertising, an e-commerce platform, hosting, and a cobranded credit card.[58]

To keep this megastore running at a fast pace, Amazon hired 115,000 employees who generated $74 billion in 2013. Target and Home Depot made a combined income of close to $74 billion in the same year, yet they employed more than 340,000 people between them in their retail stores.[59] Why does Amazon only need one third of its competitors' labor force to produce the same revenue? Like the other mega retailer, Wal-Mart, Amazon has delivered creative business solutions to their own processes to continuously increase their operating effectiveness. However, their strategy focuses on enhancing the customer shopping experience and providing excellent customer service rather than providing the lowest-priced products. To meet their customers' needs, Amazon must deliver more speed and efficiency in its giant warehouse. They use more automated work processes that reduce the company's operational costs and also increase labor efficiency and employee safety.

The quality of Amazon's warehouse labor has become the critical issue in the firm's success, and hence, hiring and retaining the best, most suitable candidates for the company's manual labor positions is a key success factor. That being said, Amazon's turnover rate at these lowest-ranked positions in the organization is high since Amazon lets go of its lowest-performing employees to make room for new, more appropriate candidates while promoting the very best. To detect the lowest- and highest-performing employees, Amazon initiated a performance evaluation system called the Organization and Leadership Review (OLR).[60]

OLR actually has two main goals: (1) finding future leaders and preparing them to be able to face the most challenging tasks presented in a fast-paced work environment; and (2) determining the 10% of employees who are the least effective and taking necessary corrective action with them. OLRs take place twice a year to grant promotions and find the least effective employees.[61] Only the top-level managers attend these meetings, where there could be two reasons why an employee's name may be mentioned. Either the employee is being considered for a promotion, or the employee's job might be at stake.

OLRs start with the attendees reading the meeting agenda. Then supervisors suggest the most deserving subordinates to be considered for promotion. All executives in the room evaluate these suggestions and then debate the alternatives. Promotions are given at the end. During the process, instead of using hard data, executives tend to evaluate employees' performance on the basis of personal, anecdotal experiences. Anyone in the meeting may deny a promotion; therefore, ambitious employees seeking a promotion should also be very friendly with their boss's peers. If an employee's supervisor cannot present that worker well enough, another's favorite subordinate will get the promotion.[62]

In terms of promotion, Amazon CEO Jeff Bezos expects the managers to set the performance bar quite high to allow only the most exceptional talent to progress.[63] Promotions are protected by well-written guidelines, which focus on delivery and impact but not on internal politics. People spend less time campaigning for their own promotions, and top performers are highly compensated based upon the quality of their work.[64] Therefore, only a few promotions are available each year, and receiving positive feedback from a supervisor is quite rare. The approval that employees get from their supervisor is not enough to earn a promotion; employees still have to "fight" for a promotion, which may not occur immediately.

Questions

1. Do you think OLRs increase employee motivation? If not, why would Amazon conduct such performance appraisals?

2. How might rater bias, stereotyping, and traits appraisal impact the accuracy of OLR? Could this be corrected? If so, how?

3. Given the differing appraisal systems described in this chapter, which appraisal systems most closely resemble OLR?

4. Given your answer to the above question, what appraisal system do you think would best meet Amazon's objectives of retaining the best employees while taking corrective action with the bottom 10%?

5. Amazon is a high-technology firm. How might it use electronic performance monitoring to supplement the OLR process?

6. What are the advantages and disadvantages of having performance reviews like OLR that only involve one-way communication, rather than MBO?

Case created by Herbert Sherman, PhD, and Theodore Vallas, Department of Management Sciences, School of Business Brooklyn Campus, Long Island University

---

● ● ● SELF-ASSESSMENT AND SKILL BUILDER 8-1 PEER AND SELF-ASSESSMENTS

This exercise includes the usual self-assessment for each chapter, plus an evaluation of peers and developing measures of performance.

Objective

To develop your skill at assessing your performance and that of your peers

To develop your skill at developing measures of performance

Skills

The primary skills developed through this exercise are as follows:

1. *HR management skill*—conceptual and design skills

2. *SHRM 2013 Curriculum Guidebook*—H: Performance management

Assignment Part 1—Self-Assessment

During your college courses, you most likely had to do some form of group assignments, and you've also done group assignments in this course. Select one group you worked with, and based on your performance in that group, do a self-evaluation using the rating scale form below.

Evaluator (you) _____
(Self-Evaluation)

	A A– Always	B+ B B– Usually	C+ C C– Frequently	D+ D D– Sometimes	F Rarely
Did a "good" analysis of project					
Developed "good" questions to ask					
Actively participated (truly interested/involved)					
Made "quality" effort and contributions					
Got along well with group members					
Displayed leadership					
List at least three of your own measures of performance here					
Class attendance—number of absences	0–1	2	3	4	5+
Attendance at group meetings to prepare group project—number of absences	0	1	2	3	4+
Managed the group's time well					

This exercise can stop with just a self-assessment, or it can continue to also include peer evaluations.

Assignment Part 2—Peer Review

1. Part 2 begins by conducting a peer evaluation using the above form for each of the other members in your group, but using this heading for the form:

   Group Member _____
   (Peer Evaluation)

   Either copy the above form for each group member, do your assessment on any sheet without using the form, or have your instructor provide you with multiple forms that you can complete for each group member.

2. Below, rank each group member (including yourself) based on their performance. The first person you list should be the best performer, and the last person you list should be the least effective performer, based on the performance appraisal above. If members are close or equal in performance, you may assign them the same rank number, but you must list the better one first.

3. To the right of each group member (including yourself), place the overall letter grade (A–F) you would assign to that member based on the performance appraisal. You may give more than one member the same grade if those individuals deserve the same grade. You may also use plus and minus grades.

Rank	Name	Grade
_____	_____	_____
_____	_____	_____
_____	_____	_____
_____	_____	_____

• • • SKILL BUILDER 8–2 DEBRIEFING THE APPRAISAL

Note: This exercise is designed for groups that have been working together for some time as part of the course requirements. It is a continuation of Skill Builder 8-1. Based on your peer evaluations, you will conduct performance appraisals for your group members.

Objective

To develop a plan to improve your team performance, and to develop your skills in conducting performance appraisals

Skills

The primary skills developed through this exercise are as follows:

1. *HR management skill*–Conceptual and design skills
2. *SHRM 2013 Curriculum Guidebook*—H: Performance management

Assignment

You will be both the evaluator and evaluatee. Get together with group members and have each member select a letter, beginning with the letter A. Pair off as follows: A and B, C and D, E and F, etc. If the group consists of an odd number of people, each member will sit out one round. A should conduct the evaluation interview for B, C should conduct the evaluation interview for D, etc., using the form in Skill Builder 8-1. The evaluators should follow up the evaluation interview with the developmental interview to give suggestions on improving B, D, and F's performance (be sure to follow the evaluative and developmental interview steps in Models 8-1 and 8-2). Make sure you are evaluators and evaluatees; do not be peers having a discussion. When you finish, or when the instructor tells you time is up, reverse roles of evaluators and evaluatees. B, D, and F will become the new evaluators for A, C, and E.

When the instructor tells you to, or when time is up, form new groups of two and decide who will be the evaluators first. Continue changing groups of two until every group member has appraised and been appraised by every other group member.

Apply It

What did I learn from this experience? How will I improve my group performance in the course? How will I use this knowledge in the future?

_____

_____

_____

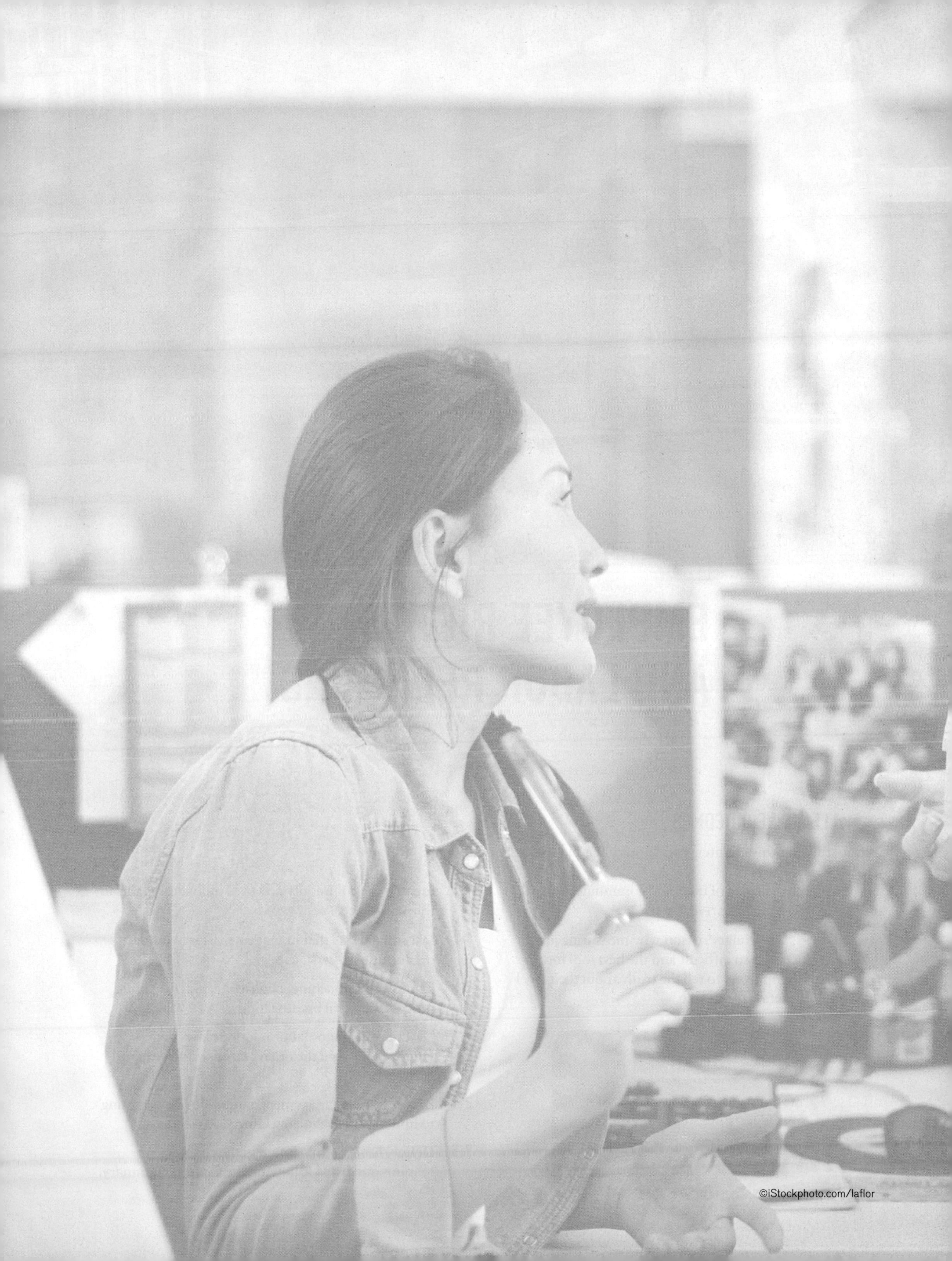

©iStockphoto.com/AnnaBryukhanova

9 EMPLOYEE RIGHTS AND LABOR RELATIONS

• • • LEARNING OUTCOMES

After studying this chapter, you should be able to do the following:

9-1 Explain the value of trust and communication in employee relations. PAGE 218

9-2 Discuss the primary reason why measuring job satisfaction is so difficult and the best tool for getting employees to tell the truth about their level of satisfaction. PAGE 220

9-3 Identify the commonly accepted individual rights in the workplace. PAGE 223

9-4 List some rights that management has in modern organizations. PAGE 225

9-5 Contrast the coaching, counseling, and discipline processes used in organizations. PAGE 226

9-6 Describe the major labor relations laws in the United States and the main reasons why we have each law. PAGE 231

9-7 Discuss what management cannot do in attempting to limit union organizing efforts. PAGE 234

9-8 Define the key terms found in the chapter margins and listed following the Chapter Summary. PAGE 239

Practitioner's Perspective

Cindy says, "If it isn't documented, it didn't happen."

That's a common expression in health care settings, and it stresses the importance of record keeping for patient care. The same holds true for management of personnel issues.

"I've had it with Jeremy!" Leonard exploded when Cindy returned his phone call one morning. "I've told him a million times how to run this report, and he won't follow my instructions! If he makes one more mistake, that's it—he's out of here."

"Whoa, Leonard," Cindy soothed. "You know our policy advises progressive discipline. Are you documenting your issues with Jeremy? Have you tried nondisciplinary counseling or a written warning?"

"I don't have time for all that nonsense," scoffed Leonard. "I should be able to fire any employee I want!"

"If you haven't been keeping records to back up your management of Jeremy's performance issues, discharge is not your first option." Cindy cautioned.

For the sake of due process in disciplinary matters, supervisors must document that an employee was informed of performance issues and given an opportunity to improve. You will find helpful information on employee versus management rights and related legal requirements in Chapter 9.

• • •

••• CHAPTER OUTLINE

Managing and Leading Your Workforce
Trust and Communication

Job Satisfaction
Measuring Job Satisfaction
Determinants of Job Satisfaction

Commonly Accepted Employee Rights
Right of Free Consent
Right to Due Process
Right to Life and Safety
Right of Freedom of Conscience (Limited)
Right to Privacy (Limited)
Right to Free Speech (Limited)

Management Rights
Codes of Conduct
Employment-at-Will

Coaching, Counseling, and Discipline
Coaching

Counseling
Disciplining

Legal Issues in Labor Relations
The Railway Labor Act (RLA) of 1926
The National Labor Relations Act (NLRA) of 1935 (Wagner Act)
The Labor Management Relations Act (LMRA) of 1947 (Taft-Hartley Act)
The Worker Adjustment and Retraining Notification Act of 1988 (WARN Act)

Unions and Labor Rights
Union Organizing
Labor Relations and Collective Bargaining
Grievances
Decertification Elections

Trends and Issues in HRM
Facebook, Twitter, etc. @ Work: Are They Out of Control?
Nonunion Worker Protection and the NLRB

LO 9-1

Explain the value of trust and communication in employee relations

WORK

APPLICATION 9-1

Select a present or past boss and describe how much you trust that person. Be sure to give specific examples of things your boss did, or didn't do, that created or destroyed your trust.

Trust Faith in the character and actions of another

MANAGING AND LEADING YOUR WORKFORCE

No matter what else happens in an organization, managers and employees have to work together to accomplish sets of goals.[1] For this to happen successfully, people in organizations must be able to communicate with each other.[2] Communication allows us to control the work environment, give and receive important information, express how we feel about a set of circumstances, and motivate ourselves and others. In addition, whenever people have to communicate to accomplish a goal, the sender and receiver must establish trust to avoid creating barriers in the communication process.[3] In this section, we begin with an overview of trust and communications and then provide details of sending and receiving messages when communicating.

Trust and Communication

Trust *is simply faith in the character and actions of another.* In other words, it is a belief that another person will do what they say they will do—every time. There is evidence of a "crisis of trust" in business today.[4] Consultant Jack Welch said trust "is enormously powerful in an organization and people won't do their best without it."[5] So how do we get others to trust us? We must do what we say we will do consistently, over a period of time. Trust is absolutely necessary to strong management-labor relations, and research shows that companies that have the trust of their employees have "lower turnover [and] higher revenue, profitability, and shareholder returns."[6]

SHRM HR CONTENT

See Appendix: *SHRM 2013 Curriculum Guidebook* for the complete list

A. Employee and Labor Relations (required)

  1. Disciplinary actions: Demotion, disciplinary termination

  8. Union membership

  9. Union-related labor laws

  10. Union/management relations

  11. Union decertification and deauthorization

  12. Collective bargaining issues

  13. Collective bargaining process

  16. Grievance management

  17. Strikes, boycotts, and work stoppages

  18. Unfair labor practices

  19. Managing union organizing policies and handbooks

  21. Attitude surveys

  22. Investigations

  27. Employee records

B. Employment Law (required)

  12. The National Labor Relations Act of 1935 (NLRA)

  13. The Labor Management Relations Act of 1947 (LMRA)

  14. The Railway Labor Act of 1926 (RLA)

  16. The Worker Adjustment and Retraining Notification Act of 1988 (WARN Act)

  19. Employee privacy

  20. Employer unfair labor practices

  30. Employment-at-will doctrine

C. Ethics (required)

  5. Guidelines and codes

  6. Behavior within ethical boundaries

H. Performance Management (required)

  8. Diagnosing problems

  9. Performance improvement programs

I. Staffing: Recruitment and Selection (required)

  14. Job offers: Employment-at-will, contracts, authorization to work

M. Workforce Planning and Talent Management (required)

  3. Retention: Involuntary turnover, outplacement counseling, alternative dispute resolution

  4. Retention: Voluntary turnover, job satisfaction, withdrawal, alternatives

Q. Organization Development (required–graduate students only)

  1. Coaching

Trust takes a while to create, but only takes an instant to lose if we don't come through for the other person. So if we want to improve others' level of trust in us, we need to be open and honest with people.[7] If people catch you in a lie, they may never trust you again. To gain and maintain trust and credibility, always get the facts straight before you communicate, and then send clear, complete messages.[8]

Communication *is the process of transmitting information and meaning.* This meaning can be transferred verbally, nonverbally, or in writing. We are expected to work well in groups and communicate with ease.[9] Open communications are needed for the organization to be successful,[10] and good managers are good communicators.[11] If you think about creating trust, open communication is a necessary part of the equation of "doing what you say you will."

Listening Skills. Listening is crucial for effective communication to occur.[12] If someone were to ask us if we are good listeners, most of us would say yes. However,

WORK
APPLICATION 9-2

Review your answers to the Listening Self-Assessment. What are your two weakest areas, and how will you improve them?

Communication The process of transmitting information and meaning

---

9-1 SELF ASSESSMENT

Listening Skills

For each statement, select the response that best describes how often you actually behave in the way described. Place the letter *A*, *U*, *F*, *O*, or *S* on the line before each statement to indicate your response.

A = almost always   U = usually   F = frequently   O = occasionally   S = seldom

_____ 1. I like to listen to people talk. I encourage others to talk by showing interest, smiling, nodding, and so forth.

_____ 2. I pay closer attention to people who are similar to me than to people who are different from me.

_____ 3. I evaluate people's words and nonverbal communication ability as they talk.

_____ 4. I avoid distractions; if it's noisy, I suggest moving to a quiet spot.

_____ 5. When people interrupt me when I'm doing something, I put what I was doing out of my mind and give them my complete attention.

_____ 6. When people are talking, I allow them time to finish. I do not interrupt, anticipate what they are going to say, or jump to conclusions.

_____ 7. I tune out people who do not agree with my views.

_____ 8. While another person is talking or a professor is lecturing, my mind wanders to personal topics.

_____ 9. While another person is talking, I pay close attention to that person's nonverbal communication so I can fully understand what they are trying to communicate.

_____ 10. I tune out and pretend to understand when the topic is difficult for me to understand.

_____ 11. When another person is talking, I think about and prepare what I am going to say in reply.

_____ 12. When I think there is something missing from or contradictory in what someone says, I ask direct questions to get the person to explain the idea more fully.

_____ 13. When I don't understand something, I let the other person know I don't understand.

_____ 14. When listening to other people, I try to put myself in their position and see things from their perspective.

_____ 15. During conversations, I repeat back to the other person, in my own words, what the other person says; I do this to be sure I understand what has been said.

If people you talk to regularly answered these questions about you, would they have the same responses that you selected? To find out, have friends answer the questions using your name rather than "I." Then compare answers.

To determine your score, do the following:

For statements 1, 4, 5, 6, 9, 12, 13, 14, and 15, give yourself 5 points for each *A*, 4 for each *U*, 3 for each *F*, 2 for each *O*, and 1 for each *S*.

For statements 2, 3, 7, 8, 10, and 11, give yourself 5 points for each *S*, 4 for each *O*, 3 for each *F*, 2 for each *U*, and 1 for each *A*.

Write your score for each letter response on the line next to the letter. Now add up your total number of points. Your score should be between 15 and 75. Note where your score falls on the continuum below. Generally, the higher your score, the better your listening skills.

Poor Listener											Good Listener	
15	20	25	30	35	40	45	50	55	60	65	70	75

9-1 APPLYING THE CONCEPT

Communications

Identify whether each strategy listed below is an effective or ineffective aid to communications.

a. effective

b. ineffective

_____ 1. When listening to instructions, if you don't understand something being said, you should not do or say anything until you have received the entire set of instructions.

_____ 2. You should repeat back what the other person said word-for-word when you paraphrase.

_____ 3. After you finish giving instructions, you should ensure understanding by asking the person, "Do you have any questions?"

_____ 4. When giving instructions, you should tell the receiver your communication objective before giving the details of what is to be done to complete the task.

_____ 5. We should multitask while receiving messages face-to-face so that we can get more than one thing done at a time.

---

unfortunately, a recent survey found that the number one thing lacking in new college grads is listening skills.[13] One of the biggest problems in the 21st century work environment is the fact that constant multitasking is degrading our ability to pay attention and listen for very long.[14] However, there are ways to improve your skills in receiving communications. Find out how good a listener you are by completing the listening skills self-assessment.

LO 9-2

Discuss the primary reason why measuring job satisfaction is so difficult and the best tool for getting employees to tell the truth about their level of satisfaction.

JOB SATISFACTION

Remember that job satisfaction is important to us because it affects many other factors, including our dependent variables from Chapter 1—productivity, absenteeism, and turnover.[15] Studies have also found that dissatisfied employees are more apt to break the rules and sabotage performance, and more than half of all US employees are unsatisfied with their jobs.[16, 17] So we need to know how satisfied our workforce is at any point in time.

SHRM

M:4

Retention: Voluntary Turnover, Job Satisfaction, Withdrawal, Alternatives

SHRM

A:21

Attitude Surveys

Measuring Job Satisfaction

Job satisfaction can be measured through an organizational development survey, but we have to remember that a survey is an indirect measurement. Since job satisfaction is an attitude, we can't directly see or measure it—we have to *ask* employees about their attitudes.

Because of questions of trust between employees and management, it's always a good idea to ensure that any job satisfaction surveys are administered

EXHIBIT 9-1   FEMALE FACES SCALE

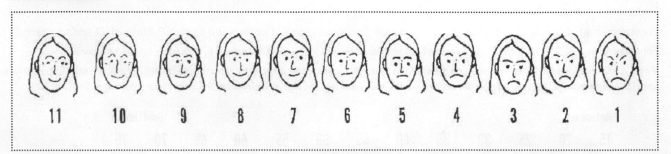

Source: "Development of a female faces scale for measuring job satisfaction" by Randall B. Dunham and Jeanne B. Herman, *Journal of Applied Psychology, 60*(5), October 1975, 629–631.

in a completely *anonymous* format because employees are much more likely to tell the truth when they take the survey. There are two common types of job satisfaction surveys or questionnaires. Let's briefly review each of them now.

The Faces Scale of Job Satisfaction Measurement. The first and simpler survey is called the "faces scale."[18] All the employee is asked to do is circle the face that most closely matches their overall satisfaction with their job. Exhibit 9-1 shows an example of the faces scale.

The Questionnaire Job Satisfaction Measurement. Take a look at Exhibit 9-2, which shows some of the questions from the Job Satisfaction Survey (JSS).[19] There are many different surveys of this type. Some firms develop their own, but the JSS is one of only a few that have been shown to be valid and reliable.[20]

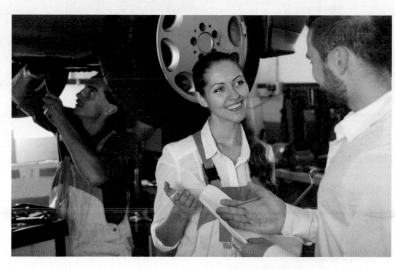

Job satisfaction effects many factors within an organization. Employers who keep tabs on their employees' levels of job satisfaction may see higher rates of productivity and lower rates of absenteeism and turnover.

Determinants of Job Satisfaction

Although compensation (pay and benefits) is important to job satisfaction, research historically has not strongly supported the idea that pay is the primary determinant of job satisfaction, or that people in high-paying jobs are more satisfied than those in low-paying jobs.[22] According to recent studies, the top reasons for job *dissatisfaction* are that employees don't like their supervisor, they feel powerless, they don't have any say in their work, and they don't feel like they get recognition for their work.[23,24] Millennials will not work for a bad boss.[25]

Seven major determinants of job satisfaction are presented in Self-Assessment 9-2: Job Satisfaction. Complete it to find out what is important to you and your own level of job satisfaction. You *can* have an overall high level of job satisfaction and still not like some aspects of your job; this is common.

WORK
APPLICATION 9-3

Identify the three most important determinants of your job satisfaction, and explain why they are important to you.

EXHIBIT 9-2 ### SAMPLE OF JOB SATISFACTION SURVEY (JSS) QUESTIONS[21]

	Disagree very much	Disagree moderately	Disagree slightly	Agree slightly	Agree moderately	Agree very much
People get ahead as fast here as they do in other places.	1	2	3	4	5	6
My supervisor shows too little interest in the feelings of subordinates.	1	2	3	4	5	6
The benefits package we have is equitable.	1	2	3	4	5	6
There are few rewards for those who work here.	1	2	3	4	5	6
I have too much to do at work.	1	2	3	4	5	6
I enjoy my coworkers.	1	2	3	4	5	6

9-2 SELF ASSESSMENT

Job Satisfaction

Select a present or past job. Identify your level of satisfaction with that job by placing a check at the appropriate position on the continuum for each determinant of job satisfaction.

1. Personality

| I have positive self-esteem. | 6 | 5 | 4 | 3 | 2 | 1 | I have negative self-esteem. |

2. Work Itself

| I enjoy doing the tasks I perform. | 6 | 5 | 4 | 3 | 2 | 1 | I do *not* enjoy doing the tasks I perform. |

3. Compensation

| I am fairly compensated (with pay and benefits). | 6 | 5 | 4 | 3 | 2 | 1 | I am *not* fairly compensated (with pay and benefits). |

4. Growth and Upward Mobility

| I have the opportunity to learn new things and get promoted to better jobs. | 6 | 5 | 4 | 3 | 2 | 1 | I have *no* opportunity to learn new things and get promoted to better jobs. |

5. Coworkers

| I like and enjoy working with my coworkers. | 6 | 5 | 4 | 3 | 2 | 1 | I do *not* like and enjoy working with my coworkers. |

6. Management

| I believe that my boss and managers are doing a good job. | 6 | 5 | 4 | 3 | 2 | 1 | I do *not* believe that my boss and managers are doing a good job. |

7. Communication

| We have open and honest communication. | 6 | 5 | 4 | 3 | 2 | 1 | We do *not* have open and honest communication. |

Overall Job Satisfaction

When determining your overall job satisfaction, you cannot simply add up a score based on the above seven determinants because they are most likely of different importance to you. Rank your top three factors below:

1. _____

2. _____

3. _____

Now, think about your job and the above factors, and rate your overall satisfaction with your job below:

| I am satisfied with my job (high level of job satisfaction). | 6 | 5 | 4 | 3 | 2 | 1 | I am dissatisfied with my job (low level of job satisfaction). |

Job Satisfaction

Correctly match each statement with its determinant of job satisfaction, writing the letter corresponding to each determinant before the statement associated with it.

a. personality

b. work itself

c. compensation

d. growth

e. coworkers

f. management

g. communications

_____ 6. There is a job opening in the metal fusion shop, and I am going to apply for the position.

_____ 7. I really enjoy fixing cars to help people get around.

_____ 8. I'm mad at my manager because he didn't give me the good performance review that I deserved.

_____ 9. Of course I can do that task for you.

_____ 10. The thing I like best about my job is the people I work with.

COMMONLY ACCEPTED EMPLOYEE RIGHTS

Providing employees with reasonable rights in the organization helps them to remain satisfied with their work. In this section, we discuss six employee rights; see Exhibit 9-3 for a list.[26] Let's break down each of the six rights individually in separate sections.

Right of Free Consent

Individuals in a modern organization have the *right of free consent*, which is the right of the individual to know what they're being asked to do and the consequences of that action to the individual or others. The organization's duty is to ensure that the individual *voluntarily agrees* to do a particular job or task for the organization, making them fully aware of everything involved.

LO 9-3

Identify the commonly accepted individual rights in the workplace.

WORK
APPLICATION 9-4

Give an example of how your present or past employer met your right to free consent. What did you consent to do on the job? Have you ever not consented to do something on the job? If yes, give an example of what you refused to do.

EXHIBIT 9-3 EMPLOYEE RIGHTS

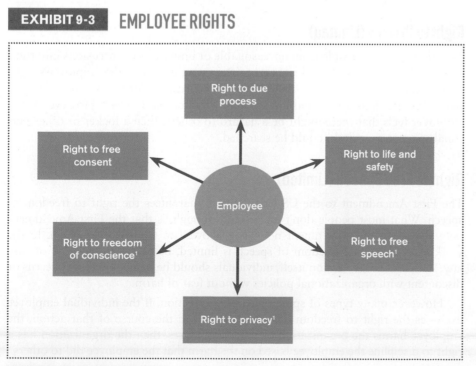

¹Note that these three rights have limitations.

©iStockphoto.com/BostjanT

Organizations have a duty to provide their employees a right to life and safety on the job.

WORK
APPLICATION 9-5

Give an example of when employees were encouraged to conduct unethical or illegal activities. Try to give an example from an organization where you work or have worked, but otherwise, give an example from another source, such as the news media.

SHRM

A:27
Employee Records

SHRM

B:19
Employee Privacy

WORK
APPLICATION 9-6

How do you feel about employees communicating negative things about the organization to outsiders? Should management monitor employee speech and take action to stop negative speech?

Right to Due Process

We have due process so that employees are not punished arbitrarily.[27] If the organization contemplates a disciplinary action, the employee has a right to know what they are accused of, to know the evidence or proof thereof, and to tell their side of what happened. We will review due process and the seven tests for Just Cause shortly, but due process is basically the concept of providing fair and reasonable disciplinary actions as consequences of an employee's behavior.

Right to Life and Safety

Every employee within the organization has a right to be protected from harm, to the best of the organization's ability. In 1948, the United Nations declared that every individual has a right to life, liberty, and security of person.[28] Security of person basically means personal safety. So the organization has a general duty to see that every employee is protected from harm when working within the organization because the individual has a right to life and safety.

Right of Freedom of Conscience (Limited)

Employees generally should not be asked to do something that violates their personal values and beliefs, *as long as these beliefs generally reflect commonly accepted societal norms*. A person's conscience determines what that person considers to be right and wrong. The organization has a general duty to avoid forcing an individual to do something that they consider to be wrong, either morally or ethically, and the individual has a right to avoid doing things within the organization that would violate their personal values and beliefs.

Right to Privacy (Limited)

This right protects people from unreasonable or unwarranted intrusions into their personal affairs. This general right to privacy would include the employee's right to have their personnel files, other employee records, and/or private areas of their workplace (such as a personal locker) kept private, *to an extent*. However, if the employer feels that there might be a hazard to others, then a locker or other personal space (e.g., a desk) could be searched.

Right to Free Speech (Limited)

The First Amendment to the US Constitution guarantees the right to freedom of speech. What most people don't understand, though, is that the First Amendment only applies to the government not being allowed to control free speech. In the workplace, individual freedom of speech is limited, based on many years of case law. Within the organization itself, individuals should be free to express concerns or discontent with organizational policies without fear of harm.

However, many types of speech have no protection. If the individual employee exercises the right to freedom of speech, and if, in the course of that action, the employee harms the organization or other employees, then the organization has a right to discipline the employee based on the harm that the employee did to others.

9-3 APPLYING THE CONCEPT

Employee Rights

Review the list of rights below and write the letter corresponding to each right before the statement involving that right.

a. free consent   d. freedom of conscience

b. due process   e. privacy

c. life and safety   f. free speech

_____ 11. The HR manager made me sign this form before I could start the job, stating that she had told me about the possible side effects from the lead paint removal.

_____ 12. I enjoy writing negative comments online about my boss and company.

_____ 13. I'm going to teach you how to use the rifle. Rule number one is to always make sure this lever is down so you don't fire the gun by accident.

_____ 14. You can't discipline me for this minor safety violation. I'm going to the labor union to stop you from doing it.

_____ 15. Let me keep working in security. I don't want to work in the bar, even though it pays better, because drinking is against my religion.

_____ 16. Get out of my locker now. You have no right to search it without my permission.

MANAGEMENT RIGHTS

Organizations, like individuals, have rights within the larger society. Organizational rights tend to be based on the necessity for the organization to protect itself and its employees from persons that might do them harm, whether intentionally or unintentionally. In cases where such harm may occur, the organization has the right to limit individual employee rights. Let's briefly discuss two additional significant management rights.

LO 9-4

List some rights that management has in modern organizations.

Codes of Conduct

Managers of organizations have a right to create and require compliance with a code of employee conduct. The code of conduct is the organization's mechanism for identifying the ethics and values of the firm, and it serves as a guide to individual action.[29] Employees are more unethical when they believe they will not get caught and punished.[30] A code of conduct gives an employee a practical tool for determining whether or not an action that they are contemplating is within the acceptable boundaries of conduct within their organization.

C:5

Guidelines and Codes

SHRM

C:6

Behavior Within Ethical Boundaries

Employment-at-Will

Currently, under common law, "employment relationships are presumed to be 'at will' in all US states except Montana."[31] The concept of **employment-at-will** *allows the company or the worker to break the work relationship at any point in time, with or without any particular reason, as long as in doing so, no law is violated.* This means the employer does not have to have *cause* (reasons) to terminate an employment relationship with an individual worker.

However, employment-at-will is in reality a fairly weak law because courts in many jurisdictions in the United States have for many years ruled that employment-at-will is limited. The courts have specifically stated that there are three *standard exceptions* to employment-at-will.[32]

Public policy exceptions include such things as being terminated for filing a legitimate worker's compensation claim, refusing to lobby for a particular political candidate just because your boss likes the candidate, or refusing to violate a professional code of ethics.

B:30

Employment-at-Will Doctrine

SHRM

I:14

Job Offers: Employment-at-Will, etc.

Employment-at-will Concept allowing the company or the worker to break the work relationship at any point in time, with or without any particular reason, as long as in doing so, no law is violated

Evidence of an *implied contract* between the employee and the employer is another exception. For instance, if the company were to note in its employee handbook that "our organization values hard work, and many of our employees who perform well have been with us for many years," that *might* be considered an implied contract stating, "If you work hard, we will continue to employ you." This implication of a contract could negate the employment-at-will rights of the employer.

A *lack of good faith and fair dealing* is the third exception. If the employer does something that will benefit them but will significantly harm the individual employee, that action would create a lack of good faith and fair dealing. For instance, we might release a 38-year-old employee citing employment-at-will shortly before they become eligible for a company-sponsored retirement plan in order to hire a younger (and cheaper) employee in the same position and thus not have to pay the retirement benefits. This would be lack of good faith and fair dealing, even though it would not be a violation of age discrimination laws.

LO 9-5

Contrast the coaching, counseling, and discipline processes used in organizations.

COACHING, COUNSELING, AND DISCIPLINE

As discussed in Chapter 8, managers need to continually coach virtually all employees to improve performance. In this section, we discuss employee development through coaching, counseling, disciplining, and (if necessary) termination.

Coaching

SHRM

H:9
Performance Improvement Programs

SHRM

Q:1
Coaching

Coaching includes a variety of behavioral techniques and methods to help improve performance.[33] Good coaching also improves communications and relationships.[34] Coaching *is the process of giving motivational feedback to maintain and improve performance.* Feedback is intended to praise progress, to redirect inappropriate behavior, and to counsel employees on how to improve.[35] Employees who are given more immediate, frequent, and direct feedback perform at higher levels than those who are not given such feedback.[36]

WORK
APPLICATION 9-7

Assess your present or past boss's coaching skills. Did the boss follow the steps in the coaching model?

The Coaching Model. Coaching is a way to provide ongoing feedback to employees about their job performance.[37] However, ask managers what they tend to put off doing, and they'll likely say that they put off advising weak employees that they must improve their performance. Procrastinating managers often hope that the employees will turn around on their own, only to find—often too late—that the situation just continues to get worse. Part of the problem is that managers don't know how to coach or are not good at coaching,[38] so we have provided a simple four-step coaching model that you can use to improve performance in Model 9-1.[39]

Counseling

When you are coaching, you are fine-tuning performance. But when you are counseling and disciplining, you are dealing with an employee who is not performing to organizational standards. Good organizations realize the need to help employees with problems.[40]

Coaching The process of giving motivational feedback to maintain and improve performance

| MODEL 9-1 | COACHING MODEL |

| 1. Describe current performance | → | 2. Describe desired performance | → | 3. Get a commitment to change | → | 4. Follow up |

When most people hear the term *counseling*, they think of psychological counseling or psychotherapy. That type of sophisticated help should not be attempted by a noncounseling professional such as a manager. Instead, **management counseling** *is the process of giving employees feedback (so they realize that a problem is affecting their job performance) and referring employees with problems that cannot be managed within the work structure to the organization's employee assistance program.*

Problem Employees. Problem employees have a negative effect on performance.[41] Good human resource management skills can help you avoid hiring problem employees,[42] but even so, you will most likely have to confront problem employees as a manager.[43] Problem employees do poor-quality work, they don't get along with coworkers, they display negative attitudes, and they frequently come in late or don't show up for work.[44]

A manager's first obligation is to the organization's performance rather than to individual employees. Not taking action with problem employees—because you feel uncomfortable confronting them, because you feel sorry for them, or because you like them—does not help you or the employee.[45] Not only do problem employees negatively affect their own productivity, but they also cause more work for managers and other employees. Problem employees also lower morale, as others resent them for not pulling their own weight. Thus, it is critical to take quick action with problem employees.[46]

Employers may use a set of standard tests—a mechanism called just cause—for providing disciplinary action.

SHRM

H:8
Diagnosing Problems

Disciplining

You should try coaching, then counseling, in dealing with a problem employee. However, if an employee is unwilling or unable to change or a rule has been broken, discipline is necessary.[47] **Discipline** *is corrective action designed to get employees to meet standards and the code of conduct.* The major objective of coaching, counseling, and disciplining is to change behavior.[48] Secondary objectives may be to let employees know that action will be taken when standing plans or performance requirements are not met, and to maintain authority when challenged.

But how do we know as managers that we are being fair in applying discipline? Let's take a look at one mechanism for determining whether or not to discipline an errant employee and what level of discipline is appropriate—Just Cause.

Just Cause is actually *a set of standard tests for fairness in disciplinary actions—tests that were originally utilized in union grievance arbitrations.* However, many other companies have adopted the tests for Just Cause in their own nonunion disciplinary processes to try to ensure fairness.

The seven tests for Just Cause are as follows:

1. Did the company give the employee forewarning or foreknowledge of the possible or probable disciplinary consequences of the employee's conduct?

   With this test, we basically want to determine whether or not the employee was given any knowledge beforehand that the action was prohibited.

Management counseling The process of giving employees feedback (so they realize that a problem is affecting their job performance) and referring employees with problems that cannot be managed within the work structure to the organization's employee assistance program

Discipline Corrective action designed to get employees to meet standards and the code of conduct

Just Cause A set of standard tests for fairness in disciplinary actions—tests that were originally utilized in union grievance arbitrations

SHRM

A:22

Investigations

2. Was the company's rule or managerial order reasonably related to (a) the orderly, efficient, and safe operation of the company's business and (b) the performance that the company might properly expect of the employee?

Here we want to find out whether the rule was reasonable. We also look at whether or not the employee should be expected to act in a certain manner in order to follow the rule or order.

3. Did the company, before administering discipline to an employee, make an effort to discover whether the employee did in fact violate or disobey a rule or order of management?

Test 3 deals with investigation of the alleged infraction. If, upon investigating, the supervisor finds that there is reasonable evidence that the individual did violate the rules, then we've passed the third test.

4. Was the company's investigation conducted fairly and objectively?

Are we utilizing facts, figures, and knowledge of the events (the OUCH test), or is the supervisor basing the investigation on some emotional reaction to the supposed infraction?

5. Upon investigation, was there substantial evidence or proof that the employee was guilty as charged?

Substantial evidence is a large body of circumstantial information showing that the individual probably committed the offense. In a disciplinary action, we don't have to meet court standards of proof of guilt. If we have *proof*, then we meet this test, but if we have substantial evidence, we *still* meet the requirements of test 5.

6. Has the company applied its rules, orders, and penalties evenhandedly and without discrimination to all employees?

Test 6 tries to identify whether or not the rule is applied in an equitable manner. If the company punishes one person for an infraction with a written reprimand and punishes another person for the same infraction with a disciplinary discharge, then the company may not have been evenhanded in its disciplinary action. Does this mean that we have to punish every person in the exact same way for the exact same infraction? The answer is no—and that is where we get into test 7.

7. Was the degree of discipline administered by the company in a particular case reasonably related to (a) the seriousness of the employee's proven offense and (b) the record of the employee's service with the company?

Test 7 is where we are allowed to provide a different punishment to different people *based on past history*. So if we have two employees who have committed the same infraction and one of the employees has never been in trouble while the other has repeatedly committed the same infraction, then we have the flexibility to provide a different punishment for the two different offenders.

Guidelines for Effective Discipline. Exhibit 9-4 lists eight guidelines for effective discipline.

Progressive Discipline. If discipline is deemed necessary after going through the Just Cause standards, what type of discipline is warranted? **Progressive discipline** *is a process in which the employer provides the employee with opportunities to correct poor behavior before terminating them*. It is typically only used in cases of minor behavioral infractions such as arriving late to work or insubordination with a superior.

WORK
APPLICATION 9-8

Assess how well your boss and the organization you work or worked for follows the Just Cause standards.

Progressive discipline A process in which the employer provides the employee with opportunities to correct poor behavior before terminating them

EXHIBIT 9-4   GUIDELINES FOR EFFECTIVE DISCIPLINE

A. Clearly communicate the standards and code of conduct to all employees.
B. Be sure that the punishment fits the crime.
C. Follow the standing plans yourself.
D. Take consistent, impartial action when the rules are broken.
E. Discipline immediately, but stay calm and get all the necessary facts before you discipline.
F. Discipline in private.
G. Document discipline.
H. When the discipline is over, resume normal relations with the employee.

The progressive disciplinary steps are (1) informal coaching talk, (2) oral warning, (3) written warning, (4) suspension, and (5) dismissal. In some *limited* cases, we may add a sixth option between suspension and dismissal. Let's briefly discuss each step in progressive discipline.

Step 1: Informal coaching talk. As we noted, the first step in progressive discipline is an *informal coaching talk*. In an informal talk, the supervisor may see an employee coming in late to work and just ask them what is going on and why they are late. Typically the manager won't even write down a recording of such conversations for their own use, although they can do so in the critical incident file (Chapter 8). They're just in an information gathering and recognition mode at this point, and they hope to avoid any further disciplinary problems.

Step 2: Oral warning. In the second step, the supervisor formally tells the employee that their behavior is currently unacceptable and also tells them what they need to do to correct the behavior. In this situation, even though the supervisor does not write a report for the individual to sign, they will keep a formal record in their own files of this conversation. The oral warning is the first of our formal methods of disciplining an employee.

Step 3: Written warning. The third step is a *written warning*. In this situation, the supervisor writes up the facts of the situation. They identify the unacceptable behavior for

WORK
APPLICATION 9-9

Describe progressive discipline where you work or have worked.

WORK
APPLICATION 9-10

Assess how well your boss and the organization where you work or have worked follows the eight guidelines for effective discipline.

9-4   APPLYING THE CONCEPT

Guidelines for Effective Discipline

Identify which guideline is being followed—or not being followed—in the following statements. Use the guidelines in Exhibit 9-4 as the answers, writing the letter of the guideline (A–H) on the line before the statement involving it.

___ 17. "Are you kidding me? Can you really fire me just for being late for work once?"

___ 18. "I didn't know that I'm not supposed to make a personal call while I'm working. Can't you let it go this one time?"

___ 19. "Some days, my boss comments about my being late, but other days, she doesn't say anything about it."

___ 20. "Let's get back to the way things were before I had to discipline you, OK?"

___ 21. "Let's go to my office so that we can discuss your rule violation now."

___ 22. "I missed it. Why was the boss yelling at Rita?"

___ 23. "The boss comes back from break late all the time and nothing happens to him; so why do I get in trouble for being late?"

___ 24. "When I come to work late, the manager reprimands me. But when Latoya is late, nothing is ever said."

___ 25. "The boss gave me a written warning for being late for work and placed it in my permanent record file."

the individual and identify ways to correct the behavior. The supervisor then speaks with the employee using the written document to assist the employee in correcting their actions. Typically here, we ask the employee to sign the written warning, acknowledging that their actions are under review and not currently acceptable. This signed paper (documentation) is then put into the employee's permanent file.[49]

Step 4: Disciplinary suspension. As a fourth step, we may move on to a *disciplinary suspension* of the employee for a period of from one day to typically a maximum of one week. Most companies use an unpaid suspension, but some companies have experimented with a paid day off as time for the employee to figure out whether or not they wish to continue working for the organization. There is *some* evidence that these paid suspensions work, although the conclusions are slightly mixed.

Other Options Before Termination. Next, we have a couple of limited options we noted at the top of this section—options that would typically not be used but might be valuable in certain cases.

We can sometimes *demote* an individual to a lower position in the organization. In some cases, this may be valuable because the employee may be overwhelmed at the higher-level position. In general, however, demotion creates even more job dissatisfaction within the individual employee, and we may see their performance deteriorate even further.

Alternatively, we may choose in some cases to *transfer* an employee from one part of the organization to another. The only time when you should use a transfer as a progressive discipline measure would be when you know that there is a personality conflict between the employee and another employee or their supervisor. Transfers should never be used simply to get rid of a problem employee from your department or division. If this is the reason for the transfer, the manager should not transfer the employee but should correct the problem behavior.

Step 5: Termination. The last resort is *discharge*. If the employee's behavior does not improve over time as a result of verbal and written warnings, suspensions, demotions, or a transfer, we may be forced to let the employee go. However, if we followed the progressive discipline process, we will have sufficient evidence to limit the employee's opportunity to bring an unlawful termination lawsuit against us.

SHRM

A:1

Disciplinary Actions: Demotion, Disciplinary Termination

SHRM

M:3

Retention: Involuntary Turnover, etc.

9-1 ETHICAL DILEMMA: WHAT WOULD YOU DO?

Disciplining Ethical Behavior

Unfortunately, some managers are unfair/unethical in coaching, counseling, and/or disciplining employees. Also, some employees are rewarded for being unethical, while others are disciplined for being ethical. For example, some auto repair shops pay a commission for work done, so mechanics are paid more if they get customers to buy parts and services they don't need. Mechanics who have a below-average number of repairs may be considered underachievers and may be pressured, through discipline, to perform unneeded repair work. Similarly, those in the medical field may push unnecessary tests or even treatments.

1. Has a manager ever been unfair/unethical in coaching, counseling, or disciplining where you work or have worked? If so, explain the situation.
2. Have you ever been in or known of a situation in which people were rewarded for being unethical and disciplined for being ethical? If so, describe the situation.
3. Is it ethical and socially responsible for firms to establish controls that reward unethical behavior and discipline ethical behavior to make more money?
4. Has anyone you know of been unfairly/unethically terminated? If so, explain the situation.

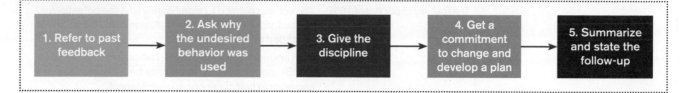

MODEL 9-2 THE DISCIPLINE MODEL

1. Refer to past feedback → 2. Ask why the undesired behavior was used → 3. Give the discipline → 4. Get a commitment to change and develop a plan → 5. Summarize and state the follow-up

The Discipline Model. There is a simple five-step discipline model that works very well. You should follow the steps of the discipline model each time you must discipline an employee. The five steps are summarized in Model 9-2.

Termination, or dismissal, is the most serious form of disciplinary action. Let's quickly look at some of the offenses that might be cause for dismissal immediately upon completion of an investigation of the facts.

Gross Negligence and Serious Misconduct. Organizations set up their own rules, listing violations that are grounds for immediate termination without progressive discipline. For example, many firms list stealing money or other assets from the organization as cause for immediate dismissal. In companies that promote open and honest communications, there might be a rule that anyone caught lying will be fired.

Two of the more common situations in which we might immediately dismiss employees would be in cases of gross negligence or serious misconduct. Gross negligence *is a serious failure to exercise care in the work environment.* It is a reckless disregard for circumstances that could cause harm to others—a lack of concern for safety or life. So if in the course of work, someone failed to exercise care in a way that would be likely to harm or kill others, then they would be guilty of gross negligence.

Serious misconduct is a little different from gross negligence. Where negligence is a failure to take care, *misconduct* is intentionally doing something that is likely to harm someone or something else. So, serious misconduct *is intentional behavior that has the potential to cause great harm to another or to the company.* An example of serious misconduct is bringing a weapon to work. These types of incidents could be cause for termination of the individual responsible—of course only after an investigation to ensure that they actually did what they are accused of.

LEGAL ISSUES IN LABOR RELATIONS

As with most management processes, a number of legal issues affect labor relations. There are laws and regulations that deal with unions; that identify what the organization has to do in the event of a layoff; that govern collective bargaining; and many government agency rulings that limit organizational rights in managing the workforce. In this section, we will introduce you to the major labor laws in the United States. See Exhibit 9-5 for a brief overview of the five major labor laws.

The Railway Labor Act (RLA) of 1926

The Railway Labor Act was originally enacted to significantly limit the potential for railroad strikes to affect interstate commerce by hindering the general public's ability to procure goods and services. Railroads were the primary means of moving the US mail as well as goods from one state to another in 1926. Airlines were added to the act in 1936 because much of the US mail was beginning to be delivered with the help of airlines, and an airline disruption would affect the delivery of the mail.

WORK
APPLICATION 9-11

Assess how well your present or past boss used the discipline model with employees.

WORK
APPLICATION 9-12

Give examples of reasons why employees can be terminated where you work or have worked.

LO 9-6

Describe the major labor relations laws in the United States and the main reasons why we have each law.

 SHRM

A:9
Union-Related Labor Laws

Gross negligence A serious failure to exercise care in the work environment

Serious misconduct Intentional behavior that has the potential to cause great harm to another or to the company

EXHIBIT 9-5 MAJOR LABOR LAWS

The Railway Labor Act of 1926 (RLA)	The act was passed to significantly limit the potential for railroad strikes to affect interstate commerce; it was later expanded to include airlines.
	In an amendment to the law, the National Mediation Board (NMB) was established to mediate between management and labor to help them come to agreement.
National Labor Relations Act of 1935 (NLRA–Wagner Act)	The act gave employees the right to unionize without fear of prosecution, as it listed unfair employer practices.
	The law also established the National Labor Relations Board (NLRB) to enforce the provisions of the act and conduct elections to determine whether employees will unionize and who will be their representative in collective bargaining.
Labor Management Relations Act of 1947 (LMRA–Taft-Hartley Act)	The act was passed to offset some of the imbalance of power given to labor by previous laws. It amended the Wagner Act (NLRA) to include a list of unfair practices by unions.
Worker Adjustment and Retraining Notification Act of 1988 (WARN)	The act was passed to give employees 60 days' advance notice in cases of plant closings or large-scale layoffs.

SHRM

B:14

The Railway Labor Act of 1926

A:10

Union/Management Relations

A:17

Strikes, Boycotts, and Work Stoppages

SHRM

B:12

The National Labor Relations Act of 1935 (NLRA)

SHRM

A:18, B:20

Employer Unfair Labor Practices

Strike A collective work stoppage by members of a union that is intended to put pressure on an employer

The act also provides protection for workers' right to join a union,[50] and it requires that in so-called *major disputes*—disputes involving rates of pay, work rules, or working conditions—management and labor must participate in a negotiation and mediation process before a labor strike may be called. A strike *is a collective work stoppage by members of a union that is intended to put pressure on an employer*. This negotiation process is designed to force the two parties to come to an agreement without resorting to a strike, in almost all cases.

The National Labor Relations Act (NLRA) of 1935 (Wagner Act)

The National Labor Relations Act (NLRA; frequently called the Wagner Act) was the first major modern law to deal with the legal issue of unions in the general workforce (workers who were not covered by special laws such as the Railway Labor Act) in the United States. In part, the act states,

> *Employees shall have the right to self-organization, to form, join, or assist labor organizations, to bargain collectively through representatives of their own choosing, and to engage in other concerted activities for the purpose of collective bargaining or other mutual aid or protection . . .*[51]

The NLRA was considered to be very one-sided by employers because it identified "unfair labor practices" (prohibitions) for employers but identified no unfair labor practices for employee unions or labor organizations.

Some *employer* unfair labor practices identified by the NLRA include the following:

1. Interfering with, restraining, or coercing employees in the exercise of the rights guaranteed in the NLRA

2. Dominating or interfering with the formation or administration of any labor organization, or contributing financial or other support to it

3. Discriminating in regard to hiring or tenure of employment or any term or condition of employment to encourage or discourage membership in any labor organization (with some specific exceptions)

4. Discharging or otherwise discriminating (retaliating) against an employee because that person has filed charges or given testimony under the NLRA

5. Refusing to bargain collectively with the legitimate representatives of employees

The NLRA is enforced by the **National Labor Relations Board (NLRB)**, which was created by the act. According to its website, the NLRB has five primary functions: conducting elections, investigating charges, seeking resolution, deciding cases, and enforcing orders.[52] For more information about the NLRB, visit its website at http://www.nlrb.gov.

The Labor Management Relations Act (LMRA) of 1947 (Taft-Hartley Act)

B:13

The Labor Management Relations Act of 1947 (LMRA)

The Labor Management Relations Act (LMRA), also called the Taft-Hartley Act, was passed as an amendment to the NLRA. Whereas the NLRA identified a series of employee rights and employer unfair labor practices, the LMRA attempted to rebalance employer and employee rights by identifying unfair labor practices on the part of unions and labor organizations. Unfair *union/labor* practices include the following:[53]

1. Restraining or coercing (a) employees in the exercise of their rights guaranteed in the NLRA or (b) an employer in the selection of his representatives for negotiations

2. Causing or attempting to cause an employer to discriminate against an employee who is not a union member

3. Refusing to bargain collectively with an employer, provided the union is the elected representative of its employees

4. Requiring dues that the NLRB finds excessive or discriminatory

5. Picketing or threatening to picket an employer for the purpose of forcing the employer to bargain with the labor organization, unless the labor organization is certified as the employees' representative

The LMRA also outlawed several types of union actions that had been used since passage of the Wagner Act. These included *jurisdictional strikes*,[54] which union members used to push companies to provide them with certain types of jobs; *wildcat strikes*,[55] where individual union members participated in strikes that were not authorized by the union; *secondary boycotts*,[56] in which a union participating in a strike against a company would pressure other unions to boycott organizations that did business with that company; and *closed shops*, which provided for "the hiring and employment of union members only."[57] In addition, the law limited *union shops*,[58] where every employee was required to become a member of the union within a certain time period. Finally, the LMRA provided that supervisors had no right to be protected if they chose to participate in union activities, so if a supervisor participated in unionizing activities, the company was allowed to terminate them.

In addition to the limitations on unions and labor, the LMRA created mechanisms for decertifying unions through an election process, and it allowed the states to pass a right-to-work law. *Right-to-work laws* work directly against union shops by declaring that every employee in a company has a right to work, even if they choose not to join the union representing the shop.[59] Union shops cannot be set up in states that pass right-to-work laws.

SHRM

B:16

The Worker Adjustment and
Retraining Notification Act of 1988
(WARN Act)

The Worker Adjustment and Retraining Notification Act of 1988 (WARN Act)

The Worker Adjustment and Retraining Notification Act was designed to protect workers in the case of a plant closing or large-scale layoff. The act requires management to give employees notice of a plant closing or layoff at least 60 days ahead of time if more than 50 people will be laid off and if there are more than 100 full-time employees at the workplace. All workers are entitled to notice under WARN, including hourly and salaried workers as well as managers.[60]

The penalty provision of the act says that an employer who fails to provide notice "is liable to each aggrieved employee for an amount including back pay and benefits for the period of violation, up to 60 days," plus a fine of up to $500 per day of violation.[61] So, if we lay people off with less than 60 days' notice (for example to avoid the possibility of sabotage), we have to pay them as if they were still employed for the 60 days anyway.

LO 9-7

Discuss what management cannot
do in attempting to limit union
organizing efforts.

UNIONS AND LABOR RIGHTS

Workers in the United States enjoy more rights and freedoms than do workers in many other countries, including the right to form and become members of unions. However, many businesses do not have labor relations as part of their HR process. Let's take a look at unions and their impact on organizations.

SHRM

A:8

Union Membership

Union Organizing

Today, most union members in the United States are public sector employees such as teachers and police officers.[62] Labor union membership in the private sector has decreased dramatically in the past 40 years in the United States, to the point where only about 6.6% of the private sector US workforce belong to a union.[63]

If employees decide they want to join a union, they will go through a union organizing process (Exhibit 9-6). In this process, employees will select a union to represent them and then ask for a vote of employees concerning whether or not they desire to be represented by the union. The primary method for union elections is a secret ballot. The NLRA is the federal law governing union organizing and elections in private firms. [64]

9-5   APPLYING THE CONCEPT

Labor Laws

Identify each statement by the law it is discussing, writing the letter corresponding to each law before the statement discussing it.

a. RLA of 1926

b. NLRA of 1935

c. LMRA of 1947

d. WARN of 1988

_____ 26.   Featherbedding is illegal. The union can't put in the contract that we have to pay for services that we really don't get. We should call in the National Labor Relations Board to investigate.

_____ 27.   I think we should call in the National Labor Relations Board to investigate the action that management is taking to stop us from unionizing.

_____ 28.   The company can't give us a notice today, with our paychecks, that our factory is being closed next week and all 500 of us will be without a job.

_____ 29.   As pilots, we shouldn't go on strike. Let's get the National Mediation Board to help us.

EXHIBIT 9-6   THE UNION ORGANIZING PROCESS

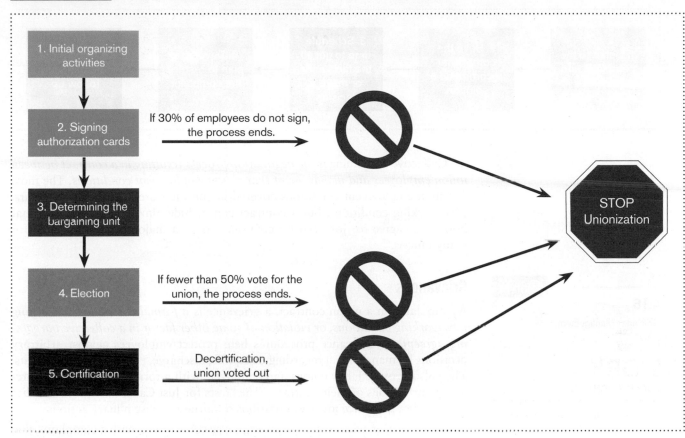

An election is authorized if at least 30% of the employees in an appropriate bargaining unit sign authorization cards allowing a union to negotiate employment terms and conditions on the employees' behalf. The union then presents these cards to the NLRB as an election petition. Once this happens, "the NLRB sharply limits what management can say and do. Violating the rules is an unfair labor practice, and the union is likely to complain to the NLRB about any such violations and use them against the employer in the union organizing campaign."[65]

The NO TIPS Rules. What practices are prohibited after providing the authorization cards to the NLRB? A lot of organizations use the acronym NO TIPS to identify what the company and its managers can't do. NO TIPS stands for no *Threats,* no *Interrogations,* no *Promises,* and no *Spying.*[66]

There is also one final limitation on actions by the organization and its managers in the last 24 hours prior to the union authorization election. Management is prohibited from holding group meetings with employees who will vote on unionization during this 24-hour period.

Once the election is held, a simple majority of those voting determines the success or failure of the campaign. In other words, if only 51 workers in a bargaining unit of 200 vote, and if 26 of the voters desire union membership, then membership in the union will be authorized.

Labor Relations and Collective Bargaining

Labor relations *are the interactions between management and unionized employees.* Since there are many more nonunionized than unionized employees, most organizations don't have to deal with labor relations as part of their human resources systems.

Labor relations The interactions between management and unionized employees

MODEL 9-3 THE EMPLOYEE COMPLAINT RESOLUTION MODEL

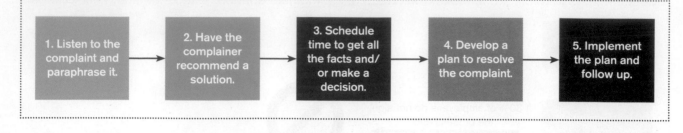

1. Listen to the complaint and paraphrase it. → 2. Have the complainer recommend a solution. → 3. Schedule time to get all the facts and/or make a decision. → 4. Develop a plan to resolve the complaint. → 5. Implement the plan and follow up.

Collective bargaining *is the negotiation process resulting in a contract between union employees and management that covers employment conditions.* The most common employment conditions covered in contracts are compensation, hours, and working conditions, but a contract can include almost any condition that both sides agree to. Job security continues to be a major bargaining issue for many unions.[67]

A:16
Grievance Management

WORK
APPLICATION 9-14

Describe a complaint that you brought to your supervisor and how it was handled. If you have never had a complaint, interview someone who has and describe the complaint and how it was handled.

SHRM

A:11
Union Decertification and Deauthorization

Collective bargaining The negotiation process resulting in a contract between union employees and management that covers employment conditions

Grievance A formal complaint concerning pay, working conditions, or violation of some other factor in a collective bargaining agreement

Grievances

As stipulated in a union contract, a **grievance** *is a formal complaint concerning pay, working conditions, or violation of some other factor in a collective bargaining agreement.* Grievance procedures help protect employees against arbitrary decisions by management regarding discipline, discharge, promotions, or benefits. They also provide labor unions and employers with a formal process for enforcing the provisions of their contracts. The "tests for Just Cause" mentioned earlier are used if a grievance involves questions of fairness in disciplinary actions.

As a manager, when you have an employee come to you with a complaint, you can follow the steps in Model 9-3: The Employee Complaint Resolution Model. Note that in step 2, you don't have to agree and implement the recommendation, and in steps 4 and 5, unless the employee is totally wrong in the complaint, you should try to resolve the complaint.

Decertification Elections

Decertification elections can be held to remove a union as the representative of company workers. This cannot happen within a year of a previous failed attempt at decertification, and management of the company can't ever bring a decertification petition up on its own. Management cannot even directly encourage this action on the part of the employees, but it can provide information to employees regarding decertification processes if they request it, "as long as the company does so without threatening its employees or promising them benefits."[68]

What happens in a decertification process? First, 30% of covered employees must sign a petition for decertification of the union. Once this happens, the election process proceeds in pretty much the same way as the process for voting *for* union representation.

TRENDS AND ISSUES IN HRM

It's time to take a look at this chapter's trends and issues. Our first issue for this chapter concerns employees' use and potential misuse of social media apps at work. Secondly, we will review some recent NLRB regulatory interpretations to protect nonunion employees.

Facebook, Twitter, etc. @ Work: Are They Out of Control?

How do social media tools create potential problems in the workplace? One of the issues with social media sites is the fact that they're almost instantaneous in their ability to broadcast information about the organization to the outside world, which can cause any number of problems, including the loss of trade secrets, harm to the company's reputation, the dissemination of inappropriate or unprofessional posts about the company, bullying or harassment, and public statements inconsistent with the company's public stance.[69] A second issue is the company time that employees can waste when participating in social media interactions rather than doing their work. If left unchecked, this can cause a serious loss of productivity within the firm.

When Walmart fired employees for not showing up for work, the NLRB charged the company for violating employees' right to strike.

So what can we do about social media at work? According to a recent SHRM article, the organization needs to ensure that it has a strict "lack of privacy policy"[70] to let employees know that they have no expectation of privacy in social media communications in association with their workplace. Guidelines on social media use should be put into a comprehensive policy that notes that the individual is responsible for their posts and that posts that harm other employees or the organization could result in disciplinary action. Social media tools add great value to the company, but they must be managed the same as any other business tools.

Nonunion Worker Protection and the NLRB

Let's take a quick look at how the NLRB is trying to become more relevant in nonunion work environments. The NLRB says that workers have a right to engage in "protected concerted activities" in the workplace and has begun to back employee actions that were historically considered illegal. One example is the series of short strikes against Walmart during the busy period leading up to the Christmas holidays. Walmart said that the employees violated company rules by not showing up for work and fired some employees for failing to follow company rules. The NLRB charged Walmart with retaliating against employees who exercised their rights under the NLRA.[71] The Board noted that workers have a right to strike, but Walmart said the intermittent nature of the employees' actions made it impossible to tell a strike from just being absent without notice.

Walmart says that such strikes are intended to interfere with its business and its customers and that the unions backing the short strikes are prohibited from taking such actions by federal law (the LMRA).[72] In some cases, state courts have agreed. However, the NLRB continues to push the issue of workers' rights to strike with the company. We will have to see how this issue will be resolved over the next few months or years, but labor rights could be significantly expanded or significantly limited based on the decisions of the administrative law judge from the NLRB and ultimately by decisions from the federal courts.

• • • CHAPTER SUMMARY

9-1   Explain the value of trust and communication in employee relations.

Trust is absolutely necessary to strong management-labor relations. Research shows that companies that have the trust of their employees have lower turnover, higher revenue, profitability, and shareholder returns. As soon as trust goes, loyalty to the company goes with it. Open communications are needed for the organization to be successful because we can't do what we say we will unless we communicate.

9-2   Discuss the primary reason why measuring job satisfaction is so difficult and the best tool for getting employees to tell the truth about their level of satisfaction.

Job satisfaction is an attitude, not a behavior. We can experience behaviors directly, while we can measure attitudes only indirectly. Because of this, we must use some form of survey and ask the employees about their job satisfaction level. When using job satisfaction surveys, we have to ensure that they are anonymous or employees will most likely not tell the truth about their satisfaction levels.

9-3   Identify the commonly accepted individual rights in the workplace.

The commonly accepted rights of individuals within the workplace include the following:

Right of free consent—the right of the individual to know what they are being asked to do, and the consequences of doing it

Right to due process—a right to not be punished arbitrarily or without reason. Generally, we use the seven tests for Just Cause to protect this right.

Right to life and safety—the right of everyone in the organization to be protected from harm while working

Right of freedom of conscience—a general right to not be forced to violate the individual's personal values and beliefs on the job

Right to privacy—a right to protection from unreasonable searches or intrusions into their personal space at work

Right to free speech—freedom to express their opinions or concerns within the organization, without fear of harming their work relationship

9-4   List some rights that management has in modern organizations.

We discussed two major management rights. Management first has a right to create and enforce an employee *code of conduct*. The organization can also identify the relationship with workers as one of *employment-at-will*, which basically allows either party to break the relationship at any time, even without stating a reason. These rights are offered based on the need for managers to be able to protect the organization and the employees from unnecessary danger or harm.

9-5   Briefly contrast the coaching, counseling, and discipline process used in organizations.

Coaching is designed to give employees feedback to improve their performance over time. This feedback in general should be designed to improve the employee's motivation to perform for the organization. The management counseling process is designed to provide employees with feedback so that they understand that their performance is not currently at an acceptable level, and it's designed to provide them with guidance on how to improve their performance over time. In cases where an employee is unwilling or unable to change or a rule has been broken, discipline is necessary. Discipline is corrective action applied in order to get employees to meet organizational standards.

9-6 Describe the major labor relations laws in the United States and the main reasons why we have each law.

1. The Railway Labor Act of 1926 was enacted to force negotiation between labor and management, first in railroads and later in the airlines, to prevent shutdown of these critical services.

2. The National Labor Relations Act of 1935 was the first major law to deal with the rights of labor to form unions in the general workforce and collectively bargain with employers. It identified unfair labor practices for management in negotiating with labor organizations.

3. The Labor Management Relations Act of 1947 was an amendment to the NLRA that focused on unfair labor practices on the part of unions and other labor organizations. It outlawed or restricted a variety of strikes and boycotts, and it also allowed the states to pass right-to-work laws.

4. The Worker Adjustment and Retraining Notification Act of 1988 required that organizations with certain qualifying characteristics should provide 60 days' notice when laying off more than 50 people or closing a plant.

9-7 Discuss what management cannot do in attempting to limit union organizing efforts.

NO TIPS is an acronym that stands for No Threats, No Interrogations, No Promises, and No Spying. This means first that employers cannot threaten to terminate employees from their jobs, threaten to close the plant, or threaten employees in any other manner during the period prior to a labor election. Secondly, employers cannot call the individual employees in question about union organizing activities on either their part or the part of others within the organization. Third, management cannot promise that if employees vote against unionization, the organization will provide them with benefits because of their votes. Finally, management cannot spy on individual employees taking part in union organizing events, either through planting individuals in such meetings or through electronic or other means.

9-8 Define the key terms found in the chapter margins and listed following the Chapter Summary.

Complete the Key Terms Review to test your understanding of this chapter's key terms.

KEY TERMS

coaching, 226
collective bargaining, 236
communication, 219
discipline, 227
employment-at-will, 225

grievance, 236
gross negligence, 231
just cause, 227
labor relations, 235
management counseling, 227

progressive discipline, 228
serious misconduct, 231
strike, 232
trust, 218

KEY TERMS REVIEW

Complete each of the following statements using one of this chapter's key terms.

1. _____ is faith in the character and actions of another.

2. _____ is the process of transmitting information and meaning.

3. _____ allows the company or the worker to break their work relationship at any point in time, with or without any particular reason, as long as in doing so, no law is violated.

4. _____ is the process of giving motivational feedback to maintain and improve performance.

5. _____ is the process of (a) giving employees feedback so they realize that a problem is affecting their job performance and (b) referring employees with problems that cannot be managed within the work structure to the organization's employee assistance program.

6. _____ is corrective action to get employees to meet standards and the code of conduct.

7. _____ is a set of standard tests for fairness in disciplinary actions; these tests were originally utilized in union grievance arbitrations.

8. _____ is a process whereby the employer provides the employee with opportunities to correct poor behavior before the individual is terminated.

9. _____ is a serious failure to exercise care in the work environment.

10. _____ is intentional employee behavior that has the potential to cause great harm to another or to the company.

11. _____ is a collective work stoppage staged by members of a union that is intended to put pressure on an employer.

12. _____ consists of the interactions between management and unionized employees.

13. _____ is the negotiation process resulting in a contract between union employees and management that covers employment conditions.

14. _____ is a formal complaint concerning pay, working conditions, or violation of some other factor in a collective bargaining agreement.

• • • COMMUNICATION SKILLS

The following critical-thinking questions can be used for class discussion and/or for written assignments to develop communication skills. Be sure to give complete explanations for all answers.

1. What actions would you consider taking, other than increasing pay, if job satisfaction survey data showed that your employees' satisfaction level was dropping significantly?

2. Do you think that organizations should provide more rights or fewer rights to employees than those listed in the chapter? If more, what would you add? If fewer, which rights do you think are unimportant?

3. Should companies make a strong attempt to never violate the privacy rights of an employee? Why or why not?

4. Do you think codes of conduct have any effect on employees' activities? What would make them more or less effective in an organization?

5. Is employment-at-will fair, or should companies have to have a legitimate reason to discharge their employees? Justify your answer.

6. Should coaching, counseling, and discipline processes be utilized by the firm, or should we just terminate the employment of workers who are not doing their job? Explain your answer.

7. Do you feel that progressive discipline processes actually work to improve employee performance in most cases? Why or why not?

8. Do you think it is ever okay for employees to strike against an employer? If so, in what circumstances? If not, why?

9. Assume that you are a fairly high-level manager in your company and that one of your employees comes to you to tell you that other employees are attempting to unionize the company. What would your initial actions be, and why?

• • • CASE 9-1 OFF-DUTY MISCONDUCT

The small Southwestern city of Happy Hollow, with a population of approximately 17,000 people, is a modern bedroom community that is located just a 15-minute drive away from a major city. Happy Hollow maintains a fire department with one fire station serving an area of 12 square miles. It is staffed with 15 full-time firefighters and 15 volunteer firefighters. The International Association of Fire Fighters (IAFF) represents all permanent, full-time employees of Happy Hollows's fire department.

Four years ago, Tim Nelson was hired as a firefighter and licensed paramedic for Happy Hollow's fire department. Previously, he worked for 3 years as a firefighter for another small city. After getting off work at 4:30 p.m. one evening, he joined a friend at a restaurant in the major city a 15- or 20-minute drive from where he lives and works. Nelson and his friend had dinner and several drinks at the restaurant and stayed there until after midnight, when Nelson drove the friend home and then started on the drive to his own home.

Upon receiving calls at 12:43 a.m. about someone driving erratically in a pickup truck at a high rate of speed,

Happy Hollow's police department dispatched a police officer to investigate. Officer Brian Jones observed someone driving the described truck at an excessive rate of speed. He followed for approximately one-half mile while observing erratic driving before stopping the truck. Officer Jones detected a strong odor of alcohol coming from the pickup truck when he approached it. Officer Jones then recognized the driver as firefighter Nelson, who appeared fatigued, with red, watery eyes. He noticed that Nelson had difficulty performing the simple task of retrieving his driver's license and proof of insurance coverage, and his speech was slurred. Officer Jones concluded that Nelson appeared to be intoxicated. Meanwhile, another Ford pickup truck and a second city patrol vehicle driven by Sgt. David Martinez arrived on the location. The driver and passenger in the other pickup advised the police officers that the truck driven by Nelson had sideswiped their vehicle before being stopped by Officer Jones, and they also said that Nelson had failed to stop after the accident. The collision caused damage to both trucks, ripping the mirrors from the passenger side of the truck driven by Nelson and the driver's side of the other truck.

Officer Jones determined that there was probable cause for arrest and advised Nelson that he was being arrested for driving under the influence (DUI) and leaving the scene of an accident. Upon arrival at the police station, Nelson elected to refuse to submit to a Breathalyzer test for measuring his blood alcohol. He was cited for a DUI and leaving the scene of an accident resulting in property damage to another vehicle. He was booked into jail and stayed for a few hours before he was released on bond.

Firefighter and paramedic Tim Nelson was subsequently placed on administrative leave with pay while the matter was being investigated. Following a 3-day investigation, the fire department held a predisciplinary hearing where Nelson had an opportunity to further describe his version of what had happened leading up to his early-morning arrest. Nelson described feeling a sudden jolt when his truck hit something while he was driving home, but he claimed that he did not know what he hit or if he hit anything at all. Nelson acknowledged that he had too much to drink that evening and that he should have had someone drive him home. He said that, although the incident had occurred while he was off duty, he was willing to do anything necessary to keep his job.

Fire department chief Calvin Moore pointed out that he had known that Nelson had been previously arrested for a DUI while working as a firefighter for the other small city but that he had hired Nelson as a firefighter for the Happy Hollow Fire Department anyway. Chief Moore explained that he had already given Nelson a second chance when he hired him, and he was unwilling to give Nelson a third chance. Chief Moore stated that Nelson had violated several rules and policies of the fire department and had failed in his obligation to the public as a firefighter and paramedic by not stopping to check to see if he had injured anyone in the collision that he caused that night. The incident also garnered significant media attention, including reports in Happy Hollow's local newspaper and on at least one news report from a local television station—thus potentially undermining the public's trust in the Happy Hollow fire department. For these reasons, Chief Moore informed Nelson that his employment was being terminated "for cause."

The union filed a grievance alleging that Nelson's punishment was too severe since the incident occurred while he was off duty. The union requested Nelson's reinstatement with punishment, such as a reasonable suspension without pay and a warning. The city's management responded that they had a duty to ensure the public trust in the fire department. They also said that the city's rules and policies, as written in the union-management labor agreement, stated, "Employees shall conduct themselves off duty in such a manner as to show respect as a member of the fire department. Conduct unbecoming a member of the Happy Hollow Fire Department will be subject to disciplinary action, up to and including dismissal."

Questions

1. May an employer take disciplinary action (including discharge) against an employee for illegal off-duty misconduct?
2. Which particular employee rights discussed in the chapter may be asserted by the employee and his labor union representative in this case?
3. What rights does the city management have in this case?
4. When conducting an investigation of an employee's off-duty misconduct, what are important factors for the investigator to consider before recommending disciplinary action?
5. When considering disciplinary action for an employee's off-duty misconduct, what difference would it make if an employee is or is not represented by a labor union?

Case created by Robert Wayland, University of Arkansas at Little Rock

• • • SKILL BUILDER 9–1 COACHING

Objective

To develop coaching skill using the coaching model

Skills

The primary skills developed through this exercise are as follows:

1. *HR management skills*—Conceptual and design
2. *SHRM 2013 Curriculum Guidebook*—L: Training and development

Procedure 1 (2–4 minutes)

Break into groups of three. Make some groups of two, if necessary. Each member selects one of the following three situations in which to be the manager and a different one in which to be the employee. In each situation, the employee knows the standing plans; the employee is not motivated to follow them. You will take turns coaching and being coached.

Three Problem Employee Situations

1. Employee 1 is a clerical worker who uses files, as do the other 10 employees in the department. The

employees all know that they are supposed to return the files when they are finished so that others can find them when they need them. Employees should have only one file out at a time. The supervisor notices that Employee 1 has five files on the desk, and another employee is looking for one of them.

2. Employee 2 is a server in an ice cream shop. The employee knows that the tables should be cleaned up quickly after customers leave so that new customers do not have to sit at dirty tables. It's a busy night. The supervisor finds dirty dishes on two of this employee's occupied tables. Employee 2 is socializing with some friends at one of the tables.

3. Employee 3 is an auto technician. All employees know that they are supposed to put a paper mat on the floor of each car so that the carpets don't get dirty. When the service supervisor got into a car Employee 3 repaired, the car did not have a mat and there was grease on the carpet.

Procedure 2 (3–7 minutes)

Prepare for coaching to improve performance. Each group member writes an outline of what they will say when coaching Employee 1, 2, or 3, following the steps below:

1. Describe current performance.
2. Describe desired performance. (Don't forget to have the employee state why it is important.)
3. Get a commitment to the change.
4. Follow up.

Round 1 (5–8 minutes)

Role-playing. The manager of Employee 1, the clerical worker, coaches that employee as planned. (Use the actual name of the group member playing Employee 1.) Talk—do not read your plan. Employee 1 should put themselves in the worker's position. Both the manager

and the employee will have to ad lib. The person not playing a role is the observer. This person makes notes as the observer for each step of the coaching model listed above. The manager should coach the employee and try to make positive comments and point out areas for improvement. The observer should give the manager alternative suggestions about what could have been said to improve the coaching session.

Feedback. The observer leads a discussion of how well the manager coached the employee. (This should be a discussion, not a lecture.) Focus on what the manager did well and how the manager could improve. The employee should also give feedback on how they felt and what might have been more effective in motivating change. Do not go on to the next interview until you are told to do so. If you finish early, wait for the others to finish.

Round 2 (5–8 minutes)

Same as Round 1, but change roles so that Employee 2, the server, is coached. The job is not much fun if you can't talk to your friends. As the supervisor, coach Employee 2. Again, the observer gives feedback after the coaching.

Round 3 (5–8 minutes)

Same as Rounds 1 and 2, but change roles so that Employee 3, the auto technician, is coached. As the supervisor, coach Employee 3. Again, the observer gives feedback after the coaching.

Apply It

What did I learn from this exercise? How will I use this knowledge in the future?

_____

_____

_____

● ● ● SKILL BUILDER 9-2 DISCIPLINING

Objective

To develop your ability to discipline an employee using the discipline model

Skills

The primary skills developed through this exercise are as follows:

1. *HR management skills*—Conceptual and design
2. *SHRM 2013 Curriculum Guidebook*—L: Training and development

Note that this is a continuation of Skill Building Exercise 9-1. Coaching didn't work, and you have to discipline the employee.

Procedure 1 (2–4 minutes)

Break into groups of three. Make some groups of two, if necessary. Each member selects one of the three situations from Skill Builder 2. Decide who will discipline Employee 1, the clerical worker; Employee 2, the ice cream shop server; and Employee 3, the auto technician. Also select different group members to play the employee being disciplined and the observer.

Procedure 2 (3–7 minutes)

Prepare for the discipline session. Write a basic outline of what you will say to Employee 1, 2, or 3; follow the steps in the discipline model below.

1. Refer to past feedback. (Assume that you have discussed the situation before, using the coaching model.)
2. Ask why the undesired behavior occurred. (The employee should make up an excuse for not changing.)
3. Administer the discipline. (Assume that an oral warning is appropriate.)
4. Get a commitment to change, and develop a plan.
5. Summarize and state the follow-up.

Round 1 (5–8 minutes)

Role-playing. The manager of Employee 1, the clerical worker, disciplines that employee as planned. (Use the actual name of the group member playing the employee.) Talk—do not read your plan. Both the manager and the employee will need to ad lib. As the supervisor, discipline Employee 1.

The person not playing a role is the observer. This person makes notes on the five steps of the discipline model above. For each of the steps, try to make a statement about the positive aspects of the discipline and a statement about how the manager could have improved. Give alternative things the manager could have said to improve the discipline session. Remember, the objective is to change behavior.

Feedback. The observer leads a discussion of how well the manager disciplined the employee. The employee should also give feedback on how they felt and what might have been more effective in motivating change. Do not go on to the next interview until you are told to do so. If you finish early, wait until the others finish or the time is up.

Round 2 (5–8 minutes)

Same as Round 1, but change roles so that Employee 2, the ice cream server, is disciplined. As Employee 2, put yourself in the worker's position. As the supervisor, discipline Employee 2. As the observer, give feedback.

Round 3 (5–8 minutes)

Same as Rounds 1 and 2, but change roles so that Employee 3, the auto technician, is disciplined. As Employee 3, put yourself in the worker's position. As the supervisor, discipline Employee 3. As the observer, give feedback.

Apply It

What did I learn from this exercise? How will I use this knowledge in the future?

_____

_____

_____

Part IV

Compensating

 10 Compensation Management

11 Employee Incentives and Benefits

PRACTITIONER'S MODEL

- ⬆ Productivity
- ⬆ Satisfaction
- ⬇ Absenteeism
- ⬇ Turnover

PART V: Protecting and Expanding Organizational Outreach
How do you PROTECT and EXPAND your Human Resources?

Chapter 12	Chapter 13	Chapter 14
Workplace Safety, Health, and Security	Organizational Ethics, Sustainability, and Social Responsibility	Global Issues for Human Resource Managers

PART IV: Compensating
How do you REWARD and MAINTAIN your Human Resources?

Chapter 10	Chapter 11
Compensation Management	Employee Incentives and Benefits

PART III: Developing and Managing
How do you MANAGE your Human Resources?

Chapter 7	Chapter 8	Chapter 9
Training, Learning, Talent Management & Development	Performance Management and Appraisal	Employee Rights and Labor Relations

PART II: Staffing
What HRM Functions do you NEED for sustainability?

Chapter 4	Chapter 5	Chapter 6
Matching Employees and Jobs	Recruiting Job Candidates	Selecting New Employees

PART I: 21st Century Human Resource Management Strategic Planning and Legal Issues
What HRM issues are CRITICAL to your organization's long-term sustainability?

Chapter 1	Chapter 2	Chapter 3
The New Human Resource Management Process	Strategy-Driven Human Resource Management	The Legal Environment and Diversity Management

©iStockphoto.com/minemero

10 COMPENSATION MANAGEMENT

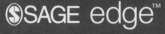

Practitioner's Perspective

Cindy tells the story of when Drew walked dejectedly into her office and flopped down in the nearest chair.

"I hear they hired a new payroll clerk—the same job I've been doing for five years—and this new person is going to be paid more than I make! I've been a loyal employee for years and haven't had a real raise since I started. Is that fair?"

Cindy couldn't fault Drew for his feelings, and she knew it was past time the company examined its compensation guidelines.

Once you have an established pay scale, is it really important to reexamine your compensation levels? What is the solution when the going market rate for a position outdistances your set pay scale? Chapter 10 answers these questions and more as it demonstrates the reasons why compensation management is so vital to attracting and retaining your best employees.

● ● ●

COMPENSATION MANAGEMENT

Compensation costs are frequently the largest part of total costs at today's firms. Compensation costs are also rising.[1] According to the US Bureau of Labor Statistics, average compensation costs rose nearly a dollar per hour from March 2013 to March 2014.[2] Compensation *is the total of an employee's pay and benefits*. A business designs and implements a compensation system to focus worker attention on the specific efforts the organization considers necessary to achieve its desired goals.[3] However, if rewards are to be useful in stimulating desired behavior, they must also meet the demands of employees whose behavior they're intended to influence.[4]

Compensation affects the process of both attracting and retaining employees.[5] A recent survey revealed that for the first time in several years, pay is now identified by employees as the top reason for job satisfaction, overtaking job security as the top driver of satisfaction in 2013. In fact, pay is currently either first or

LO 10-1

Describe expectancy and equity theories as they apply to compensation.

Compensation The total of an employee's pay and benefits

● ● ● **CHAPTER OUTLINE**

second in importance to all four major generations of employees currently in the workforce—veterans, baby boomers, generation X, and millennials—so HR must pay attention to fair and equitable compensation for company employees.[6]

The Compensation System

The compensation system of an organization includes *anything that an employee may value and desire and that the employer is willing and able to offer in exchange.* This includes the following:

1. *Compensation components.* All rewards that can be classified as monetary payments and in-kind payments constitute the compensation component.

2. *Noncompensation components.* All rewards other than monetary and in-kind payments (e.g., company cafeterias and gyms) constitute the noncompensation component.

Types of Compensation. There are four basic parts of a compensation system:

1. *Base pay.* This is typically a flat rate, either as an hourly wage or salary. Many employees consider this to be the most important part of the compensation program, and it is therefore a major factor in their decision to accept or decline the job.

2. Wage and salary add-ons. This includes overtime pay, shift differential, premium pay for working weekends and holidays, and other add-ons.

3. *Incentive pay.* Also called variable pay, *incentive pay* is pay for performance, and it commonly includes items such as piece work in production and commissioned sales. We will discuss incentives in detail in Chapter 11.

WORK
APPLICATION 10-1

Select a job. Identify the compensation you received there in detail.

Compensation system Anything that an employee may value and desire and that the employer is willing and able to offer in exchange

---

SHRM HR CONTENT

See Appendix: *SHRM 2013 Curriculum Guidebook* for the complete list

B.   Employment Law (required)

8. The Fair Labor Standards Act of 1938 (FLSA)

E.   Job Analysis/Job Design (required)

2. Job evaluation and compensation (grades, pay surveys, and pay setting)

6. Compliance with legal requirements

Equal pay (skill, effort, responsibility, and working conditions) and comparable worth

Overtime eligibility (exempt vs. nonexempt work)

G.   Outcomes: Metrics and Measurement of HR (required)

11. Benchmarking

I.   Staffing: Recruitment and Selection (required)

16. Employment brand

K.   Total Rewards (required)

A. Compensation

1. Development of a base pay system
2. Developing pay levels
3. Determining pay increases
4. Role of job analysis/job design/job descriptions in determining compensation
6. Compensation of special groups (e.g., executives, sales, contingent workers, management)
7. Internal alignment strategies
8. External competitiveness strategies
9. Legal constraints on pay issues
10. Monitoring compensation costs
11. Union role in wage and salary administration
12. Minimum wage/overtime
13. Pay discrimination and dissimilar jobs
14. Prevailing wage
15. Motivation theories: Equity theory, reinforcement theory, agency theory

10-1 APPLYING THE CONCEPT

Types of Compensation

Review the types of compensation and then write the letter corresponding to each one before the statement(s) describing it.

a. base pay

b. wage and salary add-ons

c. incentive pay

d. benefits

_____ 1. I'd like to work for a firm that will help pay for me to get my master's of business administration (MBA) degree.

_____ 2. I only get paid $11 an hour, so I'm looking for a better job.

_____ 3. I like getting paid the same each week. It helps me to budget my expenses.

_____ 4. I like being paid for every sale I make, but my pay does vary from week to week.

_____ 5. I like working nights because it pays more.

4. *Benefits.* This is indirect compensation that provides something of value to the employee. Benefits may include health insurance; payments to employees if they are unable to work because of sickness or accident; retirement pay contributions; and provision of a wide variety of desired goods and services such as cafeteria service, tuition reimbursement, and many other items. We will also discuss benefits in detail in Chapter 11.

Direct Versus Indirect Compensation. The first three compensation components—base pay, add-ons, and incentive pay—are known as *direct compensation.* These forms of compensation go directly to the employees as part of their paycheck. Benefits are *indirect compensation,* so employees don't get any funds from a benefits program. Benefits are usually paid for by the company; employees never see those funds and most don't realize how costly they are for the firm.

In for-profit businesses, we want to design the mix of direct compensation and indirect components that provide us with the best productivity return for the money spent. However, to do that, we need to understand something about the motivational value of our compensation system. Let's take a look at a few theories that help us understand how compensation systems can motivate our workers to perform to the best of their ability.

Motivation and Compensation Planning

When we look at designing compensation programs, we need to remember that we are trying to motivate the employee to do the things that we need them to do, consistently, over a period of time. Probably the most significant theories that help in compensation planning are *expectancy theory* and *equity theory.*[7]

Expectancy Theory. Expectancy theory is a *process theory* of motivation. This means that we go through a cognitive process to evaluate something or a situation. **Expectancy theory** *proposes that employees are motivated when they believe they can accomplish a task and that the rewards for doing so are worth the effort.* Expectancy theory is based on Victor Vroom's formula: Motivation = Expectancy × Instrumentality × Valence.[8]

For compensation purposes, we have intentionally simplified the theory to show how it affects a person's motivation to perform. *Expectancy* is the person's perception of their ability to accomplish or probability of accomplishing an objective. Generally, the higher one's expectancy, the better the chance for motivation. *Instrumentality* is the perception that a particular level of performance is likely to provide the individual with a desired reward. *Valence* refers to the value a person places on the outcome or reward, because not all people value the same reward.

SHRM

K:A15

Motivation Theories: Equity, Reinforcement, Agency Theories

WORK
APPLICATION 10-2

Give an example of how expectancy theory has affected your motivation or that of someone you work with or have worked with. Be sure to specify the expectancy and valence.

Expectancy theory A theory proposing that employees are motivated when they believe they can accomplish a task and that the rewards for doing so are worth the effort

EXHIBIT 10-1   EXPECTANCY THEORY AND COMPENSATION

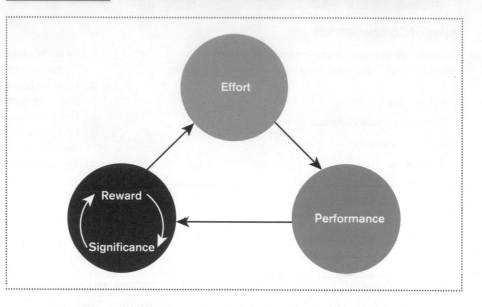

Compensation programs should be designed to motivate employees to perform consistently over a period of time.

SHRM

K:A7
Internal Alignment Strategies

SHRM

K:A8
External Competitiveness Strategies

Equity theory Theory that employees are motivated when the ratio of their perceived outcomes to inputs is at least roughly equal to that of other referent individuals

One thing that we need to remember here is that the three components of the theory—valence, instrumentality, and expectancy—are multiplicative, so if any one of the three is near zero, the motivating potential is low, and the individual has almost no motivation to perform![9] For an illustration of expectancy in action see Exhibit 10-1. Therefore, as managers, if we help employees get what they want, they will give us the work we want to help meet the organizational goals.[10]

Equity Theory. People in companies apply equity theory constantly—we all do.[11] Equity theory, particularly the version developed by J. Stacy Adams, proposes that people are motivated to seek social equity in the rewards they receive (outcomes) for their performance (input).[12] So in general, **equity theory** *proposes that employees are motivated when the ratio of their perceived outcomes to inputs is at least roughly equal to that of other referent individuals.* Employees are more motivated to achieve organizational objectives when they believe they are being treated fairly,[13] especially regarding pay equity.[14]

According to equity theory, people compare their inputs (effort, loyalty, hard work, commitment, skills, ability, experience, seniority, trust, support of colleagues, and so forth), their financial rewards (pay, benefits, and perks), and intangible outcomes (praise, recognition, status, job security, sense of advancement and achievement, etc.) to those of relevant others.[15] A *relevant other* could be a coworker or a group of employees from the same or different organizations.[16]

Notice that the definition says that employees compare their *perceived* (not actual) inputs and outcomes.[17] Equity may actually exist, but if employees believe that there is inequity, they will change their behavior to create what they consider to be equity. Employees must perceive that they are being treated fairly, relative to others. Managers can also help control employee perceptions of fairness.[18] Perceptions of inequity hurt attitudes, commitment, and cooperation, thereby decreasing individual, team, and organizational performance.[19] This perceived inequity is often used as a justification for unethical behavior.[20]

When employees perceive inequity, they are motivated to reduce it by decreasing input or increasing outcomes. A comparison with relevant others leads to one of three conclusions, which can cause problems. The employee is either underrewarded, overrewarded, or equitably rewarded.[21] When employees perceive that they are *underrewarded*, they may try to reduce the inequity by increasing outcomes (e.g., requesting a raise or committing theft), decreasing inputs (doing less work, being absent, taking long breaks, etc.), or rationalizing (finding a logical explanation for the inequity). When most employees perceive that they are *over-rewarded* they rationalize it in some way and accept it. When employees perceive that they are *equitably rewarded,* they are motivated to continue to put forth the same effort for the organization so long as they are content that inputs and outcomes are in balance.[22]

Remember this: People are generally not really motivated to work harder by equity; rather, they are demotivated if it doesn't exist. So HR managers need to understand that people will be demotivated if they feel (perceive) that they are not being treated fairly, especially regarding compensation.[23] As a result, we have to use this information when we begin to structure our compensation plan. We need to "build in" *and* advertise equity to minimize the problems associated with equity theory.

ORGANIZATIONAL PHILOSOPHY

In addition to understanding our compensation options and how they motivate employees, we need to identify what our compensation philosophy will be. Let's discuss some of these major organizational issues that we will need to evaluate before we can set up our compensation system.

Ability to Pay

Probably the first thing we need is an honest assessment of how much we can afford, or are willing to afford, to pay our employees. This means we need to complete an assessment of estimated revenues from business operations and determine what percentage of revenues can or should realistically go toward compensation costs over the long term. Why? Because if we have to cut compensation, employees may believe we broke our promises to them, and that will most likely lead to intense demotivation and potentially high rates of turnover.[24]

What Types of Compensation?

We noted earlier in the chapter that we have four basic components to compensation—base pay, wage add-ons, incentives, and benefits. We need to determine how to divide the funds available between each of the components.

There are some legal requirements for certain mandatory benefits such as Social Security, so these legal requirements have to be dealt with "off the top"—they have to be subtracted from the available funds. Once this is done, we need to determine how much direct compensation will be in the form of base pay and how much will be incentive pay.

Finally, we need to consider voluntary benefits. We need to analyze competition within the labor market and what benefits each of our close competitors provides because we will most likely have to approximately match the benefits that are provided by those competitors.[25]

WORK
APPLICATION 10-5

Select a job you have or have had. Did the firm pay for performance or longevity? Explain in detail.

Pay for Performance or Pay for Longevity?

In breaking down base pay versus incentives, we will need to look at whether our organization is going to have a *performance philosophy* or a *longevity philosophy*. Some companies pay people more for *longevity* or *seniority*, meaning accumulating years of service with the firm, by providing promotions and raises over time (assuming that we meet minimal organizational standards) regardless of performance because we have been a loyal member of the organization. Other companies, however, pay more for *performance*—for completing certain tasks or doing certain things faster or better than average, not just for being there and being loyal to the firm.[26]

Skill-Based or Competency-Based Pay?

If we decide to *use skill-based* or *competency-based* pay, we will pay members of the workforce for individual skills or competencies that they bring to work, whether or not those skills are necessary for the individuals to do their current job. *Competencies* involve the individual's level of knowledge in a particular area, while *skills* involve the ability to apply that knowledge set in that field. Examples of competencies include such things as an understanding of negotiation and collaboration, or problem-solving and decision-making expertise. Examples of skills related to these competencies would include the ability to actually negotiate contract agreements, apply principles of physics to a new equipment design, or make a high-quality decision based on good analysis of a situation. With either method, we are paying our employees for knowledge, skills, and abilities that they may not necessarily ever use in the organization, so we have to ask whether it is valuable to have people with these extra skill sets.

I:16
SHRM

Employment Brand

At, Above, or Below the Market?

The next item we must determine is whether we will pay *above market, at market,* or *below market.* We might decide to pay above market to attract better workers and enhance our employment brand. We want good employees to have a strong incentive to work for us, and one way to enhance our employment brand is to pay above the market rate.[27] We also want better productivity out of our workforce if we pay more for employees. But do better workers generally have higher levels of productivity? There is evidence supporting that this is the case. *Efficiency wage theory* says that if a company pays higher wages, it can generally hire better people who will in turn be more productive.[28] Because we have higher-quality employees, we get a productivity increase that more than offsets the higher cost of employing them.[29]

Would we necessarily get lower productivity from our workforce if we paid *below* the market? In general, yes, but not always. If our firm is in an industry where unemployment is high, it is easy to find replacement workers, and if most positions require a low-level skill set, we may be able to get away with paying less than average.

Highly successful companies like Google, Facebook, Starbucks, and Costco pay above average to hire the best, whereas most companies shoot for average, and companies like Walmart and McDonald's with lower-skilled workers tend to pay below average compared to other industries, but generally have to pay close to the same compensation as direct competitors to attract and retain employees. You may have heard that restaurant employees are pressing for a minimum wage of $15 an hour, and that companies are turning to technology/machines to replace employees that take orders and collect payment.

WORK
APPLICATION 10-6

Select a job you have or have had. Did the firm provide above-average, average, or below-average compensation? Explain how you came up with your answer, using comparisons to competitors.

Wage compression When new employees require higher starting pay than the historical norm, causing narrowing of the pay gap between experienced and new employees

Wage Compression

Wage compression is another concern in setting up and maintaining a pay structure. **Wage compression** *occurs when new employees require higher starting pay* *than the historical norm, causing narrowing of the pay gap between experienced and new employees.*[30] We bring workers into the organization in both good economic times and bad. When the economy is doing poorly and wages are depressed, people will generally accept jobs for less than they would if the economy were doing well and higher-wage jobs were available. Since raises are frequently based on an employee's initial salary or pay rate, those who start at lower pay than others may stay that way over time, and pay inequality for the same work may increase over time as well.

We may create a situation where workers with less time on the job might be paid nearly as much as, or more than, employees who have worked for us for many years.

This wage compression can weaken the desired link between pay and performance, creating significant dissatisfaction on the part of long-term employees because of the pay differential.[31] Most companies and organizations don't set out to do this—they just fall into it.[32] If we understand wage compression when creating a pay structure for the organization, we can avoid at least some of the dissatisfaction associated with the pay differentials between short-term and long-term employees.

Starbucks pays their employees above average rates. This could be to motivate employees to work harder or to create a reputation for valuing their employees.

Pay Secrecy

Recall our discussion of equity theory earlier in the chapter. One of the things some companies do to avoid equity issues is demand *pay secrecy*, which means requiring employees to not disclose their pay to anyone else. But is it legal to tell employees that they can't discuss their pay with anyone else? Over the past several years, the NLRB has consistently ruled that companies may not discipline workers who reveal information about their pay and other work conditions as long as the workers are participating in "protected, concerted activity." In addition, President Obama signed an Executive Order in 2014 (EO 13665) prohibiting pay secrecy policies in federal government contractors, with potential loss of government contracts as punishment for failure to comply. So, enforcing pay secrecy clauses is becoming more dangerous to companies.

LEGAL AND FAIRNESS ISSUES IN COMPENSATION

There are a number of federal and state laws that directly or indirectly affect pay and compensation systems. Virtually every equal employment opportunity (EEO) law identifies compensation as one of the employment actions where discrimination is prohibited if it is based on a protected characteristic. So we have to keep these laws in mind as we set up our pay system. See Exhibit 10-2 for a list of some of the major EEO laws and legal concepts that cover compensation.

Fair Labor Standards Act of 1938 (Amended)

Besides the Equal Pay Act and the other EEO laws, there are some laws that deal specifically with compensation issues. The grandfather of these laws is the Fair Labor Standards Act (FLSA). The major provisions of the FLSA cover minimum wage, overtime issues, and child labor rules for most US-based businesses.[33] Let's complete a quick review of the FLSA.

WORK
APPLICATION 10-7

Select a job you have or have had. Did people know how much other employees made, or was there pay secrecy?

LO 10-3

Discuss the three major provisions of the FLSA.

B:8

The Fair Labor Standards Act of 1938 (FLSA)

MAJOR EEO LAWS AND LEGAL CONCEPTS

Antidiscrimination legislation:
1. Equal Pay Act of 1963 (EPA)
2. Title VII of the Civil Rights Act of 1964 (CRA)
3. Age Discrimination in Employment Act of 1967 (ADEA)
4. Vietnam Era Veteran's Readjustment Act of 1974
5. Americans with Disabilities Act of 1990 (ADA)
6. CRA of 1991
7. Lilly Ledbetter Fair Pay Act of 2009 (LLFPA)

Legal concepts linking employment discrimination and pay discrimination:
1. Disparate impact
2. Disparate treatment
3. Bona fide occupational qualification (BFOQ)

SHRM

K:A12
Minimum Wage/Overtime

WORK
APPLICATION 10-8

Select a job you have or have had. What is the minimum wage in your state? Does the firm pay its lowest-level employees below, at, or above the state minimum wage?

WORK
APPLICATION 10-9

Give examples of jobs that are exempt and nonexempt. Be sure to state why they are classified as such.

Minimum wage The lowest hourly rate of pay generally permissible by federal law

Minimum Wage. The first major provision of the FLSA concerns the federal minimum wage. The **minimum wage** *is the lowest hourly rate of pay generally permissible by federal law*. The federal minimum wage in 2015 for most employees in the United States was $7.25 per hour.[34] This is adjusted periodically by Congress, but the FLSA sets the minimum wage provision. Some states and even cities have set the minimum wage higher than the federal rate. You may have noted that Seattle, Washington, recently set the city's minimum wage at $15 per hour, and several other large cities around the United States are considering similar legislation. In addition, as of this writing, the Department of Labor had recently raised the minimum wage for federal contract workers to $10.10 per hour.[35]

Exempt or Nonexempt. Does everyone get paid at least the minimum wage for their area? Not exactly. There are some exemptions to the rules.[36] If someone is *exempt*, by the definitions in the FLSA, they are exempt from the minimum wage requirement, over-time provisions, or child labor rules or possibly all three. People not meeting any of the requirements for an exemption are called *nonexempt* and must be paid minimum wage, overtime, etc.

As an example, workers who most people know are commonly exempt include restaurant servers. The current minimum wage for servers is $2.13 per hour.[37] Servers normally expect to get a large portion of their wages in tips. The FLSA says that we can pay tipped employees a minimum of $2.13 per hour as long as their tips make up the difference. So if somebody in a restaurant works 20 hours in a week and does not make an average of $5.12 an hour in tips, it is illegal to pay that person $2.13. There are also other exemptions for individuals who are live-in child care providers, newspaper carriers, seasonal workers, etc. In fact, there are hundreds of exemptions. If you would like to review some of the exemptions in the FLSA, you can go to the Department of Labor website at http://www.dol.gov/elaws/esa/flsa/screen75.asp.

There is a set of quick guidelines that can be used to determine exempt and nonexempt persons at work. If you make under $23,660, you are pretty much guaranteed to be nonexempt under the provisions of the FLSA as of June 2015.[38] "Highly compensated employees" paid $100,000 or more (*and* at least $455 per

10-2 APPLYING THE CONCEPT

Employee Exemptions

Identify each job as generally being considered exempt or not from minimum wage or overtime pay (write *a* or *b* before each job type).

a. exempt

b. nonexempt

_____ 6. Auto mechanic

_____ 7. Fruit picker

_____ 8. Worker on a foreign-flag cruise ship

_____ 9. Librarian

_____ 10. Taxi driver

_____ 11. Real estate agent

_____ 12. Bellperson at a hotel

_____ 13. Computer programmer (paid more than $27.63 per hour)

_____ 14. Hairdresser

_____ 15. Bank teller

---

week) are pretty much automatically exempt from the minimum wage and overtime rules if they regularly perform at least one of the duties of an exempt executive, administrative employee, or professional employee identified in the standard tests for exemption.[39] If an individual is paid more than $23,660 but less than $100,000, then the employee usually must meet a set of specific "duties tests" in order to fall within an exemption category (see Exhibit 10-4). There *is* a proposal by the Department of Labor to increase the minimum for exempt workers to approximately $970 per week, or around $50,000 annually, and the amount for highly compensated employees to roughly $122,000 per year, but these amounts are still in a proposed phase at the federal level.

Overtime. **Overtime** is *a higher than minimum, federally mandated wage, required for nonexempt employees if they work more than a certain number of hours in a week.* Overtime is set by the FLSA as 150% of the individual's normal wages for all hours in excess of 40 hours worked in a calendar week. With few exceptions, if a nonexempt employee works more than 40 hours in a week, that employee is eligible for overtime.

Contrary to what many people think, the FLSA has no requirement for paying anything more than time-and-a-half for any overtime work.[41] Employers are also not required to provide paid holidays, vacation, or extra pay for working on weekends or on holidays under federal law, although several states now have rules covering these situations.

Child Labor. The FLSA also has rules on the use of *child labor*, meaning workers under 18 years old. If individuals are 18 or older, we can use them in any normal employment situation. However, we can only employ 16- and 17-year-olds in *nonhazardous* jobs, although their work hours are unrestricted, and there are significantly different rules for 14- and 15-year-olds.

Minors age 14 and 15 may work outside school hours for no more than "three hours on a school day, 18 hours in a school week, eight hours on a non-school day, and 40 hours in a non-school week."[42] They can't start work before 7:00 a.m. or work after 7:00 p.m., except from June 1 through Labor Day, when they can work until 9:00 p.m. Jobs they can work are limited to retail, food service, and gasoline service at establishments specifically listed in the FLSA regulations. Employees 14 and 15 years old may not work overtime. While there are some exceptions to these rules for businesses such as family businesses or family farms, these are the general guidelines for child labor.

Employee Misclassification Under the FLSA. Misclassification of employees as exempt from minimum wage or overtime is one of the most common areas where companies get

SHRM

K:A6

Compensation of Special Groups (e.g., Executives, Sales, etc.)

SHRM

E:6

Compliance With Legal Requirements: Overtime Eligibility

WORK
APPLICATION 10-10

Select a job you have or have had. Who gets paid overtime, why, and how much?

WORK
APPLICATION 10-11

Select a job you have or have had. Does the organization hire child labor? If so, why, and what do the child laborers do?

Overtime A higher than minimum, federally mandated wage, required for nonexempt employees if they work more than a certain number of hours in a week

EXHIBIT 10-3   DUTIES TESTS FOR GENERAL EMPLOYEE EXEMPTIONS

Executive Exemption

To qualify for the *executive employee* exemption, the employee must meet all of the following criteria:

- The employee must be compensated on a salary basis (as defined in the regulations) at a rate of not less than $455 per week;

- The employee's primary duty must be managing the enterprise or managing a customarily recognized department or subdivision of the enterprise;

- The employee must customarily and regularly direct the work of at least two or more other full-time employees or their equivalent; and

- The employee must have the authority to hire or fire other employees; or the employee's suggestions and recommendations as to the hiring, firing, advancement, promotion, or any other change of status of other employees must be given particular weight.

Professional Exemption—Learned or Creative

To qualify for the *learned professional employee* exemption, the employee must meet all of the following criteria:

- The employee must be compensated on a salary or fee basis (as defined in the regulations) at a rate not less than $455 per week;

- The employee's primary duty must be the performance of work requiring advanced knowledge, defined as work that is predominantly intellectual in character and that requires the consistent exercise of discretion and judgment;

- The employee's advanced knowledge must be in a field of science or learning; and

- The employee's advanced knowledge must be customarily acquired by a prolonged course of specialized intellectual instruction.

To qualify for the *creative professional* employee exemption, the employee must meet all of the following criteria:

- The employee must be compensated on a salary or fee basis (as defined in the regulations) at a rate not less than $455 per week;

- The employee's primary duty must be the performance of work requiring invention, imagination, originality, or talent in a recognized field of artistic or creative endeavor.

Administrative Exemption

To qualify for the *administrative employee* exemption, the employee must meet all of the following criteria:

- The employee must be compensated on a salary or fee basis (as defined in the regulations) at a rate not less than $455 per week;

- The employee's primary duty must be the performance of office or nonmanual work directly related to the management or general business operations of the employer or the employer's customers; and

- The employee's primary duties must include the exercise of discretion and independent judgment with respect to matters of significance.

Outside Sales Exemption

To qualify for the *outside sales employee* exemption, the employee must meet all of the following criteria:

- The employee's primary duty must be making sales (as defined in the FLSA) or obtaining orders or contracts for services or for the use of facilities for which a consideration will be paid by the client or customer; and

- The employee must be customarily and regularly engaged away from the employer's place or places of business.

The salary requirements of the regulation do not apply to the outside sales exemption.

Computer Employee Exemption

To qualify for the *computer employee* exemption, the employee must meet all of the following criteria:

- The employee must be compensated either on a salary or fee basis at a rate of not less than $455 per week or, if compensated on an hourly basis, at a rate of not less than $27.63 an hour;

- The employee must be employed as a computer systems analyst, computer programmer, software engineer, or other similarly skilled worker in the computer field performing the duties described in the next bullet point;

- The employee's primary duty must consist of one of the following:

  1. The application of systems analysis techniques and procedures, including consulting with users to determine hardware, software, or system functional specifications;

  2. The design, development, documentation, analysis, creation, testing, or modification of computer systems or programs (including prototypes), based on and related to user or system design specifications;

  3. The design, documentation, testing, creation, or modification of computer programs related to machine operating systems; or

  4. A combination of the aforementioned duties, the performance of which requires the same level of skills.

The computer employee exemption does not include employees engaged in the manufacture or repair of computer hardware and related equipment.

Source: US Department of Labor, retrieved July 6, 2015[40]

into serious trouble. Just paying an employee a "salary" and then working that person for unlimited hours is obviously illegal under the general exemption FLSA rules noted above.

So why does misclassification occur? Obviously, companies want to save money. Many employers think that if they put you on salary, they don't have to pay overtime—so they put you on a salary and work you 70 hours per week. Another company might say, "All my people are professionals, so they are all exempt." But this is rarely possible in reality, if you look at the FLSA rules for exemption. Breaking FLSA laws can result in costly civil penalties, and repeated offenses can even land you in jail.

Pay Equity and Comparable Worth

One of the more controversial issues in compensation is comparable worth. *Comparable worth* is the principle that when jobs are distinctly different but entail similar levels of ability, responsibility, skills, and working conditions, they are of equal value and should have the same pay scale. According to the EEOC, women earn an average of 77 cents for every dollar that men earn.[43] This is one of the major reasons that comparable worth continues to be an issue in both business and government. While equal pay for equal work is the law (EPA of 1963), comparable worth is not currently federal law except in some very limited cases.

Comparable worth is simply "similar pay for similar work." While this sounds almost like the equal pay for equal work stipulated by the Equal Pay Act, the doctrine of comparable worth says that if we can compare your job with that of another person, and if the two jobs are *similar but not the same*, then we should pay you a similar wage but not necessarily exactly the same wage. So this concept is much broader than equal pay.

As we noted, though, there are a few exceptions where comparable worth is law. Some states have passed comparable worth legislation that applies to state, county, and city agencies. If individuals are employed by the state or another government agency, they are subject to comparable worth assessment

WORK
APPLICATION 10–12

Select an organization you work at or have worked at. Could comparable worth work at that organization? Why or why not?

SHRM

K:A13

Pay Discrimination and Dissimilar Jobs

Comparable worth dictates that jobs with similar levels of ability, responsibility, skills, and working conditions should offer the same pay scale.

SHRM

E:6

Compliance With Legal
Requirements: Equal Pay and
Comparable Worth

SHRM

K:A9

Legal Constraints on Pay Issues

SHRM

K:A11

Union Role in Wage and Salary
Administration

to determine their pay levels. Some states such as Washington and California have also attempted to pass comparable worth laws for businesses, but they have not succeeded yet, at least partially because of the market value factor for jobs. Let's face measurement, reliability, and validity issues. It is very difficult to compare a factory job to an office job. And as discussed, many companies are working to get more women and minorities into better paying jobs rather than trying to figure comparable worth.

Other Legal Issues

A number of other federal laws place controls on pay and benefits. Recall from Chapter 9 that the National Labor Relations Act (NLRA) allows collective bargaining on the part of workers who join a union. Since the NLRA allows employees to bargain collectively with their employers for wages, benefits, and working conditions, in limited cases the workers can agree to a workweek that is longer than 40 hours. The wages paid must be significantly higher than the minimum wage, and other conditions apply, but it is possible for the collective bargaining unit to agree to more than a 40-hour workweek.[44] Some union contracts also require mandatory overtime with pay.

Mandatory employee *pension and benefits legislation* also includes the following:

- Social Security
- Workers' compensation
- Unemployment insurance
- Family and Medical Leave Act (FMLA)
- Patient Protection and Affordable Care Act (ACA)
- Employee Retirement Income Security Act (ERISA—mandatory for employers who offer pension plans)
- Health Insurance Portability and Accountability Act (HIPAA—mandatory for employers who offer health insurance)

We will discuss each of these laws further in Chapter 11.

LO 10-4

Name the three types of job
evaluation discussed in the text
and discuss whether they are more
objective or subjective in form.

JOB EVALUATION

Deciding how much each job is worth in a company is difficult. There are two approaches to this—internal and external—though they may be used together. First we discuss the external method, followed by three internal methods.

SHRM

E:2

Job Evaluation and Compensation
(Grades, Pay Surveys, and Pay
Setting)

SHRM

K:A4

Role of Job Analysis/Job Design/
Job Descriptions in Determining
Compensation

External Method

An *external approach* involves finding out what other organizations pay for the same or similar jobs through available pay surveys, and setting pay levels based on market pricing. The vast majority of firms use this external approach to identifying pay levels.[45] On the other hand, an *internal approach* uses job evaluation. **Job evaluation** *is the process of determining the worth of each position relative to the other positions within the organization.* Organizations commonly group jobs into pay levels or grades, and the higher the grade of the job, the higher the pay. A common example of this type of grouping is the federal government's GS ratings.

How do we accomplish a job evaluation? There are several ways, but methods usually involve ranking jobs, or assigning points to activities that occur within a job and totaling the points for the job. Once this is done, we can place the job in a hierarchy, called a *job structure*, and create our pay grades. Let's discuss some of the more popular job evaluation methods.

Job evaluation The process
of determining the worth of each
position relative to the other positions
within the organization

Job Ranking Method

Job ranking is simply the process of putting jobs in order from lowest to highest, in terms of value to the company. When doing job ranking, we utilize the job descriptions that we discussed in Chapter 4 to identify the factors in each job and then rank those jobs based on their content and complexity. We usually do job ranking without assigning points to different jobs. So we might start at the top of the organization with the CEO as the highest-ranking person and then work all the way down to the lowest-skilled housekeeping job.

But if you look at this method for a second, you will see that somebody has to decide the value of each job and do so without any quantitative factors. Therefore, this determination requires judgment and is highly subjective. This means it is difficult to defend if we have to do so in court.

Point-Factor Method

A second type of job evaluation is point-factor methods, which attempt to be completely objective in form. They break a job down into components like particular skills or abilities, and then they assign a number of points to each component based on its difficulty. These components are usually referred to as *compensable factors*.

Many of the compensable factors will be common among a number of different jobs, so once we have identified the number of points the factor is worth, we can then transfer that same value to all other jobs where the factor is present. The value of the point-factor job evaluation method is that we can differentiate jobs based on the difficulty or intensity of each factor, so it becomes easier to determine the total value of the job in a quantitative form.

Factor Comparison Method

The factor comparison method combines the job ranking and point-factor methods to provide a more thorough form of job evaluation.[46] This model is somewhat similar to the point-factor method in that it assigns points to compensable factors.

10-1 ETHICAL DILEMMA: WHAT WOULD YOU DO?

Executive Compensation

In 2013, the CEO-to-worker pay ratio was 331:1 and the CEO-to-minimum-wage-worker pay ratio was 774:1. Oracle's CEO made an estimated $189,000 per hour in one year. A minimum wage full-time employee at Walmart would have to work 1,372 hours to earn as much as the Walmart CEO makes in one hour. Some say top executives are being overpaid. Fortune 500 CEOs all make millions.

However, not everyone agrees. In capitalist countries, talented CEOs, like in pro sports, are entitled to fetch their price. Top executives should be paid multimillion-dollar compensation packages; after all, if it weren't for effective CEOs, companies would not be making the millions of dollars of profits they make each year. CEOs deserve a piece of the pie they help create.

1. Do executives deserve to make 300 times more than the average worker?
2. Is it ethical for managers to take large pay increases when laying off employees?
3. Is it ethical for managers to get pay raises when their companies lose money?
4. Are companies being socially responsible when paying executives premium compensation?

Sources: Information taken from the AFL-CIO's website at http://www.aflcio.org/corporatewatch/paywatch/pay/index.cfm, accessed March 26, 2015, 2013; R. Lowenstein, "Is Any CEO Worth $189,000 per hour?" *BusinessWeek* (February 20–26, 2012), 8–9; R. Fisman and T. Sullivan, "In Defense of the CEO," *Wall Street Journal* (January 12–13, 2013), C1–C2; E.D. Smith and P. Kuntz, "Some CEOs are more equal than others," *BusinessWeek* (May 6–12, 2013), 70–73.

Job Evaluation

Review the list of job evaluation methods and then write the letter corresponding to each method before each statement below.

a. external

b. job ranking

c. point-factor

d. factor comparison

_____ 16. I use two methods together to determine how much to pay each position because I'm an HR professional.

_____ 17. I look at the job and determine the specific skills needed to do the job, and then I add up the total point value of the skills to set the pay.

_____ 18. To figure out how much to pay the data entry person, I'm checking the SHRM data.

_____ 19. I placed all the jobs in rank order, from the one that was worth the most to the one that was worth the least, in order to determine how much to pay for each position.

_____ 20. All of the companies in our industry pay essentially the same hourly wage.

WORK
APPLICATION 10-13

Select an organization. Identify and describe which of the four job evaluation methods are used in that organization to determine pay.

LO 10-5

Explain the concept of a pay structure.

SHRM

K:A1

Development of a Base Pay System

Pay structure A hierarchy of jobs and their rates of pay within the organization

However, the factor comparison method first identifies a group of benchmark jobs—positions that are identified and evaluated in a large number of organizations and that can generally be found in most pay surveys.

Examples of benchmark jobs include "Training Specialist I," "Accountant II," "Lending Officer I," or "Hotel Registration Clerk." These benchmark jobs are then analyzed in some detail based on their compensable factors. We then rank the benchmark jobs in order, and we finally compare all other jobs in the organization to the benchmark jobs to determine where each one fits in the rankings. Here again, the primary method of determining the monetary value of a job is through the analysis of the compensable factors.

DEVELOPING A PAY SYSTEM

Well, we have finally gotten to the point where we can start to develop our new pay structure. Remember, though, all of the things that we had to review and decide on first. Take a look now at Exhibit 10-4 to see how each of those items comes together to allow us to create a *pay structure* and *individual pay rates* for each job.

Job Structure and Pay Levels

A **pay structure** *is a hierarchy of jobs and their rates of pay within the organization.*[47] It allows us to identify what the pay range is for each job. Once we have completed the process of creating a pay structure, we will have the pay range for every job in the hierarchy. From that, managers can determine individual compensation levels based on the employee's performance, seniority, skills, and any other significant factors.

A pay structure is composed of both a job structure and pay levels.[48] The *job structure* is what gives us our job hierarchy. As we noted in the job evaluation section of this chapter, the job structure is the stacking up of the jobs in the organization, from the lowest to the highest level. Each of the jobs within the job structure will end up at a particular pay level. On the other hand, a *pay level* (frequently called a pay grade) can be made up of many different jobs, and each pay level has a maximum pay rate and a minimum pay rate.

EXHIBIT 10-4	**CREATION OF A PAY STRUCTURE AND INDIVIDUAL PAY RATES**

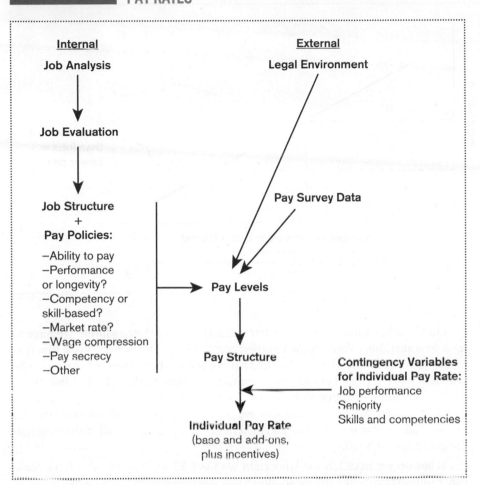

Creation of Pay Levels. To establish pay levels and determine the maximum and minimum pay rates particular jobs, we will have to look at some market factors. We look at product market competition and labor market competition because if we don't pay attention to external equity or fairness, we are going to have trouble filling many of our jobs.

Product Market Competition and Labor Market Competition. To set the minimum value for a particular pay level, we have to look at the applicable *labor market competition,* meaning labor supply versus demand for labor. If we graph compensation for a given type of work versus the number of workers in the labor market who can do that type of work, the place where the two lines cross is the average pay for that work. Per Exhibit 10-5, when the supply of labor equals the demand for that labor in the workforce, we have equilibrium. The market will pay about what the workers demand to be paid or workers who have the necessary skills won't be willing to fill the job.

What happens when there are more workers available than jobs? The market can get some of them to work for less than the normal rate (where the lines cross) because those workers need to work and earn a living. So the average compensation will most likely go down because we will have an oversupply situation. Conversely, if we have more jobs available than we have workers, we will usually have to pay more to attract the limited number of workers with the skill sets that we require. In either case, labor market competition will set the minimum pay that a worker will require in order to come to work for us—but it can be a moving target that we have to track.

EXHIBIT 10-5 SUPPLY AND DEMAND CURVE

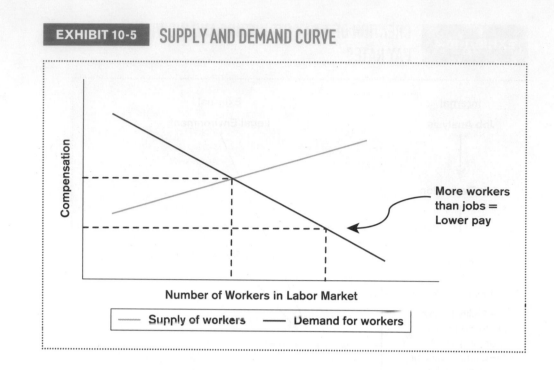

EXHIBIT 10-6 PRODUCT MARKET COMPETITION LIMITS

On the other hand, how do we determine the top of the pay level? We have to look at something called *product market competition*. This is basically a function of the value of the product or service that we sell to the customer.[49] An example will help make it clear. Let's say we manufacture utility trailers (see Exhibit 10-6). The public will pay about $500 for our 5- by 8-foot utility trailers. To make the problem simple, we will pretend that we only have a couple of components that go into making that trailer: labor and materials. Let's assume that all of the materials are going to cost $250.

What do we have left for labor? Do we have $250? No! We also have some other indirect costs like overhead, don't we? And we would like to make a profit, right? So if we estimate all of our other costs at $50, we now have $200 left. We can pay labor $200 if we only want to break even. However, if we want to make any money, we have to pay less than $200 for labor. Assume that our person who makes the trailer makes $20 per hour and it takes them 8 hours to build a trailer—$160 for the 8 hours of labor costs. So we have a $40 profit left, or about 8% before-tax profit.

Your assembler comes to you and says, "Boss, I need a raise." What do you just about have to tell the employee? "We can't pay you more." If our trailer is priced

Utility Trailer Manufacturing

$500   Sale price

– $250	Material costs
$250	= Remainder
– $50	Overhead costs
$200	= Remainder
– $160	Labor (maximum cost of labor)
$40	= Before-tax profit (8%)

at $800 and a competitor's trailer is $500, almost everyone will buy the competitor's trailer. We can't charge much more than the normal rate for a product or service. The labor is only worth so much money, because the sale price of the good or service has to cover the cost of the labor. So, *product market competition* sets the top of the pay level for most types of jobs in the company.

Exhibit 10-7, then, shows that we have a maximum and a minimum level of pay for a particular class of jobs, with labor market competition setting the bottom of the range and product market competition setting the top of the range. Remember, though, that this is a simplified example—there may be other factors involved as well.

Benchmarking Pay Survey Data. Next, we look at benchmarks from the pay survey data that we reviewed earlier and put those benchmark jobs into the pay level where they belong (the **blue** dots in Exhibit 10-7). Once we place some benchmark jobs in a plot of our pay levels, we can get a *market pay line* (sometimes called a pay curve)—a line that shows the average pay at different levels in a particular industry (see Exhibit 10-8). We use the benchmarks to see whether or not what we are doing is OK. If the range is correct, we have successfully created a pay level; if not, we have to figure out what is wrong with our range.

After going through this process for a particular pay level, we end up with a rate range, *which provides the maximum, minimum, and midpoint of pay for a certain group of jobs.* Once the range is created, we can go in and add to the range any other jobs that are at approximately the same level based on our earlier job evaluations.

Pay Structure

All right! Now we have our first pay level. So what do we do now? We start to lay pay levels out next to each other, creating a pay dispersion.[50] Again, look at Exhibit 10-8. We take our first pay level and put it down: bottom, midpoint, and top. The bottom of the range for the first level will probably be near minimum wage in most cases. Then our second tier will start, and beyond that will be the third and the fourth, and so on.

Notice that the ranges overlap each other. Why do they overlap? Take a look at the market pay line. It would have to go exactly through the corners of each pay level if the levels didn't overlap. That doesn't give us much wiggle room on which to base people's pay rates, does it? So the major reason for the overlap is to give the company some flexibility in each person's pay within a particular pay level.

SHRM

G:11
Benchmarking

SHRM

K:A14
Prevailing Wage

Rate range The maximum, minimum, and midpoint of pay for a certain group of jobs

---

EXHIBIT 10-7   **PAY LEVELS**

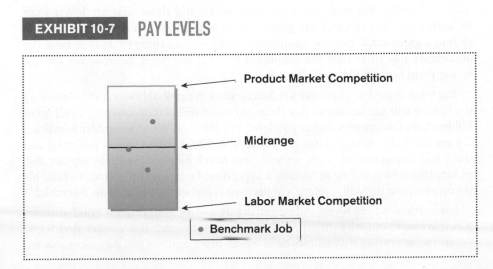

→ **Product Market Competition**

— **Midrange**

— **Labor Market Competition**

● **Benchmark Job**

EXHIBIT 10-8   PAY STRUCTURE

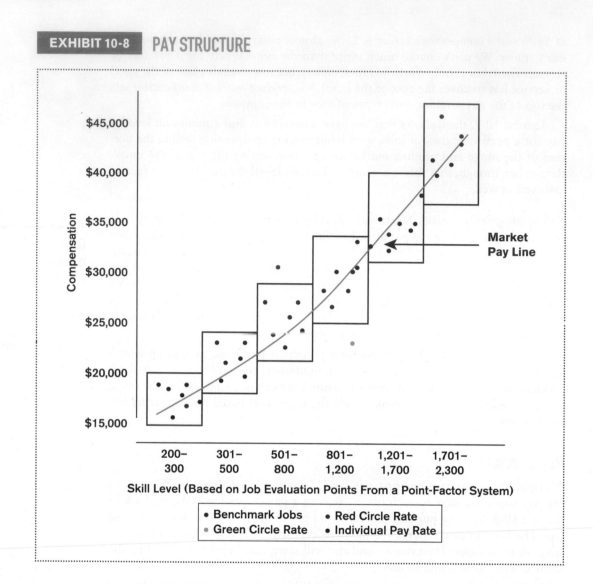

WORK
APPLICATION 10-14

Select an organization. Identify the rate range for a category of jobs.

SHRM

K:A3

Determining Pay Increases

Once we set up our pay levels, we can plot the actual pay for people in the organization. These are indicated in Exhibit 10-8 as black dots. We identify where these actual pay levels fall within the pay structure, and we will sometimes see that we have someone plotted outside our pay level ranges—either too high or too low. Individual pay rates that fall outside the pay range on the high side are called *red-circle rates* (**red** dots in Exhibit 10-8), and those that are lower than the bottom of the pay range are *green-circle rates* (green dots in Exhibit 10-8). If we find a green-circle rate for an individual, the correct thing to do is to raise the individual's pay to at least the minimum for that pay level, because we are not paying them fairly for their skill set.[51]

But what should we do about a red-circle rate? We probably won't cut someone's pay, but we will not be able to pay them any more unless they move up to a higher skill level, and therefore a higher pay level. For instance, if our assembler is making $24 per hour, the maximum for his pay level is $20, but he wants a pay raise and hasn't had one in several years, we will have to tell him no. However, we can also tell him that if he is willing to become a supervisor, he can get the chance to raise his pay rate because the skill level for a supervisor is higher than that of an assembler.

Understanding pay levels and pay structure allows us to provide good answers to employees about why their pay is set at a certain level. If a worker decides to become a supervisor, that employee is worth more and we can pay more. So we are able to tell the employee, "*The job* isn't worth any more than what you are being paid," instead of saying, "You are not worth any more than that."

Delayering and Broadbanding. A trend for many years now has been to lower the number of pay levels using one of two options—either delayering or broadbanding. **Delayering** *is the process of changing the company structure to get rid of some of the vertical hierarchy (reporting levels) in an organization.* On the other hand, **broadbanding** *is accomplished by combining multiple pay levels into one.*[52] When we lower the number of pay levels that we have to deal with, managing the pay process is simpler. It takes a long time to create, maintain, and evaluate 20 pay levels, when instead we can have just 5 broadbands. It also allows more capacity to reward outstanding performers. Because we have taller and wider levels, there is more pay flexibility while staying within the boundaries of the pay level.

Take a look at what happens to the pay structure in Exhibit 10-9 when we convert it into a broadband pay structure. The new broadband pay structure combines the first two pay levels, the third and fourth level, and finally the fifth and sixth, making three levels instead of six. This causes our red- and green-circle rates to disappear. It also creates greater ability to adjust the pay of people based on their performance and ability. Finally, it lowers the administrative burden of maintaining the compensation system.

Delayering The process of changing the company structure to get rid of some of the vertical hierarchy (reporting levels) in an organization

Broadbanding Combining multiple pay levels into one

EXHIBIT 10-9   **BROADBANDING OF MULTIPLE PAY LEVELS**

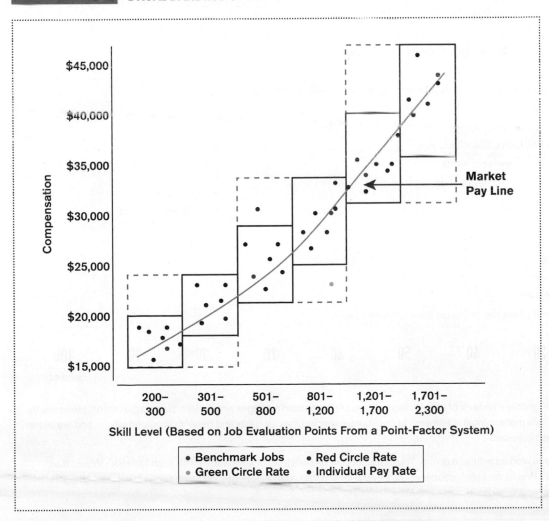

So when we are done with the pay structure, we will have created that hierarchy of jobs that we mentioned earlier—from lowest to highest. And as you have probably already guessed, much of this work is now done using computers. Once the HRIS have the necessary data, we can create most of our pay structure using existing company information. In many cases, the HRIS can identify the market pay line and provide other compensation information, too.

10-1 SELF ASSESSMENT

Compensation Management Satisfaction

This exercise is also a good review of the chapter, as it uses most of the important concepts. Select an organization that you work or have worked for and select your level of satisfaction with each of the following parts of the compensation management system, on a scale of 1 to 5.

1	2	3	4	5
Not satisfied				Satisfied

_____ 1. Base pay

_____ 2. Wage and salary add-ons

_____ 3. Incentive pay

_____ 4. Benefits

_____ 5. Meeting expectancy theory

_____ 6. Meeting equity theory

_____ 7. What the firm actually pays based on its ability to pay

_____ 8. Pay for performance vs. longevity

_____ 9. What the firm pays based on being below, at, or above market-level pay

_____ 10. Wage compression

_____ 11. Pay secrecy

_____ 12. Meeting the Fair Labor Standards Act

_____ 13. Pay equity and comparable worth

_____ 14. The system used for job evaluation

_____ 15. Job structure

_____ 16. Pay levels

_____ 17. Benchmarking

_____ 18. Pay structure

_____ 19. Pay raises

_____ 20. Benefit increases

_____ Total the points and place the score on the continuum below.

20	30	40	50	60	70	80	90	100
Not satisfied								Satisfied

The higher the score, the greater your level of satisfaction with the compensation management system of the organization. However, to most employees, what really matters most is answers to questions regarding their own pay and benefits (compensation), and we all are more satisfied when these increase.

Think about the people you worked with as a group. You can select the group's level of satisfaction with each question. Would their answers vary from yours? Would the satisfaction level vary by the level in the organization—among executives versus nonmanagers, by department, or among other groupings?

TRENDS AND ISSUES IN HRM

What trends are we seeing in the compensation of our 21st century workforce? One trend is a strong shift from base pay to variable pay components. Second, we look at how technology is allowing us to keep better track of our compensation programs.

A Shift From Base Pay to Variable Pay

As we noted earlier in this chapter, there appears to be a shift away from all or the majority of an individual's income being provided in the form of base pay toward a larger percentage of that income being provided in variable forms. What reasons do companies have for the shift toward incentive compensation? One of the biggest reasons is to lower the risk to the company when markets fail or economies go into recession.

New technology for analytic programs help companies assess their compensation programs.

How does incentive compensation do this? If a large percentage of an employee's pay comes from incentives for productivity, then when downturns occur, the company will not have to pay out as much in overall compensation as is necessary in better economic conditions since the company won't be producing as much during the recession. An illustration of this fact is the recent recession in the United States (and most of the rest of the world). In a 2010 salary survey, it was noted that "spending on variable pay as a percentage of payroll for salaried exempt workers was 11.3 percent, down from a record high of 12.0 percent in 2009." However, according to a 2013 **Aon Hewitt** report, as the economy recovered, "Ninety percent of companies offer a broad-based variable play plan and expect to spend 12.0 percent of payroll on variable pay for salaried exempt employees in 2014."[53]

This provides evidence that when companies were suffering from recession, paid-out incentives dropped, and as the economy recovered, incentives increased. So the employees, instead of employers, bear the risk of variable compensation based on changing business conditions.

The Technology of Compensation

Since compensation is typically one of the largest costs in most organizations, management needs to be mindful of what it gets for its money. As with so many other HR practices, we need to look at things like return on investment (ROI) from compensation programs. New analytical programs allow us to analyze compensation programs in more detail than has historically been possible. These programs and systems can take data from multiple sources—including external pay surveys, benchmark jobs, government databases, and company sources—and provide us with the ability to measure and monitor organizational costs and benefits.

HRIS analytical programs allow us to measure the effectiveness of incentives and compare our compensation information with industry metrics. They also help ensure compliance with various state and federal labor laws and with regulations on compensation, benefits, and medical leave. They can lower administrative costs of managing and maintaining compensation programs and can also help create higher organizational productivity, which can in turn improve employee satisfaction levels, especially when incentive programs are in place to reward productivity increases.

So given all of the capabilities of HRIS programs in compensation management, companies have to look very hard at the costs and benefits of these systems. More and more, it is becoming critical to have these tools available in order to ensure compliance and improve performance.

Get the edge on your studies at **edge.sagepub.com/fundamentalsofhrm**

Read the chapter and then take advantage of the open-access site to

- take a quiz to find out what you've mastered;
- test your knowledge with key term flashcards;
- watch videos to capture key chapter content.

REVIEW, **PRACTICE**, and **IMPROVE** your critical thinking with the tools and resources at **SAGE edge**.

$SAGE edge™

• • • CHAPTER SUMMARY

10-1 Describe expectancy and equity theories as they apply to compensation.

Expectancy theory—Employees *expect* to put forth some form of *effort* at work. This effort is *expected* to result in some level of *performance*. The performance level is then *expected* to result in some type of *reward*, and if it does, the employee *expects* to put out more effort. The reward has to be *significant* to the individual, and as long as it is, the employee will continue to put out effort. So employees will either be motivated by their outcomes, including compensation, or be demotivated by them.

Equity theory—people compare their inputs (the things they *do* in the organization) and outcomes (the things that they *receive* from the organization) to those of relevant others. If employees believe that there is inequity, they will change their work behavior to create equity. Employees must perceive that they are being treated fairly, relative to others. Compensation is obviously a large part of the perceived outcomes.

10-2 Identify the seven basic issues that make up the organizational philosophy on compensation.

1. *Ability to pay*. This is an honest assessment of how much we can afford, or are willing to afford, in order to compensate our employees.

2. *Types of compensation*. This refers to the mix of the four basic components of compensation—base pay, wage add-ons, incentives, and benefits—that we employ. We must divide available funds among the components.

3. *Pay for performance or longevity*. Will we pay people based on organizational loyalty/tenure, or will we pay based on performance in their jobs?

4. *Skill or competency-based pay*.

5. *At, above, or below the market*. What will our general pay structure look like, and why?

6. *Wage compression*. This lowers the pay differential between long-term and newly hired employees.

7. *Pay secrecy*. Will we utilize pay secrecy clauses in employment contracts? Pay secrecy may allow us to hide actual wage inequities from employees, but it has the potential to create dissatisfaction and demotivation.

10-3 Discuss the three major provisions of the FLSA.

1. Minimum wage rates identify the lowest hourly rate of pay generally allowed under the FLSA. There are many exemptions, but if a person is *nonexempt*, minimum wage will apply.

2. Overtime rates are also required for persons who are nonexempt. However, there are different exemptions for overtime than there are for minimum wage, so HR managers must check the law to determine who will have to be paid overtime.

3. Child labor requirements within the FLSA identify the jobs and allowable working hours for individuals between 14 and 18 years old. Sixteen- and 17-year-olds can only be employed in nonhazardous jobs, but their work hours are unrestricted. However, 14 and 15-year-olds can only work outside school hours, and the jobs that they are allowed to do are limited to retail and other service positions. They may not work overtime.

10-4 Name the three types of job evaluation discussed in the text and discuss whether they are more objective or subjective in form.

1. The job ranking method is simply the process of putting jobs in order from lowest to highest or vice versa, in terms of value to the company. However, it has limited usefulness because it is subjective.

2. Point-factor methods, on the other hand, attempt to be completely objective in form. They break a job down into component skills or abilities,

known as factors, and then apply points to each factor based on its difficulty.

3. The factor comparison method combines the ranking and point-factor methods to provide a more thorough form of job evaluation. It identifies benchmark jobs and then analyzes and rank-orders them. We then compare all other jobs in the organization to the benchmark jobs to determine where each one fits in the rankings.

10-5 Explain the concept of a pay structure.

A *pay structure* is created by laying out our pay levels, one next to the other. The entire group of pay levels creates the pay structure. Benchmark jobs can be plotted on the pay structure to get a *market pay line*—a line that shows the average pay at different levels in a particular industry. Once pay levels are set, we can actually plot employee rates of pay on the pay structure to see if any are plotted outside our pay level ranges, either high or low. Individuals who fall outside our pay range to the high side are paid *red-circle rates,* and those who fall outside low are paid *green-circle rates.* Each of these rates should be reviewed and corrected if necessary.

10-6 Define the key terms found in the chapter margins and listed following the Chapter Summary.

Complete the Key Terms Review to test your understanding of this chapter's key terms.

• • • KEY TERMS

broadbanding, 265
compensation, 247
compensation system, 248
delayering, 265

equity theory, 250
expectancy theory, 249
job evaluation, 258
minimum wage, 254

overtime, 255
pay structure, 260
rate range, 263
wage compression, 252

• • • KEY TERMS REVIEW

Complete each of the following statements using one of this chapter's key terms.

1. _____ is the total of an employee's pay and benefits.

2. _____ includes anything that an employee may value and desire and that the employer is willing and able to offer in exchange.

3. _____ proposes that employees are motivated when they believe they can accomplish a task and the rewards for doing so are worth the effort.

4. _____ proposes that employees are motivated when the ratio of their perceived outcomes to

inputs is at least roughly equal to that of other referent individuals.

5. _____ occurs when new employees require higher starting pay than the historical norm, causing narrowing of the pay gap between experienced and new employees.

6. _____ is the lowest hourly rate of pay generally permissible by federal law.

7. _____ is a higher than minimum, federally mandated wage, required for nonexempt employees if they work more than a certain number of hours in a week.

8. _____ is the process of determining the worth of each position relative to the other positions within the organization.

9. _____ is a hierarchy of jobs and their rates of pay within the organization.

10. _____ provides the maximum, minimum, and midpoint of pay for a certain group of jobs.

11. _____ is the process of changing the company structure to get rid of some of the vertical hierarchy (reporting levels) in an organization.

12. _____ is accomplished by combining multiple pay levels into one.

● ● ● COMMUNICATION SKILLS

The following critical-thinking questions can be used for class discussion and/or for written assignments to develop communication skills. Be sure to give complete explanations for all answers.

1. Do you believe it is always necessary to provide incentives as part of a pay structure? Why or why not?

2. As the HR manager, would you pay more attention to expectancy theory or equity theory in designing your compensation system? Why?

3. If your company had promised an incentive program right before the recession of 2007–2008, and if the recession made it impossible for the company to pay employees what they had been promised, then how would you explain this to your workforce to keep them motivated?

4. Would you rather have higher pay or better benefits? Why?

5. Would you ever consider paying below the market rate for employees if you had control of wages? Why or why not?

6. How would you approach a CEO or company president who insisted on classifying nonexempt workers as exempt? What would you say to get the CEO to stop this practice?

7. Do you think that comparable worth should be made federal law? Why or why not?

8. If you were the lead HR manager in your company, would you ever consider setting pay levels by just using external pay surveys and no internal analysis? What are the advantages and disadvantages of this?

9. As the head of HR, would you rather change narrow pay levels into broadbands? Can you think of any disadvantages to doing so?

● ● ● CASE 10-1 EMPLOYEE RED-LINING AT CVS: THE HAVE AND THE HAVE NOT

CVS Caremark is the second-largest drugstore chain in the United States (just behind **Walmart**). It employs 286,000 people in 45 states under the CVS logo, and it operates more than 7,600 drugstores. In 2013, CVS's sales exceeded $126 billion, but its net income was only around $4.6 billion, for about a 3.6% profit—about the median profit for the industry.[54]

As would any other public corporation, CVS wanted to increase its profitability for stockholders and regain its position as the industry leader. One method of increasing profits is cutting operational costs, and CVS decided to do just that. It adjusted employee annual pay raises by placing an earnings ceiling on salaries, and any employees earning the highest hourly wage in their job classification became ineligible for a raise.

Besides the obvious cost savings, why put a "red line" on wages? The main goal was to adjust the highest-paid employees' compensation to the job market average and, with these savings, provide raises to the employees who

were paid below that average. The philosophy was that as a CVS employee, one should expect lower raises (or none at all) if one is earning much more than one's colleagues. So once an employee reached the red line, that person received no additional compensation.

CVS executives knew that the new compensation policy would negatively impact some of their most loyal employees, yet the executives felt that they needed to draw a line on salaries in order to make the most of limited compensation dollars. What they did not figure was that the policy mostly hurt the employees who had been working there the longest. Worse, these same employees feared retaliation if they publicly criticized the new policy. How would it look to the other lower-paid employees (and worse, the public at large) if the highest-paid employees complained about their lack of raises?

Nationwide, the minimum wage is set at $7.25 per hour, but the wage management guidelines of CVS are different in most regions depending on the minimum wage in each state. Lowest-ranked employees with exceptional skills would receive a 4.75% raise on an annual basis if they were making minimum wage. However, if an employee with exceptional skills in the same position was already earning $12.50 an hour, that person would not receive a raise, having already crossed the red line.[55] With employment at will, the possibility of being laid off, and a tough job market, where would these employees get such high-paying jobs in the retail and service industries? It was better for them to keep quiet about their pay and stay in a company that they were comfortable with.[56]

Wage rates depend on employees' rank, and it is no secret that the CEO is going to be paid much more than the company's average worker. This is because the CEO job requires a more demanding set of skills compared to the average store job, and the workload of a CEO is much more demanding. But if the range of compensation is so great, it may discourage employees who are paid less.[57]

Some ethical and legal concerns arose when these same red-lined employees found out that this new compensation policy did not seem to apply to the top-level executives. The CEO of CVS was paid a total of $23 million in 2013, including bonuses and additional perks. He earned a 26% raise from the previous year, and that was almost 800 times more than the median income of a CVS employee. The red-lined employees saw an inequitable pay situation, with the rich getting richer because they were allowed a raise while the in-store employees had a cap on their income. The CEO's salary package was tied to the company's performance, and according to CVS spokesperson Carolyn Castel, "Last year, CVS Caremark had an outstanding year and continued to deliver strong financial results and enhanced returns to shareholders in a challenging economic environment, performing favorably against our peer group in several key areas."[58]

Questions

1. Describe the pay structure and compensation system for a CVS store employee. How might this pay structure be different from that of the CEO of the firm?

2. Define the rate range of CVS employees. How would you change the pay structure to encourage performance, especially for red-lined employees?

3. In terms of expectancy and equity theories, describe how the red-line policy will affect the motivation of employees.

4. In light of the red-line policy, what was CVS's philosophy toward employee performance, compensation, and longevity?

5. If you were CVS's CEO, knowing that you have to reduce costs and balance employee wages, what other measures would you take besides freezing raises for the highest-paid employees?

6. Why would the firm implement an HR policy that it knew would negatively affect its highest-paid employees? Did it perhaps have a hidden agenda?

Case created by Herbert Sherman, PhD, and Theodore Vallas, Department of Management Sciences, School of Business Brooklyn Campus, Long Island University

• • • SKILL BUILDER 10-1 JOB EVALUATION

Objective

To develop a better understanding of the job evaluation process

Skills

The primary skills developed through this exercise are as follows:

1. *HR management skills*—Technical, conceptual and design, and business skills
2. *SHRM 2013 Curriculum Guidebook*—K: Total rewards

Assignment

Step 1. You decided to open a restaurant and pub, and you have five job categories:

- *Owner/manager:* You are the owner, performing all the management functions and also greeting and seating people as you oversee all activities.
- *Wait staff:* They take food orders and bring food to customers.
- *Cook:* They prepare the food.
- *Helpers:* They bus tables, wash dishes, help in food preparation, and bring food to some customers.
- *Bartenders:* They make the drinks for both the dining and bar areas.

Rank the jobs from 1 to 5, with 5 being the highest-ranking job and 1 being the lowest.

Job	Mental Requirements (education, intelligence, and specialized knowledge)	Physical Requirements (effort such as standing, walking, and lifting)	Skill Requirements (specific job knowledge/ training to do work)	Responsibilities (for equipment, money, public contact, and supervision)	Working Conditions (safety, heat, ventilation, and coworkers)
Manager					
Wait Staff					
Cook					
Helper					
Bartender					
Factor Rank (1–5)					
Weight (100%)					

Step 2. Using the table below, rank each job for each of the five factors commonly used in job evaluations.

Step 3. The five factors are commonly weighted since some are more important than others.

(A) In the above table in the bottom row—Factor Rank— now rank the five factors from 1 to 5, with 5 being the most important and 1 being the least important.

(B) The five factors can also be weighted as percentages. For example, based on a total of 100%, the highest-rated factor could be weighted at 40%, then the next-highest could be rated at 30%, followed by 20%, and the other two at 5% each. So also include your percentage-based weights for each factor, like in the example.

People generally will not agree on all the rankings, and that is a major reason why there is virtually always a committee that conducts job evaluations.

Step 4 (optional due to difficulty). Assign pay values to each of the five factors and weight them to determine pay levels for each job.

Apply It

What did I learn from this experience? How will I use this knowledge in the future?

_____

_____

_____

• • • SKILL BUILDER 10–2 PRODUCT MARKET COMPETITION LIMITS

Objective

To develop a better understanding of product market competition limits

Skills

The primary skills developed through this exercise are as follows:

1. *HR management skills*—Technical and business skills
2. *SHRM 2013 Curriculum Guidebook*—K: Total rewards

Assignment

Complete the math problems below:

_____ 1. Your product sells for $1,000. Materials cost $300, labor costs $300, and overhead costs $200. What is your profit in dollars and as a percentage?

_____ 2. Your product sells for $750. Materials cost $250, labor costs $300, and overhead costs $150. What is the profit in dollars and as a percentage?

_____ 3. Your product sells for $1,000. Materials cost $300 and overhead costs $200. What is the maximum amount you can pay labor to make a $100 profit with a 10% return?

_____ 4. Your product sells for $750. Materials cost $250 and overhead costs $150. What is the maximum amount you can pay labor to make a 10% profit return on the sales price?

_____ 5. Your product sells for $800. Materials cost $300 and overhead costs $200. What is the maximum amount you can pay labor to make a 15% profit return on the sales price?

©iStockphoto.com/Georgijevic

11 EMPLOYEE INCENTIVES AND BENEFITS

••• LEARNING OUTCOMES

After studying this chapter, you should be able to do the following:

11-1 Identify the advantages and disadvantages of individual incentives. PAGE 275

11-2 Identify the advantages and disadvantages of group incentives. PAGE 278

11-3 Discuss the issue of whether or not executive compensation is too high. PAGE 291

11-4 Summarize the major statutory benefits required by federal law. PAGE 283

11-5 Name the main statutory requirements that must be followed *if* organizations choose to provide health care or retirement plans for their employees. PAGE 285

11-6 Describe the main categories of voluntary benefits available to organizations. PAGE 287

11-7 List the organization's options when providing flexible benefit plans to employees. PAGE 291

11-8 Define the key terms found in the chapter margins and listed following the Chapter Summary. PAGE 296

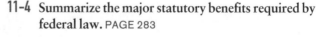

Master the content.

Use the online study tools at
edge.sagepub.com/fundamentalsofhrm
to review, practice, and improve your skills.

⑤SAGE edge™

Practitioner's Perspective

Cindy reflects: Whether the economy is up or down, your star employees can always find another job. This keeps HR departments looking for ways to keep their best employees motivated and engaged in their positions.

One of Cindy's colleagues, Terry, is a big advocate of incentive pay and good benefits packages. "We need to look at ways to reward our exceptional employees now without expanding our base labor costs into future years," Terry said at one of their strategy meetings. "I've seen evidence to support the case that employees work harder if they know they have a fair chance of being rewarded for that extra effort."

"Well, I've heard lots of complaints against incentive pay," says Bill, another member of their department. "I'm not sure we want to open our compensation program to those issues."

Are strong incentive and benefits packages a good idea? The pros and cons plus the methods of implementation are detailed for your consideration in Chapter 11.

● ● ●

THE VALUE OF INCENTIVES AND BENEFITS

We discussed the basic pay system and how our core wages or salaries are set in Chapter 10, so now we discuss incentives and benefits. Let's begin with a review of variable pay, also known as incentives. **Variable pay** *is compensation that depends on some measure of individual or group performance or results in order to be awarded.* There are two basic choices in incentive pay—individual or group-based incentives.

LO 11-1

Identify the advantages and disadvantages of individual incentives.

INDIVIDUAL INCENTIVES

Individual incentives reinforce performance of a person with a reward that is significant to that person. They are based on operant conditioning and reinforcement

Variable pay Compensation that depends on some measure of individual or group performance or results in order to be awarded

WORK
APPLICATION 11-1

Select a job. Assess the advantages and disadvantages of offering incentives for your job and whether the criteria are met for individual incentives to be effective at motivating employees.

SHRM

K:A5

Pay Programs: Merit Pay, etc.

WORK
APPLICATION 11-2

Select a job. Does the organization offer bonuses? If not, how could it offer bonuses to effectively motivate employees? Assess the advantages and disadvantages of offering bonuses at your organization. Should it offer bonuses?

theory and are designed to motivate the individual employee to do more than the minimum while on the job. We want to be able to reward our best employees so that they feel that they are being recognized,[1] and individual incentives allow us to do that.

Advantages and Disadvantages of Individual Incentives

Take a look at Exhibit 11-1 for a brief list of advantages and disadvantages of individual incentive plans.

Individual Incentive Options

There are five common options for individual incentive programs. Let's take a brief look now at each of these individual incentive options.

Bonus. A **bonus** *is a lump sum payment, typically given to an individual at the end of a time period.*[2] A bonus does not carry over from one period to the next. How would a bonus program have to be designed in order to motivate increased performance? We would need to identify specific and measurable goals that the individual could affect.[3] If they then reached the measurable goal, they would receive the bonus.

Commissions. Commissions are well-known incentive tools for sales professionals. A commission is a payment typically provided to a salesperson for selling an item to a

SHRM HR CONTENT

See Appendix: *SHRM 2013 Curriculum Guidebook* for the complete list

B. Employment Law (required)

   7. Employer Retirement Income Security Act of 1974 (ERISA)

   9. Family and Medical Leave Act of 1993 (FMLA)

  33. COBRA: Consolidated Omnibus Budget Reconciliation Act of 1985

  34. American Recovery and Reinvestment Act of 2009 (ARRA)

  37. Health Insurance Portability and Accountability Act (HIPAA) of 1996

K. Total Rewards (required)

  A. Compensation

    5. Pay programs: Merit pay, pay-for-performance, incentives/bonuses, profit sharing, group incentives/gainsharing, balanced scorecard

   15. Motivation theories: Equity theory, reinforcement theory, agency theory

  B. Employee Benefits

    1. Statutory vs. voluntary benefits

    2. Types of retirement plans (defined benefit, defined contribution, hybrid plans)

    3. Regulation of retirement plans (FLSA, ERISA, Pension Protection Act of 2006)

    4. Types of health care plans (multiple payer/single payer, universal health care systems, HMOs, PPOs, fee-for-service, consumer-directed)

    5. Regulation of health insurance programs (COBRA, HIPAA, Health Maintenance Organization Act of 1973)

    6. Federal insurance programs (Old-Age, Survivor, and Disability Insurance [OASDI], Medicare)

    7. Disability insurance

    8. Educational benefits

   10. Family-oriented benefits

   12. Life insurance

   15. Time off and other benefits

   16. Unemployment Insurance

   18. Financial benefits (gainsharing, group incentives, team awards, merit pay/bonuses)

   19. Managing employee benefits (cost control, monitoring future obligations, action planning, strategic planning)

   21. Paid leave plans

   22. Workers' compensation

EXHIBIT 11-1 INDIVIDUAL INCENTIVE PLAN ADVANTAGES AND DISADVANTAGES

Advantages	Disadvantages
Promotes the link between performance and results; pay is based on performance.	Many jobs have no direct output; measuring performance to reward is difficult.
Offers the ability to match rewards to employee desires; individuals want different rewards.	May motivate undesirable employee behaviors; individuals can use unethical behavior to achieve rewards.
Makes it easy to evaluate individual employees; individuals perform at different levels.	Record-keeping burden is high; it takes more time to evaluate and record individual performance than group performance.
May motivate less productive employees to work harder; individuals may perform at higher levels to get rewards.	May not fit organizational culture; incentives can hurt team effort of collaboration.

customer and is usually paid as a percentage of the price of an item that is sold. If you sell a $100 product and you are on a 10% commission, you would receive $10 for that sale. Salespeople sometimes work on straight commission, where they only get paid when they sell an item, or they can be paid a salary plus commission.

Merit Pay. The next incentive option is called merit pay. **Merit pay** *is a program to reward top performers with increases in their annual wage that carry over from year to year.* Merit pay works as follows: The company announces a "merit pool" available for pay increases in a given period, usually annually. The merit raises will be given to the top performers in the company based on performance evaluations. Frequently, individuals who receive either outstanding or excellent marks will get merit increases above the average, while average performers will get a lower raise and those who receive below-average marks will get no raise at all.

WORK
APPLICATION 11-3

Select a job. Does the organization offer commissions? If not, how could it offer commissions to effectively motivate employees? Assess the advantages and disadvantages of offering commissions at your organization. Should it offer commissions?

Merit pay A program to reward top performers with increases in their annual wage that carry over from year to year

11-1 APPLYING THE CONCEPT

Individual Incentive Options

Place the letter of the individual incentive on the line next to the scenario illustrating it.

a. bonus
b. commissions
c. merit pay
d. piecework
e. standard hour
f. nonmonetary awards

____ 1. I'm an auto mechanic at a dealership, and we have a set amount of time to complete each type of repair work.

I complete a job before a stated time so that I can go on to the next car and get paid extra for being faster than the average guy.

____ 2. I just sold that top-of-the-line BMW M3. I can't wait to get my pay this week.

____ 3. I'm the top producer in the entire department, so I will get an extra raise for high performance this year.

____ 4. The boss gave me a plaque and check for $5,000 in front of the entire company at our annual meeting.

____ 5. The boss just thanked me for getting a shipment that was behind schedule out on time today.

Employees paid on commission are paid based on how many sales they make. This is a common incentive tool.

Jupiterimages/Pixland/Thinkstock

Piecework Plans. Piecework or piece-rate plans are one of the simplest forms of compensation, and they can act as an incentive to produce at a higher level because the more workers produce, the more they get paid. In a "straight piece-rate" compensation system, the employee gets paid for every "piece" that they complete.[4] A "differential piece-rate" system provides the employee with a base wage to complete a certain amount of work, and if they produce more than the standard, a differential wage is paid for the extra pieces produced.

Standard Hour Plans. In a standard hour plan, each task is assigned a "standard" amount of work time for completion.[5] The individual doing the job will get paid based on the standard (expected) time to complete the job, but good workers can frequently complete the work in less than the standard amount of time. If they do, they can get paid for an hour of work while working less than an hour of time.

LO 11-2

Identify the advantages and disadvantages of group incentives.

WORK
APPLICATION 11-4

Select a job. Assess the advantages and disadvantages of offering incentives for your work group and whether the criteria are met for group incentives to be effective at motivating employees.

Social loafers Individuals who avoid providing their maximum effort in group settings because it is difficult to pick out individual performance

GROUP INCENTIVES

Individual incentive programs obviously work well in some cases. However, group incentives tend to work better in a number of other situations.

Advantages and Disadvantages of Group Incentives

What are the advantages and disadvantages of group incentive plans? See Exhibit 11-2 for a list.

Group Incentive Options

Individual incentives can work well, but can we use group incentives to motivate higher levels of performance from groups? After all, in most of our 21st century

EXHIBIT 11-2	GROUP INCENTIVE PLAN ADVANTAGES AND DISADVANTAGES

Advantages	Disadvantages
Promotes better teamwork; it promotes collaboration to work together to achieve the goal.	Social loafing can occur; loafers *avoid providing their maximum effort because it is difficult to pick out individual performance.*
Broadens individual outlook; employee better understands the relationship among jobs and departments.	Individual output may be discounted; Some individuals may feel as if they are providing most of the group's effort, and are not equitably rewarded for it.[6]
Requires less supervision; the members will enforce accepted standards of behavior and performance.	Outstanding performers may slacken efforts; faster employees may hold back performance to lower group standard level.
Is easier to develop than individual incentive programs; one incentive for a department of 20 is easier than 20 individual incentives.	Group infighting may arise; conflict can hurt group results

11-2   APPLYING THE CONCEPT

Group Advantages and Disadvantages

Identify each statement by its group advantage or disadvantage.

Advantages	Disadvantages
a. Promotes better teamwork	e. Social loafing can occur
b. Broadens individual outlook	f. Individual output may be discounted
c. Requires less supervision	g. Outstanding performers may slacken efforts
d. Is easier to develop than individual incentive programs	h. Group infighting may arise

____ 6. What happened? Latoya and Katie used to get along so well. Now they are constantly bickering.

____ 7. Katrina, you are not being fair to the rest of us by not doing your fair share of the work.

____ 8. Now that we use a team-based process, the manager doesn't check up on us like she used to.

____ 9. By assembling the product as a team, we actually increased production by 20%.

____ 10. I know I'm the best, but none of the department members work very hard, so why should I?

---

companies, groups and teams are the norm. Let's take a look at some of the more common group incentive options.

Profit Sharing Plans. **Profit sharing programs** *provide a portion of company proceeds over a specific period of time* (usually either quarterly or annually) *to the employees of the firm through a bonus payment.* The programs are designed to cause everyone in the company to focus on total organizational profitability.[7]

One major issue with profit sharing as a motivator is that it is focused on total organizational performance and profitability. If the employee doesn't know what to do in order to increase profits, what will they do differently in their job? The answer is "absolutely nothing." So profit sharing in many cases does not provide the company with the expected boost in productivity.[8]

Gainsharing Plans. An alternative to profit sharing is a gainsharing program. Gainsharing is similar to profit sharing because the "gain" is shared with the employees who helped to create the gain. However, gainsharing can be accomplished using any organizational factor that makes, or costs, the company money and that can be analyzed and modified for performance improvement.[9] Some of the more common gainsharing options are increased revenues, increased labor productivity or lower labor costs, improved safety (fewer lost-time accidents), return on assets or investment, and increased customer satisfaction.

Employee Stock Plans. There are also stock ownership plans that may work well as group incentives. The first is an *employee stock ownership plan* (ESOP). An ESOP ultimately allows at least part of the stock in the company to be earned by the employees over a period of time based on some formula.[10] For example, if you work for the company for a year, you might get 10 shares of stock, and for every additional year of employment, you would receive 10% more than the year before. An ESOP has the potential to be an incentive to the company's employees, because they become part owners of the firm.

Second, *stock options* may be offered to an employee to allow them to buy a certain number of shares of stock in the company at a specified point in the future, but at a price that is set when the option is offered.[11] The intent here

WORK
APPLICATION 11–5

Select a job at a for profit company. Does the organization offer profit sharing? If not, how could it offer a profit sharing plan to effectively motivate employees? Assess the advantages and disadvantages of offering profit sharing at your company. Should it offer a profit sharing plan?

SHRM

K:B18

Financial Benefits (Gainsharing, Group Incentives, etc.)

Profit sharing programs Programs that provide a portion of company proceeds over a specific period of time (usually either quarterly or annually) to the employees of the firm through a bonus payment

11-1   ETHICAL DILEMMA: WHAT WOULD YOU DO?

Academic Grades and Incentives

Grades are not actually pay, but they are meant to be an incentive to do well academically in college. Grade reports are based on individual performance, but in some courses part of the grade is based on group work.

Recall the Ethical Dilemma about academic standards in Chapter 8. Successful managers establish and maintain high expectations for all their employees. As Lou Holtz said, we need to set a higher standard. Today, it is generally agreed that students are doing less work while getting higher grades (grade inflation) than 10 or 20 years ago, based on a continuing trend of lowering of standards.

1. As an incentive, what affect do you believe grades have on performance, and does grade inflation affect the incentive to do well?
2. Has group work been part of your grade in any of your courses? If so, how did it affect your performance?
3. Do you believe group work should increase as part of student grading? Why or why not?
4. Do you find consistency among your professors' standards in terms of the work required in their courses and the grades given, or do some professors require a lot more work and some give lots of As and others lots of lower grades? Should colleges take action to improve consistency among professors' standards? If so, what should they do?
5. Are students who are putting in less time and getting higher grades being well prepared for a career with high standards after graduation?
6. Is it ethical and socially responsible for professors to drop standards and for colleges to award higher grades today than they did 10 or 20 years ago?
7. Should colleges take action to raise standards? If so, what should they do?

WORK
APPLICATION 11-6

Select a job at a for-profit company. Does the organization offer stock options and/ or stock ownership? If not, how could it offer one or the other to effectively motivate employees? Assess the advantages and disadvantages of offering stock options and stock ownership at your company. Should it offer stock options and/or a stock ownership plan?

is to motivate the employees to work to improve the value of the company so that when the option to buy the stock comes up at the agreed upon future date, the price of the stock has increased, giving the employee more value than what they paid for.

Lastly, *stock purchasing plans* are similar to stock options, but instead of giving you the option to buy stock in the future, they let qualifying employees buy the stock essentially anytime, usually at a discount. ESOPs, stock options, and stock purchasing give employees ownership in the company, with the intent that the employees will act more like owners of the company than simply employees.

11-3   APPLYING THE CONCEPT

Group Incentive Options

Place the letter of the group incentive option on the line next to the matching description.

a. profit sharing

b. gainsharing

c. ESOP

d. stock options

e. stock purchasing

____ 11. Our group incentive option gives us a bonus at the end of the year based on how profitable we were for the year.

____ 12. Our group incentive option plan allows me to get stock and put it in my retirement account without paying anything for it.

____ 13. Our group incentive option plan worked like this. The manager told us that if we could cut cost in our department by 5%, as a group we would get 5% of the savings to the company distributed evenly among us.

____ 14. Our group incentive option allows me to buy company stock for 10% less than the market value.

____ 15. Our group incentive option plan allows me to buy $50 shares of the company stock for only $13 apiece next year.

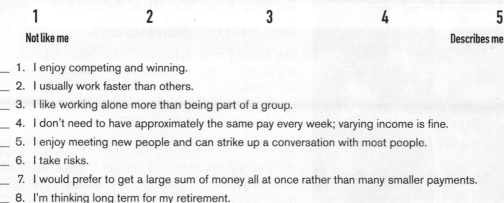

11-1 SELF ASSESSMENT

Compensation Options

Answer each question based on how well it describes you:

1	2	3	4	5
Not like me				Describes me

_____ 1. I enjoy competing and winning.

_____ 2. I usually work faster than others.

_____ 3. I like working alone more than being part of a group.

_____ 4. I don't need to have approximately the same pay every week; varying income is fine.

_____ 5. I enjoy meeting new people and can strike up a conversation with most people.

_____ 6. I take risks.

_____ 7. I would prefer to get a large sum of money all at once rather than many smaller payments.

_____ 8. I'm thinking long term for my retirement.

_____ 9. I like working toward a set of goals and being rewarded for achieving them.

_____ 10. I like knowing that I am one of the best at what I do (merit pay and praise).

There is no simple sum to add up here. Although we would all love to have a high wage or salary with lots of incentive pay on top of it, this is not the reality in most jobs today. In general, the higher your number of "describes me" statements, the more open you are to incentives versus wages/salaries. Below is an explanation of each statement.

Item 1: If you don't like competing and winning, you may be more comfortable in a job with a wage or salary; you usually have to compete for incentives like merit raises. Item 2: If you are not faster than others, piecework and standard hour incentives may not be your best option. Item 3: Commissions, piecework, and standard hours are often based on individual performance. Item 4: Wages and salaries give you a fixed income, whereas incentives provide a variable income. Item 5 is characteristic of commission salespeople. Item 6: If you don't like risk, incentives can be risky. Item 7: Getting a large sum at once tends to involve a bonus, profit sharing, or gainsharing incentives. Item 8: ESOPs are retirement plans, and stock purchases can be, too. Item 9 reflects gainsharing and bonuses. Item 10 reflects merit pay and praise.

EXECUTIVE COMPENSATION

No modern discussion of compensation is complete without at least touching on the topic of executive compensation. Executives drive organizational performance more than any other employee. CEOs like the late Steve Jobs of **Apple** have the power to make or break a company.[12] When Jobs retired in August of 2011 and died shortly thereafter, Apple stock lost nearly a third of its market value (about $120 billion!) in a year.[13] Research clearly links managerial leadership to consequences for both the individual and organizations, including financial performance. So it makes sense that executives are well paid for their managerial and decision-making skills. But has executive pay gotten out of line?

In order to even attempt to answer such a question, we need to look at what executives are paid to do. Executives are paid to make decisions for the organization and to guide it toward its goals. And the decisions that executives are paid to make are not easy decisions, such as what products to sell and where to sell them. Successful executive leadership requires a high level of inherent intelligence, knowledge, and skills to analyze so much information, and significant experience in making decisions of similar types and consequences.

Since labor is always at least partly priced based on supply and demand, and there are very few executives with the high-level skills necessary to run large firms, these individuals are always going to be worth quite a bit of money to the firm. However, this is not to say that there have not been some serious excesses in executive pay, especially when CEO pay has increased while employees were taking

LO 11-3

Discuss the issue of whether or not executive compensation is too high.

WORK
APPLICATION 11-7

Would you say the CEO of an organization you work(ed) for is overpaid, underpaid, or paid fairly for the contribution made to the firm?

Executives like Yahoo's Marissa Mayer are paid well to make major organizational decisions and guide their organization's vision and goals.

WORK
APPLICATION 11–8

Would you say the Dodd-Frank Act will help, hurt, or have no effect on an organization you work or have worked for?

SHRM

K:A15

Motivation Theories: Equity, Reinforcement, Agency Theories

Golden parachutes Provision for executives who are dismissed from a merged or acquired firm of typically large lump sum payments on dismissal

Perquisites Extra financial benefits usually provided to top employees in many businesses

pay cuts and getting laid off.[14] One result of excessive executive compensation resulted in federal legislation on executive compensation—the Dodd-Frank Wall Street Reform and Consumer Protection Act.

The Dodd-Frank Wall Street Reform and Consumer Protection Act of 2010

The Dodd-Frank Act placed new limits on executive pay in public corporations and also added requirements for reporting of both compensation and shareholder involvement with executive compensation.[15] Let's look at the major provisions of the act.

Shareholder "Say on Pay" and "Golden Parachute" Votes. Among the most significant requirements is that shareholders must be allowed to vote on compensation packages for their executive officers at least once every 3 years. This provision is called "say on pay." While the vote is non-binding, it can still put pressure on executives to maintain compensation in line with organizational performance.

Shareholders also have a vote on what's called "golden parachutes" for executives. **Golden parachutes** *provide executives who are dismissed from a merged or acquired firm with typically large lump sum payments on dismissal.* This tool is used to discourage a takeover of the firm, because the cost of the takeover becomes much higher due to the high payout to these executives.

Executive Compensation Ratios. Other provisions in Dodd-Frank include a requirement that every public company disclose the total compensation of the CEO and the total median compensation of all employees and provide a ratio of these two figures.[16] It also requires companies to provide information on the ratio between executive compensation and the *total shareholder return* of the company each year, which allows shareholders to more easily evaluate the performance of firms in which they hold stock.

The act also requires that public companies establish policies to "claw back" incentives if the company has to restate financial information that is detrimental to the firm's value.[17] In other words, if the company paid an executive incentive based on its financial statements and then had to disclose later that those statements were not accurate, company policy would require that any incentives paid out to the executives be given back to the company.

Executive Incentives

Some of the most common incentives that are used in executive compensation are *stock incentives*.[18] They are supposed to cause the executive to act to increase the value of the company over time, because if this is done, the executive's stock becomes more valuable.

Short-term and long-term bonuses attached to company performance goals are another popular incentive for executives.[19] Finally, executives generally receive compensation in the form of *perquisites* or "perks." **Perquisites** *are extra financial benefits usually provided to top employees in many businesses.* While perks are not technically incentive pay (they are generally classed as benefits), they do serve to entice top-level executives to consider accepting jobs within an organization in some cases.

STATUTORY BENEFITS

So incentives are important to employee performance, but many employees pay close attention to company-provided benefits. Some benefits are statutory (mandatory), due to federal and state laws, but some are optional, based on the desires of the firm. There are also laws that apply if the company chooses to provide certain nonmandatory benefits. Let's do a review of statutory benefits first.

Social Security and Medicare

By far the largest of the statutory programs, in both size and cost to employers (and employees), are Social Security and Medicare. The combined cost of the Old-Age, Survivors, and Disability Insurance (OASDI) and Medicare programs was over $1.4 trillion in 2015.[20]

Both employers *and* employees are required to provide funds for Social Security benefits. Since these programs are so complex, the best that we can do in this introductory text is to provide some general information on the programs.

The employer and employee jointly pay into Social Security through withholdings from the employee's paycheck and a mandatory employer payment. Each of them pays a 7.65% tax on the employee's total pay per pay period, with 6.2% going into OASDI and 1.45% of the employee's pay into the Medicare fund.

Retirement. Once an employee becomes eligible and meets the retirement age requirements, they can receive a monthly check. At what age are you eligible for Social Security retirement? If you were born in 1937 or earlier, you are eligible for retirement at age 65. If you were born in 1960 or later, your retirement age is 67. For those born between 1937 and 1960, it is based on a sliding scale.

Disability and Survivor Benefits. These components are really basically the same benefit. If an employee becomes disabled or dies and is otherwise eligible, the person, or their survivors, will get payments each month roughly equal to what the employee would have gotten in retirement based on their historical earnings.

Medicare. Finally, there is the Medicare component of Social Security. Individuals become eligible for health care through Medicare at the same time as their eligibility for Social Security retirement begins. Medicare is not completely free to the retiree though. The covered person has to pay copayments and deductibles, and there are other out-of-pocket costs involved with Medicare.

Workers' Compensation

The next statutory benefit is workers' compensation, an insurance program designed to provide medical treatment and temporary payments to employees who cannot work because of an employment-related injury or illness. "Employment-related" means that the illness or injury had to do with the worker's actions for the company, although the injury or illness didn't have to happen while the person was actually at work.

The workers' compensation program is paid for by employers and is a type of "no-fault" insurance, which means that no matter which party—the employer or the employee—was at fault in an accident- or illness-related situation, the insurance will be paid out to the party harmed. Rates are primarily determined by three factors:

1. *Occupations.* Some occupations are much more risky than others. For instance, it costs a lot more to insure firefighters, police officers, or construction workers than it does to cover office workers.

LO 11-4

Summarize the major statutory benefits required by federal law.

K:B1

Statutory vs. Voluntary Benefits

K:B19

Managing Employee Benefits

K:B10

Family-Oriented Benefits

WORK
APPLICATION 11-9

Identify the incentives the CEO of an organization you work or have worked for receives.

WORK
APPLICATION 11-10

Look at your last pay stub. How much was taken out for Social Security tax and Medicare tax? How much did your employer pay?

SHRM

K:B6

Federal Insurance Programs (OASDI, Medicare)

SHRM

K:B22

Workers' Compensation

WORK
APPLICATION 11-11

How would you rate the risk of occupational injury or illness where you work or at an organization where you have worked? Is it high, moderate, or low? Why?

SHRM

K:B16

Unemployment Insurance

2. *Experience ratings.* An **experience rating** *is a measure of how often claims are made against an insurance policy.* It is calculated on the frequency and severity of injuries that occur within that particular company. The more frequent and severe the claims are, the higher the cost of insurance. Experience ratings can significantly affect a company's workers' compensation costs.

3. *Level of benefits payable.* Injured workers will get compensated based on their state's workers' compensation rating manual. Individual states set the rates for injuries within the state's boundaries, and these rates affect the cost of workers' compensation insurance.

Unemployment Insurance

The third statutory benefit is Unemployment Insurance. Unemployment Insurance (UI) provides workers who lose their jobs with payments from UI funds for a specified period of time. The basic federal tax rate is 6.2% of wages earned (in 2011) for the first $7,000 in individual wages, but can be reduced if the employer pays state unemployment taxes on time and avoids tax delinquencies.

Here again, as in workers' compensation, the tax rate is affected by the company's "experience rating." Employers who tend to terminate more employees have a higher experience rating and, as a result, a higher UI tax rate.[21] So within the same state, some employers will pay much more in UI taxes than other employers will.

An individual becomes eligible for UI if they were terminated from employment—either through downsizing, layoff, or other processes—and in most cases if they worked in four of the last five quarters and met minimum income guidelines in each of those quarters.

What will make them *ineligible* for UI?

- The individual quit voluntarily.
- They fail to look for work.
- They were terminated "for cause" (because they did something wrong).
- They refuse suitable work (work comparable to what they were doing prior to being terminated).
- They, as a member of a union, participate in a strike against the company (in most states).
- They become self-employed.
- They fail to disclose any monies earned in a period of unemployment.

SHRM

B:9

Family and Medical Leave Act of 1993 (FMLA)

Family and Medical Leave Act of 1993 (FMLA)

The next mandatory benefit is Family and Medical Act leave (FMLA). FMLA requires that the employer provide unpaid leave for an "eligible employee" when they are faced with any of the following situations:[22]

Leave of 12 workweeks in a 12-month period for . . .

The birth of a child and to care for the newborn child within 1 year of birth

The placement with the employee of a child for adoption or foster care and to care for the newly placed child within 1 year of placement

To care for the employee's spouse, child, or parent who has a serious health condition

A serious health condition that makes the employee unable to perform the essential functions of their job

Experience rating A measure of how often claims are made against an insurance policy

Any qualifying exigency arising out of the fact that the employee's spouse, son, daughter, or parent is a covered military member on "covered active duty"

or . . .

Leave of 26 workweeks during a single 12-month period to care for a covered service member with a serious injury or illness if the eligible employee is the spouse, son, daughter, parent, or next of kin to the employee (military caregiver leave)

Any private sector employer is covered under the act if they have 50 or more

The Family and Medical Leave Act of 1993 provides unpaid leave for certain "eligible employees" to care for family issues such as births, adoptions, illnesses, and injuries.

employees who worked at least 20 weeks during the year, working within a 75-mile radius of a central location. The act exempts "salaried eligible employee(s) . . . among the highest paid 10% of the employees employed by the employer within 75 miles of the facility at which the employee is employed"[23] from job protections if they take FMLA leave, though, because loss of these individuals for as much as 12 weeks could be significantly disruptive to the company. Take a look at the US Department of Labor FMLA webpage (http://www.dol.gov/whd/fmla/) for more information on managing FMLA leave.

The Patient Protection and Affordable Care Act of 2010 (ACA)

The last mandatory benefit is the Patient Protection and Affordable Care Act of 2010. In general, this act requires that all employers with more than 50 employees provide their *full-time employees* with health care coverage or face penalties for failing to do so.[24]

One lesser-known provision of the law is that employees not covered by a health care plan at work will be *required* to go to the state health exchange where they can purchase individual coverage. Individuals who fail to gain coverage will be fined, with the maximum individual fine set at $695 in 2016. You can find out more about the ACA by going to the official site at http://www.hhs.gov/healthcare/index.html.

STATUTORY REQUIREMENTS WHEN PROVIDING CERTAIN VOLUNTARY BENEFITS

Let's take a look now at some legal requirements that apply *if* we choose to provide certain benefits to our employees. These requirements may apply if we provide our employees with health insurance or company-sponsored retirement plans.

Consolidated Omnibus Budget Reconciliation Act of 1985 (COBRA). If employers choose to provide health insurance, we have to abide by the Consolidated Omnibus Budget Reconciliation Act (COBRA). **COBRA** *is a law that requires employers to offer to maintain health insurance on individuals who leave their employment (for a period of time).* The individual former employee has to pay for the full cost of the insurance (plus up to 2% for administration of the program), but the employer is required to keep the former employee on their group insurance policy.

LO 11-5

Name the main statutory requirements that must be followed *if* organizations choose to provide health care or retirement plans for their employees.

SHRM

K:B5

Regulation of Health Insurance Programs (COBRA, HIPAA, HMO Act of 1973)

COBRA A law that requires employers to offer to maintain health insurance on individuals who leave their employment (for a period of time)

COBRA applies to companies with 20 or more full-time equivalent employees. It is required to be offered to both terminated employees and those who voluntarily quit, in most cases.

Health Insurance Portability and Accountability Act of 1996 (HIPAA). The Health Insurance Portability and Accountability Act (HIPAA) is another health insurance law that applies if the company provides health insurance to its employees. What are the general provisions of HIPAA?

First, health insurance is "*portable.*" This means that if we had group health insurance at our previous employer and *if* our new employer has health care coverage for their employees, they are required to provide us with the opportunity to participate in their health insurance plan.

Second is *accountability*. HIPAA protects "the privacy of individually identifiable health information" from being disclosed to unauthorized individuals.[25] It also provides that employers are accountable to ensure the security of personal health information. So COBRA and HIPAA are mandatory if we as an employer offer health insurance to our employees.

Employee Retirement Income Security Act of 1974 (ERISA). The first two government mandates that we discussed were contingent on firm actions in companies that choose to provide *group health insurance* to their employees. However, ERISA covers employers who provide a *group retirement plan and/or group health insurance*. Here are the major provisions of ERISA.

Eligibility. If the company provides an employee retirement plan, the guidelines in ERISA say that the plan has to be available to all employees over 21 years of age who have worked in the company for 1 year.

Vesting. A second major provision of ERISA is vesting. **Vesting** *provides for a maximum amount of time beyond which the employee will have unfettered access to their retirement funds, both employee contributions and employer contributions.* ERISA identifies the maximum amount of time that the company can retain *company* contributions to the employee's retirement account. If the employer puts money into the employee's retirement account, that employer must vest the employee in all employer contributions by one of two optional deadlines:

100% of employer contributions at the end of 5 years of contributions to the plan; or

20% of employer contributions from the end of year 3 through the end of year 7.

Portability. The portability rule allows us to take our retirement fund and move it from one employer to another qualified fund. The employer cannot require that we keep the funds with them, or under their control.

Fiduciary responsibility. ERISA also requires that administrators and managers of both retirement and health care plans meet certain fiduciary standards of conduct. Fiduciary responsibility simply means that the person has an obligation to provide sound and reasonable financial advice to the clients (employees) of these plans.

PBGC. The last big provision of ERISA is the creation of the Pension Benefit Guarantee Corporation (PBGC). The PBGC is a governmental corporation whose purpose is to insure "defined benefit" retirement funds (which we will cover shortly) from failure if employers go bankrupt or are for other reasons not able to provide promised retirement benefits. The PBGC may not fund 100% of what was promised in the specific retirement plan, but it "guarantees 'basic benefits' earned before the plan's termination date" or the employer's date of bankruptcy.[26]

WORK
APPLICATION 11-12

Which, if any, statutory requirements governing certain voluntary benefits would be mandatory where you work or have worked?

Vesting A maximum amount of time beyond which the employee will have unfettered access to their retirement funds, both employee contributions and employer contributions

PBGC A governmental corporation established within the Department of Labor whose purpose is to insure retirement funds from failure

Statutory Benefit Laws

Place the letter of the relevant statutory benefit law on the line next to the statement below.

a. FMLA

b. ACA

c. COBRA

d. HIPAA

e. ERISA

_____ 16. I don't trust my company's financial future, so I like this law because it will allow me to move my funds out of my company fund to a new account with the stockbroker of my choice.

_____ 17. I like this law because it will allow me to take time off from work to take care of my sick mother.

_____ 18. I'm going quit and look for a new job, so I like this law because I need to continue to have health insurance while I search for a new job.

_____ 19. I currently have health insurance and medical problems, but when I change jobs, the new company can't refuse to give me insurance based on any medical problems I have when I join the firm.

_____ 20. I'm out of school and almost 25, so I like this law that allows me to continue on my parents' insurance plan.

VOLUNTARY BENEFITS

In addition to mandatory benefits, almost all employers provide some group of voluntary benefits to their employees. Companies evaluate their workforce and the funds available to the company and choose the voluntary benefit packages that will best allow them to maintain a satisfied and engaged workforce. Let's discuss some of the more common voluntary benefits.

Paid Time Off

Paid time off (PTO) benefits include a group of options such as vacation time/annual leave, severance pay, personal time off, sick days, and holidays. Some companies provide an all-encompassing PTO plan that allows the employee to use their paid time off in any way they wish, whether for sick days or vacation, holidays, or for any other purpose. Others apportion the available days for vacation, sick time, holidays, and others.[27] The average cost of paid time off is $1 for every $10 in direct wages. None of the PTO benefits is mandatory based on federal law in the United States, but be aware that some states have passed, or are currently attempting to pass, mandatory sick leave and even in some cases annual leave laws. Let's do a quick review of the most common types of PTO.

Vacation or Annual Leave. The majority of US firms provide paid vacations to their employees, according to the US Bureau of Labor Statistics. In fact, about 93% of employers provide paid vacation in some form—either as a stand-alone benefit or as part of a PTO plan—to their full-time workforce.[28] The average time provided is about 10 days after 1 year of service in 2012, and 17 days after 10 years of service.[29]

Sick Leave. The next most popular PTO is sick leave. Approximately 86% of employers in the United States provide sick leave of some type to their employees.[30] Paid sick leave can offer employees relief from loss of income associated with having to miss work due to an illness.

Holiday Pay. Nearly all employers provide for at least some paid holidays with their workforce. Companies can be subject to charges of discrimination if there is cultural or religious diversity in the firm and the company does not have flexibility on days available for holiday pay. Because of these issues, some companies provide "floating" holidays so that the employee can pick which days they will observe as holidays during the work year.

LO 11-6

Describe the main categories of voluntary benefits available to organizations.

K:B15

Time Off and Other Benefits

K:B21

Paid Leave Plans

WORK
APPLICATION 11-13

Identify the paid time off benefits offered where you work or have worked.

Paid Personal Leave. Finally, many companies today provide time off for a variety of personal needs. Personal leave is an effort on the part of the organization to maintain or improve job satisfaction and organizational commitment on the part of their employees.

SHRM

K:B4

Types of Health Care Plans

Group Health Insurance

The US Bureau of Labor Statistics reported that 68% of private-industry workers receive medical care benefits and that employers offering health insurance paid an average of 81% of the cost of premiums for single coverage and 69% of the cost for family coverage in 2013,[31] and that number has grown significantly with the advent of the ACA. Let's look at the major types of group health insurance.

Traditional Plans (Also Called Fee-for-Service). **Traditional health care plans** typically cover a set percentage of fees for medical services—for either doctors or in-patient care. The most common percentage split between the insurance plan and the individual is 80/20. In other words, if the employee has to go to the hospital and is charged $10,000 for services, the insurance would pay $8,000 and the individual would be responsible for the other $2,000. Traditional plans typically do not cover preventive care, such as an annual physical exam. They do, however, give the employee a lot of choice of health care providers, but there are some serious issues with potential out-of-pocket costs, so they aren't used much anymore.

Health Maintenance Organizations (HMOs) are a health care plan that provides both health maintenance services and medical care as part of the plan. **HMOs** *are a managed care program.* This provides the patient with routine preventive care but requires that a review of specific circumstances concerning the individual and their health condition be completed before any significant medical testing, medical procedures, or hospital care is approved. Managed care plans generally require that the employee and their family use doctors and facilities that are in the managed care network.

Preferred Provider Organizations (PPOs) are a kind of hybrid between traditional fee-for-service plans and HMOs. They have some of the advantages and disadvantages as well as some of the requirements of both. PPOs have networks of physicians and medical facilities, just like HMOs. PPOs act like HMOs in that they *prefer* (but do not require) that you have a primary care physician (PCP) within their medical network and that you go to that doctor before going elsewhere for medical care. They also provide preventive care services to their insured members, similar to HMOs, and have similar copayments and annual deductibles.

However, PPOs are more similar to traditional plans in that they do not require that you have a referral from the PCP to see a specialist. They will also allow you to see any provider of care either in or outside the network, although you may be required to pay a larger percentage of the cost of care if you choose to go beyond the network of physicians and facilities.

Traditional health care plans Plans that cover a set percentage of fees for medical services—for either doctors or in-patient care

HMO A health care plan that provides both health maintenance services and medical care as part of the plan

Preferred provider organizations (PPOs) A kind of hybrid between traditional fee-for-service plans and HMOs

HSA or MSA A plan allowing the employer and employee to fund a medical savings account from which the employee can pay medical expenses each year with pretax dollars

Health or Medical Savings Accounts (HSA/MSA) are savings accounts for health care services. An **HSA or MSA** allows the employer and employee to fund a medical savings account from which the employee can pay medical expenses each year with pretax dollars. The money in this account is used to pay for medical services for the employee (and their family, if desired) over the course of that year. One of the big advantages of HSAs and MSAs is that money remaining in the account at the end of the year can usually be rolled over to future years without paying a tax penalty.[32] In an HSA, you pay the full cost of medical services used from the HSA account. There are no copayments; there are no deductibles.

HSAs are also portable, so we can take our HSA balance with us if we change employers. One of the benefits to companies using an HSA or MSA is that it causes the employee to understand the full cost of providing health care for the year because the full cost of care is coming out of the employee's pocket through the use of the HSA debit card. It is thought that they might pay more attention to unnecessary medical expenses, such as going to the doctor's office when they have a cold or cut a finger.

High-deductible health plan (HDHP). One of the problems that you can quickly see with an HSA is that medical services in a particular year could cost much more than a few thousand dollars, especially if you had surgery. However, federal rules on HSAs and MSAs require that employees who have these accounts also participate in an "HDHP." A **high-deductible health plan (HDHP)** *is a "major medical" insurance plan that protects against catastrophic health care costs and in most cases is paid for by the employer.* A very common HDHP would pay for medical costs in any given year that total more than $10,000. So if an individual exceeded the amount of money in their HSA, they would be responsible for out-of-pocket costs up to $10,000, at which time the HDHP would take over and pay all of the remaining costs of the individual's health care for the year. One of the big advantages of HSAs and MSAs is that the individual can go to any physician or medical facility. There are no HMO networks and no preferred providers.

Retirement Benefits

According to the Bureau of Labor Statistics, employer-provided retirement plans are available to 74% of all full-time workers and 37% of part-time workers in private industry.[33] Retirement benefits are categorized into two types.

Defined Benefit Versus Defined Contribution Plans. A **defined benefit plan** provides the retiree with a specific amount and type of benefits that will be available when the individual retires. For instance, a simple defined benefit plan might provide that employees who work in the company for 25 years will get 60% of the average of their two highest years of pay. In addition, they will receive 1% more for every additional year that they work. So if the same employee worked for 35 years, they would receive 70% of the average of their two highest years of pay. Because it is a defined benefit retirement plan, the employee knows exactly what their retirement payment will be.

WORK
APPLICATION 11-14

Select a company that offers health insurance and identify the type of insurance it offers.

High-deductible health plan (HDHP) A "major medical" insurance plan that protects against catastrophic health care costs and in most cases is paid for by the employer

Defined benefit plan A plan providing the retiree with a specific amount and type of benefits that will be available when the individual retires

---

11-5 **APPLYING** THE CONCEPT

Group Health Insurance

Place the letter of each type of health insurance option offered on the line next to the statement describing it.

a. Traditional

b. HMO

c. PPO

d. HSA

e. MSA

____ 21. I don't like the new insurance plan because I can only go to doctors and hospitals that are approved by the plan. I have to stop seeing my doctor and start with a new one that I'm assigned to.

____ 22. I have expensive health problems, and my insurance plan requires me to pay 20% of my health care costs, making it very expensive for me.

____ 23. I like my insurance plan because I'm healthy and pay the full cost, but I don't use it all every year and it has accumulated in case I need it someday.

____ 24. I have the same insurance deal that you have (#8), but my company only has 25 employees.

____ 25. I do have copays and deductibles, but at least I can go to any doctor or hospital I want too at an extra cost.

Employer-provided retirement plans give workers a financial cushion after they retire.

SHRM

K:B2

Types of Retirement Plans

WORK
APPLICATION 11-15

Select a company that offers retirement benefits and state the type of plan it offers. If it is a defined benefit, describe the plan. If it is a defined contribution, identify the option selected and if the employer offers any matching contributions, what they are.

Defined contribution plan A plan providing only the amount of funds that will go into a retirement account, not what the employee will receive upon retirement

Unlike a defined benefit plan, under a defined contribution plan the employee does not know what their retirement benefit will be. **Defined contribution plans** *identify only the amount of funds that will go into a retirement account, not what the employee will receive upon retirement.* If those retirement funds are invested successfully, growing significantly over time, the individual's retirement account will be able to pay much higher benefits than if the funds are not invested successfully and don't grow very much.

Shift from defined benefit to defined contribution plans. Defined benefit plans used to be the most common type of retirement plan, but they have been overtaken by defined contribution plans—some would say for legitimate business reasons. Providing a defined contribution retirement plan to employees shifts the investment risk from the company to the individual employee. Let's look at a couple of common defined contribution retirement programs.

401(k) Plans. The most well-known retirement plan in US companies today is the 401(k). 401(k) accounts, or 403(b) accounts for nonprofits, are available to nearly all employees of corporations as well as most self-employed persons. A *401(k) retirement plan* is a savings investment account.

Both the employee and the employer are allowed to contribute funds each year to the employee's 401(k) account, with the *employee* allowed to contribute up to a maximum of $17,500 (for an employee under 50 years of age in 2014).[34] Contributions are made on a "pretax basis." This means that when funds are put into the account, they do not count as taxable income for the individual. Once the individual retires and begins to remove funds from the account, they pay income taxes on the distributions from the account.

Matching contributions. Many employers that offer a 401(k) provide a matching contribution up to a set maximum. For example, an employer might allow a 100% match of employee contributions up to a $2,000 maximum. So if the employee put $2,000 of their salary into the retirement account over the course of the year, this plus the employer's matching funds would total $4,000 a year to the individual's retirement account.

IRAs and Roth IRAs. An IRA is an Individual Retirement Account. Under US law, any person who pays taxes can contribute to an IRA, and the contributions are tax-free (subject to a maximum annual income limit). In other words, they reduce your taxable income by the full amount of the contribution in the year in which they are contributed to the account.

Both IRAs and Roth IRAs can supplement the amount that an individual is contributing to a company-sponsored 401(k) account, because you are allowed to contribute to both. An individual can contribute a maximum of 100% of their income up to $5,500 per year (in 2014) into a standard, or Roth, IRA.[35]

The Roth IRA is basically the same type of account as a regular IRA with the exception that the Roth IRA "front-loads," or requires that we pay the taxes immediately for funds put into the retirement account. If we put $4,000 into a Roth IRA in 2015 and were in the 25% federal tax bracket, we would pay $1,000 in tax for 2015, but when we withdrew these funds upon retirement, they would be tax-free.

With the standard IRA, you pay no tax on the funds when you contribute them, but you pay taxes at your current tax rate when those funds are withdrawn.

Other Employee Benefits

Health insurance and retirement accounts are two of the most significant, and most expensive, benefits provided by organizations. But there are many other benefits that can be offered to a company's employees. Let's look at a few of those now.

Employee insurance options. Life Insurance. Many firms will provide group term life (GTL) insurance policies to provide for survivors of an employee who dies while employed by the company. GTL provides for a survivor payment to occur only if the employee dies during the term that is covered by the insurance policy. It is also a valuable benefit to the employer because they receive a tax deduction for up to $50,000 in coverage if it complies with IRS regulations.[36] A fairly standard benefit here would be 1 to 2 times the individual's annual compensation.

Disability Insurance. The other large-scale insurance benefit in many companies is disability insurance. This insurance can be either short- or long-term in nature, and some companies offer both options.

Short-term disability is insurance against being unable to work for up to 6 months due to illness or injury. This is valuable because most *long*-term disability policies do not provide replacement income until the employee completes a 180-day "elimination period" (a period during which they are unable to work). Short-term coverage closes this 6-month gap.

Long-term disability policies cover employees who are unable to work for more than 6 months due to illness or injury. Long-term disability is designed to replace a portion of the disabled employee's income (*typically* 50%–60%) for extended periods of time, or even permanently.[37]

Employee Services. Companies may provide a wide variety of employee services as benefits for their workforce. *Educational (or tuition) assistance* is one common benefit in this group. In 2013, roughly 60% of all companies provided some form of educational assistance to their employees.[38]

Other common employee services include on-site child care or child care vouchers; elder care assistance; company-provided fitness facilities or vouchers for memberships outside the business; organization-sponsored sports teams; services to mitigate commuting costs or public or private transportation vouchers; cafeterias or meal vouchers; plus too many others to name.

Employee services are provided in order to minimize disruptions to the employee's work life. If the employee isn't worried about their children (because the company has a day care facility on site), they can concentrate on work. If they don't have to deal with figuring out where they can park downtown, they are less stressed when they start their day. Companies don't provide these services because they like to give money away. They provide employee services to lower stress and allow employees to concentrate on the job.

Before we go on to discuss how to administer and communicate benefits, let's review the list of benefits discussed so far in Exhibit 11-3. Note that there are an unlimited number of voluntary benefits, but only some major ones are listed here.

FLEXIBLE BENEFIT (CAFETERIA) PLANS

In a survey, 87% of respondents said that flexibility in the offered benefits package would be extremely or very important in deciding whether to take a new job

SHRM
K:B12
Life Insurance

SHRM
K:B7
Disability Insurance

SHRM
K:B8
Educational Benefits

WORK
APPLICATION 11-16

Select a company that offers voluntary benefits. Besides paid time off, retirement, and health and employee insurance, what other benefits does it offer?

LO 11-7

List the organization's options when providing flexible benefit plans to employees.

EXHIBIT 11-3   EMPLOYEE BENEFITS

Statutory Benefits	Voluntary Benefits
Social Security and Medicare	Paid time off
Workers' compensation	Group health insurance
Unemployment Insurance	Retirement benefits
Family and Medical Leave Act (FMLA)	Employee insurance coverage
The Patient Protection and Affordable Care Act (ACA)	Employee services
	Educational (or tuition) assistance
Statutory requirements when providing certain voluntary benefits	On-site child care or child care vouchers
Consolidated Omnibus Budget Reconciliation Act (COBRA)	Elder care assistance
	Company-provided fitness facilities or vouchers for memberships
Health Insurance Portability and Accountability Act (HIPAA)	Organization-sponsored sports teams
Employee Retirement Income Security Act (ERISA)	Services to mitigate commuting costs including work shuttles, company-provided or paid parking, "green" vehicle allowances, public or private transportation vouchers
	Free or low-cost meals

11-2   SELF ASSESSMENT

Selecting Employee Benefits

Assume you are graduating with your college degree and getting your first or a new full-time job. The organization gives you the list below and asks you to rank order the list of employee benefits from 1 (the most important to you) to 11 (the least important to you).

_____   Paid time off (vacations, sick and personal days, holidays)

_____   Health insurance (traditional, HMO, PPO, HSA/MSA)

_____   Retirement benefits (401[k] or 403[b], IRA or Roth IRA, SEP)

_____   Employee insurance coverage (life, disability, others)

_____   Educational (or tuition) assistance (getting your MBA or other degree or some type of certification or license like the PHR and SPHR, CPA, or FICF)

_____   Child care (on-site or vouchers)

_____   Elder care (on-site or vouchers)

_____   Fitness (organization-provided fitness facilities or vouchers for memberships)

_____   Organization-sponsored sports teams (softball, basketball, bowling, golf, etc.)

_____   Commuting (work shuttles, company-provided or paid parking, "green" vehicle allowances, public or private transportation vouchers)

_____   Meals (free or low-cost meals on site or meal vouchers)

There is no scoring as this is a personal choice. Think about your selection today. Will your priority ranking change in 5, 10, 15, or 20 years?

or not.[39] We need to allow at least some flexibility in our benefits system so that it can be partially tailored to the needs of the worker. What is a flexible benefits plan, commonly known as a *cafeteria* plan? Most cafeteria plans fall into one of three categories—each with its own advantages and disadvantages.

Modular Plans. The employee has several basic modules from which they can choose to provide a set of benefits that match their life and family circumstances. Each module has a different mix of insurance, employee services, and retirement options. The employee chooses a module that most closely meets their needs. There may be a module for young single employees that maximizes work flexibility with more time off for personal activities, but has minimal or no benefits in areas such as family health plans, child care, or dental. Another module might be designed for families with young children, while a third might be set up for older workers whose children are grown.

Core-Plus Plans. In a *core-plus plan*, we have a base set of benefits, called the *core*, that are provided to everyone, and then employees are allowed to choose other options to meet personal needs and desires. The core benefits provide basic protection for all of the company's employees in areas such as health and life insurance, and maybe a minimum amount of retirement funding. The remaining benefits are available for the employee to pick and choose other options that match their personal needs.

Full-Choice Plans. The full-choice plans provide complete flexibility to the organizational member. Each employee can choose exactly the set of benefits that they desire, within specified monetary limitations. This is truly a cafeteria plan in that employees can choose any offered benefit they want without a modular or core set of benefits. However, there are some significant problems with full-choice plans for both the individual and the organization. Employees may choose the wrong mix of benefits, or they may try to manipulate the system by only choosing a benefit – such as dental care – in a year when they know they will have a significant expense in that area. Through this manipulation of the benefits system, the overall cost to the organization for providing these benefits can go up significantly.

The bottom line is that flexible plans are really gaining ground because our workforce is much more diverse than it used to be. Benefits need to match the needs of our workers, but we have to remember that the more flexible the plan, the more expensive it is.

WORK
APPLICATION 11-17

Select a company that offers a flexible benefit plan. Identify its type and describe the major benefit options within that category of flexibility.

11-6 APPLYING THE CONCEPT

Flexible Benefit Plans

Place the letter of the type of flexible plan on the line next to statement that describes it.

a. modular

b. core-plus

c. full-choice

____ 26. I don't think our benefit plan is fair because I use my spouse's health insurance plan and I just lose the benefit. To be fair, I should be able to use the money for other benefits I want.

____ 27. I sure wish we got more of our compensation in benefits, but at least with my benefit package, I can choose any benefit I want to every year.

____ 28. My benefit plan has five packages, and I get to pick any one of them that I want every year. But it's difficult to select one.

____ 29. I definitely want to get health care and retirement benefits, and it's nice to have the option of selecting a few other benefits with a set dollar value.

____ 30. The hard part about my benefit plan is that there are oo many options to choose from that I have a hard time selecting the ones I may really need.

TRENDS AND ISSUES IN HRM

Here we explore how incentive pay can cause unethical actions on the part of managers and employees and the trend toward personalization of employee healthcare plans.

Incentives to Act Unethically?

What caused the greatest recession of the last 80 years? That is what a lot of people were asking when the financial crisis hit the United States in 2008–2009. Well, at least part of it was caused by incentive programs. Recall that any incentive program is designed to cause people to be motivated to act a certain way because they want a reward. So how did this contribute to the financial crisis?

Mortgage incentives both to individuals looking to buy homes and to banks and other financial firms created a "housing bubble" around 2005–2006. Mortgage brokers encouraged, and in some cases even coached, individuals to apply for loans that were of greater than normal risk because of historically low interest rates and because the brokers received incentive bonuses for providing the loans.[40]

This was the case in many large banks, and as a result, they made riskier and riskier loans to individual mortgage applicants. This was assisted by relaxation of documentation requirements at the federal level, but it was driven primarily by the bonus payments attached to "writing" the mortgages. Many executives in the large international banks also had their annual incentive bonuses based on assets under their control instead of based on long-term increases in the value of the firm. This put further pressure on employees to write loans that increased the value of the assets under the bank's control.

This was, without a doubt, one of the contributing factors to the meltdown. Bonus payments created a situation where rational individuals acted unethically because of the incentives they received for taking such actions. Incentive payments have the potential to lead to such unethical actions, so we always have to guard against them when we design our incentive programs.

Personalization of Health Care

"The health care system in the United States will change more in the next five to seven years than it has in the last 50," according to Jeff Bauer, a "health futurist."[41] By all available evidence, he is correct. Individuals will continue to gain more control over their own health and their health care planning over the next several years. From apps to health services shopping, and finally to managing ongoing health care costs, the individual will continue to gain power as they become closer to the health care provider by using technology.

Smartphone apps continue to evolve as a mechanism for managing personal health care. We now have apps for checking symptoms; apps for checking and tracking heart rate, blood pressure, and other vital information; apps to interface directly with medical service providers without going into a doctor's office; and many others that help us manage our health—and the number and types of these tools continues to grow at a rapid rate.[42]

Shopping for the best plans for you as an individual will also continue to get easier as information becomes more readily available online. And managing cost will also become easier as more of us move to HSA/MSA and HDHPs, where we directly control medical expenditures.

This trend toward individualization of health care will continue to expand in the future. There doesn't appear to be any evidence that we are going to go back to the days when your health care decisions were made completely by other people. So company employees will need to become more knowledgeable about their health care options, which means HR will have to educate them.

• • • CHAPTER SUMMARY

11-1 **Identify the advantages and disadvantages of individual incentives.**

Individual incentives make it easy to evaluate each individual employee; they provide the ability to choose rewards that match employee desires; they promote a link between performance and results; and they may motivate less productive workers to work harder. Disadvantages include the fact that many jobs have no direct outputs, making it hard to identify individual objectives; we may motivate undesirable behaviors; there is a higher record-keeping burden than in group incentives; and individual rewards may not fit in the organizational culture.

11-2 **Identify the advantages and disadvantages of group incentives.**

Group incentives help foster more teamwork; they broaden the individual's outlook by letting them see how they affect others. They also require less supervision and are easier to develop than individual incentives. Disadvantages include the potential for social loafing; the possibility that we will discount individual efforts and output; the fact that outstanding performers may lessen their efforts; and the potential for group infighting.

11-3 **Discuss the issue of whether or not executive compensation is too high.**

There is no doubt that in some cases, executive compensation has gotten out of control. There is evidence that at the highest levels, it can be more than 200 times the average employee's pay. However, research shows that overall executive pay only runs about 5.4 times the pay of an average employee in most firms, which means that as a general rule, executive pay is probably not out of line, considering the pressure on executives to perform at the highest level all the time.

11-4 **Summarize the major statutory benefits required by federal law.**

Social Security and Medicare—Social Security is composed of Old-Age, Survivors, and Disability Insurance (OASDI) programs, and Medicare is the national health care program for the elderly or disabled.

Workers' compensation is a program to provide medical treatment and temporary payments to employees who are injured on the job or become ill because of their job.

Unemployment Insurance is a federal program managed by each state to provide payments for a fixed period of time to workers who lose their jobs.

FMLA is leave that must be provided by the employer to eligible employees when they or their immediate family members are faced with various medical issues. The leave is unpaid, but the employer must maintain health coverage for the employee while they are on leave.

ACA requires that all employers with more than 50 employees provide health insurance for their full-time employees or face significant penalties levied by the federal government.

11-5 **Name the main statutory requirements that must be followed if organizations choose to provide health care or retirement plans for their employees.**

COBRA is a law that requires employers to offer continuation of health insurance on individuals who leave their employment for up to 18 to 36 months, if the employee is willing to pay the premium cost of the insurance policy.

HIPAA requires that, if the employee had health insurance at their old job and the new company provides health insurance as a benefit, it must be offered to the employee. In other words, the individual's health insurance is "portable." HIPAA also requires that companies take care to protect the health information of employees from unauthorized individuals.

ERISA lays out requirements that must be followed if the employer provides a retirement or health care plan. ERISA determines who is eligible to participate and when they are eligible, provides rules for "vesting" of the employee's retirement funds, requires portability of those funds, and requires that the funds are managed "prudently" by the fiduciary that maintains them.

11-6   **Describe the main categories of voluntary benefits available to organizations.**

Major voluntary benefits include paid time off, group health insurance, retirement plans, other insurance coverage, and employee services. Paid time off comes in various forms, such as sick leave, vacation time, holidays, and personal days. Group health insurance provides employees with health care coverage, and retirement plans allow them to save for their own retirement, sometimes with some help from the organization. Other insurance includes group term life insurance, short- and long-term disability policies, dental and vision insurance,

group automobile and homeowners insurance, and many more. Finally, employee services can include a massive range of options from educational assistance to child or adult day care, gyms, cafeterias, and too many others to list.

11-7   **List the organization's options when providing flexible benefit plans to employees.**

Companies can choose modular plans, core-plus plans, or full-choice plans. Modular plans provide several basic modules from which each employee chooses. There is no other option outside one of the modules. Core-plus plans provide a base set of benefits to all employees (the core) and then other options that the employee can choose from freely to meet their personal desires and needs. Full-choice plans allow the employee complete freedom of choice, but they come with some potential problems such as "moral hazard," "adverse selection," and high management costs.

11-8   **Define the key terms found in the chapter margins and listed following the Chapter Summary.**

Complete the Key Terms Review to test your understanding of this chapter's key terms.

• • • KEY TERMS

COBRA, 285
defined benefit plan, 289
defined contribution plan, 290
experience rating, 284
golden parachutes, 282
high-deductible health plan
 (HDHP), 289

HMO, 288
HSA or MSA, 288
merit pay, 277
PBGC, 286
perquisites, 282
preferred provider organizations
 (PPOs), 288

profit sharing programs, 279
social loafers, 278
traditional health care plans, 288
variable pay, 275
vesting, 286

• • • KEY TERMS REVIEW

Complete each of the following statements using one of this chapter's key terms:

1. _____ is compensation that depends on some measure of individual or group performance or results in order to be awarded.

2. _____ is a program to reward top performers with increases in their annual wage that carry over from year to year.

3. _____ are individuals who avoid providing their maximum effort in group settings because it is difficult to pick out individual performance.

4. _____ provide a portion of company proceeds over a specific period of time (usually either

quarterly or annually) to the employees of the firm through a bonus payment.

5. _____ provide executives who are dismissed from a merged or acquired firm of typically large lump sum payments on dismissal.

6. _____ are extra financial benefits usually provided to top employees in many businesses.

7. _____ is a measure of how often claims are made against an insurance policy.

8. _____ is a law that requires employers to offer to maintain health insurance on individuals who leave their employment (for a period of time).

9. _____ provides for a maximum amount of time beyond which the employee will have unfettered

access to their retirement funds, both employee contributions and employer contributions.

10. _____ is a governmental corporation established within the Department of Labor whose purpose is to insure retirement funds from failure.

11. _____ are plans that cover a set percentage of fees for medical services—for either doctors or in-patient care.

12. _____ is a health care plan that provides both health maintenance services and medical care as part of the plan.

13. _____ are a kind of hybrid between traditional fee-for-service plans and HMOs.

14. _____ allows the employer and employee to fund a medical savings account from which the employee can pay medical expenses each year with pretax dollars.

15. _____ is a "major medical" insurance plan that protects against catastrophic health care costs and in most cases is paid for by the employer.

16. _____ provide the retiree with a specific amount and type of benefits that will be available when the individual retires.

17. _____ identify only the amount of funds that will go into a retirement account, not what the employee will receive upon retirement.

• • • COMMUNICATION SKILLS

The following critical-thinking questions can be used for class discussion and/or for written assignments to develop communication skills. Be sure to give complete explanations for all answers.

1. Would you rather be given the opportunity to receive incentives based on individual performance or group performance? Does it depend on the situation? Why?

2. Would you rather work on a commission basis if you were in sales, or would you rather have a salary—or a combination of both? Why?

3. Would you personally rather participate in a profit sharing plan or a gainsharing plan? Why?

4. Do you think incentive programs in general really work? Why or why not?

5. Would you rather have better benefits and a modest salary or a high salary and lower levels of benefits? Why?

6. Based on what is in the chapter, should the ACA federal health care legislation remain in its current form, or should we rescind the requirement that employers and/or employees have to pay a fine if the employee is not covered by a health care plan? Explain your answer.

7. Is the vesting requirement in ERISA too long, too short, or just about right? Why did you answer the way that you did?

8. Should the United States mandate a certain amount of paid time off per year as many other countries currently do? Why or why not?

9. Do you think that in today's workforce it is becoming necessary to have a "full-choice" flexible benefits plan? Why or why not?

• • • CASE 11–1 GOOGLE SEARCHES SAS FOR THE BUSINESS SOLUTION TO HOW TO CREATE AN AWARD–WINNING CULTURE

Statistical Analysis System Institute Inc. (SAS) is a privately held company that develops software to provide business solutions for their clients. As of 2013, they employed more than 14,000 people and reported revenues of $3 billion. Founded in 1976, they have maintained high profits during the five recessions since then. They have also maintained a growth rate of more than 10% per year from 1980 to 2000.[43] Besides posting impressive growth, SAS has made it onto the Fortune "Best Companies to Work For" list for almost two decades. Google has made it to the top of this list for the past 3 years, but they do not hesitate to confess that they implemented SAS's model in their HR practices. Yet why would Google, a very successful firm in its own right, copy SAS?[44]

Perhaps Google mimics SAS because the company's achievements are built upon a culture that keeps their employees satisfied and motivated. Feeling ecstatic about the company's cultural environment, SAS employees are highly motivated, intensely loyal, and very dedicated to delivering only the highest performance results. Why? According to the CEO/cofounder, James Goodnight, SAS functions like a triangle where happy employees are essential for great customer service and great customer service is the key to a successful business. Employees know that SAS will provide anything that will increase productivity or inspire their imagination. For example, more than 3,000 pieces of art are displayed throughout its premises, and two full-time artists are employed to keep the environment updated.[45] By testing their perks, SAS realized that these types of benefits are key factors to their highly profitable business.

One advantage of running a private business is that CEO James Goodnight does not have the obligation to answer to shareholders, a board of directors, or anyone on Wall Street and therefore can take some calculated risks when it comes to building that cutting-edge culture, a culture that focuses on creating an environment that fosters originality and innovation and keeps employees' minds sharp. Software development is a mentally challenging business, and therefore the proper environment is needed to foster creativity and thinking outside the box. The goal of SAS is to create a stress-free environment for their employees so they enjoy being at work, and SAS does this by providing a work environment with as much comfort and convenience as possible.[46] What are the foundations of a stress-free environment?

SAS provides their employees competitive pay, discretionary bonuses, medical care, retirement plans (401[k]), profit sharing, and disability benefits. SAS also provides a vast amount of what are called "convenience benefits," which are very appealing to job applicants. These new benefits began with free M&Ms every Wednesday and later included a no dress code policy and no specific working hours when employees have to clock in or clock out.[47]

In addition, the main headquarters in North Carolina provides employees with an on-site, state-of-the-art fitness center, a swimming pool, tennis courts, and even a golf course. The following no-cost amenities are also available: dry-cleaning, car detailing, day care programs for employees' children, and a cafeteria that serves 2,500 meals per lunch with no reserved room for executives. In SAS there is a work/life center that provides care for the elderly, helps manage financial debts, and handles personal problems like divorce. SAS provides in-house health benefits and amenities free to all their employees. They only require an employee to pay 20% of the bill when seeing an outside specialist.

SAS's culture and benefits programs have led to a remarkably low employee turnover rate of 3%.[48] But good luck landing a job there: They receive more than 15,000 applications per year![49]

Questions

1. What are the statutory benefits SAS must offer every employee? What defined benefits do they offer beyond those requirements?

2. SAS offers an array of employee benefits, especially at their main headquarters. What might be their rationale for providing such services to their employees?

3. What would you suggest if utilization analysis indicated that only a few employees used those additional benefits, such as the work/life center?

4. What seems to be the weakest part of SAS's benefits package? What would you do instead of offering that particular benefit?

5. What additional amenities might SAS offer their employees? Why?

6. How does their 3% turnover rate impact training and recruiting expenses?

Case created by Herbert Sherman, PhD, and Theodore Vallas, Department of Management Sciences, School of Business Brooklyn Campus, Long Island University

• • • SKILL BUILDER 11–1 DEVELOPING A COMPENSATION WITH INCENTIVE PLAN

Objective

To develop a better understanding of creating motivational incentives.

Skills

The primary skills developed through this exercise are:

1. HR *Management skill*—Technical, conceptual and design, and business skills
2. *SHRM 2013 Curriculum Guidebook*—K: Total rewards

After a few years of selling new cars, you managed to get the funding to start your own small new car dealership as a sole proprietorship. Your starting staffing of 10 employees will be as follows:

- **You** are the **owner manager** and will oversee everything. You will also be the **sales manager** and do some selling.
- **Sales staff**. Three sales people reporting directly to you.
- **Service and Parts Manager**. You will have one person supervise the mechanics and detailer.
- **Mechanics**. Three mechanics to work on the cars.
- **Detailer**. One person to clean the cars, help out the mechanics, and work in parts.
- **Office staff**. Two people to answer phones, greet customers, make up the bills and collect money from sales and service, and do other paperwork including bookkeeping. They will report to you.

Preparing for Exercise 11-1—Develop an incentive system

1. What type of compensation will each classification of employee receive for their work? Will you give them a wage, salary, or incentive pay (commissions, piece-work, or standard hour)?

2. Will you give incentives (recognition and other non-monetary incentives, merit pay, bonuses, profit sharing, gainsharing, ESOPs, stock option and/or stock purchase plans)?

3. As the only executive, what will your compensation package include?

• • • SKILL BUILDER 11–2 DEVELOPING FLEXIBLE EMPLOYEE BENEFIT PLANS

Objective

To develop your skill at designing flexible benefits.

Skills

The primary skills developed through this exercise are:

1. HR *Management skill*—Technical, conceptual and design, and business skills
2. *SHRM 2010 Curriculum Guidebook*—K: Total rewards—Employee Benefits

Assignment

1. Using Exhibit 11-3: Employee Benefits, the "Voluntary Benefits" column, as the HR benefits manager, select the benefits to be offered in three different modular plans. Be sure to identify the target group for each of the three modules.

2. Again using Exhibit 11-3, as the HR benefits manager, develop a core-plus benefits plan.

• • • SKILL BUILDER 11–3 SELECTING FLEXIBLE EMPLOYEE BENEFIT PLANS

Objective

To develop your skill at selecting flexible benefits.

Skills

The primary skills developed through this exercise are:

1. HR *Management skill*—Technical, conceptual and design, and business skills

2. *SHRM 2010 Curriculum Guidebook*—K: Total rewards—Employee Benefits

Assignment

As an employee, rank order the voluntary benefits from 1 being most important to 9 being the least important to you in Self-Assessment Exercise 13-1.

Part V
Protecting and Expanding Organizational Outreach

12 Workplace Safety, Health, and Security

13 Organizational Ethics, Sustainability, and Social Responsibility

14 Global Issues for Human Resource Managers

PRACTITIONER'S MODEL

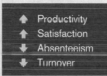

| ↑ Productivity |
| ↑ Satisfaction |
| ↓ Absenteeism |
| ↓ Turnover |

PART V: Protecting and Expanding Organizational Outreach How do you PROTECT and EXPAND your Human Resources?		
Chapter 12 Workplace Safety, Health, and Security	Chapter 13 Organizational Ethics, Sustainability, and Social Responsibility	Chapter 14 Global Issues for Human Resource Managers

PART IV: Compensating How do you REWARD and MAINTAIN your Human Resources?	
Chapter 10 Compensation Management	Chapter 11 Employee Incentives and Benefits

PART III: Developing and Managing How do you MANAGE your Human Resources?		
Chapter 7 Training, Learning, Talent Management & Development	Chapter 8 Performance Management and Appraisal	Chapter 9 Employee Rights and Labor Relations

PART II: Staffing What HRM Functions do you NEED for sustainability?		
Chapter 4 Matching Employees and Jobs	Chapter 5 Recruiting Job Candidates	Chapter 6 Selecting New Employees

PART I: 21st Century Human Resource Management Strategic Planning and Legal Issues What HRM issues are CRITICAL to your organization's long-term sustainability?		
Chapter 1 The New Human Resource Management Process	Chapter 2 Strategy-Driven Human Resource Management	Chapter 3 The Legal Environment and Diversity Management

©iStockphoto.com/mumininan

12 WORKPLACE SAFETY, HEALTH, AND SECURITY

• • • **LEARNING OUTCOMES**

After studying this chapter, you should be able to do the following:

Master the content.

Use the online study tools at
edge.sagepub.com/fundamentalsofhrm
to review, practice, and improve your skills.

Practitioner's Perspective

Describing her workplace, Cindy says: We believe a safe and healthy workplace is a right—whether you work in a factory or an office. Is it also an employer's responsibility to provide for their employees' mental health? Not everyone may see it as an obligation, but there is great benefit in assisting an employee whose personal issues may be impacting their job performance.

"I think I am going to have to take time off," Nancy confessed the other day. "I just can't seem to manage everything going on in my life, and I can't concentrate at work."

"I know things are tough with the divorce—but can you really afford to miss work right now?" her coworker Chloe queried. "Have you seen the information HR posted about the Employee Assistance Program? Let's get the contact information. It's completely confidential and available to you and your family. Perhaps they can help. In the meantime, you can talk to your supervisor about the new flexible work hours until things are better."

Could this level of support "save" a good employee? Learn more about the issues and ethics behind workplace health, safety, and security in Chapter 12.

● ● ●

WORKPLACE SAFETY AND OSHA

We now have a workforce that is fairly compensated, well trained, and productive. The next major management concern is to keep them safe and healthy so that they can continue to perform at high levels. This chapter will first focus on federal workplace safety laws and regulations as well as the governing agencies for industrial safety and health. Later in the chapter, we will cover employee health issues—including employee assistance and employee wellness programs, and stress—and how they affect our employees. Finally, we cover the increasingly important topic of workplace security.

LO 12-1

Identify the responsibilities of both employers and employees under the general duties clause of the OSH Act.

● ● ● **CHAPTER OUTLINE**

Workplace Safety and OSHA
The Occupational Safety and Health Act (OSH Act)

The Occupational Safety and Health Administration (OSHA)
National Institute of Occupational Safety and Health (NIOSH)

Employee Health
Employee Assistance Programs (EAPs) and Employee Wellness Programs (EWPs)
Ergonomics and Musculoskeletal Disorders (MSDs)
Safety and Health Management and Training

Stress
Functional and Dysfunctional Stress

Stress Management
The Stress Tug-of-War

Workplace Security
Cyber Security
General Security Policies, Including Business Continuity and Recovery

Workplace Violence
Social Media for Workplace Safety and Security
Employee Selection and Screening

Trends and Issues in HRM
Employee Wellness
Bullying in the Workplace

B:26

The Occupational Safety and Health Act of 1970 (OSH)

The Occupational Safety and Health Act (OSH Act)

Safety affects recruitment and retention,[1] and it is a major problem globally as hundreds of employees die on the job each year.[2] To help protect employees, the Occupational Safety and Health Act (OSH Act) of 1970 requires employers to pursue workplace safety. Workplace safety *deals with the physical protection of people from injury or illness while on the job*. Employers must meet all Occupational Safety and Health Administration (OSHA) safety standards, maintain records of injuries and deaths due to workplace accidents, and submit to on-site inspections when notified. Those who do not comply are subject to citations and penalties, usually in the form of fines.[3]

Did you know that employers can go to prison for willfully failing to maintain safe work environments? You may have heard that the walls of a building that was being demolished in Philadelphia in 2013 caved in on a Salvation Army store, killing six people. The company in that case, **Campbell Construction**, has been cited for *willful violations* (we will discuss this term shortly) of the OSH Act, and the general contractor, Griffin Campbell, has personally been charged with third-degree murder in that case and could be jailed for failing to follow a series of safety procedures. Willful violations of the OSH Act that cause a death are directly punishable with a fine of up to $500,000 for the organization and $250,000 and up to 6 months in prison for an individual who is found culpable.

Today, the HR department commonly has responsibility for ensuring the health and safety of employees. HRM works closely with other departments and maintains health and safety records along with managing safety training programs. It is critical that you know the safety rules, be sure your employees know them, and enforce them to prevent accidents. In addition to many specific requirements in the act, the *general duties clause* in OSHA that *covers all employers* states that each employer[4]

Workplace safety The physical protection of people from injury or illness while on the job

SHRM HR CONTENT

See Appendix: *SHRM 2013 Curriculum Guidebook* for the complete list

B. Employment Law (required)

    26. The Occupational Safety and Health Act of 1970 (OSHA)

C. Ethics (required)

    6. Behavior within ethical boundaries

    14. Abusive behavior–Workplace bullying

E. Job Analysis/Job Design (required)

    6. Compliance with legal requirements

    Ergonomics and workplace safety (work hazards and mitigation)

K. Total Rewards (required)

    B. Employee Benefits

      9. Employee assistance/wellness programs

      17. Wellness programs

X. Workplace Health, Safety, and Security (secondary)

    1. OSHA citations and penalties (required)

    2. Disaster preparation, continuity, and recovery planning

    3. Employee health

    4. Inspection

    5. Protection from retaliation

    6. Safety management

    7. Security concerns at work

    9. Data security

    11. Ergonomics

1. shall furnish a place of employment that is free from recognized hazards that are causing or are likely to cause death or serious physical harm to employees;

2. shall comply with occupational safety and health standards and all rules, regulations, and orders issued pursuant to this Act which are applicable to his own actions and conduct.

The general duties clause also states that *each employee* has a *duty to comply* with occupational safety standards, rules, and regulations.

In 1970, the year that OSHA was passed, job-related accidents accounted for more than 14,000 worker deaths in the United States.[5] The good news is that the rate of fatal work injuries has fallen, but the bad news is that in 2013, there were still 4,585 fatalities[6] and about 3 million injuries or illnesses, half of which required time away from work.[7] This is a rate of almost 3.4 per 100 equivalent full-time workers. Recall from Chapter 1 that absenteeism is one of the major concerns of all managers, and by allowing injuries and occupational illnesses to occur, we are contributing to that absenteeism. So, losing this many workdays, as well as nearly 4,600 lives, has to be a concern to all of us.

THE OCCUPATIONAL SAFETY AND HEALTH ADMINISTRATION (OSHA)

LO 12-2

Describe the types of violations that OSHA looks for in inspections.

OSHA is the division within the Department of Labor that is charged with overseeing the OSH Act. It was created to "assure safe and healthful working conditions by setting and enforcing standards and by providing training, outreach, education and assistance."[8] OSHA has broad authority to investigate complaints and impose citations and penalties on employers who violate the OSH Act.

What Does OSHA Do?

OSHA is responsible for setting federal safety and health standards and promulgating those standards to employers. OSHA is also responsible for occupational safety and health inspections. Inspections are made *without any advance notice* to the employer and are done based on the following issues (in priority order):[9]

- Imminent danger

- Catastrophes (fatalities or hospitalizations of more than three employees)

- Worker complaints and referrals

- Targeted inspections (such as companies with high injury rates)

- Follow-up inspections

Inspectors must identify themselves and tell the employer the reason for the inspection upon arrival at the worksite. The employer *can* decide not to allow the inspection without an *inspection warrant* (a court order establishing OSHA's probable cause for the inspection).

WORK
APPLICATION 12-1

Identify any unsafe or unhealthy working conditions that you have observed in any organization (business, sports, school, etc.).

Employer and Employee Rights and Responsibilities Under OSHA

General rights of employers and employees are shown in Exhibit 12-1. We want to make sure that company management always stays within their rights in interactions with OSHA.

SHRM

Employer Rights. During an inspection, the employer has a right to get the inspector's credentials, including their name and badge number, and to receive information on the reason for the inspection—either the employee complaint or the program inspection information. The employer also has the right to refuse to allow the inspection without a warrant being provided, but this is generally not a very good idea on a number of levels. Besides making it look like the company might have something to hide, it wastes time, and the inspector will be less likely to assist the employer in immediately correcting discrepancies that might be found during the inspection—*which will ultimately occur anyway* after the warrant is provided. In general, it makes more sense to allow the inspection to go on, in accordance with OSHA rules.[10]

EXHIBIT 12-1   EMPLOYER AND EMPLOYEE RIGHTS AND RESPONSIBILITIES UNDER OSHA

Employer Rights[11]	Employee Rights[12]
OSHA inspections should be conducted "reasonably"	Working conditions free from unnecessary hazards
Have an opening conference/know the reason for inspection visits	Receipt of information and training on workplace hazards
Accompany inspectors when on site	File a complaint about hazardous working conditions and request an inspection
Contest OSHA citations	Maintain anonymity when filing a complaint
Know the names of employees interviewed in an inspection	Use their rights without fear of retaliation or discrimination
Take notes on what is inspected and any discrepancies	Object to the time frame for correction of discrepancies
Employer Responsibilities	**Employee Responsibilities**
General Duty Clause	Follow employer safety and health rules and keep the workplace free from hazards
Find and correct safety/health hazards	Comply with OSHA standards and regulations
Inform and train employees about existing hazards in the workplace	Report hazardous conditions to their supervisor
Notify OSHA within 8 hours if a fatality occurs or if 3 or more workers are hospitalized	Report job-related injuries or illnesses to their supervisor
Provide personal protective equipment necessary to do the job at no cost to workers	Tell the truth if interviewed by an OSHA inspector
Keep accurate records of work-related injuries or illnesses	
Avoid retaliation against workers who exercise their rights under the OSH Act	

Source: OSHA

12-1 APPLYING THE CONCEPT

Employer Rights and Responsibilities Under OSHA

Respond yes or no to each question regarding employer rights and responsibilities.

a. Yes

b. No

_____ 1. Is it permissible to ask the inspector the reason for the inspection?

_____ 2. Henry got us into trouble with OSHA, so is it OK to demote him?

_____ 3. Is it OK to take some notes during the OSHA inspection?

_____ 4. Does OSHA require us to inform and train employees about existing hazards in the workplace?

_____ 5. Does OSHA require us to keep records of work-related injuries or illnesses?

_____ 6. Does a member of the HR staff have to accompany the OSHA inspector during the site visit?

_____ 7. Can we require employees to buy their own safety equipment?

So assuming that the inspection is allowed, we need to be aware of some things that we have a right to and should do during the inspection. If the inspection is being conducted due to a worker complaint, we have the right to get a copy of the complaint (without the employee's name), and we want to do so because we want to know what is being alleged. Secondly, we have a right to have a company representative accompany inspectors as they go through their site visit, and we, as the HR representative, want to accompany them.

There are a few reasons to accompany the inspector. First, we want to understand any violations that the inspector finds and notes because sometimes, no matter how hard a person tries to describe a problem, it will be unclear unless we see it ourselves. Secondly, in many cases we can immediately fix a discrepancy such as loose lines or hoses strung across a workspace. Although the discrepancy will almost surely still be noted, the inspector will see that we are willing to comply with the law and OSHA regulations quickly and to the best of our ability. This willingness can keep minor infractions from becoming major infractions. Third, we want to make sure that the inspection stays within the scope noted in the complaint or the program inspection guidelines. We don't really want the OSHA representative wandering all over the worksite, and we have a right to limit their movements to only cover the inspection scope.

An employer representative also has a right to be present when the inspector is interviewing employees (unless the interview is private by request of the employee being interviewed) and the right to stop interviews that are becoming confrontational or disturbing the work environment.

The employer also has a right to inform the employees of their rights during the inspection. The inspector will provide the employer with a list of discrepancies upon completion of their inspection. After an inspection, employers have a right to contest any citations that they receive through OSHA.

Employee Rights. Employee rights during inspections include the right to refuse to be interviewed, or if an employee agrees to an interview, they can request that an employer representative be present *or* that the interview be held in private. The employee also has the right to legal representation during the interview if they request it, and they can end the interview at any point in time just by requesting that the interview be discontinued. Finally, employees have a right against company retaliation for taking part in an interview with the inspector and telling the truth.

Hazard Communication Standards. OSHA requires that all employers maintain information at each work site that describes any chemical hazards that may be present on-site. A new set of Hazard Communication Standards (HCS) was established in

SHRM

X:5

Protection From Retaliation

APPLYING THE CONCEPT

Employee Rights and Responsibilities Under OSHA

Respond yes or no to each question regarding employee rights and responsibilities.

a. Yes

b. No

____ 8. Is it OK to object to the time frame for correction of discrepancies of OSHA standards?

____ 9. Can OSHA make my employer maintain working conditions free from any hazards?

____ 10. If I see hazardous conditions, does OSHA state that I have to tell my supervisor?

____ 11. Do I have to wear this back brace? It is heavy and uncomfortable, and I can't move as well with it on.

____ 12. If I report hazardous conditions to HR, do I have to tell them who I am?

____ 13. If an OSHA inspector interviews me, can I cover up for the company and say we followed OSHA guidelines so we don't get into trouble?

____ 14. Do I have to tell my supervisor I just got hurt? I don't want him to be mad at me for making him do all the paperwork.

2012 and can be found on the OSHA website (http://www.osha.gov). Under federal law, "All employers with hazardous chemicals in their workplaces are required to have a hazard communication program, including container labels, safety data sheets, and employee training."[13] **Safety Data Sheets (SDS)** *are documents that provide information on a hazardous chemical and its characteristics.* The OSHA-required SDS format is provided in Exhibit 12-2. The SDS provides employees with a quick reference to the hazards of working with a particular chemical compound. Electronic versions of SDS are acceptable, as long as there are no barriers to immediate access at the worksite.

Safety Data Sheets Documents that provide information on a hazardous chemical and its characteristics

EXHIBIT 12-2   SAFETY DATA SHEETS (SDS) FORMAT[14]

OSHA now requires that Hazard Communication SDS follow the following 16-section format.

Section 1, Identification includes product identifier; manufacturer or distributor name, address, phone number; emergency phone number; recommended use; restrictions on use.

Section 2, Hazard(s) identification includes all hazards regarding the chemical.

Section 3, Composition/information on ingredients includes information on chemical ingredients.

Section 4, First-aid measures includes important symptoms/effects (acute, delayed) and required treatment.

Section 5, Fire-fighting measures lists suitable extinguishing techniques, equipment; chemical hazards from fire.

Section 6, Accidental release measures lists emergency procedures; protective equipment; proper methods of containment and cleanup.

Section 7, Handling and storage lists precautions for safe handling and storage.

Section 8, Exposure controls/personal protection lists OSHA's Permissible Exposure Limits (PELs); Threshold Limit Values (TLVs); appropriate engineering controls; personal protective equipment (PPE).

Section 9, Physical and chemical properties lists the chemical's characteristics.

Section 10, Stability and reactivity lists chemical stability and possibility of hazardous reactions.

Section 11, Toxicological information includes routes of exposure; related symptoms, acute and chronic effects.

Section 12, Ecological information includes ecotoxicity (aquatic and terrestrial); persistence and degradability; bioaccumulative potential; mobility in soil.

Section 13, Disposal considerations includes description of waste residues and information on their safe handling and methods of disposal.

Section 14, Transport information includes transport hazard class(es); environmental hazards; special precautions which a user needs to be aware of, or needs to comply with, in connection with transport.

Section 15, Regulatory information includes safety, health, and environmental regulations specific for the product in question.

Section 16, Other information, includes the date of preparation or last revision.

Source: OSHA

Violations, Citations, and Penalties. OSHA violations include the following:[15]

- *Willful*—a violation in which the employer knew that a hazardous condition existed but made no effort to eliminate the hazard

- *Serious*—a violation where the hazard could cause injury or illness that would most likely result in death or significant physical harm

- *Other than serious*—a violation where any illness or injury likely to result from the hazard is unlikely to cause death or serious physical harm, but the violation does have a direct impact on employees' safety and health

- *De minimis*—violations that have no direct or immediate safety or health danger. This does not result in citations or penalties.

- *Failure to abate*—violations where the employer has not corrected a previous violation for which a citation was issued and the settlement date has passed

- *Repeated*—violations where the employer has been previously cited for the same type of violation within the previous 5 years

Willful and repeated violations can bring the employer up to a $70,000 fine for each violation, even without a serious injury occurring because of the violation. *Failure to abate* violations can cost the employer as much as $7,000 per day while the violation continues to exist, and *serious* violations can also cost the employer a $7,000 fine.

National Institute of Occupational Safety and Health (NIOSH)

NIOSH works under the umbrella of the Centers for Disease Control and Prevention (CDC). NIOSH was also created as part of the 1970 OSH Act, and its mission is global in scope. "[NIOSH] is the federal agency that conducts research and makes recommendations to prevent worker injury and illness."[16] NIOSH notes three major goals in its strategic plan:[17]

©NationalInstituteforOccupationalSafetyandHealth(NIOSH)/ CreativeCommons/Wikimedia Commons

The National Institute of Occupational Safety and Health (NIOSH) works on a global scale to understand and preserve workplace safety by conducting research and providing recommendations on workplace safety measures.

- Conduct research to reduce work-related illnesses and injuries.

- Promote safe and healthy workplaces through interventions, recommendations, and capacity building.

- Enhance international workplace safety and health through global collaborations.

NIOSH routinely works with worldwide government health laboratories and other member nations in the World Health Organization (WHO) to identify workplace issues that can cause illness or injury and to create standards for the WHO member countries. NIOSH also works hand in hand with OSHA to identify workplace illnesses and to track diseases that can be passed from one person to another in the work environment. It does research on occupational safety and health topics from ergonomics (we will discuss this shortly) to MRSA (methicillin-resistant *Staphylococcus aureus*) infections and workplace violence. NIOSH research frequently provides the data that OSHA uses to create new workplace standards and regulations.

LO 12-3

Discuss EAPs and EWPs and what their value is to companies and employees.

SHRM

X:3

Employee Health

SHRM

K:B9

Employee Assistance/Wellness Programs

SHRM

K:B17

Wellness Programs

Employee health The state of physical and psychological wellness in the workforce

EAP A set of counseling and other services provided to employees that help them to resolve personal issues that may affect their work

EWP Plans designed to cater to the employee's physical, instead of psychological, welfare through education and training programs

EMPLOYEE HEALTH

Meeting OSHA requirements is necessary, but there are many other aspects to maintaining good employee health. **Employee health** *is the state of physical and psychological wellness in the workforce*. We have to consider both physical *and* psychological health in order to have a strong workforce. We need to provide our employees with the ability to maintain both. In this section, we are going to complete a quick review of some of the other physical and psychological issues in today's workplace.

Employee Assistance Programs (EAP) and Employee Wellness Programs (EWP)

Two significant employee services that can assist with employee mental and physical health are Employee Assistance Programs (EAPs) and Employee Wellness Programs (EWPs), also known as Workplace Wellness Programs (WWPs). EAPs and EWPs continue to grow in popularity in the United States and other countries around the world, most likely because companies are seeing benefits from the use of such programs.[18]

EAPs. An **EAP** is *a set of counseling and other services provided to employees that help them to resolve personal issues that may affect their work*. More than half of private sector workers have access to an employee assistance plan (EAP).[19] An EAP is designed to assist employees in confronting and overcoming problems in their personal life such as marital problems or divorce, financial problems, substance addictions, emotional problems, and many other issues. Employers pay for these services because they help retain valuable employees and, as a result, save the company money.[20,21]

EAPs are confidential services. The employee can contact the EAP and receive counseling and/or treatment. In some cases, EAPs may be regulated by federal laws, including the requirements of ERISA and COBRA, so HR personnel need to be aware of this fact.

EWPs. **EWPs** *are designed to cater to the employee's physical, instead of psychological, welfare through education and training programs*. Wellness programs offer health education, training and fitness, weight and lifestyle management, and health risk assessment services to employees. The obvious goal is improving the health of our workforce, but why? Companies like **Johnson & Johnson** claim EWPs have succeeded in slowing health care cost increases.[22] EWPs can return from $2 to $6 in lower health care and lost productivity costs for every dollar spent.[23] Another interesting effect of EWPs appears to be lower turnover: "Healthy employees stay with your company."[24] So wellness programs provide employers with high return on investment and help with productivity, absenteeism, and turnover. No wonder companies continue to institute these programs.

Ergonomics and Musculoskeletal Disorders (MSDs)

According to OSHA, "**Ergonomics** *is the science of fitting workplace conditions and job demands to the capabilities of the working population.*"[25] The CDC identifies the goal of ergonomics as being to "reduce stress and eliminate injuries and disorders associated with the overuse of muscles, bad posture, and repeated tasks."[26] Workplace ergonomics focuses on design of jobs and workspaces to limit the repetitive stresses that employees face in doing their daily work. OSHA provides employers with a set of voluntary guidelines on ergonomics in the workplace. These voluntary guidelines took the place of an earlier set of more rigid rules from OSHA on ergonomics that were rescinded by Congress in 2001.[27]

Several industries do still have specific sets of guidelines provided by OSHA though. Other industries have the general set of voluntary guidelines published by OSHA.[28] It is wise for the organization to know OSHA's voluntary guidelines for your industry, even though the earlier ergonomics rule was rescinded, because "under the OSH Act's General Duty Clause, employers must keep their workplaces free from recognized serious hazards, including ergonomic hazards. This requirement exists whether or not there are voluntary guidelines."[29]

It just makes sense to pay attention to ergonomics. Musculoskeletal disorders (MSDs) "affect the body's muscles, joints, tendons, ligaments, and nerves"[30] and can occur in many different work environments. They can take a toll on employee productivity when workers suffer from these issues. MSDs include a commonly known *repetitive stress injury (RSI)* called *carpal tunnel syndrome* where the nerves in the wrist become inflamed and painful, making movement difficult.

But a large number of other problems fall under the MSD category, including other RSIs like rotator cuff syndrome, tennis elbow, carpet layer's knee, and many others.[31] All of these problems have the potential to cost the organization money in the form of lost productivity as well as workers' compensation claims. So paying attention to ergonomics at work can both improve productivity and save the company money.

Review the Cornell University ergonomics program called **CUErgo** if you have an interest in ergonomics. The site has a large number of tools to help design jobs that are less stressful on employees; for a listing, go to its website at http://ergo.human.cornell.edu.

Safety and Health Management and Training

HR managers need to understand OSHA rules and standards in order to be able to make the workplace as safe as possible, and offering EAPs and EWPs and stress management training (our next section) is part of safety and health management.

By keeping the number of accidents and incidents low, we lower absenteeism plus increase job satisfaction. By improving two of our four most important variables at work—absenteeism and job satisfaction—we are almost assured of increasing productivity over time. This is yet another way that HRM can assist in reaching organizational goals while using the least amount of organizational resources possible.

WORK
APPLICATION 12-3

Select an organization that offers an Employee Assistance Program (EAP) and Employee Wellness Program (EWP). Describe the program offerings.

E:6
Compliance With Legal Requirements: Ergonomics and Workplace Safety

SHRM

X:11
Ergonomics

WORK
APPLICATION 12-4

Identify potential ergonomics and musculoskeletal disorders (MSDs) in an industry that you work in or want to work in.

X:6
Safety Management

Ergonomics According to OSHA, "the science of fitting workplace conditions and job demands to the capabilities of the working population"

LO 12-4

Compare functional and
dysfunctional stress and how to
manage dysfunctional stress.

WORK
APPLICATION 12-5

*Describe any safety, health, and stress
training offered by an organization,
preferably one you work or have
worked for.*

WORK
APPLICATION 12-6

*Assess your ability to deal with stress.
Identify when you tend to get stressed
and the negative consequences you
experience from dysfunctional stress.*

STRESS

People often have internal reactions to external environmental stimuli. Stress *is
the body's reaction to environmental demands.* This reaction can be emotional
and/or physical. According to *Forbes,* 35% of Americans have thought about
leaving a job because of stress at work, and 42% have *actually done so!*[32] As
stated in Chapter 1, absenteeism is costly, and there is a significant relationship
between absenteeism and workplace stress.[33] In this section, we discuss functional
and dysfunctional stress, how to manage it, and the stress tug-of-war.

Functional and Dysfunctional Stress

What's the difference between functional and dysfunctional stress and the consequences of dysfunctional stress?

Functional Stress. Stress is *functional* (also called acute stress) when it helps improve
performance by challenging and motivating people to meet objectives. People perform best under some pressure. When deadlines are approaching, adrenaline flows
and people rise to the occasion. Stress actually provides greater strength and focus
than we think we are capable of—so long as we are in control of it.[34]

Dysfunctional Stress. On the other hand, too much stress is dysfunctional because it
decreases performance. Stressors *are factors that may, if extreme, cause people to feel
overwhelmed by anxiety, tension, and/or pressure.* Stress that is constant, chronic,
and severe can lead to burnout over a period of time.[35] **Burnout** *is a constant lack of
interest and motivation to perform one's job.* Burnout results from too much stress.
Stress that is severe enough to lead to burnout is dysfunctional stress.[36] But stress is
an individual matter. Some people are better at handling stress than others.[37]

Causes of Stress. Here are six common reasons for workplace stress: Personality
(complete Self-Assessment 12-1 to determine if you are a Type A or Type B),
Organizational Culture and Change (highly competitive cultures and change are
stressful), Management (a bad boss can stress employees), Type of work (some jobs
are more stressful), and Relationships (jerks can cause you stress). The causes of
stress are also listed in Exhibit 12-4, the Stress Tug of War.

Negative Consequences of Dysfunctional Stress. HR managers need to understand and
be able to recognize the symptoms of stress, and especially dysfunctional stress,
because it causes mental and physical health problems.[38] More than 80% of
Americans said they were less productive at work because of stress. Stress costs
an estimated $300 billion a year in absenteeism; decreased productivity; employee
turnover; accidents; and medical, legal, and insurance fees.[39] Stress causes head-
aches, depression, and illness.[40] Here are some other things dysfunctional stress
does to us: It weakens our immune system, it makes us sick more often, it ages us
so we look older, it makes us fatter, it decreases our sex drive, it ruins our sleep,
and it can even kill us.[41] Stress, like perception, is an individual matter. In the same
situation, one person may be very comfortable and stress-free, while another feels
stressed to the point of burnout.

Stress The body's reaction to
environmental demands

Stressors Factors that may,
if extreme, cause people to feel
overwhelmed by anxiety, tension, and/
or pressure

Burnout Constant lack of interest
and motivation to perform one's job

Stress Management

When we continually feel pressured and fear that we will miss deadlines or fail,
we are experiencing stress. We *can* limit job stress,[42] and many firms are making
wellness a top priority through training employees in stress management.[43] EWPs
frequently provide stress management programs for employees. *Stress management* is the process of reducing stress and making it functional. Here are *six stress
management techniques* that have proven valuable in stress reduction.[44]

Personality Type A or B and Stress

Identify how frequently each item applies to you at work or school. Place a number from 1 to 5 on the line before each statement.

5 = usually   4 = often   3 = occasionally   2 = seldom   1 = rarely

_____ 1. I enjoy competition, and I work/play to win.

_____ 2. I skip meals or eat fast when there is a lot of work to do.

_____ 3. I'm in a hurry.

_____ 4. I do more than one thing at a time.

_____ 5. I'm aggravated and upset.

_____ 6. I get irritated or anxious when I have to wait.

_____ 7. I measure progress in terms of time and performance.

_____ 8. I push myself to work to the point of getting tired.

_____ 9. I work on days off.

_____ 10. I set short deadlines for myself.

_____ 11. I'm not satisfied with my accomplishments for very long.

_____ 12. I try to outperform others.

_____ 13. I get upset when my schedule has to be changed.

_____ 14. I consistently try to get more done in less time.

_____ 15. I take on more work when I already have plenty to do.

_____ 16. I enjoy work/school more than other activities.

_____ 17. I talk and walk fast.

_____ 18. I set high standards for myself and work hard to meet them.

_____ 19. I'm considered a hard worker by others.

_____ 20. I work at a fast pace.

_____ Total. Add up the numbers you assigned to all 20 items. Your score will range from 20 to 100. Indicate where your score falls on the continuum below.

Type A   **Type B**

100_____90_____80_____70_____60_____50_____40_____30_____20

The higher your score, the more characteristic you are of the Type A personality. The lower your score, the more characteristic you are of the Type B personality.

The *Type A personality* is characterized as fast-moving, hard-driving, time-conscious, competitive, impatient, and preoccupied with work. The Type B personality is pretty much the opposite of Type A. In general, people with Type A personalities experience more stress than people with Type B personalities. If you have a Type A personality, you could end up with some of the problems associated with dysfunctional stress.

Time Management. Generally, people with good time management skills experience less job stress. Vince Lombardi, the famous football coach, said, "Plan your work and work your plan." Remember that procrastinating gives us more time to think about what we have to do and to get stressed before starting, so starting earlier lowers stress. It's a huge relief when we finish the task.[45] If we are perfectionists, we may do a high-quality job, but perfectionism stresses us as we perform the work, so sometimes it's OK to define what is "good enough" and stop there.

Relaxation. Relaxation is an excellent stress management technique, and we should relax both on and off the job. *Laughter* releases stress-reducing endorphins that

Aerobic exercise is an effective way to mitigate stress and tame anxiety.

WORK
APPLICATION 12-7

Identify your major causes of stress; then select stress management techniques you will use to help overcome the causes of your stress.

lower blood pressure, relax muscles, stimulate our brain, improve our mood, and increase our oxygen intake—so laugh it up.[46] In addition, understand that each of us has our own way of relaxing. It doesn't matter *how* you relax, as long as you relax in a way that is soothing to you. Exhibit 12-3 lists muscle relaxation exercises that we can do almost anywhere.

Nutrition. Good health is essential to everyone's performance, and nutrition is a major factor in health. Underlying stress can lead to overeating and compulsive dieting, and being overweight is stressful on the body. Unfortunately, around 34% of Americans are obese, while another 32% are overweight.[47] Men with a waist over 40 inches, and women over 35 inches, are twice as likely to die a premature death.[48] Obesity costs US businesses about $45 billion a year in medical expenses and lost productivity.[49]

We should watch our intake of junk foods, which contain fat (fried meat and vegetables, including French fries and chips), sugar (pastry, candy, fruit drinks, and soda), caffeine (coffee, tea, soda), and salt. Eat more fruits and vegetables and whole grains, and drink water and pure juices. Realize that poor nutrition; overeating; and the use of tobacco, alcohol, and drugs to reduce stress often create other stressful problems over a period of time.

EXHIBIT 12-3   RELAXATION EXERCISES

Forehead: Wrinkle forehead by trying to make eyebrows touch hairline; hold for 5 seconds.

Eyes, nose: Close eyes tightly for 5 seconds.

Lips, cheeks, jaw: Draw corners of the mouth back tightly in a grimace; hold for 5 seconds.

Neck: Drop chin to chest, slowly rotate head without tilting it back.

Shoulders: Lift shoulders up to the ears and tighten for 5 seconds.

Upper arms: Bend elbows and tighten upper arm muscles for 5 seconds.

Forearms: Extend arms out against an invisible wall and push forward with hands for 5 seconds.

Hands: Extend arms to front; clench fists tightly for 5 seconds.

Stomach: Suck in and tighten stomach muscles for 5 seconds.

Back: Lie on back on the floor or a bed and arch back up off the floor, while keeping shoulders and buttocks on the floor; tighten for 5 seconds.

Hips, buttocks: Tighten buttocks for 5 seconds.

Thighs: Press thighs together and tighten for 5 seconds.

Feet, ankles: Flex feet with toes pointing up as far as possible and hold position for 5 seconds; then point feet down and hold for 5 seconds.

Toes: Curl toes under and tighten for 5 seconds; then wiggle toes to relax them.

12-1 ETHICAL DILEMMA: WHAT WOULD YOU DO?

Obesity and Smoking

Being overweight and smoking places stress on the body, and poor nutrition contributes to obesity. Obesity is on the increase, and it is a major contributor to the rising cost of health care, as is smoking. Health officials are trying to persuade Americans to quit smoking and lose weight. The government has released public service ads to convince people to stop smoking and get in shape and eat right.

1. Is there prejudice and discrimination against obese people and/or smokers at work?
2. Is it ethical and socially responsible for the government to try to get people to stop smoking and lose weight through ads and other methods?
3. Should tax money be spent on ads to promote not smoking, exercise, and healthy eating?
4. What is the reason for the increase in obesity in the United States? Some people blame restaurant owners (like McDonald's and its prior super-size it) and other food marketers (Coke and Pepsi, Frito-Lay) for the obesity problem. Some say consumers love junk food, just want to overeat, they don't care about being obese, and are too lazy to exercise. What do you think?
5. Should the government pass laws to require junk food to be healthier? If so, what should the laws require?
6. Should the government pass laws to restrict where people can smoke and/or prevent people from smoking? If so, what should the laws require?

Exercise. Contrary to the belief of many, proper exercise increases our energy level rather than depleting it. If we are stressed for any reason, the fastest way to tame our anxiety can be physical activity. In fact, exercise is usually more effective than antidepressants in making moderate depression disappear.[50]

Aerobic exercise, in which we increase the heart rate and maintain it for 30 minutes, is generally considered the most beneficial type of exercise for stress reduction. Fast walking or jogging, biking, swimming, and aerobic dance or exercise fall into this category. Playing sports and weight lifting are also beneficial and can be aerobic if we don't take many breaks and we cross-train by mixing weights with other aerobic exercises.

Positive Thinking. People with an optimistic personality and attitude generally have less stress than pessimists because thoughts of gloom and doom (which are often distorted anyway) lead to stress.[51] Once we start having doubts about our ability to do what we have to do, we become stressed. Make statements to yourself in the affirmative, such as "This is easy," and "I will do it." Repeating positive statements while doing deep breathing helps us relax and increase performance.

Support Network. Reaching out to supportive family, friends, and colleagues in our network can help reduce stress.[52] So we can find a confidant at work, or people outside of the workplace, and talk things through.[53] Being out of work-life balance is stressful, so cultivate a supportive network of family, friends, and colleagues to help maintain that critical work-life balance.[54]

The Stress Tug-of-War

Think of stress as a tug-of-war with you in the center, as illustrated in Exhibit 12-4. On the left are causes of stress trying to pull you toward burnout. On the right are stress management techniques you use to keep you in the center. If the stress becomes too powerful, it will pull us off center to the left, and we may suffer burnout and dysfunctional stress with low performance. If there is no stress, we tend to move to the right and just take it easy and perform at low levels. The stress tug of war is an ongoing game. Our main objective is to stay in the center with functional stress, which leads to high levels of performance.[55]

EXHIBIT 12-4   THE STRESS TUG-OF-WAR

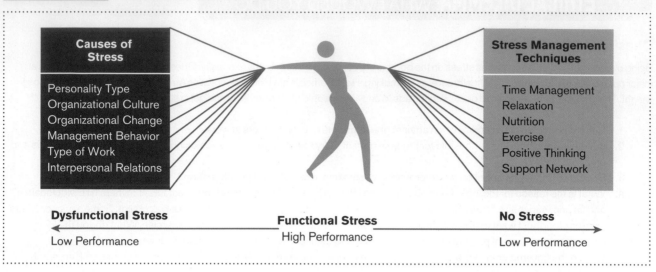

If we try stress management but still experience long-term burnout, we should seriously consider getting out of the situation. Ask yourself two questions: Is my long-term health important? Is this situation worth hurting my health for? If you answer yes and no respectively, a change of situations may be advisable. Career changes are often made for this reason.

LO 12-5

List the top concerns for security in the workplace today.

Workplace security The management of personnel, equipment, and facilities in order to protect them

WORKPLACE SECURITY

Workplace security *is the management of personnel, equipment, and facilities in order to protect them.* While workplace safety deals with the issue of minimizing occupational illness and injury, workplace security covers topics such as violence in the workplace, bomb threats, management of natural and man-made disasters, risk to company computer systems and intranets, and many other issues. Workplace security is concerned with mitigating these risks to the organization and its members. **Securitas Security Services USA**, a large security firm, identified cyber security, workplace violence, business continuity planning, and employee selection and screening as the top security threats to businesses. Prior to 2010,

12-3 APPLYING THE CONCEPT

Stress Management Techniques

Put the letter of the technique being used on the line next to the corresponding statement.

a. time management

b. relaxation

c. nutrition

d. exercise

e. positive thinking

f. support network

____ 15. "I've been stressed out, so I have been praying more lately."

____ 16. "I've been working on positive affirmations, so I have been repeating to myself that 'I can meet the deadline.'"

____ 17. "I'm not too organized, so I've started using a to-do list."

____ 18. "I've been taking a walk at lunchtime with Latoya."

____ 19. "I've been getting up earlier and eating a healthy breakfast."

____ 20. "I have a bad boss, so I've been talking to my colleague Tom about her."

workplace violence had been the number one concern for more than 10 years, but cyber security replaced it as the number one concern in 2010.[56] Let's take a brief look at some of these major workplace security issues in order of concern.

Cyber Security

Let's do a quick review of some of the issues companies face today with cyber security, for non-IS experts. Cyber security *is the use of tools and processes to protect organizational computer systems and networks.* This topic has been in the news constantly for the past several years, with concerns that amateur and professional hackers, hacktivists, terrorist organizations, and even some governments are working to break into company computer systems for a variety of purposes. The US attorney general recently accused hackers working for the Chinese government of hacking US companies, including **Westinghouse, Alcoa,** and the **United Steel Workers Union**.[57] Every company has to be concerned with this issue and do what it can to prevent becoming a victim.

HRM is especially concerned with outsiders penetrating company computer systems that have sensitive employee information on them, such as information on medical records, payroll and banking data, and other personal data. HR managers must work with company security managers to put up strong roadblocks to outsiders who seek to enter systems with this type of data. While there are no foolproof systems, we have to do the best that we can to make it as hard as possible for hackers or other unauthorized users to find and exploit employee data. Obviously, the HR manager won't be the person to research and implement this type of computer security, but we do need to know that it is an issue and work with our company's computer security managers to make it as hard as possible to get access from unauthorized users.

General Security Policies, Including Business Continuity and Recovery

Common disasters and emergencies might include such events as fires, floods, earthquakes, severe weather, tsunamis, terrorist attacks, bomb threats, and many others. Some are dependent on the company's geographic location, while others are universal possibilities. One thing is sure, though—disasters and emergencies happen without warning, creating a situation in which the normal organizational services can become overwhelmed or even disappear. You may remember the nuclear crisis in Fukushima, Japan, when a tsunami wiped out electrical power to a nuclear plant and then, because there was no power to pump water, several of the reactors melted down.

During such a crisis, companies require a set of processes that address the needs of emergency response and recovery operations. The Japanese power company, **TEPCO**, did not have sufficient processes for such a disaster. To address these types of emergencies, the company should establish an emergency response plan, which provides guidelines for immediate actions and operations required to respond to an emergency or disaster, and these guidelines need to take into consideration *everything* that a company can think of in order to provide the appropriate plan.

The overall *priorities* of any plan in any emergency or disaster should be these:

- Protect human life; prevent/minimize personal injury.

- Preserve physical assets.

- Protect the environment.

- Restore programs and return operations to normal.

X:7
Security Concerns at Work

X:9
Data Security

X:2
Disaster Preparation, Continuity, and Recovery Planning

Cyber security The use of tools and processes to protect organizational computer systems and networks

But what part does the HRM professional play in this planning process? HRM should be part of the management team that determines the goals of the plan. Once the goals are determined, HR can again help operational management to staff the various key positions in the disaster recovery teams by understanding the types of people that are necessary to do these jobs under crisis circumstances.

Additionally, HR is typically responsible for the training function in the company, and everyone in the organization needs to be trained on the plan and its processes. The training should also become part of the new employee orientation (Chapter 7) so that all personnel are aware of the correct responses to potential emergencies. There are many examples of good emergency response and business recovery plans out there on the Internet for free. All the company needs to do is find a good sample and modify it for their particular circumstances and the likely disasters that would occur based on their geographic locations.

One final thing that HRM needs to determine is where extra assistance might come from if needed because of a disaster or emergency. For instance, if severe weather were to kill and injure a number of company employees, grief counseling services might become necessary. Most companies don't routinely have grief counselors on hand, but in this type of situation may need access to such counselors very quickly. HRM can think of likely situations and their aftermaths and determine where these types of services might be procured if the need presented itself. One potential provider in at least some cases might be the vendor that services the company EAP. Recall that EAPs are services for the psychological well-being of our employees. Therefore, they may have the needed personnel to handle the psychological aftermath of a disaster.

LO 12-6

Explain ways in which companies can make the workplace safer for employees.

WORKPLACE VIOLENCE

HR managers report increasing violence between employees, stating it can happen anywhere. And don't think that this is just an issue of violent men. Women commit nearly a quarter of all threats or attacks. There has also been an increase in violence between outsiders and employees, such as customers shooting employees and other customers. More than one in 10 workplace fatalities is from homicide, and homicide is the leading cause of death for women in the workplace.[58] The key to preventing workplace violence is to recognize and handle suspicious behavior before it turns violent.[59]

Signs of Potential Violence. Workplace violence is rarely spontaneous; it is more commonly passive-aggressive behavior in rising steps, related to an unresolved conflict. Employees do give warning signs that violence is possible, so it can be prevented if we look for these signs and take action to defuse the anger before it becomes violent.[60]

- Take verbal threats seriously. Most violent people do make a threat of some kind before they act. If we hear a threat, or hear about a threat from someone else, talk to the person who made the threat and try to resolve the issue.

- Watch nonverbal communication. Behavior such as yelling, gestures, or other body language that conveys anger can also indicate a threat of violence. Talk to the person to find out what's going on.

- Watch for stalking and harassment. It usually starts small, but it can lead to violence. Put a stop to it.

- Watch for damage to property. If an employee kicks a desk, punches a wall, and so on, talk to the person to get to the reason for the behavior. People who damage property can become violent to coworkers.

- Watch for indications of alcohol and drug use. People can be violent if under their influence. Get them out of the workplace and get them professional help from the EAP if it's a recurring problem.

- Include the isolated employee. It is common for violent people to be employees who don't fit in, especially if they are picked on or harassed by coworkers. Reach out to this employee and help them fit in or get them to a place where they do.

- Look for the presence of weapons or objects that might be used as weapons. You may try talking to the person if you feel safe, but get security involved if you feel the least bit unsafe.

Security is of concern to organizations today.

Organizational Prevention of Violence. The number one preventive method is to train all employees to deal with anger and prevent violence,[61] which is what you are learning now. However, the starting place is with a written policy addressing workplace violence, and a zero-tolerance policy is the best preventive policy. From the HR manager's perspective, it is very important to take quick disciplinary action against employees who are violent at work. Otherwise, aggression will spread in the organization, and it will be more difficult to stop. Managers especially need to avoid using aggression at work because employees more readily copy managers' behavior than other employees'.

As discussed in Chapter 9, the organization should have a system for dealing with grievances, and it should also track incidents of violence as part of its policy. Organizations can also screen job applicants for past or potential violence so that they are not hired. They should also develop a good work environment addressing the issues listed above as causes of violence. Demotions, firing, and layoffs should be handled in a humane way following the guidelines to deal with anger, and outplacement services to help employees find new jobs can help cut down on violence.

Social Media for Workplace Safety and Security

Organizations around the world are establishing security alert systems to be used in the case of a company emergency of any type, including a violent individual or group on organization property. The systems use existing technology like **Twitter** and text messaging to provide immediate warnings to all persons who are signed up to receive alerts, and they can even give them information on what steps to take to remain safe in such situations. These systems have already undoubtedly saved lives in violent incidents in many companies, and it's not that expensive, so any company without such a system should probably look at installing the capability as soon as feasible.

Employee Selection and Screening

We discussed tools concerning employee selection and screening in Chapter 6, but we need to be reminded of some of them again here because of their importance to company security. The first tool that we want to make sure that we use in employee screening is background checks. Recall that we can be held liable for monetary damages if we are guilty of a "negligent hire." One way to guard against such a hire is through the consistent use of criminal background checks that specifically look for a history of violent actions or threats of violence on the part of an applicant or employee.

Web searches can sometimes turn up negative information on an applicant that may show that they are a potential security risk, even when criminal checks do not. In addition, credit checks might show evidence of a history of unethical behavior that would make it more likely that an applicant might be unscrupulous, and might even intentionally harm other employees if hired. So we do have some tools available, as long as the state in which the company is located allows such checks.

In addition to background checks, substance abuse testing can provide us with a tool to minimize the security dangers in our company. As we noted in Chapter 6, "Most employers have the right to test for a wide variety of substances in the workplace,"[62] and the former head of the White House Office of National Drug Control Policy has said that the "issue of drugs in the workplace is an understated crisis that results in $200 billion in lost productivity annually."[63] According to SHRM, "Substance abuse prevention is an essential element of an effective workplace safety and security program. Properly implemented preventive programs—including drug and alcohol testing—protect the business from liability."[64] The US Department of Justice noted that "the link between drug use and crime has been well-documented in recent years."[65] Screening out substance abusers in the applicant stage can minimize security threats to the organization because there is strong evidence that at least some substance abusers will commit crimes, including violent crimes at work in many cases.

TRENDS AND ISSUES IN HRM

What are some of the significant trends and issues in workplace safety and health? First, we are going to explore employee wellness in a bit more detail. Then we will take a look at one significant problem in modern workplaces—bullying behavior.

Employee Wellness

There is strong evidence that Americans (and people in many other countries) do not exercise enough. More than a third of Americans are obese, with many more overweight.[66] Employee wellness programs (EWPs) work to help our employees become more healthy and fit and to lower the incidence of these types of health problems, so companies are promoting them.

Any exercise is better than none. Getting people up and moving is valuable to organizations because "sitting is the smoking of our generation."[67] A research study by the National Institutes of Health says that "sitting for prolonged periods can compromise metabolic health" and that "too much sitting is distinct from too little exercise."[68]

Although EWPs are beneficial, current research states that at least some of the benefits that have been reported are not valid measures. Still, companies should consider wellness programs for their workforce—even if the cost-benefit relationship is basically 1:1. The peripheral benefits of lower absenteeism and higher productivity and job satisfaction will likely lead to at least an indirect benefit from such programs.

Bullying in the Workplace

SHRM

C:6
Behavior Within Ethical Boundaries

Have you ever been the victim of a bully—on the school playground or at work? The year 2013 was an eye-opening year for both employers and employees who are concerned with, or have been victims of, bullying.

Bullying behaviors have been found to be four times more common than sexual harassment,[69] but there are still no laws at the *national level* in the United States that deal *directly* with bullying as an offense.[70] There are certainly ways in which managers can use existing laws when bullying behaviors are based on protected class characteristics (e.g., race, religion, disability, etc.) or other illegal actions such as assault or sexual harassment, but there is no federal law directly associated with workplace bullying.

HR managers need to know the state and local laws that can be used for bullying behaviors, but they also need to address the issue in company handbooks and provide training on processes that should be used if someone suspects bullying behaviors or are themselves a victim of such behavior. Here is a basic set of steps that we need to put into place in order to stop bullying in our company:

1. Develop a policy on bullying, defining the concept and making it clear that bullying behavior will not be tolerated.

2. Train all employees on the policy on a routine basis—typically at least once per year and upon hiring of new employees.

3. Develop mechanisms for reporting bullying behaviors that are outside the normal chain of command, since bullying frequently occurs with supervisors who have control over other employees.

4. Investigate all reported incidents of bullying using the Just Cause procedures that we discussed in Chapter 9.

5. Take prompt, fair disciplinary action with those individuals who have been found to be guilty of bullying behaviors, whether senior members of the organization or subordinate individuals.

SHRM

C:14

Abusive Behavior—Workplace Bullying

Get the edge on your studies at edge.sagepub.com/fundamentalsofhrm

Read the chapter and then take advantage of the open-access site to

- take a quiz to find out what you've mastered;
- test your knowledge with key term flashcards;
- watch videos to capture key chapter content.

REVIEW, PRACTICE, and **IMPROVE** your critical thinking with the tools and resources at **SAGE edge.**

$SAGE edge™

• • • CHAPTER SUMMARY

12-1 Identify the responsibilities of both employers and employees under the general duties clause of the OSH Act.

Employers have to provide employees with a place of employment free from recognized hazards that are causing or are likely to cause death or serious physical harm and are required to comply with occupational safety and health standards identified in the act.

Employees also have a duty to comply with occupational safety standards, rules, and regulations in all cases while at work.

12-2 Describe the types of violations that OSHA looks for in inspections.

Violations include the following:

Willful—where the employer knew that a hazardous condition existed but made no effort to eliminate the hazard

Serious—where the hazard could cause injury or illness that would most likely result in death or significant physical harm

Other than serious—where any illness or injury incurred is unlikely to cause death or serious physical harm, but the violation does have a direct impact on safety and health

De minimis—violations that have no direct or immediate safety or health danger

Failure to abate—where the employer has not corrected a previous violation for which a citation was issued and the settlement date has passed

Repeated—the employer has been cited for the same type of violation within 5 years

12-3   Discuss EAPs and EWPs and what their value is to companies and employees.

EAPs and EWPs both help employees with their work-life balance. EAPs provide confidential counseling and other personal services to employees to help them cope with stress created by personal issues related to either work or home life. EWPs help employees with their physical wellness. They provide programs to employees such as health education, training and fitness programs, weight management, and health risk assessments.

12-4   Compare functional and dysfunctional stress and how to manage dysfunctional stress.

Functional stress helps to improve performance by challenging and motivating people to meet organizational objectives. People perform better under some pressure. However, too much stress is dysfunctional. Dysfunctional stress may cause people to feel overwhelmed by anxiety, tension, or pressure and can lead to burnout.

Stress management techniques include good time management skills, the ability to relax once in a while (in whatever form you choose), good nutrition,

moderate amounts of exercise, positive thinking skills, and a strong personal support network. All of these tools help us cope with stress successfully.

12-5   List the top concerns for security in the workplace today.

The four biggest concerns of employers today are cyber security, workplace violence, business continuity planning, and employee selection and screening. Cyber security deals with the company's computer and network security. Workplace violence is another major issue because of the continuing rise in incidents of workplace violence. Third, business continuity planning has become a much more significant issue to most employers in the past 10 years, partly because of terrorism threats but also because of a number of large-scale environmental and natural disasters worldwide. Finally, employee selection and screening have become more of an issue because of the problem of negligent hires and the possibility for increased workplace violence if we allow individuals who have a history of violence into our organization.

12-6   Explain ways in which companies can make the workplace safer for employees.

The first thing that needs to happen is we have to train everyone to deal with anger and prevent violence. Next, we need to have, and follow, written policies on workplace violence. A zero-tolerance policy is the best preventive policy. When violence occurs, take swift disciplinary action against violent employees. We also need to have a strong system for dealing with employee grievances that should also allow us to track incidents of violence. Finally, demotions, firing, and layoffs should be handled in a humane way to prevent displaced anger.

12-7   Define the key terms found in the chapter margins and listed following the Chapter Summary.

Complete the Key Terms Review to test your understanding of this chapter's key terms.

• • • KEY TERMS

burnout, 312
cyber security, 317
EAP, 310
employee health, 310

ergonomics, 311
EWP, 310
Safety Data Sheets, 308
stress, 312

stressors, 312
workplace safety, 304
workplace security, 316

• • • KEY TERMS REVIEW

Complete each of the following statements using one of this chapter's key terms.

1. _____ is the physical protection of people from injury or illness while on the job.

2. _____ are documents that provide information on a hazardous chemical and its characteristics.

3. _____ is the state of physical and psychological wellness in the workforce.

4. _____ is a set of counseling and other services provided to employees that help them to resolve personal issues that may affect their work.

5. _____ are designed to cater to the employee's physical, instead of psychological, welfare through education and training programs.

6. _____ is the science of fitting workplace conditions and job demands to the capabilities of the working population.

7. _____ is the body's reaction to environmental demands.

8. _____ are factors that may, if extreme, cause people to feel overwhelmed by anxiety, tension, and/or pressure.

9. _____ is a constant lack of interest and motivation to perform one's job.

10. _____ is the management of personnel, equipment, and facilities in order to protect them.

11. _____ is the use of tools and processes to protect organizational computer systems and networks.

• • • COMMUNICATION SKILLS

The following critical-thinking questions can be used for class discussion and/or for written assignments to develop communication skills. Be sure to give complete explanations for all answers.

1. Are some number of occupational illnesses and injuries an acceptable part of doing business? Why or why not? Explain your answers.

2. Do you foresee a situation in which you would ever refuse to allow an OSHA inspector on your worksite? Why or why not?

3. What actions would you take if you were the company representative accompanying an OSHA inspector who found a serious violation in your company? Explain your answer.

4. Do you think the OSHA and NIOSH occupational safety and health requirements generally make sense? Why or why not?

5. If you were in charge, would you put an EAP into place at your company? How about an EWP? Why or why not?

6. Do you think that you suffer from too much stress? Name a few things that you could do to minimize the dysfunctional stress in your life.

7. Go through the process of how you would train your employees on a new business continuity and disaster recovery plan. What do you think the most important part of the training would be? Why?

8. Should smoking be banned in all buildings where smokers and nonsmokers have to work together? Why or why not?

9. What programs would you put into effect as a leader in order to make your employees understand that occupational safety and health are critical to a modern company?

• • • CASE 12–1 NIKE: TAKING A RUN AT FIXING OUTSOURCED WORKER SAFETY

During the past two decades, manufacturing companies have relied more than ever on low-wage workers in the Far East as an alternative to high labor costs in order to remain competitive in world markets. However, these multinational companies have been criticized for their insensitivity toward their subcontracted employees' working conditions. A Bangladeshi minimum wage of about $38 a month is appealing to major corporations as it helps them expand internationally at low cost; they spent about $1 trillion on outsourcing there in 2014. However, Bangladesh's worker safety record poses a big threat to the reputations of the companies that conduct business in this country. Even the companies that effectively made efforts toward improving safety conditions are now at risk, as the problems in Bangladesh are widespread and rising throughout the garment industry—a case in point being the footwear giant Nike.[71]

In 2014, Nike was worth $66 billion and manufactured goods in more than 740 factories worldwide with sales of $24 billion.[72] Founded in 1971, Nike became the industry leader in designing and manufacturing shoes, apparel, equipment, and accessories because they manufactured high-quality, high-priced goods with low manufacturing costs. These costs were kept low by contracting overseas low-cost labor, an idea that the cofounder and chairman of the company, Phillip H. Knight, came up with when he was pursuing his MBA. Nike set the industry trend for outsourcing manufacturing; back in 1971, 4% of US footwear was made overseas, but as of 2014, that had risen to 98%.[73]

Nike grew rapidly in the 1970s with their strength in high-quality, low-cost products, but soon the company became a target for protestors. In the 1990s, many consumers rallied against Nike's horrendous overseas factory work conditions. As reported by the press, Nike took no responsibility for these factory employees' work surroundings, stating that since their manufacturing was outsourced and they did not own these factories, they therefore could not be held accountable for the safety problems or labor conditions there.[74]

Mere protests that began with Nike's sweatshops in the early 1990s continued up until the two fatal incidents that took place in Bangladesh. In November 2012, 112 workers were killed by a fire in a Nike-contracted factory because they were trapped behind locked doors. Then in April 2013, another 1,129 deaths occurred after an outsourced factory collapsed on top of its workers due to an unstable infrastructure. Companies who outsourced production overseas to these factories did not accept responsibility for their actions (except for **Walt Disney Co.**); these firms claimed that they were in fact surprised to see that their branded apparel was found in the factory rubble. These calamities epitomized the worst characteristics of subcontracting and indicated the need for a thorough overhaul of the entire industry, including factory owners, labor unions, and related government agencies.[75] The Bangladeshi garment association met with the representatives of these firms to discuss a solution strategy; however, only two major brands were willing to sign any agreement. The rest of the companies found it too costly to implement the suggested changes and decided to fix the problems on their own.[76]

Nike fortunately implemented their own work-safety program, Project Rewire, even before the incidents had occurred. This program gave Nike control over their subcontracted employees' work environments. Initially, Nike started by removing hazardous materials, such as toxic solvents and molecular gases, from their products, thereby reducing possible exposure health issues. This also targeted their concern about global warming and the environment. They then examined their supply chain in order to minimize worker safety issues. They eliminated excessive overtime for factory workers, increased the hours of safety training, and reevaluated their contracts with the factories, continuing to do business only with those firms that were committed to worker safety and the environment.[77]

Nike isn't "doing it" just yet. The Worker Rights Consortium, a nonprofit group partially funded by universities that monitor factories producing college athletic gear, has published reports on 16 of Nike's suppliers since 2006 alleging violations of overtime and worker abuse. In August of 2013, the Consortium sent an email to Nike asking why it didn't take action after it was told one of its suppliers in Bangalore, India, hadn't raised wages for its 10,000 workers after a government-mandated increase. A Nike spokesperson confirmed the factory had failed to comply with wage rules and said workers were compensated later.[78]

Questions

1. Nike products are made by over 1,000,000 workers in 744 factories worldwide. How can the company monitor worker safety and health issues at all of these locations?

2. If Nike was manufacturing their products in the United States in the same way they were being made in overseas factories, which OSHA laws would have been violated?

3. In terms of Employee Wellness Programs, how did Nike improve working conditions for overseas employees?

4. What ergonomic principles might be applied to factory working conditions to improve operational settings and reduce employee stress?

5. Project Rewire represents a major commitment by Nike to improve outsourced employee working conditions. What more should the company do, in your opinion, to increase workplace safety for these factory workers?

6. For many firms, "the bottom line" is the driving force behind many strategic decisions. How does being a "differentiator" help Nike determine how much they should spend on overseas worker safety?

Case created by Herbert Sherman, PhD, and Theodore Vallas, Department of Management Sciences, School of Business Brooklyn Campus, Long Island University

• • • SKILL BUILDER 12–1 DEVELOPING A STRESS MANAGEMENT PLAN

Objective

To develop your skill at managing stress

Skills

The primary skills developed through this exercise are as follows:

1. *HR management skills*—Conceptual and design
2. *SHRM 2013 Curriculum Guidebook*—X: Workplace health, safety, and security

Assignment

Write out the answers to these questions:

1. Identify your major causes of stress.
2. How do you currently manage stress?
3. Select stress management techniques you will use to help overcome the causes of your stress.

©iStockphoto.com/stevecoleimages

13 ORGANIZATIONAL ETHICS, SUSTAINABILITY, AND SOCIAL RESPONSIBILITY

● ● ● **LEARNING OUTCOMES**

After studying this chapter, you should be able to do the following:

13-1 Discuss the term *ethics*, including common elements of the definition PAGE 327

13-2 Identify and discuss each factor required in a good code of ethics PAGE 333

13-3 Describe the "business case" for corporate social responsibility (CSR) PAGE 337

13-4 Review the concept of sustainability in a business context PAGE 340

13-5 Define the key terms found in the chapter margins and listed following the Chapter Summary PAGE 346

Practitioner's Perspective

Reflecting on ethics, Cindy says: There are many definitions of *ethics* and many shades of gray in their interpretations. Some decisions may be legal but not "fair," justifiable but not "correct," and sometimes it is hard to determine who should even be setting the standards. I prefer to compare ethical behavior to behaving with integrity. My definition is C. S. Lewis's observation: "Integrity is doing the right thing, even when no one is watching." Business does not always behave with integrity, as we know from scandals since the turn of the century. In 2002, a lack of integrity was exemplified by Enron and its accounting misrepresentations; in 2007, it was the banking industry and the subprime mortgage morass. Each time new rules and regulations are put into place to prevent such ethical abuses from ever happening again. But it takes more than reactive rules and regulations. To really make a difference in business behavior, we need to begin with ourselves—we can chart the course for a better future. Chapter 13 takes an in-depth look at what you need to know about business ethics.

• • •

ETHICAL ORGANIZATIONS

Does it pay to be ethical? The simple answer is yes. Research shows a positive relationship between ethical behavior and leadership effectiveness.[1] Most highly successful people are ethical.[2] Being ethical may be difficult, but it has its rewards.[3] It actually makes you feel better.[4] Honest people have fewer mental health and physical complaints, less anxiety and back pain, and better social interactions.[5] On the reverse side, unethical behavior is costly, as it contributed to the 2007–2008 financial crisis that resulted in the world economies going into recession.[6] It has long-term negative consequences for companies, including loss of reputation, legal fees, and fines.[7] Also, sales declines, increasing cost of capital, market share deterioration, and network partner loss can all be the result of unethical corporate behavior.[8] Some companies have even gone out of business.

Thus, there have been strong and recurring calls for more ethical business practices globally. To improve ethics, business schools have doubled the number of ethics-related courses to help students prepare to face ethical dilemmas during their careers.[9] But what is ethics, and what business practices are, or should be, considered "ethical"?

LO 13-1

Discuss the term *ethics*, including common elements of the definition.

WORK
APPLICATION 13-1

Thinking of business leaders, preferably where you work or have worked, do you trust them to act ethically? Why or why not?

SHRM

R:2
Ethics

Ethics Defined

Before we define ethics, complete Self-Assessment 13-1 to determine how ethical your behavior is.

Ethics has been defined in many books and articles. Let's do a quick review here of some of the common definitions of *ethics* and then see if we can apply those definitions to business ethics.

- "Ethics is a reflection on morality, that is, a reflection on what constitutes right or wrong behavior."[10]

- "[Ethics is] the principles, values and beliefs that define right and wrong decisions and behavior."[11]

- "Ethics is a set of moral principles or values which is concerned with the righteousness or wrongness of human behavior and which guides your conduct in relation to others."[12]

You might notice that these definitions all have some common elements: morals, values, beliefs, principles of conduct. So for our purposes, ethics *is the application of a set of values and principles in order to make the right, or good, choice*. So ethics also must include personal integrity and trust in the character and behavior of others. *Integrity* means being honest. So lying, cheating, and stealing are unethical behaviors. If you are not honest, the truth will eventually catch up with you.[13] And when it does, you will lose the trust of people and hurt your relationships for a very long time before you will be able to earn their trust back—if you ever can.[14] Remember the common elements above as we review some factors contributing to unethical behavior and learn about a few ethical approaches.

Contributing Factors to Unethical Behavior

Let's discuss some of the reasons why unethical behavior occurs—or why do good people do bad things?

Ethics The application of a set of values and principles in order to make the right, or good, choice

Personality Traits and Attitudes. You probably already realize that some people have a higher level of ethics than others, as integrity is considered a personality trait.

SHRM HR CONTENT

See Appendix: *SHRM 2013 Curriculum Guidebook* for the complete list

C. Ethics (required)
1. Rules of conduct
2. Moral principles
4. Organizational values
7. Facing and solving ethical dilemmas
9. Compliance and laws
11. Conflicts of interest
12. Use of company assets
13. Acceptance or providing of gifts, gratuities, and entertainment

F. Managing a Diverse Workforce (required)
3. Aging workforce
10. Gay, lesbian, bisexual, transgender (GLBT)/sexual orientation issues

R. Corporate/Social Responsibility and Sustainability (secondary)
2. Ethics
8. Community/employee engagement
10. The business case for CSR

13-1   SELF ASSESSMENT

How Ethical Is Your Behavior?

For this exercise, you will respond to the same set of statements twice. The first time you read them, focus on your own behavior and the frequency with which you behave in certain ways. On the line before each statement number, place a number from 1 to 4 that represents how often you do that behavior (or how likely you would be to do it) according to the following scale:

Frequently			Never
1	**2**	**3**	**4**

The numbers allow you to determine your level of ethics. You can be honest, as you will not tell others in class your score. *Sharing ethics scores is not part of the exercise.*

Next, go through the list of statements a second time, focusing on other people in an organization that you work for now or one you have worked for. Place an *O* on the line after the number of each statement if you have observed someone doing this behavior; place an *R* on the line if you reported this behavior within the organization or externally: *O* = observed, *R* = reported.

In College

_____ 1. _____ Cheating on homework assignments

_____ 2. _____ Cheating on exams

_____ 3. _____ Submitting as your own work papers that were completed by someone else

On the Job

_____ 4. _____ Lying to others to get what you want or to stay out of trouble

_____ 5. _____ Coming to work late, leaving work early, taking long breaks/lunches and getting paid for them

_____ 6. _____ Socializing, goofing off, or doing personal work rather than doing the work that you are getting paid to do

_____ 7. _____ Calling in sick to get a day off when you are not sick

_____ 8. _____ Using an organization's phone, computer, Internet access, copier, mail, or car for personal use

_____ 9. _____ Taking home company tools or equipment without permission for personal use

_____ 10. _____ Taking home organizational supplies or merchandise

_____ 11. _____ Giving company supplies or merchandise to friends or allowing friends to take them without saying anything

_____ 12. _____ Applying for reimbursement for expenses for meals, travel, or other expenses that weren't actually incurred

_____ 13. _____ Taking a spouse or friends out to eat or on business trips and charging their expenses to the organizational account

_____ 14. _____ Accepting gifts from customers/suppliers in exchange for giving them business

_____ 15. _____ Cheating on your taxes

_____ 16. _____ Misleading a customer to make a sale, such as promising rapid delivery dates

_____ 17. _____ Misleading competitors to get information to use to compete against them, such as pretending to be a customer/supplier

_____ 18. _____ Taking credit for another employee's accomplishments

_____ 19. _____ Selling more of a product than the customer needs in order to get the commission

_____ 20. _____ Spreading rumors about coworkers or competitors to make yourself look better, so as to advance professionally or to make more sales

_____ 21. _____ Lying for your boss when asked or told to do so

_____ 22. _____ Deleting information that makes you look bad or changing information to make yourself look better

_____ 23. _____ Allowing yourself to be pressured, or pressuring others, to sign off on documents that contain false information

_____ 24. _____ Allowing yourself to be pressured, or pressuring others, to sign off on documents you haven't read, knowing they may contain information or describe decisions that might be considered inappropriate

_____ 25. _____ If you were to give this assessment to a coworker with whom you do not get along, would she or he agree with your answers? If your answer is yes, write a 4 on the line before the statement number; if your answer is no, write a 1 on the line.

(Continued)

(Continued)

After completing the second phase of the exercise (indicating whether you have observed or reported any of the behaviors), list any other unethical behaviors you have observed. Indicate if you reported the behavior, using *R*.

26. _____
27. _____
28. _____

Note: This self-assessment is not meant to be a precise measure of your ethical behavior. It is designed to get you thinking about ethics and about your behavior and that of others from an ethical perspective. All of these actions are considered unethical behavior in most organizations.

Another ethical aspect of this exercise is your honesty when rating your behavior. How honest were you?

Scoring: To determine your ethics score, add up the numbers for all 25 statements. Your total will be between 25 and 100. Place the number that represents your score on the continuum below. The higher your score, the more ethical your behavior.

25	30	40	50	60	70	80	90	100
Unethical								**Ethical**

Unfortunately, a culture of lying and dishonesty is infecting American business and society as these behaviors have become more common and accepted.[15] Some people lie deliberately, based on the attitude that lying is no big deal; some people don't even realize that they are liars.[16]

Moral Development. This refers to distinguishing right from wrong and choosing to do the right thing.[17] Our ability to make ethical choices is related to our level of moral development.[18] There are three levels of personal moral development. At the first level, the *preconventional* level, a person chooses right and wrong behavior based on self-interest and the likely consequences of the behavior (reward or punishment). This preconventional level is: It's all about me—I'll take advantage of you to get what I want. Those whose ethical reasoning has advanced to the second, *conventional* level seek to maintain expected standards and live up to the expectations of others. Most people are on this level and do as the others in their group do—they easily give in to peer pressure to act ethically or unethically. Those at the third level,

13-1 APPLYING THE CONCEPT

Level of Moral Development

Place the letter of the level of moral development on the line next to the statement that illustrates it.

a. preconventional level

b. conventional level

c. postconventional level

_____ 1. I lie to customers to sell more products because the others sales reps do it, too.

_____ 2. I lie to customers so that I can sell more products and get larger commission checks.

_____ 3. I don't lie to customers because it is unethical to lie.

_____ 4. Carl says to John, "You're not selling as much as the rest of us. You really should lie to customers like we do. If the boss asks why you aren't selling as much as the rest of us, you'd better not tell him we lie, or you will be sorry."

_____ 5. Karen says to John, "Telling lies to customers is no big deal—we're helping them buy a good product."

the *postconventional* level, make an effort to define moral principles for themselves; regardless of leaders or group ethics, they do the right thing. People can be on different levels for different issues and situations.[19]

The Situation. In certain situations, it can be tempting to be unethical,[20] such as when you are negotiating.[21] Unsupervised people in highly competitive situations are more likely to engage in unethical behavior. Unethical behavior occurs more often when there is no formal ethics policy or code of ethics and when unethical behavior is not punished. In other words, people are more unethical when they believe they will not get caught.[22] Unethical behavior is also more likely when performance falls below aspirational levels. People are also less likely to report unethical behavior (blow the whistle) when they perceive the violation as not being serious or when they are friends of the offender. It takes high moral responsibility to be a *whistle-blower*.

Justification of Unethical Behavior. Most people understand right and wrong behavior and have a conscience. So why do good people do bad things? Most often, when people behave unethically, it is not because they have some type of character flaw or were born bad. Just about everyone has the capacity to be dishonest.[23] We respond to "incentives" and can usually be manipulated to behave ethically or unethically, if you find the right incentives.[24] The incentive can be personal gain or to avoid getting into trouble.[25]

Few people see themselves as unethical. We all want to view ourselves in a positive manner. Therefore, when we do behave unethically, we justify the behavior to protect our *self-concept* so that we don't have to feel bad.[26] If we only cheat a little, we can still feel good about our sense of integrity.[27] Take a look at some common justifications for our unethical behavior:

- Everyone else does it—we all pad the expense account.

- I did it for the good of others or the company—I cooked the books so the company looks good.

- I was only following orders—my boss made me do it.

- I'm not as bad as the others—I only call in sick when I'm not sick once in a while.

- Disregard or distortion of consequences—No one will be hurt if I inflate the figures, and I will not get caught. And if I do, I'll just get a slap on the wrist anyway.

WORK
APPLICATION 13-2

Give an example of unethical business behavior from your personal experience or the news and the reason given to justify it.

13-2 APPLYING THE CONCEPT

Justifying Unethical Behavior

Place the letter of the justification given for engaging in unethical behavior on the line next to the statement exemplifying it.

a. Everyone else does it.

b. I did it for the good of others or the company.

c. I was only following orders.

d. I'm not as bad as the others.

e. Disregard or distortion of consequences.

____ 6. Don't blame me. It was the boss's idea to do it. I just went along with it.

____ 7. It's no big deal that I lie to customers because no one gets hurt. In fact, I'm helping them buy a good product.

____ 8. I changed the numbers so the department will look good on our quarterly report to top management.

____ 9. Yes. I do lie to customers, but it's the way we do business here.

____ 10. I do take some of the company product home, but I take a lot less than the others.

©iStockphoto.com/skynesher

Following guides to ethical behavior will help you address issues in the workplace in the best way possible.

SHRM

C:7

Facing and Solving Ethical Dilemmas

WORK
APPLICATION 13-3

Describe any guidelines you use, or will use in the future, to help you make ethical decisions.

Ethical Approaches

Several common ethical approaches, or guidelines, exist to help you make ethical choices. Understanding some of the common approaches will help you resolve ethical dilemmas that you will certainly face at work. Let's discuss four guides to ethical behavior below.

Golden Rule. "Do unto others as you would have them do unto you." Most successful people live by the Golden Rule.[28] This is a moral principle in virtually every religious text in the world. Following the golden rule will help you to be ethical. The world could literally be changed overnight if people would follow this simple rule.

Four-Way Test. Rotary International uses a four-way test to determine ethical behavior:[29] (1) Is it the truth? (2) Is it fair to all concerned? (3) Will it build goodwill and better friendship? (4) Will it be beneficial to all concerned? If the answers are yes, then the action is probably ethical.

Stakeholders' Approach to Ethics. The stakeholders' approach tries to create win-win results for all stakeholders affected by the decision. This is the approach put forth by Warren Buffett at Berkshire Hathaway, known as one of the most ethical organizations in business today. Exhibit 13-1 gives the statement taken from Berkshire's Code of Business Conduct and Ethics.

So, if you are comfortable telling people who are affected by your decision what you have decided, it is probably ethical. But if you keep rationalizing the decision and try to hide it from others, it is quite likely unethical—at least to some of the affected stakeholders. You can't always create a win for everyone, but you can try.

Discernment and Advice. Research shows that making a decision without using an ethical guide leads to less ethical choices.[31] Using ethical guides at the point of making a decision helps keep you honest.[32] If you are unsure whether a decision is ethical, you can check the company code of ethics/conduct and talk to your boss, higher-level managers, and other people with high ethical standards. If you are reluctant to ask others for advice on an ethical decision because you may not like their answers, the decision may not be ethical.

Each of the above approaches should cue you to think about some concepts that we have previously discussed in this text—trust, integrity, and consistency. If you recall our conversation about trust in Chapter 9, you will remember that trust is "faith in the character and actions of another." Does that sound familiar when you take a look at the definitions of *ethics* above? Without trust, we cannot

EXHIBIT 13-1	BERKSHIRE HATHAWAY CODE OF BUSINESS CONDUCT AND ETHICS[30]

When in doubt, remember Warren Buffett's rule of thumb:

"I want employees to ask themselves whether they are willing to have any contemplated act appear the next day on the front page of their local paper—to be read by their spouses, children and friends—with the reporting done by an informed and critical reporter."

13-3 APPLYING THE CONCEPT

Ethical Approach

Place the letter of the approach to making ethical decisions on the line next to the statement that illustrates it.

a. Golden Rule

b. Four-way test

c. Stakeholders' approach

d. Discernment and advice

e. Code of ethics

____ 11. I'm a member of Rotary International, and I use its approach when I make decisions.

____ 12. When I make decisions, I follow the guidelines the company gave all of us to use to make sure I'm doing the right thing.

____ 13. I try to make sure that everyone affected by my decisions gets a fair deal.

____ 14. I try to treat people the way I want them to treat me.

____ 15. Hi, Latoya. What do you think of my decision about how to handle this customer's complaint?

successfully manage in the organization for very long, so we have to do what we said we would do *consistently* over time in order to get our stakeholders to trust us—the OUCH test helps.

Integrity (honestly doing what you say you will do) and trust (the expectation that you will continue to do so) are important to managers in the firm because research shows that companies who have the trust of employees have lower turnover and higher revenue, profitability, and shareholder returns. Rewarding personal relationships are also based on integrity and trust. But how do we get others to be trustworthy and make decisions based on principles, values, beliefs, and character? Most organizations (like Buffet's **Berkshire Hathaway**) today use a *code of ethics*, sometimes called a code of conduct, to project the values and beliefs of the organization to their employees.

CODES OF ETHICS

Every culture endorses an ethical way to live.[33] Following the code of ethics is actually an ethical approach. The *Houston Chronicle* provides a good template on their http://chron.com website for an organizational code of ethics that includes the following factors listed and quoted:[34]

Values *are our basic concepts of good and bad, or right and wrong.* Values come from our society and culture. Every culture has concepts of right and wrong, although these values do vary some from culture to culture (we will discuss this further in Chapter 14). The *Chronicle* article notes that "a primary objective of the code of ethics is to define what the company is about and make it clear that the company is based on honesty and fairness."

Principles are a *basic application of our values.* We *apply* principles to specific situations in order to come up with a set of actions that we consider to be ethical. An example would be to *maintain personal integrity.* This is obviously based on the application of the values of honesty and integrity. Another example would be the principle to *treat all employees fairly*, which would match up with the value of equality.

Management support, and especially top management support, is absolutely critical to a successful code of ethics. If senior managers pay no attention to the code of ethics, subordinate managers and employees will pay no attention as well. In addition, we need to encourage reporting of unethical behavior to management. The open-door policies and processes that allow

LO 13-2

Identify and discuss each factor required in a good code of ethics.

C:4

Organizational Values

C:2

Moral Principles

Values Our basic concepts of good and bad, or right and wrong

Principles Basic application of our values

the anonymous reporting of ethics issues should be included in the code. These processes help management maintain and uphold the code across the organization.

Personal Responsibility. This is the concept that everyone in the organization is responsible for the ethical conduct of business, not just "the boss." Personal responsibility also refers to accountability for one's own actions, so we need to identify the consequences to an employee if they violate the code of ethics. We have a personal responsibility to report others' violations of the code to the appropriate authority.

Compliance. The compliance factor can identify applicable laws or industry regulations that must be adhered to as part of the code of ethics. Certainly, the OSH Act, the Sarbanes-Oxley Act, and the Dodd-Frank Act would apply to pretty much all public companies, but other laws and regulations apply to certain industries and groups, so we need to note them in the code as well. This is just another reinforcement of the annual training that we have to do regarding each law or regulation that covers our business and industry.

Remember that the code of ethics is important because a culture of misconduct can result in higher turnover and lower productivity and profitability,[35] as well as costly legal problems. Management always has to take the lead in being ethical, or employees will not perform.

Creating and Maintaining Ethical Organizations

The code of ethics is a first strong step in maintaining an ethical organization, but as already noted, managers must lead ethically. However, is the right (ethical) choice always the obvious choice? Unfortunately, it is not that easy. People that we interact with continually give us the opportunity to be unethical by providing us with personal advantages that help us but do not help the organization—for instance, by offering us gifts. In order to understand what managers should do in such situations, we need to look at what they can do, based on authority, responsibility, and accountability. Let's look at these concepts in an organizational setting.

Authority. **Authority** *is the right to give orders, enforce obedience, make decisions, and commit resources toward completing organizational goals.* So authority allows managers to tell people who work for them what to do and to how to use organizational resources.

Responsibility. **Responsibility** *is the obligation to answer for something/someone—the duty to carry out an assignment to a satisfactory conclusion.* So responsibility means that, when we are given authority, we have to accept a position-based obligation to use those resources that we are given to help the organization meet its goals.

Accountability. **Accountability** is *the personal duty to someone else (a higher-level manager or the organization itself) for the effective use of resources to complete an assignment.* In other words, the manager can be held *personally* liable for failing to use resources in the way that they should to help the organization. Unethical behavior often has personal negative consequences,[36] such as getting into trouble at work, being fired, and even going to jail. If you get away with unethical behavior, it can be contagious and lead to more and larger transgressions.[37] On a personal level, this tends to happen with cheating on personal income taxes. People start cheating just a little, and when they don't get caught, they continue to increase the cheating. When they eventually get audited by the IRS, they pay large fines and interest charges, and even criminal charges for fraud.

People who cook the books often start by believing that it is no big deal, they will hit the numbers the next quarter/year and make it up and no one will ever

C:1
Rules of Conduct

C:11
Conflicts of Interest

WORK
APPLICATION 13-4

Describe a code of ethics, preferably where you work or have worked. Provide a copy if possible.

Authority The right to give orders, enforce obedience, make decisions, and commit resources toward completing organizational goals

Responsibility The obligation to answer for something/someone—the duty to carry out an assignment to a satisfactory conclusion

Accountability The personal duty to someone else (a higher-level manager or the organization itself) for the effective use of resources to complete an assignment

know (we will not get caught), and no one will get hurt. But in most cases, as happened at Enron, you never catch up. So be careful not to start down the road using unethical behavior because you may not be able to make a U-turn. You will most likely eventually get caught, and you too can end up fired and even in jail.

Peter Drucker, the noted management author, said, "Whoever claims authority thereby assumes responsibility."[38] In order to be *allowed to use* the authority given, the person must *accept* responsibility. Both of these concepts are tied to the *position* of the manager in the organization. In other words, if you have the position of HR manager, you may be given some types of authority (for instance, authority to require annual EEO and sexual harassment training programs). However, you have to accept the responsibility to carry out these training programs—the buck stops here, with you. If you do not accept the responsibility for doing so, then the authority needs to be rescinded (you need to be taken out of the position of HR manager).

Authority and responsibility always need to be balanced. This is one of the most common failures in organizations. An example would be a CEO who requires subordinate managers to take responsibility for their department's expenditures but doesn't give them authority to veto purchases. This is requiring the subordinate to accept responsibility without commensurate authority. Or consider the sales manager who uses their authority to require subordinates to complete minor tasks that take up large amounts of time and then provides these subordinates with a poor evaluation for failure to sell. This is using positional authority without taking responsibility. So we have to try to make sure that these factors are balanced and that the person accepts their responsibilities.

If you accept responsibility, you become accountable (personally liable) for the effective completion of the action. In the case above of the HR manager and training, you would have *personal accountability* even if someone else who works for you actually does the training. Accountability goes beyond an obligation to do something for the organization. It now requires that the person be held to account for their actions—that they give reasons why they did or did not do a certain thing and justify how their actions helped the organization reach its goals. So authority and responsibility give managers rights and obligations based on their job in the company, but accountability concerns when they can be punished—in some cases even go to prison—if they do not exercise their authority in a responsible manner.

As we noted above, we constantly have the opportunity to make decisions that will benefit us as an individual but do harm to the organization, peers, or our subordinates. If you apply the concept of responsibility to the situation (an obligation to use those resources to benefit the organization), then it is easy to see that you are being unethical. If you then continue anyway, the consequences of your actions might cause you to be held accountable by the organization and potentially disciplined or even fired if you misuse resources to a great extent.

Managers face ethical questions on a daily basis. Should you choose a favorite employee to do overtime work instead of the employee who is best for the job because you know your favorite needs extra money? Should you tell the manager of another department a lie because you haven't completed a project yet? We have to learn to apply the concepts of authority, responsibility, and accountability constantly in order to avoid unethical actions, and in doing so, we will gain the trust of others in the organization. We have to know the appropriate use of company assets and what constitutes misuse of those assets as well. What are some of the most *common ethical issues* that both managers and their companies have to deal with on an ongoing basis?

Bribery. A bribe is a payment meant to cause someone to make decisions that may help a person or an organization but do significant harm to other organizations or other

SHRM
C:13
Acceptance or Providing of Gifts, Gratuities, and Entertainment

SHRM
C:12
Use of Company Assets

13-1 ETHICAL DILEMMA: WHAT WOULD YOU DO?

Bribes

An American businessperson working in a foreign country complained to a local telephone manager that the technician showed up and asked for a bribe before installing the phone. The businessperson refused, so the telephone worker left without installing the phone. The telephone company manager told the businessperson that the matter would be investigated, for a fee (bribe).

1. Is it ethical and socially responsible to pay bribes?
2. Should the businessperson have paid the bribe to get the phone installed?
3. Are you aware of any bribes in the work place? If so, describe the situation without listing the real names of people and companies to protect their identity.

stakeholders in the decision. In a recent case where a US company *was* determined to be acting illegally, clothing company **Ralph Lauren** agreed to pay a $1.6 million fine for bribing Argentinian officials from 2005 to 2009.[39]

Corrupt payments to government officials. This type of payment is designed to allow the company to avoid scrutiny of their actions by government agencies or to facilitate a desired company action, such as building a new factory in an environmentally sensitive area. Corruption at the highest government levels was common for many years under the regime of President Suharto of Indonesia; if you were going to do business in Indonesia, you had to pay bribes to government officials and members of the Suharto family. But it has since been cleaned up to a significant extent by the leaders that have followed him.

Employment and personnel issues. Who to fire or hire, promotions, and changes in compensation and working conditions all can be affected by managerial decisions, which in turn will affect productivity, absenteeism, and turnover in the company. **Walmart** is a good example of a company that has been identified as having managers that use bias in making personnel decisions.[40] In addition, in many countries, practices such as the use of child labor and forced labor by convicts are common, and many other discriminatory labor practices occur, but many of these practices are not only unethical but illegal in other countries.

Marketing practices. Dishonest marketing practices can ruin corporate reputations and even cause them to fail.[41] **Countrywide Financial** is an excellent example of a company that made billions of dollars by unethical marketing of low-documentation and no-documentation loans to individuals during the housing boom of the early 2000s, and it was still in danger of bankruptcy, even after being purchased by **Bank of America,** as late as 2013.[42]

Impact on the economy and environment. Unethical practices on the part of many financial firms (including Countrywide) are thought to be the main cause of the massive recession that started in late 2007. In addition, past practices in many industries have had a long-lasting (if not permanent) effect on the environment around the world. Examples include the use of asbestos long after we knew the health hazards, strip-mining leading to massive flooding in many countries, or recent concerns that some pesticide producers are possibly creating "superbugs" that will be pesticide resistant.[43]

Employee and customer privacy. Due to advancements in technology, the ability to gather and maintain large amounts of personal data has become common in organizations. Use of such data must be for legitimate business purposes only. You may recall that **Facebook** received a huge number of complaints when they decided to experiment on their users by showing them happier or sadder newsfeeds on their personal pages.[44]

Many of these customers felt as though this was not done for a legitimate business purpose. There are also many companies who now monitor all employee communication on company computers and other devices. Is this universal monitoring ethical, or is it an invasion of employee privacy?

Of course, all of the information that we have discussed does no good unless and until the manager makes the choice to do the right thing—makes the ethical decision. And this is not always easy. In many cases, there is no single right or wrong decision— it is *shades of gray*. One decision may be more ethical, but it still harms some stakeholders, while the other decision harms more people and has fewer beneficiaries.

The question to ask yourself isn't whether the ethical guidelines presented help in making ethical choices; rather, will you use the ethical guidelines to make the right decisions? Here is the simplest takeaway that we can provide you: If you don't think about making the ethical decision *before* a situation arises that requires you to have integrity, you will probably make the expedient decision (the decision that gives you the greatest benefit or does you the least personal harm) and not the ethical decision, and you will *know* this because you rationalize the decision and will not be willing to tell others what is going on and what decision you have made. So following the ethical approaches including the code of ethics does help us make ethical decisions.

The founder of athletic apparel company Lululemon blamed their customers for a perceived flaw in their product, bringing the company's corporate social reponsibility into question.

CORPORATE SOCIAL RESPONSIBILITY (CSR)

Ethics and corporate social responsibility (CSR) are closely related, as being socially responsible means going beyond legal and economic obligations to do the right things by acting in ways that benefit society. CSR is an umbrella term for exploring the responsibilities of business and its role in society.[45] CSR has been in the news constantly for the past several years. Many of the business problems that have occurred—from the early-2000s financial crisis to **Walmart**'s recent bribery scandal[46] to the **Lululemon** founder blaming women with big thighs for his too-sheer yoga pants[47]—have been caused at least in part by a lack of corporate social responsibility. Let's review this concept and then take a look at some of the stakeholders that are affected by CSR.

CSR Defined

The concept of corporate social responsibility is based on the belief that "companies have some responsibilities to society beyond that of making profits for the shareholders."[48] So **corporate social responsibility** *is the concept that organizations have a duty to all societal stakeholders to operate in a manner that takes each of their needs into account*. In other words, companies need to look at their effects on society and all corporate stakeholders, not just shareholders. They must provide *employees* with safe working conditions and with adequate pay and benefits. Companies must provide safe products and services to *customers*. For *society*, the company should improve the quality of life, or at least not destroy the *environment*. The company must compete fairly with *competitors* and work with *suppliers* in a cooperative manner. It must abide by the laws and regulations

LO 13-3

Describe the "business case" for corporate social responsibility (CSR).

Corporate social responsibility The concept that organizations have a duty to all societal stakeholders to operate in a manner that takes each of their needs into account

of *government*. At the same time, the company must provide *shareholders* with a reasonable profit. Without profits, it is difficult to be socially responsible.

SHRM

R:10

The Business Case for CSR

The Business Case for CSR. Does it pay to be socially responsible? The answer is yes. If it didn't, would virtually all of the Fortune 500 companies have formal CSR programs?[49] CSR can improve stock returns.[50] With a choice of two products of similar price and quality, 80% of surveyed customers said they are willing to buy the more sustainable option.[51] Being socially irresponsible also has negative consequences, as it gives the company a negative reputation that leads to more difficulty in attracting customers, investors, and employees, and it can lead to costly lawsuits.[52] Money can be made again, but a negative reputation can take years to improve, and a good reputation may be lost forever.[53] Visit your favorite large corporation's website and you will most likely find a link stating how the firm engages in CSR; it is even included in most companies' annual reports, where it is often called a *social audit* because it is a measure of social behavior.

SHRM

R:8

Community/Employee Engagement

So the business case for CSR is based on the ability of the organization to help or harm various stakeholder groups and the ability of all stakeholder groups to help or harm the company. Each stakeholder group has different—and sometimes competing—interests, but the organization must balance these "social responsibilities" among all of the groups. If we help shareholders make more money to the detriment of society, government stakeholders will step in and sanction the company. If we help customers by sourcing items from questionable suppliers, the community may get angry with us and put pressure on customers to stop doing business with us. Every group has to be thought of in a modern company, much more so than ever in history.

Finally, for those of you who are considering "whether or not all of this CSR is really necessary," remember that it is "hard to hide" now with the immediate availability of mountains of information. Even if you try to bury information inside the organization, it is quite likely to get out because of the power of the Web and its ability to connect people who may be interested in what your company is doing. Think about how rapidly **Twitter** forwards information to users and how comprehensive **LinkedIn** is when it covers company issues. So if you think the information won't get out, you may want to think again.

SHRM

C:9

Compliance and Laws

Stakeholders and CSR

In addition to being good public practice, CSR is also being codified more often in law in the United States and in other countries. There are a number of corporate compliance laws written by state and federal government stakeholders, many of which we have already discussed. The Dodd-Frank Wall Street Reform and Consumer Protection Act (Chapter 11), the OSH Act (Chapter 12), the Fair Labor Standards Act (Chapter 10), and many others have already been covered, and we will briefly review another significant compliance law in Chapter 14 called the US Foreign Corrupt Practices Act. You will have to become familiar with each of the major compliance laws as well as those other compliance regulations in your state or country as you begin your career.

Many employee stakeholder subgroups are also beginning to receive much more attention than has historically been the case. Among these groups are older workers, women and minorities in management and the executive suite, lesbian/gay/bi/transgender (LGBT) employees, and a more racially and ethnically diverse employee pool. Public pressure has contributed to the interests of these and other groups in organizations, and therefore companies are having to figure out how to meet the needs of these stakeholders in the organization.

Increasing Diversity. It is now true: The majority group in the United States is a minority in at least one area. The birthrate of Caucasian children is now less than 50% of the total birthrate.[54] In 10 states, white children are a minority, and in 23 states, minorities now make up more than 40% of the child population.[55] One in 12 children (8%) born in America is the offspring of illegal immigrants, and those children are US citizens.[56] The total Caucasian population throughout the world, including America, is decreasing as there are more deaths than births,[57] and the percentage of the population that is Caucasian is decreasing.[58] By around 2040, less than one half of the total US population will be Caucasian.[59] By 2060, it is estimated that Caucasians will be 43% of the US population and 1 in 3 people will be Hispanic.[60] What does this shift mean to the organization? It means that employee diversity will continue to grow and we will have to become better at managing that diversity than we have been in the past.

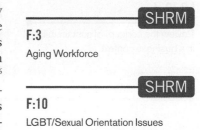

F:3

Aging Workforce

F:10

LGBT/Sexual Orientation Issues

Levels of Corporate Social Responsibility

Clearly, in today's society, the question is not whether business should be socially responsible and take all stakeholder groups into account. Instead, the question is, *at what level of CSR should the business operate?* Businesses do vary greatly in their social responsibility activities based on the overall level of CSR at which they decide to operate.[61] Managers can choose to operate the business at one of three levels of CSR. See Exhibit 13-2 for an illustration of the three levels.

1. *Legal CSR* focuses on maximizing profits while obeying the law; it focuses on increasing sales and cutting costs to maximize returns to stockholders. In dealings with market stakeholders, these firms meet all of their legal responsibilities, such as fulfilling contract obligations and providing legally safe products while honoring guarantees and warranties. They do what it takes to beat the competition legally. In dealing with nonmarket stakeholders (society and government), they obey all the laws and regulations, such as not polluting more than the legal limits and meeting all OSHA standards.

2. *Ethical CSR* focuses on profitability and doing what is right, just, and fair. Providing ethical leadership and avoiding questionable practices mean doing more than is required in dealing with market stakeholders, such as treating employees right and paying them fair wages, providing safer products, not squeezing suppliers, and competing to win business ethically. These companies meet reasonable societal expectations and exceed government laws and regulations to be just and fair to stakeholders.

3. *Benevolent CSR* focuses on profitability and helping society through philanthropy. This highest level of CSR is also called "good corporate citizenship." Benevolent firms are *philanthropic*, giving gifts of money, or other resources, to charitable causes. Employees are expected, encouraged, and rewarded for being active volunteers in the community, often on company time.

WORK

APPLICATION 13-5

Select a business, preferably one you work or have worked for, and identify how it is socially responsible on a specific issue.

WORK

APPLICATION 13-6

Select a business, preferably one you work or have worked for, and identify its level of corporate social responsibility. Be sure to explain your answer with examples of specific things it does.

EXHIBIT 13-2   LEVELS OF CORPORATE SOCIAL RESPONSIBILITY

3. Benevolent CSR. Focus on profitability and helping society through philanthropy.

2. Ethical CSR. Focus on profitability and going beyond the law to do what is right, just, and fair.

1. Legal CSR. Focus on maximizing profits while obeying the law.

LO 13-4

Review the concept of sustainability in a business context.

SUSTAINABILITY

Sustainability practices are part of CSR. **Sustainability** *involves meeting the needs of the current generation without compromising the ability of future generations to meet their needs.*[62] *Sustainability* is now a common business term,[63] and based on the gravity of environmental problems, it is an important topic for all countries.[64] Countries and businesses are realizing that economic growth and environmental sustainability can work together.[65] Some people even refer to the triple bottom line: concern for profit, society, and the environment.

Society expects sustainability and for managers to use resources wisely and responsibly; protect the environment; minimize the amount of air, water, energy, minerals, and other materials found in the final goods we consume; recycle and reuse these goods to the extent possible rather than drawing on nature to replenish them; respect nature's calm, tranquility, and beauty; and eliminate toxins that harm people in the workplace and communities.[66] Thus, including sustainability in managing the business is being socially responsible.

What does business need to do in order to be considered sustainable? Organizations use up resources in the course of their operations. Any resource that is used must be replenished or it disappears forever. In years past, it was thought that resources were so abundant that we could never use them up, but we now know better. There are already shortages of some critical items necessary for the survival of people, and other species, over the long term—shortages of good drinking water in some areas, for instance. As this is written, the state of California is suffering from a severe drought, and it is becoming more difficult to get water resources into the hands of the state's population of more than 39 million people, or about one eighth of the entire US population. So for sustainability, ocean water is being converted to fresh drinking water, but not fast enough yet.

HR and Organizational Sustainability

Organizations have to practice sustainability in today's business environment. We cannot afford to waste resources that are difficult to replace.

Sustainability Practices and Green Companies. Sustainability issues influence activities in the business world.[67] A *green company* acts in a way that minimizes damage to the environment. With the current worldwide environmental problems, many new ventures have been created in green management.[68] Social entrepreneurs are taking advantage of sustainability for new businesses. Large corporations are also engaging in sustainability practices in a big way. A new corporate title has emerged—chief sustainability officer (CSO). CSOs are in charge of the corporation's environmental programs. Nearly all of the 150 world's largest companies have a sustainability officer with the rank of vice president or higher.[69]

Walmart is a leader in sustainability. Back in 2010, it stated that it would cut some 20 million metric tons of greenhouse gas emissions from its supply chain by the end of 2015.[70] Walmart's requirements of reduced waste from packaging have created industry-wide reforms.[71] It essentially pressures all of its thousands of suppliers to meet its sustainability standards. Even the greenest companies tout their close ties to Walmart in their promotional materials.[72] Walmart is also working with truck manufacturers to build energy-efficient trucks. However, many companies are not yet doing what they should in terms of sustainable business practices.[73]

The Need for Management Commitment. Sustainable practices require a strong commitment by companies in order to create the necessary follow-through at all levels of the company. As with any other ethical issue, we have to get the most senior level

WORK

APPLICATION 13-7

Select an organization, preferably one you work or have worked for. Describe its sustainability practice efforts.

Sustainability Meeting the needs of the current generation without compromising the ability of future generations to meet their needs

of management to commit to sustainability and walk the talk. The process of sustainable design requires that everyone think about what resources are being used in every action that the company takes.

Sustainability goals and objectives tied to the company strategy are an essential part of the efforts to "green the company," and HR must play its part in these efforts. *Performance evaluations* of all managers should contain items relating to their sustainability efforts, and in many cases part of their *incentive compensation* may be tied to those efforts. It takes tenacity to make any program take hold in an organization, and the effort to become sustainable is no different than with any other program. HR managers also need to implement *sustainability training* to inform and guide all employees in their sustainability efforts. Let's take a look at sustainability training now.

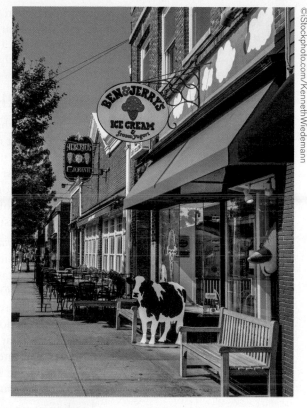

Ben & Jerry's has a long-term reputation for being concerned with sustainability and CSR issues.

Sustainability Training

Look back just a few years and you would probably find that there were very few sustainability training programs in major corporations. Fortunately for all of us, this is no longer the case. While a very small number of organizations have been concerned with CSR and sustainability for many years (for example **Ben and Jerry's Ice Cream**, founded in 1978), most larger businesses didn't become concerned with sustainability programs until about the turn of the 21st century. However, the concept of sustainability is increasingly viewed as providing value to "the so called triple bottom line of economic, social, and environmental performance."[74]

Organizations with sustainability programs tend to gain the trust of their customers and surrounding communities. By doing so, these organizations may gain competitive advantage over their rivals who are less oriented to the sustainability of the community and the environment. Because a sustainable organization embodies the values of its customers and community, those customers and community members become willing to provide reciprocal concern for the organization. This can create significant loyalty to the organization and its brands.

However, it can be extremely difficult for organizations to embed the concept of CSR and sustainability throughout the firm. A sustainability mind-set must be incorporated into the corporate culture, and that can only typically happen from the top of the organization down.[75] So any organizational sustainability training program must begin at the top and change the culture of the executives and managers. Strong organizational cultures that have sustainability as one of their core concepts can begin to create a collective commitment to CSR and sustainability within the entire workforce. But how do corporations disseminate this culture of sustainability down into the employee ranks?

Certainly, training that involves identification of the concept of sustainability and how the organization can affect its environment plays a large part in disseminating this information. In addition, the organization may choose to provide all employees with information in the company code of conduct/ethics that identifies sustainability as one of the core principles of the firm.

In conjunction with the training and code of conduct, the organization must measure the impact of their sustainability programs to allow modifications to those programs if necessary. Changes in company policies and procedures, as well as organizational structure, may also assist in improving sustainability within the

WORK
APPLICATION 13-8

Select an organization, preferably one you work or have worked for. Describe how it is using training and development to meet the challenges of sustainability.

organization. Again though, *training* on the changes in policies, procedures, and structure must occur in order to modify those employees' behaviors. If the organization succeeds in these training efforts, corporate sustainability efforts will be likely to significantly improve over time.

The Sustainable 21st Century Organization

There is evidence that more than 4 out of 5 customers are concerned with sustainability and that more of them today are willing to avoid doing business with companies who do not pay attention to their CSR and sustainability. So what will our sustainable 21st century company look like? What do organizational leaders need to know? Unfortunately, there is no single answer to this question. However, we do know some of the things that companies need to think about in their quest to become more sustainable.

MIT Sloan Management Review and The Boston Consulting Group research business sustainability on an annual basis. According to this research, 86% of companies say that sustainability initiatives are necessary in order to be competitive in today's markets.[76] Other articles note that "the concept of sustainability is moving from 'nice to have' to 'need to have,'"[77] and that "there is an entire ecosystem of stakeholders who care. Governments care. Investors care. Employees care."[78] Evidence shows that companies are going to have to become more transparent in their efforts to create sustainable products, because social media is going to cause those companies to be held more responsible and accountable for their decisions that affect the environment.

Leading companies are already starting to put their sustainability efforts out in full view of their customers as well as their detractors to show what they are doing. In some cases, they are even asking, "What else can we do?" **Patagonia** is doing this through "The Footprint Chronicles," which, according to their website, "examines Patagonia's life and habits as a company. The goal is to use transparency about our supply chain to help us reduce our adverse social and environmental impacts."[79] But what can your company do if it has not yet jumped on the transparency bandwagon?

The World Business Council for Sustainable Development (WBCSD) provides a reasonably compact set of takeaways in its "Action 2020" document:[80]

1. Get business to buy into long-term goals for sustainability.

2. Change the nature of the debate from attacks and counterattacks on company sustainability initiatives to the science behind the need for sustainable business practices.

3. Speak the right language—the language of business. This means putting the information into the business cycle of "plan, do, check, act."

4. Work toward building partnerships and collaboration, because that is the only way to have a large-scale effect on the environment.

5. Make solutions "open source" and allow all entities who can benefit from them to use them.

Where can you go for more information? There are many good sources for data and information on corporate environmental impact and sustainability. Exhibit 13-3 provides you with information on some of the major sites hosting this information.

Now that you have some working knowledge of ethics, CSR, and sustainability and where to find more information, let's move on to this chapter's trends and issues.

EXHIBIT 13-3	INTERNET RESOURCES FOR CORPORATE SUSTAINABILITY

World Business Council for Sustainable Development (WBCSD): http://www.wbcsd.org

Provides a platform for business collaboration around the "Vision to Action" model for sustainable business.

International Organization for Standardization (ISO): http://www.iso.org

The ISO 14000 series of standards address environmental management in organizations, providing "practical tools for companies . . . looking to identify and control their environmental impact."[81]

International Institute for Sustainable Development (IISD): http://www.iisd.org

The IISD champions sustainability development around the world through innovation, partnerships, research, and communications.

United Nations Global Compact: http://www.unglobalcompact.org

Provides "supply chain sustainability" information based on 10 principles that drive the Global Compact efforts.[82]

International Organization for Sustainable Development (IOSD): http://www.iosd.org

A United Nations registered site, IOSD provides a number of white papers on sustainability issues around the world.

World Economic Forum (WEF): http://www.weforum.org

"The World Economic Forum is an international institution committed to improving the state of the world through public-private cooperation."[83] They provide sustainability information on everything from climate to food insecurity at http://www.weforum.org/issues/sustainability/

National Association of Environmental Managers (NAEM): http://www.naem.org

NAEM is a membership organization that focuses on environmental health and safety, including sustainability as part of its environmental health mission.

Corporate Social Responsibility Newswire (CSRwire): http://www.csrwire.com

CSR Wire is a newswire service that provides "the latest news, views and reports in corporate social responsibility (CSR) and sustainability."[84] This is a very good site that gathers news and information on CSR and sustainability issues.

TRENDS AND ISSUES IN HRM

Let's take a look at some sustainability-based benefits available in organizations today, followed by a look at the value of diversity training.

Sustainability-Based Benefits

One area that has seen recent interest is sustainability-based benefit programs. A number of companies are looking at options for providing benefits to their employees that assist with improving environmental stability and sustainability over the long term. These programs can range from providing "credits" to employees for riding bicycles or public transportation to work all the way to sharing the costs of cars or home appliances that lower energy usage.

Benefits that will lower the employee's individual "carbon footprint" help the environment and help the employee because such benefits almost always lower the employee's cost of living. An example is a program called HEAL Arkansas. This program was started by the **Addison Shoe Factory** when they learned that many of their employees spent *up to half of their income* on energy bills.[85] The HEAL program is now offered through the state of Arkansas to selected businesses and provides "facility audits and zero interest retrofit financing of energy efficiency improvements for their facilities."[86] The companies in turn must use part of their energy savings to help employees with home audits and retrofitting of appliances, windows, and other energy-saving items by providing the employees with zero-interest loans for such improvements.

Companies may also provide a variety of other "green" subsidies so that employees can help the environment. These might include assistance to employees with purchasing renewable energy options for their homes such as solar cells or hybrid, electric, or alternative fuel vehicles. Even telecommuting can be a sustainability benefit because it lowers the number of employees commuting to work. So employers just need to use a bit of imagination and a good search engine to find ways in which they can encourage sustainable practices on the part of their employees as well as practices that they can put into effect within the company.

Does Diversity Training Work?

Competitive organizations always need to work to maximize the talent pool from which they can draw recruits. If, in fact, the organization arbitrarily limits the number and types of recruits through artificial limits on organizational diversity, it restricts its ability to draw on the best talent available from the at-large workforce. However, most organizations today accept the fact that *unmanaged* diversity can decrease employee commitment and engagement, lower job satisfaction, increase turnover, and increase conflict. Organizations must create a *cultural change* in order for diversity training to be successful. But since cultural change is very difficult, many organizations try to shortcut the process and as a result end up with failed programs.[87]

How can organizations create and deliver a diversity training process that has a chance of being successful? Common diversity initiatives include such things as diversity recruitment, diversity training, and formal mentoring programs. However, plugging these programs into organizational training without providing a process by which they can be integrated into the daily activities of the members of the organization will likely lead to minimal, if any, success.

Diversity training has been around in some form since the 1960s. In its earlier days, diversity training primarily focused on organizational *compliance* with equal opportunity laws. Later on, diversity training moved through a sequence of options—from attempting to *assimilate* different individuals into an organizational culture; through attempting to make employees sensitive to others and their differences; and more recently to trying to create *inclusion* of all individuals, from all backgrounds, into the organization.[88]

It is important for organizations to manage workplace diversity, but taking shortcuts in diversity training is not the answer.

Throughout each phase of diversity training's existence, its effectiveness has been questioned by many organizations and researchers. Evidence, though, appears to be growing that diversity training does add value to the organization, both sociologically and economically.[89,90] The bottom line is that most major corporations believe that diversity adds significant value to their organizations, both from the perspective of providing different viewpoints and solutions to problems, and from the perspective of providing the organization with a larger talent pool in a period when qualified applicants are becoming less and less available in the at-large workforce.

WORK
APPLICATION 13-10

Select an organization, preferably one you work or have worked for. Describe how it is using training and development to meet the challenges of an increasingly diversified world.

Get the edge on your studies at **edge.sagepub.com/fundamentalsofhrm**

Read the chapter and then take advantage of the open-access site to

- take a quiz to find out what you've mastered;
- test your knowledge with key term flashcards;
- watch videos to capture key chapter content.

REVIEW, PRACTICE, and **IMPROVE** your critical thinking with the tools and resources at **SAGE edge.**

\$SAGE edge™

• • • CHAPTER SUMMARY

13-1 Discuss the term ethics, including common elements of the definition.

There are many definitions of *ethics*, but they all have some common elements. The common elements include the concepts of morals, values, beliefs, and principles. These in turn lead to the need for personal integrity and trust in the character of another, or we won't believe that they will act ethically if they have an opportunity for self-enrichment at the expense of others.

13-2 Identify and discuss each factor required in a good code of ethics.

Values are the first factor. They "define what the company is about and make it clear that the company is based on honesty and fairness." *Principles* apply our values to specific situations to identify actions that we consider ethical. *Management support* is critical because if senior managers do not pay attention to the code, others will not either. *Personal responsibility* identifies the fact that everyone is personally accountable for their own behavior and is expected to act ethically. Finally, *compliance* identifies applicable laws and regulations that guide ethical behavior in specific industries.

13-3 Describe the "business case" for CSR.

CSR says that organizations have a duty to all stakeholders to operate in a manner that takes each of their needs into account. All stakeholders means *all*—not just shareholders or executives. The business case for CSR is based on the ability of the organization to help or harm various stakeholder groups and of those stakeholder groups in turn to help or harm the company. Each stakeholder group has different—and sometimes competing—interests, but the organization must balance these "social responsibilities" among all of the groups in order to succeed.

13-4 Review the concept of sustainability in a business context.

Sustainability means meeting the needs of the current generation without compromising the ability of future generations to meet their own needs. Business must practice sustainability today because so many resources are being overused to the point where they cannot be replenished and will ultimately disappear unless we quickly change our practices. Sustainability goals must be created and managed like any other organizational goal in order to improve business sustainability.

13-5 Define the key terms found in the chapter margins and listed following the Chapter Summary

Complete the Key Terms Review to test your understanding of this chapter's key terms.

••• KEY TERMS

accountability, 334
authority, 334
corporate social responsibility, 337

ethics, 328
principles, 333
responsibility, 334

sustainability, 340
values, 333

••• KEY TERMS REVIEW

Complete each of the following statements using one of this chapter's key terms.

1. _____ is the application of a set of values and principles in order to make the right, or good, choice.

2. _____ are our basic concepts of good and bad, or right and wrong.

3. _____ are a basic application of our values.

4. _____ is the right to give orders, enforce obedience, make decisions, and commit resources toward completing organizational goals.

5. _____ is the obligation to answer for something/someone or the duty to carry out an assignment to a satisfactory conclusion.

6. _____ is the personal duty to someone else for the effective use of resources to complete an assignment.

7. _____ is the concept that organizations have a duty to all societal stakeholders to operate in a manner that takes each of their needs into account.

8. _____ involves meeting the needs of the current generation without compromising the ability of future generations to meet their needs.

••• COMMUNICATION SKILLS

The following critical-thinking questions can be used for class discussion and/or for written assignments to develop communication skills. Be sure to give complete explanations for all answers.

1. Do you think the term *ethics* is overused in today's business environment? Justify your answer.

2. Will applying the Golden Rule always result in a decision that you can defend as "ethical"? Why or why not?

3. Can you think of situations where someone might violate the code of ethics in a company but should not be punished for it? Give examples.

4. Using the concepts of authority, responsibility, and accountability, can you explain what should happen to an individual who misuses company resources for personal gain? Provide an example.

5. Do you agree that companies have a duty to stakeholders other than their shareholders? If so, justify who else they are obligated to and why.

6. Can you identify one case where you think the government (state or federal) is the most important stakeholder of a firm (do not use the government as a customer but as another external stakeholder)? Explain your answer.

7. Is sustainability just a marketing tool to get people to "think green," or is it a necessary business tool? Defend your answer.

8. How would you motivate people in your organization to practice sustainability? Be specific with the managerial tools that you would use.

••• CASE 13-1 MICROSOFT, NOKIA, AND THE FINNISH GOVERNMENT: A PROMISE MADE, A PROMISE BROKEN?

At the turn of the 21st century, Microsoft seemed invincible as both a firm and an operating system, and controlled the tech industry by completely overshadowing its nemesis, Apple. After launching successful operating systems like Windows XP and 2000, the company gained wealth, recognition, and power by creating a near monopoly over personal computing devices.[91] Although they were not the pioneers of user-friendly operating systems (accolades to Apple for developing the first mass merchandised system), they were enjoying a 97% market share. In 2000, personal computers were the only available noncommercial computing devices and Microsoft dominated them all.[92]

As of 2005, the demand for smartphones started to increase and the market increased opportunities for new entrants. Microsoft's decline started in 2007 after Apple introduced the first iPhone. The market was moving away from Microsoft's products; compared to Apple's Mac operating system, Windows Vista was barely holding up and was considered inferior to its predecessor, Windows XP. Apple showed tremendous growth over the next decade and Wall Street announced that Apple was valued higher than Microsoft in 2010. Google then introduced its Android system to compete with Apple's iPhone OS. This new system was adopted by the other half of the smartphone industry. As a late entrant, Microsoft introduced their first Windows Phone in 2010 and the next year, they announced their commitment to Finnish expertise in the telecommunications sector by partnering with Nokia and functioning as one team. This arrangement permitted all Nokia devices to use Microsoft operating systems, which reintroduced Microsoft to the smartphone market.[93]

By 2013, there were approximately 2.5 billion computing devices, including tablets, that were dominated by three companies: Microsoft, Google, and Apple. The total number of personal computer sales had yet to reach 500 million, but smartphones had already sold more than 1.5 billion units over a decade.[94] Smart phones had dominated the tech industry as the major item in the personal computer market. Apple's iPhone was a huge success, which created billions of dollars' worth of supplementary revenue from mobile applications. In this respect, Apple's iTunes and Samsung's alignment with Google enhanced user experiences with smartphones. Microsoft, on the other hand, was not prepared for the sudden shift in the market, and although still a tech giant, they were clearly caught off guard.

With its market cap at 20%, Microsoft desperately wanted to regain market share. They installed a new CEO who was tasked with realigning the company under the "One Microsoft" vision. The company was ready to change its business model, to increase the speed of innovation, increase efficiency, and rebuild the company culture. To that end they announced Office 2013, a new operating system called Windows 8.1, and Xbox One, their new gaming console.[95]

In 2013, the agreement between Microsoft and Nokia became more than a partnership as Microsoft bid to acquire Nokia in a $7.2 billion deal. Founded in 1865, Nokia is a Finnish telecommunications and technology company that engaged more than 90,000 employees and reported around $12 billion in annual revenues. This was a big move for Microsoft since Nokia had experienced its own declines as indicated by its stocks dropping by 80% in the prior few years. Both companies had ignored the winds of change and both paid the price for letting their competitors slide past them.[96]

The acquisition of Nokia, however, was delayed by numerous legal issues with the Finnish government, who approved the deal with the understanding that layoffs would not be forthcoming. The purchase was finally approved by the numerous international governmental regulatory agencies in the first quarter of 2014. With purchase in hand, Microsoft felt they now had good access to the mobile phone industry with $50 billion in annual sales. Three months after the deal was inked, Microsoft's first major action was to lay off 18,000 people in their work force. This was the largest layoff in the tech industry, but it helped Microsoft save about $600 million a year.[97]

Finnish Prime Minister Alexander Stubb received a call in July 2014 from Stephen Elop, the head of Microsoft Corp.'s device business and a former Nokia Corp. chief executive. Elop alerted him that Microsoft would cut 1,100 of the 4,700 jobs in Finland that came with its purchase of Nokia's mobile phone operations. Mr. Stubb called the layoffs "extremely regrettable" and said the government would do all it could to cushion the blow to those affected. Finnish politicians issued statements calling on Microsoft to show social responsibility and offer retraining and generous severance packages to the people it was dismissing, something that Nokia has done in the past in Finland and abroad. Some went further and accused Microsoft of reneging on the promises it supposedly made about job security and Finland's place in its strategy. "You can say we were betrayed," said Finland's newly minted minister of finance, Antti Rinne, a Social Democrat.[98]

Questions

1. Who are Microsoft's key stakeholders in this case? Why?

2. Using the five forces model from Chapter 2, describe how the changes in the computer technology industry impacted Microsoft's ability to compete. Which force most negatively impacted Microsoft? Why?

3. What seems to be Microsoft's ethical approach? How does this approach seem to impact their human resource management decisions?

4. Describe the conflict between stakeholders' interests and the Finnish government's perception of Microsoft's lack of social responsibility to Nokia's employees. Whom do you side with and why?

5. Instead of layoffs, what if Microsoft decided to decrease the total compensation to Nokia employees. What part of that package would you decrease and why?

6. Besides changing the compensation package, what other human resource management options might Microsoft consider rather than layoffs?

Case created by Herbert Sherman, PhD, and Theodore Vallas, Department of Management Sciences, School of Business Brooklyn Campus, Long Island University

••• SKILL BUILDER 13-1 ETHICS AND WHISTLE-BLOWING

Objective

To determine your level of ethics

Skills

The primary skills developed through this exercise are as follows:

1. *HR management skills*—Conceptual and design skills
2. *SHRM 2013 Competencies*—C: Ethics

Assignment

For this exercise, first complete Self-Assessment 13-1 in the chapter (page 329).

Discussion Questions

1. Who is harmed and who benefits from the unethical behaviors in items 1 through 3?

2. For items 4 to 24, select the three (circle their numbers) you consider the most unethical. Who is harmed by and who benefits from these unethical behaviors?

3. If you observed unethical behavior but didn't report it, why didn't you report the behavior? If you did blow the whistle, what motivated you to do so? What was the result?

4. As a manager, it is your responsibility to uphold ethical behavior. If you know employees are doing any of these unethical behaviors, will you take action to enforce compliance with ethical standards?

5. What can you do to prevent unethical behavior?

6. As part of the class discussion, share any of the other unethical behaviors you observed and listed.

You may be asked to present your answers to the class or share them in small groups in class or online.

••• SKILL BUILDER 13-2 CODE OF ETHICS AND CORPORATE SOCIAL RESPONSIBILITY

Objective

To better understand a business's ethics and CSR

Skills

The primary skills developed through this exercise are as follows:

1. *HR management skills*—Conceptual and design skills
2. *SHRM 2013 Competencies*—C: Ethics

Assignment

Select a specific business. It can be one you work for or, better yet, one you would like to work for in the future.

Make sure the company you select meets the following criteria: It must have a written code of ethics and operate at the benevolent level of CSR.

Go online to the company's website and get a copy of its code of ethics and its report on its corporate social responsibility programs. Be sure to identify any of its sustainability practices—this information may be at a separate link.

Be prepared to make a report on your company's code of ethics and CSR to the entire class or in a small group.

©iStockphoto.com/zhudifeng

14 GLOBAL ISSUES FOR HUMAN RESOURCE MANAGERS

••• LEARNING OUTCOMES

After studying this chapter, you should be able to do the following:

14-1 Discuss the reasons for increasing business globalization. PAGE 351

14-2 Describe the five dimensions of Hofstede's Model of Culture. PAGE 357

14-3 Name the advantages and disadvantages of parent-country, host-country, and third-country nationals for international assignments. PAGE 360

14-4 Explain the two major types of training that you should generally provide before expatriate assignments. PAGE 362

14-5 Define the options for compensation of expatriate workers. PAGE 364

14-6 Define the key terms found in the chapter margins and listed following the Chapter Summary. PAGE 369

Master the content.

Use the online study tools at **edge.sagepub.com/fundamentalsofhrm** to review, practice, and improve your skills.

Practitioner's Perspective

Cindy says: One of the biggest changes in business has been the explosion of the global marketplace. Business doesn't compete across the country, but around the world. Americans tend to be Eurocentric (the viewpoint that Western civilization is superior). We must recognize that foreign cultures deserve to be valued in the same manner as a diverse workforce is valued, and that what is acceptable behavior in the United States can be anything but in another country.

Zac is an assistant manager for Kawasaki Heavy Industries, a global company with US manufacturing plants. After escorting US employees to company meetings in Japan, Zac has some amusing stories to tell. His favorite is about the fellow who went around waving and saying "Hi" to everyone. Hi in Japanese means yes, so imagine how strange this literal "yes-man" appeared. Another interesting difference is giving and receiving business cards. In the United States, one would usually put a business card away after receiving it, but in Japan, that would be considered extremely rude. There one must leave the card lying on the table until all business is concluded.

What will you discover about global issues in Chapter 14?

● ● ●

GLOBALIZATION OF BUSINESS AND HRM

We live in a world that is dynamically globally interconnected.[1] The major factor increasing the complexity of the environment is the globalization of markets.[2] Think about the complexity of **FedEx**'s environment, delivering to more than 220 countries and territories.[3] Therefore, it has to follow the rules and regulations of different governments in countries with different economies, labor forces, societies, and so on. There are significant cultural differences between countries and regions. In fact, in many cases, there are multiple cultures in a single country. All of this makes global business more challenging. Clearly, to be successful, companies need global leaders.[4] Today's managers—and students of management—cannot afford to underestimate the importance of the global environment to business.[5] Let's take a look at how HRM has to be managed differently in global firms.

LO 14-1

Discuss the reasons for increasing business globalization.

● ● ● CHAPTER OUTLINE

SHRM

0:1

Global Business Environment

Reasons for Business Globalization

Over the past 40 years, our environment has conspired to make it easier to move both goods and people, along with abstract ideas and concrete knowledge, across borders and around the world. In turn, business must adapt to this new environment. There are many reasons why business is having to adapt to globalization on a scale never seen before. Let's quickly review some of the major reasons for this.

Increase Business. Let's face it: Most large corporations want to continue to grow. If you are a major corporation like Coca-Cola, is there anyplace in America to expand? No, the market is saturated. Also, the US population is only 318.74 million, a small fraction of the world's population of 7.19 billion.[6] So if large corporations want to grow, they have to globalize. However, businesses of all sizes also have growth potential if they go global, so many smaller businesses are conducting international business.

The Global Village. The global village refers to companies conducting business worldwide without boundaries. The word village implies something small and emphasizes that the world, although very large, is becoming smaller through technology. Technology and the Internet have changed the way business is conducted in the global village. In its first 30 days, **Amazon.com** went global, recording sales in all 50 US states and 45 other countries.[7]

Declining Trade Barriers and the WTO. The World Trade Organization's (WTO) "… primary purpose is to open trade for the benefit of all."[8] It is a forum for governments to negotiate trade agreements as the WTO enforces a system of trade rules among its 161 member governments.[9] Visit http://www.wto.org for updated information about the WTO. Because the WTO and its predecessors have been so effective at lowering trade barriers, international trade has opened up to businesses that would not have been able to compete internationally before these organizations and agreements existed.

Declining Barriers of Distance and Culture. In the 1950s, it was difficult to transport goods across country borders and over oceans. It was also difficult to communicate between one location and another. But—things have changed! Communication to most parts of the world is nearly instantaneous. You can dial up your friend in China, or get on the Internet and use a webcam to see exactly what is wrong with your production equipment in Shanghai, China, and provide instructions on how to

SHRM HR CONTENT

See Appendix: *SHRM 2013 Curriculum Guidebook* for the complete list

fix it in a few minutes. If you need to send experts to the plant, they can be anywhere in the world in about a day.

The Rise of Trade Blocs. **Trade blocs** *are groups of countries who form an association for the purpose of facilitating movement of goods across national borders.* These trade blocs allow free, or low-cost, passage of goods among member nations to encourage companies to specialize in certain types of goods to become more efficient and therefore lower the cost of those goods to all member countries. See Exhibit 14-1 for a list of major trade agreements.

If you are not part of the bloc, trade barriers tend to be significant, and they will raise your cost of doing business with the countries in the bloc. One method of getting around the barriers is to become part of the bloc. This is usually accomplished by having business operations in at least one country within the bloc, which will make your company a de facto member of the bloc and reduce or eliminate this barrier. So companies will now frequently build factories, assembly facilities, component plants, or other facilities within the bloc in order to overcome the trade barrier associated with that trade bloc.

To Remain Competitive! The last reason for business globalization is simple:

Global corporations vs. Domestic organizations = One-sided competition

In many cases, if a domestic firm is competing head-to-head with a global firm, the competition is seriously one-sided. The global firm will source all of its resources from wherever they are the most efficient. If the global company sources raw materials from one country for half the cost, component production in another country for 75% of the cost, and labor from a third country for 25% of the cost of the domestic competitor, who is going to win the battle for the customers? The domestic firm is at an absolute cost disadvantage versus the global firm. The customer *will not* pay double the price for the same good of the same quality, no matter where it is made! Buy American products is a good slogan, but most people don't even know the country of ownership of most products. Complete Self-Assessment 14-1 to find out how knowledgeable you are.

WORK
APPLICATION 14-1

Identify a global business, one you have worked for if possible. Discuss the reasons it went global.

WORK
APPLICATION 14-2

Select a business, preferably one you work(ed) for or want to work for, and identify reasons why it is a global business.

Trade blocs Groups of countries who form an association for the purpose of facilitating movement of goods across national borders

EXHIBIT 14-1   MAJOR TRADE AGREEMENTS

Agreement	Members	Website
North American Free Trade Agreement (NAFTA)	3 North American countries (Canada, USA, Mexico)	http://www.naftanow.org/
Dominican Republic-Central American Free Trade Agreement (CAFTA-DR)	6 Beneficiary countries	http://www.caftadr.net
Union of South American Nations (UNASUR)	12 South American countries	http://www.unasursg.org/
European Union (EU)– Maastricht Treaty of Europe	28 European member states	http://europa.eu
Association of Southeast Asian Nations (ASEAN)	10 Asian and Pacific Rim countries	http://www.asean.org
Asia-Pacific Economic Cooperation (APEC)	21 Pacific Rim countries	http://www.apec.org

| 14-1 | **SELF** ASSESSMENT |

Products by Country of Origin

For each item, determine the country of origin. If your answer is the United States, place a check in the left-hand column. If it's another country, write the name of the country in the right-hand column.

Product	United States	Other (list country)
1. Shell gasoline	_____	_____
2. Nestlé hot cocoa	_____	_____
3. Unilever Dove soap	_____	_____
4. Nokia cell phones	_____	_____
5. L'Oreal cosmetics	_____	_____
6. Johnson & Johnson baby powder	_____	_____
7. Burger King fast food	_____	_____
8. Samsung televisions	_____	_____
9. Bayer aspirin	_____	_____
10. Anheuser-Busch beer	_____	_____
11. Volvo cars	_____	_____
12. AMC theaters	_____	_____

1. Shell is owned by Royal Dutch Shell of the Netherlands. 2. Nestlé is headquartered in Switzerland. 3. Unilever is British. 4. Nokia was a Finnish company but was acquired by US Microsoft in September 2013. 5. L'Oreal is French. 6. Johnson & Johnson is a US company. 7. Burger King is Brazilian owned. 8. Samsung is South Korean. 9. Bayer is German. 10. Anheuser-Busch InBev is Belgian owned. 11. Volvo and 12. AMC are both Chinese owned.

How many did you get correct?

Is HRM Different in Global Firms?

"To function effectively in a multicultural global business environment, individuals and organizations must be capable of adapting smoothly and successfully across cultural boundaries."[10] This means that as the organization expands beyond its original borders, employees need to learn to change their personal perceptions from a local focus toward a broader concept of society. They need to become capable cultural chameleons—able to change on the fly as necessary in order to interact with other employees, customers, vendors, and any other stakeholders—to manage the business. Yet, the evidence shows that this is one of the most significant weaknesses of individuals who have a business degree but have little work experience.[11]

Companies nearly always start out small and local—they have one shop or store in one town in a single country. When managing this "simple" organization structure, the complexity is minimal. Generally, all decisions are made by the boss. As we get larger and more complex, management in the organization has to change and adapt to that complexity by loosening up on centralized authority so that things can get done in a reasonable time frame.

Ultimately, in many industries at least, the company will consider international operations of some type to gain an advantage over its competitors. And along with the creation of an international presence, the complexity of the firm goes up even more. This is the point at which HR must become a different and more complex department. International operations require us to rethink every major function in HRM. For example:

- *Staffing.* Home-country, host-country, and third-party employees all require different sourcing, training, disciplinary actions, and compensation and may require many other differences in management.

- *Training.* From orientation to culture and religion, to language problems and managing infrastructure, training will need to be modified. For instance, safety training will need to be provided in multiple languages in many cases, and it will have to be accomplished so as to comply with multiple country laws and regulations.

- *Employee and labor relations.* Different countries' laws concerning employee relations require HR to become competent in legal issues where the company operates. Many countries' labor laws are strongly oriented toward protection of the individual employee—much more so than in the United States—and the HR manager must become competent in all of these legal differences. In addition, cultural attitudes and national laws also affect when and how employees are disciplined.

- *Compensation.* Should the company pay local average wages, home-country average wages, or other wage levels? How do incentives work with employees from different cultures?

Global organizations are more effective if employees from different cultures are able to interact with each other in meaningful ways.

These are just a few of the many issues that must be taken into account as we move from a single-country business to a global firm. Throughout the rest of this chapter, you will learn more about global HRM functions.

LEGAL, ETHICAL, AND CULTURAL ISSUES

> "If you see in any given situation only what everybody else can see, you can be said to be so much a representative of your culture that you are a victim of it."
>
> —*US Senator S. I. Hayakawa*

14-1   ETHICAL DILEMMA: WHAT WOULD YOU DO?

Buy American

You most likely have heard the slogan "Buy American." Many labor unions urge Americans to buy products made in the United States because that helps retain jobs for American workers. On the other hand, some Americans ask why they should buy American products if they cost more or their quality or style is not as good as that of foreign-made products. But as you've seen, it isn't always easy for consumers to know the country of ownership of many products they buy.

1. Is it ethical and socially responsible to ask people to buy American?
2. Is it ethical and socially responsible to buy foreign products?
3. Do you attempt to buy American? Why or why not?

Legal, ethical, and especially cultural issues also have to be examined by companies considering global operations. The HR department has responsibility for many of these issues, including international labor laws, organizational ethics policies, and cultural training—for both national culture adaptation and corporate culture orientation.

International Labor Laws

As the company begins to operate in more than one country's market, the managers, including HR managers, have to ensure that the company complies with each country's legal requirements. The major HR laws tend to be in the areas of staffing, labor relations, and disciplinary action/termination. Employment and labor law in different countries is highly complex. Your organization will need to do significant research before moving any operations into another country to avoid violating that country's labor laws.

US Law

You know that most organizations within the United States are subject to a variety of EEO laws. But are employees of foreign companies working in the United States subject to the same laws, and are employees of US companies operating in other countries subject to these laws? Again, the EEOC gives us guidance on these situations.

According to the EEOC,

All employees who work in the U.S. or its territories . . . are protected by EEO laws, regardless of their citizenship or work authorization status. Employees who work in the U.S. or its territories are protected whether they work for a U.S. or foreign employer.[12]

So if you are in the United States or a US territory, you are covered by US EEO laws.

But what about Americans working outside the United States? According to the EEOC, "U.S. citizens who are employed outside the U.S. by a U.S. employer— or a foreign company controlled by a U.S. employer—are protected by Title VII, the ADEA, and the ADA." However, "U.S. employers are not required to comply with the requirements of Title VII, the ADEA, or the ADA if adherence to that requirement would violate a law of the country where the workplace is located."[13] Finally, if you are employed by a foreign company in a country other than the United States, the laws of that country would apply, so you would not have the protection of US EEO laws in such a case.

The United States also has a law specifically addressing corruption and bribery by US national companies while operating in other countries. The **Foreign Corrupt Practices Act (FCPA)** *bars US-based or US-listed companies from bribing foreign officials in exchange for business*. The FCPA also requires companies to keep accurate books and records concerning their foreign operations. However, it is sometimes hard to tell the difference between a legitimate business expense and a bribe.[14] So global companies need to clarify the difference in their code of ethics, top managers must set a good example, and penalties for unethical and illegal behavior must be enforced.

Remember that different countries have different employment laws based on that country's values, principles, and ethics which must be obeyed. So think about the complexity facing the HR executive working for a multinational company doing business in more than 100 countries! Thus, multinationals need HR legal specialists in each country.

SHRM

C:17

Foreign Corrupt Practices Act

WORK
APPLICATION 14-3

Do you believe in buying American products? Do you try to buy only American products, and should you?

Foreign Corrupt Practices Act Law barring US-based or US-listed companies from bribing foreign officials in exchange for business

National Culture

Recall that we discussed organizational culture in Chapter 2. All of that information also applies to national culture, but national culture is even more powerful in many cases. It is what people have known their entire lives, and like the old adage about a fish in water not knowing that there *is* any other possible environment, people who have lived their lives in one culture many times don't even realize that there *are* other options for values, beliefs, and culture. This view of the world is called **parochialism**—*a narrow-minded view of the world with an inability to recognize individual differences.* Managers in global organizations cannot survive with a parochial view of the world.

Differences in national culture influence the effectiveness of different managerial behaviors. These cultural differences require responses that are based on the country in which you are doing business. For instance, singling out and praising an individual worker in Japan is tantamount to yelling at an American employee on the shop floor. Japan, as a highly collectivist culture (we will discuss this momentarily), does not single out the individual for either praise or discipline in a public setting.

In another context, would you manage female employees the same way in a Muslim country such as Iran as you would in the United States? Would female managers lead others in the same way as male managers in this case? Would they manage male subordinates in the same way as their US counterpart? It's necessary for managers (in all countries, and all organizations) to understand the need to adjust their methods and their style to the region/country/community in which they will be operating.

So if you are going to have to manage in an international setting, you will need to understand the cultures that you are dealing with. But how do expatriate employees know how to act in another culture?

Hofstede's Model of National Culture. Let's look at a way that we can classify country cultures in order to determine how to train managers to successfully work with employees in that culture—*Hofstede's model of national culture.*

In the 1960s Geert Hofstede identified five dimensions—each of which allows a country culture to be plotted along a continuum. Each dimension was measured on a scale of 0 to 100, with 100 being the highest exhibition of that dimension. (More countries were added to Hofstede's model in later years, resulting in some scores moving above 100.) Let's look at the dimensions of the model in Exhibit 14-2.

What is the value in knowing that Russian culture is oriented toward the short term, Japan is highly masculine, and India is moderately collectivist? The *value* in the model is in knowing how significant the differences are between two countries' cultures. The greater the difference in the two cultures on each of the dimensions, the more difficult it is to bring employees from one culture into the other to work together effectively.

Similarly, putting employees from these two cultures together to accomplish any task is likely to fail unless they are given cultural training before working together. The HR department is typically charged with cross-cultural training of employees who will be working outside their native culture. (On a side note: If you ever get bored and want to watch a pretty good movie about extreme culture clash, watch a film from the 1980s called *Gung-Ho* with Michael Keaton. You will quickly see why cultural differences matter in business.)

SHRM

F:13

Cultural Competence

LO 14-2

Describe the five dimensions of Hofstede's model of culture.

SHRM

C:3

Individual Versus Group Behavior

WORK
APPLICATION 14-4

Give an example of cultural diversity you have encountered, preferably at work.

Parochialism A narrow-minded view of the world with an inability to recognize individual differences

EXHIBIT 14-2   HOFSTEDE'S MODEL OF NATIONAL CULTURE[15]

1. *Power-Distance (low vs. high)*—The degree to which societies accept that inequalities in power and well-being among members of the society are the result of differences in their individual abilities, both physical and intellectual, and their social status. In societies where these inequalities are allowed to continue or even grow, we consider the society to be a high power-distance culture. In societies where the differential value of rich and poor, intelligent and less intelligent, manager and employee is not an accepted part of the culture, we say that they exhibit low power-distance.

2. *Individualism (vs. Collectivism)*—The basis of this dimension is the degree to which individuals are integrated into groups. Individualist cultures value individual freedom and self-expression and believe that people should be judged on their personal achievements. Collectivist cultures believe that the group is the primary unit of value, and the individual only has value insofar as he or she assists the group in reaching its overall goals.

3. *Masculinity (vs. Femininity) or Assertiveness (vs. Nurturing)*—Hofstede used the terms *masculinity* versus *femininity* back in the 1960s. However, for political correctness, these terms have been changed to *assertiveness* versus *nurturing*. Masculine or assertive societies value performance/winning, assertiveness, competition, and success. Masculine societies value heroes and material rewards. Feminine or nurturing cultures, on the other hand, value relationships with others, interaction over winning, quality of life, and concern for others. So in a masculine society, you might see a sign saying "He who dies with the most toys wins," but a feminine option might be "The best things in life are free."

4. *Uncertainty Avoidance (high vs. low)*—Societies, like individuals, differ in their tolerance of risk. The uncertainty avoidance dimension "expresses the degree to which the members of a society feel uncomfortable with uncertainty and ambiguity." Societies that are high in uncertainty avoidance will make attempts to avoid uncertainty—at least as much as possible. Cultures with low uncertainty avoidance can tolerate significant risk within their society and will not spend as much societal effort to protect their citizens.

5. *Long-Term Orientation (vs. Short-Term Orientation)*—This dimension was not part of the original Hofstede model, but he added it after it became apparent that different cultures had differing concepts of past, present, and future. Cultures with a long-term orientation value saving, thrift, and persistence in working toward and reaching future goals. In cultures with a short-term orientation, we will see little intent to save for the future and a focus on immediate, or at least relatively quick, results.

Hofstede's dimensions with country examples:[16]

Low Power-Distance		High Power-Distance
←————————————————————————————————→		
Denmark (18)	Italy (50)	Panama (95)
Collectivist		Individualist
←————————————————————————————————→		
Colombia (13)	India (48)	USA (91)
Feminine/Nurturing		Masculine/Assertiveness
←————————————————————————————————→		
Sweden (5)	Turkey (45)	Japan (95)
Low Uncertainty Avoidance		High Uncertainty Avoidance
←————————————————————————————————→		
Jamaica (13)	Philippines (44)	Belgium (94)
Short-Term		Long-Term
←————————————————————————————————→		
Russia (10)	Singapore (48)	Hong Kong (91)

Source: The Hofstede Centre

14-1 APPLYING THE CONCEPT

Globe Dimensions

Place the letter of the Hofstede dimension of cultural diversity on the line next to the statement exemplifying it.

a. Power-Distance (low vs. high)

b. Individualism (vs. Collectivism)

c. Masculinity (vs. Femininity) or Assertiveness (vs. Nurturing)

d. Uncertainty Avoidance (high vs. low)

e. Long-Term Orientation (vs. Short-Term Orientation)

_____ 1. The people seem to prefer sports like soccer and basketball to sports like golf and track-and-field.

_____ 2. Managers place great importance on status symbols such as the executive dining room, reserved parking spaces, and big offices.

_____ 3. Managers provide poor working conditions to maximize profits.

_____ 4. Employees get nervous and stressed when changes are made.

_____ 5. Managers focus on quarterly and annual earnings to meet analysis expectations.

GLOBAL STAFFING

As you can see, operating a business on a global scale requires some complex skills. How are we going to staff the organization with people who have both the ability and the desire to work in this type of environment? We will need to recruit people with specific skills. We will also have to make some choices about what types of employees we are going to recruit, and from which countries. Then we will have to determine what training is necessary for them to be successful. These choices by the HRM can determine the success or failure of our global organization.

Skills and Traits for Global Managers

Going back to Chapter 1, you probably remember that all "managers require a mix of technical, human relations, conceptual and design, and business skills in order to successfully carry out their jobs." In international assignments, all of these skill sets can differ from what a manager or employee would typically learn in order to do their job. The way work is carried out—for instance in a high power-distance culture where employees expect to receive and carry out orders without question—may affect the way a manager does their job, so an American manager going into a high power-distance culture would need different technical skills than normal. Certainly with multiple cultures, probably speaking multiple languages, managers will need very strong human relations skills, and even conceptual and design skills may need to vary from what the manager would consider "normal" in different cultures. And finally, as we have already noted, business skills can be significantly different due to the variance in laws, regulations, and business structures in different countries (think of the *keiretsu* and *chaebol* partnerships in some Asian countries).

But what else do we need to take into account before sending someone to another country to work with or manage others? Companies may want *previous international experience* in the employees that they are considering sending on assignments outside of their home country. The feeling is that people who have made the adjustment before will have an easier time adjusting to yet another environment. This is not always true, but it can help to have a history of living in different cultures. Culture shock (we will discuss this shortly) is

©iStockphoto.com/XavierArnau

When staffing a global organization, managers need to look for candidates with specific skills that lend themselves to operating on an international scale.

WORK
APPLICATION 14-5

How would you assess your personality fit, family situation, and language ability in terms of an overseas assignment? Are you interested in working in another country? If so, in which country(ies) would you like to work?

SHRM

F:5

Language Issues

thought to decrease as people are exposed to, and live in, multiple different cultures. This can be advantageous to both the individual and the organization because the individual can settle in and become more productive sooner if they do not have to learn how to behave within the culture.

We noted in Chapter 8 that it is sometimes necessary to evaluate *individual traits* when evaluating our employees. This is one of those cases where it is indeed necessary. "Personality traits have been widely regarded as among the most important potential factors leading to expatriate adjustment,"[17] so a global assignment is one situation in which we will need to attempt to assess the traits of the people we are considering sending to another country to live. Some very strong evidence says that expatriates will fit into a culture better if their personality traits match up well with the culture's most significant characteristics.[18]

Suitability of immediate family who will accompany the employee is also important. We have to consider the entire family when making an international assignment unless the assignment will be "unaccompanied," or without the family. If they do accompany the employee, they will need to be assessed for suitability and disposition as well as being trained right along with the employee.

All of the assessment that we will accomplish prior to sending an individual on an international assignment is designed to identify the "fit" of the individual with the assignment. Remember that we also discussed *personality-job fit* and *person-organization fit* along with ability-job fit in Chapter 6. Personality-job fit and person-organization fit will need to be measured and analyzed in conjunction with a potential international assignment just as if we were hiring the person into the organization from the outside world. They will have to adapt to the organization and the job in a very different environment from the one that they are coming from, and there is a high risk of failure in the job if we don't do the analysis successfully.

Finally, *language ability* is something that may need to be taken into consideration. This will depend on the assignment, the difficulty of learning the language, the benefits of language training, and other considerations, but we do have to at least identify the possible need for the employee to speak the native language of the people in the assignment location.

LO 14-3

Name the advantages and disadvantages of parent-country, host-country, and third-country nationals for international assignments.

Staffing Choice: Home-, Host-, or Third-Country Employees

Our next consideration is where we will source the individual from for an international assignment. We have three generic options, each of which may be the best in some circumstances:

- *Parent- (home-) country nationals*—People who work for the organization in the country where the organization is headquartered

- *Host-country nationals*—People who live in a different country where a work assignment will take place

- *Third-country nationals*—People who happen to have a skill set needed for an international assignment but who are not citizens of either the home or host country

Each of the three staffing options has advantages and disadvantages.[19] Let's identify what you might need to know in order to consider each option in Exhibit 14-3.

Outsourcing as an Alternative to International Expansion

As an alternative to expanding the home organization, outsourcing is one way in which organizations can manage work without creating a direct international subsidiary. **Outsourcing** *is the process of hiring another organization to do work that was previously done within the host organization.* In quite a few cases, the organization to which we outsource a particular process will be located in another

Outsourcing The process of hiring another organization to do work that was previously done within the host organization

EXHIBIT 14-3	ADVANTAGES AND DISADVANTAGES OF PARENT, HOST, AND THIRD-COUNTRY NATIONALS		
	Parent-country	**Host-country**	**Third-country**
Advantages	• Generally have a better understanding of the organization, strategy, structure, and culture of the business • Allows managers to gain international experience • More effective communication with parent-country management	• Minimizes language and culture problems • Compensation is generally easier and is based on local pay scale • Less expensive than moving someone to the country • Better understanding of local business laws, culture, and customs	• Can hire the best talent from wherever they are located • May be less expensive than either parent- or host-country managers • May be more advantageous than parent-country managers due to similar culture and/or language with host
Disadvantages	• Language differences may be a problem • Compensation may be more of a problem than with host-country nationals • Country culture may create barriers to success for employee and family • Income and other tax rules can be complex	• Company culture and ways of doing business may create problems • May create more problems communicating with the parent office • Loyalty to the country may outweigh loyalty to the company	• Still may have company culture and business process issues • Host-country government may create barriers to third-party managers • Income and other tax rules can be complex

Source: Dörrenbächer, C., Gammelgaard, J., McDonald, F., Stephan, A., & Tüselmann, H. (2013). Staffing foreign subsidiaries with parent country nationals or host country nationals? Insights from European subsidiaries (No. 74). Working Papers of the Institute of Management Berlin at the Berlin School of Economics and Law (HWR Berlin).

country. In this case, the outsourcing is often referred to as *offshoring*. Nike outsources making all of its products, as it doesn't own any manufacturing facilities.

On the other hand, in the United States and many other developed countries, there has been a recent governmental push to return jobs that have been offshored to the home country. This is called onshoring (you may also see the terms *inshoring* and *reshoring*). Onshoring *is the process of shuttering operations in other countries and bringing work back to the home country* to increase employment there. In some cases this onshoring makes sense, but in others it may not. However, it is also an ethical question in the minds of a significant number of home-country citizens.

The ethical question in each of these cases first involves the potential for job loss or gain within the home organization because of shipping jobs overseas. In the case of offshoring, the firm may cut entire divisions' worth of employees and send that work to the offshore organization. Many US firms did this with customer service operations in the early 2000s, but you may also recall that several high-profile failures occurred in offshoring, such as **Dell** moving several thousand jobs back to the United States after significant customer complaints about support. Secondarily, companies have to be concerned with doing what is best for their shareholders and in fact have a fiduciary responsibility to do so. As a result, even when there is pressure from governments to reshore jobs, companies have to consider this option very carefully before taking that step because making some products at home costs too much to compete globally.

DEVELOPING AND MANAGING GLOBAL HUMAN RESOURCES

Once we have determined that we are going to expand internationally, we need to ensure that our employees will be able to successfully integrate into another country culture and complete their assignments. We need to select the right types

SHRM

K:B14
Outsourcing

O:7
Offshoring/Outsourcing

O:6
Inshoring

WORK
APPLICATION 14-6

Select a global business. Does it produce products in its home country? Should it have more inshoring?

SHRM

O:3
Cross-Border HR Management

Onshoring The process of shuttering operations in other countries and bringing work back to the home country

Because hiring an expatriate employee comes with significant cost to the organization, it is important to provide expatriates with cultural and communnication training so they are able to do their jobs well.

of individuals, train them appropriately, and support them during their international assignments. Finally, we will have to make sure that they reintegrate into the home-country operations once they return from the assignment. Let's look at some details on how we can do that.

Recruiting and Selection

We mentioned the problems with finding knowledge workers in Chapter 1. This continuing issue is causing more and more companies to source employees, including managers, from wherever they can find them. If they have to build a facility in another country to find enough of these workers, then that is what they will do. In today's world economy, where those low-skilled jobs are going away and we are constantly searching for knowledge workers, we have seen a shift to sourcing skilled employees from any country where they can be found and moving them to the locations where they are most needed. Many of the "lesser-developed economies" are now developing at a rapid rate and have become *sources* of talented knowledge workers.[20]

SHRM

0:2

Managing Expatriates in Global Markets

Expatriate Training and Preparation

Carlos Ghosn, the CEO of **Renault-Nissan Alliance**, said in a recent interview:

> You have to know how to motivate people who speak different languages, who have different cultural contexts, who have different sensitivities and habits. You have to get prepared to deal with teams who are multicultural, to work with people who do not all think the same way as you do.[21]

An **expatriate** *is an employee who leaves their home country to go work in another country*. As discussed, they can be home-, host-, or third-country employees. The cost of expatriates is very high, so we have to carefully select and develop these employees.[22]

LO 14-4

Explain the two major types of training that you should generally provide before expatriate assignments.

Cultural Training. Preparing employees for expatriate assignments will primarily be a training process, and the biggest training issue will usually be cross-cultural training. *Culture shock* can occur when we move from one culture to another. This culture shock can cause significant problems for the expatriate employee, and in fact, there is evidence that up to 50% of employees fail to complete their international assignment, with the major reason being an inability (on the part of the employee or family members) to adapt to cultural differences.[23] This inability to adapt may be because the parent company does not support the employee and family members in learning the culture that they will have to live in for an extended period of time.[24] Alternately, it may be due to a bad selection process, as we noted above in the section on personality traits.[25] Regardless, culture shock is one of the main reasons for early termination of an international assignment. But what is culture shock? Look at a diagram in Exhibit 14-4 to help explain.

Expatriate An employee who leaves their home country to go work in another country

If people know what to expect and have some training in how to adapt, the problems associated with hostility and depression (month 4-7+) can be lessened.

They will *not* go away, but they can be lessened, and this lessening may be enough to allow employees to ultimately adapt and be able to finish their assignment. "Effective pre-departure training is essential to support the employee to adapt to a new culture and country—as well as a new job."[26]

Communication Training. Expats frequently require both language training and other communication training (verbal, nonverbal, and symbolic). Communication can be difficult even when everyone is speaking the same language. It becomes much more difficult when there is more than one language being spoken and also when you have different nonverbal and symbolic cues based on different cultures. So individuals need to be trained on how to manage their body language and other nonverbal cues.

EXHIBIT 14-4   **CULTURE SHOCK**

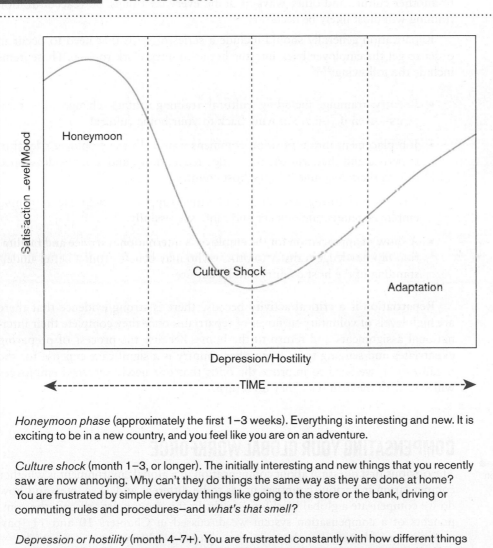

Honeymoon phase (approximately the first 1–3 weeks). Everything is interesting and new. It is exciting to be in a new country, and you feel like you are on an adventure.

Culture shock (month 1–3, or longer). The initially interesting and new things that you recently saw are now annoying. Why can't they do things the same way as they are done at home? You are frustrated by simple everyday things like going to the store or the bank, driving or commuting rules and procedures—and *what's that smell?*

Depression or hostility (month 4–7+). You are frustrated constantly with how different things are. You may even be depressed and not want to go outside and interact with people. You may avoid doing anything that requires that you involve yourself in the culture of the country.

Adaptation (month 7+). You start to accept the cultural norms and can interact with others successfully. You are now accustomed to the way things are done and the normal way to act in common situations. You feel "normal" in your everyday activities.

WORK
APPLICATION 14-7

Assume you were going to become an expatriate. What questions would you have about going to live and work in another country, and what specific training would you like to have?

SHRM

0:4

Repatriating Employees Post International Assignment

Symbolic communication is using items that we surround ourselves with. It can be a type of clothing or hat; it can be a crucifix necklace; it can be jewelry or body piercings, or even the type of vehicle that you drive. Everything that we surround ourselves with that then conveys meaning to others is part of symbolic communication, and it can have very different meanings in different cultures. You would not want to have a visible crucifix in many Muslim countries. If you drive a large SUV in other countries, you may be considered to be a drug dealer. So our employees need training on the various forms of symbolic communication.

Repatriation After Foreign Assignments

Would you care to guess what is likely to happen after a lengthy international assignment when an individual (and possibly their family, too) returns to their home country? They are going to go through another culture shock. The same adjustment will be necessary as they return home because they have adapted to another culture and other ways of doing everyday things. So reacculturation training will most likely be necessary.

Repatriation generally should include a series of steps that need to occur in order to get the employee back into the home-country work routine. These items include the following:[27,28]

- Reentry training, including cultural training (things change in several years—even if you are moving back to your home culture!)

- Job placement into a position commensurate with the employee's level of expertise and that will use their knowledge, skills, and abilities developed during their assignment in the host country

- Possibly mentoring assistance and other support to help the returning employee reintegrate quicker and more successfully

- A show of appreciation for the employee's international service and facilitation of knowledge transfer to others who may benefit from a better understanding of the host country and its culture

Repatriation is a critical activity because there is strong evidence that there are high levels of voluntary turnover of repatriates once they complete their international assignments and return to the home. Because the process of preparing expatriates and sending them to another country is a significant expense for the organization, we need to improve the odds that our newly returned employees will stay with the firm once they do return.

LO 14-5

Define the options for compensation of expatriate workers.

COMPENSATING YOUR GLOBAL WORKFORCE

The obvious first question about compensation in a global environment is whether compensation in various countries needs to be different and, if so, why and how do we compensate a global workforce fairly. In this section, let's discuss the components of a compensation system we discussed in Chapters 10 and 11 (pay, incentives, and benefits) as they relate to a global workforce.

Pay

We need to compensate differently globally because each country has a different standard and cost of living. If we want to keep high-quality managers and workers in our organization while asking them to work in countries around the world, we need to compensate them fairly. But what is fair? Is it fair to take a manager from a high-cost country and send them to a location that has a lower cost of living (United States to China), and once there lower their pay to match the local norm? If you were the manager, would you accept this?

Conversely, if we bring a manager from a low-cost economy to a higher-cost environment, we probably need to increase their pay to match the country or region in which they will be working. However, if we return them to their home country or location, should we lower their pay back to the original rate? Another question concerns the currency in which the employee will be paid. Should we pay our employees in their home currency, or should we pay them in the local currency where they are assigned?

Compensating a global workforce can be a difficult task.

As you can see, compensation of a global workforce becomes pretty complex very quickly. Let's discuss some options for paying expatriates.

Balance Sheet Approach. Using the balance sheet approach, the organization continues to pay the individual at a rate equivalent to their home-country salary while providing allowances during an overseas assignment to enable that employee to maintain their normal standard of living. Obviously, this is only necessary when an individual is moving to a higher-cost environment and out of their home country.

Split-Pay Approach. A variant on the balance sheet approach is to use *split pay.*[29] In fact, about half the organizations in a recent survey said that they use split pay as part of their compensation strategy.[30] Split pay is a process where the organization pays the individual partly in home-country currency and partly in the currency of their work location. This allows the individual to lower currency exchange rate risks in moving money from one location to another and to pay obligations in both their home location and their work location much easier than if all their pay were in one currency.

Other Approaches. Other options for compensating employees on international assignments include a *negotiation approach*, where the employer and employee mutually agree on a compensation package; a *localization approach*, where the expatriate's compensation is based on local (host-country) norms; and a *lump sum option*, which pays the expatriate a lump sum of money to use on items such as taxes, vehicles, housing, and similar items during their assignment.[31]

Compensation where workers are operating all over the world is a very difficult process. However, HR must play a part in the analysis and implementation of a compensation system that will allow the company to attract and retain high-quality managers and employees for their facilities. The only way to do this, based on our discussions of operant conditioning and reinforcement as well as equity and expectancy theories, is to provide reasonable and fair returns to those employees for the job that they do.

Incentives in Global Firms

Effective global leaders are a vital asset that can offer a competitive advantage within organizations today.[32] Former CEO Mike Duke of **Walmart** said that his biggest challenge was to continue to develop the leadership talent to grow the company around the world.[33] But do incentive programs work the same worldwide?

WORK
APPLICATION 14-8

Assume you were going to become an expatriate. What questions would you have about your pay, and which pay method would you want to have?

14-2 APPLYING THE CONCEPT

Global Compensation

Place the letter of the type of compensation on the line next to the corresponding example.

a. balance sheet

b. split-pay

c. negotiation

d. localization

e. lump sum

_____ 6. I'm going overseas for a 6-month assignment, and they are giving half the money in US dollars and half in euros.

_____ 7. I'm going overseas for a 6-month assignment, and they are paying me in the other country's currency, the euro.

_____ 8. I'm going overseas for a 6-month assignment, and they are continuing to pay me in euros, but they are also giving me a US dollar allowance for the higher cost of living in New York.

_____ 9. I'm going overseas for a 6-month assignment, and we are having a meeting to discuss my compensation for while I'm away.

_____ 10. I'm going overseas for a 6-month assignment, and they are giving me one check to pay for the entire time I'm away.

WORK
APPLICATION 14-9

Assume you were going to become an expatriate. Would you prefer straight salary or to have incentives? What type of incentive would entice you to take an overseas assignment?

The answer, briefly, is "No, but they are becoming more similar over time." In fact, in some emerging-market countries, variable pay is a higher proportion of overall compensation than in most developed markets.[34] However, in other countries, variable pay still has negative connotations, especially as an *individual* incentive. Many countries' cultures do not mesh well with individual incentive programs, and some do not readily accept even group incentive programs.[35]

The main thing that compensation professionals need to understand is that we cannot provide the same types of incentives to employees regardless of the organizational and country culture and structure. We have to understand the function of "significance" in expectancy theory and always make sure that our system rewards are significant and acceptable to our employees.

SHRM

K:B11

Global Employee Benefits

Benefit Programs Around the World

If we just think about it, benefit programs must adapt to the part of the world in which our employees work and live. For one thing, some countries mandate certain benefits that are not required in other countries, and we have no choice but to offer them. In other cases, the living conditions may be such that different benefit packages just make sense. Let's take a look at some examples of differences that we might see in benefit programs in various parts of the world.

Due to government laws, companies in many of the European Union countries have to provide more benefits than in the United States. Retirement benefits vary among countries, with some governments providing a strong centralized retirement system (Australia is a good example) and others providing very little in the way of centralized retirement planning and savings. Even in countries where there is a strong central government plan, most employees are concerned that they have not saved enough for retirement. One reason for this is that people are living longer today than ever before—all across the globe. Another issue is that in most countries, the population is planning on retiring at an earlier age than has historically been the case. This combination of living longer and retiring earlier is creating the potential for a gap in retirement plan funding. More and more companies are working with employees to narrow this gap through a series of options.

A significant trend is the move by companies toward offering more, and a larger variety of, voluntary benefits that are fully paid by the employee, instead of the employer providing at least part of the money to cover the cost of such benefits. In Brazil, for example, almost a third of female employees expressed interest in accident and pension funds for which they would pay 100% of the cost. Likewise, in Mexico, 56% of workers said that they would like a wider choice of voluntary benefits, and about one fourth said that they would pay the *full cost* for life, disability, and health insurance.[36]

Even if there are some significant differences in benefit plans around the world due to differing government policies, the consensus is that a good benefit package is a powerful force in employee satisfaction and retention—and employees globally like flexible benefits so that they can choose the benefits they want and need the most. Employers worldwide would be well served to start formal communications with their employees to find out what types of benefits will best serve to improve satisfaction and retention in their organizations.

TRENDS AND ISSUES IN HRM

In this section, we will take a look at a couple of globalization issues. The first issue is whether or not globalization is a fading trend and what managers need to do about it. The second is how labor organizations are increasingly affecting employee relations in the global environment.

Globalization of Business *Is* a Trend!

We have been talking about the effect of globalization on HRM for an entire chapter now, but is it really all that important to the companies that *you* will be working for? The evidence says that it is. *Forbes* magazine noted that "the major cause of [business model] disruption is the rapid advancement of technology and globalization, which allows new business models to be introduced at an ever-increasing rate and with rapidly declining costs."[37] A recent Deloitte Consulting report also notes that the BRIC economies "collectively quadrupled their GDP" in the first decade of the 21st century, compared to an 18% increase in the United States and the United Kingdom and an increase of less than 10% in Germany and Japan.[38]

At the same time, though, evidence is also pretty strong that some developed countries are retrenching a bit when it comes to international operations. Governments are putting pressure on business to reshore some of their operations after the recession of 2007–2008, and global trade has actually shrunk to just over half of what it was as a percentage of global GDP before the recession occurred.[39] At the same time, instability of some countries has made doing business in those locations much more risky, so there is evidence of some companies pulling back here as well. But don't think global business is going to go away anytime soon. Even with retrenchment of businesses in the developed economies after the recent recession, 59% of 1,200 CEOs in another survey said that they plan to increase the number of their international assignments as part of their HR strategy.[40]

So the bottom line is that while companies may retrench some jobs back to their home countries, it appears that some production and service jobs will continue to be moved out of home countries to other locations around the world to take advantage of capital cost savings. This means that managers, including HR managers, are going to have to continue getting more capable in training and preparing employees for international assignments.

The Worldwide Labor Environment

In the global village, developing-country unionization is just beginning, and it is expanding quickly. For example, in China angry migrant workers have used the Internet to organize. China has 348 million users, which is more than the total population of the United States at around 309 million,[41] and it has 787 million mobile phones available to help workers organize. Let's take a quick look at two countries around the world and how unions can affect work processes.

WORK
APPLICATION 14-10

Do you want to have a global assignment as part of your career?

Brazil. Brazil's labor regulations tend to favor the employee over the employer and provide strong protection for unions. While union membership has fallen over the years in the United States, Brazil has seen a significant increase in unionized workers in the past several years. The number of unionized workers stood at 18.35% in 2005, up from 16.73% in 2001.[42] Labor is also guaranteed the right to strike in the constitution, and labor agreements can either be in writing "or may be implied from the relationship between an individual and the company."[43] Labor laws in Brazil also require any disputes between management and workers "to be settled in labor tribunals rather than in the companies involved, so little space is left for direct negotiations between employers and employees."[44]

South Korea. South Korea's laws concerning labor relations are similar to those in the United States. The South Korean Trade Union Act allows workers to organize, collectively bargain, and act in concert to achieve labor goals. However, for many years the government had direct control of the major labor union in the country. This is not so any longer, and as a matter of fact, South Korea passed legislation that allows multiple unions to represent different workers within the same organization. South Korean employers are concerned that relations with employees will deteriorate due to this multiple unions system.[45]

As we can quickly see from the sample of countries above, union influence affects relationships between labor and management in significantly different ways in different countries. For those working in a business that operates in multiple countries, these differences in labor laws will be significant. You may have to become well informed on the differing laws concerning labor relations and union representation in each of the countries in which your firm works.

Get the edge on your studies at **edge.sagepub.com/fundamentalsofhrm**

Read the chapter and then take advantage of the open-access site to

- take a quiz to find out what you've mastered;
- test your knowledge with key term flashcards;
- watch videos to capture key chapter content.

REVIEW, PRACTICE, and **IMPROVE** your critical thinking with the tools and resources at **SAGE edge**.

⑤SAGE edge™

• • • CHAPTER SUMMARY

14-1 Discuss the reasons for increasing business globalization.

The main reason is to increase business, which is aided by the world becoming a global village where goods, ideas, services, and knowledge flow freely across national borders, creating greater demand for products. Barriers to trade have been minimized compared to historical norms, even though there is a series of trade blocs that operate

in multiple countries. Barriers to transportation, communication, and culture have also lessened. But the biggest reason for globalization is to remain competitive.

14-2 Describe the five dimensions of Hofstede's model of culture.

Power-distance is the degree to which societies accept that people will have different power because of their abilities and social status. Individualist cultures believe in the value of the individual and judge the individual, while collectivist cultures believe that the group is the unit of value in society, not the individual. Masculine societies value performance, winning, competition, and success, while feminine societies value relationships between members and quality of life more than winning. High-uncertainty avoidance cultures will do whatever they can to minimize risks to members of the society, and low-uncertainty avoidance cultures will not try to mitigate these risks nearly as much. Finally, short-term societies focus on immediate or short-term outcomes, while long-term societies focus on saving for the future, thrift, and persistence.

14-3 Name the advantages and disadvantages of parent-country, host-country, and third-country nationals for international assignments.

Parent-country members usually know the organization better, know the strategy and structure, and communicate better. However, language, compensation issues, cultural barriers, and national laws on income may be disadvantages. Host-country nationals present advantages with respect to the language, culture, compensation issues, and local laws and regulations, but they may not have the company knowledge that is needed, may be less loyal to the firm, and could have problems communicating with the home office. Third-country nationals allow us to hire the best person for a job and may be less expensive in some cases. They may also share a language or similar culture with the host-country office. Disadvantages include host-country laws concerning third-party employees, income and other tax rules, and potential lack of knowledge of company procedures and culture.

14-4 Explain the two major types of training that you should generally provide before expatriate assignments.

The two types of training are cultural training and communication training. Cultural training shows the employee what culture shock is and how to manage it during an expatriate assignment. Inability to adapt to another culture is one of the major reasons that employees fail to complete foreign assignments. Communication training, including language training if necessary, helps to overcome some of the problems associated with international assignments. Training in nonverbal and symbolic communication is especially important.

14-5 Define the options for compensation of expatriate workers.

The *balance sheet* approach is one of the most common methods. This is where the employee is paid their home salary, but allowances are provided to "balance" the different costs associated with the overseas assignment. Another option is *split-pay*, where part of the compensation is paid based on the home-country norm and part is paid in the assignment-country currency to minimize exchange rate risk. We can also use a straight *negotiation* approach, where the compensation package is agreed to upfront; a *localization* approach, where compensation is based on the host-country standards; or a *lump sum* approach, where a set amount of money is given to the employee to use on unique expenses associated with an assignment to a particular country.

14-6 Define the key terms found in the chapter margins and listed following the Chapter Summary.

Complete the Key Terms Review to test your understanding of this chapter's key terms.

• • • KEY TERMS

expatriate, 362
Foreign Corrupt Practices Act, 356

onshoring, 361
outsourcing, 360

parochialism, 357
trade blocs, 353

• • • KEY TERMS REVIEW

Complete each of the following statements using one of this chapter's key terms:

1. _____ are groups of countries who form an association for the purpose of facilitating movement of goods across national borders.

2. _____ bars US-based or US-listed companies from bribing foreign officials in exchange for business.

3. _____ is a narrow-minded view of the world with an inability to recognize individual differences.

4. _____ is hiring another organization to do work that was previously done within the host organization.

5. _____ is the process of shuttering operations in other countries and bringing work back to the home country.

6. _____ is an employee who leaves their home country to go work in another country.

• • • COMMUNICATION SKILLS

The following critical-thinking questions can be used for class discussion and/or for written assignments to develop communication skills. Be sure to give complete explanations for all answers.

1. Do you expect that globalization of business will continue to expand? Why or why not?

2. Is it fair to utilize the least expensive "capital resources," no matter where they come from? Why?

3. Should tariffs and other trade barriers be increased in order to protect jobs in the home country? Why or why not?

4. Do you believe that Hofstede's culture model is accurate? If not, what would you change to make it more useful in training people to work in a different culture?

5. Is knowing the local language always necessary when working internationally? Why?

6. Who would you rather assign to manage a foreign office of *your* business? Would you rather have a home-country, host-country, or third-country national? Why?

7. Should companies reshore more jobs that have been moved overseas? What are the pros and cons of doing so?

8. Would you ever consider sending someone to work in another country without cultural training if you were the HR manager? If so, in what circumstances?

9. Which option for compensation would you want if you were assigned by your company to work in another country? Why?

• • • CASE 14-1 IBM (I'VE BEEN MOVED) AT HSBC: KEEPING COMPENSATION COMPETITIVE WITH ECA INTERNATIONAL

HSBC is one of the world's largest banking groups by assets (and the leader in customer deposits, with more than $1 trillion), with HSBC Holdings owning subsidiaries throughout Europe, Hong Kong, and the rest of the Asia/Pacific region, the Middle East and Africa, and the Americas. All told, the company has some 7,200 locations in more than 80 countries. Its activities include consumer and commercial banking, credit cards, private banking, investment banking, and leasing. Its North American operations include HSBC USA, HSBC Bank Canada, HSBC Bank Bermuda, and Grupo Financiero HSBC in Mexico.[46]

With around 9,500 offices in 85 countries and territories, employee work and life balance satisfaction is an international enterprise and requires constant vigilance. Employees at HSBC are extremely consistent in highlighting the enormous benefits that the company's HR policies and work experiences bring to their careers. They indicate that the global nature of the bank brings tremendous international exposure to the role of employees at the bank, right from the start. "The makeup and strategy of the bank allows you to have constant exposure to interesting and complex international operations," explains one employee. "The best thing about this job is seeing how intrinsically linked the global economy is to everything that we do here at HSBC," says another. This also allows for endless international travel opportunities, with HSBC employees wayfaring to almost anywhere in the globe; they should expect to relocate at least twice in their career if they wish to climb the corporate ladder.[47]

Job mobility is an integral part of HSBC's operations, and tracking employee salaries is a key factor in their HRM success formula. HSBC typically pays its employees 5% above market value, with competitive firms such as JP Morgan Chase and Citibank paying only 3% above market.[48] Benefits include health insurance (medical, dental, vision), life insurance, retirement and savings programs including a 401(k) match, and other employee services including adoption assistance, time-off programs, and concierge services.[49] The challenge for HSBC then was how to ensure that they would continue to pay their employees a premium salary and benefits package worldwide, especially when employees are constantly being switched from one location to another where salaries and benefits may vary drastically.

HSBC quickly realized that such a large operation required expert advice and counsel. HSBC contracted with ECA International to design and implement a new assignment salary and benefits management system to help them with their 1,400 long-term assignees in 50 locations.[50] ECA is one of the world's leaders in the development and provision of solutions for the management and assignment of employees around the world. Their highly skilled teams help to ensure that businesses' international assignments operate efficiently and cost-effectively. Delivering data, expertise, systems, and support in formats that suit its clients, ECA's offer includes a complete "outsource" package of calculations, advice, and services for companies with little international assignment management experience or resource; subscriptions to comprehensive online information and software systems for companies with larger requirements; and custom policy and system development projects for companies that manage thousands of international assignees around the world.[51]

The key objectives of the project was to improve efficiency, accuracy, consistency, and transparency of calculation and data storage of salary and benefits information while reducing operational costs and allowing HSBC to react quickly to international opportunities. The new system needed to be able to incorporate all elements of HSBC's HR policies for consistency of application while accommodating the inevitable policy deviations experienced country by country, and it had to be accessible from HSBC's three regional hubs and be completely secure.

ECA's software team prototyped a new solution for HSBC based on ECAEnterprise, a comprehensive, data-populated, web-enabled salary and benefits calculator and database, and then developed the prototype in close collaboration with HSBC through a shared website. HSBC worked with both ECA's client services and software experts, who advised on both policy and technical matters, ensuring the system fulfilled HSBC's policy objectives and user needs.

On time and on budget, the customized, hosted version allowed for a seamless transition between the old and the new operating systems. At the time the new web-enabled tool became operational, users in all three of HSBC's hubs had been trained on-site by ECA staff.

Harry Lister, senior manager of benefits and international mobility, is pleased with the new system. "HSBCEnterprise fulfills all of the business goals we set out to achieve," Lister says. "We can now calculate and store salary and benefits packages for all of the Group's international assignees efficiently and with a transparency that our previous legacy systems did not allow."[52]

Questions

1. Describe some of the ethical and legal issues HSBC should be cognizant of given the breadth of their international operation. What might be some key HR issues for this firm?

2. HSBC has numerous office locations and subsidiaries. What seems to be the firm's generic business strategy?

3. Given your answer to question 2, how does the firm's policy regarding employee travel, job mobility, and relocation support HSBC's generic strategy? Why?

4. HSBC is a global firm with nearly 9,500 offices in 85 countries. In such a large international operation, why would tracking employee salaries and benefits be such a key factor in the HRM success formula? How does this formula support the firm's generic strategy?

5. ECA develops and implements solutions for the management and assignment of employees around the world for global firms. What other HRM functions might be included in those services? Why?

6. HSBC has offices in the Middle East. What HR concerns might HSBC have regarding employees working in that particular region, especially expatriates?

Case created by Herbert Sherman, PhD, and Theodore Vallas, Department of Management Sciences, School of Business Brooklyn Campus, Long Island University

---

••• SKILL BUILDER 14-1 THE GLOBAL HRM ENVIRONMENT

Objective

To develop your global HRM awareness

Skills

The primary skills developed through this exercise are as follows:

1. HR *management skills*—Conceptual and design, and business skills

2. *SHRM 2013 Curriculum Guidebook*—Parts of multiple guides including Question 3—B: Employment Law, Question 4—F: Managing a Diverse Workforce, Question 5—I. Staffing: Recruitment and Selection, Question 6—L: Training and Development, Questions 7 and 8—K: Total Reward, Question 9—C: Ethics

Assignment

For this exercise, select a company that conducts business as an MNC or a transnational global corporation, preferably one you work or would like to work for. You will most likely need to conduct some research to get the answers to the questions below, such as visiting the company's website and talking to HR professionals.

1. Explain the stage of corporate globalization.

2. List at least five countries it conducts business in and the trade agreements these countries participate in.

3. Identify some of the key differences in laws among the five countries.

4. Compare the company's five Hofstede's Model of National Culture dimensions for the five countries it does business in.

5. Explain how it recruits and selects expatriate employees.

6. Describe how it trains its expatriates and families.

7. Discuss the method(s) of compensation for its expatriates.

8. Compare the compensation (pay, incentives, and benefits) among the five countries.

9. Does the company have any specific code of ethics for conducting business in other countries, and if so, describe the code.

Your professor may or may not require you to answer all nine questions. You may be asked to pass in this assignment, present your answers to the class, and/or discuss your answers in small groups or online.

• • • SKILL BUILDER 14-2 CULTURAL DIVERSITY AWARENESS

Objective

To develop your global cultural awareness

Skills

The primary skills developed through this exercise are as follows:

1. *HR management skills*—Human relations skills
2. *SHRM 2013 Curriculum Guidebook*—F: Managing a Diverse Workforce

Assignment

Procedure 1 (4–6 minutes)

You and your classmates will share your international experience and nationalities. Start with people who have lived in another country, then move to those who have visited another country, and follow with discussion of nationality (e.g., "I am half French and half Irish but have never been to either country"). The instructor or a recorder will write the countries on the board until several countries/nationalities are listed or the time is up.

Procedure 2 (10–30 minutes)

You and your classmates will share your knowledge of cultural differences between the country in which the course is being taught and those listed on the board. This is a good opportunity for international students and those who have visited other countries to share their experiences. You may also discuss cultural differences within the country.

• • • SKILL BUILDER 14-3 THE MOST IMPORTANT THINGS I GOT FROM THIS COURSE

Objective

To review your course learning, critical thinking, and skill development

Skills

The primary skills developed through this exercise are as follows:

1. *HR management skills*—Conceptual and design
2. *SHRM 2013 Curriculum Guidebook*—The guide will vary with student answers

Assignment

Think about and write/type the three or four most important things you learned or skills you developed through this course and how they are helping or will help you in your personal and/or professional life.

You may be asked to pass in this assignment, present your answers to the class, and/or discuss your answers in small groups or online.

Appendix

SHRM 2013 CURRICULUM GUIDEBOOK

Required and Secondary HR Content Areas

(Reordered and numbered for reference)

The Society for Human Resources Management (SHRM), the world's largest Human Resource Management association, periodically puts out guidance on college and university curricula for human resource management (HRM) programs (what they think we need to teach you). The latest version of their guidebook is provided below for your information and use. This guidance provides information on what SHRM considers to be critical in the study of HRM. If you choose to pursue human resource management as a career choice, this information will help you with the process of certification through the Human Resource Certification Institute (HRCI) or through SHRM's new internal accreditation program. Even if you don't decide to pursue HRM as a career, this is the information that will be most pertinent to your success as a manager in any field of business.

It makes sense that an introductory textbook would introduce you to each of the areas that are critical in that field of study. As a result, in this textbook we've chosen to discuss all "Required Content" for undergraduate HR programs from the most recent version (2013) of the Curriculum Guide. As far as we know, no other introductory HRM textbook does this. This has been done to introduce you to each of the topics that SHRM considers to be critical. We have reordered the information from the SHRM curriculum guide to emphasize the required content first, and then the secondary and graduate content areas, but the content itself is identical to the guidelines from SHRM. You can call up the guide itself at http://www.shrm.org/Education/hreducation/Documents/2013_SHRM%20 HR%20Curriculum%20Guidelines%20and%20Templates_View%20Only_ FINAL.pdf.

This appendix is designed to link back to each of the chapters and identify where each of the required content areas is discussed within the textbook. When you see a box in the chapter titled *SHRM Guide*, it will have an alphanumeric reference. That alphanumeric reference ties to this appendix by Section (the capital letter) and Subtopic (the numeral). For example, if you see the box in the margin here, it would lead you to Section A (Employee and Labor Relations), Subtopic 5 (Employee Involvement). Next to each of the subtopics is the page number on which the topic is discussed. This should help if you are looking for information on a particular topic within the chapters.

SHRM

A:5

Employee Involvement

REQUIRED CONTENT: UNDERGRADUATE CURRICULUM

A. Employee and Labor Relations

1. Disciplinary actions: Demotion, disciplinary termination
[Chapter 9, p. 230]

3. Managing/creating a positive organizational culture
[Chapter 2, p. 40]

4. Employee engagement [Chapter 1, p. 6]

5. Employee involvement [Chapter 1, p. 5]

6. Employee retention [Chapter 1, p. 8]

8. Union membership [Chapter 9, p. 234]

9. Union-related labor laws [Chapter 9, p. 231]

10. Union/management relations [Chapter 9, p. 232]

11. Union decertification and deauthorization [Chapter 9, p. 236]

12. Collective bargaining issues [Chapter 9, p. 235]

13. Collective bargaining process [Chapter 9, p. 235]

16. Grievance management [Chapter 9, p. 236]

17. Strikes, boycotts, and work stoppages [Chapter 9, p. 232]

18. Unfair labor practices [Chapter 9, p. 232]

19. Managing union organizing policies and handbooks [Chapter 9, p. 235]

20. Attendance [Chapter 1, p. 8]

21. Attitude surveys [Chapter 9, p. 220]

22. Investigations [Chapter 9, p. 228]

27. Employee records [Chapter 9, p. 224]

B. Employment Law

1. Age Discrimination in Employment Act of 1967 [Chapter 3, p. 62]

2. Americans with Disabilities Act of 1990 and as amended in 2008 [Chapter 3, p. 62]

3. Equal Pay Act of 1963 [Chapter 3, p. 59]

4. Pregnancy Discrimination Act of 1978 [Chapter 3, p. 62]

5. Title VII of the Civil Rights Act of 1964 and 1991 [Chapter 3, p. 60, 63]

6. Executive Order 11246 (1965) [Chapter 3, p. 68]

7. Employer Retirement Income Security Act of 1974 (ERISA) [Chapter 11, p. 286]

8. Fair Labor Standards Act of 1938 (FLSA) [Chapter 10, p. 253]

9. Family and Medical Leave Act of 1993 (FMLA) [Chapter 11, p. 284]

12. National Labor Relations Act of 1935 (NLRA) [Chapter 9, p. 232]

13. Labor Management Relations Act of 1947 (LMRA) [Chapter 9, p. 233]

14. Railway Labor Act of 1926 (RLA) [Chapter 9, p. 232]

15. Uniformed Services Employment and Reemployment Rights Act of 1994 (USERRA) [Chapter 3, p. 64]

16. Worker Adjustment and Retraining Notification Act of 1988 (WARN Act) [Chapter 9, p. 234]

17. Enforcement agencies (EEOC, OFCCP) [Chapter 3, p. 66]

19. Employee privacy [Chapter 9, p. 224]

20. Employer unfair labor practices [Chapter 14, p. 232]

21. Professional liability [Chapter 1, p. 19]

24. Disparate impact [Chapter 3, p. 60]

25. Disparate treatment [Chapter 3, p. 60]

26. The Occupational Safety and Health Act of 1970 (OSHA) [Chapter 12, p. 304]

   Citations and penalties

27. Unlawful harassment [Chapter 3, p. 66]

   Sexual

   Religious

   Disability

   Race

   Color

   Nation of origin

28. Whistle-blowing/retaliation [Chapter 3, p. 66]

29. Reasonable accommodation [Chapter 3, p. 62, 74]

    ADA

    Religious

30. Employment-at-will doctrine [Chapter 9, p. 225]

31. Lilly Ledbetter Fair Pay Act [Chapter 3, p. 65]

32. Genetic Information Nondiscrimination Act (GINA) [Chapter 3, p. 65, Chapter 6, p. 143]

33. COBRA: Consolidated Omnibus Budget Reconciliation Act of 1985 [Chapter 11, p. 286]

34. American Recovery and Reinvestment Act of 2009 (ARRA) [Chapter 11, p. 286]

36. Fair Credit Reporting Act (FCRA) [Chapter 6, p. 150]

37. Health Insurance Portability and Accountability Act (HIPAA) of 1996 [Chapter 11, p. 286]

39. Negligent hiring [Chapter 6, p. 137]

C. Ethics

1. Rules of conduct [Chapter 13, p. 334]

2. Moral principles [Chapter 13, p. 333]

3. Individual versus group behavior [Chapter 2, p. 40; Chapter 14, p. 357]

4. Organizational values [Chapter 13, p. 333]

5. Guidelines and codes [Chapter 9, p. 225]

6. Behavior within ethical boundaries [Chapter 9, p. 225; Chapter 12, p. 320]

7. Facing and solving ethical dilemmas [Chapter 13, p. 332]

8. Codes of ethics [Chapter 1, p. 11]

   General value system

   Ethical principles

   Ethical rules

9. Compliance and laws [Chapter 13, p. 338]

11. Conflicts of interest [Chapter 13, p. 334]

12. Use of company assets [Chapter 13, p. 335]

13. Acceptance or providing of gifts, gratuities, and entertainment [Chapter 13, p. 335]

14. Abusive behavior [Chapter 12, p. 321]

    Workplace bullying

17. Foreign Corrupt Practices Act [Chapter 14, p. 356]

D. HR's Role in Organizations

1. It is generally expected that faculty will discuss HR's role with regard to each of the individual HR disciplines whenever an individual discipline is taught. This may take the form of describing HR's role in developing human capital, its effect on the organization's success, or the interplay among the various disciplines— meaning how decisions in one HR discipline affect other HR disciplines. [Chapter 1, p. 15]

E. Job Analysis/Job Design

1. Job/role design (roles, duties, and responsibilities) [Chapter 4, p. 92]

2. Job evaluation and compensation (grades, pay surveys, and pay setting) [Chapter 10, p. 258]

3. Employment practices (recruitment, selection, and placement) [Chapter 6, p. 137]

4. Performance management (performance criteria and appraisal) [Chapter 8, p. 191]

5. Training and development [Chapter 7, p. 164, 167]

   Vocational and career counseling

   Needs assessment

   Career pathing

6. Compliance with legal requirements [Chapter 3, p. 66. Chapter 10, p. 255, 258, Chapter 12, p. 311]

   Equal employment (job-relatedness, bona fide occupational qualifications, and the reasonable accommodation process)

   Equal pay (skill, effort, responsibility, and working conditions) and comparable worth

   Overtime eligibility (exempt vs. nonexempt work)

   Ergonomics and workplace safety (work hazards and mitigation)

7. HR planning (skill inventories and supply/demand forecasting) [Chapter 4, p. 99]

8. Work management (work processes and outsourcing) [Chapter 4, p. 86, 104]

9. Organization design (missions, functions, and other aspects of work units for horizontal and vertical differentiation) [Chapter 2, p. 39]

F. Managing a Diverse Workforce

1. Equal employment opportunity (EEO) [Chapter 3, p. 66]

2. Affirmative action (AA) [Chapter 3, p. 68]

3. Aging workforce [Chapter 13, p. 339]

4. Individuals with disabilities [Chapter 3, p. 62]

5. Language issues [Chapter 14, p. 360]

6. Racial/ethnic diversity [Chapter 3, p. 69]

7. Religion [Chapter 3, p. 74]

8. Reverse discrimination [Chapter 1, p. 21]

9. Sex/gender issues [Chapter 3, p. 70]

10. Gay, lesbian, bisexual, transgender (GLBT)/sexual orientation issues [Chapter 13, p. 339]

12. Business case for diversity [Chapter 3, p. 69]

13. Cultural competence [Chapter 14, p. 357]

G. Outcomes: Metrics and Measurement of HR

1. Economic value added [Chapter 2, p. 45]

5. Trend and ratio analysis projections [Chapter 4, p. 100]

6. Calculating and interpreting yield ratios [Chapter 5, p. 124]

7. Return on investment (ROI) [Chapter 2, p. 45]

10. Quantitative analysis [Chapter 4, p. 100]

11. Benchmarking [Chapter 10, p. 263]

12. Analyzing and interpreting metrics [Chapter 4, p. 100]

13. Forecasting [Chapter 4, p. 99]

H. Performance Management

1. Identifying and measuring employee performance [Chapter 8, p. 197]

2. Sources of information (e.g., managers, peers, clients) [Chapter 8, p. 200]

3. Rater errors in performance measurement [Chapter 8, p.203]

5. Performance appraisals [Chapter 8, p. 196]

6. Appraisal feedback [Chapter 8, p. 206]

7. Managing performance [Chapter 8, p. 194]

8. Diagnosing problems [Chapter 9, p. 227]

9. Performance improvement programs [Chapter 9, p. 226]

I. Staffing: Recruitment and Selection

1. Employment relationship: Employees, contractors, temporary workers [Chapter 4, p. 104]

2. External influences on staffing: Labor markets, unions, economic conditions, technology [Chapter 5, p. 114]

3. External recruitment: Recruiters, open vs. targeted recruitment, recruitment sources, applicant reactions, medium (electronic, advertisement), fraud/misrepresentation [Chapter 5, p. 118]

6. Initial assessment methods: Résumés, cover letters, application blanks, biographical information, reference/background checks, genetic screening, initial interviews, minimum qualifications [Chapter 6, p. 141]

7. Discretionary assessment methods [Chapter 6, p. 137]

8. Ability/job knowledge tests, assessment centers [Chapter 6, p. 145]

9. Noncognitive assessments (e.g., personality assessments, integrity tests, situational judgment tests, interest inventories) [Chapter 6, p. 144]

10. Structured interviews [Chapter 6, p. 147]

11. Contingent assessment methods: Drug testing, medical exams [Chapter 6, p. 146]

12. Measurement concepts: Predictors/criteria, reliability, validity [Chapter 6, p. 140]

13. Selection decisions: Ranking, grouping/banding, random selection [Chapter 6, p. 153]

14. Job offers: Employment-at-will, contracts, authorization to work [Chapter 9, p. 225]

15. Bona fide occupational qualifications (BFOQs) [Chapter 3, p. 61]

16. Employment brand [Chapter 10, p. 252]

J. Strategic HR

1. Strategic management [Chapter 2, p. 34]

2. Enhancing firm competitiveness [Chapter 2, p. 39]

3. Strategy formulation [Chapter 2, p. 39]

5. Sustainability/corporate social responsibility [Chapter 1, p.11]

6. Internal consulting (required for graduate students only) [Chapter 1, p. 15]

7. Competitive advantage [Chapter 2, p. 35]

8. Competitive strategy [Chapter 2, p. 33]

9. Ethics [Chapter 1, p. 11]

10. Linking HR strategy to organizational strategy [Chapter 2, p. 39]

11. Organizational effectiveness [Chapter 1, p. 7]

12. Trends and forecasting in HR [Chapter 4, p. 100]

13. Mission and vision [Chapter 2, p. 35]

K. Total Rewards

obligations, action planning, strategic planning) [Chapter 11, p. 283]

21. Paid leave plans [Chapter 11, p. 287]
22. Workers' compensation [Chapter 11, p. 283]

L. Training and Development

1. Needs assessment [Chapter 7, p. 167]
3. Learning theories: Behaviorism, constructivism, cognitive models, adult learning, knowledge management [Chapter 7, p. 168]
4. Training evaluation: Kirkpatrick's model [Chapter 7, p. 175]
5. E-learning and use of technology in training [Chapter 7, p. 175]
6. On-the-job training (OJT) [Chapter 7, p. 173]
7. Outsourcing (secondary) [Chapter 7, p. 181]
8. Transfer of training: Design issues, facilitating transfer [Chapter 7, p. 176]
9. Employee development: Formal education, experience, assessment [Chapter 7, p. 177]
11. The role of training in succession planning [Chapter 7, p. 166]

M. Workforce Planning and Talent Management

1. Downsizing/rightsizing (secondary) [Chapter 4, p. 102]
2. Planning: Forecasting requirements and availabilities, gap analysis, action planning, core/flexible workforce [Chapter 4, p. 99]
3. Retention: Involuntary turnover, outplacement counseling, alternative dispute resolution [Chapter 9, p. 230]
4. Retention: Voluntary turnover, job satisfaction, withdrawal, alternatives [Chapter 9, p. 220]
6. Labor supply and demand [Chapter 4, p. 102]

REQUIRED CONTENT: GRADUATE CURRICULUM

N. Change Management

1. Stages of change management
   Indifference
   Rejection
   Doubt
   Neutrality
   Experimentation
   Commitment
2. Dimensions of change
   Culture
   Coaching
   Direction
   Communication
   Accountability
   Resilience
   Skills and knowledge
   Recognition
   Managing projects
   Involvement
3. Communication
4. Building trust
5. Creating a foundation for problem solving
6. Leading change
7. Planning change strategy
8. Implementing change
9. Coping strategies for employees
10. Adjusting to change within the organization

O. Globalization

1. Global business environment
2. Managing expatriates in global markets
3. Cross-border HR management
4. Repatriating employees post international assignment
5. Global security and terrorism
6. Inshoring
7. Offshoring/outsourcing
8. Global labor markets
9. Cross-cultural effectiveness

P. Internal Consulting

1. Assess customers' needs
2. Influence cross-departmentally
3. Identify areas for HR intervention and design intervention
4. Advise management and colleagues cross-divisionally
5. Analyze and recommend solutions to business problems
6. Analyze data and prepare reports to inform business decisions
7. Recommend changes for process improvement
8. Conduct periodic audits
9. Lead special and cross-functional project teams

Q. Organizational Development

1. Coaching
2. Developing human resources
3. Emotional intelligence
4. Equipping the organization for present and future talent needs
5. Improving organizational effectiveness
6. Knowledge management
7. Leadership development
8. Measurement systems
9. Ongoing performance and productivity initiatives
10. Organizational effectiveness
11. Organizational learning
12. Organizational structure and job design
13. Outsourcing employee development
14. Social networking
15. Succession planning
16. Training employees to meet current and future job demands

SECONDARY CONTENT

R. Corporate/Social Responsibility and Sustainability

1. Corporate philanthropy
2. Ethics
3. Diversity
4. Financial transparency
5. Employee relations and employment practices
   Participative decision making
6. Supply chain management
7. Governance
8. Community/employee engagement
9. Green management
10. The business case for CSR
11. Reputation and brand enhancement
12. Accountability and transparency
13. Risk management
14. Linking organizational culture and corporate values

S. Downsizing/Rightsizing

1. Employment downsizing
2. Alternatives to employment downsizing
3. Strategies for long-term success
4. Why downsizing happens
5. When downsizing is the answer
6. Effectively managing a downsizing effort
7. Alternatives to downsizing
8. Consequences of employment downsizing
9. Approaches to reducing staff size
10. Identifying and eliminating unnecessary work
11. Prioritizing jobs for combining, streamlining, or eliminating
12. Identifying selection criteria for making downsizing/rightsizing decisions
13. Importance of focusing on individual jobs vs. individual staff members
14. Layoffs
15. Reductions in force

T. HR Career Planning

1. Definition of a career
2. Balancing work and life
3. Career management systems
4. Company policies to accommodate work and nonwork activities
5. Coping with job loss
6. Developing leader skills
   Authentic leadership
   Contingency theory
   Ethical decision making
   Leader-member exchange
   theory
   Path-goal theory
   Situational approach
   Skills approach
   Style approach
   Team leadership
   Trait approach
   Transformational leadership
7. Plateauing
8. Skills obsolescence
9. Career development

U. HR Information Systems

1. Conducting systems needs assessments
2. Determining system specifications
3. Selecting an HR information system
4. Using HR data for enterprise management
5. Issues to consider when selecting HRIS software

V. Mergers and Acquisitions

1. Conducting HR due diligence
2. Integrating HR systems
3. Assimilating work cultures
4. Integrating compensation and benefits structures
5. Merging workplace cultures
6. Integrating performance management systems
7. Cultural compatibility
   Address cultural differences
   Degree of internal integration
   Autonomy
   Adaptability
   Employee trust
   Diversity
8. Integration

Communication

Employee anxiety

Rumors

Redundancy

Downsizing

Morale

W. Outsourcing

1. Creating an outsourcing strategy
2. Preparing a request for information (RFI) or request for proposal (RFP)
3. Identifying third-party providers (contractors)
4. Evaluating proposals from contractors
5. Conducting cost-benefit analyses
6. Negotiating contract terms
7. Retaining management rights
8. Importance of legal review of contracts
9. Managing vendor/staff relationships
10. Managing a vendor's performance under the contract terms
11. Managing communications and deliverables
12. Evaluating effectiveness of outsourcing efforts

X. Workplace Health, Safety, and Security

1. OSHA citations and penalties (required)
2. Disaster preparation, continuity, and recovery planning
3. Employee health
4. Inspection
5. Protection from retaliation
6. Safety management
7. Security concerns at work
8. Communicable diseases
9. Data security
10. Testing for substance abuse
11. Ergonomics
12. Monitoring, surveillance, privacy

Glossary

absenteeism The failure of an employee to report to the workplace as scheduled.

accountability The personal duty to someone else (a higher-level manager or the organization itself) for the effective use of resources to complete an assignment.

active listening The intention and ability to listen to others, use the content and context of the communication, and respond appropriately.

adverse employment action Any action such as firings, demotions, schedule reductions, or changes that would harm the individual employee.

affirmative action A series of policies, programs, and initiatives that have been instituted by various entities within both government and the private sector that are designed to prefer hiring of individuals from protected groups in certain circumstances, in an attempt to mitigate past discrimination.

assessment center A place where job applicants undergo a series of tests, interviews, and simulated experiences to determine their potential for a particular job.

authority The right to give orders, enforce obedience, make decisions, and commit resources toward completing organizational goals.

behaviorally anchored rating scale (BARS) form A performance appraisal that provides a description of each assessment along a continuum.

behaviors The actions taken by an individual.

bias A personality-based tendency, either toward or against something.

biological job design Designing jobs by focusing on minimizing the physical strain on the worker by structuring the physical work environment around the way the body works.

bona fide occupational qualification (BFOQ) A qualification that is absolutely required in order for an individual to be able to successfully do a particular job.

broadbanding Combining multiple pay levels into one.

burnout Constant lack of interest and motivation to perform one's job.

business necessity When a particular practice is necessary for the safe and efficient operation of the business and when there is a specific business purpose for applying a particular standard that may, in fact, be discriminatory.

business skills The analytical and quantitative skills—including in-depth knowledge of how the business works and its budgeting and strategic planning processes—that are necessary for a manager to understand and contribute to the profitability of the organization.

career As defined by Douglas Hall, the individually perceived sequence of attitudes and behaviors associated with work-related experiences and activities over the span of the person's life.

centralization Degree to which decision making is concentrated within the organization.

coaching The process of giving motivational feedback to maintain and improve performance.

COBRA A law that requires employers to offer to maintain health insurance on individuals who leave their employment (for a period of time).

cognitive ability test An assessment of general intelligence or of some type of aptitude for a particular job.

cohesiveness An intent and desire for group members to stick together in their actions.

collective bargaining The negotiation process resulting in a contract between union employees and management that covers employment conditions.

communication The process of transmitting information and meaning.

compensation The total of an employee's pay and benefits

compensation system Anything that an employee may value and desire and that the employer is willing and able to offer in exchange.

compensatory damages Monetary damages awarded by the court that compensate the injured person for losses.

compensatory selection model Model allowing an individual to do poorly on one test but make up for that poor grade by doing exceptionally well on other tests.

complexity Degree to which different parts of the organization are segregated from one another.

conceptual and design skills The ability to evaluate a situation, identify alternatives, select a reasonable alternative, and make a decision to implement a solution to a problem.

conflict The act of being opposed to another.

construct validity An assessment that measures a theoretical concept or trait that is not directly observable.

constructive discharge When an employee is put under such extreme pressure by management that continued employment becomes intolerable and, as a result, the employee quits, or resigns from the organization.

content validity An assessment of whether a test measures knowledge or understanding of the items it is supposed to measure.

corporate social responsibility The concept that organizations have a duty to all societal stakeholders to operate in a manner that takes each of their needs into account.

cost center A division or department that brings in no revenue or profit for the organization—running this function only costs the organization money.

creativity A basic ability to think in unique and different ways and apply those thought processes to existing problems.

criterion-related validity An assessment of the ability of a test to measure some other factor related to the test.

critical incidents method A performance appraisal method in which a manager keeps a written record of the positive and negative performance of employees throughout the performance period.

cyber security The use of tools and processes to protect organizational computer systems and networks.

data analytics Process of accessing large amounts of data in order to analyze those data and gain insight into significant trends or patterns within organizations or industries.

defined benefit plan A plan providing the retiree with a specific amount and type of benefits that will be available when the individual retires.

defined contribution plan A plan providing only the amount of funds that will go into a retirement account, not what the employee will receive upon retirement.

delayering The process of changing the company structure to get rid of some of the vertical hierarchy (reporting levels) in an organization.

disability A physical or mental impairment that substantially limits one or more major life activities, a record of having such an impairment, or being regarded as having such an impairment.

discipline Corrective action designed to get employees to meet standards and the code of conduct.

discrimination The act of making distinctions or choosing one thing over another; in HR, it is making distinctions among people.

disparate impact When an officially neutral employment practice disproportionately excludes the members of a protected group; it is generally considered to be unintentional, but intent is irrelevant.

disparate treatment When individuals in similar situations are intentionally treated differently and the different treatment is based on an individual's membership in a protected class.

divergent thinking The ability to find many possible solutions to a particular problem, including unique, untested solutions.

diversity The existence of differences—in HRM, it deals with different types of people in an organization.

EAP A set of counseling and other services provided to employees that help them to resolve personal issues that may affect their work.

economic value added (EVA) Measure of profits that remain after the cost of capital has been deducted from operating profits.

effectiveness A function of getting the job done whenever and however it must be done.

efficiency A function of how many organizational resources we used in getting the job done.

empathy Being able to put yourself in another person's place—to understand not only what that person is saying but why the individual is communicating that information to you.

employee development Ongoing education to improve knowledge and skills for present and future jobs.

employee engagement A combination of job satisfaction, ability, and a willingness to perform for the organization at a high level and over an extended period of time.

employee health The state of physical and psychological wellness in the workforce.

employment-at-will Concept allowing the company or the worker to break the work relationship at any point in time, with or without any particular reason, as long as in doing so, no law is violated.

equity theory Theory that employees are motivated when the ratio of their perceived outcomes to inputs is at least roughly equal to that of other referent individuals.

ergonomics According to OSHA, "the science of fitting workplace conditions and job demands to the capabilities of the working population."

essential functions The fundamental duties of the position.

ethics The application of a set of values and principles in order to make the right, or good, choice.

EWP Plans designed to cater to the employee's physical, instead of psychological, welfare through education and training programs.

expatriate An employee who leaves their home country to go work in another country.

expectancy theory A theory proposing that employees are motivated when they believe they can accomplish a task and that the rewards for doing so are worth the effort.

experience rating A measure of how often claims are made against an insurance policy.

external recruiting The process of engaging individuals from the labor market outside the firm to apply for a job.

extinction The lack of response, either positive or negative, in order to avoid reinforcing an undesirable behavior.

fitness-for-duty test A test identifying whether or not an employee is physically capable at a particular point in time of performing a specific type of work.

Foreign Corrupt Practices Act Law barring US-based or US-listed companies from bribing foreign officials in exchange for business.

formalization Degree to which jobs are standardized within an organization, meaning the degree to which we have created policies, procedures, and rules that "program" the jobs of the employees.

Four-Fifths Rule A test used by various federal courts, the Department of Labor, and the EEOC to determine whether disparate impact exists in an employment test.

golden parachutes Provision for executives who are dismissed from a merged or acquired firm of typically large lump sum payments on dismissal.

graphic rating scale form A performance appraisal checklist form on which a manager simply rates performance on a continuum such as excellent, good, average, fair, and poor.

grievance A formal complaint concerning pay, working conditions, or violation of some other factor in a collective bargaining agreement.

gross negligence A serious failure to exercise care in the work environment.

high-deductible health plan (HDHP) A "major medical" insurance plan that protects against catastrophic health care costs and in most cases is paid for by the employer.

HMO A health care plan that provides both health maintenance services and medical care as part of the plan.

hostile work environment Harassment that occurs when someone's behavior at work creates an environment that is sexual in nature and that makes it difficult for someone of a particular sex to work in that environment.

hoteling When an organization uses a software program that allows employees to "reserve" office space for particular parts of the workweek when they will need it.

HR forecasting Identifying the estimated supply and demand for the different types of human resources in the organization over some future period, based on analysis of past and present demand.

HSA or MSA A plan allowing the employer and employee to fund a medical savings account from which the employee can pay medical expenses each year with pretax dollars.

human relations skills The ability to understand, communicate, and work well with individuals and groups through developing effective relationships.

human resource information systems (HRIS) Interacting database systems that aim at generating and delivering HR information and allow us to automate some human resource management functions.

human resources (HR) The people within an organization.

illegal discrimination The act of making distinctions that harm people and that are based on those people's membership in a protected class.

Information Age An era that began around 1980, in which information became one of the main products used in organizations; it is characterized by exponential increases in available information in all industries.

innovation The act of creating useful processes or products based on creative thought processes.

interest test A test measuring a person's intellectual curiosity and motivation in a particular field.

internal recruiting Filling job openings with current employees or people the employees know.

job analysis The process used to identify the work performed and the working conditions for each of the jobs within our organizations.

job characteristics model A conceptual framework for designing or enriching jobs based on core job characteristics.

job description Identification of the major tasks, duties, and responsibilities that are components of a job.

job design The process of identifying tasks that each employee is responsible for completing, as well as identifying how those tasks will be accomplished.

job evaluation The process of determining the worth of each position relative to the other positions within the organization.

job expansion The process of making jobs broader, with less repetition. Jobs can be expanded through rotation, enlargement, and enrichment.

job relatedness When a test for employment is a legitimate measure of an individual's ability to do the essential functions of a job.

job satisfaction The feeling of well-being that we experience in our jobs—basically whether or not we like what we do and the immediate environment surrounding us and our jobs.

job simplification The process of eliminating or combining tasks and/or changing the work sequence to improve performance.

job specification Identification of the qualifications of a person who should be capable of doing the job tasks noted in the job description.

Just Cause A set of standard tests for fairness in disciplinary actions—tests that were originally utilized in union grievance arbitrations.

knowledge workers Workers who "use their head more than their hands" and who gather and interpret information to improve a product or process for their organizations.

labor market The external pool of candidates from which we draw our recruits.

labor relations The interactions between management and unionized employees.

layoff A process of terminating a group of employees, usually due to some business downturn or perhaps a technological change, with intent to improve organizational efficiency and effectiveness.

learning Any relatively permanent change in behavior that occurs as a result of experience or practice.

line managers The individuals who create, manage, and maintain the people and organizational processes that create whatever it is that the business sells.

management by objectives (MBO) method A process in which managers and employees jointly set objectives for the employees, periodically evaluate performance, and reward employees according to the results.

management counseling The process of giving employees feedback (so they realize that a problem is affecting their job performance) and referring employees with problems that cannot be managed within the work structure to the organization's employee assistance program.

marginal job functions Those functions that may be performed on the job but need not be performed by all holders of the job.

mechanistic job design Designing jobs around the concepts of task specialization, skill simplification, and repetition.

merit pay A program to reward top performers with increases in their annual wage that carry over from year to year.

minimum wage The lowest hourly rate of pay generally permissible by federal law.

mission statement A statement laying out our expectation of what we're going to do in order to become the organization that we have envisioned.

motivation The willingness to achieve organizational objectives.

motivational job design Designing jobs by focusing on the job characteristics that affect the psychological meaning and motivational potential of the job; this approach views attitudinal variables as the most important outcomes of job design.

multiple-hurdle selection model Model requiring that each applicant must pass a particular selection test in order to go on to the next test.

narrative method or form Method in which the manager is required to write a statement about the employee's performance.

needs assessment The process of analyzing the difference between what is currently occurring within a job or jobs and what is required— either now or in the future— based on the organization's operations and strategic goals.

negative reinforcement Withdrawal of a harmful thing from the environment in response to a positive action on the part of the subject.

negligent hire A legal concept that says if the organization hires someone who may pose a danger to coworkers, customers, suppliers, or other third parties, and if that person then harms someone else in the course of working for the company, then the company can be held liable for the individual's actions.

objectives Statements of what is to be accomplished in singular, specific, and measurable terms, with a target date.

onshoring The process of shuttering operations in other countries and bringing work back to the home country.

organizational culture The values, beliefs, and assumptions about appropriate behavior that members of an organization share.

organizational structure The way in which an organization groups its resources to accomplish its mission.

orientation The process of introducing new employees to the organization and their jobs.

OUCH test A rule of thumb rule used whenever you are contemplating any employment action, to maintain fairness and equity for all of your employees or applicants.

outsourcing The process of hiring another organization to do work that was previously done within the host organization.

overtime A higher than minimum, federally mandated wage, required for nonexempt employees if they work more than a certain number of hours in a week.

parochialism A narrow-minded view of the world with an inability to recognize individual differences.

pattern or practice discrimination When a person or group engages in a sequence of actions over a significant period of time that is intended to deny the rights provided by Title VII of the 1964 CRA to a member of a protected class.

pay structure A hierarchy of jobs and their rates of pay within the organization.

PBGC A governmental corporation established within the Department of Labor whose purpose is to insure retirement funds from failure.

perceptual-motor job design Designing jobs with tasks that remain within the worker's normal mental capabilities and limitations.

performance appraisal The ongoing process of evaluating employee performance.

performance management The process of identifying, measuring, managing, and developing the performance of the human resources in an organization.

386   FUNDAMENTALS OF HUMAN RESOURCE MANAGEMENT

perquisites Extra financial benefits usually provided to top employees in many businesses.

personality test A test measuring the psychological traits or characteristics of applicants to determine suitability for performance in a specific type of job.

physical test A test designed to ensure that applicants are capable of performing on the job in ways defined by the job specification and description.

positive reinforcement Providing a reward in return for a constructive action on the part of the subject.

preferred provider organizations (PPOs) A kind of hybrid between traditional fee-for-service plans and HMOs.

principles Basic application of our values.

productivity The amount of output that an organization gets per unit of input, with human input usually expressed in terms of units of time.

productivity center A revenue center that enhances the profitability of the organization through enhancing the productivity of the people within the organization.

profit sharing programs Programs that provide a portion of company proceeds over a specific period of time (usually either quarterly or annually) to the employees of the firm through a bonus payment.

progressive discipline A process in which the employer provides the employee with opportunities to correct poor behavior before terminating them.

punishment The application of an adverse consequence, or the removal of a reward, in order to decrease an unwanted behavior.

punitive damages Monetary damages awarded by the court that are designed to punish an injuring party that has intentionally inflicted harm on others.

qualitative forecasting The use of nonquantitative methods to forecast the future, usually based on the knowledge of a pool of experts in a subject or an industry.

quantitative forecast Utilizing mathematics to forecast future events based on historical data.

quid pro quo harassment Harassment that occurs when some type of benefit or punishment is made contingent upon the employee submitting to sexual advances.

race norming When different groups of people have different scores designated as "passing" grades on a test for employment.

ranking A performance appraisal method that is used to evaluate employee performance from best to worst.

rate range The maximum, minimum, and midpoint of pay for a certain group of jobs.

ratio analysis The process of reviewing historical data and calculating specific proportions between a business factor (such as production) and the number of employees needed.

realistic job preview (RJP) A review of all of the tasks and requirements of the job, both good and bad.

reasonable accommodation An accommodation made by an employer to allow someone who is disabled but otherwise qualified to do the essential functions of a job to be able to perform that job.

reasonable person The "average" person who would look at the situation and its intensity to determine whether the accused person was wrong in their actions.

recruiting The process of creating a reasonable pool of qualified candidates for a job opening.

regression analysis A statistical technique that identifies the relationship between a series of variable data points for use in forecasting future variables.

reliability The consistency of a test measurement.

remediation The correction of a deficiency or failure in a process or procedure.

responsibility The obligation to answer for something/someone—the duty to carry out an assignment to a satisfactory conclusion.

results A measure of the goals achieved through a work process.

retaliation A situation where the organization takes an "adverse employment action" against an employee because the employee brought discrimination charges against the organization or supported someone who brought discrimination charges against the company.

return on investment (ROI) Measure of the financial return we receive because of something that we do to invest in our organization or its people.

revenue centers Divisions or departments that generate monetary returns for the organization.

reverse discrimination Discrimination against members of the majority group by an organization, generally resulting from affirmative action policies within an organization.

right-to-sue A notice from the EEOC, issued if it elects not to prosecute an individual discrimination complaint within the agency, that gives the recipient the right to go directly to the courts with the complaint.

Safety Data Sheets Documents that provide information on a hazardous chemical and its characteristics.

selection The process of choosing the best-qualified applicant who was recruited for a given job.

self-efficacy Whether or not a person believes that they have the capability to do something or attain a particular goal.

serious misconduct Intentional behavior that has the potential to cause great harm to another or to the company.

sexual harassment "Unwelcome sexual advances, requests for sexual favors, and other verbal or physical conduct of a sexual nature constitutes sexual harassment when submission to or rejection of this conduct explicitly or implicitly affects an individual's employment, unreasonably interferes with an individual's work performance or creates an intimidating, hostile or offensive work environment."

simulation A test where a candidate is put into a high-pressure situation in a controlled environment so that the danger and cost are limited.

skills test An assessment instrument designed to determine if you have the ability to apply a particular knowledge set.

social loafers Individuals who avoid providing their maximum effort in group settings because it is difficult to pick out individual performance.

Society for Human Resource Management (SHRM) The largest and most recognized of the HRM advocacy organizations in the United States.

staff managers Individuals who advise line managers in some field of expertise.

stereotyping Mentally classifying a person into an affinity group and then identifying the person as having the same assumed characteristics as the group.

strategy A plan of action designed to achieve a particular set of objectives.

stress The body's reaction to environmental demands.

stressors Factors that may, if extreme, cause people to feel overwhelmed by anxiety, tension, and/or pressure.

strike A collective work stoppage by members of a union that is intended to put pressure on an employer.

sustainability Meeting the needs of the current generation without compromising the ability of future generations to meet their needs.

technical skills The ability to use methods and techniques to perform a task.

360-degree evaluation An evaluation that analyzes individuals' performance from all sides—from their supervisor's viewpoint, from their subordinates' viewpoint, from their customers (if applicable), from their peers, and from their own self-evaluation.

trade blocs Groups of countries who form an association for the purpose of facilitating movement of goods across national borders.

traditional health care plans Plans that cover a set percentage of fees for medical services—for either doctors or in-patient care.

training The process of teaching employees the skills necessary to perform a job.

traits The physical or psychological characteristics of a person.

trend analysis A process of reviewing historical items such as revenues and relating changes in those items to some business factor to form a predictive chart.

trust Faith in the character and actions of another.

turnover The permanent loss of workers from the organization.

undue hardship When the level of difficulty for an organization to provide accommodations, determined by looking at the nature and cost of the accommodation and the overall financial resources of the facility, becomes a significant burden on the organization.

Uniform Guidelines on Employee Selection Procedures (UGESP) Guidelines that provide information that can be used to avoid discriminatory hiring practices as well as discrimination in other employment decisions.

validity The extent to which a test measures what it claims to measure.

values Our basic concepts of good and bad, or right and wrong.

variable pay Compensation that depends on some measure of individual or group performance or results in order to be awarded.

vesting A maximum amount of time beyond which the employee will have unfettered access to their retirement funds, both employee contributions and employer contributions.

vision What we expect to become as an organization at a particular point in time in the future.

wage compression When new employees require higher starting pay than the historical norm, causing narrowing of the pay gap between experienced and new employees.

work sample A test conducted by providing a sample of the work that the candidate would perform on the job and asking the candidate to perform the tasks under some type of controlled conditions.

workflow analysis The tool that we use to identify what has to be done within the organization to produce a product or service.

workplace safety The physical protection of people from injury or illness while on the job.

workplace security The management of personnel, equipment, and facilities in order to protect them.

yield ratio A calculation of how many people make it through the recruiting step to the next step in the hiring process.

●●● Notes

CHAPTER 1

1. A.C. Cosper, "How to Be Great," *Entrepreneur* (March 2010), p. 12.
2. J.C. Santora, "Quality Management and Manufacturing Performance: Does Success Depend on Firm Culture?" *Academy of Management Perspective* (2009), 23(2), pp. 103–105.
3. R.S. Rubin, E.C. Dierdorff, "On the Road to Abilene: Time to Manage Agreement About MBA Curricular Relevance," *Academy of Management Learning & Education* (2011), 10(1), pp. 148–161.
4. G. Colvin, "Ignore These Insights at Your Peril," *Fortune* (October 28, 2013), p. 85.
5. B.A. Campbell, R. Coff, D. Kryscynski, "Rethinking Sustained Competitive Advantage From Human Capital," *Academy of Management Review* (2012), 37(3), pp. 376–395.
6. I.S. Fulmer, R.E. Ployhart, "Our Most Important Asset: A Multidisciplinary/Multilevel Review of Human Capital Valuation for Research and Practice," *Journal of Management* (2014), 40(1), pp. 161–192.
7. A. Bryant, "Google's Quest to Build a Better Boss," *The New York Times* (March 13, 2011), p. BU-1.
8. A. Fox, "Raising Engagement," *HR Magazine* (May 2010), p. 36.
9. A. Edmans, "Does the Stock Market Fully Value Intangibles? Employee Satisfaction and Equity Prices," *Journal of Financial Economics* (September 2009), 101(3), pp. 621–640.
10. R. Rubin, E. Dierdorff, "Building a Better MBA: From a Decade of Critique Toward a Decennium of Creation," *Academy of Management Learning and Education* (2013), 12(1), pp. 125–141.
11. T.T. Baldwin, J.R. Pierce, R.C. Joines, S. Farouk, "The Elusiveness of Applied Management Knowledge: A Critical Challenge for Management Educators," *Academy of Management Learning & Education* (2011), 10(4), pp. 583–605. doi:10.5465/amle.2010.0045
12. R. Grossman, E. Salas, D. Pavlas, M.A. Rosen, "Using Instructional Features to Enhance Demonstration-Based Training in Management Education," *Academy of Management Learning & Education* (2013), 12(2), pp. 219–243. doi:10.5465/amle.2011.0527
13. K.W. Mossholder, H.A. Richardson, R.P. Settoon, "Human Resource Systems and Helping in Organizations: A Relational Perspective," *Academy of Management Review* (2011), 36(1), pp. 33–52.
14. "HR Departments Get New Star Power at Some Firms," *The Wall Street Journal*, http://online.wsj.com/news/articles/SB121417392782995251 (retrieved December 26, 2013).
15. http://www.successfactors.com/en_us/company/press-releases/2013/companies-with-chief-hr-officers-consistently-outperform-peers.html (retrieved January 20, 2014).
16. http://www.shrm.org/Research/SurveyFindings/Articles/Documents/SHRM-Challenges-Facing-HR-Future-2022-FINAL.pptx (retrieved December 26, 2013).
17. J.G. Proudfoot, P.J. Corr, D.E. Guest, G. Dunn, "Cognitive-Behavioural Training to Change Attributional Style Improves Employee Well-being, Job Satisfaction, Productivity, and Turnover," *Personality and Individual Differences* (2009), 46(2), pp. 147–153.
18. P.E. Spector, *Job Satisfaction: Application, Assessment, Causes and Consequences* (London, UK: Blackwell, 1997).
19. http://www.shrm.org/hrdisciplines/staffingmanagement/Articles/Pages/More-Voluntary-Exits (retrieved January 20, 2014).
20. A.J. Nyberg, R.E. Ployhart, "Context-Emergent Turnover (CED) Theory: A Theory of Collective Turnover." *Academy of Management Review* (2013), 38(1), pp. 109–131. doi:10.5465/amr.2011.0201
21. M.S. Christian, A.J. Ellis, "Examining the Effects of Sleep Deprivation on Workplace Deviance: A Self-Regulatory Perspective," *Academy of Management Journal* (2011), 54(5), pp. 913–934. doi:10.5465/amj.2010.0179
22. https://www.shrm.org/Publications/hrmagazine/EditorialContent/2011/0911/Pages/0911grossman.aspx (retrieved January 20, 2014).
23. http://www.gallup.com/poll/150026/unhealthy-workers-absenteeism-costs-153-billion.aspx (retrieved January 20, 2014).
24. H. Nguyen, M. Groth, A. Johnson, "When the Going Gets Tough, the Tough Keep Working: Impact of Emotional Labor on Absenteeism," *Journal of Management* (2013), published online. doi:10.1177/0149206313490026
25. R. Rubin, E. Dierdorff, "On the Road to Abilene: Time to Manage Agreement About MBA Curricular Relevance," *Academy of Management Learning & Education* (2011), 10(1), pp. 148–161.
26. E.E. Gordon, *The 2010 Meltdown: Solving the Impending Jobs Crisis* (Westport, CT: Praeger, 2005).
27. B. Eversole, D. Venneberg, C. Crowder, "Creating a Flexible Organizational Culture to Attract and Retain Talented Workers Across Generations," *Advances in Developing Human Resources* (2012), 14(4), pp. 607–625.
28. S.A. Mohrman, E.E. Lawler I, "Generating Knowledge That Drives Change," *Academy of Management Perspectives* (2012), 26(1), pp. 41–51. doi:10.5465/amp.2011.0141
29. C. Phillipson, "Commentary: The Future of Work and Retirement," *Human Relations* (January 2013), 66, pp.143–153.
30. http://www.bls.gov/opub/ted/2012/ted_20120501.htm (retrieved January 24, 2014).
31. H.J. Walker, T. Bauer, M. Cole, J. Bernerth, H. Feild, J. Short, "Is This How I Will Be Treated? Reducing Uncertainty Through Recruitment Interactions," *Academy of Management Journal* (2013), 56(5), pp. 1325–1347.
32. Definition developed by the Brundtland Commission. Cited from Colvin Interview of Linda Fisher, *Fortune* (November 23, 2009), pp. 45–50.
33. R.S. Rubin, E.C. Dierdorff, "On the Road to Abilene: Time to Manage Agreement About MBA Curricular Relevance," *Academy of Management Learning & Education* (2011), 10(1), pp. 148–161.
34. D.R. Laker, J.L. Powell, "The Differences Between Hard and Soft Skills and Their Relative Impact on Training Transfer," *Human Resource Development Quarterly* (2011), 22(1), pp. 111–122.
35. A.C. Cosper, "How to Be Great," *Entrepreneur* (March 2010), p. 12.
36. E.M. Wong, M.E. Ormiston, P.E. Tetlock, "The Effects of Top Management Team Integrative Complexity and Decentralized Decision Making on Corporate Social Performance," *Academy of Management Journal* (2011), 54(6), pp. 1207–1228.
37. R.S. Rubin, E.C. Dierdorff, "How Relevant Is the MBA? Assessing the Alignment of Required Curricula and Required Managerial Competencies," *Academy of Management Learning & Education* (2009), 8(5), pp. 208–224.
38. http://www.shrm.org/about/pages/default.aspx (retrieved December 30, 2013).

39. http://www.shrm.org/about/pressroom/PressReleases/Pages/AssuranceofLearningAssessment.aspx (retrieved December 30, 2013).

40. Association for Talent Development, http://www.astd.org (retrieved December 30, 2013).

41. WorldatWork, www.worldatwork.org (retrieved May 28, 2010).

42. http://www.gallup.com/strategicconsulting/163007/state-american-workplace.aspx (retrieved January 20, 2014).

43. S. Abraham, "Job Satisfaction as an Antecedent to Employee Engagement," SIES Journal of Management (2012), 8(2), pp. 27–36.

44. http://go.globoforce.com/rs/globoforce/images/WP_Engagement_Globoforce.pdf (retrieved January 21, 2014).

45. http://go.globoforce.com/rs/globoforce/images/WP_Engagement_Globoforce.pdf (retrieved January 21, 2014).

46. K. Wollard, "'Quiet Desperation': Another Perspective on Employee Engagement," Advances in Developing Human Resources (2011), 13(4), pp. 526–537.

47. R. Berger Levinson, "Gender-Based Affirmative Action and Reverse Gender Bias: Beyond Gratz, Parents Involved, and Ricci," Harvard Journal of Law and Gender (2010), 34.

48. E. Rusli, "Zynga's Tough Culture Risks a Talent Drain," The New York Times, http://dealbook.nytimes.com/2011/11/27/zyngas-tough-culture-risks-a-talent-drain/?_r=0 (retrieved December 29, 2013).

49. Ibid.

50. Ibid.

51. Ibid.

CHAPTER 2

1. P. Ghemawat, "Finding Your Strategy in the New Landscape," Harvard Business Review (2010), 88(3), pp. 54–60.

2. H. Steenhuis, E. De Bruijn, H. Heerkens, "New Entrants and Overcapacity: Lessons From Regional Aircraft Manufacturing," International Journal of Technology Transfer and Commercialisation (2010), 9(4), pp. 342–372. doi:10.1504/IJTTC.2010.0354

3. Institute for Energy Research, "Overcapacity Plagues Solar Industry" (January 3, 2012), http://www.instituteforenergyresearch.org/2012/01/03/overcapacity-plagues-solar-industry (retrieved September 23, 2014).

4. J. Hökerberg, "China Infected With Overcapacity" (July 26, 2013), http://brightmarketinsight.com/headlines/china-infected-with-overcapacity (retrieved September 23, 2014).

5. C. Dibrell, J. Craig, D. Neubaum, "Linking the Formal Strategic Planning Process, Planning Flexibility, and Innovativeness to Firm Performance," Journal of Business Research (2014), 67, http://www.academia.edu/7908997/Linking_the_formal_strategic_planning_process_planning_flexibility_and_innovativeness_to_firm_performance (retrieved September 23, 2014). doi:10.1016/j.jbusres.2013.10.011

6. W. Zheng, B. Yang, G. McLean, "Linking Organizational Culture, Structure, Strategy, and Organizational Effectiveness: Mediating Role of Knowledge Management," Journal of Business Research (2010), 63(7), pp. 763–771. doi:10.1016/j.jbusres.2009.06.005

7. J. Shin, M.S. Taylor, M.G. Seo, "Resources for Change: The Relationships of Organizational Inducements and Psychological Resilience to Employees' Attitudes and Behaviors Toward Organizational Change," Academy of Management Journal (2012), 55(3), pp. 727–748.

8. M. Kibbeling, H. van der Bij, A. van Weele, "Market Orientation and Innovativeness in Supply Chains: Supplier's Impact on Customer Satisfaction," Journal of Product Innovation Management (2013), 30(3), pp. 500–515.

9. S. Droege, M. Lane, M. Casile, "A Tumultuous Decade in Thailand: Competitive Dynamics Among Domestic Banks and Multi-national Entrants in an Emerging Market," International Journal of Business and Emerging Markets (2013), 5(4), pp. 371–387. doi:10.1504/IJBEM.2013.056814

10. R. King, "War for Tech Talent Heats Up," The Wall Street Journal blog (July 23, 2012), http://blogs.wsj.com/cio/2012/07/23/war-for-tech-talent-heats-up/.

11. K.D. Dea Roglio, G. Light, "Executive MBA Programs: The Development of the Reflective Executive," Academy of Management Learning & Education (2009), 8(2), pp. 156–173.

12. H.R. Huhman, "As War for Talent Heats Up, So Does Employee Poaching," Business Insider (March 11, 2011).

13. Inc., "LivingSocial" [company profile], http://www.inc.com/profile/livingsocial/ (retrieved February 28, 2014).

14. M.J. Canyan, "Executive Compensation and Incentives," Academy of Management Perspectives (2006), 20(1), pp. 25–44.

15. E.M. Wong, M.E. Ormiston, P.E. Tetlock, "The Effects of Top Management Team Integrative Complexity and Decentralized Decision Making on Corporate Social Performance," Academy of Management Journal (2011), 54(6), pp. 1207–1228.

16. D. Charles, "Pepsi Pressured to Fight Big Sugar's 'Land Grab,'" NPR blog (November 23, 2013), http://www.npr.org/blogs/thesalt/2013/11/23/246753281/pepsi-pressured-to-fight-big-sugar-s-land-grab/.

17. A. McWilliams, D. Siegel, "Corporate Social Responsibility: A Theory of the Firm Perspective," Academy of Management Review (2001), (26)1, pp. 117–127.

18. G.F. Keller, "The Influence of Military Strategies on Business Planning," International Journal of Business and Management (May 2008), p. 129.

19. C. Wolf, S. Floyd, "Strategic Planning Research: Toward a Theory-Driven Agenda," Journal of Management, published online (March 26, 2013), doi:10.1177/0149206313478185

20. P.M. Wright, G.C. McMahan, "Exploring Human Capital: Putting 'Human' Back Into Strategic Human Resource Management," Human Resource Management Journal (2011), 21(2), pp. 93–104.

21. I. Ugboro, K. Obeng, O. Spann, "Strategic Planning as an Effective Tool of Strategic Management in Public Sector Organizations: Evidence From Public Transit Organizations," Administration and Society (2011), 43(1), pp. 87–123.

22. J. Welch, S. Welch, "Inventing the Future Now," Businessweek (May 11, 2009), p. 76.

23. W. Bennis, "Acting the Part of a Leader," Businessweek (September 14, 2009), p. 80.

24. University of Arkansas Little Rock, http://http://ualr.edu/cob/about-us/mission/ (retrieved March 1, 2014).

25. The American Heritage College Dictionary (New York: Houghton Mifflin, 1993).

26. University of Arkansas Little Rock, http://ualr.edu/cob/about-us/mission/ (retrieved March 1, 2014).

27. I. Jacobs, J. Jaffe, P.L. Hegaret. (2012). How the Open Web Platform Is Transforming Industry. IEEE internet computing, 16(6).

28. G. Hirst, D. Van Knippenberg, J. Zhou, "A Cross-Level Perspective on Employee Creativity: Goal Orientation, Team Learning Behavior, and Individual Creativity," Academy of Management Journal (2009), Vol. 52, No. 2, pp. 280-293.

29. L. Dragoni, P.E. Tesluk, J.E.A. Russell, I. Oh, "Understanding Managerial Development: Integrating Developmental Assignments, Learning Orientation, and Access to Developmental Opportunities in Predicting Managerial Competencies," Academy of Management Journal (2009), Vol. 52, No. 4, pp. 731-742.

30. http://world.honda.com/investors/policy/ceo/ (retrieved March 1, 2014).

31. http://nikeinc.com/news/nike-inc-announces-target-for-fy17-revenues-of-36-billion-2nd-release (retrieved March 1, 2014).

32. "Dell," *Wall Street Journal* (February 27, 2009), p. A1.

33. K. Stock, "Company News: Corporate Inversions, Jimmy Choo, Tesco, Philips, General Motors." *BusinessWeek* (September 25, 2014), online. http://www.bloomberg.com/bw/articles/2014-09-25/company-news-corporate-inversions-jimmy-choo-tesco-philips-general-motors.

34. Burger King Website (www.burgerking.com) (retrieved January 5, 2015).

35. M. Porter, *Competitive Strategy: Techniques for Analyzing Industries and Competitors* (New York, NY: Free Press, 1980), p. 15.

36. G. Anderson, "Can Walmart Beat Dollar Stores on Their Own Turf?" Forbes blog (May 14, 2013), http://www.forbes.com/sites/retailwire/2013/05/14/can-walmart-beat-dollar-stores-on-their-own-turf/.

37. http://www.brandchannel.com/home/post/Tata-Nano-Overhaul-101513.aspx (retrieved March 1, 2014).

38. H.L. Smith, R. Discenza, K.G. Baker, "Building Sustainable Success in Art Galleries: An Exploratory Study of Adaptive Strategies," *Journal of Small Business Strategy* (2005/2006), 16(2), pp. 29–41.

39. N. Byrnes, "Why Dr. Pepper Is in the Pink of Health," *Businessweek* (October 26, 2009), p. 59.

40. Y.H. Hsieh, H.M. Chen, "Strategic Fit Among Business Competitive Strategy, Human Resource Strategy, and Reward System," *Academy of Strategic Management Journal* (2011), 10(2).

41. Ibid.

42. J.H. Marler, "Strategic Human Resource Management in Context: A Historical and Global Perspective," *The Academy of Management Perspectives* (2012), 26(2), pp. 6–11.

43. M.S. Wood, "Does One Size Fit All? The Multiple Organizational Forms Leading to Successful Academic Entrepreneurship," *Entrepreneurship Theory and Practice* (2009), 33(4), pp. 929–947.

44. P. Fiss, E. Zajac, "The Symbolic Management of Strategic Change: Sensegiving via Framing and Decoupling," *Academy of Management Journal* (2006), 49(6), pp. 1173–1193.

45. R. Adhikari, "Nadella Begins Microsoft Leadership Transformation," *E-Commerce Times* (March 3, 2014), http://www.ecommercetimes.com/story/80075.html.

46. M.K. Fiegener, "Matching Business-Level Strategic Controls to Strategy: Impact on Control System Effectiveness," *Journal of Applied Business Research (JABR)* (2011), 10(1), pp. 25–34.

47. Ibid.

48. M. Guadalupe, H. Li, J. Wulf, "Who Lives in the C-Suite? Organizational Structure and the Division of Labor in Top Management," *Management Science* (2013).

49. P.M. Figueroa, "Risk Communication Surrounding the Fukushima Nuclear Disaster: An Anthropological Approach," *Asia Europe Journal* (2013), 11(1), pp. 53–64.

50. B. Gates, "The Best Advice I Ever Got," *Fortune* (July 6, 2009), p. 43.

51. P. Drucker, *Management: Tasks, Responsibilities, Practices* (Oxford, UK: Butterworth-Heinemann, 1999), p. 546.

52. Lashinsky, "Microsoft Culture Must Change, Chairman Says," *Fortune* (February 27, 2014), http://tech.fortune.cnn.com/2014/02/27/microsoft-culture-must-change-chairman-says/.

53. L.Z. Wu, H.K. Kwan, F.H.K. Yim, R. Chiu, X. He, "CEO Ethical Leadership and Corporate Social Responsibility: A Moderated Mediation Model," *Journal of Business Ethics* (February 2014), published online.

54. D. West, lecture at Springfield College (November 23, 2009).

55. P. Bolton, M.K. Brennermeier, L. Veldkamp, "Leadership, Coordination, and Corporate Culture," *Review of Economic Studies* (2013), 80(2), pp. 512–537.

56. M.J. Culnan, P.J. McHugh, J.I. Zubillaga, "How Large U.S. Companies Can Use Twitter and Other Social Media to Gain Business Value," *MIS Quarterly Executive* (2010), 9(4), pp. 243–259.

57. M.W. DiStaso, T. McCorkindale, D.K. Wright, "How Public Relations Executives Perceive and Measure the Impact of Social Media in Their Organizations," *Public Relations Review* (2011), 37(3), pp. 325–328.

58. K. Steinmetz, "Obama Asks Celebs to Tweet About ObamaCare," *Time* (October 2, 2013), http://swampland.time.com/2013/10/02/obama-asks-celebs-to-tweet-about-obamacare/.

59. M. Lim, "Clicks, Cabs, and Coffee Houses: Social Media and Oppositional Movements in Egypt, 2004–2011," *Journal of Communication* (2012), 62(2), pp. 231–248.

60. S. Cleland, "Google's 'Infringenovation' Secrets," *Forbes* (October 3, 2011), http://www.forbes.com/sites/scottcleland/2011/10/03/googles-infringenovation-secrets/.

61. S. Lohr, "Big Data, Trying to Build Better Workers," *The New York Times* (April 21, 2013), p. BU4.

62. "Big Data: The Next Frontier for Innovation, Competition, and Productivity," *McKinsey Global Institute* (June 2011), p. 23.

63. S. Lohr, "Big Data, Trying to Build Better Workers," *The New York Times* (April 21, 2013), p. BU4.

64. McAfee, E. Brynjolfsson, "Big Data: The Management Revolution," *Harvard Business Review* (October 2012), p. 4.

65. Ibid.

66. J. Schramm, "Future Focus: The Trouble With Algorithms," *HR Magazine* (November 2013), 58(11), p. 80.

67. M. L. Brosnan, C. S. Farley, D. Gartside, H. Tambe, "How Well Do You Know Your Workforce?" Accenture (October 2013), http://www.accenture.com/us-en/outlook/Pages/outlook-journal-2013-how-well-do-you-know-your-workforce-analytics.aspx.

68. Chartered Institute of Personnel and Development, *Talent Analytics and Big Data—The Challenge for HR* (London, UK: CIPD, 2013), p. 2, http://www.oracle.com/us/products/applications/human-capital-management/talent-analytics-and-big-data-2063584.pdf.

69. S. Lohr, "Big Data, Trying to Build Better Workers," *The New York Times* (April 21, 2013), p. BU4.

70. Ibid.

71. http://www.shrm.org/hrdisciplines/staffingmanagement/articles/pages/tapping-talent-analytics-potential.aspx (retrieved March 15, 2014).

72. Boston Consulting Group, "People Management Translates Into Superior Economic Performance," [press release] (August 2, 2012), http://www.bcg.com/media/PressReleaseDetails.aspx?id=tcm:12-110525/.

73. K.W. Mossholder, H.A. Richardson, R.P. Settoon, "Human Resource Systems and Helping in Organizations: A Relational Perspective," *Academy of Management Review* (2011), 36(1), pp. 33–52.

74. D. Mueller, S. Strohmeier, C. Gasper, "HRIS Design Characteristics: Towards a General Research Framework," *3rd European Academic Workshop on Electronic Human Resource Management* (May 2010).

75. S. Pande, P. Khanna, "Leveraging Human Resource Information Systems: Alignment of Business With Technology," *International Journal of Computer Applications* (2012), p. 56.

76. Society for Human Resource Management, http://www.shrm.org/Publications/hrmagazine/EditorialContent/Pages/0808hrsolutions.aspx (retrieved, July 7, 2010).

77. J. Walker, "Companies Trade in Hunch-Based Hiring for Computer Modeling," *The New York Times* (September 20, 2012), p. B1.

78. Wikipedia. (2014). Netflix. Retrieved June 15, 2014 from http://en.wikipedia.org/wiki/Netflix.
79. P. McCord, "How Netflix Reinvented HR," *Harvard Business Review* 92(1/2), pp. 70–76.
80. P. Sikka, Netflix Will Raise Its Prices After Better-Than-Expected Earnings, *MarketRealist.com*. Retrieved from http://marketrealist.com/2014/04/netflix-will-raise-prices-better-expected-earnings/.
81. P. McCord, "How Netflix Reinvented HR," *Harvard Business Review*, 92(1/2), pp. 70–76.
82. Ibid.
83. Ibid.
84. Ibid.

CHAPTER 3

1. S. Nkomo, J. Hoobler, "A Historical Perspective on Diversity Ideologies in the United States: Reflections on Human Resource Management Research and Practice," *Human Resource Management Review* (April 2014), p. 24.
2. J. Hendon, "Hiring and the OUCH Test," *Arkansas Business* (May 3, 2010).
3. http://www.eeoc.gov/policy/docs/qanda_clarify_procedures.html (retrieved May 24, 2014).
4. http://uniformguidelines.com/uniformguidelines.html#18/ (retrieved May 24, 2014).
5. http://www.eeoc.gov/policy/docs/factemployment_procedures.html (retrieved May 24, 2014).
6. http://www.eeoc.gov/laws/statutes/epa.cfm (retrieved July 20, 2010).
7. Ibid.
8. http://www.eeoc.gov/laws/statutes/titlevii.cfm (retrieved May 24, 2014).
9. http://www.eeoc.gov/policy/docs/factemployment_procedures.html (retrieved May 24, 2014).
10. http://www.eeoc.gov/policy/docs/factemployment_procedures.html (retrieved May 24, 2014).
11. http://www.eeoc.gov/laws/statutes/titlevii.cfm (retrieved July 21, 2010).
12. http://www3.ce9.uscourts.gov/jury-instructions/node/182/ (retrieved May 24, 2014).
13. http://www.eeoc.gov/laws/statutes/titlevii.cfm (retrieved May 24, 2014).
14. http://www.eeoc.gov/laws/statutes/titlevii.cfm (retrieved May 24, 2014).
15. http://www.dol.gov/compliance/laws/comp-vevraa.htm (retrieved May 24, 2014).
16. http://www.eeoc.gov/facts/fs-preg.html (retrieved May 24, 2014).
17. http://www.ada.gov/pubs/adastatute08.htm (retrieved May 24, 2014).
18. Ibid.
19. http://www.ada.gov/employmt.htm (retrieved May 24, 2014).
20. http://www.ada.gov/pubs/adastatute08.htm (retrieved May 24, 2014).
21. http://www.eeoc.gov/eeoc/statistics/enforcement/charges.cfm (retrieved May 24, 2014).
22. Civil Rights Act of 1991–Public Law 102-166.
23. http://www.eeoc.gov/employers/remedies.cfm (retrieved May 24, 2014).
24. http://www.eeoc.gov/eeoc/history/35th/thelaw/cra_1991.html (retrieved May 24, 2014).
25. http://www.dol.gov/vets/usc/vpl/usc38.htm#4301/ (retrieved May 24, 2014).
26. http://www.dol.gov/elaws/vets/userra/userra.asp (retrieved May 24, 2014).
27. http://www.dol.gov/vets/usc/vpl/usc38.htm#4301/ (retrieved May 24, 2014).
28. http://www.dol.gov/vets/regs/fedreg/final/2005023960.htm#regs/ (retrieved May 24, 2014).
29. http://www.eeoc.gov/laws/statutes/gina.cfm (retrieved May 24, 2014).
30. http://www.eeoc.gov/laws/statutes/gina.cfm (retrieved May 24, 2014).
31. http://eeoc.gov/eeoc/ (retrieved May 24, 2014).
32. http://eeoc.gov/eeoc/ (retrieved May 24, 2014).
33. http://www.eeoc.gov/employers/eeo1survey/faq.cfm (retrieved May 21, 2014).
34. http://www.eeoc.gov/laws/statutes/titlevii.cfm (retrieved May 24, 2014).
35. http://eeoc.gov/eeoc/statistics/enforcement/charges.cfm (retrieved May 21, 2014).
36. *Pennsylvania State Police v. Suders* (03-95), 542 U.S. 129 (2004), 325 F.3d 432.
37. http://ecfr.gpoaccess.gov/cgi/t/text/text-idx?c=ecfr&tpl=/ecfrbrowse/Title29/29cfr1608_main_02.tpl (retrieved July 21, 2010).
38. http://www.shrm.org/templatestools/hrqa/pages/whenisanaapneeded.aspx (retrieved May 24, 2014).
39. 41 CFR Part 60-1.
40. Ibid.
41. http://www.supremecourt.gov/opinions/12pdf/11-345_l5gm.pdf (retrieved May 25, 2014).
42. http://www.nytimes.com/2014/04/23/us/supreme-court-michigan-affirmative-action-ban.html?_r=0 (retrieved May 25, 2014).
43. Z.T. Kalinoski, D. Steele-Johnson, E.J. Peyton, K.A. Leas, J. Steinke, N.A. Bowling, "A Meta-Analytic Evaluation of Diversity Training Outcomes," *Journal of Organizational Behavior* (2013), 34(8), pp. 1076–1104.
44. A. Joshi, H. Roh, "The Role of Context in Work Team Diversity Research: A Meta-Analytic Review," *Academy of Management Journal* (2009), 52(3), pp. 599–627.
45. E. Kearney, D. Gebert, S.C. Voelpel, "When and How Diversity Benefits Teams: The Importance of Team Members' Need for Cognition," *Academy of Management Journal* (2009), 52(3), pp. 581–598.
46. C.L. Holladay, M.A. Quiñones, "The Influence of Training Focus and Trainer Characteristics on Diversity Training Effectiveness," *Academy of Management Learning & Education* (2008), 7(3), pp. 343–354.
47. S.D. Sidle, "Building a Committed Global Workforce: Does What Employees Want Depend on Culture?" *Academy of Management Perspectives* (2009), 23(1), pp. 79–80.
48. S. Bell et al., "Getting Specific About Demographic Diversity Variable and Team Performance Relationships: A Meta-Analysis," *Journal of Management* (2011), 37(3), pp. 709–743.
49. A.N. Pieterse, D. van Knippenberg, D. van Dierendonck, "Cultural Diversity and Team Performance: The Role of Team Member Goal Orientation," *Academy of Management Journal* (2013), 56(3), pp. 782–804.
50. M. Mayfield, J. Mayfield, "Developing a Scale to Measure the Creative Environment Perceptions: A Questionnaire for Investigating Garden Variety Creativity," *Creativity Research Journal* (2010), 22(2), pp. 162–169.
51. M.A. Runco, S. Acar, "Divergent Thinking as an Indicator of Creative Potential," *Creativity Research Journal* (2012), 24(1), pp. 66–75.
52. F. Stevens, V. Plaut, J. Sanchez-Burks, "Unlocking the Benefits of Diversity," *Journal of Applied Behavioral Science* (2008), 44(1), pp. 116–133.
53. S. Benard, L. Doan, "The Conflict-Cohesion Hypothesis: Past, Present, and Possible Futures," *Advances in Group Processes* (2011), 28, pp. 189–225.
54. E.A. Okoro, M.C. Washington, "Workforce Diversity and Organizational Communication: Analysis of Human Capital Performance and Productivity," *Journal of Diversity Management* (2012), 7(1), pp. 57–62.
55. S.D. Sidle, "Building a Committed Global Workforce: Does What Employees Want Depend on Culture?" *Academy of Management Perspectives* (2009), 23(1), pp. 79–80.
56. http://www.eeoc.gov/facts/fs-sex.html (retrieved May 24, 2014).
57. http://caselaw.lp.findlaw.com/scripts/getcase.pl?court=US&vol=477&invol=57 (retrieved May 24, 2014).
58. http://www.eeoc.gov/policy/docs/current issues.html (retrieved May 24, 2014).
59. http://www.law.cornell.edu/supct/html/96-568.ZO.html (retrieved May 24, 2014).

60. Ibid.
61. Ibid.
62. Ibid.
63. http://www.shrm.org/legalissues/federalresources/pages/headscarf-accommodation-muslim-applicant.aspx (retrieved May 23, 2014).
64. Ibid.
65. http://www.eeoc.gov/eeoc/newsroom/release/4-4-06.cfm (retrieved May 24, 2014).
66. http://www.eeoc.gov/eeoc/plan/2013parhigh_discussion.cfm (retrieved May 24, 2014).
67. http://www.eeoc.gov/eeoc/systemic/ (retrieved May 24, 2014).
68. Ibid.
69. http://www.insidecounsel.com/2012/02/06/labor-increased-litigation-under-the-adaaa/ (retrieved May 23, 2014).
70. Ibid.
71. http://www1.eeoc.gov/eeoc/newsroom/release/5-15-13.cfm (retrieved May 23, 2014).
72. http://www.eeoc.gov/eeoc/newsroom/release/7-30-13a.cfm (retrieved May 23, 2014).

CHAPTER 4

1. A.L. Kallenbert, "The Mismatched Worker: When People Don't Fit Their Jobs," *Academy of Management Perspectives* (2008), 22(1), pp. 24–40.
2. T. Barmby, A. Bryson, B. Eberth, "Human Capital, Matching and Job Satisfaction," *Economics Letters* (2012), 117(3), pp. 548–551.
3. H.C.W. Lau, G.T.S. Ho, K.F. Chu, W. Ho, C.K.M. Lee, "Development of an Intelligent Quality Management System Using Fuzzy Association Rules," *Expert Systems With Applications* (2009), 36(2), pp. 1801–1815.
4. Y. Gil, V. Ratnakar, J. Kim, P.A. González-Calero, P. Groth, J. Moody, E. Deelman, "Wings: Intelligent Workflow-Based Design of Computational Experiments," *IEEE Intelligent Systems* (2011), 26(1), pp. 62–72.
5. A.H. Memon, I.A. Rahman, A.A. Aziz, K. Ravish, N.M. Hanas, "Identifying Construction Resource Factors Affecting Construction Cost: Case of Johor," in *Malaysian Technical Universities International Conference on Engineering & Technology* (2011).
6. O. Henry, "Organisational Conflict and Its Effects on Organisational Performance," *Research Journal of Business Management* (2009), 2(1), pp. 16–24.
7. P. Singh, "Job Analysis for a Changing Workplace," *Human Resource Management Review* (2008), 18(2), pp. 87–89.
8. J.I. Sanchez, E.L. Levine, "The Rise and Fall of Job Analysis and the Future of Work Analysis," *Annual Review of Psychology* (2012), 63, pp. 397–425.
9. http://www.onetcenter.org/overview.html (retrieved March 22, 2015).
10. M. Robinson, "Work Sampling: Methodological Advances and New Applications," *Human Factors and Ergonomics in Manufacturing & Service Industries* (2010), 20(1), pp. 42–60.
11. S.G. Gibson, "Generalized Work Dimension Analysis," in *The Handbook of Work Analysis: Methods, Systems, Applications and Science of Work Measurement in Organizations*, edited by M.A. Wilson, W. Bennett, S.G. Gibson, G.M. Alliger (New York, NY: Taylor & Francis, 2012), pp. 215–230.
12. J. Kilgour, "Job Evaluation Revisited: The Point Factor Method; The Point Factor Method of Job Evaluation Consists of a Large Number of Discretionary Decisions That Result in Something That Appears to Be Entirely Objective and, Even, Scientific," *Compensation & Benefits Review* (July/August 2008), 40, pp. 37–46.
13. S.G. Gibson, "Generalized Work Dimension Analysis," in *The Handbook of Work Analysis: Methods, Systems, Applications and Science of Work Measurement in Organizations*, edited by M.A. Wilson, W. Bennett, S.G. Gibson, G.M. Alliger (New York, NY: Taylor & Francis, 2012), pp. 215–230.
14. M. Robinson, "Work Sampling: Methodological Advances and New Applications," *Human Factors and Ergonomics in Manufacturing & Service Industries* (2010), 20(1), pp. 42–60.
15. S.H. Yun, "Enterprise Human Resource Matching Model Based on Job Analysis and Quality Assessment," in *The 19th International Conference on Industrial Engineering and Engineering Management* (Heidelberg, Germany: Springer, 2013), pp. 761–771.
16. A.C. Keller, N.K. Semmer, "Changes in Situational and Dispositional Factors as Predictors of Job Satisfaction," *Journal of Vocational Behavior* (2013), 83(1), pp. 88–98.
17. J. Lahart, "Moment of Truth for Productivity Boom," *The Wall Street Journal* (May 6, 2010), pp. A1, A16.
18. G.R. Oldham, J.R. Hackman, "Not What It Was and Not What It Will Be: The Future of Job Design Research," *Journal of Organizational Behavior* (2010), 31(2–3), pp. 463–479.
19. F.P. Morgeson, G.J. Medsker, M.A. Campion, "Job and Team Design," in *Handbook of Human Factors and Ergonomics* (2012), edited by Gabriel Salvendy (Hoboken, NJ: Wiley, 2006), pp. 428–457.
20. G.P. McClelland, D.J. Leach, C.W. Clegg, I. McGowan, "Collaborative Crafting in Call Centre Teams," *Journal of Occupational and Organizational Psychology* (2014).
21. R.W. Proctor, K.P.L. Vu, "Cumulative Knowledge and Progress in Human Factors, *Annual Review of Psychology* (2010), 61, pp. 623–651.
22. J.H. Batchelor, K.A. Abston, K. Lawlor, G.F. Burch, "The Job Characteristics Model: An Extension to Entrepreneurial Motivation," *Small Business Institute® Journal* (2014), 10(1), pp. 1–10.
23. D. Liu, T.R. Mitchell, T.W. Lee, B.C. Holtom, T.R. Hinkin, "How Employees Are Out of Step With Coworkers: How Job Satisfaction Trajectory and Dispersion Influence Individual- and Unit-Level Voluntary Turnover," *Academy of Management Journal* (2012), 55(6), pp. 1360–1380.
24. A.M. Grant, "Giving Time, Time After Time: Work Design and Sustained Employee Participation in Corporate Volunteering," *Academy of Management Review* (2012), 37(4), pp. 589–615.
25. S.K. Parker, "Beyond Motivation: Job and Work Design for Development, Health, Ambidexterity, and More," *Annual Review of Psychology* (2014), 65, pp. 661–691.
26. Generations website (www.generations.com) accessed April 9, 2015.
27. T. Woods, "The Best Advice I Ever Got," *Fortune* (July 6, 2009), p. 43.
28. A. Jagoda, "Deskilling as the Dark Side of the Work Specialization," *International Journal of Academic Research* (2013), 5(3).
29. K. Swisher, "A Question of Management," *The Wall Street Journal* (June 2, 2009), p. R4.
30. A.M. Grant, "Giving Time, Time After Time: Work Design and Sustained Employee Participation in Corporate Volunteering," *Academy of Management Review* (2012), 37(4), pp. 589–615.
31. C. Tuna, "Micromanagers Miss Bull's-Eye," *The Wall Street Journal* (November 3, 2008), p. B4.
32. M.R. Barrick, M.K. Mount, N. Li, "The Theory of Purposeful Work Behavior: The Role of Personality, Higher-Order Goals, and Job Characteristics," *Academy of Management Review* (2013), 38(1), pp. 132–153.
33. L. McNall, A. Masuda, J. Nicklin, "Flexible Work Arrangements, Job Satisfaction, and Turnover Intentions: The Mediating Role of Work-to-Family Enrichment," *The Journal of Psychology: Interdisciplinary and Applied Issue* (2010), 144(1), pp. 61–81.
34. A.D. Masuda, S.A. Poelmans, T.D. Allen, P.E. Spector, L.M. Lapierre, C.L. Cooper, . . . I. Moreno-Velazquez, "Flexible Work Arrangements Availability and Their Relationship With

Work-to-Family Conflict, Job Satisfaction, and Turnover Intentions: A Comparison of Three Country Clusters," *Applied Psychology* (2012), 61(1), pp. 1–29.

35. Society for Human Resource Management, "Sample Policy: Flextime," http://www.shrm.org/templatestools/samples/policies/pages/cms_007473.aspx (retrieved March 27, 2015).

36. US Office of Personnel Management, "Performance Management: Performance Management Cycle," http://www.opm.gov/perform/articles/2001/win01-1.asp (retrieved March 28, 2015).

37. S. Mayer, "Strategic Human Resource Management Practices of High Performance Organizations," http://www.innovativehumandynamics.com [newsletter (2008)], pp. 1–4.

38. http://www.referenceforbusiness.com/management/Gr-Int/Human-Resource-Information-Systems.html (retrieved March 28, 2015).

39. S. Strohmeier, F. Piazza, "Domain Driven Data Mining in Human Resource Management: A Review of Current Research," *Expert Systems With Applications* (2013), 40(7), pp. 2410–2420.

40. J.I. Hancock, D.G. Allen, F.A. Bosco, K.R. McDaniel, C.A. Pierce, "Meta-Analytic Review of Employee Turnover as a Predictor of Firm Performance," *Journal of Management* (2013), 39(3), pp. 573–603.

41. M. Levinson, "Nine Things Managers and Employees Need to Know About Layoffs," *CIO* (March 18, 2008), http://www.cio.com/article/198702/Nine_Things_Managers_and_Employees_Need_to_Know_About_Layoffs/.

42. F. Gandolfi, "HR Strategies That Can Take the Sting out of Downsizing-Related Layoffs," *Ivey Business Journal* (July/August 2008), http://iveybusinessjournal.com/topics/strategy/hr-strategies-that-can-take-the-sting-out-of-downsizing-related-layoffs#.U4oRwygkTv4/.

43. Ibid.

44. F. Gandolfi, "HR Strategies That Can Take the Sting out of Downsizing-Related Layoffs," *Ivey Business Journal* (July/August 2008), http://iveybusinessjournal.com/topics/strategy/hr-strategies-that-can-take-the-sting-out-of-downsizing-related-layoffs#.U4oRwygkTv4/.

45. K.M. Day, A.A. Armenakis, H.S. Feild, D.R. Norris, "Other Organizations Are Doing It, Why Shouldn't We? A Look at Downsizing and Organizational Identity Through an Institutional Theory Lens," *Journal of Change Management* (2012), 12(2), pp. 165–188.

46. E. Krell, "Make It Easier to Say Goodbye," *HR Magazine* (2012), 57(10), pp. 40–44.

47. US Department of Labor, Wage and Overtime Division, "Overtime Pay," http://www.dol.gov/whd/overtime_pay.htm (retrieved August 22, 2014).

48. M.A. Tipgoes, J.P. Trebby, "Job-Related Stresses and Strains in Management Accounting," *Journal of Applied Business Research* (2011), 3(3), pp. 8–14.

49. M.J. Bidwell, F. Briscoe, "Who Contracts? Determinants of the Decision to Work as an Independent Contractor Among Information Technology Workers," *Academy of Management Journal* (2009), 52(6), pp. 1148–1166.

50. M.E. Lapalme, G. Simard, M. Tremblay, "The Influence of Psychological Contract Breach on Temporary Workers' Commitment and Behaviors: A Multiple Agency Perspective," *Journal of Business and Psychology* (2011), 26(3), pp. 311–324.

51. M.J. Chambel, F. Sobral, "Training Is an Investment With Return in Temporary Workers: A Social Exchange Perspective," *Career Development International* (2011), 16(2), pp. 161–177.

52. R.W. Wood, "New Crackdown on Using Independent Contractors," *Forbes* (November 15, 2012), http://www.forbes.com/sites/robertwood/2012/11/15/new-crackdown-on-using-independent-contractors/.

53. B. Izzo, P Narancic, "Vizcaino v. Microsoft Raises the Stakes on Worker Classification; Other Major Changes Give Guidance to Employers," http://corporate.findlaw.com/human-resources/vizcaino-v-microsoft-raises-the-stakes-on-worker-classification.html (retrieved March 28, 2015).

54. Reuters, "IRS says Fedex owed $319 mln in Back Taxes-Filing" http://www.reuters.com/article/2007/12/24/idUSN2129616020071224 (retrieved March 27, 2015).

55. G. Jericho, "Alleviating Skills Shortages Takes Time (and Lots of It)," *The Drum* (June 6, 2012), http://www.abc.net.au/unleashed/4053438.html.

56. M.C. Davidson, Y. Wang, "Sustainable Labor Practices? Hotel Human Resource Managers' Views on Turnover and Skill Shortages," *Journal of Human Resources in Hospitality & Tourism* (2011), 10(3), pp. 235–253.

57. J.I. Hancock, D.G. Allen, F.A. Bosco, K.R. McDaniel, C.A. Pierce, "Meta-Analytic Review of Employee Turnover as a Predictor of Firm Performance," *Journal of Management* (2013), 39(3), pp. 573–603.

58. O*Net Resource Center, "O*Net Toolkit for Business," http://www.onetcenter.org/toolkit.html (retrieved March 30, 2015).

59. O*Net Resource Center, http://www.onetonline.org (retrieved March 30, 2015).

60. J.H. Spangenberg, A. Fuad-Luke, K. Blincoe, "Design for Sustainability (DfS): The Interface of Sustainable Production and Consumption," *Journal of Cleaner Production* (2010), 18(15), pp. 1485–1493.

61. N. Landrum, S. Edwards, *Sustainable Business, An Executive's Primer* (New York, NY: Business Expert Press, 2009).

62. Ibid.

63. Cote, D. M. (2013, June). Honeywell's CEO on how he avoided layoffs. *Harvard Business Review.* Retrieved from http://hbr.org/2013/06/honeywells-ceo-on-how-he-avoided-layoffs/.

64. Hoover's Inc. (2014). *Honeywell International, Inc.* [Hoover's Company Records: In-Depth Records]. Retrieved July 3, 2014, from Long Island University Academic Database.

65. Cote, D. M. (2013, June). Honeywell's CEO on how he avoided layoffs. *Harvard Business Review.* Retrieved from http://hbr.org/2013/06/honeywells-ceo-on-how-he-avoided-layoffs/.

CHAPTER 5

1. S.D. Maurer, D.P. Cook, "Using Company Web Sites to E-Recruit Qualified Applicants: A Job Marketing–Based Review of Theory-Based Research," *Computers in Human Behavior* (2011), 27(1), pp. 106–117.

2. D.G. Allen, P.C. Bryant, J.M. Vardaman, "Retaining Talent: Replacing Misconceptions With Evidence-Based Strategies," *Academy of Management Perspectives* (2010), 24(2), 2010, pp. 48–64.

3. D. Autor, L. Katz, M. Kearney, "Trends in U.S. Wage Inequality: Revising the Revisionists," *The Review of Economics and Statistics* (2008), 90(2), pp. 300–323.

4. E. Glazer, "Problems and Solutions—We Asked HR Executives: What's Your Biggest Challenge?" *The Wall Street Journal* (October 24, 2011), p. R-2.

5. S. Sorenson, J. Mattingly, F. Lee, "Decoding the Signal Effects of Job Candidate Attraction to Corporate Social Practices," *Business and Society Review* (2010), 115(2), pp. 173–204.

6. J.M. Henderson, "Job Stability vs. Job Satisfaction? Millennials May Have to Settle for Neither," *Forbes* blog (December 22, 2012), http://www.forbes.com/sites/jmaureenhenderson/2012/12/22/job-stability-vs-job-satisfaction-millennials-may-have-to-settle-for-neither/.

7. K. Lundby (Ed.), *Going Global: Practical Applications and Recommendations for HR and OD Professionals in the Global Workplace* (San Francisco, CA: Jossey-Bass, 2010), pp. 114–115.

8. S. Raice, "Friend—and Possible Employee," *The Wall Street Journal* (October 24, 2011), p. A-2.

9. J. Barrett-Poindexter, "How to Find Out What a Company's Culture Is Really Like," *Glassdoor* blog (July 22, 2013), http://www.glassdoor.com/blog/find-companys-culture/.

10. G. Segal, "The Real Way to Build a Network," *Fortune* (February 6, 2013), pp. 23–32.

11. J. Valentino-Devries, "Social Media and Bias in Hiring," *The Wall Street Journal*, (November 21, 2013), p. B-4.

12. V. Elmer, "Hiring Without a Net: Groupon's Recruiter Speaks," *Fortune* (July 25, 2011), p. 34.

13. J.I. Hancock, D.G. Allen, F.A. Bosco, K.R. McDaniel, C.A. Pierce, "Meta-Analytic Review of Employee Turnover as a Predictor of Firm Performance," *Journal of Management* (2013), 39(3), pp. 573–603.

14. R. Bonet, P. Cappelli, M. Hamori, "Labor Market Intermediaries and the New Paradigm for Human Resources," *The Academy of Management Annals* (2013), 7(1), pp. 341–392.

15. E. Parry, S. Tyson, "An Analysis of the Use and Success of Online Recruitment Methods in the UK," *Human Resource Management Journal* (2008), 18(3), pp. 257–274.

16. W-C. Tsai, I. W-F. Yang, "Does Image Matter to Different Job Applicants? The Influences of Corporate Image and Applicant Individual Differences on Organizational Attractiveness," *International Journal of Selection and Assessment* (2010), 18(1), pp. 48–63.

17. D.R. Earnest, D.G. Allen, R.S. Landis, "Mechanisms Linking Realistic Job Previews With Turnover: A Meta-Analytic Path Analysis," *Personnel Psychology* (2011), 64(4), pp. 865–897.

18. Ibid.

19. C.C. Chen, C.S. Hsu, P.S. Tsai, "The Process Mechanisms Linking Recruiter Positive Moods and Organizational Attraction," *International Journal of Selection and Assessment* (2013), 21(4), pp. 376–387.

20. S. Overman, "Help Recruiters Vault Ahead," *Staffing Management Magazine* (2006), 2(2), pp. 32–35.

21. C.B. Felsen, E.K. Shaw, J.M. Ferrante, L.J. Lacroix, B.F. Crabtree, "Strategies for In-Person Recruitment: Lessons Learned From a New Jersey Primary Care Research Network (NJPCRN) Study," *The Journal of the American Board of Family Medicine* (2010), 23(4), pp. 523–533.

22. H. Weger Jr., G. Castle Bell, E.M. Minei, M.C. Robinson, "The Relative Effectiveness of Active Listening in Initial Interactions," *International Journal of Listening* (2014), 28(1), pp. 13–31.

23. C.C. Chen, C.S. Hsu, P.S. Tsai, "The Process Mechanisms Linking Recruiter Positive Moods and Organizational Attraction," *International Journal of Selection and Assessment* (2013), 21(4), pp. 376–387.

24. Society for Human Resource Management, "Cost per Hire" [spreadsheet template], http://www.shrm.org/templatestools/samples/metrics/documents/cost%20per%20hire.xls. (retrieved June 10, 2014).

25. D.G. Allen, P.C. Bryant, J.M. Vardaman, "Retaining Talent: Replacing Misconceptions With Evidence-Based Strategies," *Academy of Management Perspectives* (2010), 24(2), pp. 48–64.

26. D. De Leon, K. LaVelle, S. Cantrell, "Trends Reshaping the Future of HR: Tapping Skills Anywhere, Anytime," *Accenture* (January 22, 2013), p. 3.

27. HR executives are also projecting significant worker shortages in many professions in ten major industries by 2020 and 2030.

28. P. Cappelli, J.R. Keller, "Classifying Work in the New Economy," *Academy of Management Review* (2013), 38(4), pp. 575–596.

29. D. Gartside et al., "Trends Reshaping the Future of HR: The Rise of the Extended Workforce," *Accenture* (January 22, 2013), p. 3.

30. D. De Leon, K. LaVelle, S. Cantrell, "Trends Reshaping the Future of HR: Tapping Skills Anywhere, Anytime," *Accenture* (January 22, 2013), p. 5.

31. P. Cappelli, J.R. Keller, "Classifying Work in the New Economy," *Academy of Management Review* (2013), 38(4), pp. 575–596.

32. D. Gartside et al., "Trends Reshaping the Future of HR: The Rise of the Extended Workforce," *Accenture* (January 22, 2013), p. 4.

33. Hoover's Inc. (2014). *LinkedIn* [Hoover's Company Records: In-Depth Records]. Retrieved July 17, 2014, from Long Island University Academic Database.

34. G. Anders, "Insider trading for talent," *Forbes* (November 18, 2013), 192(7), p. 1-1.

35. LinkedIn Corporation. (2014). *About LinkedIn*. Retrieved June 3, 2014, from http://press.linkedin.com/about/.

36. Ibid.

CHAPTER 6

1. CareerBuilder, "Bad Hires Can Be Costly," *HR Magazine* (February 2013), p. 18.

2. Z. Syed, W. Jamal, "Universalistic Perspective of HRM and Organisational Performance: Meta-Analytical Study," *International Bulletin of Business Administration ISSN* (2012).

3. P. Moen, J. Lam, S. Ammons, E.L. Kelly, "Time Work by Overworked Professionals: Strategies in Response to the Stress of Higher Status," *Work and Occupations* (2013), 40(2), pp. 79–114.

4. V. Elmer, "Hiring Without a Net: Groupon's Recruiter Speaks," *Fortune* (July 25, 2011), p. 34.

5. L.B. Hollinshead, "Social-Media Privacy and Protection Laws," *Employment Relations Today* (2013), 40(3), pp. 73–82.

6. T. Jefferson, *The Declaration of Independence*, http://www.archives.gov/exhibits/charters/declaration_transcript.html.

7. M.T. Iqbal, W. Latif, W. Naseer, "The Impact of Person Job Fit on Job Satisfaction and Its Subsequent Impact on Employees' Performance," *Mediterranean Journal of Social Sciences* (2012), 3(2), pp. 523–530.

8. J.L. Burnette, J.M. Pollack, "Implicit Theories of Work and Job Fit: Implications for Job and Life Satisfaction," *Basic and Applied Social Psychology* (2013), 35(4), pp. 360–372.

9. D.G. Allen, P.C. Bryant, J.M. Vardaman, "Retaining Talent: Replacing Misconceptions With Evidence-Based Strategies," *Academy of Management Perspectives* (2010), 24(2), pp. 48–64.

10. E.M. Nolan, M.J. Morley, "A Test of the Relationship Between Person-Environment Fit and Cross Cultural Adjustment Among Self-Initiated Expatriates," *The International Journal of Human Resource Management* (2014), 25(11), published online.

11. US Equal Employment Opportunity Commission, "Employment Tests and Selection Procedures (September 23, 2010), http://www.eeoc.gov/policy/docs/factemployment_procedures.html (retrieved June 9, 2014).

12. US Office of Personnel Management, "Frequently Asked Questions: Assessment Policy," https://www.opm.gov/FAQs/QA.aspx?fid=a6da6c2e-e1cb-4841-b72d-53eb4adf1ab1&pid=402c2b0c-bb5c-44e9-acbc-39cc6149ad36 (retrieved June 9, 2014).

13. US Code of Federal Regulations, "Title 29: Labor, Part 1607: Uniform Guidelines on Employee Selection Procedures (1978)," http://www.gpo.gov/fdsys/pkg/CFR-2011-title29-vol4/xml/CFR-2011-title29-vol4-part1607.xml (retrieved June 9, 2014).

14. Ibid.

15. "Title 29: Labor," http://www.gpo.gov/fdsys/pkg/CFR-2011-title29-vol4/xml/CFR-2011-title29-vol4-part1607.xml (retrieved June 9, 2014).

16. Uniform Guidelines on Employee Selection Procedures, "III. General Questions Concerning Validity and the

Use of Selection Procedures" (2013), http://www.uniformguidelines.com/questionandanswers.html#3 (retrieved June 9, 2014).

17. Uniform Guidelines on Employee Selection Procedures, "III. General Questions Concerning Validity and the Use of Selection Procedures" (2013), http://www.uniformguidelines.com/questionandanswers.html#3 (retrieved June 9, 2014).

18. US Equal Employment Opportunity Commission, http://www.eeoc.gov (retrieved July 9, 2013).

19. D.G. Allen, P.C. Bryant, J.M. Vardaman, "Retaining Talent: Replacing Misconceptions With Evidence-Based Strategies," *Academy of Management Perspectives* (2010), 24(2), pp. 48–64.

20. V. Elmer, "Hiring Without a Net: Groupon's Recruiter Speaks," *Fortune* (July 25, 2011), p. 34.

21. K. Connell, "AccuScreen CEO Will Discuss Résumé Lying on Fox 13 News Tampa Bay" (January 14, 2009), http://www.accuscreen.com/index.php?s=lying+on +resumes/.

22. M. Henricks, "Interview for Integrity," *Entrepreneur* (April 2009), p. 22.

23. Uniform Guidelines on Employee Selection Procedures, "IV. A. Criterion-Related Validity" (2013), http://www.uniformguidelines.com/questionandanswers.html#5 (retrieved June 10, 2014).

24. US Department of Labor, "Employee Polygraph Protection Act of 1988." (Pub. L. 100-347, July 27, 1988), http://www.dol.gov/whd/regs/statutes/poly01.pdf.

25. National Human Genome Research Institute, "Genetic Information Nondiscrimination Act of 2008," http://www.genome.gov/10002328/ (retrieved January 27, 2014).

26. M.Y. Alsabbah, H.I. Ibrahim, "Recruitment and Selection Process and Employee Competence Outcome: An Important Area for Future Research," *Human Resource Management Research* (2013), 3(3), pp. 82–90.

27. http://smallbusiness.foxbusiness.com/biz-on-main/2011/03/04/businesses-hire-based-personality/ (retrieved June 10, 2014).

28. J.M. McCarthy, C.H. Van Iddekinge, F. Lievens, M.C. Kung, E.F. Sinar, M.A. Campion, "Do Candidate Reactions Relate to Job Performance or Affect Criterion-Related Validity? A Multistudy Investigation of Relations Among Reactions, Selection Test Scores, and Job Performance," *Journal of Applied Psychology* (2013), 98(5), p. 701.

29. *Watson v. Fort Worth Bank & Trust*, 487 US 977 (1988), http://supreme.justia.com/cases/federal/us/487/977/case.html.

30. D.S. Ones, C. Viswesvaran, F.L. Schmidt, "Integrity Tests Predict Counterproductive Work Behaviors and Job Performance Well: Comment on Van Iddekinge, Roth, Raymark, and Odle-Dusseau," *Journal of Applied Psychology* (2012), 97(3), pp. 537–542.

31. Science Clarified, "Chapter 3: The Virtual Classroom: Virtual Reality in Training and Education," in *Virtual Reality,* http://www.scienceclarified.com/scitech/Virtual-Reality/The-Virtual-Classroom-Virtual-Reality-in-Training-and-Education.html (retrieved October 10, 2010).

32. US Department of Labor, "Drug-Free Workplace Policy Builder: Section 7–Drug Testing," http://www.dol.gov/elaws/asp/drugfree/drugs/screen92.asp (retrieved June 10, 2014).

33. J.E. Kenney, S. Hoffman, "Substance Abuse Program Administrators Association (SAPAA) Position Paper on Medical Marijuana" (September 4, 2013), http://www.sapaa.com/resource/resmgr/sapaa_med_marijuana_white_p.docx.

34. C. Sargent, D. Darwent, S.A. Ferguson, G.D. Roach, "Can a Simple Balance Task Be Used to Assess Fitness for Duty?" *Accident Analysis & Prevention* (2012), 45, pp. 74–79.

35. US Equal Opportunity Commission, "ADA: FMLA; Reasonable Accommodation–Leave; Medical Exams and Inquiries," http://www.eeoc.gov/eeoc/foia/letters/2008/ada_fmla_reasonableaccommodation_leave.html.

36. A. Lashinsky, "Larry Page Interview," *Fortune* (February 6, 2012), pp. 98–99.

37. H. Ismail, S. Karkoulian, "Interviewers' Characteristics and Post-hire Attitudes and Performance," *Contemporary Management Research* (2013), 9(4).

38. J. Alsever, "How to Get a Job: Show, Don't Tell," *Fortune* (March 19, 2012), pp. 29–31.

39. D. Meinert, "Cultural Similarities Influence Hiring Decisions," *HR Magazine* (February 2013), p. 18.

40. T. Lytle, "Streamline Hiring," *HR Magazine* (April 2013), pp. 63–65.

41. A. Bryant, "In Head-Hunting, Big Data May Not Be Such a Big Deal," *The New York Times* (June 19, 2013), http://www.nytimes.com/2013/06/20/business/in-head-hunting-big-data-may-not-be-such-a-big-deal.html.

42. http://www.shrm.org/templatestools/samples/interviewquestions/pages/competenciesksa%E2%80%99s.aspx (retrieved June 7, 2014).

43. M. Henricks, "Interview for Integrity," *Entrepreneur* (April 2009), p. 22.

44. US Equal Employment Opportunity Commission and Federal Trade Commission, "Background Checks: What Employers Need to Know," http://www.eeoc.gov/eeoc/publications/background_checks_employers.cfm (June 8, 2014).

45. D.B. Weisenfeld, "Colorado Becomes 9th State to Limit Employer Credit Checks" (April 30, 2013), http://www.xperthr.com/news/colorado-becomes-9th-state-to-limit-employer-credit-checks/9819/.

46. Federal Trade Commission, "Employment Background Checks" (February 2013), http://www.consumer.ftc.gov/articles/0157-employment-background-checks/.

47. A. Preston, "Disney Sued for Misusing Background Checks" (November 20, 2013), http://www.shrm.org/hr disciplines/safetysecurity/articles/pages/disney-sued-background-checks.aspx.

48. "11 U.S. Code § 525: Protection Against Discriminatory Treatment," http://www.law.cornell.edu/uscode/text/11/525/ (retrieved June 10, 2014).

49. B. Yuille, "Four New Job-Search Trends," *Forbes* (February 23, 2010), http://www.forbes.com/2010/02/23/job-search-trends-personal-finance-resume.html.

50. R. McHale, "Using Facebook to Screen Potential Hires Can Get You Sued," *Fast Company* (July 20, 2012), http://www.fastcompany.com/1843142/using-facebook-screen-potential-hires-can-get-you-sued/.

51. K. Schoening, K. Kleisinger, "Off-Duty Privacy: How Far Can Employers Go?" *Northern Kentucky Law Review* (2010), 37, p. 287.

52. G.M. Saylin, T.C. Horrocks, "The Risks of Pre-employment Social Media Screening" (July 18, 2013), http://www.shrm.org/hrdisciplines/staffingmanagement/articles/pages/preemployment-social-media-screening.aspx.

53. http://www.nolo.com/legal-encyclopedia/sexual-orientation-discrimination-rights-29541.html (retrieved August 2, 2014).

54. http://www.whitehouse.gov/the-press-office/2014/07/21/executive-order-further-amendments-executive-order-11478-equal-employment/ (retrieved August 3, 2014).

55. *Forbes.* (n.d.). *The World's Billionaires: #46 Brian Acton.* Retrieved July 17, 2014, from http://www.forbes.com/profile/brian-acton/.

56. Wikipedia. (2014). WhatsApp. Retrieved July 17, 2014, from http://en.wikipedia.org/wiki/WhatsApp.

57. G. Anders. (2014, February 19). He wanted a job; Facebook said "no"—in a $3 billion mistake. *Forbes.* Retrieved http://www.forbes.com/sites/.georgeanders/2014/02/19/he-wanted-a-job-facebook-said-no-in-a-3-billion-mistake/.

58. C. Gordon (2012, October 5). Getting a job at Facebook: Inside the "Meritocratic" hiring process. Retrieved from the AOL website at http://jobs.aol

.com/articles/2012/10/05/want-to-get-a-job-at-facebook-weve-demystified-the-hiring-proc/.

59. C. Bueno (2012, July 20). Get that job at Facebook. Retrieved from the Facebook Engineering page at https://www.facebook.com/notes/facebook-engineering/get-that-job-at-facebook/101509 64382448920/.

60. Ibid.

61. Ibid.

62. *Forbes*. (n.d.). *The World's Billionaires: #46 Brian Acton*. Retrieved July 17, 2014, from http://www.forbes.com/profile/brian-acton/.

63. Wikipedia. (2014). WhatsApp. Retrieved July 17, 2014, from http://en.wikipedia.org/wiki/WhatsApp.

CHAPTER 7

1. R.C. Rose, N. Kumar, O.B. Pak, "The Effect of Organizational Learning on Organizational Commitment, Job Satisfaction and Work Performance, *Journal of Applied Business Research* (2011), 25(6).

2. D.G. Allen, P.C. Bryant, J.M. Vardaman, "Retaining Talent: Replacing Misconceptions With Evidence-Based Strategies," *Academy of Management Perspectives* (2010), 24(2), pp. 48–64.

3. K. Pajo, A. Coetzer, N. Guenole, "Formal Development Opportunities and Withdrawal Behavior by Employees in Small and Medium-Sized Enterprises," *Journal of Small Business Management* (2010), 48(3), pp. 281–301.

4. S.K. Johnson, L.O. Garrison, G.H. Broome, J.W. Fleenor, J.L. Steed, "Go for the Goals: Relationships Between Goal Setting and Transfer of Training Following Leadership Development," *Academy of Management Learning & Education* (2012), 11(4), pp. 555–569.

5. M. Festing, "Strategic Human Resource Management in Germany," *Academy of Management Perspectives* (2012), 26(2), pp. 37–54.

6. A. Fox, "Help Managers Shine," *HR Magazine* (February 2013), pp. 43–46.

7. B. Schyns, T. Kiefer, R. Kerschreiter, A. Tymon, "Teaching Implicit Leadership Theories to Develop Leaders and Leadership: How and Why It Can Make a Difference," *Academy of Management Learning & Education* (2011), 10(3), pp. 397–408.

8. S.K. Johnson, L.O. Garrison, G.H. Broome, J.W. Fleenor, J.L. Steed, "Go for the Goals: Relationships Between Goal Setting and Transfer of Training Following Leadership Development, *Academy of Management Learning & Education* (2012), 11(4), pp. 555–569.

9. http://www.entrepreneur.com/article/224440/ (retrieved June 14, 2014).

10. T. Sitzmann, K. Ely, K.G. Brown, K.N. Bauer, "Self-Assessment of Knowledge: A Cognitive Learning or Affective Measure?" *Academy of Management Learning & Education* (2010), (9)2, pp. 169–191.

11. D.G. Allen, P.C. Bryant, J.M. Vardaman, "Retaining Talent: Replacing Misconceptions With Evidence-Based Strategies," *Academy of Management Perspectives* (2010), 24(2), pp. 48–64.

12. D.M. Sluss, R.E. Ployhart, M.G. Cobb, B.E. Ashforth, "Generalizing Newcomers' Relational and Organizational Identifications: Process and Prototypicality," *Academy of Management Journal* (2012), 55(4), pp. 949–975.

13. R.E. Silverman, "First Day on Job: Not Just Paperwork," *The Wall Street Journal* (May 28, 2013), p. D1.

14. D.G. Allen, L.R. Shanock, "Perceived Organizational Support and Embeddedness as Key Mechanisms Connecting Socialization Tactics to Commitment and Turnover Among New Employees," *Journal of Organizational Behavior* (2013), 34(3), pp. 350–369.

15. C. Tschopp, G. Grote, M. Gerber, "How Career Orientation Shapes the Job Satisfaction–Turnover Intention Link," *Journal of Organizational Behavior* (2014), 35(2), pp. 151–171.

16. D.G. Allen, P.C. Bryant, J.M. Vardaman, "Retaining Talent: Replacing Misconceptions With Evidence-Based Strategies," *Academy of Management Perspectives* (2010), 24(2), pp. 48–64.

17. Ibid.

18. C.B. Cox, M.F. Beier, "Too Old to Train or Reprimand: The Role of Intergroup Attribution Bias in Evaluating Older Workers," *Journal of Business and Psychology* (2013), pp. 1–10.

19. S. Robbins, M. Coulter, *Management* (Saddle River, NJ: Pearson Education, 2014), p. 466.

20. P.E. Kennedy, S.Y. Chyung, D.J. Winiecki, R.O. Brinkerhoff, "Training Professionals' Usage and Understanding of Kirkpatrick's Level 3 and Level 4 Evaluations," *International Journal of Training and Development* (2014), 18(1), pp. 1–21.

21. D.S. Chiaburu, J.L. Huang, H.M. Hutchins, R.G. Gardner, "Trainees' Perceived Knowledge Gain Unrelated to the Training Domain: The Joint Action of Impression Management and Motives," *International Journal of Training and Development* (2014), 18(1), pp. 37–52.

22. Ibid.

23. D.T. Hall, *Careers in and out of Organizations* (Thousand Oaks, CA: SAGE, 2002).

24. C. Hu, S. Wang, C.C. Yang, T.Y. Wu, "When Mentors Feel Supported: Relationships With Mentoring Functions

and Protégés' Perceived Organizational Support," *Journal of Organizational Behavior* (2014), 35(1), pp. 22–37.

25. S. Humphrey, F. Morgeson, M. Mannor, "Developing a Theory of the Strategic Core of Teams: A Role Composition Model of Team Performance," *Journal of Applied Psychology* (2009), (94)1, pp. 48–61.

26. D. Super, D. Hall, "Career Development: Exploration and Planning," *Annual Review of Psychology* (1978), 29, pp. 333–372.

27. http://business.financialpost.com/2014/01/09/gamification-newest-tool-in-corporate-training-arsenal/ (retrieved June 11, 2014).

28. ADP (Ed.), "Outsourcing and the Future of HR," *ADP* (2012), p. 3.

29. Jon Hay (Ed.), "HR Outsourcing Trends and Insights 2009," *Hewitt Associates* (2009), p. 10.

30. Hoover's Inc. (2014). Google Inc. [Hoover's Company Records: In-Depth Records]. Retrieved July 19, 2014, from Long Island University Academic Database.

31. I. Lapowsky (2014, July 1). Google and Square recruit girls early to tackle tech's gender problem. *Wired.com*. Retrieved from http://www.wired.com/2014/07/girls-coding/.

32. S. Warnes (2014, July 1). 70% male, 50% white: Why Silicon Valley needs to diversify. *Mirror*. Retrieved from http://ampp3d.mirror.co.uk/2014/07/01/70-male-50-white-why-silicon-valley-needs-to-diversity/.

33. P. Mejia (2014, July 11). Codes, not bros: Google pledges $50 million to ladies in tech. *Newsweek*. Retrieved from http://www.newsweek.com/codes-not-bros-google-pledges-50-million-ladies-tech-258298/.

34. S. Warnes (2014, July 1). 70% male, 50% white: Why Silicon Valley needs to diversify. *Mirror*. Retrieved from http://ampp3d.mirror.co.uk/2014/07/01/70-male-50-white-why-silicon-valley-needs-to-diversify/.

35. P. Mejia (2014, July 11). Codes, not bros: Google pledges $50 million to ladies in tech. *Newsweek*. Retrieved from http://www.newsweek.com/codes-not-bros-google-pledges-50-million-ladies-tech-258298/.

36. Ibid.

37. V. Jones (2014, July 8). How to hook up tech sector with talent. *CNN.com*. Retrieved from http://www.cnn.com/2014/07/08/opinion/jones-tech-minorities/.

38. P. Mejia (2014, July 11). Codes, not bros: Google pledges $50 million to ladies in tech. *Newsweek*. Retrieved from http://www.newsweek.com/codes-not-bros-google-pledges-50-million-ladies-tech-258298/.

CHAPTER 8

1. J. Welch, S. Welch, "Dealing With the Morning-After Syndrome at Facebook," *Fortune* (March 19, 2012), p. 92.

2. M.K. Duffy, K.L. Scott, J.D. Shaw, B.J. Tepper, K. Aquino, "A Social Context Model of Envy and Social Undermining," *Academy of Management Journal* (2012), 55(3), pp. 643–666.

3. S.K. Johnson, L.O. Garrison, G.H. Broome, J.W. Fleenor, J.L. Steed, "Go for the Goals: Relationships Between Goal Setting and Transfer of Training Following Leadership Development," *Academy of Management Learning & Education* (2012), 11(4), pp. 555–569.

4. "Master Class," *Businessweek* (May 6–12, 2013), p. 83.

5. K. Gurchiek, "New HR Standard on Performance Management," *HR Magazine* (April 2013), p. 74.

6. C.O. Longenecker, "How the Best Motivate Workers," *Industrial Management* (2011), 53(1), pp. 8–13.

7. S.A. Culbert, "Get Rid of the Performance Review," *The Wall Street Journal* (October 20, 2008), p. R4.

8. D.G. Allen, P.C. Bryant, J.M. Vardaman, "Retaining Talent: Replacing Misconceptions With Evidence-Based Strategies," *Academy of Management Perspectives* (2010), 24(2), pp. 48–64.

9. A.S. DeNisi, "Managing Performance to Change Behavior," *Journal of Organizational Behavior Management* (2011), 31(4), pp. 262–276.

10. I.A. Scott, G. Phelps, C. Brand, "Assessing Individual Clinical Performance: A Primer for Physicians," *Internal Medicine Journal* (2011), 41(2), pp. 144–155.

11. Ibid.

12. http://www.shrm.org/templatestools/toolkits/pages/managingemployeeperformance.aspx (retrieved June 20, 2014).

13. Society for Human Resource Management, *Performance Management Survey* (2000), http://www.shrm.org/Research/SurveyFindings/Documents/Performance%20Management%20Survey.pdf, p. 7.

14. http://www.shrm.org/hrdisciplines/employeerelations/articles/Pages/UsedtoMotivateWeedOut.aspx (retrieved June 20, 2014).

15. P.F. Buller, G.M. McEvoy, "Strategy, Human Resource Management and Performance: Sharpening Line of Sight," *Human Resource Management Review* (2012), 22(1), pp. 43–56.

16. K. Blanchard, D. Hudson, E. Wills, *The One Minute Entrepreneur* (New York, NY: Currency, 2008).

17. G. Blickle, J.A. Meurs, A. Wihler, C. Ewen, A. Plies, S. Günther, "The Interactive Effects of Conscientiousness, Openness to Experience, and Political Skill on Job Performance in Complex Jobs: The Importance of Context," *Journal of Organizational Behavior* (2013), 34(8), pp. 1145–1164.

18. P. Mussel, "Introducing the Construct Curiosity for Predicting Job Performance," *Journal of Organizational Behavior* (2013), 34(4), pp. 453–472.

19. K. Blanchard, D. Hudson, E. Wills, *The One Minute Entrepreneur* (New York, NY: Currency, 2008).

20. J. Goodale, "Behaviorally-Based Rating Scales: Toward an Integrated Approach to Performance Appraisal," *Contemporary Problems in Personnel* (Chicago, IL: St. Clair Press, 1977), p. 247.

21. K. Blanchard, D. Hutson, E. Wills, *The One Minute Entrepreneur* (New York, NY: Currency, 2008).

22. Ibid.

23. D.G. Allen, P.C. Bryant, J.M. Vardaman, "Retaining Talent: Replacing Misconceptions With Evidence-Based Strategies," *Academy of Management Perspectives* (2010), 24(2), pp. 48–64.

24. A. Cohen, "When Do You Do Your Best Thinking?" M. Buckley response, *BusinessWeek* (May 14, 2015), p. 78.

25. H.K. Fulk, R.L. Bell, N. Bodie, "Team Management by Objectives: Enhancing Developing Teams' Performance," *Journal of Management Policy and Practice* (2011), 12(3), pp. 17–26.

26. Wikipedia.com (retrieved January 17, 2011). The first known uses of the term SMART goals occur in the November 1981 issue of *Management Review* by George T. Doran.

27. E. Gibson, "The Stop-Managing Guide to Management," *Businessweek* (June 15, 2009), p. 73.

28. H.K. Fulk, R.L. Bell, N. Bodie, "Team Management by Objectives: Enhancing Developing Teams' Performance," *Journal of Management Policy and Practice* (2011), 12(3), pp. 17–26.

29. S. McCartney, "How US Airways Vaulted to First Place," *The Wall Street Journal* (July 22, 2009), p. D3.

30. http://www.shrm.org/publications/hrnews/pages/announcements-on-stack-rankings-touch-off-debate.aspx (retrieved June 22, 2014).

31. S. Ovide, "Microsoft Abandons Dreaded Stack," *The Wall Street Journal* (November 13, 2013), p. B1.

32. R. Karlgaad, "Do Jerks Always Win?" *Forbes* (December 29, 2014), p. 44.

33. K. Blanchard, D. Hutson, E. Wills, *The One Minute Entrepreneur* (New York, NY: Currency, 2008).

34. M. Ohland, M. Loughry, D. Woehr, C. Finelli, L. Bullard, R. Felder, . . . D. Schmucker, "The Comprehensive Assessment of Team Member Effectiveness: Development of a Behaviorally Anchored Rating Scale for Self and Peer Evaluation," *Academy of Management Learning & Education* (2012).

35. A. Sudarsan, "Concurrent Validity of Peer Appraisal of Group Work for Administrative Purposes," *The IUP Journal of Organizational Behavior* (2010), 9(1 & 2), pp. 73–86.

36. S. Brutus, M. Donia, S. Ronen, "Can Business Students Learn to Evaluate Better? Evidence From Repeated Exposure to a Peer Evaluation Process," *Academy of Management Learning & Education* (2012).

37. http://www.shrm.org/hrdisciplines/employeerelations/articles/Pages/ManagerEmployeePerceptions.aspx (retrieved June 20, 2014).

38. N. Castle, H. Garton, G. Kenward, "Confidence vs. Competence: Basic Life Support Skills of Health Professionals," *British Journal of Nursing* (2007), 16, pp. 664–666.

39. M. Matthews, S. Beal, "Assessing Situation Awareness in Field Training Exercises," *U.S. Army Research Institute for the Behavioral and Social Sciences Research Report 1795* (2002).

40. K. Sullivan, C. Hall, "Introducing Students to Self-Assessment," *Assessment & Evaluation in Higher Education* (1997), 22, pp. 289–305.

41. B. McKinstry, H. Peacock, D. Blaney, "Can Trainers Accurately Assess Their Training Skills Using a Detailed Checklist? A Questionnaire-Based Comparison of Trainer Self-Assessment and Registrar Assessment of Trainers' Learning Needs," *Education for Primary Care* (2003), 14, pp. 426–430.

42. H. Han, S.S. Hyun, "Image Congruence and Relationship Quality in Predicting Switching Intention Conspicuousness of Product Use as a Moderator Variable," *Journal of Hospitality & Tourism Research* (2013), 37(3), pp. 303–329.

43. R.J. Ely, H. Ibarra, D.M. Kolb, "Taking Gender Into Account: Theory and Design for Women's Leadership Development Programs," *Academy of Management Learning & Education* (2011), 10(3), p. 474.

44. E.M. Mone, M. London, *Employee Engagement Through Effective Performance Management: A Practical Guide for Managers* (New York, NY: Routledge/Taylor & Francis, 2011).

45. H. Aguinas, *Performance Management* (Upper Saddle River, NJ: Pearson Education, 2007), p. 184.

46. A. Thomas, J. Palmer, J. Feldman, "Examination and Measurement of Halo via Curvilinear Regression: A New Approach to Halo," *Journal of Applied Social Psychology* (February 2009), 39(2), pp. 350–358.

47. A.N. Esfahani, M. Abzari, S. Dezianian, "Analyzing the Effect of Performance Appraisal Errors on Perceived Organizational Justice," *International Journal of Academic Research in Accounting, Finance and Management Sciences* (2014), 4(1), pp. 36–40.

48. K. Blanchard, D. Hutson, E. Wills, *The One Minute Entrepreneur* (New York, NY: Currency, 2008).

49. R. Albergotti, "At Facebook, Boss is a Dirty Word," *The Wall Street Journal* (December 26, 2014), pp. B1, B2.

50. C. Dusterhoff, J.B. Cunningham, J.N. MacGregor, "The Effects of Performance Rating, Leader-Member Exchange, Perceived Utility, and Organizational Justice on Performance Appraisal Satisfaction: Applying a Moral Judgment Perspective," *Journal of Business Ethics* (2014), 119(2), pp. 265–273.

51. J. McGregor, "Job Review in 140 Keystrokes," *Businessweek* (March 23 & 30, 2009), p. 58.

52. D.G. Allen, P.C. Bryant, J.M. Vardaman, "Retaining Talent: Replacing Misconceptions With Evidence-Based Strategies," *Academy of Management Perspectives* (2010), 24(2), pp. 48–64.

53. E. Gibson, "The Stop-Managing Guide to Management," *Businessweek* (June 15, 2009), p. 73.

54. Ibid.

55. D.G. Allen, P.C. Bryant, J.M. Vardaman, "Retaining Talent: Replacing Misconceptions With Evidence-Based Strategies," *Academy of Management Perspectives* (2010), 24(2), pp. 48–64.

56. T. Gutner, "Ways to Make the Most of a Negative Job Review," *The Wall Street Journal* (January 13, 2009), p. D4.

57. Ibid.

58. Hoover's Inc. (2014). *Amazon.com, Inc.* [Hoover's Company Records–Competitive Landscape/In-Depth Records]. Retrieved July 13, 2014 from Long Island University Academic Database.

59. Ibid.

60. B. Stone, "Why It's So Difficult to Climb Amazon's Corporate Ladder," *Bloomberg BusinessWeek* (October 15, 2013). Retrieved from http://www.businessweek.com/articles/2013-10-15/careers-at-amazon-why-its-so-hard-to-climb-jeff-bezoss-corporate-ladder/.

61. Ibid.

62. Ibid.

63. Ibid.

64. T. Soper, "Here's What Employees Love and Hate About Working at Amazon, Microsoft," *Geek Wire* (December 13, 2012). Retrieved from http://www.geekwire.com/2012/employees-love-hate-working-amazon-microsoft/.

CHAPTER 9

1. N. Saif, N. Razzaq, S.U. Rehman, A. Javed, U. Ahmad, "The Role of Workplace Partnership Strategies in Employee Management Relations," *Information and Knowledge Management* (2013), 3(6), pp. 34–39.

2. M.W. Kramer, R.J. Meisenbach, G.J. Hansen, "Communication, Uncertainty, and Volunteer Membership," *Journal of Applied Communication Research* (2013), 41(1), pp. 18–39.

3. D.B. Arnett, C.M. Wittmann, "Improving Marketing Success: The Role of Tacit Knowledge Exchange Between Sales and Marketing," *Journal of Business Research* (2014), 67(3), pp. 324–331.

4. R. Hurley, "Trust Me," *The Wall Street Journal* (October 24, 2011), p. R4.

5. "Jack Welch's Lessons for Success," *Fortune* (1993), 127(2), pp. 86–93.

6. R. Hurley, "Trust Me," *The Wall Street Journal* (October 24, 2011), p. R4.

7. D. Dowell, T. Heffernan, M. Morrison, "Trust Formation at the Growth Stage of a Business-to-Business Relationship: A Qualitative Investigation," *Qualitative Market Research: An International Journal* (2013), 16(4), pp. 436–451.

8. P.H. Kim, K. Dirks, C.D. Cooper, "The Repair of Trust: A Dynamic Bilateral Perspective and Multilevel Conceptualization," *Academy of Management Review* (2009), 34(3), pp. 401–422.

9. J. Paskin, "Finding the 'I' in Team," *Businessweek* (February 18–24, 2013), p. 78.

10. Dreamworks, http://www.dreamworksstudios.com (retrieved May 16, 2011).

11. J. Birkinshaw, "Why Good Management Is So Difficult," *Strategic HR Review* (2014), 13(2).

12. E. Bernstein, "The Hidden Benefits of Chitchat," *The Wall Street Journal* (August 13, 2013), pp. D1–D2.

13. Public Radio News Broadcast, WFCR 88.5 (May 28, 2010).

14. J. Robinson, "E-mail Is Making You Stupid?" *Entrepreneur* (March 2010), pp. 61–63.

15. L.E. Sears, Y. Shi, C.R. Coberley, J.E. Pope, "Overall Well-Being as a Predictor of Health Care, Productivity, and Retention Outcomes in a Large Employer," *Population Health Management* (2013), 16(6), pp. 397–405.

16. B.A. Scott, C.M. Barnes, D.T. Wagner, "Chameleonic or Consistent? A Multilevel Investigation of Emotional Labor Variability and Self-Monitoring," *Academy of Management Journal* (2012), 55(4), pp. 905–926.

17. K. Hannon, "It's Never Too Late to Love Your Job," *AARP Magazine* (May 2013), pp. 44–45.

18. R. Dunham, J. Herman, "Development of a Female Faces Scale for Measuring Job Satisfaction," *Journal of Applied Psychology* (1975), 60(5), pp. 629–631.

19. P. Spector, "Measurement of Human Service Staff Satisfaction: Development of the Job Satisfaction Survey," *American Journal of Community Psychology* (1985), 13(6), pp. 693–713.

20. C. Ai-Hong, J.S. Nafisah, M.N.A. Rahim, "Comparison of Job Satisfaction Among Eight Health Care Professions in Private (Non-government) Settings," *The Malaysian Journal of Medical Sciences* (2012), 19(2), p. 19.

21. P. Spector, "Measurement of Human Service Staff Satisfaction: Development of the Job Satisfaction Survey," *American Journal of Community Psychology* (1985), 13(6), pp. 693–713.

22. D.C. Wyld, "Does More Money Buy More Happiness on the Job?" *Academy of Management Perspective* (2011), 25(1), pp. 101–102.

23. http://www.shrm.org/hrdisciplines/employeerelations/articles/pages/miserable-workers.aspx (retrieved June 25, 2014).

24. T. Lytle, "Employee Relations: Give Employees a Say; How to Encourage Ideas From Employees–and Pick the Best Ones to Act on," *HR Magazine–Alexandria* (2011), 56(10), p. 68.

25. R. Reuteman, "Generation Gaps," *Entrepreneur* (March 2015), pp. 42–48.

26. G.F. Cavanagh, D.J. Moberg, M. Velasquez, "The Ethics of Organizational Politics," *Academy of Management Review* (1981), 6(3), pp. 363–374.

27. J. Hughes, C. Babcock, F. Bass, "You're Fired, Now Get Back to Work," *Businessweek* (August 1–7, 2011), pp. 31–32.

28. United Nations, *Universal Declaration of Human Rights* (adopted by the General Assembly December 10, 1948), UN Doc. GA/RES/217 A (III).

29. S.S. Wiltermuth, F.J. Flynn, "Power, Moral Clarity, and Punishment in the Workplace," *Academy of Management Journal* (2013), 56(4), pp. 1002–1023.

30. D. Ariely, "Why We Lie," *The Wall Street Journal* (May 26–27, 2012), pp. C1–C2.

31. http://www.sba.gov/community/blogs/community-blogs/business-law-advisor/how-fire-employee-and-stay-within-law retrieved (June 23, 2014).

32. C.J. Muhl, "Employment-at-Will Doctrine: Three Major Exceptions," *The Monthly Labor Review*, 124(3), pp. 3–11.

33. J. Segers, D. Vloeberghs, E. Henderickx, I. Inceoglu, "Structuring and Understanding the Coaching Industry:

The Coaching Cube," *Academy of Management Learning & Education* (2011), 2(2), pp. 204–221.

34. "Need Coaching?" *HR Magazine* (February 2013), p. 66.

35. S.K. Johnson, L.O. Garrison, G.H. Broome, J.W. Fleenor, J.L. Steed, "Go for the Goals: Relationships Between Goal Setting and Transfer of Training Following Leadership Development," *Academy of Management Learning & Education* (2012), 11(4), pp. 555–569.

36. B. Menguc, S. Auh, M. Fisher, A. Haddad, "To Be Engaged or Not to Be Engaged: The Antecedents and Consequences of Service Employee Engagement," *Journal of Business Research* (2013), 66(11), pp. 2163–2170.

37. G. Colvin, "Why Talent Is Over Rated," *Fortune* (October 27, 2008), pp. 138–147.

38. J. Segers, D. Vloeberghs, E. Henderickx, I. Inceoglu, "Structuring and Understanding the Coaching Industry: The Coaching Cube," *Academy of Management Learning & Education* (2011), 2(2), pp. 204–221.

39. E. De Haan, C. Bertie, A. Day, C. Sills, "Clients' Critical Moments of Coaching: Toward a 'Client Model' of Executive Coaching," *Academy of Management Learning & Education* (2010), 9(4), pp. 607–621.

40. N. Tocher, M.W. Rutherford, "Perceived Acute Human Resource Management Problems in Small and Medium Firms: An Empirical Examination," *Entrepreneurship Theory and Practice* (2009), 33(2), pp. 455–479.

41. S. Shellenbarger, "Meet the Meeting Killers," *The Wall Street Journal* (May 16, 2012), pp. D1, D3.

42. CareerBuilder, "Bad Hires Can Be Costly," *HR Magazine* (February 2013), p. 18.

43. J.R. Detert, A.C. Edmondson, "Implicit Voice Theories: Taken-for-Granted Rules of Self-Censorship at Work," *Academy of Management Journal* (2011), 54(3), pp. 461–488.

44. CareerBuilder, "Bad Hires Can Be Costly," *HR Magazine* (February 2013), p. 18.

45. M. Voronov, R. Vince, "Integrating Emotions Into the Analysis of Institutional Work," *Academy of Management Review* (2012), 37(1), pp. 58–81.

46. CareerBuilder, "Bad Hires Can Be Costly," *HR Magazine* (February 2013), p. 18.

47. R.E. Kidwell, "A Strategic Deviance Perspective on the Franchise Form of Organizing," *Entrepreneurship Theory and Practice* (2011), 35(3), pp. 467–482.

48. M. Goldsmith, "What Got You Here Won't Get You There: How Successful People Became Even More Successful," *Academy of Management Perspective* (2009), 23(3), pp. 103–105.

49. A.R. Gardner, "No Finding of Race Discrimination in Failure-to-Promote Case," *HR Magazine* (April 2013), p. 74.

50. http://www.nmb.gov/resources/docs/the-railway-labor-act/ (retrieved June 28, 2014).

51. http://www.nlrb.gov/national-labor-relations-act/ (retrieved June 28, 2014).

52. http://www.nlrb.gov/what-we-do/ (retrieved June 28, 2014).

53. http://www.nlrb.gov/resources/national-labor-relations-act/ (retrieved June 28, 2014).

54. http://law.justia.com/cases/california/cal2d/49/625.html (retrieved June 28, 2014).

55. http://www.perb.ca.gov/csmcs/glossary.pdf (retrieved June 28, 2014).

56. http://www.dol.gov/oasam/programs/history/glossary.htm (retrieved April 9, 2011).

57. Ibid.

58. Ibid.

59. Collins, B. *Right to Work Laws: Legislative Background and Empirical Research* (Washington, DC: Congressional Research Service, 2012), http://fas.org/sgp/crs/misc/R42575.pdf.

60. http://doleta.gov/programs/factsht/warn.htm (retrieved June 26, 2014).

61. http://doleta.gov/programs/factsht/warn.htm (retrieved June 26, 2014).

62. http://www.bls.gov/news.release/union2.nr0.htm (retrieved June 24, 2015).

63. Ibid.

64. http://www.nlrb.gov/resources/national-labor-relations-act/ (retrieved June 25, 2014).

65. http://www.velaw.com/uploadedFiles/VEsite/Resources/UnionOrganization Process(5-501-0280).pdf (retrieved June 25, 2014).

66. http://www.velaw.com/uploadedFiles/VEsite/Resources/UnionOrganization Process (5-501-0280).pdf (retrieved June 25, 2014).

67. M. Valdez, "Boeing Machinists OK Contract Tied to 777x," Associated Press (January 4, 2014).

68. http://www.shrm.org/TemplatesTools/hrqa/Pages/decertifyaunion.aspx (retrieved June 25, 2014).

69. S. Sobell, "Social Networking @ Work," *The Costco Connection* (June 2011), p. 21.

70. J. Deschenaux, "Employee Use of Social Media: Laws Fail to Keep Pace With Technology," http://www.shrm.org/LegalIssues/FederalResources/Pages/EmployeeUseofSocialMedia.aspx (retrieved March 20, 2011).

71. M. Trottman, "U.S. Admonishes Wal-Mart," *The Wall Street Journal* (November 19, 2013), p. B2.

72. http://thehill.com/blogs/congress-blog/labor/208512-courts-agree-unions-latest-tactics-are-illegal/ (retrieved June 28, 2014).

CHAPTER 10

1. M. Philips, "Wage Growth May Signal Inflation Ahead," *Bloomberg Businessweek* (January 21–27, 2013), pp. 13–15.

2. http://www.bls.gov/news.release/pdf/ecec.pdf (retrieved July 5, 2014).

3. J. DeVaro, "A Theoretical Analysis of Relational Job Design and Compensation," *Journal of Organizational Behavior* (2010), 31 (2–3), pp. 279–301.

4. R. E. Johnson, C.D. Chang, L.O. Yang, "Commitment and Motivation at Work: The Relevance of Employee Identity and Regulatory Focus," *Academy of Management Review* (2010), 35(2), pp. 226–245.

5. G.O. Trevor, G. Reilly, B. Gerhart, "Reconsidering Pay Dispersion's Effect on the Performance of Interdependent Work: Reconciling Sorting and Pay Inequality," *Academy of Management Journal* (2012), 55(3), pp. 585–610.

6. http://www.shrm.org/research/surveyfindings/documents/14-0028%20JobSatEngage_Report_FULL_FNL.pdf (retrieved July 5, 2014).

7. J. DeVaro, "A Theoretical Analysis of Relational Job Design and Compensation," *Journal of Organizational Behavior* (2010), 31(2–3), pp. 279–301.

8. V. Vroom, *Work and Motivation* (New York: John Wiley & Sons, 1964).

9. M. Renko, K.G. Kroeck, A. Bullough, "Expectancy Theory and Nascent Entrepreneurship," *Small Business Economics* (2012), 39(3), pp. 667–684.

10. R.L. Purvis, T.J. Zagenczyk, G.E. McCray, "What's in It for Me? Using Expectancy Theory and Climate to Explain Stakeholder Participation, Its Direction and Intensity," *International Journal of Project Management* (2014).

11. http://knowledge.wharton.upenn.edu/article/balancing-the-pay-scale-fair-vs-unfair/ (retrieved July 5, 2014).

12. J. S. Adams, "Toward an Understanding of Inequity," *Journal of Abnormal and Social Psychology* (1963), 67, pp. 422–436.

13. C.P. Long, C. Bendersky, C. Morrill, "Fairness Monitoring: Linking Managerial Controls and Fairness Judgments in Organizations," *Academy of Management Journal* (2011), 54(5), pp. 1045–1068.

14. A. Edmans, "The Link Between Job Satisfaction and Firm Value, With Implications for Corporate Social Responsibility, *Academy of Management Perspectives* (2012), 26(4), pp. 1–19.

15. http://www.mindtools.com/pages/article/newLDR_96.htm (retrieved July 9, 2014).

16. M.K. Duffy, K.L. Scott, J.D. Shaw, B.J. Tepper, K. Aquino, "A Social Context

Model of Envy and Social Undermining," *Academy of Management Journal* (2012), 55(3), pp. 643–666.

17. S.A. Samaha, R.W. Palmatier, R.P. Dant, "Poisoning Relationships: Perceived Unfairness in Channels of Distribution," *Journal of Marketing* (2011), 75(3), pp. 99–117.

18. C.P. Long, C. Bendersky, C. Morrill, "Fairness Monitoring: Linking Managerial Controls and Fairness Judgments in Organizations," *Academy of Management Journal* (2011), 54(5), pp. 1045–1068.

19. G.O. Trevor, G. Reilly, B. Gerhart, "Reconsidering Pay Dispersion's Effect on the Performance of Interdependent Work: Reconciling Sorting and Pay Inequality," *Academy of Management Journal* (2012), 55(3), pp. 585–610.

20. K. Leavitt, S.J. Reynolds, C.M. Barnes, P. Schilpzan, S.T. Hannah, "Different Hats, Different Obligations: Plural Occupational Identities and Situated Moral Judgments," *Academy of Management Journal* (2012), 55(6), pp. 1316–1333.

21. R.L. Bell, J.S. Martin, "The Relevance of Scientific Management and Equity Theory in Everyday Managerial Communication Situations," *Journal of Management Policy and Practice* (2012), 13(3), pp. 106–115.

22. http://www.mindtools.com/pages/article/newLDR_96.htm (retrieved July 9, 2014).

23. C.O. Trevor, G. Reilly, B. Gerhart, "Reconsidering Pay Dispersion's Effect on the Performance of Interdependent Work: Reconciling Sorting and Pay Inequality," *Academy of Management Journal* (2012), 55(3), pp. 585–610.

24. H. Yang, "Efficiency Wages and Subjective Performance Pay," *Economic Inquiry* (2008), 46(2), pp. 179–196.

25. http://blog.roberthalf.com/are-you-staying-competitive-with-employment-benefits (retrieved July 9, 2014).

26. P. M. Madhani, "Rebalancing Fixed and Variable Pay in a Sales Organization: A Business Cycle Perspective," *Compensation Benefits Review* (2010), 42(3), pp. 179–189.

27. J. Helyar, D. MacMillan, "In Tech, Poaching Is the Sincerest Form of Flattery," *Businessweek* (March 7–13, 2011), pp. 17–18.

28. G.N. Stock, C. McDermott, M. McDermott, "The Effects of Capital and Human Resource Investments on Hospital Performance," *Hospital Topics* (2014), 92(1), pp. 14–19.

29. C.N. Halaby, "Supervision, Pay, and Effort," *Social Forces* (2014), 92(3), pp. 1135–1158.

30. D.H. Bradley, *The Federal Minimum Wage: In Brief* (Washington, DC: Congressional Research Service, 2013), http://fas.org/sgp/crs/misc/R43089.pdf.

31. B. Bartling, F.A. von Siemens, "The Intensity of Incentives in Firms and Markets: Moral Hazard With Envious Agents," *Labour Economics* (2010), 17(3), pp. 598–607.

32. http://www.shrm.org/hrdisciplines/compensation/articles/pages/salary-compression-lid.aspx (retrieved July 6, 2014).

33. http://www.dol.gov/whd/regs/statutes/0002.fair.pdf (retrieved July 9, 2014).

34. http://www.dol.gov/compliance/guide/minwage.htm (retrieved July 9, 2014).

35. http://www.dol.gov/opa/media/press/whd/WHD20141131.htm (retrieved July 7, 2014).

36. http://www.dol.gov/compliance/guide/minwage.htm (retrieved July 9, 2014).

37. Ibid.

38. http://www.dol.gov/whd/regs/compliance/fairpay/fs17g_salary.htm (retrieved July 6, 2014).

39. http://www.dol.gov/whd/regs/compliance/fairpay/fs17h_highly_comp.pdf (retrieved July 6, 2014).

40. http://www.dol.gov/whd/regs/compliance/fairpay/fs17g_salary.htm (retrieved July 6, 2014).

41. http://www.dol.gov/elaws/faq/esa/flsa/016.htm (retrieved July 9, 2014).

42. http://www.dol.gov/compliance/guide/childlbr.htm (retrieved July 9, 2014).

43. http://www.eeoc.gov/eeoc/newsroom/equal_pay_day_2014.cfm (retrieved July 7, 2014).

44. http://www.dol.gov/oasam/programs/history/flsa1938.htm (retrieved July 9, 2014).

45. http://www.worldatwork.org/adim Link?id=74254 (retrieved July 8, 2014).

46. http://www.shrm.org/Research/Articles/Articles/Pages/Compensation_20 Series_20Part_20II__20Job_ 20 Evaluation.aspx (retrieved July 9, 2014).

47. http://www.shrm.org/Education/hreducation/Pages/DesigningaPay StructureACaseStudyandIntegrated Exercises.aspx (retrieved July 9, 2014).

48. http://www.shrm.org/Education/hreducation/Pages/DesigningaPay StructureACaseStudyandIn tegrated Exercises.aspx (retrieved July 9, 2014).

49. M. Guadalupe, J. Wulf, "The Flattening Firm and Product Market Competition: The Effect of Trade Liberalization on Corporate Hierarchies," *American Economic Journal: Applied Economics* (2010), 2(4), pp. 105–127.

50. G.O. Trevor, G. Reilly, B. Gerhart, "Reconsidering Pay Dispersion's Effect on the Performance of Interdependent Work: Reconciling Sorting and Pay Inequality," *Academy of Management Journal* (2012), 55(3), pp. 585–610.

51. http://www.shrm.org/TemplatesTools/HowtoGuides/Pages/HowtoEstablishSalaryRanges.aspx (retrieved July 9, 2014).

52. http://www.shrm.org/hrdisciplines/compensation/Articles/Pages/CMS_000067.aspx (retrieved July 9, 2014).

53. http://aon.mediaroom.com/2013-08-29-Aon-Hewitt-Survey-Shows-2014-Salary-Increases-to-Reach-Highest-Levels-Since-2008 (retrieved July 9, 2014).

54. Hoover's Inc. (2014). *CVS Caremark Corporation* [Hoover's Company Records: In-Depth Records]. Retrieved July 12, 2014, from Long Island University Academic Database.

55. D. Lazarus, "At CVS, Only the Very Rich Get Much Richer," *Los Angeles Times,* http://www.latimes.com/business/la-fi-lazarus-20140627-column.html (June 26, 2014).

56. Ibid.

57. Ibid.

58. J. Kell, "CVS Caremark CEO's Pay Jumps 44%," *Wall Street Journal,* http://online.wsj.com/news/articles/SB10001 42412788732350100457839038392 9384430 (March 29, 2013).

CHAPTER 11

1. R. E. Johnson, C.D. Chang, L.O. Yang, "Commitment and Motivation at Work: The Relevance of Employee Identity and Regulatory Focus," *Academy of Management Review* (2010), 35(2), pp. 226–245.

2. J.J. Martocchio, *Strategic Compensation: A Human Resource Management Approach* (Upper Saddle River, NJ: Prentice Hall, 2015), p. 86.

3. C.S. Jung, "Extending the Theory of Goal Ambiguity to Programs: Examining the Relationship Between Goal Ambiguity and Performance," *Public Administration Review* (2014), 74(2), pp. 205–219.

4. L.A. Myers Jr., "One Hundred Years Later: What Would Frederick W. Taylor Say?" *International Journal of Business and Social Science* (2011), 2(20), pp. 8–11.

5. H. Young Shin, W. Lee, "How Can We Introduce the Most Effective Incentive Plan for Non-exempt Employees?" (2013), http://digitalcommons.ilr.cornell.edu/student/18/.

6. S. Anand, P.R. Vidyarthi, R.C. Linden, D.M. Rousseau, "Good Citizens in Poor-Quality Relationships: Idiosyncratic Deals as a Substitute for Relationship Quality," *Academy of Management Journal* (2010), 53(5), pp. 970–988.

7. J.J. Martocchio, *Strategic Compensation: A Human Resource Management Approach* (Upper Saddle River, NJ: Prentice Hall, 2015), p. 92.

8. Ibid.

9. D. Kruse, R.B. Freeman, J.R. Blasi, *Shared Capitalism at Work: Employee Ownership, Profit and Gain Sharing, and*

Broad-Based Stock Options (Chicago, IL: University of Chicago Press, 2010).

10. J. Blasi, D. Kruse, D. Weltmann, "Firm Survival and Performance in Privately Held ESOP Companies," *Advances in the Economic Analysis of Participatory & Labor-Managed Firms* (2013), 14, pp. 109–124.

11. D.C. Wyld, "Do Employees View Stock Options the Same Way as Their Bosses Do?" *Academy of Management Perspectives* (2011), 25(4), pp. 91–92.

12. S. Gustin, "Two Years After Steve Jobs' Death, Is Apple a Different Company?" *TIME Magazine* (October 4, 2013).

13. http://ycharts.com/companies/AAPL/market_cap/ (retrieved July 13, 2014).

14. M. Krantz, B. Hansen, "CEO Pay Soars While Worker's Pay Stalls," *USA Today* (April 1, 2011), pp. B1–B2.

15. "Executive Compensation Group Advisory," *Vedder Price P.C.* (July 2010).

16. http://www.bloomberg.com/news/2013-09-17/ceo-to-worker-pay-ratio-disclosure-proposal-to-be-issued-by-sec.html (retrieved July 13, 2014).

17. "Executive Compensation Group Advisory," *Vedder Price P.C.* (July 2010).

18. http://www.shrm.org/hrdisciplines/compensation/Articles/Pages/CMS_014050.aspx (retrieved July 15, 2014).

19. Ibid.

20. https://www.whitehouse.gov/sites/default/files/omb/budget/fy2016/assets/tables.pdf (retrieved July 12, 2015).

21. Ibid.

22. http://www.dol.gov/whd/fmla/index.htm (retrieved July 2, 2011).

23. http://www.dol.gov/whd/fmla/fmlaAmended.htm#SEC_101_DEFINITIONS (retrieved July 22, 2014).

24. http://www.littler.com/publication-press/publication/employer-mandate-delay-beware-ignoring-aca/ (retrieved July 22, 2014).

25. http://www.hhs.gov/ocr/privacy/ (retrieved July 23, 2014).

26. http://www.pbgc.gov/wr/benefits/guaranteed-benefits.html (retrieved July 23, 2014).

27. Society for Human Resources Management, *Examining Paid Leave in the Workplace* (Alexandria, VA: SHRM, 2008), http://www.shrm.org/research/survey findings/articles/documents/09-0228_paid_leave_sr_fnl.pdf.

28. Society for Human Resources Management, "2013 Employee Benefits," (Alexandria, VA: SHRM, 2013), p. 30, http://www.shrm.org/research/surveyfindings/articles/documents/13-0245%202013_empbenefits_fnl.pdf.

29. http://www.bls.gov/opub/ted/2013/ted_20130730.htm (retrieved July 23, 2014).

30. Society for Human Resources Management, "2013 Employee Benefits" (Alexandria, VA: SHRM, 2013), p. 31, http://www.shrm.org/research/surveyfindings/articles/documents/13-0245%202013_empbenefits_fnl.pdf.

31. http://www.bls.gov/ncs/ebs/benefits/2013/ownership/civilian/table06a.htm (retrieved July 23, 2014).

32. http://www.irs.gov/pub/irs-pdf/p969.pdf (retrieved July 23, 2014).

33. http://www.bls.gov/ncs/ebs/benefits/2013/ownership/private/table02a.htm (retrieved July 23, 2014).

34. http://www.irs.gov/Retirement-Plans/Plan-Participant-Employee/Retirement-Topics-401k-and-Profit-Sharing-Plan-Contribution-Limits (retrieved July 23, 2014).

35. http://www.irs.gov/Retirement-Plans/Plan-Participant-Employee/Retirement-Topics-IRA-Contribution-Limits (retrieved July 23, 2014).

36. http://www.irs.gov/Government-Entities/Federal-State-&-Local-Governments/Group-Term-Life-Insurance (retrieved July 24, 2014).

37. http://pueblo.gsa.gov/cic_text/employ/lt-disability/insurance.htm (retrieved July 24, 2014).

38. Society for Human Resources Management, "2013 Employee Benefits" (Alexandria, VA: SHRM, 2013), p. 25, http://www.shrm.org/research/surveyfindings/articles/documents/13-0245%202013_empbenefits_fnl.pdf.

39. Ibid.

40. http://graphics8.nytimes.com/packages/pdf/business/20110428-docs/allstate.pdf (retrieved July 15, 2014).

41. http://www.shrm.org/hrdisciplines/benefits/articles/pages/transform-health-care.aspx (retrieved July 26, 2014).

42. Ibid.

43. R. Leung, "Working the Good Life," CBSNews. Retrieved from http://www.cbsnews.com/news/working-the-good-life/ (April 18, 2013).

44. M. Crowley," How SAS Became the World's Best Place to Work," *Fast Company & Inc.* Retrieved from http://www.fastcompany.com/3004953/how-sas-became-worlds-best-place-work/ (January 22, 2013).

45. M. Weitzner. "The Royal Treatment," *60 Minutes.* Retrieved from YouTube at https://www.youtube.com/watch?v=N-ebIGpZIWI.

46. Ibid.

47. R. Leung, "Working the Good Life," CBSNews. Retrieved from http://www.cbsnews.com/news/working-the-good-life/.

48. Ibid.

49. M. Weitzner, "The Royal Treatment," *60 Minutes*," Retrieved from YouTube at https://www.youtube.com/watch?v=N-ebIGpZIWI (September 15, 2007).

CHAPTER 12

1. K. Jiang, D.P. Lepak, J. Hu, J.C. Baer, "How Does Human Resource Management Influence Organizational Outcomes? A Meta-Analytic Investigation of Mediating Mechanisms," *Academy of Management Journal* (2012), 55(6), pp. 1264–1294.

2. R. Maurer, "Corporations Urged to Push Suppliers on Worker Safety," *HR Magazine* (February 2013), p. 15.

3. http://www.osha.gov (retrieved July 10, 2013).

4. http://www.osha.gov/pls/oshaweb/owadisp.show_document?p_id=2743&p_table=OSHACT (retrieved July 20, 2011).

5. http://www.osha.gov/doc/outreachtraining/htmlfiles/introsha.html (retrieved July 20, 2011).

6. http://www.bls.gov/iif/oshwc/cfoi/cfoi_revised12.pdf (retrieved July 26, 2014).

7. http://www.bls.gov/news.release/osh.nr0.htm (retrieved July 26, 2014).

8. http://www.osha.gov/about.html (retrieved July 26, 2014).

9. http://www.osha.gov/Publications/3439at-a-glance.pdf (retrieved July 26, 2014).

10. http://www.shrm.org/legalissues/federalresources/pages/osha-inspectors.aspx (retrieved July 26, 2014).

11. http://www.shrm.org/legalissues/federalresources/pages/osha-inspectors.aspx (retrieved July 27, 2014).

12. https://www.osha.gov/Publications/3439at-a-glance.pdf (retrieved July 27, 2014).

13. https://www.osha.gov/FedReg_osha_pdf/FED20120326.pdf (retrieved July 27, 2014).

14. https://www.osha.gov/dsg/hazcom/hazcom-appendix-d.html (retrieved July 27, 2014).

15. http://www.osha.gov/Publications/osha3000.pdf (retrieved July 27, 2014).

16. http://cdc.gov/niosh/about.html (retrieved July 27, 2014).

17. http://www.cdc.gov/niosh/docs/strategic/ (retrieved July 27, 2014).

18. D.A. Sharar, J. Pompe, R. Lennox, "Evaluating the Workplace Effects of EAP Counseling," *Journal of Health & Productivity* (2012), 6(12), pp. 5–14.

19. http://www.bls.gov/ncs/ebs/benefits/2010/ebbl0046.pdf (retrieved July 27, 2014).

20. G. Hargrave et al., "EAP Treatment Impact on Presenteeism and Absenteeism: Implications for Return on Investment," *Journal of Workplace Behavioral Health* (2008), 23(3), pp. 283–293.

21. M. Attridge, P. Herlihy, P. Sharar, T. Amaral, T. McPherson, et al., "EAP Effectiveness and ROI," *EASNA Research Notes* (2009), 1(3).

22. M.E. Porter, M.R. Kramer, "Creating Shared Value," *Harvard Business Review*, 89(1/2), pp. 62–77.

23. L. Berry, A. Mirabito, W. Baun, "What's the Hard Return on Employee Wellness Programs?" *Harvard Business Review* (2010), 88(12), pp. 104–112.

24. Ibid.

25. http://www.cdc.gov/workplace healthpromotion/evaluation/topics/disorders.html (retrieved July 27, 2014).

26. Ibid.

27. http://www.osha.gov/ergonomics/FAQs-external.html (retrieved July 29, 2014).

28. https://www.osha.gov/SLTC/ergonomics/index.html (retrieved July 29, 2014).

29. Ibid.

30. http://www.ncbi.nlm.nih.gov/pmc/articles/PMC3736412/ (retrieved October 2, 2015).

31. http://ehs.okstate.edu/kopykit/Office%20Ergonomics1.PDF (retrieved July 29, 2014).

32. http://www.forbes.com/sites/kathryndill/2014/04/18/survey-42-of-employees-have-changed-jobs-due-to-stress/ (retrieved July 27, 2014).

33. M.L. Marzec, A.F. Scibelli, D.W. Edington, "Examining Individual Factors According to Health Risk Appraisal Data as Determinants of Absenteeism Among US Utility Employees," *Journal of Occupational and Environmental Medicine* (2013), 55(7), pp. 732–740.

34. R.C. Deb, S.K. Biswas, "Stress Management: A Critical View," *European Journal of Business and Management* (2011), 3(4), pp. 205–212.

35. M.F. Marin, C. Lord, J. Andrews, R.P. Juster, S. Sindi, G. Arsenault-Lapierre, . . . S.J. Lupien, "Chronic Stress, Cognitive Functioning and Mental Health," *Neurobiology of Learning and Memory* (2011), 96(4), pp. 583–595.

36. C.R. Wanberg, J. Zhu, R. Kanfer, Z. Zhang, "After the Pink Slip: Applying Dynamic Motivation Frameworks to the Job Search Experience," *Academy of Management Journal* (2012), 55(2), pp. 261–284.

37. S. Shellenbarger, "Are You Hard-Wired to Boil Over From Stress?" *The Wall Street Journal* (February 13, 2013), p. D3.

38. C.R. Wanberg, J. Zhu, R. Kanfer, Z. Zhang, "After the Pink Slip: Applying Dynamic Motivation Frameworks to the Job Search Experience," *Academy of Management Journal* (2012), 55(2), pp. 261–284.

39. http://www.corporatewellnessmagazine.com/issue-24/worksite-wellness-issue-24/workplace-stress-strains-organizations-bottom-lines/ (retrieved July 27, 2014).

40. A.E. Nixon, J.J. Mazzola, J. Bauer, J.R. Krueger, P.E. Spector, "Can Work Make You Sick? A Meta-Analysis of the Relationships Between Job Stressors and Physical Symptoms," *Work & Stress* (2011), 25(1), pp. 1–22.

41. "Preserve Your Health Like Your Wealth," *The Wall Street Journal* (April 15, 2009), pp. D5–D6.

42. E. Monsen, R.W. Boss, "The Impact of Strategic Entrepreneurship Inside the Organization: Examining Job Stress and Employee Retention," *Entrepreneurship Theory and Practice* (2009), 33(1), pp. 71–104.

43. K.E. Spaeder, "Time to De-stress," *Entrepreneur* (October 2008), p. 24.

44. "Preserve Your Health Like Your Wealth," *The Wall Street Journal* (April 15, 2009), pp. D5–D6.

45. Ibid.

46. Ibid.

47. Staff, "Over 34% of Americans," *The Wall Street Journal* (January 10–11, 2009), p. A1.

48. R. Tomsho, "Bulging Waist Carries Risk," *The Wall Street Journal* (November 13, 2008), p. D4.

49. C. Arnst, "Taxing the Rich–Food, That Is," *Businessweek* (February 23, 2009), p. 62.

50. "Preserve Your Health Like Your Wealth," *The Wall Street Journal* (April 15, 2009), pp. D5–D6.

51. S.D. Sidle, "Workplace Stress Management Interventions: What Works Best?" *Academy of Management Perspective* (2008), 22(3), pp. 111–112.

52. J. Welch, S. Welch, "Finding Your Inner Courage," *Businessweek* (February 23, 2009), p. 84.

53. "Preserve Your Health Like Your Wealth," *The Wall Street Journal* (April 15, 2009), pp. D5–D6.

54. S. Covey, "Time Management," *Fortune* (September 19, 2009), pp. 28–29.

55. S. Shellenbarger, "When Stress Is Good for You," *The Wall Street Journal* (January 24, 2012), pp. D1, D5.

56. "Top Security Threats and Management Issues Facing Corporate America: 2012 Survey of Fortune 1000 Companies," *Securitas Security Services USA* (2013), p. 6.

57. http://www.cnn.com/2014/05/19/justice/china-hacking-charges/ (retrieved July 27, 2014).

58. https://www.osha.gov/SLTC/workplaceviolence/ (retrieved October 1, 2015).

59. R. Lussier, "Dealing With Anger and Preventing Workplace Violence," *Clinical Leadership & Management Review* (2004), 18(2), pp. 117–119.

60. Ibid.

61. Ibid.

62. http://www.dol.gov/elaws/asp/drugfree/drugs/screen92.asp.

63. http://www.shrm.org/hrdisciplines/safetysecurity/articles/pages/drugs-workplace-crisis.aspx (retrieved July 27, 2014).

64. http://www.shrm.org/templatestools/toolkits/pages/introsafety andsecurity.aspx (retrieved July 27, 2014).

65. http://www.ojp.usdoj.gov/newsroom/pdfs/ojp_resource_guide_08.pdf (retrieved July 27, 2014).

66. http://www.cdc.gov/nchs/fastats/obesity-overweight.htm (retrieved July 28, 2014).

67. http://blogs.hbr.org/2013/01/sitting-is-the-smoking-of-our-generation/ (retrieved July 28, 2014).

68. N. Owen, G.N. Healy, C.E. Matthews, D.W. Dunstan, "Too Much Sitting: The Population-Health Science of Sedentary Behavior," *Exercise and Sport Sciences Reviews* (2010), 38(3), p. 105.

69. http://www.shrm.org/hrdisciplines/global/articles/pages/workplace-bullying-protections-differ-globally.aspx (retrieved July 29, 2014).

70. http://www.stopbullying.gov/laws/federal/index.html (retrieved July 29, 2014).

71. S. Banjo, "Inside Nike's Struggle to Balance Cost and Worker Safety in Bangladesh," *The Wall Street Journal* (April 21, 2014). Retrieved from http://online.wsj.com/news/articles/SB10001 424052702303873604579493502231 397942/.

72. Hoover's Inc., *Nike, Inc.* [Hoover's company records: In-depth records] (June 23, 2014). Retrieved June 24, 2014, from Long Island University Academic Database.

73. S. Banjo, "Inside Nike's Struggle to Balance Cost and Worker Safety in Bangladesh," *The Wall Street Journal* (April 21, 2014). Retrieved from http://online.wsj.com/news/articles/SB10001 424052702303873604579493502231 397942/.

74. Ibid.

75. S. Cendrowski, "Can Outsourcing Be Improved?" *Fortune*, 167(8). Retrieved from http://scottcendrowski.com/can-outsourcing-be-improved/ (June 10, 2013).

76. S. Greenhouse, "Major Retailers Join Bangladesh Safety Plan," *The New York Times* (May 13, 2013). Retrieved from http://www.nytimes.com/2013/05/14/business/global/hm-agrees-to-bangladesh-safety-plan.html?_r=0.

77. S. Banjo, Nike CEO on Bangladesh: 'Is it a Perfect Situation? No.' [Interview with Mike Parker]. *The Wall Street Journal*. (April 22, 2014). Retrieved from http://blogs.wsj.com/corporate-intelligence/2014/04/22/nike-ceo-on-bangladesh-is-it-a-perfect-situation-no/.

78. S. Banjo, "Inside Nike's Struggle to Balance Cost and Worker Safety in Bangladesh," *The Wall Street Journal* (April 21, 2014). Retrieved from http: //online.wsj.com/news/articles/SB1000 1424052702303873604579493502231 397942/.

CHAPTER 13

1. R.L. Hughes, R.C. Ginnett, G.J. Curphy, *Leadership: Enhancing the Lessons of Experience*, 7th ed. (Burr Ridge, IL: McGraw-Hill, 2011).
2. R. Murphree, "Visionary Leader: Gospel Is Key to Unlimited Success," *AFA Journal* (March 2013), p. 11.
3. C. Bonanos, "The Lies We Tell at Work," *Businessweek* (February 4–10, 2013), pp. 71–73.
4. P. Zak, *The Moral Molecule* (New York, NY: Penguin, 2012).
5. C. Downs, "Liar, Liar—Back's on Fire," *AARP Magazine* (October/November 2012), p. 22.
6. K. Leavitt, S.J. Reynolds, C.M. Barnes, P. Schilpzan, S.T. Hannah, "Different Hats, Different Obligations: Plural Occupational Identities and Situated Moral Judgments," *Academy of Management Journal* (2012), 55(6), pp. 1316–1333.
7. B.C. Gunia, L. Wang, L. Huang, J. Wang, J.K. Murnighan, "Contemplation and Conversation: Subtle Influences on Moral Decision Making," *Academy of Management Journal* (2012), 55(1), pp. 13–33.
8. D. Lange, N.T. Washburn, "Understanding Attributions of Corporate Social Irresponsibility," *Academy of Management Journal* (2012), 37(2), pp. 300–326.
9. A. Rasche, K.U. Gilbert, I. Schedel, "Cross-Disciplinary Ethics Education in MBA Programs: Rhetoric or Reality?" *Academy of Management Learning & Education* (2013), 12(1), pp. 71–85.
10. C. Besio, A. Pronzini, "Morality, Ethics, and Values Outside and Inside Organizations: An Example of the Discourse on Climate Change," *Journal of Business Ethics* (2014), 119(3), pp. 287–300.
11. S. Robbins, M. Coulter, *Management* (Upper Saddle River, NJ: Pearson, 2014), p. 136.
12. R. Chandra, *Business Ethics* (Self-published, 2013).
13. C.A. Rusnak, "Are You Confusing People With Your Leadership Style?" *Costco Connection* (March 2012), p. 11.
14. J. Geisler, "Forgive? Forget? Not Likely," *Costco Connection* (December 2012), p. 10.
15. C. Bonanos, "The Lies We Tell at Work," *Businessweek* (February 4–10, 2013), pp. 71–73.
16. D. Ariely, "Why We Lie," *The Wall Street Journal* (May 26–27, 2012), pp. C1–C2.
17. M.K. Duffy, K.L. Scott, J.D. Shaw, B.J. Tepper, K. Aquino, "A Social Context Model of Envy and Social Undermining," *Academy of Management Journal* (2012), 55(3), pp. 643–666.
18. D.M. Mayer, K. Aquino, R.L. Greenbaum, M. Kuenzi, "Who Displays Ethical Leadership, and Why Does It Matter? An Examination of Antecedents and Consequences of Ethical Leadership," *Academy of Management Journal* (2011), 55(1), pp. 151–171.
19. M.K. Duffy, K.L. Scott, J.D. Shaw, B.J. Tepper, K. Aquino, "A Social Context Model of Envy and Social Undermining," *Academy of Management Journal* (2012), 55(3), pp. 643–666.
20. B.C. Gunia, L. Wang, L. Huang, J. Wang, J.K. Murnighan, "Contemplation and Conversation: Subtle Influences on Moral Decision Making," *Academy of Management Journal* (2012), 55(1), pp. 13–33.
21. C. Bonanos, "The Lies We Tell at Work," *Businessweek* (February 4–10, 2013), pp. 71–73.
22. D. Ariely, "Why We Lie," *The Wall Street Journal* (May 26–27, 2012), pp. C1–C2.
23. Ibid.
24. S.D. Levitt, S.J. Dubner, "SuperFreakonomics: Global Cooling, Patriotic Prostitutes, and Why Suicide Bombers Should Buy Life Insurance," *Academy of Management Perspectives* (2011), 25(2), pp. 86–87.
25. D. Ariely, "Why We Lie," *The Wall Street Journal* (May 26–27, 2012), pp. C1–C2.
26. K. Leavitt, S.J. Reynolds, C.M. Barnes, P. Schilpzan, S.T. Hannah, "Different Hats, Different Obligations: Plural Occupational Identities and Situated Moral Judgments," *Academy of Management Journal* (2012), 55(6), pp. 1316–1333.
27. D. Ariely, "Why We Lie," *The Wall Street Journal* (May 26–27, 2012), pp. C1–C2.
28. Ibid.
29. https://www.rotary.org/myrotary/en/learning-reference/about-rotary/history-rotary-international/ (retrieved August 5, 2014).
30. http://www.berkshirehathaway.com/govern/corpgov.pdf (retrieved August 5, 2014).
31. B.C. Gunia, L. Wang, L. Huang, J. Wang, J.K. Murnighan, "Contemplation and Conversation: Subtle Influences on Moral Decision Making," *Academy of Management Journal* (2012), 55(1), pp. 13–33.
32. D. Ariely, "Why We Lie," *The Wall Street Journal* (May 26–27, 2012), pp. C1–C2.
33. P. Zak, *The Moral Molecule* (New York, NY: Penguin, 2012).
34. http://smallbusiness.chron.com/key-components-code-ethics-business-244.html (retrieved August 1, 2014).
35. D. Meinert, "Creating an Ethical Culture," *HR Magazine* (April 2014), pp. 22–27.
36. J.R. Detert, M.C. Edmondson, "Implicit Voice Theories: Taken-for-Granted Rules of Self-Censorship at Work," *Academy of Management Journal* (2011), 54(3), pp. 461–488.
37. D. Ariely, "Why We Lie," *The Wall Street Journal* (May 26–27, 2012), pp. C1–C2.
38. P. Drucker, *Management* (New York, NY: Routledge, 2012).
39. http://dealbook.nytimes.com/2013/04/22/ralph-lauren-pays-1-6-million-to-resolve-bribery-case/ (retrieved August 2, 2014).
40. http://blog.thomsonreuters.com/index.php/judge-dismisses-class-discrimination-claims-against-wal-mart/ (retrieved August 5, 2014).
41. D. Lange, N.T. Washburn, "Understanding Attributions of Corporate Social Irresponsibility," *Academy of Management Journal* (2012), 37(2), pp. 300–326.
42. http://www.reuters.com/article/2013/06/10/us-bofa-mbs-idUSBRE95916M20130610/ (retrieved August 2, 2014).
43. http://www.forbes.com/sites/nathanielparishflannery/2011/09/03/monsantos-pesticide-problems-raise-awareness-for-corporate-environmental-responsibility/ (retrieved August 2, 2014).
44. http://online.wsj.com/articles/furor-erupts-over-facebook-experiment-on-users-1404085840/ (retrieved August 5, 2014).
45. D. Lange, N.T. Washburn, "Understanding Attributions of Corporate Social Irresponsibility," *Academy of Management Journal* (2012), 37(2), pp. 300–326.
46. http://www.bloomberg.com/news/2014-03-26/wal-mart-says-bribery-probe-cost-439-million-in-past-two-years.html (retrieved August 5, 2014).
47. http://abcnews.go.com/US/lululemon-founder-chip-wilson-blames-womens-bodies-yoga/story?id=20815278 (retrieved August 5, 2014).
48. A.B. Carroll, K.M. Shabana, "The Business Case for Corporate Social Responsibility: A Review of Concepts, Research and Practice," *International Journal of Management Reviews* (2010), 12(1), pp. 85–105.
49. A.M. Grant, "Giving Time, Time After Time: Work Design and Sustained Employee Participation in Corporate Volunteering," *Academy of Management Review* (2012), 37(4), pp. 589–615.
50. Edmans, "The Link Between Job Satisfaction and Firm Value, With Implications for Corporate Social Responsibility," *Academy of Management Perspectives* (2012), 26(4), pp. 1–19.
51. "Master Class," *Businessweek* (May 6–12, 2013), p. 83.
52. D. Lange, N.T. Washburn, "Understanding Attributions of Corporate Social Irresponsibility," *Academy of Management Journal* (2012), 37(2), pp. 300–326.

53. R. Cohen, "Five Lessons From the Banana Man, *The Wall Street Journal* (June 2–3, 2012), p. C2.

54. http://www.huffingtonpost.com/sally-steenland/americans-see-opportunity_b_4177762.html (retrieved August 2, 2014).

55. C. Dougherty, "New Faces of Childhood," *The Wall Street Journal* (April 6, 2011), p. A3.

56. M. Jordan, "Illegals Estimated to Account for 1 in 12 U.S. Births," *The Wall Street Journal* (August 12, 2010), pp. A1–A2.

57. "More White Americans Died," *The Wall Street Journal* (June 13, 2013), pp. A1, A8.

58. C. Dougherty, "U.S. Nears Racial Milestone," *The Wall Street Journal* (June 11, 2010), p. A3.

59. S. Reddy, "Latinos Fuel Growth in Decade," *The Wall Street Journal* (March 25, 2011), p. A2.

60. U.S. Census Bureau, reported in *The Wall Street Journal* (December 13, 2012), p. A3.

61. "Corporate Social Responsibility: Good Citizenship or Investor Rip-off?" *The Wall Street Journal* (January 9, 2006), p. R6.

62. J. Morelli, "Environmental Sustainability: A Definition for Environmental Professionals," *Journal of Environmental Sustainability* (2013), 1(1), p. 2.

63. A. Nadim, R.N. Lussier, "Sustainability as a Small Business Competitive Strategy," *Journal of Small Strategy* (2012), 21(2), pp. 79–95.

64. S.B. Banerjee, "Embedding Sustainability Across the Organization: A Critical Perspective," *Academy of Management Learning & Education* (2011), 10(4), pp. 719–731.

65. H. Paulson, "Fortune Global Forum," *Fortune* (April 29, 2013), p. 20.

66. A.A. Marcus, A.R. Fremeth, "Green Management Matters Regardless," *Academy of Management Perspectives* (2009), 23(3), pp. 17–26.

67. K.K. Dhanda, P.J. Murphy, "The New Wild West Is Green: Carbon Offset Markets, Transactions, and Providers," *Academy of Management Perspectives* (2011), 25(4), pp. 37–49.

68. A. Nadim, R.N. Lussier, "Sustainability as a Small Business Competitive Strategy," *Journal of Small Strategy* (2012), 21(2), pp. 79–95.

69. http://en.wikipedia.org/wiki/Chief_sustainability_officer/ (retrieved May 22, 2013).

70. http://www.walmart.com (retrieved May 22, 2013).

71. Briefs: Wal-Mart, *Businessweek* (February 13–19, 2012), p. 28.

72. K. Weise, "Sustainability: I'm With Wal-Mart," *Businessweek* (November 28–December 2, 2011), p. 60.

73. http://www.theguardian.com/sustainable-business/blog/best-practices-sustainability-us-corporations-ceres (retrieved August 3, 2014).

74. M. Porter, M. Kramer, "Strategy & Society: The Link Between Competitive Advantage and Corporate Social Responsibility," *Harvard Business Review* (December 2006), 84(12), pp. 78–92.

75. O. Branzei, A. Nadkarni, "The Tata Way: Evolving and Executing Sustainable Business Strategies," *Ivey Business Journal* (March/April 2008), 72(2), pp. 1–8.

76. MIT Sloan Management Review, *Findings From the 2013 Sustainability & Innovation Global Executive Study and Research Project* (Boston, MA: MIT Sloan Management Review/Boston Consulting Group, 2013), p. 15.

77. http://www.environmentalleader.com/2014/04/23/spotlight-on-the-hows-and-whys-of-sustainable-products/ (retrieved August 5, 2014).

78. https://www.linkedin.com/today/post/article/20140220123325-60894986-how-should-a-business-leader-understand-sustainability (retrieved August 5, 2014).

79. http://www.patagonia.com/us/footprint/ (retrieved August 5, 2014).

80. www3.weforum.org/.../WEF_GAC_GovernanceSustainability_GreenLight_January_Report_2014.pdf (retrieved August 4, 2014).

81. http://www.iso.org/iso/home/standards/management-standards/iso14000.htm (retrieved August 5, 2014).

82. http://www.unglobalcompact.org/AboutTheGC/TheTenPrinciples/index.html (retrieved August 5, 2014).

83. http://www.weforum.org (retrieved August 5, 2014).

84. http://www.csrwire.com/pages/about_us (retrieved August 5, 2014).

85. N. Landrum, S. Edwards, *Sustainable Business: An Executive's Primer* (New York, NY: Business Expert Press, 2009), p. 32.

86. http://arkansasenergy.org/industry/incentives-and-programs/home-energy-assistance-loan-%28heal%29-program.aspx (retrieved July 28, 2011).

87. A. Brief (Ed.), *Diversity at Work* (Cambridge, UK: Cambridge University Press, 2008), pp. 265–267.

88. R. Anand, M. Winters, "A Retrospective View of Corporate Diversity Training From 1964 to the Present," *Academy of Management Learning & Education* (2008), 7(3), pp. 356–372.

89. Ibid.

90. C. Holladay, M. Quinones, "The Influence of Training Focus and Trainer Characteristics on Diversity Training Effectiveness," *Academy of Management Learning & Education* (2008), 7(3), pp. 343–354.

91. H. Blodget, "In Case You Don't Appreciate How Fast the 'Windows Monopoly' Is Getting Destroyed...," *Business Insider*. Retrieved August 13, 2014, from http://www.businessinsider.com/windows-monopoly-is-getting-destroyed-2013-7

92. T. Worstall, "Microsoft's Market Share Drops From 97% to 20% in Just Over a Decade *Forbes*. Retrieved August 13, 2014 from http://www.forbes.com/sites/timworstall/2012/12/13/microsofts-market-share-drops-from-97-to-20-in-just-over-a-decade/.

93. J. Yarow, "Chart of the Day: The Collapse of Microsoft's Monopoly," *Business Insider*. Retrieved August 13, 2014, from http://www.businessinsider.com/chart-of-the-day-consumer-compute-shift-2012-12?nr_email_referer=1&utm_source=Triggermail&utm_medium=email&utm_term=SAI%20Chart%20Of%20The%20Day&utm_campaign=SAI_COTD_120712

94. H. Leonard, "There Will Soon Be One Smartphone for Every Five People in the World," *Business Insider*. Retrieved August 13, 2014, from http://www.businessinsider.com/15-billion-smartphones-in-the-world-22013-2.

95. J. Callaham, "The Top 10 Microsoft News Stories of 2013," *Neowin*. Retrieved August 13, 2014, from http://www.neowin.net/news/the-top-10-microsoft-news-stories-of-2013.

96. "Nokia," in *Wikipedia*. Retrieved August 14, 2014, from http://on.wikipedia.org/wiki/Nokia.

97. J. Rossi, "Microsoft Layoffs Hit Finland Staff Hard," *Wall Street Journal*. Retrieved August 14, 2014, from http://online.wsj.com/articles/microsoft-layoffs-hit-nokias-finland-1405624498.

98. Ibid.

CHAPTER 14

1. M. Li, W.H. Mobley, A. Kelly, "When Do Global Leaders Learn Best to Develop Cultural Intelligence? An Investigation of the Moderating Role of Experiential Learning Styles," *Academy of Management Education & Learning* (2013), 12(1), pp. 32–50.

2. S.T. Hannah, B.J. Avolio, D.R. May, "Moral Maturation and Moral Conations: A Capacity Approach to Explaining Moral Thought and Action," *Academy of Management Review* (2011), 36(4), pp. 663–685.

3. http://www.fedex.com (retrieved May 16, 2013).

4. M. Li, W.H. Mobley, A. Kelly, "When Do Global Leaders Learn Best to Develop Cultural Intelligence? An Investigation of the Moderating Role of Experiential Learning Styles," *Academy of Management Education & Learning* (2013), 12(1), pp. 32–50.

5. J.H. Marler, "Strategic Human Resource Management in Context," *Academy of Management Perspectives* (2012), 26(2), pp. 6–11.

6. http://www.census.gov/popclock (retrieved August 25, 2014).

7. Amazon.com website, www.amazon.com, accessed April 7, 2015.

8. http://www.wto.org/english/thewto_e/whatis_e/wto_dg_stat_e.htm (retrieved August 12, 2014).

9. Information taken from the World Trade Organization's website, http://www.wto.org, accessed April 7, 2015.

10. A. Molinsky, "The Psychological Processes of Cultural Retooling," *Academy of Management Journal* (2010).

11. M. Mendenhall, A. Arnardottir, G. Oddou, L. Burke, "Developing Cross-Cultural Competencies in Management Education Via Cognitive-Behavior Therapy," *Academy of Management Learning & Education* (2013).

12. http://www.eeoc.gov/facts/multi-employees.html (retrieved July 22, 2010).

13. Ibid.

14. J. Palazzolo, "Is It a Bribe . . . or Not?" *The Wall Street Journal* (July 22, 2013), p. R3.

15. http://geert-hofstede.com/dimensions.html (retrieved August 13, 2014).

16. home.sandiego.edu/~dimon/CulturalFrameworks.pdf

17. T.J. Huang, S.C. Chi, J.J. Lawler, "The Relationship Between Expatriates' Personality Traits and Their Adjustment to International Assignments," *The International Journal of Human Resource Management* (2005), 16(9), pp. 1656–1670.

18. S. Mor, M. Morris, J. Joh, "Identifying and Training Adaptive Cross-Cultural Management Skills: The Crucial Role of Cultural Metacognition," *Academy of Management Learning & Education* (2013).

19. C. Dörrenbächer, J. Gammelgaard, F. McDonald, A. Stephan, H. Tüselmann, "Staffing Foreign Subsidiaries With Parent Country Nationals or Host Country Nationals? Insights From European Subsidiaries (No. 74)," Working Papers of the Institute of Management Berlin at the Berlin School of Economics and Law (HWR Berlin, 2013).

20. R. Maurer. "Emerging Markets Drive Global Talent Strategy Shift," http://www.shrm.org/hrdisciplines/global/articles/pages/emerging-markets-global-talent-strategy.aspx (retrieved August 21, 2014).

21. G.K. Stahl, M.Y. Brannen, "Building Cross-Cultural Leadership Competence: An Interview With Carlos Ghosn," *Academy of Management Learning & Education* (2013), 12(3), pp. 494–502.

22. http://www.shrm.org/education/hreducation/documents/international_hrm_presentation.pptx (retrieved August 23, 2014).

23. R.L. Minter, "Preparation of Expatriates for Global Assignments: Revisited," *Journal of Diversity Management* (2011), 3(2), pp. 37–42.

24. N. Cole, K. Nesbeth, "Why Do International Assignments Fail? The Expatriate Families Speak," *International Studies of Management and Organization* (2014), 44(3).

25. K. van der Zee, J.P. van Oudenhoven, "Culture Shock or Challenge? The Role of Personality as a Determinant of Intercultural Competence," *Journal of Cross-Cultural Psychology* (2013), 44(6), pp. 928–940.

26. http://www.shrm.org/education/hreducation/documents/international_hrm_presentation.pptx (retrieved August 23, 2014).

27. Society for Human Resource Management, "Repatriation: How Can My Company Best Retain Repatriated Employees?" http://www.shrm.org/templatestools/hrqa/pages/howcanmycompanybestretainrepatriatedemployees.aspx (retrieved August 23, 2014).

28. C. Bailey, L. Dragoni, "Repatriation After Global Assignments: Current HR Practices and Suggestions for Ensuring Successful Repatriation," *People & Strategy Journal* (2013), 36(1), pp. 48–57.

29. T. Shelton, "Global Compensation Strategies: Managing and Administering Split Pay for an Expatriate Workforce," *Compensation and Benefits Review* (Jan/Feb 2008), 40, pp. 56–60.

30. ORC Worldwide, 2006 Worldwide Survey of International Assignment Policies and Practices, (New York, NY: ORC, 2007).

31. Society for Human Resource Management, "'Global: Expatriate': How Should We Compensate an Employee on a Foreign Assignment?" (December 11, 2012), http://www.shrm.org/templatestools/hrqa/pages/howshouldwecompensateanemployeeona foreignassignment.aspx.

32. K.Y. Ng, L.V. Dyne, S. Ang, "From Experience to Experiential Learning: Cultural Intelligence as a Learning Capability for Global Leader Development," *Academy of Management Learning & Education* (2009), 8(1), pp. 511–526.

33. C. Rose, "Charlie Rose Talks to Mike Duke," *Businessweek* (December 2–6, 2010), p. 30.

34. "Work on Your Winning Strategy," *Global Management Consultancy Hay Group* (2010).

35. M. Segalla, D. Rouzies, M. Besson, B. Weitz, "A Cross-National Investigation of Incentive Sales Compensation," *International Journal of Research in Marketing* (2006), 23(4), pp. 419–433.

36. Ibid.

37. http://www.forbes.com/sites/johnkotter/2013/04/03/how-to-lead-through-business-disruption/ (retrieved August 24, 2014).

38. E. Kelly, *Business Trends 2014: Navigating the Next Wave of Globalization* (Westlake, TX: Deloitte University Press, 2014), p.6, http://dupress.com/periodical/trends/business-trends-2014/?id=us:el:dc:bt14:awa.

39. Ibid. p. 3.

40. C. Bailey, L. Dragoni, "Repatriation After Global Assignments: Current HR Practices and Suggestions for Ensuring Successful Repatriation," *People & Strategy Journal* (2013), 36(1), pp. 48–57.

41. http://www.wikipedia.com (retrieved May 19, 2011).

42. http://www.wharton.universia.net/index.cfm?fa=viewArticle&id=1349&language=english (retrieved May 11, 2011).

43. "Brazil: Labor Relations," *TozziniFriere Advogados* (2007), p. 1.

44. J. Almeida, *Brazil in Focus* (New York, NY: Nova Science, 2008), pp. 124–125.

45. "75% of Employers Expect Worse Labor Relations in 2011," *The Korea Times* (December 19, 2010), http://www.koreatimes.co.kr/www/news/nation/nation_view.asp?newsIdx=78249&categoryCode=113 Korea Times (retrieved May 11, 2011).

46. Hoover's Inc. *HSBC Holdings PLC* [Hoover's company records: In-depth records] (2014). Retrieved July 30, 2014, from Long Island University Academic Database.

47. The JobCrowd, *HSBC Bank PLC Job Reviews*. Retrieved August 4, 2014, from http://www.thejobcrowd.com/employer/hsbc-bank-plc/overview/.

48. PayScale, *Average Salary for HSBC Employees*. Retrieved August 4, 2014, from http://www.payscale.com/research/US/Employer=HSBC/Salary.

49. HSBC, *Benefits and Rewards*. Retrieved August 4, 2014, from http://www.us.hsbc.com/1/2/home/about/careers/benefits-rewards/.

50. ECA International, *Case Study: HSBC; Design and Implementation of a Custom Salary Management Programme*. Retrieved July 30, 2014, from http://www.eca-international.com/about_eca/our_clients/case_study_hsbc.

51. ECA International, *What We Do*. Retrieved July 30, 2014, from http://www.eca-international.com/about_eca/what_we_do.

52. ECA International, *Case Study: HSBC; Design and Implementation of a Custom Salary Management Programme*. Retrieved July 30, 2014, from http://www.eca-international.com/about_eca/our_clients/case_study_hsbc.

 # Index